Primitive Culture (

Researches into the development of my
religion, language, art, and

Edward B. Tylor

Alpha Editions

This edition published in 2024

ISBN 9789362095367

Design and Setting By

Alpha Editions

www.alphaedis.com

Email - info@alphaedis.com

As per information held with us this book is in Public Domain.
This book is a reproduction of an important historical work.
Alpha Editions uses the best technology to reproduce historical work
in the same manner it was first published to preserve its original nature.
Any marks or number seen are left intentionally to preserve.

Contents

PREFACE TO THE FIRST EDITION. ....- 1 -

PREFACE TO THE SECOND EDITION. ....- 2 -

PREFACE TO THE THIRD EDITION ....- 3 -

PREFACE TO THE FOURTH EDITION. ....- 4 -

CHAPTER I. THE SCIENCE OF CULTURE. ....- 5 -

CHAPTER II. THE DEVELOPMENT OF CULTURE. ....- 22 -

CHAPTER III. SURVIVAL IN CULTURE. ....- 51 -

CHAPTER IV. SURVIVAL IN CULTURE (continued). ....- 77 -

CHAPTER V. EMOTIONAL AND IMITATIVE LANGUAGE. .... - 108 -

CHAPTER VI. EMOTIONAL AND IMITATIVE LANGUAGE (continued). .... - 133 -

CHAPTER VII. THE ART OF COUNTING. .... - 160 -

CHAPTER VIII. MYTHOLOGY. .... - 181 -

CHAPTER IX. MYTHOLOGY (continued). .... - 209 -

CHAPTER X. MYTHOLOGY (continued) .... - 241 -

CHAPTER XI. ANIMISM. .... - 271 -

PREFACE TO THE FIRST EDITION.

The present volumes, uniform with the previous volume of 'Researches into the Early History of Mankind' (1st Ed. 1865; 2nd Ed. 1870), carry on the investigation of Culture into other branches of thought and belief, art and custom. During the past six years I have taken occasion to bring tentatively before the public some of the principal points of new evidence and argument here advanced. The doctrine of survival in culture, the bearing of directly-expressive language and the invention of numerals on the problem of early civilization, the place of myth in the primitive history of the human mind, the development of the animistic philosophy of religion, and the origin of rites and ceremonies, have been discussed in various papers and lectures,[1] before being treated at large and with a fuller array of facts in this work.

The authorities for the facts stated in the text are fully specified in the foot-notes, which must also serve as my general acknowledgment of obligations to writers on ethnography and kindred sciences, as well as to historians, travellers, and missionaries. I will only mention apart two treatises of which I have made especial use: the 'Mensch in der Geschichte,' by Professor Bastian, of Berlin, and the 'Anthropologie der Naturvölker,' by the late Professor Waitz, of Marburg.

In discussing problems so complex as those of the development of civilization, it is not enough to put forward theories accompanied by a few illustrative examples. The statement of the facts must form the staple of the argument, and the limit of needful detail is only reached when each group so displays its general law, that fresh cases come to range themselves in their proper niches as new instances of an already established rule. Should it seem to any readers that my attempt to reach this limit sometimes leads to the heaping up of too cumbrous detail, I would point out that the theoretical novelty as well as the practical importance of many of the issues raised, make it most unadvisable to stint them of their full evidence. In the course of ten years chiefly spent in these researches, it has been my constant task to select the most instructive ethnological facts from the vast mass on record, and by lopping away unnecessary matter to reduce the data on each problem to what is indispensable for reasonable proof.

E. B. T.

March, 1871.

PREFACE TO THE SECOND EDITION.

Since the publication of this work in 1871, translations have appeared in German and Russian. In the present edition the form of page has been slightly altered, for convenience of re-issue at once in England and America. The matter, however, remains substantially the same. A few passages have been amplified or altered for greater clearness, and on some points additional or improved evidence has been put in. Among the anthropologists whose published reviews or private communications have enabled me to correct or strengthen various points, I will only mention by name Professor Felix Liebrecht, of Liége, Mr. Clements R. Markham, Professor Calderwood, Mr. Ralston, and Mr. Sebastian Evans.

It may have struck some readers as an omission, that in a work on civilization insisting so strenuously on a theory of development or evolution, mention should scarcely have been made of Mr. Darwin and Mr. Herbert Spencer, whose influence on the whole course of modern thought on such subjects should not be left without formal recognition. This absence of particular reference is accounted for by the present work, arranged on its own lines, coming scarcely into contact of detail with the previous works of these eminent philosophers.

An objection made by several critics as to the accumulation of evidence in these volumes leads me to remark, with sincere gratification, that this objection has in fact been balanced by solid advantage. The plan of collecting wide and minute evidence, so that readers may have actually before them the means of judging the theory put forward, has been justified by the reception of the book, even in circles to whose views many of its arguments are strongly adverse, and that in matters of the first importance. Writers of most various philosophical and theological schools now admit that the ethnological facts are real, and vital, and have to be accounted for. It is not too much to say that a perceptible movement of public opinion has here justified the belief that the English mind, not readily swayed by rhetoric, moves freely under the pressure of facts.

E. B. T.

September, 1873.

PREFACE TO THE THIRD EDITION.

In this edition, while I have not found it needful to alter the general argument, the new information which has become available during the last twenty years has made it necessary to insert further details of evidence, and to correct some few statements. For convenience of reference, the paging of the last edition is kept to.

E. B. T.

September, 1891.

PREFACE TO THE FOURTH EDITION.

For ordinary purposes the present edition may be taken as substantially unchanged. In only a few passages noticeable alterations have been made, (see vol. i. p. 167, vocal tone; vol. ii. pp. 234-7, totemism).

E. B. T.

October, 1903.

CHAPTER I.
THE SCIENCE OF CULTURE.

> Culture or Civilization—Its phenomena related according to definite Laws—Method of classification and discussion of the evidence—Connexion of successive stages of culture by Permanence, Modification, and Survival—Principal topics examined in the present work.

Culture or Civilization, taken in its wide ethnographic sense, is that complex whole which includes knowledge, belief, art, morals, law, custom, and any other capabilities and habits acquired by man as a member of society. The condition of culture among the various societies of mankind, in so far as it is capable of being investigated on general principles, is a subject apt for the study of laws of human thought and action. On the one hand, the uniformity which so largely pervades civilization may be ascribed, in great measure, to the uniform action of uniform causes: while on the other hand its various grades may be regarded as stages of development or evolution, each the outcome of previous history, and about to do its proper part in shaping the history of the future. To the investigation of these two great principles in several departments of ethnography, with especial consideration of the civilization of the lower tribes as related to the civilization of the higher nations, the present volumes are devoted.

Our modern investigators in the sciences of inorganic nature are foremost to recognize, both within and without their special fields of work, the unity of nature, the fixity of its laws, the definite sequence of cause and effect through which every fact depends on what has gone before it, and acts upon what is to come after it. They grasp firmly the Pythagorean doctrine of pervading order in the universal Kosmos. They affirm, with Aristotle, that nature is not full of incoherent episodes, like a bad tragedy. They agree with Leibnitz in what he calls 'my axiom, that nature never acts by leaps (la nature n'agit jamais par saut),' as well as in his 'great principle, commonly little employed, that nothing happens without sufficient reason.' Nor again, in studying the structure and habits of plants and animals, or in investigating the lower functions even of man, are these leading ideas unacknowledged. But when we come to talk of the higher processes of human feeling and action, of thought and language, knowledge and art, a change appears in the prevalent tone of opinion. The world at large is scarcely prepared to accept the general study of human life as a branch of natural science, and to carry out, in a large sense, the poet's injunction, to 'Account for moral as for natural things.' To many educated minds there seems something presumptuous and repulsive in the view that the history of mankind is part and parcel of the history of nature, that our thoughts, wills, and actions accord with laws as definite as those which govern the motion of waves, the combination of acids and bases, and the growth of plants and animals.

The main reasons of this state of the popular judgment are not far to seek. There are many who would willingly accept a science of history if placed before them with substantial definiteness of principle and evidence, but who not unreasonably reject the systems offered to them, as falling too far short of a scientific standard. Through resistance such as this, real knowledge always sooner or later makes its way, while the habit of opposition to novelty does such excellent service against the invasions of speculative dogmatism, that we may sometimes even wish it were stronger than it is. But other obstacles to the investigation of laws of human nature arise from considerations of metaphysics and theology. The popular notion of free human will involves not only freedom to act in accordance with motive, but also a power of breaking loose from continuity and acting without cause,—a combination which may be roughly illustrated by the simile of a balance sometimes acting in the usual way, but also possessed of the faculty of turning by itself without or against its weights. This view of an anomalous action of the will, which it need hardly be said is incompatible with scientific argument, subsists as an opinion patent or latent in men's minds, and strongly affecting their theoretic views of history, though it is not, as a rule, brought prominently forward in systematic reasoning. Indeed the definition of human will, as strictly according with motive, is the only possible scientific basis in such enquiries. Happily, it is not needful to add here yet another to the list of dissertations on supernatural intervention and natural causation, on liberty, predestination, and accountability. We may hasten to escape from the regions of transcendental philosophy and theology, to start on a more hopeful journey over more practicable ground. None will deny that, as each man knows by the evidence of his own consciousness, definite and natural cause does, to a great extent, determine human action. Then, keeping aside from considerations of extra-natural interference and causeless spontaneity, let us take this admitted existence of natural cause and effect as our standing-ground, and travel on it so far as it will bear us. It is on this same basis that physical science pursues, with ever-increasing success, its quest of laws of nature. Nor need this restriction hamper the scientific study of human life, in which the real difficulties are the practical ones of enormous complexity of evidence, and imperfection of methods of observation.

Now it appears that this view of human will and conduct as subject to definite law, is indeed recognised and acted upon by the very people who oppose it when stated in the abstract as a general principle, and who then complain that it annihilates man's free will, destroys his sense of personal responsibility, and degrades him to a soulless machine. He who will say these things will nevertheless pass much of his own life in studying the motives which lead to human action, seeking to attain his wishes through them, framing in his mind theories of personal character, reckoning what are likely to be the effects of new combinations, and giving to his reasoning the crowning character of true scientific enquiry, by taking it for granted that in so far as his calculation turns out wrong, either his evidence must have been false or incomplete, or his judgment upon it unsound. Such a one will sum up the experience of years spent in complex relations with society, by declaring his persuasion that there is a reason for everything in life, and that where events look unaccountable, the rule is to wait and watch in hope that the key to the problem may some day be found. This man's observation may have been as narrow as his inferences are crude and prejudiced, but nevertheless he has been an inductive philosopher 'more than forty years without knowing it.' He has practically acknowledged definite laws of human thought and action, and has simply thrown out of account in his own studies of life the whole fabric of motiveless will and uncaused spontaneity. It is assumed here that they should be just so thrown out of account in wider studies, and that the true philosophy of history lies in extending and improving the methods of the plain people who form their judgments upon facts, and check them upon new facts. Whether the doctrine be wholly or but partly true, it accepts the very condition under which we search for new knowledge in the lessons of experience, and in a word the whole course of our rational life is based upon it.

'One event is always the son of another, and we must never forget the parentage,' was a remark made by a Bechuana chief to Casalis the African missionary. Thus at all times historians, so far as they have aimed at being more than mere chroniclers, have done their best to show not merely succession, but connexion, among the events upon their record. Moreover, they have striven to elicit general principles of human action, and by these to explain particular events, stating expressly or taking tacitly for granted the existence of a philosophy of history. Should any one deny the possibility of thus establishing historical laws, the answer is ready with which Boswell in such a case turned on Johnson: 'Then, sir, you would reduce all history to no better than an almanack.' That nevertheless the labours of so many eminent thinkers should have as yet brought history only to the threshold of science, need cause no wonder to those who consider the bewildering complexity of the problems which come before the general historian. The evidence from which he is to draw his conclusions is at once so multifarious and so doubtful, that a full and distinct view of its bearing on a particular question is hardly to be attained, and thus the temptation becomes all but irresistible to garble it in support of some rough and ready theory of the course of events. The philosophy of history at large, explaining the past and predicting the future phenomena of man's life in the world by reference to general laws, is in fact a subject with which, in the present state of knowledge, even genius aided by wide research seems but hardly able to cope. Yet there are departments of it which, though difficult enough, seem comparatively accessible. If the field of enquiry be narrowed from History as a whole to that branch of it which is here called Culture, the history, not of tribes or nations, but of the condition of knowledge, religion, art, custom, and the like among them, the task of investigation proves to lie within far more moderate compass. We suffer still from the same kind of difficulties which beset the wider argument, but they are much diminished. The evidence is no longer so wildly heterogeneous, but may be more simply classified and compared, while the power of getting rid of extraneous matter, and treating each issue on its own proper set of facts, makes close reasoning on the whole more available than in general history. This may appear from a brief preliminary examination of the problem, how the phenomena of Culture may be classified and arranged, stage by stage, in a probable order of evolution.

Surveyed in a broad view, the character and habit of mankind at once display that similarity and consistency of phenomena which led the Italian proverb-maker to declare that 'all the world is one country,' 'tutto il mondo è paese.' To general likeness in human nature on the one hand, and to general likeness in the circumstances of life on the other, this similarity and consistency may no doubt be traced, and they may be studied with especial fitness in comparing races near the same grade of civilization. Little respect need be had in such comparisons for date in history or for place on the map; the ancient Swiss lake-dweller may be set beside the mediæval Aztec, and the Ojibwa of North America beside the Zulu of South Africa. As Dr. Johnson contemptuously said when he had read about Patagonians and South Sea Islanders in Hawkesworth's Voyages, 'one set of savages is like another.' How true a generalization this really is, any Ethnological Museum may show. Examine for instance the edged and pointed instruments in such a collection; the inventory includes hatchet, adze, chisel, knife, saw, scraper, awl, needle, spear and arrow-head, and of these most or all belong with only differences of detail to races the most various. So it is with savage occupations; the wood-chopping, fishing with net and line, shooting and spearing game, fire-making, cooking, twisting cord and plaiting baskets, repeat themselves with wonderful uniformity in the museum shelves which illustrate the life of the lower races from Kamchatka to Tierra del Fuego, and from Dahome to Hawaii. Even when it comes to comparing barbarous hordes with civilized nations, the consideration thrusts itself upon our minds, how far item after item of the life of the lower races passes into analogous proceedings of the higher, in forms not too far changed to be recognized, and sometimes hardly changed at all. Look at the modern European peasant using his hatchet and his hoe, see his food boiling or roasting over the log-fire, observe the exact place which beer holds in his calculation of happiness, hear his tale of the ghost in the nearest haunted house, and of the farmer's niece who was bewitched with knots in her inside till she fell into fits and died. If we choose out in this way things which have altered little in a long course of centuries, we may draw a picture where there shall be scarce a hand's breadth difference between an English ploughman and a negro of Central Africa. These pages will be so crowded with evidence of such correspondence among mankind, that there is no need to dwell upon its details here, but it may be used at once to override a problem which would complicate the argument, namely, the question of race. For the present purpose it appears both possible and desirable to eliminate considerations of hereditary varieties or races of man, and to treat mankind as homogeneous in nature, though placed in different grades of civilization. The details of the enquiry will, I think, prove that stages of culture may be compared without taking into account how far tribes who use the same implement, follow the same custom, or believe the same myth, may differ in their bodily configuration and the colour of their skin and hair.

A first step in the study of civilization is to dissect it into details, and to classify these in their proper groups. Thus, in examining weapons, they are to be classed under spear, club, sling, bow and arrow, and so forth; among textile arts are to be ranged matting, netting, and several grades of making and weaving threads; myths are divided under such headings as myths of sunrise and sunset, eclipse-myths, earthquake-myths, local myths which account for the names of places by some fanciful tale, eponymic myths which account for the parentage of a tribe by turning its name into the name of an imaginary ancestor; under rites and ceremonies occur such practices as the various kinds of sacrifice to the ghosts of the dead and to other spiritual beings, the turning to the east in worship, the purification of ceremonial or moral uncleanness by means of water or fire. Such are a few miscellaneous examples from a list of hundreds, and the ethnographer's business is to classify such details with a view to making out their distribution in geography and history, and the relations which exist among them. What this task is like, may be almost perfectly illustrated by comparing these details of culture with the species of plants and animals as studied by the naturalist. To the ethnographer the bow and arrow is a species, the habit of flattening children's skulls is a species, the practice of reckoning numbers by tens is a species. The geographical distribution of these things, and their transmission from region to region, have to be studied as the naturalist studies the geography of his botanical and zoological, species. Just as certain plants and animals are peculiar to certain districts, so it is with such instruments as the Australian boomerang, the Polynesian stick-and-groove for fire-making, the tiny bow and arrow used as a lancet or phleme by tribes about the Isthmus of Panama, and in like manner with many an art, myth, or custom, found isolated in a particular field. Just as the catalogue of all the species of plants and animals of a district represents its Flora and Fauna, so the list of all the items of the general life of a people represents that whole which we call its culture. And just as distant regions so often produce vegetables and animals which are analogous, though by no means identical, so it is with the details of the civilization of their inhabitants. How good a working analogy there really is between the diffusion of plants and animals and the diffusion of civilization, comes well into view when we notice how far the same causes have produced both at once. In district after district, the same causes which have introduced the cultivated plants and domesticated animals of civilization, have brought in with them a corresponding art and knowledge. The course of events which carried horses and wheat to America carried with them the use of the gun and the iron hatchet, while in return the whole world received not only maize, potatoes, and turkeys, but the habit of tobacco-smoking and the sailor's hammock.

It is a matter worthy of consideration, that the accounts of similar phenomena of culture, recurring in different parts of the world, actually supply incidental proof of their own authenticity. Some years since, a question which brings out this point was put to me by a great historian— 'How can a statement as to customs, myths, beliefs, &c., of a savage tribe be treated as evidence where it depends on the testimony of some traveller or missionary, who may be a superficial observer, more or less ignorant of the native language, a careless retailer of unsifted talk, a man prejudiced or even wilfully deceitful?' This question is, indeed, one which every ethnographer ought to keep clearly and constantly before his mind. Of course he is bound to use his best judgment as to the trustworthiness of all authors he quotes, and if possible to obtain several accounts to certify each point in each locality. But it is over and above these measures of precaution that the test of recurrence comes in. If two independent visitors to different countries, say a mediæval Mohammedan in Tartary and a modern Englishman in Dahome, or a Jesuit missionary in Brazil and a Wesleyan in the Fiji Islands, agree in describing some analogous art or rite or myth among the people they have visited, it becomes difficult or impossible to set down such correspondence to accident or wilful fraud. A story by a bushranger in Australia may, perhaps, be objected to as a mistake or an invention, but did a Methodist minister in Guinea conspire with him to cheat the public by telling the same story there? The possibility of intentional or unintentional mystification is often barred by such a state of things as that a similar statement is made in two remote lands, by two witnesses, of whom A lived a century before B, and B appears never to have heard of A. How distant are the countries, how wide apart the dates, how different the creeds and characters of the observers, in the catalogue of facts of civilization, needs no farther showing to any one who will even glance at the footnotes of the present work. And the more odd the statement, the less likely that several people in several places should have made it wrongly. This being so, it seems reasonable to judge that the statements are in the main truly given, and that their close and regular coincidence is due to the cropping up of similar facts in various districts of culture. Now the most important facts of ethnography are vouched for in this way. Experience leads the student after a while to expect and find that the phenomena of culture, as resulting from widely-acting similar causes, should recur again and again in the world. He even mistrusts isolated statements to which he knows of no parallel elsewhere, and waits for their genuineness to be shown by corresponding accounts from the other side of the earth, or the other end of history. So strong, indeed, is this means of authentication, that the ethnographer in his library may sometimes presume to decide, not only whether a particular explorer is a shrewd, honest observer, but also whether what he reports is conformable to the general rules of civilization. 'Non quis, sed quid.'

To turn from the distribution of culture in different countries, to its diffusion within these countries. The quality of mankind which tends most to make the systematic study of civilization possible, is that remarkable tacit consensus or agreement which so far induces whole populations to unite in the use of the same language, to follow the same religion and customary law, to settle down to the same general level of art and knowledge. It is this state of things which makes it so far possible to ignore exceptional facts and to describe nations by a sort of general average. It is this state of things which makes it so far possible to represent immense masses of details by a few typical facts, while, these once settled, new cases recorded by new observers simply fall into their places to prove the soundness of the classification. There is found to be such regularity in the composition of societies of men, that we can drop individual differences out of sight, and thus can generalize on the arts and opinions of whole nations, just as, when looking down upon an army from a hill, we forget the individual soldier, whom, in fact, we can scarce distinguish in the mass, while we see each regiment as an organized body, spreading or concentrating, moving in advance or in retreat. In some branches of the study of social laws it is now possible to call in the aid of statistics, and to set apart special actions of large mixed communities of men by means of taxgatherers' schedules, or the tables of the insurance office. Among modern arguments on the laws of human action, none have had a deeper effect than generalizations such as those of M. Quetelet, on the regularity, not only of such matters as average stature and the annual rates of birth and death, but of the recurrence, year after year, of such obscure and seemingly incalculable products of national life as the numbers of murders and suicides, and the proportion of the very weapons of crime. Other striking cases are the annual regularity of persons killed accidentally in the London streets, and of undirected letters dropped into post-office letter-boxes. But in examining the culture of the lower races, far from having at command the measured arithmetical facts of modern statistics, we may have to judge of the condition of tribes from the imperfect accounts supplied by travellers or missionaries, or even to reason upon relics of prehistoric races of whose very names and languages we are hopelessly ignorant. Now these may seem at the first glance sadly indefinite and unpromising materials for scientific enquiry. But in fact they are neither indefinite nor unpromising, but give evidence that is good and definite so far as it goes. They are data which, for the distinct way in which they severally denote the condition of the tribe they belong to, will actually bear comparison with the statistician's returns. The fact is that a stone arrow-head, a carved club, an idol, a grave-mound where slaves and property have been buried for the use of the dead, an account of a sorcerer's rites in making rain, a table of numerals, the conjugation of a verb, are things which each express the state of a people as to one particular point of culture, as truly as the tabulated numbers of deaths by poison, and of chests of tea imported, express in a different way other partial results of the general life of a whole community.

That a whole nation should have a special dress, special tools and weapons, special laws of marriage and property, special moral and religious doctrines, is a remarkable fact, which we notice so little because we have lived all our lives in the midst of it. It is with such general qualities of organized bodies of men that ethnography has especially to deal. Yet, while generalizing on the culture of a tribe or nation, and setting aside the peculiarities of the individuals composing it as unimportant to the main result, we must be careful not to forget what makes up this main result. There are people so intent on the separate life of individuals that they cannot grasp a notion of the action of a community as a whole—such an observer, incapable of a wide view of society, is aptly described in the saying that he 'cannot see the forest for the trees.' But, on the other hand, the philosopher may be so intent upon his general laws of society as to neglect the individual actors of whom that society is made up, and of him it may be said that he cannot see the trees for the forest. We know how arts, customs, and ideas are shaped among ourselves by the combined actions of many individuals, of which actions both motive and effect often come quite distinctly within our view. The history of an invention, an opinion, a ceremony, is a history of suggestion and modification, encouragement and opposition, personal gain and party prejudice, and the individuals concerned act each according to his own motives, as determined by his character and circumstances. Thus sometimes we watch individuals acting for their own ends with little thought of their effect on society at large, and sometimes we have to study movements of national life as a whole, where the individuals co-operating in them are utterly beyond our observation. But seeing that collective social action is the mere resultant of many individual actions, it is clear that these two methods of enquiry, if rightly followed, must be absolutely consistent.

In studying both the recurrence of special habits or ideas in several districts, and their prevalence within each district, there come before us ever-reiterated proofs of regular causation producing the phenomena of human life, and of laws of maintenance and diffusion according to which these phenomena settle into permanent standard conditions of society, at definite stages of culture. But, while giving full importance to the evidence bearing on these standard conditions of society, let us be careful to avoid a pitfall which may entrap the unwary student. Of course the opinions and habits belonging in common to masses of mankind are to a great extent the results of sound judgment and practical wisdom. But to a great extent it is not so. That many numerous societies of men should have believed in the influence of the evil eye and the existence of a firmament, should have sacrificed slaves and goods to the ghosts of the departed, should have handed down traditions of giants slaying monsters and men turning into beasts—all this is ground for holding that such ideas were indeed produced in men's minds by efficient causes, but it is not ground for holding that the rites in question are profitable, the beliefs sound, and the history authentic. This may seem at the first glance a truism, but, in fact, it is the denial of a fallacy which deeply affects the minds of all but a small critical minority of mankind. Popularly, what everybody says must be true, what everybody does must be right—'Quod ubique, quod semper, quod ab omnibus creditum est, hoc est vere proprieque Catholicum'—and so forth. There are various topics, especially in history, law, philosophy, and theology, where even the educated people we live among can hardly be brought to see that the cause why men do hold an opinion, or practise a custom, is by no means necessarily a reason why they ought to do so. Now collections of ethnographic evidence bringing so prominently into view the agreement of immense multitudes of men as to certain traditions, beliefs, and usages, are peculiarly liable to be thus improperly used in direct defence of these institutions themselves, even old barbaric nations being polled to maintain their opinions against what are called modern ideas. As it has more than once happened to myself to find my collections of traditions and beliefs thus set up to prove their own objective truth, without proper examination of the grounds on which they were actually received, I take this occasion of remarking that the same line of argument will serve equally well to demonstrate, by the strong and wide consent of nations, that the earth is flat, and nightmare the visit of a demon.

It being shown that the details of Culture are capable of being classified in a great number of ethnographic groups of arts, beliefs, customs, and the rest, the consideration comes next how far the facts arranged in these groups are produced by evolution from one another. It need hardly be pointed out that the groups in question, though held together each by a common character, are by no means accurately defined. To take up again the natural history illustration, it may be said that they are species which tend to run widely into varieties. And when it comes to the question what relations some of these groups bear to others, it is plain that the student of the habits of mankind has a great advantage over the student of the species of plants and animals. Among naturalists it is an open question whether a theory of development from species to species is a record of transitions which actually took place, or a mere ideal scheme serviceable in the classification of species whose origin was really independent. But among ethnographers there is no such question as to the possibility of species of implements or habits or beliefs being developed one out of another, for development in Culture is recognized by our most familiar knowledge. Mechanical invention supplies apt examples of the kind of development which affects civilization at large. In the history of fire-arms, the clumsy wheel-lock, in which a notched steel wheel revolved by means of a spring against a piece of pyrites till a spark caught the priming, led to the invention of the more serviceable flint-lock, of which a few still hang in the kitchens of our farm-houses for the boys to shoot small birds with at Christmas; the flint-lock in time passed by modification into the percussion-lock, which is just now changing its old-fashioned arrangement to be adapted from muzzle-loading to breech-loading. The mediæval astrolabe passed into the quadrant, now discarded in its turn by the seaman, who uses the more delicate sextant, and so it is through the history of one art and instrument after another. Such examples of progression are known to us as direct history, but so thoroughly is this notion of development at home in our minds, that by means of it we reconstruct lost history without scruple, trusting to general knowledge of the principles of human thought and action as a guide in putting the facts in their proper order. Whether chronicle speaks or is silent on the point, no one comparing a long-bow and a cross-bow would doubt that the cross-bow was a development arising from the simpler instrument. So among the fire-drills for igniting by friction, it seems clear on the face of the matter that the drill worked by a cord or bow is a later improvement on the clumsier primitive instrument twirled between the hands. That instructive class of specimens which antiquaries sometimes discover, bronze celts modelled on the heavy type of the stone hatchet, are scarcely explicable except as first steps in the transition from the Stone Age to the

Bronze Age, to be followed soon by the next stage of progress, in which it is discovered that the new material is suited to a handier and less wasteful pattern. And thus, in the other branches of our history, there will come again and again into view series of facts which may be consistently arranged as having followed one another in a particular order of development, but which will hardly bear being turned round and made to follow in reversed order. Such for instance are the facts I have here brought forward in a chapter on the Art of Counting, which tend to prove that as to this point of culture at least, savage tribes reached their position by learning and not by unlearning, by elevation from a lower rather than by degradation from a higher state.

Among evidence aiding us to trace the course which the civilization of the world has actually followed, is that great class of facts to denote which I have found it convenient to introduce the term 'survivals.' These are processes, customs, opinions, and so forth, which have been carried on by force of habit into a new state of society different from that in which they had their original home, and they thus remain as proofs and examples of an older condition of culture out of which a newer has been evolved. Thus, I know an old Somersetshire woman whose hand-loom dates from the time before the introduction of the 'flying shuttle,' which new-fangled appliance she has never even learnt to use, and I have seen her throw her shuttle from hand to hand in true classic fashion; this old woman is not a century behind her times, but she is a case of survival. Such examples often lead us back to the habits of hundreds and even thousands of years ago. The ordeal of the Key and Bible, still in use, is a survival; the Midsummer bonfire is a survival; the Breton peasants' All Souls' supper for the spirits of the dead is a survival. The simple keeping up of ancient habits is only one part of the transition from old into new and changing times. The serious business of ancient society may be seen to sink into the sport of later generations, and its serious belief to linger on in nursery folk-lore, while superseded habits of old-world life may be modified into new-world forms still powerful for good and evil. Sometimes old thoughts and practices will burst out afresh, to the amazement of a world that thought them long since dead or dying; here survival passes into revival, as has lately happened in so remarkable a way in the history of modern spiritualism, a subject full of instruction from the ethnographer's point of view. The study of the principles of survival has, indeed, no small practical importance, for most of what we call superstition is included within survival, and in this way lies open to the attack of its deadliest enemy, a reasonable explanation. Insignificant, moreover, as multitudes of the facts of survival are in themselves, their study is so effective for tracing the course of the historical development through which alone it is possible to understand their meaning, that it becomes a vital point of ethnographic research to gain the clearest possible insight into their nature. This importance must justify the detail here devoted to an examination of survival, on the evidence of such games, popular sayings, customs, superstitions, and the like, as may serve well to bring into view the manner of its operation.

Progress, degradation, survival, revival, modification, are all modes of the connexion that binds together the complex network of civilization. It needs but a glance into the trivial details of our own daily life to set us thinking how far we are really its originators, and how far but the transmitters and modifiers of the results of long past ages. Looking round the rooms we live in, we may try here how far he who only knows his own time can be capable of rightly comprehending even that. Here is the 'honeysuckle' of Assyria, there the fleur-de-lis of Anjou, a cornice with a Greek border runs round the ceiling, the style of Louis XIV, and its parent the Renaissance share the looking-glass between them. Transformed, shifted, or mutilated, such elements of art still carry their history plainly stamped upon them; and if the history yet farther behind is less easy to read, we are not to say that because we cannot clearly discern it there is therefore no history there. It is thus even with the fashion of the clothes men wear. The ridiculous little tails of the German postilion's coat show of themselves how they came to dwindle to such absurd rudiments; but the English clergyman's bands no longer so convey their history to the eye, and look unaccountable enough till one has seen the intermediate stages through which they came down from the more serviceable wide collars, such as Milton wears in his portrait, and which gave their name to the 'band-box' they used to be kept in. In fact, the books of costume, showing how one garment grew or shrank by gradual stages and passed into another, illustrate with much force and clearness the nature of the change and growth, revival and decay, which go on from year to year in more important matters of life. In books, again, we see each writer not for and by himself, but occupying his proper place in history; we look through each philosopher, mathematician, chemist, poet, into the background of his education,—through Leibnitz into Descartes, through Dalton into Priestley, through Milton into Homer. The study of language has, perhaps, done more than any other in removing from our view of human thought and action the ideas of chance and arbitrary invention, and in substituting for them a theory of development by the co-operation of individual men, through processes ever reasonable and intelligible where the facts are fully known. Rudimentary as the science of culture still is, the symptoms are becoming very strong that even what seem its most spontaneous and motiveless phenomena will, nevertheless, be shown to come within the range of distinct cause and effect as certainly as the facts of mechanics. What would be popularly thought more indefinite and uncontrolled than the products of the imagination in myths and fables? Yet any systematic investigation of mythology, on the basis of a wide collection of evidence, will show plainly enough in such efforts of fancy at once a development from stage to stage, and a production of uniformity of result from uniformity of cause. Here, as elsewhere, causeless spontaneity is seen to recede farther and farther into shelter within the dark precincts of ignorance; like chance, that still holds its place among the vulgar as a real cause of events otherwise unaccountable, while to educated men it has long consciously meant nothing but this ignorance itself. It is only when men fail to see the line of connexion in events, that they are prone to fall upon the notions of arbitrary impulses, causeless freaks, chance and nonsense and indefinite unaccountability. If childish games, purposeless customs, absurd superstitions, are set down as spontaneous because no one can say exactly how they came to be, the assertion may remind us of the like effect that the eccentric habits of the wild rice-plant had on the philosophy of a Red Indian tribe, otherwise disposed to see in the harmony of nature the effects of one controlling personal will. The Great Spirit, said these Sioux theologians, made all things except the wild rice; but the wild rice came by chance.

'Man,' said Wilhelm von Humboldt, 'ever connects on from what lies at hand (der Mensch knüpft immer an Vorhandenes an).' The notion of the continuity of civilization contained in this maxim is no barren philosophic principle, but is at once made practical by the consideration that they who wish to understand their own lives ought to know the stages through which their opinions and habits have become what they are. Auguste Comte scarcely overstated the necessity of this study of development when he declared at the beginning of his 'Positive Philosophy' that 'no conception can be understood except through its history,' and his phrase will bear extension to culture at large. To expect to look modern life in the face and comprehend it by mere inspection, is a philosophy whose weakness can easily be tested. Imagine any one explaining the trivial saying, 'a little bird told me,' without knowing of the old belief in the language of birds and beasts, to which Dr. Dasent, in the introduction to the Norse Tales, so reasonably traces its origin. Attempts to explain by the light of reason things which want the light of history to show their meaning, may be instanced from Blackstone's Commentaries. To Blackstone's mind, the very right of the commoner to turn his beast out to graze on the common, finds its origin and explanation in the feudal system. 'For, when lords of manors granted out parcels of land to tenants, for services either done or to be done, these tenants could not plough or manure the land without beasts; these beasts could not be sustained without pasture; and pasture could not be had but in the lord's wastes, and on the uninclosed fallow grounds of themselves and the other tenants. The law therefore annexed this right of common, as inseparably incident, to the grant of the lands; and this was the original of common appendant,' &c.[2] Now though there is nothing irrational in this explanation, it does not agree at all with the Teutonic land-law which prevailed in England long before the Norman Conquest, and of which the remains have never wholly disappeared. In the old village-community even the arable land, lying in the great common fields which may still be traced in our country, had not yet passed into separate property, while the pasturage in the fallows and stubbles and on the waste belonged to the householders in common. Since those days, the change from communal to individual ownership has mostly transformed this old-world system, but the right which the peasant enjoys of pasturing his cattle on the common still remains, not as a concession to feudal tenants, but as possessed by the commoners before the lord ever claimed the ownership of the waste. It is always unsafe to detach a custom from its hold on past events, treating it as an isolated fact to be simply disposed of by some plausible explanation.

In carrying on the great task of rational ethnography, the investigation of the causes which have produced the phenomena of culture, and of the laws to which they are subordinate, it is desirable to work out as systematically as possible a scheme of evolution of this culture along its many lines. In the following chapter, on the Development of Culture, an attempt is made to sketch a theoretical course of civilization among mankind, such as appears on the whole most accordant with the evidence. By comparing the various stages of civilization among races known to history, with the aid of archæological inference from the remains of prehistoric tribes, it seems possible to judge in a rough way of an early general condition of man, which from our point of view is to be regarded as a primitive condition, whatever yet earlier state may in reality have lain behind it. This hypothetical primitive condition corresponds in a considerable degree to that of modern savage tribes, who, in spite of their difference and distance, have in common certain elements of civilization, which seem remains of an early state of the human race at large. If this hypothesis be true, then, notwithstanding the continual interference of degeneration, the main tendency of culture from primæval up to modern times has been from savagery towards civilization. On the problem of this relation of savage to civilized life, almost every one of the thousands of facts discussed in the succeeding chapters has its direct bearing. Survival in Culture, placing all along the course of advancing civilization way-marks full of meaning to those who can decipher their signs, even now sets up in our midst primæval monuments of barbaric thought and life. Its investigation tells strongly in favour of the view that the European may find among the Greenlanders or Maoris many a trait for reconstructing the picture of his own primitive ancestors. Next comes the problem of the Origin of Language. Obscure as many parts of this problem still remain, its clearer positions lie open to the investigation whether speech took its origin among mankind in the savage state, and the result of the enquiry is that consistently with all known evidence, this may have been the case. From the examination of the Art of Counting a far more definite consequence is shown. It may be confidently asserted, that not only is this important art found in a rudimentary state among savage tribes, but that satisfactory evidence proves numeration to have been developed by rational invention from this low stage up to that in which we ourselves possess it. The examination of Mythology contained in the first volume, is for the most part made from a special point of view, on evidence collected for a special purpose, that of tracing the relation between the myths of savage tribes and their analogues among more civilized nations. The issue of such enquiry goes far to prove that the earliest myth-maker arose and flourished among savage hordes, setting on foot an art which his more cultured successors would carry on, till its results came to be fossilized in superstition, mistaken for history, shaped and draped in poetry, or cast aside as lying folly.

Nowhere, perhaps, are broad views of historical development more needed than in the study of religion. Notwithstanding all that has been written to make the world acquainted with the lower theologies, the popular ideas of their place in history and their relation to the faiths of higher nations are still of the mediæval type. It is wonderful to contrast some missionary journals with Max Müller's Essays, and to set the unappreciating hatred and ridicule that is lavished by narrow hostile zeal on Brahmanism, Buddhism, Zoroastrism, besides the catholic sympathy with which deep and wide knowledge can survey those ancient and noble phases of man's religious consciousness; nor, because the religions of savage tribes may be rude and primitive compared with the great Asiatic systems, do they lie too low for interest and even for respect. The question really lies between understanding and misunderstanding them. Few who will give their minds to master the general principles of savage religion will ever again think it ridiculous, or the knowledge of it superfluous to the rest of mankind. Far from its beliefs and practices being a rubbish-heap of miscellaneous folly, they are consistent and logical in so high a degree as to begin, as soon as even roughly classified, to display the principles of their formation and development; and these principles prove to be essentially rational, though working in a mental condition of intense and inveterate ignorance. It is with a sense of attempting an investigation which bears very closely on the current theology of our own day, that I have set myself to examine systematically, among the lower races, the development of Animism; that is to say, the doctrine of souls and other spiritual beings in general. More than half of the present work is occupied with a mass of evidence from all regions of the world, displaying the nature and meaning of this great element of the Philosophy of Religion, and tracing its transmission, expansion, restriction, modification, along the course of history into the midst of our own modern thought. Nor are the questions of small practical moment which have to be raised in a similar attempt to trace the development of certain prominent Rites and Ceremonies—customs so full of instruction as to the inmost powers of religion, whose outward expression and practical result they are.

In these investigations, however, made rather from an ethnographic than a theological point of view, there has seemed little need of entering into direct controversial argument, which indeed I have taken pains to avoid as far as possible. The connexion which runs through religion, from its rudest forms up to the status of an enlightened Christianity, may be conveniently treated of with little recourse to dogmatic theology. The rites of sacrifice and purification may be studied in their stages of development without entering into questions of their authority and value, nor does an examination of the successive phases of the world's belief in a future life demand a discussion of the arguments adduced for or against the doctrine itself. The ethnographic results may then be left as materials for professed theologians, and it will not perhaps be long before evidence so fraught with meaning shall take its legitimate place. To fall back once again on the analogy of natural history, the time may soon come when it will be thought as unreasonable for a scientific student of theology not to have a competent acquaintance with the principles of the religions of the lower races, as for a physiologist to look with the contempt of past centuries on evidence derived from the lower forms of life, deeming the structure of mere invertebrate creatures matter unworthy of his philosophic study.

Not merely as a matter of curious research, but as an important practical guide to the understanding of the present and the shaping of the future, the investigation into the origin and early development of civilization must be pushed on zealously. Every possible avenue of knowledge must be explored, every door tried to see if it is open. No kind of evidence need be left untouched on the score of remoteness or complexity, of minuteness or triviality. The tendency of modern enquiry is more and more towards the conclusion that if law is anywhere, it is everywhere. To despair of what a conscientious collection and study of facts may lead to, and to declare any problem insoluble because difficult and far off, is distinctly to be on the wrong side in science; and he who will choose a hopeless task may set himself to discover the limits of discovery. One remembers Comte starting in his account of astronomy with a remark on the necessary limitation of our knowledge of the stars: we conceive, he tells us, the possibility of determining their form, distance, size, and movement, whilst we should never by any method be able to study their chemical composition, their mineralogical structure, &c. Had the philosopher lived to see the application of spectrum analysis to this very problem, his proclamation of the dispiriting doctrine of necessary ignorance would perhaps have been recanted in favour of a more hopeful view. And it seems to be with the philosophy of remote human life somewhat as with the study of the nature of the celestial bodies. The processes to be made out in the early stages of our mental evolution lie distant from us in time as the stars lie distant from us in space, but the laws of the universe are not limited with the direct observation of our senses. There is vast material to be used in our enquiry; many workers are now busied in bringing this material into shape, though little may have yet been done in proportion to what remains to do; and already it seems not too much to say that the vague outlines of a philosophy of primæval history are beginning to come within our view.

CHAPTER II.
THE DEVELOPMENT OF CULTURE.

Stages of culture, industrial, intellectual, political, moral—Development of culture in great measure corresponds with transition from savage through barbaric to civilized life—Progression-theory—Degeneration-theory—Development-theory includes both, the one as primary, the other as secondary—Historical and traditional evidence not available as to low stages of culture—Historical evidence as to principles of Degeneration—Ethnological evidence as to rise and fall in culture from comparison of different levels of culture in branches of the same race—Extent of historically recorded antiquity of civilization—Prehistoric Archæology extends the antiquity of man in low stages of civilization—Traces of Stone Age, corroborated by megalithic structures, lake dwellings, shell-heaps, burial-places, &c., prove original low culture throughout the world—Stages of Progressive Development in industrial arts.

In taking up the problem of the development of culture as a branch of ethnological research, a first proceeding is to obtain a means of measurement. Seeking something like a definite line along which to reckon progression and retrogression in civilization, we may apparently find it best in the classification of real tribes and nations, past and present. Civilization actually existing among mankind in different grades, we are enabled to estimate and compare it by positive examples. The educated world of Europe and America practically settles a standard by simply placing its own nations at one end of the social series and savage tribes at the other, arranging the rest of mankind between these limits according as they correspond more closely to savage or to cultured life. The principal criteria of classification are the absence or presence, high or low development, of the industrial arts, especially metal-working, manufacture of implements and vessels, agriculture, architecture, &c., the extent of scientific knowledge, the definiteness of moral principles, the condition of religious belief and ceremony, the degree of social and political organization, and so forth. Thus, on the definite basis of compared facts, ethnographers are able to set up at least a rough scale of civilization. Few would dispute that the following races are arranged rightly in order of culture:—Australian, Tahitian, Aztec, Chinese, Italian. By treating the development of civilization on this plain ethnographic basis, many difficulties may be avoided which have embarrassed its discussion. This may be seen by a glance at the relation which theoretical principles of civilization bear to the transitions to be observed as matter of fact between the extremes of savage and cultured life.

From an ideal point of view, civilization may be looked upon as the general improvement of mankind by higher organization of the individual and of society, to the end of promoting at once man's goodness, power, and happiness. This theoretical civilization does in no small measure correspond with actual civilization, as traced by comparing savagery with barbarism, and barbarism with modern educated life. So far as we take into account only material and intellectual culture, this is especially true. Acquaintance with the physical laws of the world, and the accompanying power of adapting nature to man's own ends, are, on the whole, lowest among savages, mean among barbarians, and highest among modern educated nations. Thus a transition from the savage state to our own would be, practically, that very progress of art and knowledge which is one main element in the development of culture.

But even those students who hold most strongly that the general course of civilization, as measured along the scale of races from savages to ourselves, is progress towards the benefit of mankind, must admit many and manifold exceptions. Industrial and intellectual culture by no means advances uniformly in all its branches, and in fact excellence in various of its details is often obtained under conditions which keep back culture as a whole. It is true that these exceptions seldom swamp the general rule; and the Englishman, admitting that he does not climb trees like the wild Australian, nor track game like the savage of the Brazilian forest, nor compete with the ancient Etruscan and the modern Chinese in delicacy of goldsmith's work and ivory carving, nor reach the classic Greek level of oratory and sculpture, may yet claim for himself a general condition above any of these races. But there actually have to be taken into account developments of science and art which tend directly against culture. To have learnt to give poison secretly and effectually, to have raised a corrupt literature to pestilent perfection, to have organized a successful scheme to arrest free enquiry and proscribe free expression, are works of knowledge and skill whose progress toward their goal has hardly conduced to the general good. Thus, even in comparing mental and artistic culture among several peoples, the balance of good and ill is not quite easy to strike.

If not only knowledge and art, but at the same time moral and political excellence, be taken into consideration, it becomes yet harder to reckon on an ideal scale the advance or decline from stage to stage of culture. In fact, a combined intellectual and moral measure of human condition is an instrument which no student has as yet learnt properly to handle. Even granting that intellectual, moral, and political life may, on a broad view, be seen to progress together, it is obvious that they are far from advancing with equal steps. It may be taken as man's rule of duty in the world, that he shall strive to know as well as he can find out, and to do as well as he knows how. But the parting asunder of these two great principles, that separation of intelligence from virtue which accounts for so much of the wrong-doing of mankind, is continually seen to happen in the great movements of civilization. As one conspicuous instance of what all history stands to prove, if we study the early ages of Christianity, we may see men with minds pervaded by the new religion of duty, holiness, and love, yet at the same time actually falling away in intellectual life, thus at once vigorously grasping one half of civilization, and contemptuously casting off the other. Whether in high ranges or in low of human life, it may be seen that advance of culture seldom results at once in unmixed good. Courage, honesty, generosity, are virtues which may suffer, at least for a time, by the development of a sense of value of life and property. The savage who adopts something of foreign civilization too often loses his ruder virtues without gaining an equivalent. The white invader or colonist, though representing on the whole a higher moral standard than the savage he improves or destroys, often represents his standard very ill, and at best can hardly claim to substitute a life stronger, nobler, and purer at every point than that which he supersedes. The onward movement from barbarism has dropped behind it more than one quality of barbaric character which cultured modern men look back on with regret, and will even strive to regain by futile attempts to stop the course of history, and to restore the past in the midst of the present. So it is with social institutions. The slavery recognised by savage and barbarous races is preferable in kind to that which existed for centuries in late European colonies. The relation of the sexes among many savage tribes is more healthy than among the richer classes of the Mohammedan world. As a supreme authority of government, the savage councils of chiefs and elders compare favourably with the unbridled despotism under which so many cultured races have groaned. The Creek Indians, asked concerning their religion, replied that where agreement was not to be had, it was best to 'let every man paddle his canoe his own way:' and after long ages of theological strife and persecution, the modern world seems coming to think these savages not far wrong.

Among accounts of savage life, it is not, indeed, uncommon to find details of admirable moral and social excellence. To take one prominent instance, Lieut. Bruijn Kops and Mr. Wallace have described, among the rude Papuans of the Eastern Archipelago, a habitual truthfulness, rightfulness, and kindliness which it would be hard to match in the general moral life of Persia or India, to say nothing of many a civilized European district.[3] Such tribes may count as the 'blameless Ethiopians' of the modern world, and from them an important lesson may be learnt. Ethnographers who seek in modern savages types of the remotely ancient human race at large, are bound by such examples to consider the rude life of primæval man under favourable conditions to have been, in its measure, a good and happy life. On the other hand, the pictures drawn by some travellers of savagery as a kind of paradisiacal state may be taken too exclusively from the bright side. It is remarked as to these very Papuans, that Europeans whose intercourse with them has been hostile become so impressed with the wild-beast-like cunning of their attacks, as hardly to believe in their having feelings in common with civilized men. Our Polar explorers may well speak in kindly terms of the industry, the honesty, the cheerful considerate politeness of the Esquimaux; but it must be remembered that these rude people are on their best behaviour with foreigners, and that their character is apt to be foul and brutal where they have nothing to expect or fear. The Caribs are described as a cheerful, modest, courteous race, and so honest among themselves that if they missed anything out of a house they said quite naturally: 'There has been a Christian here.' Yet the malignant ferocity with which these estimable people tortured their prisoners of war with knife and fire-brand and red pepper, and then cooked and ate them in solemn debauch, gave fair reason for the name of Carib (Cannibal) to become the generic name of man-eaters in European languages.[4] So when we read descriptions of the hospitality, the gentleness, the bravery, the deep religious feeling of the North American Indians, we admit their claims to our sincere admiration; but we must not forget that they were hospitable literally to a fault, that their gentleness would pass with a flash of anger into frenzy, that their bravery was stained with cruel and treacherous malignity, that their religion expressed itself in absurd belief and useless ceremony. The ideal savage of the 18th century may be held up as a living reproof to vicious and frivolous London; but in sober fact, a Londoner who should attempt to lead the atrocious life which the real savage may lead with impunity and even respect, would be a criminal only allowed to follow his savage models during his short intervals out of gaol. Savage moral standards are real enough, but they are far looser and weaker than ours. We may, I think, apply the often-repeated comparison of savages to children as fairly to their moral as to their intellectual condition. The better savage social life seems in but unstable equilibrium, liable to be easily upset by a touch of distress, temptation, or violence, and then it becomes the worse savage life, which we know by so many dismal and hideous examples. Altogether, it may be admitted that some rude tribes lead a life to be envied by some barbarous races, and even by the outcasts of higher nations. But that any known savage tribe would not be improved by judicious civilization, is a proposition which no moralist would dare to make; while the general tenour of the evidence goes far to justify the view that on the whole the civilized man is not only wiser and more capable than the savage, but also better and happier, and that the barbarian stands between.

It might, perhaps, seem practicable to compare the whole average of the civilization of two peoples, or of the same people in different ages, by reckoning each, item by item, to a sort of sum-total, and striking a balance between them, much as an appraiser compares the value of two stocks of merchandise, differ as they may both in quantity and quality. But the few remarks here made will have shown how loose must be the working-out of these rough-and-ready estimates of culture. In fact, much of the labour spent in investigating the progress and decline of civilization has been misspent, in premature attempts to treat that as a whole which is as yet only susceptible of divided study. The present comparatively narrow argument on the development of culture at any rate avoids this greatest perplexity. It takes cognizance principally of knowledge, art, and custom, and indeed only very partial cognizance within this field, the vast range of physical, political, social, and ethical considerations being left all but untouched. Its standard of reckoning progress and decline is not that of ideal good and evil, but of movement along a measured line from grade to grade of actual savagery, barbarism, and civilization. The thesis which I venture to sustain, within limits, is simply this, that the savage state in some measure represents an early condition of mankind, out of which the higher culture has gradually been developed or evolved, by processes still in regular operation as of old, the result showing that, on the whole, progress has far prevailed over relapse.

On this proposition, the main tendency of human society during its long term of existence has been to pass from a savage to a civilized state. Now all must admit a great part of this assertion to be not only truth, but truism. Referred to direct history, a great section of it proves to belong not to the domain of speculation, but to that of positive knowledge. It is mere matter of chronicle that modern civilization is a development of mediæval civilization, which again is a development from civilization of the order represented in Greece, Assyria, or Egypt. Thus the higher culture being clearly traced back to what may be called the middle culture, the question which remains is whether this middle culture may be traced back to the lower culture, that is, to savagery. To affirm this, is merely to assert that the same kind of development in culture which has gone on inside our range of knowledge has also gone on outside it, its course of proceeding being unaffected by our having or not having reporters present. If any one holds that human thought and action were worked out in primæval times according to laws essentially other than those of the modern world, it is for him to prove by valid evidence this anomalous state of things, otherwise the doctrine of permanent principle will hold good, as in astronomy or geology. That the tendency of culture has been similar throughout the existence of human society, and that we may fairly judge from its known historic course what its prehistoric course may have been, is a theory clearly entitled to precedence as a fundamental principle of ethnographic research.

Gibbon in his 'Roman Empire' expresses in a few vigorous sentences his theory of the course of culture, as from savagery upward. Judged by the knowledge of nearly a century later, his remarks cannot, indeed, pass unquestioned. Especially he seems to rely with misplaced confidence on traditions of archaic rudeness, to exaggerate the lowness of savage life, to underestimate the liability to decay of the ruder arts, and in his view of the effect of high on low civilization, to dwell too exclusively on the brighter side. But, on the whole, the great historian's judgment seems so substantially that of the unprejudiced modern student of the progressionist school, that I gladly quote the passage here at length, and take it as a text to represent the development theory of culture:—'The discoveries of ancient and modern navigators, and the domestic history, or tradition, of the most enlightened nations, represent the *human savage* naked both in mind and body, and destitute of laws, of arts, of ideas, and almost of language. From this abject condition, perhaps the primitive and universal state of man, he has gradually arisen to command the animals, to fertilise the earth, to traverse the ocean, and to measure the heavens. His progress in the improvement and exercise of his mental and corporeal faculties has been irregular and various; infinitely slow in the beginning, and increasing by degrees with redoubled velocity: ages of laborious ascent have been followed by a moment of rapid downfall; and the several climates of the globe have felt the vicissitudes of light and darkness. Yet the experience of four thousand years should enlarge our hopes, and diminish our apprehensions: we cannot determine to what height the human species may aspire in their advances towards perfection; but it may safely be presumed, that no people, unless the face of nature is changed, will relapse into their original barbarism. The improvements of society may be viewed under a threefold aspect. 1. The poet or philosopher illustrates his age and country by the efforts of a *single* mind; but these superior powers of reason or fancy are rare and spontaneous productions; and the genius of Homer, or Cicero, or Newton, would excite less admiration, if they could be created by the will of a prince, or the lessons of a preceptor. 2. The benefits of law and policy, of trade and manufactures, of arts and sciences, are more solid and permanent; and *many* individuals may be qualified, by education and discipline, to promote, in their respective stations, the interest of the community. But this general order is the effect of skill and labour; and the complex machinery may be decayed by time, or injured by violence. 3. Fortunately for mankind, the more useful, or, at least, more necessary arts, can be performed without superior talents, or national subordination;

without the powers of *one*, or the union of *many*. Each village, each family, each individual, must always possess both ability and inclination, to perpetuate the use of fire and of metals; the propagation and service of domestic animals; the methods of hunting and fishing; the rudiments of navigation; the imperfect cultivation of corn, or other nutritive grain; and the simple practice of the mechanic trades. Private genius and public industry may be extirpated; but these hardy plants survive the tempest, and strike an everlasting root into the most unfavourable soil. The splendid days of Augustus and Trajan were eclipsed by a cloud of ignorance; and the barbarians subverted the laws and palaces of Rome. But the scythe, the invention, or emblem of Saturn, still continued annually to mow the harvests of Italy; and the human feasts of Læstrigons have never been renewed on the coast of Campania. Since the first discovery of the arts, war, commerce, and religious zeal, have diffused, among the savages of the Old and New World, these inestimable gifts: they have been successively propagated; they can never be lost. We may therefore acquiesce in the pleasing conclusion, that every age of the world has increased, and still increases, the real wealth, the happiness, the knowledge, and perhaps the virtue, of the human race.'[5]

This progression-theory of civilization may be contrasted with its rival, the degeneration-theory, in the dashing invective of Count Joseph de Maistre, written toward the beginning of the 19th century. 'Nous partons toujours,' he says, 'de l'hypothèse banale que l'homme s'est élevé graduellement de la barbarie à la science et à la civilisation. C'est le rêve favori, c'est l'erreur-mère, et comme dit l'école le proto-pseudes de notre siècle. Mais si les philosophes de ce malheureux siècle, avec l'horrible perversité que nous leur avons connue, et qui s'obstinent encore malgré les avertissements qu'ils ont reçus, avaient possédé de plus quelques-unes de ces connaissances qui ont dû nécessairement appartenir aux premiers hommes, &c.'[6] The degeneration-theory, which this eloquent antagonist of 'modern ideas' indeed states in an extreme shape, has received the sanction of men of great learning and ability. It has practically resolved itself into two assumptions, first, that the history of culture began with the appearance on earth of a semi-civilized race of men, and second, that from this stage culture has proceeded in two ways, backward to produce savages, and forward to produce civilized men. The idea of the original condition of man being one of more or less high culture, must have a certain prominence given to it on account of its considerable hold on public opinion. As to definite evidence, however, it does not seem to have any ethnological basis whatever. Indeed, I scarcely think that a stronger counter-persuasion could be used on an intelligent student inclined to the ordinary degeneration-theory than to induce him to examine critically and impartially the arguments of the advocates on his own side. It must be borne in mind, however, that the grounds on which this theory has been held have generally been rather theological than ethnological. The strength of the position it has thus occupied may be well instanced from the theories adopted by two eminent French writers of the 18th century, which in a remarkable way piece together a belief in degeneration and an argument for progression. De Brosses, whose whole intellectual nature turned to the progression-theory, argued that by studying what actually now happens 'we may trace men upward from the savage state to which the flood and dispersion had reduced them.'[7] And Goguet, holding that the pre-existing arts perished at the deluge, was thus left free to work out on the most thorough-going progressionist principles his theories of the invention of fire, cooking, agriculture, law, and so forth, among tribes thus reduced to a condition of low savagery.[8] At the present time it is not unusual for the origin of civilization to be treated as matter of dogmatic theology. It has happened to me more than once to be assured from the pulpit that the theories of ethnologists who consider man to have risen from a low original condition are delusive fancies, it being revealed truth that man was originally in a high condition. Now as a matter of Biblical criticism it must be remembered that a large proportion of modern theologians are far from accepting such a dogma. But in investigating the problem of early civilization, the claim to ground scientific opinion upon a basis of revelation is in itself objectionable. It would be, I think, inexcusable if students who have seen in Astronomy and Geology the unhappy results of attempting to base science on religion, should countenance a similar attempt in Ethnology.

By long experience of the course of human society, the principle of development in culture has become so ingrained in our philosophy that ethnologists, of whatever school, hardly doubt but that, whether by progress or degradation, savagery and civilization are connected as lower and higher stages of one formation. As such, then, two principal theories claim to account for their relation. As to the first hypothesis, which takes savage life as in some sort representing an early human state whence higher states were, in time, developed, it has to be noticed that advocates of this progression-theory are apt to look back toward yet lower original conditions of mankind. It has been truly remarked that the modern naturalist's doctrine of progressive development has encouraged a train of thought singularly accordant with the Epicurean theory of man's early existence on earth, in a condition not far removed from that of the lower animals. On such a view, savage life itself would be a far advanced condition. If the advance of culture be regarded as taking place along one general line, then existing savagery stands directly intermediate between animal and civilized life; if along different lines, then savagery and civilization may be considered as at least indirectly connected through their common origin. The method and evidence here employed are not, however, suitable for the discussion of this remoter part of the problem of civilization. Nor is it necessary to enquire how, under this or any other theory, the savage state first came to be on earth. It is enough that, by some means or other, it has actually come into existence; and so far as it may serve as a guide in inferring an early condition of the human race at large, so far the argument takes the very practicable shape of a discussion turning rather on actual than imaginary states of society. The second hypothesis, which regards higher culture as original, and the savage condition as produced from it by a course of degeneration, at once cuts the hard knot of the origin of culture. It takes for granted a supernatural interference, as where Archbishop Whately simply refers to miraculous revelation that condition above the level of barbarism which he considers to have been man's original state.[9] It may be incidentally remarked, however, that the doctrine of original civilization bestowed on man by divine intervention, by no means necessarily involves the view that this original civilization was at a high level. Its advocates are free to choose their starting-point of culture above, at, or below the savage condition, as may on the evidence seem to them most reasonable.

The two theories which thus account for the relation of savage to cultured life may be contrasted according to their main character, as the progression-theory and the degradation-theory. Yet of course the progression-theory recognizes degradation, and the degradation-theory recognizes progression, as powerful influences in the course of culture. Under proper limitations the principles of both theories are conformable to historical knowledge, which shows us, on the one hand, that the state of the higher nations was reached by progression from a lower state, and, on the other hand, that culture gained by progression may be lost by degradation. If in this enquiry we should be obliged to end in the dark, at any rate we need not begin there. History, taken as our guide in explaining the different stages of civilization, offers a theory based on actual experience. This is a development-theory, in which both advance and relapse have their acknowledged places. But so far as history is to be our criterion, progression is primary and degradation secondary; culture must be gained before it can be lost. Moreover, in striking a balance between the effects of forward and backward movement in civilization, it must be borne in mind how powerfully the diffusion of culture acts in preserving the results of progress from the attacks of degeneration. A progressive movement in culture spreads, and becomes independent of the fate of its originators. What is produced in some limited district is diffused over a wider and wider area, where the process of effectual 'stamping out' becomes more and more difficult. Thus it is even possible for the habits and inventions of races long extinct to remain as the common property of surviving nations; and the destructive actions which make such havoc with the civilizations of particular districts fail to destroy the civilization of the world.

The enquiry as to the relation of savagery to barbarism and semi-civilization lies almost entirely in præ-historic or extra-historic regions. This is of course an unfavourable condition, and must be frankly accepted. Direct history hardly tells anything of the changes of savage culture, except where in contact with and under the dominant influence of foreign civilization, a state of things which is little to our present purpose. Periodical examinations of low races otherwise left isolated to work out their own destinies, would be interesting evidence to the student of civilization if they could be made; but unfortunately they cannot. The lower races, wanting documentary memorials, loose in preserving tradition, and ever ready to clothe myth in its shape, can seldom be trusted in their stories of long-past ages. History is oral or written record which can be satisfactorily traced into contact with the events it describes; and perhaps no account of the course of culture in its lower stages can satisfy this stringent criterion. Traditions may be urged in support either of the progression-theory or of the degradation-theory. These traditions may be partly true, and must be partly untrue; but whatever truth or untruth they may contain, there is such difficulty in separating man's recollection of what was from his speculation as to what might have been, that ethnology seems not likely to gain much by attempts to judge of early stages of civilization on a traditional basis. The problem is one which has occupied the philosophic mind even in savage and barbaric life, and has been solved by speculations asserted as facts, and by traditions which are, in great measure, mere realized theories. The Chinese can show, with all due gravity, the records of their ancient dynasties and tell us how in old times their ancestors dwelt in caves, clothed themselves with leaves, and ate raw flesh, till, under such and such rulers, they were taught to build huts, prepare skins for garments, and make fire.[10] Lucretius can describe to us, in his famous lines, the large-boned, hardy, lawless, primæval race of man, living the roving life of the wild beasts which they overcame with stones and heavy clubs, devouring berries and acorns, ignorant as yet of fire, and agriculture, and the use of skins for clothing. From this state the Epicurean poet traces up the development of culture, beginning outside but ending inside the range of human memory.[11] To the same class belong those legends which, starting from an ancient savage state, describe its elevation by divine civilizers: this, which may be called the supernatural progression-theory, is exemplified in the familiar culture-traditions of Peru and Italy.

But other minds, following a different ideal track from the present to the past, have seen in a far different shape the early stages of human life. Those men whose eyes are always turned to look back on the wisdom of the ancients, those who by a common confusion of thought ascribe to men of old the wisdom of old men, those who hold fast to some once-honoured scheme of life which new schemes are superseding before their eyes, are apt to carry back their thought of present degeneration into far-gone ages, till they reach a period of primæval glory. The Parsi looks back to the happy rule of King Yima, when men and cattle were immortal, when water and trees never dried up and food was inexhaustible, when there was no cold nor heat, no envy nor old age.[12] The Buddhist looks back to the age of glorious soaring beings who had no sin, no sex, no want of food, till the unhappy hour when, tasting a delicious scum that formed upon the surface of the earth, they fell into evil, and in time became degraded to eat rice, to bear children, to build houses, to divide property, and to establish caste. In after ages, record preserves details of the continuing course of degeneration. It was King Chetiya who told the first lie, and the citizens who heard of it, not knowing what a lie was, asked if it were white, black or blue. Men's lives grew shorter and shorter, and it was King Maha Sâgara who, after a brief reign of 252,000 years, made the dismal discovery of the first grey hair.[13]

Admitting the imperfection of the historical record as regards the lowest stages of culture, we must bear in mind that it tells both ways. Niebuhr, attacking the progressionists of the 18th century, remarks that they have overlooked the fact 'that no single example can be brought forward of an actually savage people having independently become civilized.'[14] Whately appropriated this remark, which indeed forms the kernel of his well-known Lecture on the Origin of Civilisation: 'Facts are stubborn things,' he says, 'and that no authenticated instance can be produced of savages that ever *did* emerge, unaided, from that state is no *theory*, but a statement, hitherto never disproved, of a matter of *fact*.' He uses this as an argument in support of his general conclusion, that man could not have risen independently from a savage to a civilized state, and that savages are degenerate descendants of civilized men.[15] But he omits to ask the counter-question, whether we find one recorded instance of a civilized people falling independently into a savage state? Any such record, direct and well vouched, would be of high interest to ethnologists, though, of course, it would not contradict the development-theory, for proving loss is not disproving previous gain. But where is such a record to be found? The defect of historical evidence as to the transition between savagery and higher culture is a two-sided fact, only half taken into Archbishop Whately's one-sided argument. Fortunately the defect is by no means fatal. Though history may not account directly for the existence and explain the position of savages, it at least gives evidence which bears closely on the matter. Moreover, we are in various ways enabled to study the lower course of culture on evidence which cannot have been tampered with to support a theory. Old traditional lore, however untrustworthy as direct record of events, contains most faithful incidental descriptions of manners and customs; archæology displays old structures and buried relics of the remote past; philology brings out the undesigned history in language, which generation after generation have handed down without a thought of its having such significance; the ethnological survey of the races of the world tells much; the ethnographical comparison of their condition tells more.

Arrest and decline in civilization are to be recognised as among the more frequent and powerful operations of national life. That knowledge, arts, and institutions should decay in certain districts, that peoples once progressive should lag behind and be passed by advancing neighbours, that sometimes even societies of men should recede into rudeness and misery—all these are phenomena with which modern history is familiar. In judging of the relation of the lower to the higher stages of civilization, it is essential to gain some idea how far it may have been affected by such degeneration. What kind of evidence can direct observation and history give as to the degradation of men from a civilized condition towards that of savagery? In our great cities, the so-called 'dangerous classes' are sunk in hideous misery and depravity. If we have to strike a balance between the Papuans of New Caledonia and the communities of European beggars and thieves, we may sadly acknowledge that we have in our midst something worse than savagery. But it is not savagery; it is broken-down civilization. Negatively, the inmates of a Whitechapel casual ward and of a Hottentot kraal agree in their want of the knowledge and virtue of the higher culture. But positively, their mental and moral characteristics are utterly different. Thus, the savage life is essentially devoted to gaining subsistence from nature, which is just what the proletarian life is not. Their relations to civilized life—the one of independence, the other of dependence—are absolutely opposite. To my mind the popular phrases about 'city savages' and 'street Arabs' seem like comparing a ruined house to a builder's yard. It is more to the purpose to notice how war and misrule, famine and pestilence, have again and again devastated countries, reduced their population to miserable remnants, and lowered their level of civilization, and how the isolated life of wild country districts seems sometimes tending towards savagery. So far as we know, however, none of these causes have ever really reproduced a savage community. For an ancient account of degeneration under adverse circumstances, Ovid's mention of the unhappy colony of Tomi on the Black Sea is a case in point, though perhaps not to be taken too literally. Among its mixed Greek and barbaric population, harassed and carried off into slavery by the Sarmatian horsemen, much as the Persians till lately were by the Turkomans, the poet describes the neglect of the gardener's craft, the decay of textile arts, the barbaric clothing of hides.

'Nec tamen hæc loca sunt ullo pretiosa metallo:

Hostis ab agricola vix sinit illa fodi.

Purpura sæpe tuos fulgens prætexit amictus:

Sed non Sarmatico tingitur illa mari.

Vellera dura ferunt pecudes, et Palladis uti

Arte Tomitanæ non didicere nurus.

Femina pro lana Cerialia munera frangit,

Suppositoque gravem vertice portat aquam.

Non hic pampineis amicitur vitibus ulmus:

Nulla premunt ramos pondere poma suo.

Tristia deformes pariunt absinthia campi,

Terraque de fructu quam sit amara docet.'[16]

Cases of exceptionally low civilization in Europe may perhaps be sometimes accounted for by degeneration of this kind. But they seem more often the relics of ancient unchanged barbarism. The evidence from wild parts of Ireland two or three centuries ago is interesting from this point of view. Acts of Parliament were passed against the inveterate habits of fastening ploughs to the horses' tails, and of burning oats from the straw to save the trouble of threshing. In the 18th century Ireland could still be thus described in satire:—

'The Western isle renowned for bogs,

For tories and for great wolf-dogs,

For drawing hobbies by the tails,

And threshing corn with fiery flails.'[17]

Fynes Moryson's description of the wild or 'meere' Irish about 1600, is amazing. The very lords of them, he says, dwelt in poor clay houses, or cabins of boughs covered with turf. In many parts men as well as women had in very winter time but a linen rag about the loins and a woollen mantle on their bodies, so that it would turn a man's stomach to see an old woman in the morning before breakfast. He notices their habit of burning oats from the straw, and making cakes thereof. They had no tables, but set their meat on a bundle of grass. They feasted on fallen horses, and seethed pieces of beef and pork with the unwashed entrails of beasts in a hollow tree, lapped in a raw cow's hide, and so set over the fire, and they drank milk warmed with a stone first cast into the fire.[18] Another district remarkable for a barbaric simplicity of life is the Hebrides. Till of late years, there were to be found there in actual use earthen vessels, unglazed and made by hand without the potter's wheel, which might pass in a museum as indifferent specimens of savage manufacture. These 'craggans' are still made by an old woman at Barvas for sale as curiosities. Such a modern state of the potter's art in the Hebrides fits well with George Buchanan's statement in the 16th century that the islanders used to boil meat in the beast's own paunch or hide.[19] Early in the 18th century Martin mentions as prevalent there the ancient way of dressing corn by burning it dexterously from the ear, which he notices to be a very quick process, thence called 'graddan' (Gaelic, *grad*=quick).[20] Thus we see that the habit of burning out the grain, for which the 'meere Irish' were reproached, was really the keeping up of an old Keltic art, not without its practical use. So the appearance in modern Keltic districts of other widespread arts of the lower culture—hide-boiling, like that of the Scythians in Herodotus, and stone-boiling, like that of the Assinaboins of North America—seems to fit not so well with degradation from a high as with survival from a low civilization. The Irish and the Hebrideans had been for ages under the influence of comparatively high civilization, which nevertheless may have left unaltered much of the older and ruder habit of the people.

Instances of civilized men taking to a wild life in outlying districts of the world, and ceasing to obtain or want the appliances of civilization, give more distinct evidence of degradation. In connexion with this state of things takes place the nearest known approach to an independent degeneration from a civilized to a savage state. This happens in mixed races, whose standard of civilization may be more or less below that of the higher race. The mutineers of the Bounty, with their Polynesian wives, founded a small but not savage community on Pitcairn's Island.[21] The mixed Portuguese and native races of the East Indies and Africa lead a life below the European standard, but not a savage life.[22] The Gauchos of the South American Pampas, a mixed European and Indian race of equestrian herdsmen, are described as sitting about on ox-skulls, making broth in horns with hot cinders heaped round, living on meat without vegetables, and altogether leading a foul, brutal, comfortless, degenerate, but not savage life.[23] One step beyond this brings us to the cases of individual civilized men being absorbed in savage tribes and adopting the savage life, on which they exercise little influence for improvement; the children of these men may come distinctly under the category of savages. These cases of mixed breeds, however, do not show a low culture actually produced as the result of degeneration from a high one. Their theory is that, given a higher and a lower civilization existing among two races, a mixed race between the two may take to the lower or an intermediate condition.

Degeneration probably operates even more actively in the lower than in the higher culture. Barbarous nations and savage hordes, with their less knowledge and scantier appliances, would seem peculiarly exposed to degrading influences. In Africa, for instance, there seems to have been in modern centuries a falling off in culture, probably due in a considerable degree to foreign influence. Mr. J. L. Wilson, contrasting the 16th and 17th century accounts of powerful negro kingdoms in West Africa with the present small communities, with little or no tradition of their forefathers' more extended political organization, looks especially to the slave-trade as the deteriorating cause.[24] In South-East Africa, also, a comparatively high barbaric culture, which we especially associate with the old descriptions of the kingdom of Monomotapa, seems to have fallen away, not counting the remarkable ruins of buildings of hewn stone fitted without mortar which indicate the intrusion of more civilized foreigners into the gold region![25] In North America, Father Charlevoix remarks of the Iroquois of the last century, that in old times they used to build their cabins better than other nations, and better than they do themselves now; they carved rude figures in relief on them; but since in various expeditions almost all their villages have been burnt, they have not taken the trouble to restore them in their old condition.[26] The degradation of the Cheyenne Indians is matter of history. Persecuted by their enemies the Sioux, and dislodged at last even from their fortified village, the heart of the tribe was broken. Their numbers were thinned, they no longer dared to establish themselves in a permanent abode, they gave up the cultivation of the soil, and became a tribe of wandering hunters, with horses for their only valuable possession, which every year they bartered for a supply of corn, beans, pumpkins, and European merchandise, and then returned into the heart of the prairies.[27] When in the Rocky Mountains, Lord Milton and Dr. Cheadle came upon an outlying fragment of the Shushwap race, without horses or dogs, sheltering themselves under rude temporary slants of bark or matting, falling year by year into lower misery, and rapidly dying out; this is another example of the degeneration which no doubt has lowered or destroyed many a savage people.[28] There are tribes who are the very outcasts of savage life. There is reason to look upon the miserable Digger Indians of North America and the Bushmen of South Africa as the persecuted remnants of tribes who have seen happier days.[29] The traditions of the lower races of their ancestors' better life may sometimes be real recollections of a not far distant past. The Algonquin Indians look back to old days as to a golden age when life was better than now, when they had better laws and leaders, and manners less rude.[30] And indeed, knowing what we do of their history, we may admit that they have cause to remember in misery happiness gone by. Well, too, might the rude Kamchadal declare that the world is growing worse and worse, that men are becoming fewer and viler, and food scarcer, for the hunter, and the bear, and the reindeer are hurrying away from here to the happier life in the regions below.[31] It would be a valuable contribution to the study of civilization to have the action of decline and fall investigated on a wider and more exact basis of evidence than has yet been attempted. The cases here stated are probably but part of a long series which might be brought forward to prove degeneration in culture to have been, by no means indeed the primary cause of the existence of barbarism and savagery in the world, but a secondary action largely and deeply affecting the general development of civilization. It may perhaps give no unfair idea to compare degeneration of culture, both in its kind of operation and in its immense extent, to denudation in the geological history of the earth.

In judging of the relations between savage and civilized life, something may be learnt by glancing over the divisions of the human race. For this end the classification by families of languages may be conveniently used, if checked by the evidence of bodily characteristics. No doubt speech by itself is an insufficient guide in tracing national descent, as witness the extreme cases of Jews in England, and three-parts negro races in the West Indies, nevertheless speaking English as their mother-tongue. Still, under ordinary circumstances, connexion of speech does indicate more or less connexion of ancestral race. As a guide in tracing the history of civilization, language gives still better evidence, for common language to a great extent involves common culture. The race dominant enough to maintain or impose its language, usually more or less maintains or imposes its civilization also. Thus the common descent of the languages of Hindus, Greeks, and Teutons is no doubt due in great measure to common ancestry, but is still more closely bound up with a common social and intellectual history, with what Professor Max Müller well calls their 'spiritual relationship.' The wonderful permanence of language often enables us to detect among remotely ancient and distant tribes the traces of connected civilization. How, on such grounds, do savage and civilized tribes appear to stand related, within the various groups of mankind connected historically by the possession of kindred languages?

The Semitic family, which represents one of the oldest known civilizations of the world, includes Arabs, Jews, Phœnicians, Syrians, &c., and has an earlier as well as a later connexion in North Africa. This family takes in some rude tribes, but none which would be classed as savages. The Aryan family has existed in Asia and Europe certainly for many thousand years, and there are well-known and well-marked traces of its early barbaric condition, which has perhaps survived with least change among secluded tribes in the valleys of the Hindu Kush and Himalaya. There seems, again, no known case of any full Aryan tribe having become savage. The Gypsies and other outcasts are, no doubt, partly Aryan in blood, but their degraded condition is not savagery. In India there are tribes Aryan by language, but whose physique is rather of indigenous type, and whose ancestry is mainly from indigenous stocks with more or less mixture of the dominant Hindu. Some tribes coming under this category, as among the Bhils and Kulis of the Bombay Presidency, speak dialects which are Hindi in vocabulary at least, whether or not in grammatical structure, and yet the people themselves are lower in culture than some Hinduized nations who have retained their original Dravidian speech, the Tamils for instance. But these all appear to stand at higher stages of civilization than any wild forest tribes of the peninsula who can be reckoned as nearly savages; all such are non-Aryan both in blood and speech.[32] In Ceylon, however, we have the remarkable phenomenon of men leading a savage life while speaking an Aryan dialect. This is the wild part of the race of Veddas or 'hunters,' of whom a remnant still inhabit the forest land. These people are dark-skinned and flat-nosed, slight of frame, and very small of skull, and five feet is an average man's height. They are a shy, harmless, simple people, living principally by hunting; they lime birds, take fish by poisoning the water, and are skilful in getting wild honey; they have bows with iron-pointed arrows, which, with their hunting-dogs, are their most valuable possessions. They dwell in caves or bark huts, and their very word for a house is Singhalese for a hollow tree (*rukula*); a patch of bark was formerly their dress, but now a bit of linen hangs to their waist-cords; their planting of patches of ground is said to be recent. They count on their fingers, and produce fire with the simplest kind of fire-drill twirled by hand. They are most truthful and honest. Their monogamy and conjugal fidelity contrast strongly with the opposite habits of the more civilized Singhalese. A remarkable Vedda marriage custom sanctioned a man's taking his younger (not elder) sister as his wife; sister-marriage existing among the Singhalese, but being confined to the royal family. Mistaken statements have been made as to the Veddas having no religion, no personal names, no language. Their religion, in fact, corresponds with the animism of the ruder tribes of India; some of their names are remarkable as being Hindu, but not in use among the modern Singhalese; their language is a Singhalese dialect. There is no doubt attaching to the usual opinion that the Veddas are in the main descended from the 'yakkos' or demons; i.e. from the indigenous tribes of the island. Legend and language concur to make probable an admixture of Aryan blood accompanying the adoption of Aryan speech, but the evidence of bodily characteristics shows the Vedda race to be principally of indigenous pre-Aryan type.[33]

The Tatar family of Northern Asia and Europe (Turanian, if the word be used in a restricted sense) displays evidence of quite a different kind. This wide-lying group of tribes and nations has members nearly or quite touching the savage level in ancient and even modern times, such as Ostyaks, Tunguz, Samoyeds, Lapps, while more or less high ranges of culture are represented by Mongols, Turks, and Hungarians. Here, however, it is unquestionable that the rude tribes represent the earlier condition of the Tatar race at large, from which its more mixed and civilized peoples, mostly by adopting the foreign culture of Buddhist, Moslem, and Christian nations, and partly by internal development, are well known to have risen. The ethnology of South-Eastern Asia is somewhat obscure; but if we may classify under one heading the native races of Siam, Burma, &c., the wilder tribes may be considered as representing earlier conditions, for the higher culture of this region is obviously foreign, especially of Buddhist origin. The Malay race is also remarkable for the range of civilization represented by tribes classed as belonging to it. If the wild tribes of the Malayan peninsula and Borneo be compared with the semi-civilized nations of Java and Sumatra, it appears that part of the race survives to represent an early savage state, while part is found in possession of a civilization which the first glance shows to have been mostly borrowed from Hindu and Moslem sources. Some forest tribes of the peninsula seem to be representatives of the Malay race at its lowest level of culture, how far original and how far degraded it is not easy to say. Among them the very rude Orang Sabimba, who have no agriculture and no boats, give a remarkable account of themselves, that they are descendants of shipwrecked Malays from the Bugis country, but were so harassed by pirates that they gave up civilization and cultivation, and vowed not to eat fowls, which betrayed them by their crowing. So they plant nothing, but eat wild fruit and vegetables, and all animals but the fowl. This, if at all founded on fact, is an interesting case of degeneration. But savages usually invent myths to account for peculiar habits, as where, in the same district, the Biduanda Kallang account for their not cultivating the ground by the story that their ancestors vowed not to make plantations. Another rude people of the Malay peninsula are the Jakuns, a simple, kindly race, among whom some trace their pedigree to a pair of white monkeys, while others declare that they are descendants of white men; and indeed there is some ground for supposing these latter to be really of mixed race, for they use a few Portuguese words, and a report exists of some refugees having settled up the country.[34] The Melanesians, Papuans, and Australians represent grades of savagery spread each over its own vast area in a comparatively homogeneous way. Lastly, the relations of savagery to higher conditions are remarkable, but obscure, on the American continents. There are several great linguistic families whose members were discovered in a savage state throughout; such are the Esquimaux, Algonquin, and Guarani groups. On the other hand there were three apparently unconnected districts of semi-civilization reaching a high barbaric level, viz., in Mexico and Central America, Bogota, and Peru. Between these higher and lower conditions were races at the level of the Natchez of Louisiana and the Apalaches of Florida. Linguistic connexion is not unknown between the more advanced peoples and the lower races around them.[35] But definite evidence showing the higher culture to have arisen from the lower, or the lower to have fallen from the higher, is scarcely forthcoming. Both operations may in degree have happened.

It is apparent, from such general inspection of this ethnological problem, that it would repay a far closer study than it has as yet received. As the evidence stands at present, it appears that when in any race some branches much excel the rest in culture, this more often happens by elevation than by subsidence. But this elevation is much more apt to be produced by foreign than by native action. Civilization is a plant much oftener propagated than developed. As regards the lower races, this accords with the results of European intercourse with savage tribes during the last three or four centuries; so far as these tribes have survived the process, they have assimilated more or less of European Culture and risen towards the European level, as in Polynesia, South Africa, South America. Another important point becomes manifest from this ethnological survey. The fact, that during so many thousand years of known existence, neither the Aryan nor the Semitic race appears to have thrown off any direct savage offshoot, tells, with some force, against the probability of degradation to the savage level ever happening from high-level civilization.

With regard to the opinions of older writers on early civilization, whether progressionists or degenerationists, it must be borne in mind that the evidence at their disposal fell far short of even the miserably imperfect data now accessible. Criticizing an 18th century ethnologist is like criticizing an 18th century geologist. The older writer may have been far abler than his modern critic, but he had not the same materials. Especially he wanted the guidance of Prehistoric Archæology, a department of research only established on a scientific footing within the last few years. It is essential to gain a clear view of the bearing of this newer knowledge on the old problem.

Chronology, though regarding as more or less fictitious the immense dynastic schemes of the Egyptians, Hindus, and Chinese, passing as they do into mere ciphering-book sums with years for units, nevertheless admits that existing monuments carry back the traces of comparatively high civilization to a distance of above five thousand years. By piecing together Eastern and Western documentary evidence it seems that the great religious divisions of the Aryan race, to which modern Brahmanism, Zarathustrism, and Buddhism are due, belong to a period of remotely ancient history. Even if we cannot hold, with Professor Max Müller, in the preface to his translation of the 'Rig Veda,' that this collection of Aryan hymns 'will take and maintain for ever its position as the most ancient of books in the library of mankind,' and if we do not admit the stringency of his reckonings of its date in centuries B.C., yet we must grant that he shows cause to refer its composition to a very ancient period, where it then proves that a comparatively high barbaric culture already existed. The linguistic argument for the remotely ancient common origin of the Indo-European nations, in a degree as to their bodily descent, and in a greater degree as to their civilization, tends toward the same result. So it is again with Egypt. The calculations of Egyptian dynasties in thousands of years, however disputable in detail, are based on facts which at any rate authorize the reception of a long chronology. To go no further than the identification of two or three Egyptian names mentioned in Biblical and Classical history, we gain a strong impression of remote antiquity. Such are the names of Shishank; of the Psammitichos line, whose obelisks are to be seen in Rome; of Tirhakah, King of Ethiopia, whose nurse's coffin is in the Florence Museum; of the city of Rameses, plainly connected with that great Ramesside line which Egyptologists call the 19th Dynasty. Here, before classic culture had arisen, the culture of Egypt culminated, and behind this time lies the somewhat less advanced age of the Pyramid kings, and behind this again the indefinite lapse of ages which such a civilization required for its production. Again, though no part of the Old Testament can satisfactorily prove for itself an antiquity of composition approaching that of the earliest Egyptian hieroglyphic inscriptions, yet all critics must admit that the older of the historical books give on the one hand contemporary documents showing considerable culture in the Semitic world at a date which in comparison with classic history is ancient; while on the other hand they afford evidence by way of chronicle, carrying back ages farther the record of a somewhat advanced barbaric civilization. Now if the development-theory is to account for phenomena such as these, its chronological demand must be no small one, and the more so when it is admitted that in the lower ranges of culture progress would be extremely slow in comparison with that which experience shows among nations already far advanced. On these conditions of the first appearance of the middle civilization being thrown back to distant antiquity, and of slow development being required to perform its heavy task in ages still more remote, Prehistoric Archæology cheerfully takes up the problem. And, indeed, far from being dismayed by the vastness of the period required on the narrowest computation, the prehistoric archæologist shows even too much disposition to revel in calculations of thousands of years, as a financier does in reckonings of thousands of pounds, in a liberal and maybe somewhat reckless way.

Prehistoric Archæology is fully alive to facts which may bear on degeneration in culture. Such are the colossal human figures of hewn stone in Easter Island, which may possibly have been shaped by the ancestors of the existing islanders, whose present resources, however, are quite unequal to the execution of such gigantic works.[36] A much more important case is that of the former inhabitants of the Mississippi Valley. In districts where the native tribes known in modern times rank as savages, there formerly dwelt a race whom ethnologists call the Mound-Builders, from the amazing extent of their mounds and enclosures, of which there is a single group occupying an area of four square miles. The regularity of the squares and circles and the repetition of enclosures similar in dimensions, raise interesting questions as to the methods by which these were planned out. To have constructed such works the Mound-Builders must have been a numerous population, mainly subsisting by agriculture, and indeed vestiges of their ancient tillage are still to be found. They did not however in industrial arts approach the level of Mexico. For instance, their use of native copper, hammered into shape for cutting instruments, is similar to that of some of the savage tribes farther north. On the whole, judging by their earthworks, fields, pottery, stone implements and other remains, they seem to have belonged to those high savage or barbaric tribes of the Southern States, of whom the Creeks and Cherokees, as described by Bartram, may be taken as typical.[37] If any of the wild roving hunting tribes now found living near the huge earthworks of the Mound-Builders are the descendants of this somewhat advanced race, then a very considerable degradation has taken place. The question is an open one. The explanation of the traces of tillage may perhaps in this case be like that of the remains of old cultivation-terraces in Borneo, the work of Chinese colonists whose descendants have mostly been merged in the mass of the population and follow the native habits.[38] On the other hand, the evidence of locality may be misleading as to race. A traveller in Greenland, coming on the ruined stone buildings at Kakortok, would not argue justly that the Esquimaux are degenerate descendants of ancestors capable of such architecture, for in fact these are the remains of a church and baptistery built by the ancient Scandinavian settlers.[39] On the whole it is remarkable how little of colourable evidence of degeneration has been disclosed by archæology. Its negative evidence tells strongly the other way. As an instance may be quoted Sir John Lubbock's argument against the idea that tribes now ignorant of metallurgy and pottery formerly possessed but have since lost these arts. 'We may also assert, on a general proposition, that no weapons or instruments of metal have ever been found in any country inhabited by savages wholly ignorant of metallurgy. A still stronger case is afforded by pottery. Pottery is not easily destroyed; when known at all it is always abundant, and it possesses two qualities, namely, those of being easy to break and yet difficult to destroy, which render it very valuable in an archæological point of view. Moreover, it is in most cases associated with burials. It is, therefore, a very significant fact, that no fragment of pottery has ever been found in Australia, New Zealand, or in the Polynesian Islands.'[40] How different a state of things the popular degeneration-theory would lead us to expect is pointedly suggested by Sir Charles Lyell's sarcastic sentences in his 'Antiquity of Man.' Had the original stock of mankind, he argues, been really endowed with superior intellectual powers and inspired knowledge, while possessing the same improvable nature as their posterity, how extreme a point of advancement would they have reached. 'Instead of the rudest pottery or flint tools, so irregular in form as to cause the unpractised eye to doubt whether they afford unmistakable evidence of design, we should now be finding sculptured forms surpassing in beauty the masterpieces of Phidias or Praxiteles; lines of buried railways or electric telegraphs from which the best engineers of our day might gain invaluable hints; astronomical instruments and microscopes of more advanced construction than any known in Europe, and other indications of perfection in the arts and sciences, such as the nineteenth century has not yet witnessed. Still farther would the triumphs of inventive genius be found to have been carried, when the later deposits, now assigned to the ages of bronze and iron, were formed. Vainly should we be straining our imaginations to guess the possible uses and meaning of such relics— machines, perhaps, for navigating the air or exploring the depths of the ocean, or for calculating arithmetical problems beyond the wants or even the conceptions of living mathematicians.'[41]

The master-key to the investigation of man's primæval condition is held by Prehistoric Archæology. This key is the evidence of the Stone Age, proving that men of remotely ancient ages were in the savage state. Ever since the long-delayed recognition of M. Boucher de Perthes' discoveries (1841 and onward) of the flint implements in the Drift gravels of the Somme Valley, evidence has been accumulating over a wide European area to show that the ruder Stone Age, represented by implements of the Palæolithic or Drift type, prevailed among savage tribes of the Quaternary period, the contemporaries of the mammoth and the woolly rhinoceros, in ages for which Geology asserts an antiquity far more remote than History can avail to substantiate for the human race. Mr. John Frere had already written in 1797 respecting such flint instruments discovered at Hoxne in Suffolk. 'The situation in which these weapons were found may tempt us to refer them to a very remote period indeed, even beyond that of the present world.'[42] The vast lapse of time through which the history of London has represented the history of human civilization, is to my mind one of the most suggestive facts disclosed by archæology. There the antiquary, excavating but a few yards deep, may descend from the débris representing our modern life, to relics of the art and science of the Middle Ages, to signs of Norman, Saxon, Romano-British times, to traces of the higher Stone Age. And on his way from Temple Bar to the Great Northern Station he passes near the spot ('opposite to black Mary's near Grayes inn lane') where a Drift implement of black flint was found with the skeleton of an elephant by Mr. Conyers, about a century and a half ago, the relics side by side of the London mammoth and the London savage.[43] In the gravel-beds of Europe, the laterite of India, and other more superficial localities, where relics of the Palæolithic Age are found, what principally testifies to man's condition is the extreme rudeness of his stone implements, and the absence of even edge-grinding. The natural inference that this indicates a low savage state is confirmed in the caves of Central France. There a race of men, who have left indeed really artistic portraits of themselves and the reindeer and mammoths they lived among, seem, as may be judged from the remains of their weapons, implements, &c., to have led a life somewhat of Esquimaux type, but lower by the want of domesticated animals. The districts where implements of the rude primitive Drift type are found are limited in extent. It is to ages later in time and more advanced in development, that the Neolithic or Polished Stone Period belonged, when the manufacture of stone instruments was much improved, and grinding and polishing were generally introduced. During the long period of prevalence of this state of things, Man appears to have spread almost over the whole habitable earth. The examination of district after district of the world has now all but established a universal rule that the Stone Age (bone or shell being the occasional substitutes for stone) underlies the Metal Age everywhere. Even the districts famed in history as seats of ancient civilization show, like other regions, their traces of a yet more archaic Stone Age. Asia Minor, Egypt, Palestine, India, China, furnish evidence from actual specimens, historical mentions, and survivals, which demonstrate the former prevalence of conditions of society which have their analogues among modern savage tribes.[44] The Duke of Argyll, in his 'Primeval Man,' while admitting the Drift implements as having been the ice hatchets and rude knives of low tribes of men inhabiting Europe toward the end of the Glacial Period, concludes thence 'that it would be about as safe to argue from these implements as to the condition of Man at that time in the countries of his Primeval Home, as it would be in our own day to argue from the habits and arts of the Eskimo as to the state of civilization in London or in Paris.'[45] The progress of Archæology for years past, however, has been continually cutting away the ground on which such an argument as this can stand, till now it is all but utterly driven off the field. Where now is the district of the earth that can be pointed to as the 'Primeval Home' of Man, and that does not show by rude stone implements buried in its soil the savage condition of its former inhabitants? There is scarcely a known province of the world of which we cannot say certainly, savages once dwelt here, and if in such a case an ethnologist asserts that these savages were the descendants or successors of a civilized nation, the burden of proof lies on him. Again, the Bronze Age and the Iron Age belong in great measure to history, but their relation to the Stone Age proves the soundness of the judgement of Lucretius, when, attaching experience of the present to memory and inference from the past, he propounded what is now a tenet of archæology, the succession of the Stone, Bronze, and Iron Ages:

'Arma antiqua manus ungues dentesque fuerunt,

Et lapides et item silvarum fragmina rami

Posterius ferri vis est ærisque reperta,

Et prior æris erat quam ferri cognitus usus.'[46]

Throughout the various topics of Prehistoric Archæology, the force and convergence of its testimony upon the development of culture are overpowering. The relics discovered in gravel-beds, caves, shell-mounds, terramares, lake-dwellings, earthworks, the results of an exploration of the superficial soil in many countries, the comparison of geological evidence, of historical documents, of modern savage life, corroborate and explain one another. The megalithic structures, menhirs, cromlechs, dolmens, and the like, only known to England, France, Algeria, as the work of races of the mysterious past, have been kept up as matters of modern construction and recognized purpose among the ruder indigenous tribes of India. The series of ancient lake-settlements which must represent so many centuries of successive population fringing the shores of the Swiss lakes, have their surviving representatives among the rude tribes of the East Indies, Africa, and South America. Outlying savages are still heaping up shell-mounds like those of far-past Scandinavian antiquity. The burial mounds still to be seen in civilized countries have served at once as museums of early culture and as proofs of its savage or barbaric type. It is enough, without entering farther here into subjects fully discussed in modern special works, to claim the general support given to the development-theory of culture by Prehistoric Archæology. It was with a true appreciation of the bearings of this science that one of its founders, the venerable Professor Sven Nilsson, declared in 1843 in the Introduction to his 'Primitive Inhabitants of Scandinavia,' that we are 'unable properly to understand the significance of the antiquities of any individual country without at the same time clearly realizing the idea that they are the fragments of a progressive series of civilization, and that the human race has always been, and still is, steadily advancing in civilization.'[47]

Enquiry into the origin and early development of the material arts, as judged of by comparing the various stages at which they are found existing, leads to a corresponding result. Not to take this argument up in its full range, a few typical details may serve to show its general character. Amongst the various stages of the arts, it is only a minority which show of themselves by mere inspection whether they are in the line of progress or of decline. Most such facts may be compared to an Indian's canoe, stem and stern alike, so that one cannot tell by looking at it which way it is set to go. But there are some which, like our own boats, distinctly point in the direction of their actual course. Such facts are pointers in the study of civilization, and in every branch of the enquiry should be sought out. A good example of these pointer-facts is recorded by Mr. Wallace. In Celebes, where the bamboo houses are apt to lean with the prevalent west wind, the natives have found out that if they fix some crooked timbers in the sides of the house, it will not fall. They choose such accordingly, the crookedest they can find, but they do not know the rationale of the contrivance, and have not hit on the idea that straight poles fixed slanting would have the same effect in making the structure rigid.[48] In fact, they have gone halfway toward inventing what builders call a 'strut.' but have stopped short. Now the mere sight of such a house would show that the plan is not a remnant of higher architecture, but a half-made invention. This is a fact in the line of progress, but not of decline. I have mentioned elsewhere a number of similar cases; thus the adaptation of a cord to the fire-drill is obviously an improvement on the simpler instrument twirled by hand, and the use of the spindle for making thread is an improvement on the clumsier art of hand-twisting;[49] but to reverse this position, and suppose the hand-drill to have come into use by leaving off the use of the cord of the cord-drill, or that people who knew the use of the spindle left it off and painfully twisted their thread by hand, is absurd. Again, the appearance of an art in a particular locality where it is hard to account for it as borrowed from elsewhere, and especially if it concerns some special native product, is evidence of its being a native invention. Thus, what people can claim the invention of the hammock, or the still more admirable discovery of the extraction of the wholesome cassava from the poisonous manioc, but the natives of the South American and West Indian districts to which these things belong? As the isolated possession of an art goes to prove its invention where it is found, so the absence of an art goes to prove that it was never present. The onus probandi is on the other side; if anyone thinks that the East African's ancestors had the lamp and the potter's wheel, and that the North American Indians once possessed the art of making beer from their maize like the Mexicans, but that these arts have been lost, at any rate let him show cause for such an opinion. I need not, perhaps, go so far as a facetious ethnological friend of mine, who argues that the existence of savage tribes who do not kiss their women is a proof of primæval barbarism, for, he says, if they had ever known the practice they could not possibly have forgotten it. Lastly and principally, as experience shows us that arts of civilized life are developed through successive stages of improvement, we may assume that the early development of even savage arts came to pass in a similar way, and thus, finding various stages of an art among the lower races, we may arrange these stages in a series probably representing their actual sequence in history. If any art can be traced back among savage tribes to a rudimentary state in which its invention does not seem beyond their intellectual condition, and especially if it may be produced by imitating nature or following nature's direct suggestion, there is fair reason to suppose the very origin of the art to have been reached.

Professor Nilsson, looking at the remarkable similarity of the hunting and fishing instruments of the lower races of mankind, considers them to have been contrived instinctively by a sort of natural necessity. As an example he takes the bow and arrow.[50] The instance seems an unfortunate one, in the face of the fact that the supposed bow-and-arrow-making instinct fails among the natives of Tasmania, to whom it would have been very useful, nor have the Australians any bow of their own invention. Even within the Papuan region, the bow so prevalent in New Guinea is absent, or almost so, from New Caledonia. It seems to me that Dr. Klemm, in his dissertations on Implements and Weapons, and Colonel Lane Fox, in his lectures on Primitive Warfare, take a more instructive line in tracing the early development of arts, not to a blind instinct, but to a selection, imitation, and gradual adaptation and improvement of objects and operations which Nature, the instructor of primæval man, sets before him. Thus Klemm traces the stages by which progress appears to have been made from the rough stick to the finished spear or club, from the natural sharp-edged or rounded stone to the artistically fashioned celt, spear-head, or hammer.[51] Lane Fox traces connexion through the various types of weapons, pointing out how a form once arrived at is repeated in various sizes, like the spear-head and arrow-point; how in rude conditions of the arts the same instrument serves different purposes, as where the Fuegians use their arrow-heads also for knives, and Kafirs carve with their assagais, till separate forms are adopted for special purposes; and how in the history of the striking, cutting, and piercing instruments used by mankind, a continuity may be traced, which indicates a gradual progressive development from the rudest beginnings to the most advanced improvements of modern skill. To show how far the early development of warlike arts may have been due to man's imitative faculty, he points out the analogies in methods of warfare among animals and men, classifying as defensive appliances hides, solid plates, jointed plates, scales; as offensive weapons, the piercing, striking, serrated, poisoned kinds, &c.; and under the head of stratagems, flight, concealment, leaders, outposts, war-cries, and so forth.[52]

The manufacture of stone implements is now almost perfectly understood by archæologists. The processes used by modern savages have been observed and imitated. Sir John Evans, for instance, by blows with a pebble, pressure with a piece of stag's horn, sawing with a flint-flake, boring with a stick and sand, and grinding on a stone surface, succeeds in reproducing all but the finest kinds of stone implements.[53] On thorough knowledge we are now able to refer in great measure the remarkable similarities of the stone scrapers, flake-knives, hatchets, spear- and arrow-heads, &c., as found in distant times and regions, to the similarity of natural models, of materials, and of requirements which belong to savage life. The history of the Stone Age is clearly seen to be one of development. Beginning with the natural sharp stone, the transition to the rudest artificially shaped stone implement is imperceptibly gradual, and onward from this rude stage much independent progress in different directions is to be traced, till the manufacture at last arrives at admirable artistic perfection, by the time that the introduction of metal is superseding it. So with other implements and fabrics, of which the stages are known through their whole course of development from the merest nature to the fullest art. The club is traced from the rudest natural bludgeon up to the weapon of finished shape and carving. Pebbles held in the hand to hammer with, and cutting-instruments of stone shaped or left smooth at one end to be held in the hand, may be seen in museums, hinting that the important art of fixing instruments in handles was the result of invention, not of instinct. The stone hatchet, used as a weapon, passes into the battle-axe. The spear, a pointed stick or pole, has its point hardened in the fire, and a further improvement is to fix on a sharp point of horn, bone, or chipped stone. Stones are flung by hand, and then by the sling, a contrivance widely but not universally known among savage tribes. From first to last in the history of war the spear or lance is grasped as a thrusting weapon. Its use as a missile no doubt began as early, but it has hardly survived so far in civilization. Thus used, it is most often thrown by the unaided arm, but a sling for the purpose is known to various savage tribes. The short cord with an eye used in the New Hebrides, and called a 'becket' by Captain Cook, and a whip-like instrument noticed in New Zealand, are used for spear-throwing. But the more usual instrument is a wooden handle, a foot or two long. This spear-thrower is known across the high northern districts of North America, among some tribes of South America, and among the Australians. These latter, it has been asserted, could not have invented it in their present state of barbarism. But the remarkable feature of the matter is that the spear-thrower belongs especially to savagery, and not to civilization. Among the higher nations the nearest approach to it seems to have been the classic amentum, a thong attached to the middle of the shaft of the javelin to throw it with. The highest people known to have used the spear-thrower proper were the nations of Mexico and Central America. Its existence among them is vouched for by representations in the mythological pictures, by its Mexican name 'atlatl,' and by a beautifully artistic specimen of the thing itself in the Christy Museum; but we do not hear of it as in practical use after the Spanish Conquest. In fact the history of the instrument seems in absolute opposition to the degradation-theory, representing as it does an invention belonging to the lower civilization, and scarcely able to survive beyond. Nearly the same may be said of the blow-tube, which as a serious weapon scarcely ranges above rude tribes of the East Indies and South America, though kept up in sport at higher levels. The Australian boomerang has been claimed as derived from some hypothetical high culture, whereas the transition-stages through which it is connected with the club are to be observed in its own country, while no civilized race possesses the weapon.

The use of spring traps of boughs, of switches to fillip small missiles with, and of the remarkable darts of the Pelew Islands, bent and made to fly by their own spring, indicate inventions which may have led to that of the bow, while the arrow is a miniature form of the javelin. The practice of poisoning arrows, after the manner of stings and serpents' fangs, is no civilized device, but a characteristic of lower life, which is generally discarded even at the barbaric stage. The art of narcotizing fish, remembered but not approved by high civilization, belongs to many savage tribes, who might easily discover it in any forest pool where a suitable plant had fallen in. The art of setting fences to catch fish at the ebb of the tide, so common among the lower races, is a simple device for assisting nature quite likely to occur to the savage, in whom sharp hunger is no mean ally of dull wit. Thus it is with other arts. Fire-making, cooking, pottery, the textile arts, are to be traced along lines of gradual improvement.[54] Music begins with the rattle and the drum, which in one way or another hold their places from end to end of civilization, while pipes and stringed instruments represent an advanced musical art which is still developing. So with architecture and agriculture. Complex, elaborate, and highly-reasoned as are the upper stages of these arts, it is to be remembered that their lower stages begin with mere direct imitation of nature, copying the shelters which nature provides, and the propagation of plants which nature performs. Without enumerating to the same purpose the remaining industries of savage life, it may be said generally that their facts resist rather than require a theory of degradation from higher culture. They agree with, and often necessitate, the same view of development which we know by experience to account for the origin and progress of the arts among ourselves.

In the various branches of the problem which will henceforward occupy our attention, that of determining the relation of the mental condition of savages to that of civilized men, it is an excellent guide and safeguard to keep before our minds the theory of development in the material arts. Throughout all the manifestations of the human intellect, facts will be found to fall into their places on the same general lines of evolution. The notion of the intellectual state of savages as resulting from decay of previous high knowledge, seems to have as little evidence in its favour as that stone celts are the degenerate successors of Sheffield axes, or earthen grave-mounds degraded copies of Egyptian pyramids. The study of savage and civilized life alike avail us to trace in the early history of the human intellect, not gifts of transcendental wisdom, but rude shrewd sense taking up the facts of common life and shaping from them schemes of primitive philosophy. It will be seen again and again, by examining such topics as language, mythology, custom, religion, that savage opinion is in a more or less rudimentary state, while the civilized mind still bears vestiges, neither few nor slight, of a past condition from which savages represent the least, and civilized men the greatest advance. Throughout the whole vast range of the history of human thought and habit, while civilization has to contend not only with survival from lower levels, but also with degeneration within its own borders, it yet proves capable of overcoming both and taking its own course. History within its proper field, and ethnography over a wider range, combine to show that the institutions which can best hold their own in the world gradually supersede the less fit ones, and that this incessant conflict determines the general resultant course of culture. I will venture to set forth in mythic fashion how progress, aberration, and retrogression in the general course of culture contrast themselves in my own mind. We may fancy ourselves looking on Civilization, as in personal figure she traverses the world; we see her lingering or resting by the way, and often deviating into paths that bring her toiling back to where she had passed by long ago; but, direct or devious, her path lies forward, and if now and then she tries a few backward steps, her walk soon falls into a helpless stumbling. It is not according to her nature, her feet were not made to plant uncertain steps behind her, for both in her forward view and in her onward gait she is of truly human type.

CHAPTER III.
SURVIVAL IN CULTURE.

> Survival and Superstition—Children's games—Games of chance—Traditional sayings—Nursery poems—Proverbs—Riddles—Significance and survival in Customs: sneezing-formula, rite of foundation-sacrifice, prejudice against saving a drowning man.

When a custom, an art, or an opinion is fairly started in the world, disturbing influences may long affect it so slightly that it may keep its course from generation to generation, as a stream once settled in its bed will flow on for ages. This is mere permanence of culture; and the special wonder about it is that the change and revolution of human affairs should have left so many of its feeblest rivulets to run so long. On the Tatar steppes, six hundred years ago, it was an offence to tread on the threshold or touch the ropes in entering a tent, and so it appears to be still.[55] Eighteen centuries ago Ovid mentions the vulgar Roman objection to marriages in May, which he not unreasonably explains by the occurrence in that month of the funeral rites of the Lemuralia:—

'Nec viduæ tædis eadem nec virginis apta

Tempora. Quæ nupsit, non diuturna fuit.

Hac quoque de causa, si te proverbia tangunt,

Mense malas Maio nubere volgus ait.'[56]

The saying that marriages in May are unlucky survives to this day in England, a striking example how an idea, the meaning of which has perished for ages, may continue to exist simply because it has existed.

Now there are thousands of cases of this kind which have become, so to speak, landmarks in the course of culture. When in the process of time there has come general change in the condition of a people, it is usual, notwithstanding, to find much that manifestly had not its origin in the new state of things, but has simply lasted on into it. On the strength of these survivals, it becomes possible to declare that the civilization of the people they are observed among must have been derived from an earlier state, in which the proper home and meaning of these things are to be found; and thus collections of such facts are to be worked as mines of historic knowledge. In dealing with such materials, experience of what actually happens is the main guide, and direct history has to teach us, first and foremost, how old habits hold their ground in the midst of a new culture which certainly would never have brought them in, but on the contrary presses hard to thrust them out. What this direct information is like, a single example may show. The Dayaks of Borneo were not accustomed to chop wood, as we do, by notching out V-shaped cuts. Accordingly, when the white man intruded among them with this among other novelties, they marked their disgust at the innovation by levying a fine on any of their own people who should be caught chopping in the European fashion; yet so well aware were the native wood-cutters that the white man's plan was an improvement on their own, that they would use it surreptitiously when they could trust one another not to tell.[57] The account is twenty years old, and very likely the foreign chop may have ceased to be an offence against Dayak conservatism, but its prohibition was a striking instance of survival by ancestral authority in the very teeth of common sense. Such a proceeding as this would be usually, and not improperly, described as a superstition; and, indeed, this name would be given to a large proportion of survivals, such for instance as may be collected by the hundred from books of folk-lore and occult science. But the term superstition now implies a reproach, and though this reproach may be often cast deservedly on fragments of a dead lower culture embedded in a living higher one, yet in many cases it would be harsh, and even untrue. For the ethnographer's purpose, at any rate, it is desirable to introduce such a term as 'survival,' simply to denote the historical fact which the word 'superstition' is now spoiled for expressing. Moreover, there have to be included as partial survivals the mass of cases where enough of the old habit is kept up for its origin to be recognizable, though in taking a new form it has been so adapted to new circumstances as still to hold its place on its own merits.

Thus it would be seldom reasonable to call the children's games of modern Europe superstitions, though many of them are survivals, and indeed remarkable ones. If the games of children and of grown-up people be examined with an eye to ethnological lessons to be gained from them, one of the first things that strikes us is how many of them are only sportive imitations of the serious business of life. As children in modern civilized times play at dining and driving horses and going to church, so a main amusement of savage children is to imitate the occupations which they will carry on in earnest a few years later, and thus their games are in fact their lessons. The Esquimaux children's sports are shooting with a tiny bow and arrow at a mark, and building little snow-huts, which they light up with scraps of lamp-wick begged from their mothers.[58] Miniature boomerangs and spears are among the toys of Australian children; and even as the fathers keep up as a recognized means of getting themselves wives the practice of carrying them off by violence, so playing at such Sabine marriage has been noticed as one of the regular games of the little native boys and girls.[59] Now it is quite a usual thing in the world for a game to outlive the serious practice of which it is an imitation. The bow and arrow is a conspicuous instance. Ancient and widespread in savage culture, we trace this instrument through barbaric and classic life and onward to a high mediæval level. But now, when we look on at an archery meeting, or go by country lanes at the season when toy bows and arrows are 'in' among the children, we see, reduced to a mere sportive survival, the ancient weapon which among a few savage tribes still keeps its deadly place in the hunt and the battle. The cross-bow, a comparatively late and local improvement on the longbow, has disappeared yet more utterly from practical use; but as a toy it is in full European service, and likely to remain so. For antiquity and wide diffusion in the world, through savage up to classic and mediæval times, the sling ranks with the bow and arrow. But in the middle ages it fell out of use as a practical weapon, and it was all in vain that the 15th century poet commended the art of slinging among the exercises of a good soldier:—

'Use eek the cast of stone, with slynge or honde:

It falleth ofte, yf other shot there none is,

Men harneysed in steel may not withstonde,

The multitude and mighty cast of stonys;

And stonys in effecte, are every where,

And slynges are not noyous for to beare.'[60]

Perhaps as serious a use of the sling as can now be pointed out without the limits of civilization is among the herdsmen of Spanish America, who sling so cleverly that the saying is they can hit a beast on either horn and turn him which way they will. But the use of the rude old weapon is especially kept up by boys at play, who are here again the representatives of remotely ancient culture.

As games thus keep up the record of primitive warlike arts, so they reproduce, in what are at once sports and little children's lessons, early stages in the history of childlike tribes of mankind. English children delighting in the imitations of cries of animals and so forth, and New Zealanders playing their favourite game of imitating in chorus the saw hissing, the adze chipping, the musket roaring, and the other instruments making their proper noises, are alike showing at its source the imitative element so important in the formation of language.[61] When we look into the early development of the art of counting, and see the evidence of tribe after tribe having obtained numerals through the primitive stage of counting on their fingers, we find a certain ethnographic interest in the games which teach this earliest numeration. The New Zealand game of 'ti' is described as played by counting on the fingers, a number being called by one player, and he having instantly to touch the proper finger; while in the Samoan game one player holds out so many fingers, and his opponent must do the same instantly or lose a point.[62] These may be native Polynesian games, or they may be our own children's games borrowed. In the English nursery the child learns to say how many fingers the nurse shows, and the appointed formula of the game is '*Buck, Buck*, how many horns do I hold up?' The game of one holding up fingers and the others holding up fingers to match is mentioned in Strutt. We may see small schoolboys in the lanes playing at the guessing-game, where one gets on another's back and holds up fingers, the other must guess how many. It is interesting to notice the wide distribution and long permanence of these trifles in history when we read the following passage from Petronius Arbiter, written in the time of Nero:—'Trimalchio, not to seem moved by the loss, kissed the boy and bade him get up on his back. Without delay the boy climbed on horseback on him, and slapped him on the shoulders with his hand, laughing and calling out '*bucca, bucca*, quot sunt hic?'[63] The simple counting-games played with the fingers must not be confounded with the addition-game, where each player throws out a hand, and the sum of all the fingers shown has to be called, the successful caller scoring a point; each should call the total before he sees his adversary's hand, so that the skill lies especially in shrewd guessing. This game affords endless amusement to Southern Europe, where it is known in Italian as 'morra,' and in French as 'mourre,' and it is popular in China under the name of *ts'ai mei*, or 'guess how many!' So peculiar a game would hardly have been invented twice over in Europe and Asia, and as the Chinese term does not appear to be ancient, we may take it as likely that the Portuguese merchants introduced the game into China, as they certainly did into Japan. The ancient Egyptians, as their sculptures show, used to play at some kind of finger-game, and the Romans had their finger-flashing, 'micare digitis,' at which butchers used to gamble with their customers for bits of meat. It is not clear whether these were morra or some other games.[64]

When Scotch lads, playing at the game of 'tappie-tousie,' take one another by the forelock and say, 'Will ye be my man?'[65] they know nothing of the old symbolic manner of receiving a bondman which they are keeping up in survival. The wooden drill for making fire by friction, which so many rude or ancient races are known to have used as their common household instrument, and which lasts on among the modern Hindus as the time-honoured sacred means of lighting the pure sacrificial flame, has been found surviving in Switzerland as a toy among the children, who made fire with it in sport, much as Equimaux would have done in earnest.[66] In

Gothland it is on record that the ancient sacrifice of the wild boar has actually been carried on into modern time in sportive imitation, by lads in masquerading clothes with their faces blackened and painted, while the victim was personated by a boy rolled up in furs and placed upon a seat, with a tuft of pointed straws in his mouth to imitate the bristles of the boar.[67] One innocent little child's sport of our own time is strangely mixed up with an ugly story of about a thousand years ago. The game in question is thus played in France:—The children stand in a ring, one lights a spill of paper and passes it on to the next, saying, 'petit bonhomme vit encore,' and so on round the ring, each saying the words and passing on the flame as quickly as may be, for the one in whose hands the spill goes out has to pay a forfeit, and it is then proclaimed that 'petit bonhomme est mort.' Grimm mentions a similar game in Germany, played with a burning stick, and Halliwell gives the nursery rhyme which is said with it when it is played in England:—

'Jack's alive and in very good health,

If he dies in your hand you must look to yourself.'

Now, as all readers of Church history know, it used to be a favourite engine of controversy for the adherents of an established faith to accuse heretical sects of celebrating hideous orgies as the mysteries of their religion. The Pagans told these stories of the Jews, the Jews told them of the Christians, and Christians themselves reached a bad eminence in the art of slandering religious opponents whose moral life often seems in fact to have been exceptionally pure. The Manichæans were an especial mark for such aspersions, which were passed on to a sect considered as their successors— the Paulicians, whose name reappears in the middle ages, in connexion with the Cathari. To these latter, apparently from an expression in one of their religious formulas, was given the name of Boni Homines, which became a recognized term for the Albigenses. It is clear that the early Paulicians excited the anger of the orthodox by objecting to sacred images, and calling those who venerated them idolaters; and about A.D. 700, John of Osun, Patriarch of Armenia, wrote a diatribe against the sect, urging accusations of the regular anti-Manichæan type, but with a peculiar feature which brings his statement into the present singular connexion. He declares that they blasphemously call the orthodox 'image-worshippers;' that they themselves worship the sun; that, moreover, they mix wheaten flour with the blood of infants and therewith celebrate their communion, and 'when they have slain by the worst of deaths a boy, the first-born of his mother, thrown from hand to hand among them by turns, they venerate him in whose hand the child expires, as having attained to the first dignity of the sect.' To explain the correspondence of these atrocious details with the nursery sport, it is perhaps the most likely supposition, not that the game of 'Petit Bonhomme' keeps up a recollection of a legend of the Boni Homines, but that the game was known to the children of the eighth century much as it is now, and that the Armenian Patriarch simply accused the Paulicians of playing at it with live babes.[68]

It may be possible to trace another interesting group of sports as survivals from a branch of savage philosophy, once of high rank though now fallen into merited decay. Games of chance correspond so closely with arts of divination belonging already to savage culture, that there is force in applying to several such games the rule that the serious practice comes first, and in time may dwindle to the sportive survival. To a modern educated man, drawing lots or tossing up a coin is an appeal to chance, that is, to ignorance; it is committing the decision of a question to a mechanical process, itself in no way unnatural or even extraordinary, but merely so difficult to follow that no one can say beforehand what will come of it. But we also know that this scientific doctrine of chance is not that of early civilization, which has little in common with the mathematician's theory of probabilities, but much in common with such sacred divination as the choice of Matthias by lot as a twelfth apostle, or, in a later age, the Moravian Brethren's rite of choosing wives for their young men by casting lots with prayer. It was to no blind chance that the Maoris looked when they divined by throwing up lots to find a thief among a suspected company;[69] or the Guinea negroes when they went to the fetish-priest, who shuffled his bundle of little strips of leather and gave his sacred omen.[70] The crowd with uplifted hands pray to the gods, when the heroes cast lots in the cap of Atreides Agamemnon, to know who shall go forth to do battle with Hektor and help the well-greaved Greeks.[71] With prayer to the gods, and looking up to heaven, the German priest or father, as Tacitus relates, drew three lots from among the marked fruit-tree twigs scattered on a pure white garment, and interpreted the answer from their signs.[72] As in ancient Italy oracles gave responses by graven lots,[73] so the modern Hindus decide disputes by casting lots in front of a temple, appealing to the gods with cries of 'Let justice be shown! Show the innocent!'[74]

The uncivilized man thinks that lots or dice are adjusted in their fall with reference to the meaning he may choose to attach to it, and especially he is apt to suppose spiritual beings standing over the diviner or the gambler, shuffling the lots or turning up the dice to make them give their answers. This view held its place firmly in the middle ages, and later in history we still find games of chance looked on as results of supernatural operation. The general change from mediæval to modern notions in this respect is well shown in a remarkable work published in 1619, which seems to have done much toward bringing the change about. Thomas Gataker, a Puritan minister, in his treatise 'Of the Nature and Use of Lots,' states, in order to combat them, the following among the current objections made against games of chance:—'Lots may not be used but with great reverence, because the disposition of them commeth immediately from God' ... 'the nature of a Lot, which is affirmed to bee a worke of Gods speciall and immediate providence, a sacred oracle, a divine judgement or sentence: the light use of it therefore to be an abuse of Gods name; and so a sinne against the third Commandement.' Gataker, in opposition to this, argues that 'to expect the issue and event of it, as by ordinarie meanes from God, is common to all actions: to expect it by an immediate and extraordinarie worke is no more lawfull here than elsewhere, yea is indeed mere superstition.'[75] It took time, however, for this opinion to become prevalent in the educated world. After a lapse of forty years, Jeremy Taylor could still bring out a remnant of the older notion, in the course of a generally reasonable argument in favour of games of chance when played for refreshment and not for money. 'I have heard,' he says, 'from them that have skill in such things, there are such strange chances, such promoting of a hand by fancy and little arts of geomancy, such constant winning on one side, such unreasonable losses on the other, and these strange contingencies produce such horrible effects, that it is not improbable that God hath permitted the conduct of such games of chance to the devil, who will order them so where he can do most mischief; but, without the instrumentality of money, he could do nothing at all.'[76] With what vitality the notion of supernatural interference in games of chance even now survives in Europe, is well shown by the still flourishing arts of gambler's magic. The folk-lore of our own day continues to teach that a Good Friday's egg is to be carried for luck in gaming, and that a turn of one's chair will turn one's fortune; the Tyrolese knows the charm for getting from the devil the gift of winning at cards and dice; there is still a great sale on the continent for books which show how to discover, from dreams, good numbers for the lottery; and the Lusatian peasant will even hide his lottery-tickets under the altar-cloth that they may receive the blessing with the sacrament, and so stand a better chance of winning.[77]

Arts of divination and games of chance are so similar in principle, that the very same instrument passes from one use to the other. This appears in the accounts, very suggestive from this point of view, of the Polynesian art of divination by spinning the 'niu' or coco-nut. In the Tongan Islands, in Mariner's time, the principal purpose for which this was solemnly performed was to enquire if a sick person would recover; prayer was made aloud to the patron god of the family to direct the nut, which was then spun, and its direction at rest indicated the intention of the god. On other occasions, when the coco-nut was merely spun for amusement, no prayer was made, and no credit given to the result. Here the serious and the sportive use of this rudimentary teetotum are found together. In the

Samoan Islands, however, at a later date, the Rev. G. Turner finds the practice passed into a different stage. A party sit in a circle, the coco-nut is spun in the middle, and the oracular answer is according to the person towards whom the monkey-face of the fruit is turned when it stops; but whereas formerly the Samoans used this as an art of divination to discover thieves, now they only keep it up as a way of casting lots, and as a game of forfeits.[78] It is in favour of the view of serious divination being the earlier use, to notice that the New Zealanders, though they have no coco-nuts, keep up a trace of the time when their ancestors in the tropical islands had them and divined with them; for it is the well-known Polynesian word 'niu,' i.e. coco-nut, which is still retained in use among the Maoris for other kinds of divination, especially that performed with sticks. Mr. Taylor, who points out this curiously neat piece of ethnological evidence, records another case to the present purpose. A method of divination was to clap the hands together while a proper charm was repeated; if the fingers went clear in, it was favourable, but a check was an ill omen; on the question of a party crossing the country in war-time, the locking of all the fingers, or the stoppage of some or all, were naturally interpreted to mean clear passage, meeting a travelling party, or being stopped altogether. This quaint little symbolic art of divination seems now only to survive as a game; it is called 'puni-puni.'[79] A similar connexion between divination and gambling is shown by more familiar instruments. The hucklebones or astragali were used in divination in ancient Rome, being converted into rude dice by numbering the four sides, and even when the Roman gambler used the tali for gambling, he would invoke a god or his mistress before he made his throw.[80] Such implements are now mostly used for play, but, nevertheless, their use for divination was by no means confined to the ancient world, for hucklebones are mentioned in the 17th century among the fortune-telling instruments which young girls divined for husbands with,[81] and Negro sorcerers still throw dice as a means of detecting thieves.[82] Lots serve the two purposes equally well. The Chinese gamble by lots for cash and sweetmeats, whilst they also seriously take omens by solemn appeals to the lots kept ready for the purpose in the temples, and professional diviners sit in the market-places, thus to open the future to their customers.[83] Playing-cards are still in European use for divination. That early sort known as 'tarots' which the French dealer's license to sell 'cartes et tarots' still keeps in mind, is said to be preferred by fortune-tellers to the common kind; for the tarot-pack, with its more numerous and complex figures, lends itself to a greater variety of omens. In these cases, direct history fails to tell us whether the use of the instrument for omen or play came first. In this respect, the history of the Greek 'kottabos' is instructive. This art of divination consisted in flinging wine out of a cup into a metal basin some distance off without spilling any, the thrower saying or thinking his mistress's name, and judging from the clear or dull splash of the wine on the metal what his fortune in love would be; but in time the magic passed out of the process, and it became a mere game of dexterity played for a prize.[84] If this be a typical case, and the rule be relied on that the serious use precedes the playful, then games of chance may be considered survivals in principle or detail from corresponding processes of magic—as divination in sport made gambling in earnest.

Seeking more examples of the lasting on of fixed habits among mankind, let us glance at a group of time-honoured traditional sayings, old saws which have a special interest as cases of survival. Even when the real signification of these phrases has faded out of men's minds, and they have sunk into sheer nonsense, or have been overlaid with some modern superficial meaning, still the old formulas are handed on, often gaining more in mystery than they lose in sense. We may hear people talk of 'buying a pig in a poke,' whose acquaintance with English does not extend to knowing what a poke is. And certainly those who wish to say that they have a great mind to something, and who express themselves by declaring that they have 'a month's mind' to it, can have no conception of the hopeless nonsense they are making of the old term of the 'month's mind,' which was really the monthly service for a dead man's soul, whereby he was kept in mind or remembrance. The proper sense of the phrase 'sowing his wild oats' seems generally lost in our modern use of it. No doubt it once implied that these ill weeds would spring up in later years, and how hard it would then be to root them out. Like the enemy in the parable, the Scandinavian Loki, the mischief-maker, is proverbially said in Jutland to sow his oats ('nu saaer Lokken sin havre'), and the name of 'Loki's oats' (Lokeshavre) is given in Danish to the wild oats (avena fatua).[85] Sayings which have their source in some obsolete custom or tale, of course lie especially open to such ill-usage. It has become mere English to talk of an 'unlicked cub' who 'wants licking into shape,' while few remember the explanation of these phrases from Pliny's story that bears are born as eyeless, hairless, shapeless lumps of white flesh, and have afterwards to be licked into form.[86]

Again, in relics of old magic and religion, we have sometimes to look for a deeper sense in conventional phrases than they now carry on their face, or for a real meaning in what now seems nonsense. How an ethnographical record may become embodied in a popular saying, a Tamil proverb now current in South India will show perfectly. On occasions when A hits B, and C cries out at the blow, the bystanders will say, "Tis like a Koravan eating asafœtida when his wife lies in!' Now a Koravan belongs to a low race in Madras, and is defined as 'gipsy, wanderer, ass-driver, thief, eater of rats, dweller in mat tents, fortune-teller, and suspected character;' and the explanation of the proverb is, that whereas native women generally eat asafœtida as strengthening medicine after childbirth, among the Koravans it is the husband who eats it to fortify himself on the occasion. This, in fact, is a variety of the world-wide custom of the 'couvade,' where at childbirth the husband undergoes medical treatment, in many cases being put to bed for days. It appears that the Koravans are among the races practising this quaint custom, and that their more civilized Tamil neighbours, struck by its oddity, but unconscious of its now-forgotten meaning, have taken it up into a proverb.[87] Let us now apply the same sort of ethnographical key to dark sayings in our own modern language. The maxim, a 'hair of the dog that bit you' was originally neither a metaphor nor a joke, but a matter-of-fact recipe for curing the bite of a dog; one of the many instances of the ancient homœopathic doctrine, that what hurts will also cure: it is mentioned in the Scandinavian Edda, 'Dog's hair heals dog's bite.'[88] The phrase 'raising the wind' now passes as humorous slang, but it once, in all seriousness, described one of the most dreaded of the sorcerer's arts, practised especially by the Finland wizards, of whose uncanny power over the weather our sailors have not to this day forgotten their old terror. The ancient ceremony or ordeal of passing through a fire or leaping over burning brands has been kept up so vigorously in the British Isles, that Jamieson's derivation of the phrase 'to haul over the coals' from this rite appears in no way far-fetched. It is not long since an Irishwoman in New York was tried for killing her child; she had made it stand on burning coals to find out whether it was really her own or a changeling.[89] The English nurse who says to a fretful child, 'You got out of bed wrong foot foremost this morning,' seldom or never knows the meaning of her saying; but this is still plain in the German folk-lore rule, that to get out of bed left foot first will bring a bad day,[90] one of the many examples of that simple association of ideas which connects right and left with good and bad respectively. To conclude, the phrase 'cheating the devil' seems to belong to that familiar series of legends where a man makes a compact with the fiend, but at the last moment gets off scot-free by the interposition of a saint, or by some absurd evasion—such as whistling the gospel he has bound himself not to say, or refusing to complete his bargain at the fall of the leaf, on the plea that the sculptured leaves in the church are still on their boughs. One form of the mediæval compact was for the demon, when he had taught his black art to a class of scholars, to seize one of them for his professional fee, by letting them all run for their lives and catching the last—a story obviously connected with another popular saying: 'devil take the hindmost.' But even at this game the stupid fiend may be cheated, as is told in the folk-lore of Spain and Scotland, in the legends of the Marqués de Villano and the Earl of Southesk, who attended the Devil's magic schools at Salamanca and Padua. The apt scholar only leaves the master his shadow to clutch as following hindmost in the race, and with this unsubstantial payment the demon must needs be satisfied, while the new-made magician goes forth free, but ever after shadowless.[91]

It seems a fair inference to think folk-lore nearest to its source is where it has its highest place and meaning. Thus, if some old rhyme or saying has in one place a solemn import in philosophy or religion, while elsewhere it lies at the level of the nursery, there is some ground for treating the serious version as the more original, and the playful one as its mere lingering survival. The argument is not safe, but yet is not to be quite overlooked. For instance, there are two poems kept in remembrance among the modern Jews, and printed at the end of their book of Passover services in Hebrew and English. One is that known as גדיא חד (Chad gadyâ): it begins, 'A kid, a kid, my father bought for two pieces of money;' and it goes on to tell how a cat came and ate the kid, and a dog came and bit the cat, and so on to the end.—'Then came the Holy One, blessed be He! and slew the angel of death, who slew the butcher, who killed the ox, that drank the water, that quenched the fire, that burnt the stick, that beat the dog, that bit the cat, that ate the kid, that my father bought for two pieces of money, a kid, a kid.' This composition is in the 'Sepher Haggadah,' and is looked on by some Jews as a parable concerning the past and future of the Holy Land. According to one interpretation, Palestine, the kid, is devoured by Babylon the cat; Babylon is overthrown by Persia, Persia by Greece, Greece by Rome, till at last the Turks prevail in the land; but the Edomites (i.e. the nations of Europe) shall drive out the Turks, the angel of death shall destroy the enemies of Israel, and his children shall be restored under the rule of Messiah. Irrespectively of any such particular interpretation, the solemnity of the ending may incline us to think that we really have the composition here in something like its first form, and that it was written to convey a mystic meaning. If so, then it follows that our familiar nursery tale of the old woman who couldn't get her kid (or pig) over the stile, and wouldn't get home till midnight, must be considered a broken-down adaptation of this old Jewish poem. The other composition is a counting-poem, and begins thus:

'Who knoweth one? I (saith Israel) know One:

One is God, who is over heaven and earth.

Who knoweth two? I (saith Israel) know two:

Two tables of the covenant; but One is our God who is over the heavens and the earth.'

(And so forth, accumulating up to the last verse, which is—)

'Who knoweth thirteen? I (saith Israel) know thirteen: Thirteen divine attributes, twelve tribes, eleven stars, ten commandments, nine months preceding childbirth, eight days preceding circumcision, seven days of the week, six books of the Mishnah, five books of the Law, four matrons, three patriarchs, two tables of the covenant; but One is our God who is over the heavens and the earth.'

This is one of a family of counting-poems, apparently held in much favour in mediæval Christian times, for they are not yet quite forgotten in country places. An old Latin version runs: 'Unus est Deus,' &c., and one of the still-surviving English forms begins, 'One's One all alone, and evermore shall be so,' thence reckoning on as far as 'Twelve the twelve apostles.' Here both the Jewish and Christian forms are or have been serious, so it is possible that the Jew may have imitated the Christian, but the nobler form of the Hebrew poem here again gives it a claim to be thought the earlier.[92]

The old proverbs brought down by long inheritance into our modern talk are far from being insignificant in themselves, for their wit is often as fresh, and their wisdom as pertinent, as it ever was. Beyond these practical qualities, proverbs are instructive for the place in ethnography which they occupy. Their range in civilization is limited; they seem scarcely to belong to the lowest tribes, but appear first in a settled form among some of the higher savages. The Fijians, who were found a few years since living in what archæologists might call the upper Stone Age, have some well-marked proverbs. They laugh at want of forethought by the saying that 'The Nakondo people cut the mast first' (i.e. before they had built the canoe); and when a poor man looks wistfully at what he cannot buy, they say, 'Becalmed, and looking at the fish.'[93] Among the list of the New Zealanders' 'whakatauki,' or proverbs, one describes a lazy glutton: 'Deep throat, but shallow sinews;' another says that the lazy often profit by the work of the industrious: 'The large chips made by Hardwood fall to the share of Sit-still;' a third moralizes that 'A crooked part of a stem of toetoe can be seen; but a crooked part in the heart cannot be seen.'[94] Among the Basutos of South Africa, 'Water never gets tired of running' is a reproach to chatterers; 'Lions growl while they are eating,' means that there are people who never will enjoy anything; 'The sowing-month is the headache-month,' describes those lazy folks who make excuses when work is to be done; 'The thief eats thunderbolts,' means that he will bring down vengeance from heaven on himself.[95] West African nations are especially strong in proverbial philosophy; so much so that Captain Burton amused himself through the rainy season at Fernando Po in compiling a volume of native proverbs,[96] among which there are hundreds at about as high an intellectual level as those of Europe. 'He fled from the sword and hid in the scabbard,' is as good as our 'Out of the frying-pan into the fire;' and 'He who has only his eyebrow for a cross-bow can never kill an animal,' is more picturesque, if less terse than our 'Hard words break no bones.' The old Buddhist aphorism, that 'He who indulges in enmity is like one who throws ashes to windward, which come back to the same place and cover him all over,' is put with less prose and as much point in the negro saying, 'Ashes fly back in the face of him who throws them.' When someone tries to settle an affair in the absence of the people concerned, the negroes will object that 'You can't shave a man's head when he is not there,' while, to explain that the master is not to be judged by the folly of his servant, they say, 'The rider is not a fool because the horse is.' Ingratitude is alluded to in 'The sword knows not the head of the smith' (who made it), and yet more forcibly elsewhere, 'When the calabash had saved them (in the famine), they said, let us cut it for a drinking-cup.' The popular contempt for poor men's wisdom is put very neatly in the maxim, 'When a poor man makes a proverb it does not spread,' while the very mention of making a proverb as something likely to happen, shows a land where proverb-making is still a living art. Transplanted to the West Indies, the African keeps up this art, as witness these sayings: 'Behind dog it is dog, but before dog it is Mr. Dog;' and 'Toute cabinette tini maringouin'—'Every cabin has its mosquito.'

The proverb has not changed its character in the course of history; but has retained from first to last a precisely definite type. The proverbial sayings recorded among the higher nations of the world are to be reckoned by tens of thousands, and have a large and well-known literature of their own. But though the range of existence of proverbs extends into the highest levels of civilization, this is scarcely true of their development. At the level of European culture in the middle ages, they have indeed a vast importance in popular education, but their period of actual growth seems already at an end. Cervantes raised the proverb-monger's craft to a pitch it never surpassed; but it must not be forgotten that the incomparable Sancho's wares were mostly heirlooms; for proverbs were even then sinking to remnants of an earlier condition of society. As such, they survive among ourselves, who go on using much the same relics of ancestral wisdom as came out of the squire's inexhaustible budget, old saws not to be lightly altered or made anew in our changed modern times. We can collect and use the old proverbs, but making new ones has become a feeble, spiritless imitation, like our attempts to invent new myths or new nursery rhymes.

Riddles start near proverbs in the history of civilization, and they travel on long together, though at last towards different ends. By riddles are here meant the old-fashioned problems with a real answer intended to be discovered, such as the typical enigma of the Sphinx, but not the modern verbal conundrums set in the traditional form of question and answer, as a way of bringing in a jest à propos of nothing. The original kind, which may be defined as 'sense-riddles,' are found at home among the upper savages, and range on into the lower and middle civilization; and while their growth stops at this level, many ancient specimens have lasted on in the modern nursery and by the cottage fireside. There is a plain reason why riddles should belong only to the higher grades of savagery; their making requires a fair power of ideal comparison, and knowledge must have made considerable advance before this process could become so familiar as to fall from earnest into sport. At last, in a far higher state of culture, riddles begin to be looked on as trifling, their growth ceases, and they only survive in remnants for children's play. Some examples chosen among various races, from savagery upwards, will show more exactly the place in mental history which the riddle occupies.

The following are specimens from a collection of Zulu riddles, recorded with quaintly simple native comments on the philosophy of the matter:— *Q.* 'Guess ye some men who are many and form a row; they dance the wedding-dance, adorned in white hip-dresses?' *A.* 'The teeth; we call them men who form a row, for the teeth stand like men who are made ready for a wedding-dance, that they may dance well. When we say, they are "adorned with white hip-dresses," we put that in, that people may not at once think of teeth, but be drawn away from them by thinking, "It is men who put on white hip-dresses," and continually have their thoughts fixed on men,' &c. *Q.* 'Guess ye a man who does not lie down at night: he lies down in the morning until the sun sets; he then awakes, and works all night; he does not work by day; he is not seen when he works?' *A.* 'The closing-poles of the cattle-pen.' *Q.* 'Guess ye a man whom men do not like to laugh, for it is known that his laughter is a very great evil, and is followed by lamentation, and an end of rejoicing. Men weep, and trees, and grass; and everything is heard weeping in the tribe where he laughs; and they say the man has laughed who does not usually laugh?' *A.* 'Fire. It is called a man that what is said may not be at once evident, it being concealed by the word "man." Men say many things, searching out the meaning in rivalry, and missing the mark. A riddle is good when it is not discernible at once,' &c.[97] Among the Basutos, riddles are a recognized part of education, and are set like exercises to a whole company of puzzled children. *Q.* 'Do you know what throws itself from the mountain top without being broken?' *A.* 'A waterfall.' *Q.* 'There is a thing that travels fast without legs or wings, and no cliff, nor river, nor wall can stop it?' *A.* 'The voice.' *Q.* 'Name the ten trees with ten flat stones on the top of them.' *A.* 'The fingers.' *Q.* 'Who is the little immovable dumb boy who is dressed up warm in the day and left naked at night?' *A.* 'The bed-clothes' peg.'[98] From East Africa, this Swahili riddle is an example: *Q.* 'My hen has laid among thorns?' *A.* 'A pineapple.'[99] From West Africa, this Yoruba one: 'A long slender trading woman who never gets to market?' *A*. 'A canoe (it stops at the landing-place).'[100] In Polynesia, the Samoan Islanders are given to riddles. *Q*. 'There are four brothers, who are always bearing about their father?' *A*. 'The Samoan pillow,' which is a yard of three-inch bamboo resting on four legs. *Q*. 'A white-headed man stands above the fence, and reaches to the heavens?' *A*. 'The smoke of the oven.' *Q*. 'A man who stands between two ravenous fish?' *A*. 'The tongue.'[101] (There is a Zulu riddle like this, which compares the tongue to a man living in the midst of enemies fighting.) The following are old Mexican enigmas: *Q*. 'What are the ten stones one has at his sides?' *A*. 'The finger-nails.' *Q*. 'What is it we get into by three parts and out of by one?' *A*. 'A shirt.' *Q*. 'What goes through a valley and drags its entrails after it?' *A*. 'A needle.'[102]

These riddles found among the lower races do not differ at all in nature from those that have come down, sometimes modernized in the setting, into the nursery lore of Europe. Thus Spanish children still ask, 'What is the dish of nuts that is gathered by day, and scattered by night?' (the stars.) Our English riddle of the pair of tongs: 'Long legs, crooked thighs, little head, and no eyes,' is primitive enough to have been made by a South Sea Islander. The following is on the same theme as one of the Zulu riddles: 'A flock of white sheep, On a red hill; Here they go, there they go; Now they stand still?' Another is the very analogue of one of the Aztec specimens: 'Old Mother Twitchett had but one eye, And a long tail which she let fly; And every time she went over a gap, She left a bit of her tail in a trap?'

So thoroughly does riddle-making belong to the mythologic stage of thought, that any poet's simile, if not too far-fetched, needs only inversion to be made at once into an enigma. The Hindu calls the Sun Saptâsva, i.e. 'seven-horsed,' while, with the same thought, the old German riddle asks, 'What is the chariot drawn by the seven white and seven black horses?' (the year, drawn by the seven days and nights of the week.[103]) Such, too, is the Greek riddle of the two sisters, Day and Night, who gave birth each to the other to be born of her again:

Εἰσὶ κασίγνηται διτταί, ὧν ἡ μία τίκτει

Τὴν ἑτέραν, αὐτὴ δὲ τεκοῦσ ὑπὸ τῆσδε τεκνοῦται;

and the enigma of Kleoboulos, with its other like fragments of rudimentary mythology:

Εἷς ὁ πατήρ, παῖδες δὲ δυώδεκα· τῶν δέ γ' ἑκάστῳ

Παῖδες ἔασι τριήκοντ' ἄνδιχα εἶδος ἔχουσαι·

Ἡι μὲν λευκαὶ ἔασιν ἰδεῖν, ἧ δ' αὖτε μέλαιναι·
Ἀθάνατοι δέ τ' ἐοῦσαι ἀποφθίνουσιν ἅπασαι.

'One is the father, and twelve the children, and, born unto each one,
Maidens thirty, whose form in twain is parted asunder,
White to behold on the one side, black to behold on the other,
All immortal in being, yet doomed to dwindle and perish.'[104]

Such questions as these may be fairly guessed now as in old times, and must be distinguished from that scarcer class which require the divination of some unlikely event to solve them. Of such the typical example is Samson's riddle, and there is an old Scandinavian one like it. The story is that Gestr found a duck sitting on her nest in an ox's horned skull, and thereupon propounded a riddle, describing with characteristic Northman's metaphor the ox with its horns fancied as already made into drinking-horns. The following translation does not exaggerate the quaintness of the original:—'Joying in children the bill-goose grew, And her building-timbers together drew; The biting grass-shearer screened her bed, With the maddening drink-stream overhead.'[105] Many of the old oracular responses are puzzles of precisely this kind. Such is the story of the Delphic oracle, which ordered Temenos to find a man with three eyes to guide the army, which injunction he fulfilled by meeting a one-eyed man on horseback.[106] It is curious to find this idea again in Scandinavia, where Odin sets King Heidrek a riddle, 'Who are they two that fare to the Thing with three eyes, ten feet, and one tail?' the answer being, the one-eyed Odin himself on his eight-footed horse Sleipnir.[107]

The close bearing of the doctrine of survival on the study of manners and customs is constantly coming into view in ethnographic research. It seems scarcely too much to assert, once for all, that meaningless customs must be survivals, that they had a practical, or at least ceremonial, intention when and where they first arose, but are now fallen into absurdity from having been carried on into a new state of society, where their original sense has been discarded. Of course, new customs introduced in particular ages may be ridiculous or wicked, but as a rule they have discernible motives. Explanations of this kind, by recourse to some forgotten meaning, seem on the whole to account best for obscure customs which some have set down to mere outbreaks of spontaneous folly. A certain Zimmermann, who published a heavy 'Geographical History of Mankind' in the 18th century, remarks as follows on the prevalence of similar nonsensical and stupid customs in distant countries:—'For if two clever heads may, each for himself, hit upon a clever invention or discovery, then it is far likelier, considering the much larger total of fools and blockheads, that like fooleries should be given to two far-distant lands. If, then, the inventive fool be likewise a man of importance and influence, as is, indeed, an extremely frequent case, then both nations adopt a similar folly, and then, centuries after, some historian goes through it to extract his evidence for the derivation of these two nations one from the other.'[108]

Strong views as to the folly of mankind seem to have been in the air about the time of the French Revolution, Lord Chesterfield was no doubt an extremely different person from our German philosopher, but they were quite at one as to the absurdity of customs. Advising his son as to the etiquette of courts, the Earl writes thus to him:—'For example, it is respectful to bow to the King of England, it is disrespectful to bow to the King of France; it is the rule to courtesy to the Emperor; and the prostration of the whole body is required by Eastern Monarchs. These are established ceremonies, and must be complied with; but why they were established, I defy sense and reason to tell us. It is the same among all ranks, where certain customs are received, and must necessarily be complied with, though by no means the result of sense and reason. As for instance, the very absurd, though almost universal custom of drinking people's healths. Can there be anything in the world less relative to any other man's health, than my drinking a glass of wine? Common sense, certainly, never pointed it out, but yet common sense tells me I must conform to it.'[109] Now, though it might be difficult enough to make sense of the minor details of court etiquette, Lord Chesterfield's example from it of the irrationality of mankind is a singularly unlucky one. Indeed, if any one were told to set forth in few words the relations of the people to their rulers in different states of society, he might answer that men grovel on their faces before the King of Siam, kneel on one knee or uncover before a European monarch, and shake the hand of the President of the United States as though it were a pump-handle. These are ceremonies at once intelligible and significant. Lord Chesterfield is more fortunate in his second instance, for the custom of drinking healths is really of obscure origin. Yet it is closely connected with an ancient rite, practically absurd indeed, but done with a conscious and serious intention which lands it quite outside the region of nonsense. This is the custom of pouring out libations and drinking at ceremonial banquets to gods and the dead. Thus the old Northmen drank the 'minni' of Thor, Odin, and Freya, and of kings likewise at their funerals. The custom did not die out with the conversion of the Scandinavian and Teutonic nations. Such formulas as 'God's minne!' 'a bowl to God in heaven!' are on record, while in like manner Christ, Mary, and the Saints were drunk to in place of heathen gods and heroes, and the habit of drinking to the dead and the living at the same feast and in similar terms goes far to prove here a common origin for both ceremonies. The 'minne' was at once love, memory, and the thought of the absent, and it long survived in England in the 'minnying' or 'mynde' days, on which the memory of the dead was celebrated by services or banquets. Such evidence as this fairly justifies the writers, older and newer, who have treated these ceremonial drinking usages as in their nature sacrificial.[110] As for the practice of simply drinking the health of living men, its ancient history reaches us from several districts inhabited by Aryan nations. The Greeks in symposium drank to one another, and the Romans adopted the habit (προπίνειν, propinare, Græco more bibere). The Goths cried 'hails!' as they pledged each other, as we have it in the curious first line of the verses 'De conviviis barbaris' in the Latin Anthology, which sets down the shouts of a Gothic drinking-bout of the fifth century or so, in words which still partly keep their sense to an English ear.

'Inter *eils* Goticum *scapiamatziaia drincan*

Non audet quisquam dignos educere versus.'

As for ourselves, though the old drinking salutation of 'wæs hæl?' is no longer vulgar English, the formula remains with us, stiffened into a noun. On the whole, there is presumptive though not conclusive evidence that the custom of drinking healths to the living is historically related to the religious rite of drinking to the gods and the dead.

Let us now put the theory of survival to a somewhat severe test, by seeking from it some explanation of the existence, in practice or memory, within the limits of modern civilized society, of three remarkable groups of customs which civilized ideas totally fail to account for. Though we may not succeed in giving clear and absolute explanations of their motives, at any rate it is a step in advance to be able to refer their origins to savage or barbaric antiquity. Looking at these customs from the modern practical point of view, one is ridiculous, the others are atrocious, and all are senseless. The first is the practice of salutation on sneezing, the second the rite of laying the foundations of a building on a human victim, the third the prejudice against saving a drowning man.

In interpreting the customs connected with sneezing, it is needful to recognize a prevalent doctrine of the lower races, of which a full account will be given in another chapter. As a man's soul is considered to go in and out of his body, so it is with other spirits, particularly such as enter into patients and possess them or afflict them with disease. Among the less cultured races, the connexion of this idea with sneezing is best shown among the Zulus, a people firmly persuaded that kindly or angry spirits of the dead hover about them, do them good or harm, stand visibly before them in dreams, enter into them, and cause diseases in them. The following particulars are abridged from the native statements taken down by Dr. Callaway:—When a Zulu sneezes, he will say, 'I am now blessed. The Idhlozi (ancestral spirit) is with me; it has come to me. Let me hasten and praise it, for it is it which causes me to sneeze!' So he praises the manes of his family, asking for cattle, and wives, and blessings. Sneezing is a sign that a sick person will be restored to health; he returns thanks after sneezing, saying, 'Ye people of ours, I have gained that prosperity which I wanted. Continue to look on me with favour!' Sneezing reminds a man that he should name the Itongo (ancestral spirit) of his people without delay, because it is the Itongo which causes him to sneeze, that he may perceive by sneezing that the Itongo is with him. If a man is ill and does not sneeze, those who come to him ask whether he has sneezed or not; if he has not sneezed, they murmur, saying, 'The disease is great!' If a child sneezes, they say to it, 'Grow!' it is a sign of health. So then, it is said, sneezing among black men gives a man strength to remember that the Itongo has entered into him and abides with him. The Zulu diviners or sorcerers are very apt to sneeze, which they regard as an indication of the presence of the spirits, whom they adore by saying, 'Makosi!' (i.e. lords or masters). It is a suggestive example of the transition of such customs as these from one religion to another, that the Amakosa, who used to call on their divine ancestor Utixo when they sneezed, since their conversion to Christianity say, 'Preserver, look upon me!' or, 'Creator of heaven and earth!'[111] Elsewhere in Africa, similar ideas are mentioned. Sir Thomas Browne, in his 'Vulgar Errors,' made well known the story that when the King of Monomotapa sneezed, acclamations of blessing passed from mouth to mouth through the city; but he should have mentioned that Godigno, from whom the original account is taken, said that this took place when the king drank, or coughed, or sneezed.[112] A later account from the other side of the continent is more to the purpose. In Guinea, in the last century, when a principal personage sneezed, all present fell on their knees, kissed the earth, clapped their hands, and wished him all happiness and prosperity.[113] With a different idea, the negroes of Old Calabar, when a child sneezes, will sometimes exclaim, 'Far from you!' with an appropriate gesture as if throwing off some evil.[114] Polynesia is another region where the sneezing salutation is well marked. In New Zealand, a charm was said to prevent evil when a child sneezed;[115] if a Samoan sneezed, the bystanders said, 'Life to you!'[116] while in the Tongan group a sneeze on the starting of an expedition was a most evil presage.[117] A curious American instance dates from Hernando de Soto's famous expedition into Florida, when Guachoya, a native chief, came to pay him a visit. 'While this was going on, the cacique Guachoya gave a great sneeze; the gentlemen who had come with him and were lining the walls of the hall among the Spaniards there all at once bowing their heads, opening their arms, and closing them again, and making other gestures of great veneration and respect, saluted him with different words, all directed to one end, saying, "The Sun guard thee, be with thee, enlighten thee, magnify thee, protect thee, favour thee, defend thee, prosper thee, save thee," and other like phrases, as the words came, and for a good space there lingered the murmur of these words among them, whereat the governor wondering said to the gentlemen and captains with him, "Do you not see that all the world is one?" This matter was well noted among the Spaniards, that among so barbarous a people should be used the same ceremonies, or greater, than among those who hold themselves to be very civilized. Whence it may be believed that this manner of salutation is natural among all nations, and not caused by a pestilence, as is vulgarly said,' &c.[118]

In Asia and Europe the sneezing superstition extends through a wide range of race, age, and country.[119] Among the passages relating to it in the classic ages of Greece and Rome, the following are some of the most characteristic,—the lucky sneeze of Telemachos in the Odyssey;[120] the soldier's sneeze and the shout of adoration to the god which rose along the ranks, and which Xenophon appealed to as a favourable omen;[121] Aristotle's remark that people consider a sneeze as divine (τὸν ηὲν πταρμὸν θεὸν ἡγούμεθα εἶναι), but not a cough,[122] &c.; the Greek epigram on the man with the long nose, who did not say Ζεῦ σῶσον when he sneezed, for the noise was too far off for him to hear;[123] Petronius Arbiter's mention of the custom of saying 'Salve!' to one who sneezed;[124] and Pliny's question, 'Cur sternutamentis salutamus?' apropos of which he remarks that even Tiberius Cæsar, that saddest of men, exacted this observance.[125] Similar rites of sneezing have long been observed in Eastern Asia.[126] When a Hindu sneezes, bystanders say, 'Live!' and the sneezer replies, 'With you!' It is an ill omen, to which among others the Thugs paid great regard on starting on an expedition, and which even compelled them to let the travellers with them escape.[127]

The Jewish sneezing formula is, 'Tobim chayim!' i.e. 'Good life!'[128] The Moslem says, 'Praise to Allah!' when he sneezes, and his friends compliment him with proper formulas, a custom which seems to be conveyed from race to race wherever Islam extends.[129] Lastly, the custom ranges through mediæval into modern Europe. To cite old German examples, 'Die Heiden nicht endorften niesen, dâ man doch sprichet "Nu helfiu Got?"' 'Wir sprechen, swer niuset, Got helfe dir.'[130] For a Norman French instance in England, the following lines (A.D. 1100) may serve, which show our old formula 'waes hæl!' ('may you be well!'—'wassail!') used also to avert being taken ill after a sneeze:—

'E pur une feyze esternuer

Tantot quident mal trouer,

Si *uesbeil* ne diez aprez.'[131]

In the 'Rules of Civility' (A.D. 1685, translated from the French) we read:—'If his lordship chances to sneeze, you are not to bawl out, "God bless you, sir," but, pulling off your hat, bow to him handsomely, and make that obsecration to yourself.'[132] It is noticed that Anabaptists and Quakers rejected these with other salutations, but they remained in the code of English good manners among high and low till half a century or so ago, and are so little forgotten now, that most people still see the point of the story of the fiddler and his wife, where his sneeze and her hearty 'God bless you!' brought about the removal of the fiddle case. 'Got hilf!' may still be heard in Germany, and 'Felicità!' in Italy.

It is not strange that the existence of these absurd customs should have been for ages a puzzle to curious enquirers. Especially the legend-mongers took the matter in hand, and their attempts to devise historical explanations are on record in a group of philosophic myths,—Greek, Jewish, Christian. Prometheus prays for the preservation of his artificial man, when it gives the first sign of life by a sneeze; Jacob prays that man's soul may not, as heretofore, depart from his body when he sneezes; Pope Gregory prays to avert the pestilence, in those days when the air was so deadly that he who sneezed died of it; and from these imaginary events legend declares that the use of the sneezing formulas was handed down. It is more to our purpose to notice the existence of a corresponding set of ideas and customs connected with gaping. Among the Zulus, repeated yawning and sneezing are classed together as signs of approaching spiritual possession.[133] The Hindu, when he gapes, must snap his thumb and finger, and repeat the name of some God, as Rama: to neglect this is a sin as great as the murder of a Brahman.[134] The Persians ascribe yawning, sneezing, &c., to demoniacal possession. Among the modern Moslems generally, when a man yawns, he puts the back of his left hand to his mouth, saying, 'I seek refuge with Allah from Satan the accursed!' but the act of yawning is to be avoided, for the Devil is in the habit of leaping into a gaping mouth.[135] This may very likely be the meaning of the Jewish proverb, 'Open not thy mouth to Satan!' The other half of this idea shows itself clearly in Josephus' story of his having seen a certain Jew, named Eleazar, cure demoniacs in Vespasian's time, by drawing the demons out through their nostrils, by means of a ring containing a root of mystic virtue mentioned by Solomon.[136] The account of the sect of the Messalians, who used to spit and blow their noses to expel the demons they might have drawn in with their breath,[137] the records of the mediæval exorcists driving out devils through the patients' nostrils,[138] and the custom, still kept up in the Tyrol, of crossing oneself when one yawns, lest something evil should come into one's mouth,[139] involve similar ideas. In comparing the modern Kafir ideas with those of other districts of the world, we find a distinct notion of a sneeze being due to a spiritual presence. This, which seems indeed the key to the whole matter, has been well brought into view by Mr. Haliburton, as displayed in Keltic folk-lore, in a group of stories turning on the superstition that any one who sneezes is liable to be carried off by the fairies, unless their power be counteracted by an invocation, as 'God bless you!'[140] The corresponding idea as to yawning is to be found in an Iceland folk-lore legend, where the troll, who has transformed herself into the shape of the beautiful queen, says, 'When I yawn a little yawn, I am a neat and tiny maiden; when I yawn a half-yawn, then I am as a half-troll; when I yawn a whole yawn, then am I as a whole troll.'[141] On the whole, though the sneezing superstition makes no approach to universality among mankind, its wide distribution is highly remarkable, and it would be an interesting problem to decide how far this wide distribution is due to independent growth in several regions, how far to conveyance from race to race, and how far to ancestral inheritance. Here it has only to be maintained that it was not originally an arbitrary and meaningless custom, but the working out of a principle.[142] The plain statement by the modern Zulus fits with the hints to be gained from the superstition and folk-lore of other races, to connect the notions and practices as to sneezing with the ancient and savage doctrine of pervading and invading spirits, considered as good or evil, and treated accordingly. The lingering survivals of the quaint old formulas in modern Europe seem an unconscious record of the time when the explanation of sneezing had not yet been given over to physiology, but was still in the 'theological stage.'

There is current in Scotland the belief that the Picts, to whom local legend attributes buildings of prehistoric antiquity, bathed their foundation-stones with human blood; and legend even tells that St. Columba found it necessary to bury St. Oran alive beneath the foundation of his monastery, in order to propitiate the spirits of the soil who demolished by night what was built during the day. So late as 1843, in Germany, when a new bridge was built at Halle, a notion was abroad among the people that a child was wanted to be built into the foundation. These ideas of church or wall or bridge wanting human blood or an immured victim to make the foundation steadfast, are not only widespread in European folk-lore, but local chronicle or tradition asserts them as matter of historical fact in district after district. Thus, when the broken dam of the Nogat had to be repaired in 1463, the peasants, on the advice to throw in a living man, are said to have made a beggar drunk and buried him there. Thuringian legend declares that to make the castle of Liebenstein fast and impregnable, a child was bought for hard money of its mother and walled in. It was eating a cake while the masons were at work, the story goes, and it cried out, 'Mother, I see thee still;' then later, 'Mother, I see thee a little still;' and, as they put in the last stone, 'Mother, now I see thee no more.' The wall of Copenhagen, legend says, sank as fast as it was built; so they took an innocent little girl, set her on a chair at a table of toys and eatables, and, as she played and ate, twelve master-masons closed a vault over her; then, with clanging music, the wall was raised, and stood firm ever after. Thus Italian legend tells of the bridge of Arta, that fell in and fell in till they walled in the master-builder's wife, and she spoke her dying curse that the bridge should tremble like a flower-stalk henceforth. The Slavonic chiefs founding Detinez, according to old heathen custom, sent out men to take the first boy they met and bury him in the foundation. Servian legend tells how three brothers combined to build the fortress of Skadra (Scutari); but, year after year, the demon (vila) razed by night what the three hundred masons built by day. The fiend must be appeased by a human sacrifice, the first of the three wives who should come bringing food to the workmen. All three brothers swore to keep the dreadful secret from their wives; but the two eldest gave traitorous warning to theirs, and it was the youngest brother's wife who came unsuspecting, and they built her in. But she entreated that an opening should be left for her to suckle her baby through, and for a twelve-month it was brought. To this day, Servian wives visit the tomb of the good mother, still marked by a stream of water which trickles, milky with lime, down the fortress wall. Lastly, there is our own legend of Vortigern, who could not finish his tower till the foundation-stone was wetted with the blood of a child born of a mother without a father. As is usual in the history of sacrifice, we hear of substitutes for such victims; empty coffins walled up in Germany, a lamb walled in under the altar in Denmark to make the church stand fast, and the churchyard in like manner handselled by burying a live horse first. In modern Greece an evident relic of the idea survives in the superstition that the first passer-by after a foundation-stone is laid will die within the year, wherefore the masons will compromise the debt by killing a lamb or a black cock on the stone. With much the same idea German legend tells of the bridge-building fiend cheated of his promised fee, a soul, by the device of making a cock run first across; and thus German folk-lore says it is well, before entering a new house, to let a cat or dog run in.[143] From all this it seems that, with due allowance for the idea having passed into an often-repeated and varied mythic theme, yet written and unwritten tradition do preserve the memory of a bloodthirsty barbaric rite, which not only really existed in ancient times, but lingered long in European history. If now we look to less cultured countries, we shall find the rite carried on in our own day with a distinctly religious purpose, either to propitiate the earth-spirits with a victim, or to convert the soul of the victim himself into a protecting demon.

In Africa, in Galam, a boy and girl used to be buried alive before the great gate of the city to make it impregnable, a practice once executed on a large scale by a Bambarra tyrant; while in Great Bassam and Yarriba such sacrifices were usual at the foundation of a house or village.[144] In Polynesia, Ellis heard of the custom, instanced by the fact that the central pillar of one of the temples at Maeva was planted upon the body of a human victim.[145] In Borneo, among the Milanau Dayaks, at the erection of the largest house a deep hole was dug to receive the first post, which was then suspended over it; a slave girl was placed in the excavation; at a signal the lashings were cut, and the enormous timber descended, crushing the girl to death, a sacrifice to the spirits. St. John saw a milder form of the rite performed, when the chief of the Quop Dayaks set up a flagstaff near his house, a chicken being thrown in to be crushed by the descending pole.[146] More cultured nations of Southern Asia have carried on into modern ages the rite of the foundation-sacrifice. A 17th century account of Japan mentions the belief there that a wall laid on the body of a willing human victim would be secure from accident; accordingly, when a great wall was to be built, some wretched slave would offer himself as foundation, lying down in the trench to be crushed by the heavy stones lowered upon him.[147] When the gates of the new city of Tavoy, in Tenasserim, were built about 1780, as Mason relates on the evidence of an eye-witness, a criminal was put in each post-hole to become a protecting demon. Thus it appears that such stories as that of the human victims buried for spirit watchers under the gates of Mandalay, of the queen who was drowned in a Burmese reservoir to make the dyke safe, of the hero whose divided body was buried under the fortress of Thatung to make it impregnable, are the records, whether in historical or mythical form, of the actual customs of the land.[148] Within our own dominion, when Rajah Sala Byne was building the fort of Sialkot in the Punjab, the foundation of the south-east bastion gave way so repeatedly that he had recourse to a soothsayer, who assured him that it would never stand until the blood of an only son was shed there, wherefore the only son of a widow was sacrificed.[149] It is thus plain that hideous rites, of which Europe has scarcely kept up more than the dim memory, have held fast their ancient practice and meaning in Africa, Polynesia, and Asia, among races who represent in grade, if not in chronology, earlier stages of civilization.

When Sir Walter Scott, in the 'Pirate,' tells of Bryce the pedlar refusing to help Mordaunt to save the shipwrecked sailor from drowning, and even remonstrating with him on the rashness of such a deed, he states an old superstition of the Shetlanders. 'Are you mad?' says the pedlar; 'you that have lived sae lang in Zetland, to risk the saving of a drowning man? Wot ye not, if you bring him to life again, he will be sure to do you some capital injury?' Were this inhuman thought noticed in this one district alone, it might be fancied to have had its rise in some local idea now no longer to be explained. But when mentions of similar superstitions are collected among the St. Kilda islanders and the boatmen of the Danube, among French and English sailors, and even out of Europe and among less civilized races, we cease to think of local fancies, but look for some widely accepted belief of the lower culture to account for such a state of things. The Hindu does not save a man from drowning in the sacred Ganges, and the islanders of the Malay archipelago share the cruel notion.[150] Of all people the rude Kamchadals have the prohibition in the most remarkable form. They hold it a great fault, says Kracheninnikow, to save a drowning man; he who delivers him will be drowned himself.[151] Steller's account is more extraordinary, and probably applies only to cases where the victim is actually drowning: he says that if a man fell by chance into the water, it was a great sin for him to get out, for as he had been destined to drown he did wrong in not drowning, wherefore no one would let him into his dwelling, nor speak to him, nor give him food or a wife, but he was reckoned for dead; and even when a man fell into the water while others were standing by, far from helping him out, they would drown him by force. Now these barbarians, it appears, avoided volcanoes because of the spirits who live there and cook their food; for a like reason, they held it a sin to bathe in hot springs; and they believed with fear in a fish-like spirit of the sea, whom they called Mitgk.[152] This spiritualistic belief among the Kamchadals is, no doubt, the key to their superstition as to rescuing drowning men. There is even to be found in modern European superstition, not only the practice, but with it a lingering survival of its ancient spiritualistic significance. In Bohemia, a recent account (1864) says that the fishermen do not venture to snatch a drowning man from the waters. They fear that the 'Waterman' (i.e. water-demon) would take away their luck in fishing, and drown themselves at the first opportunity.[153] This explanation of the prejudice against saving the water-spirit's victim may be confirmed by a mass of evidence from various districts of the world. Thus, in discussing the doctrine of sacrifice, it will appear that the usual manner of making an offering to a well, river, lake, or sea, is simply to cast property, cattle, or men into the water, which personally or by its indwelling spirit takes possession of them.[154] That the accidental drowning of a man is held to be such a seizure, savage and civilized folk-lore show by many examples. Among the Sioux Indians, it is Unk-tahe the water-monster that drowns his victims in flood or rapid;[155] in New Zealand huge supernatural reptile-monsters, called Taniwha, live in river-bends, and those who are drowned are said to be pulled under by them;[156] the Siamese fears the Pnük or water-spirit that seizes bathers and drags them under to his dwelling;[157] in Slavonic lands it is Topielec (the ducker) by whom men are always drowned;[158] when some one is drowned in Germany, people recollect the religion of their ancestors, and say, 'The river-spirit claims his yearly sacrifice,' or, more simply, 'The nix has taken him:'[159]—

'Ich glaube, die Wellen verschlingen,

Am Ende Fischer und Kahn;

Und das hat mit ihrem Singen

Die Lorelei gethan.'

From this point of view it is obvious that to save a sinking man is to snatch a victim from the very clutches of the water-spirit, a rash defiance of deity which would hardly pass unavenged. In the civilized world the rude old theological conception of drowning has long been superseded by physical explanation; and the prejudice against rescue from such a death may have now almost or altogether disappeared. But archaic ideas, drifted on into modern folk-lore and poetry, still bring to our view an apparent connexion between the primitive doctrine and the surviving custom.

As the social development of the world goes on, the weightiest thoughts and actions may dwindle to mere survival. Original meaning dies out gradually, each generation leaves fewer and fewer to bear it in mind, till it falls out of popular memory, and in after-days ethnography has to attempt, more or less successfully, to restore it by piecing together lines of isolated or forgotten facts. Children's sports, popular sayings, absurd customs, may be practically unimportant, but are not philosophically insignificant, bearing as they do on some of the most instructive phases of early culture. Ugly and cruel superstitions may prove to be relics of primitive barbarism, for in keeping up such Man is like Shakespeare's fox,

'Who, ne'er so tame, so cherish'd, and lock'd up,

Will have a wild trick of his ancestors.'

CHAPTER IV.
SURVIVAL IN CULTURE (*continued*).

Occult Sciences—Magical powers attributed by higher to lower races—Magical processes based on Association of Ideas—Omens—Augury, &c.—Oneiromancy—Haruspication, Scapulimancy, Chiromancy, &c.—Cartomancy, &c.—Rhabdomancy, Dactyliomancy, Coscinomancy, &c.—Astrology—Intellectual conditions accounting for the persistence of Magic—Survival passes into Revival—Witchcraft, originating in savage culture, continues in barbaric civilization; its decline in early mediæval Europe followed by revival; its practices and counter-practices belong to earlier culture—Spiritualism has its source in early stages of culture, in close connexion with witchcraft—Spirit-rapping and Spirit-writing—Rising in the air—Performances of tied mediums—Practical bearing of the study of Survival.

In examining the survival of opinions in the midst of conditions of society becoming gradually estranged from them, and tending at last to suppress them altogether, much may be learnt from the history of one of the most pernicious delusions that ever vexed mankind, the belief in Magic. Looking at Occult Science from this ethnographic point of view, I shall instance some of its branches as illustrating the course of intellectual culture. Its place in history is briefly this. It belongs in its main principle to the lowest known stages of civilization, and the lower races, who have not partaken largely of the education of the world, still maintain it in vigour. From this level it may be traced upward, much of the savage art holding its place substantially unchanged, and many new practices being in course of time developed, while both the older and newer developments have lasted on more or less among modern cultured nations. But during the ages in which progressive races have been learning to submit their opinions to closer and closer experimental tests, occult science has been breaking down into the condition of a survival, in which state we mostly find it among ourselves.

The modern educated world, rejecting occult science as a contemptible superstition, has practically committed itself to the opinion that magic belongs to a lower level of civilization. It is very instructive to find the soundness of this judgment undesignedly confirmed by nations whose education has not advanced far enough to destroy their belief in magic itself. In any country an isolated or outlying race, the lingering survivor of an older nationality, is liable to the reputation of sorcery. It is thus with the Lavas of Burma, supposed to be the broken-down remains of an ancient cultured race, and dreaded as man-tigers;[160] and with the Budas of Abyssinia, who are at once the smiths and potters, sorcerers and werewolves, of their district.[161] But the usual and suggestive state of things is that nations who believe with the sincerest terror in the reality of the magic art, at the same time cannot shut their eyes to the fact that it more essentially belongs to, and is more thoroughly at home among, races less civilized than themselves. The Malays of the Peninsula, who have adopted Mohammedan religion and civilization, have this idea of the lower tribes of the land, tribes more or less of their own race, but who have remained in their early savage condition. The Malays have enchanters of their own, but consider them inferior to the sorcerers or poyangs belonging to the rude Mintira; to these they will resort for the cure of diseases and the working of misfortune and death to their enemies. It is, in fact, the best protection the Mintira have against their stronger Malay neighbours, that these are careful not to offend them for fear of their powers of magical revenge. The Jakuns, again, are a rude and wild race, whom the Malays despise as infidels and little higher than animals, but whom at the same time they fear extremely. To the Malay the Jakun seems a supernatural being, skilled in divination, sorcery, and fascination, able to do evil or good according to his pleasure, whose blessing will be followed by the most fortunate success, and his curse by the most dreadful consequences; he can turn towards the house of an enemy, at whatever distance, and beat two sticks together till that enemy will fall sick and die; he is skilled in herbal physic; he has the power of charming the fiercest wild beasts. Thus it is that the Malays, though they despise the Jakuns, refrain, in many circumstances, from ill-treating them.[162] In India, in long-past ages, the dominant Aryans described the rude indigenes of the land by the epithets of 'possessed of magical powers,' 'changing their shape at will.'[163] To this day, Hindus settled in Chota-Nagpur and Singbhum firmly believe that the Mundas have powers of witchcraft, whereby they can transform themselves into tigers and other beasts of prey to devour their enemies, and can witch away the lives of man and beast; it is to the wildest and most savage of the tribe that such powers are generally ascribed.[164] In Southern India, again, we hear in past times of Hinduized Dravidians, the Sudras of Canara, living in fear of the demoniacal powers of the slave-caste below them.[165] In our own day, among Dravidian tribes of the Nilagiri district, the Todas and Badagas are in mortal dread of the Kurumbas, despised and wretched forest outcasts, but gifted, it is believed, with powers of destroying men and animals and property by witchcraft.[166] Northern Europe brings the like contrast sharply into view. The Finns and Lapps, whose low Tatar barbarism was characterized by sorcery such as flourishes still among their Siberian kinsfolk, were accordingly objects of superstitious fear to their Scandinavian neighbours and oppressors. In the middle ages the name of

Finn was, as it still remains among sea-faring men, equivalent to that of sorcerer, while Lapland witches had a European celebrity as practitioners of the black art. Ages after the Finns had risen in the social scale, the Lapps retained much of their old half-savage habit of life, and with it naturally their witchcraft, so that even the magic-gifted Finns revered the occult powers of a people more barbarous than themselves. Rühs writes thus early in the last century: 'There are still sorcerers in Finland, but the skilfullest of them believe that the Lapps far excel them; of a well-experienced magician they say, "That is quite a Lapp," and they journey to Lapland for such knowledge.'[167] All this is of a piece with the survival of such ideas among the ignorant elsewhere in the civilized world. Many a white man in the West Indies and Africa dreads the incantations of the Obi-man, and Europe ascribes powers of sorcery to despised outcast 'races maudites,' Gypsies and Cagots. To turn from nations to sects, the attitude of Protestants to Catholics in this matter is instructive. It was remarked in Scotland: 'There is one opinion which many of them entertain, ... that a popish priest can cast out devils and cure madness, and that the Presbyterian clergy have no such power.' So Bourne says of the Church of England clergy, that the vulgar think them no conjurers, and say none can lay spirits but popish priests.[168] These accounts are not recent, but in Germany the same state of things appears to exist still. Protestants get the aid of Catholic priests and monks to help them against witchcraft, to lay ghosts, consecrate herbs, and discover thieves;[169] thus with unconscious irony judging the relation of Rome toward modern civilization.

The principal key to the understanding of Occult Science is to consider it as based on the Association of Ideas, a faculty which lies at the very foundation of human reason, but in no small degree of human unreason also. Man, as yet in a low intellectual condition, having come to associate in thought those things which he found by experience to be connected in fact, proceeded erroneously to invert this action, and to conclude that association in thought must involve similar connexion in reality. He thus attempted to discover, to foretell, and to cause events by means of processes which we can now see to have only an ideal significance. By a vast mass of evidence from savage, barbaric, and civilized life, magic arts which have resulted from thus mistaking an ideal for a real connexion, may be clearly traced from the lower culture which they are of, to the higher culture which they are in.[170] Such are the practices whereby a distant person is to be affected by acting on something closely associated with him—his property, clothes he has worn, and above all cuttings of his hair and nails. Not only do savages high and low like the Australians and Polynesians, and barbarians like the nations of Guinea, live in deadly terror of this spiteful craft—not only have the Parsis their sacred ritual prescribed for burying their cut hair and nails, lest demons and sorcerers should do mischief with them, but the fear of leaving such clippings and parings about lest their former owner should be harmed through them, has by no means died out of European folk-lore, and the German peasant, during the days between his child's birth and baptism, objects to lend anything out of the house, lest witchcraft should be worked through it on the yet unconsecrated baby.[171] As the negro fetish-man, when his patient does not come in person, can divine by means of his dirty cloth or cap instead,[172] so the modern clairvoyant professes to feel sympathetically the sensations of a distant person, if communication be made through a lock of his hair or any object that has been in contact with him.[173] The simple idea of joining two objects with a cord, taking for granted that this communication will establish connexion or carry influence, has been worked out in various ways in the world. In Australia, the native doctor fastens one end of a string to the ailing part of the patient's body, and by sucking at the other end pretends to draw out blood for his relief.[174] In Orissa, the Jeypore witch lets down a ball of thread through her enemy's roof to reach his body, that by putting the other end in her own mouth she may suck his blood.[175] When a reindeer is sacrificed at a sick Ostyak's tent door, the patient holds in his hand a cord attached to the victim offered for his benefit.[176] Greek history shows a similar idea, when the citizens of Ephesus carried a rope seven furlongs from their walls to the temple of Artemis, thus to place themselves under her safeguard against the attack of Crœsus; and in the yet more striking story of the Kylonians, who tied a cord to the statue of the goddess when they quitted the asylum, and clung to it for protection as they crossed unhallowed ground; but by ill-fate the cord of safety broke and they were mercilessly put to death.[177] And in our own day, Buddhist priests in solemn ceremony put themselves in communication with a sacred relic, by each taking hold of a long thread fastened near it and around the temple.[178]

Magical arts in which the connexion is that of mere analogy or symbolism are endlessly numerous throughout the course of civilization. Their common theory may be readily made out from a few typical cases, and thence applied confidently to the general mass. The Australian will observe the track of an insect near a grave, to ascertain the direction where the sorcerer is to be found, by whose craft the man died.[179] The Zulu may be seen chewing a bit of wood, in order, by this symbolic act, to soften the heart of the man he wants to buy oxen from, or of the woman he wants for a wife.[180] The Obi-man of West Africa makes his packet of grave-dust, blood, and bones, that this suggestive representation of death may bring his enemy to the grave.[181] The Khond sets up the iron arrow of the War-god in a basket of rice, and judges from its standing upright that war must be kept up also, or from its falling that the quarrel may be let fall too; and when he tortures human victims sacrificed to the Earth-goddess, he rejoices to see them shed plentiful tears, which betoken copious showers to fall upon his land.[182] These are fair examples of the symbolic magic of the lower races, and they are fully rivalled in superstitions which still hold their ground in Europe. With quaint simplicity, the German cottager declares that if a dog howls looking downward, it portends a death; but if upward, then a recovery from sickness.[183] Locks must be opened and bolts drawn in a dying man's house, that his soul may not be held fast.[184] The Hessian lad thinks that he may escape the conscription by carrying a baby-girl's cap in his pocket—a symbolic way of repudiating manhood.[185] Modern Servians, dancing and singing, lead about a little girl dressed in leaves and flowers, and pour bowls of water over her to make the rain come.[186] Sailors becalmed will sometimes whistle for a wind; but in other weather they hate whistling at sea, which raises a whistling gale.[187] Fish, says the Cornishman, should be eaten from the tail towards the head, to bring the other fishes' heads towards the shore, for eating them the wrong way turns them from the coast.[188] He who has cut himself should rub the knife with fat, and as it dries, the wound will heal; this is a lingering survival from days when recipes for sympathetic ointment were to be found in the Pharmacopœia.[189] Fanciful as these notions are, it should be borne in mind that they come fairly under definite mental law, depending as they do on a principle of ideal association, of which we can quite understand the mental action, though we deny its practical results. The clever Lord Chesterfield, too clever to understand folly, may again be cited to prove this. He relates in one of his letters that the king had been ill, and that people generally expected the illness to be fatal, because the oldest lion in the Tower, about the king's age, had just died. 'So wild and capricious is the human mind,' he exclaims, by way of comment. But indeed the thought was neither wild nor capricious, it was simply such an argument from analogy as the educated world has at length painfully learnt to be worthless; but which, it is not too much to declare, would to this day carry considerable weight to the minds of four-fifths of the human race.

A glance at those magical arts which have been systematized into pseudo-sciences, shows the same underlying principle. The art of taking omens from seeing and meeting animals, which includes augury, is familiar to such savages as the Tupis of Brazil[190] and the Dayaks of Borneo,[191] and extends upward through classic civilization. The Maoris may give a sample of the character of its rules: they hold it unlucky if an owl hoots during a consultation, but a council of war is encouraged by prospect of victory when a hawk flies overhead; a flight of birds to the right of the war-sacrifice is propitious if the villages of the tribe are in that quarter, but if the omen is in the enemy's direction the war will be given up.[192] Compare these with the Tatar rules, and it is obvious that similar thoughts lie at the source of both. Here a certain little owl's cry is a sound of terror, although there is a white owl which is lucky; but of all birds the white falcon is most prophetic, and the Kalmuk bows his thanks for the good omen when one flies by on the right, but seeing one on the left turns away his face and expects calamity.[193] So to the negro of Old Calabar, the cry of the great kingfisher bodes good or evil, according as it is heard on the right or left.[194] Here we have the obvious symbolism of the right and left hand, the foreboding of ill from the owl's doleful note, and the suggestion of victory from the fierce swooping hawk, a thought which in old Europe made the bird of prey the warrior's omen of conquest. Meaning of the same kind appears in the 'Angang,' the omens taken from meeting animals and people, especially on first going out in the morning, as when the ancient Slaves held meeting a sick man or an old woman to bode ill-luck. Any one who takes the trouble to go into this subject in detail, and to study the classic, mediæval, and oriental codes of rules, will find that the principle of direct symbolism still accounts for a fair proportion of them, though the rest may have lost their early significance, or may have been originally due to some other reason, or may have been arbitrarily invented (as a considerable proportion of such devices must necessarily be) to fill up the gaps in the system. It is still plain to us why the omen of the crow should be different on the right or left hand, why a vulture should mean rapacity, a stork concord, a pelican piety, an ass labour, why the fierce conquering wolf should be a good omen, and the timid hare a bad one, why bees, types of an obedient nation, should be lucky to a king, while flies, returning however often they are driven off, should be signs of importunity and impudence.[195] And as to the general principle that animals are ominous to those who meet them, the German peasant who says a flock of sheep is lucky but a herd of swine unlucky to meet, and the Cornish miner who turns away in horror when he meets an old woman or a rabbit on his way to the pit's mouth, are to this day keeping up relics of early savagery as genuine as any flint implement dug out of a tumulus.

The doctrine of dreams, attributed as they are by the lower and middle races to spiritual intercourse, belongs in so far rather to religion than to magic. But oneiromancy, the art of taking omens from dreams by analogical interpretation, has its place here. Of the leading principle of such mystical explanation, no better types could be chosen than the details and interpretations of Joseph's dreams (Genesis xxxvii., xl., xli.), of the sheaves and the sun and moon and eleven stars, of the vine and the basket of meats, of the lean and fat kine, and the thin and full corn-ears. Oneiromancy, thus symbolically interpreting the things seen in dreams, is not unknown to the lower races. A whole Australian tribe has been known to decamp because one of them dreamt of a certain kind of owl, which dream the wise men declared to forebode an attack from a certain other tribe.[196] The Kamchadals, whose minds ran much on dreams, had special interpretations of some; thus to dream of lice or dogs betokened a visit of Russian travellers, &c.[197] The Zulus, experience having taught them the fallacy of expecting direct fulfilment of dreams, have in some cases tried to mend matters by rushing to the other extreme. If they dream of a sick man that he is dead, and they see the earth poured into the grave, and hear the funeral lamentation, and see all his things destroyed, then they say, 'Because we have dreamt of his death he will not die.' But if they dream of a wedding-dance, it is a sign of a funeral. So the Maoris hold that a kinsman dreamt of as dying will recover, but to see him well is a sign of death.[198] Both races thus work out, by the same crooked logic that guided our own ancestors, the axiom that 'dreams go by contraries.' It could not be expected, in looking over the long lists of precepts of classic, oriental, and modern popular dream-interpretation, to detect the original sense of all their readings. Many must turn on allusions intelligible at the time, but now obscure. The Moslem dream-interpretation of eggs as concerning women, because of a saying of Mohammed about women being like an egg hidden in a nest, is an example which will serve as well as a score to show how dream-rules may turn on far-fetched ideas, not to be recognized unless the key happens to have been preserved. Many rules must have been taken at random to fill up lists of omens, and of contingencies to match them. Why should a dream of roasting meat show the dreamer to be a back-biter, or laughter in sleep presage difficult circumstances, or a dream of playing on the clavicord the death of relatives? But the other side of the matter, the still apparent nonsensical rationality of so many dream omens, is much more remarkable. It can only be considered that the same symbolism that lay at the root of the whole delusion, favoured the keeping up and new making of such rules as carried obvious meaning. Take the Moslem ideas that it is a good omen to dream of something white or green, or of water, but bad to dream of black or red, or of fire; that a palm-tree indicates an Arab, and a peacock a king; that he who dreams of devouring the stars will live free at some great man's table. Take the classic rules as in the 'Oneirocritica' of Artemidorus, and pass on through the mediæval treatises down to such a dream-dictionary as servant-maids still buy in penny chap-books at the fair, and it will be seen that the ancient rules still hold their places to a remarkable extent, while half the mass of precepts still show their original mystic significance, mostly direct, but occasionally according to the rule of contraries. An offensive odour signifies annoyance; to wash the hands denotes release from anxieties; to embrace one's best beloved is very fortunate; to have one's feet cut off prevents a journey; to weep in sleep is a sign of joy; he who dreams he hath lost a tooth shall lose a friend; and he that dreams that a rib is taken out of his side shall ere long see the death of his wife; to follow bees, betokens gain; to be married signifies that some of your kinsfolk are dead; if one sees many fowls together, that shall be jealousy and chiding; if a snake pursue him, let him be on his guard against evil women; to dream of death, denotes happiness and long life; to dream of swimming and wading in the water is good, so that the head be kept above water; to dream of crossing a bridge, denotes you will leave a good situation to seek a better; to dream you see a dragon is a sign that you shall see some great lord your master, or a magistrate.[199]

Haruspication belongs, among the lower races, especially to the Malays and Polynesians,[200] and to various Asiatic tribes.[201] It is mentioned as practised in Peru under the Incas.[202] Captain Burton's account from Central Africa perhaps fairly displays its symbolic principle. He describes the mganga or sorcerer taking an ordeal by killing and splitting a fowl and inspecting its inside: if blackness or blemish appears about the wings, it denotes the treachery of children and kinsmen; the backbone convicts the mother and grandmother; the tail shows that the criminal is the wife, &c.[203] In ancient Rome, where the art held so great a place in public affairs, the same sort of interpretation was usual, as witness the omen of Augustus, where the livers of the victims were found folded, and the diviners prophesied him accordingly a doubled empire.[204] Since then, haruspication has died out more completely than almost any magical rite, yet even now a characteristic relic of it may be noticed in Brandenburg; when a pig is killed and the spleen is found turned over, there will be another overthrow, namely a death in the family that year.[205] With haruspication may be classed the art of divining by bones, as where North American Indians would put in the fire a certain flat bone of a porcupine, and judge from its colour if the porcupine hunt would be successful.[206] The principal art of this kind is divination by a shoulder-blade, technically called scapulimancy or omoplatoscopy. This art, related to the old Chinese divination by the cracks of a tortoise-shell on the fire, is especially found in vogue in Tartary. Its simple symbolism is well shown in the elaborate account with diagrams given by Pallas. The shoulder-blade is put on the fire till it cracks in various directions, and then a long split lengthwise is reckoned as the 'way of life,' while cross-cracks on the right and left stand for different kinds and degrees of good and evil fortune; or if the omen is only taken as to some special event, then lengthwise splits mean going on well, but crosswise ones stand for hindrance, white marks portend much snow, black ones a mild winter, &c.[207] To find this quaint art lasting on into modern times in Europe, we can hardly go to a better place than our own country; a proper English term for it is 'reading the speal-bone' (*speal = espaule*). In Ireland, Camden describes the looking through the blade-bone of a sheep, to find a dark spot which foretells a death, and Drayton thus commemorates the art in his Polyolbion:—

'By th' shoulder of a ram from off the right side par'd,

Which usually they boile, the spade-bone being bar'd,

Which when the wizard takes, and gazing therupon

Things long to come foreshowes, as things done long agone.'[208]

Chiromancy, or palmistry, seems much like this, though it is also mixed up with astrology. It flourished in ancient Greece and Italy as it still does in India, where to say, 'It is written on the palms of my hands,' is a usual way of expressing a sense of inevitable fate. Chiromancy traces in the markings of the palm a line of fortune and a line of life, finds proof of melancholy in the intersections on the saturnine mount, presages sorrow and death from black spots in the finger-nails, and at last, having exhausted the powers of this childish symbolism, it completes its system by details of which the absurdity is no longer relieved by even an ideal sense. The art has its modern votaries not merely among Gypsy fortune-tellers, but in what is called 'good society.'[209]

It may again and again thus be noticed in magic arts, that the association of ideas is obvious up to a certain point. Thus when the New Zealand sorcerer took omens by the way his divining sticks (guided by spirits) fell, he quite naturally said it was a good omen if the stick representing his own tribe fell on top of that representing the enemy, and vice versâ. Zulu diviners still work a similar process with their magical pieces of stick, which rise to say yes and fall to say no, jump upon the head or stomach or other affected part of the patient's body to show where his complaint is, and lie pointing towards the house of the doctor who can cure him. So likewise, where a similar device was practised ages ago in the Old World, the responses were taken from staves which (by the operation of demons) fell backward or forward, to the right or left.[210] But when processes of this kind are developed to complexity, the system has, of course, to be completed by more arbitrary arrangements. This is well shown in one of the divinatory arts mentioned in the last chapter for their connexion with games of chance. In cartomancy, the art of fortune-telling with packs of cards, there is a sort of nonsensical sense in such rules as that two queens mean friendship and four mean chattering, or that the knave of hearts prophesies a brave young man who will come into the family to be useful, unless his purpose be reversed by his card being upside down. But of course the pack can only furnish a limited number of such comparatively rational interpretations, and the rest must be left to such arbitrary fancy as that the seven of diamonds means a prize in the lottery, and the ten of the same suit an unexpected journey.[211]

A remarkable group of divining instruments illustrates another principle. In South-East Asia, the Sgau Karens, at funeral feasts, hang a bangle or metal ring by a thread over a brass basin, which the relatives of the dead approach in succession and strike on the edge with a bit of bamboo; when the one who was most beloved touches the basin, the dead man's spirit responds by twisting and stretching the string till it breaks and the ring falls into the cup, or at least till it rings against it.[212] Nearer Central Asia, in the north-east corner of India, among the Bodo and Dhimal, the professional exorcist has to find out what deity has entered into a patient's body to punish him for some impiety by an attack of illness; this he discovers by setting thirteen leaves round him on the ground to represent the gods, and then holding a pendulum attached to his thumb by a string, till the god in question is persuaded by invocation to declare himself, making the pendulum swing towards his representative leaf.[213] These mystic arts (not to go into the question how these tribes came to use them) are rude forms of the classical dactyliomancy, of which so curious an account is given in the trial of the conspirators Patricius and Hilarius, who worked it to find out who was to supplant the emperor Valens. A round table was marked at the edge with the letters of the alphabet, and with prayers and mystic ceremonies a ring was held suspended over it by a thread, and by swinging or stopping towards certain letters gave the responsive words of the oracle.[214] Dactyliomancy has dwindled in Europe to the art of finding out what o'clock it is by holding a ring hanging inside a tumbler by a thread, till, without conscious aid by the operator, it begins to swing and strikes the hour. Father Schott, in his 'Physica Curiosa' (1662), refrains with commendable caution from ascribing this phenomenon universally to demoniac influence. It survives among ourselves in child's play, and though we are 'no conjurers,' we may learn something from the little instrument, which remarkably displays the effects of insensible movement. The operator really gives slight impulses till they accumulate to a considerable vibration, as in ringing a church-bell by very gentle pulls exactly timed. That he does, though unconsciously, cause and direct the swings, may be shown by an attempt to work the instrument with the operator's eyes shut, which will be found to fail, the directing power being lost. The action of the famous divining-rod with its curiously versatile sensibility to water, ore, treasure, and thieves, seems to belong partly to trickery by professional Dousterswivels, and partly to more or less conscious direction by honester operators. It is still known in England, and in Germany they are apt to hide it in a baby's clothes, and so get it baptized for greater efficiency.[215] To conclude this group of divinatory instruments, chance or the operator's direction may determine the action of one of the most familiar of classic and mediæval ordeals, the so-called coscinomancy, or, as it is described in Hudibras, 'th' oracle of sieve and shears, that turns as certain as the spheres.' The sieve was held hanging by a thread, or by the points of a pair of shears stuck into its rim, and it would turn, or swing, or fall, at the mention of a thief's name, and give similar signs for other purposes. Of this ancient rite, the Christian ordeal of the Bible and key, still in frequent use, is a variation: the proper way to detect a thief by this is to read the 50th Psalm to the apparatus, and when it hears the verse, 'When thou sawest a thief, then thou consentedst with him,' it will turn to the culprit.[216]

Count de Maistre, with his usual faculty of taking an argument up at the wrong end, tells us that judicial astrology no doubt hangs to truths of the first order, which have been taken from us as useless or dangerous, or which we cannot recognize under their new forms.[217] A sober examination of the subject may rather justify the contrary opinion, that it is on an error of the first order that astrology depends, the error of mistaking ideal analogy for real connexion. Astrology, in the immensity of its delusive influence on mankind, and by the comparatively modern period to which it remained an honoured branch of philosophy, may claim the highest rank among the occult sciences. It scarcely belongs to very low levels of civilization, although one of its fundamental conceptions, namely, that of the souls or animating intelligences of the celestial bodies, is rooted in the depths of savage life. Yet the following Maori specimen of astrological reasoning is as real an argument as could be found in Paracelsus or Agrippa, nor is there reason to doubt its being home-made. When the siege of a New Zealand 'pa' is going on, if Venus is near the moon, the natives naturally imagine the two as enemy and fortress; if the planet is above, the foe will have the upper hand; but if below, then the men of the soil will be able to defend themselves.[218] Though the early history of astrology is obscure, its great development and elaborate systematization were undoubtedly the work of civilized nations of the ancient and mediæval world. As might be well supposed, a great part of its precepts have lost their intelligible sense, or never had any, but the origin of many others is still evident. To a considerable extent they rest on direct symbolism. Such are the rules which connect the sun with gold, with the heliotrope and pæony, with the cock which heralds day, with magnanimous animals, such as the lion and bull; and the moon with silver, and the changing chamæleon, and the palm-tree, which was considered to send out a monthly shoot. Direct symbolism is plain in that main principle of the calculation of nativities, the notion of the 'ascendant' in the horoscope, which reckons the part of the heavens rising in the east at the moment of a child's birth as being connected with the child itself, and prophetic of its future life.[219] It is an old story, that when two brothers were once taken ill together, Hippokrates the physician concluded from the coincidence that they were twins, but Poseidonios the astrologer considered rather that they were born under the same constellation: we may add, that either argument would be thought reasonable by a savage. One of the most instructive astrological doctrines which has kept its place in modern popular philosophy, is that of the sympathy of growing and declining nature with the waxing and waning moon. Among classical precepts are these: to set eggs under the hen at new moon, but to root up trees when the moon is on the wane, and after midday. The Lithuanian precept to wean boys on a waxing, but girls on a waning moon, no doubt to make the boys sturdy and the girls slim and delicate, is a fair match for the Orkney islanders' objection to marrying except with a growing moon, while some even wish for a flowing tide. The following lines, from Tusser's 'Five Hundred Points of Husbandry,' show neatly in a single case the two contrary lunar influences:—

'Sowe peason and beans in the wane of the moone

Who soweth them sooner, he soweth too soone:

That they, with the planet, may rest and rise,

And flourish with bearing, most plentiful wise.'[220]

The notion that the weather changes with the moon's quarterings is still held with great vigour in England. Yet the meteorologists, with all their eagerness to catch at any rule which at all answers to facts, quite repudiate this one, which indeed appears to be simply a maxim belonging to popular astrology. Just as the growth and dwindling of plants became associated with the moon's wax and wane, so changes of weather became associated with changes of the moon, while, by astrologer's logic, it did not matter whether the moon's change were real, at new and full, or imaginary, at the intermediate quarters. That educated people to whom exact weather records are accessible should still find satisfaction in the fanciful lunar rule, is an interesting case of intellectual survival.

In such cases as these, the astrologer has at any rate a real analogy, deceptive though it be, to base his rule upon. But most of his pseudo-science seems to rest on even weaker and more arbitrary analogies, not of things, but of names. Names of stars and constellations, of signs denoting regions of the sky and periods of days and years, no matter how arbitrarily given, are materials which the astrologer can work upon, and bring into ideal connexion with mundane events. That astronomers should have divided the sun's course into imaginary signs of the zodiac, was enough to originate astrological rules that these celestial signs have an actual effect on real earthly rams, bulls, crabs, lions, virgins. A child born under the sign of the Lion will be courageous; but one born under the Crab will not go forward well in life; one born under the Waterman is likely to be drowned, and so forth. Towards 1524, Europe was awaiting in an agony of prayerful terror a second deluge, prophesied for February in that year. As the fatal month drew nigh, dwellers by the waterside moved in crowds to the hills, some provided boats to save them, and the President Aurial, at Toulouse, built himself a Noah's Ark. It was the great astrologer Stoefler (the originator, it is said, of the weather-prophecies in our almanacks) who foretold this cataclysm, and his argument has the advantage of being still perfectly intelligible—at the date in question, three planets would be together in the aqueous sign of Pisces. Again, simply because astronomers chose to distribute among the planets the names of certain deities, the planets thereby acquired the characters of their divine namesakes. Thus it was that the planet Mercury became connected with travel, trade, and theft, Venus with love and mirth, Mars with war, Jupiter with power and 'joviality.' Throughout the East, astrology even now remains a science in full esteem. The condition of mediæval Europe may still be perfectly realized by the traveller in Persia, where the Shah waits for days outside the walls of his capital till the constellations allow him to enter, and where on the days appointed by the stars for letting blood, it literally flows in streams from the barbers' shops into the street. Professor Wuttke declares that there are many districts in Germany where the child's horoscope is still regularly kept with the baptismal certificate in the family chest. We scarcely reach this pitch of conservatism in England, but I happen to myself live within a mile of an astrologer, and I lately saw a grave paper on nativities, offered in all good faith to the British Association. The piles of 'Zadkiel's Almanack' in the bookseller's windows in country towns about Christmas are a symptom how much yet remains to be done in popular education. As a specimen at once of the survival and of the meaning of astrologic reasoning, I cannot do better than quote a passage from a book published in London in 1861, and entitled 'The Hand-Book of Astrology, by Zadkiel Tao-Sze.' At page 72 of his first volume, the astrologer relates as follows: 'The Map of the heavens given at page 45 was drawn on the occasion of a young lady having been arrested on a charge of the murder of her infant brother. Having read in a newspaper, at twenty-four minutes past noon on the 23rd July, 1860, that Miss C. K. had been arrested on a charge of the murder of her young brother, the author felt desirous to ascertain whether she were guilty or not, and drew the map accordingly. Finding the moon in the twelfth house, she clearly signifies the prisoner. The moon is in a moveable sign, and moves in the twenty-four hours, 14° 17′. She is, therefore, swift in motion. These things indicated that the prisoner would be very speedily released. Then we find a moveable sign in the cusp of the twelfth, and its ruler, ♀, in a moveable sign, a further indication of speedy release. Hence it was judged and declared to many friends that the prisoner would be immediately released, which was the fact. We looked to see whether the prisoner were guilty of the deed or not, and finding the Moon in Libra, a humane sign, and having just past the ☐ aspect of the Sun and ♃, both being on the M. C. we felt assured that she was a humane, feeling, and honourable girl, and that it was quite impossible she could be guilty of any such atrocity. We declared her to be perfectly innocent, and as the Moon was so well aspected from the tenth house, we declared that her honour would be very soon perfectly established.' Had the astrologer waited a few months longer, to have read the confession of the miserable Constance Kent, he would perhaps have put a different sense on his moveable signs, just balances, and sunny and jovial aspects. Nor would this be a difficult task, for these fancies lend themselves to endless variety of new interpretation. And on such fancies and such interpretations, the great science of the stars has from first to last been based.

Looking at the details here selected as fair samples of symbolic magic, we may well ask the question, is there in the whole monstrous farrago no truth or value whatever? It appears that there is practically none, and that the world has been enthralled for ages by a blind belief in processes wholly irrelevant to their supposed results, and which might as well have been taken just the opposite way. Pliny justly saw in magic a study worthy of his especial attention, 'for the very reason that, being the most fraudulent of arts, it had prevailed throughout the world and through so many ages' (eo ipso quod fraudulentissima artium plurimum in toto terrarum orbe plurimisque seculis valuit). If it be asked how such a system could have held its ground, not merely in independence but in defiance of its own facts, a fair answer does not seem hard to give. In the first place, it must be borne in mind that occult science has not existed entirely in its own strength. Futile as its arts may be, they are associated in practice with other proceedings by no means futile. What are passed off as sacred omens, are often really the cunning man's shrewd guesses at the past and future. Divination serves to the sorcerer as a mask for real inquest, as when the ordeal gives him invaluable opportunity of examining the guilty, whose trembling hands and equivocating speech betray at once their secret and their utter belief in his power of discerning it. Prophecy tends to fulfil itself, as where the magician, by putting into a victim's mind the belief that fatal arts have been practised against him, can slay him with this idea as with a material weapon. Often priest as well as magician, he has the whole power of religion at his back; often a man in power, always an unscrupulous intriguer, he can work witchcraft and statecraft together, and make his left hand help his right. Often a doctor, he can aid his omens of life or death with remedy or poison, while what we still call 'conjurers' tricks' of sleight of hand have done much to keep up his supernatural prestige. From the earliest known stages of civilization, professional magicians have existed, who live by their craft, and keep it alive. It has been said, that if somebody had endowed lecturers to teach that two sides of a triangle are together equal to the third, the doctrine would have a respectable following among ourselves. At any rate, magic, with an influential profession interested in keeping it in credit and power, did not depend for its existence on mere evidence.

And in the second place, as to this evidence. Magic has not its origin in fraud, and seems seldom practised as an utter imposture. The sorcerer generally learns his time-honoured profession in good faith, and retains his belief in it more or less from first to last; at once dupe and cheat, he combines the energy of a believer with the cunning of a hypocrite. Had occult science been simply framed for purposes of deception, mere nonsense would have answered the purpose, whereas, what we find is an elaborate and systematic pseudo-science. It is, in fact, a sincere but fallacious system of philosophy, evolved by the human intellect by processes still in great measure intelligible to our own minds, and it had thus an original standing-ground in the world. And though the evidence of fact was dead against it, it was but lately and gradually that this evidence was brought fatally to bear. A general survey of the practical working of the system may be made somewhat thus. A large proportion of successful cases belong to natural means disguised as magic. Also, a certain proportion of cases must succeed by mere chance. By far the larger proportion, however, are what we should call failures; but it is a part of the magician's profession to keep these from counting, and this he does with extraordinary resource of rhetorical shift and brazen impudence. He deals in ambiguous phrases, which give him three or four chances for one. He knows perfectly how to impose difficult conditions, and to lay the blame of failure on their neglect. If you wish to make gold, the alchemist in Central Asia has a recipe at your service, only, to use it, you must abstain three days from thinking of apes; just as our English folk-lore says, that if one of your eyelashes comes out, and you put it on your thumb, you will get anything you wish for, if you can only avoid thinking of foxes' tails at the fatal moment. Again, if the wrong thing happens, the wizard has at least a reason why. Has a daughter been born when he promised a son, then it is some hostile practitioner who has turned the boy into a girl; does a tempest come just when he is making fine weather, then he calmly demands a larger fee for stronger ceremonies, assuring his clients that they may thank him as it is, for how much worse it would have been had he not done what he did. And even setting aside all this accessory trickery, if we look at honest but unscientific people practising occult science in good faith, and face to face with facts, we shall see that the failures which condemn it in our eyes carry comparatively little weight in theirs. Part escape under the elastic pretext of a 'little more or less,' as the loser in the lottery consoles himself that his lucky number came within two of a prize, or the moon-observer points out triumphantly that a change of weather has come within two or three days before or after a quarter, so that his convenient definition of near a moon's quarter applies to four or six days out of every seven. Part escape through incapacity to appreciate negative evidence, which allows one success to outweigh half-a-dozen failures. How few there are even among the educated classes now, who have taken in the drift of that memorable passage in the beginning of the 'Novum Organum:'—'The human understanding, when any proposition has been once laid down (either from general admission and belief, or from the pleasure it affords), forces everything else to add fresh support and confirmation; and although most cogent and abundant instances may exist to the contrary, yet either does not observe or despises them, or gets rid of and rejects them by some distinction, with violent and injurious prejudice, rather than sacrifice the authority of its first conclusions. It was well answered by him who was shown in a temple the votive tablets suspended by such as had escaped the peril of shipwreck, and was pressed as to whether he would then recognize the power of the gods, by an inquiry, "But where are the portraits of those who have perished in spite of their vows?"'[221]

On the whole, the survival of symbolic magic through the middle ages and into our own times is an unsatisfactory, but not a mysterious fact. A once-established opinion, however delusive, can hold its own from age to age, for belief can propagate itself without reference to its reasonable origin, as plants are propagated from slips without fresh raising from the seed.

The history of survival in cases like those of the folk-lore and occult arts which we have been considering, has for the most part been a history of dwindling and decay. As men's minds change in progressing culture, old customs and opinions fade gradually in a new and uncongenial atmosphere, or pass into states more congruous with the new life around them. But this is so far from being a law without exception, that a narrow view of history may often make it seem to be no law at all. For the stream of civilization winds and turns upon itself, and what seems the bright onward current of one age may in the next spin round in a whirling eddy, or spread into a dull and pestilential swamp. Studying with a wide view the course of human opinion, we may now and then trace on from the very turning-point the change from passive survival into active revival. Some well-known belief or custom has for centuries shown symptoms of decay, when we begin to see that the state of society, instead of stunting it, is favouring its new growth, and it bursts forth again with a vigour often as marvellous as it is unhealthy. And though the revival be not destined to hold on indefinitely, and though when opinion turns again its ruin may be more merciless than before, yet it may last for ages, make its way into the inmost constitution of society, and even become a very mark and characteristic of its time.

Writers who desire to show that, with all our faults, we are wiser and better than our ancestors, dwell willingly on the history of witchcraft between the middle and modern ages. They can quote Martin Luther, apropos of the witches who spoil the farmers' butter and eggs, 'I would have no pity on these witches; I would burn them all.' They can show the good Sir Matthew Hale hanging witches in Suffolk, on the authority of scripture and the consenting wisdom of all nations; and King James presiding at the torture of Dr. Fian for bringing a storm against the king's ship on its course from Denmark, by the aid of a fleet of witches in sieves, who carried out a christened cat to sea. In those dreadful days, to be a blear-eyed wizened cripple was to be worth twenty shillings to a witch-finder; for a woman to have what this witch-finder was pleased to call the devil's mark on her body was presumption for judicial sentence of death; and not to bleed or shed tears or sink in a pond was torture first and then the stake. Reform of religion was no cure for the disease of men's minds, for in such things the Puritan was no worse than the Inquisitor, and no better. Papist and Protestant fought with one another, but both turned against that enemy of the human race, the hag who had sold herself to Satan to ride upon a broomstick, and to suck children's blood, and to be for life and death of all creatures the most wretched. But with new enlightenment there came in the very teeth of law and authority a change in European opinion. Toward the end of the seventeenth century the hideous superstition was breaking down among ourselves; Richard Baxter, of the 'Saint's Rest,' strove with fanatic zeal to light again at home the witch-fires of New England, but he strove in vain. Year by year the persecution of witches became more hateful to the educated classes, and though it died hard, it died at last down to a vestige. In our days, when we read of a witch being burnt at Camargo in 1860, we point to Mexico as a country miserably in the rear of civilization. And if in England it still happens that village boors have to be tried at quarter-sessions for ill-using some poor old woman, who they fancy has dried a cow or spoiled a turnip crop, we comment on the tenacity with which the rustic mind clings to exploded follies, and cry out for more schoolmasters.

True as all this is, the ethnographer must go wider and deeper in his enquiry, to do his subject justly. The prevailing belief in witchcraft that sat like a nightmare on public opinion from the 13th to the 17th centuries, far from being itself a product of mediævalism, was a revival from the remote days of primæval history. The disease that broke out afresh in Europe had been chronic among the lower races for how many ages we cannot tell. Witchcraft is part and parcel of savage life. There are rude races of Australia and South America whose intense belief in it has led them to declare that if men were never bewitched, and never killed by violence, they would not die at all. Like the Australians, the Africans will inquire of their dead what sorcerer slew them by his wicked arts, and when they have satisfied themselves of this, blood must atone for blood. In West Africa, it has been boldly asserted that the belief in witchcraft costs more lives than the slave trade ever did. In East Africa, Captain Burton, a traveller apt to draw his social sketches in a few sharp lines, remarks that what with slavery and what with black-magic, life is precarious among the Wakhutu, and 'no one, especially in old age, is safe from being burnt at a day's notice;' and, travelling in the country of the Wazaramo, he tells us of meeting every few miles with heaps of ashes and charcoal, now and then such as seemed to have been a father and mother, with a little heap hard by that was a child.[222] Even in districts of British India a state of mind ready to produce horrors like these is well known to exist, and to be kept down less by persuasion than by main force. From the level of savage life, we trace witchcraft surviving throughout the barbarian and early civilized world. It was existing in Europe in the centuries preceding the 10th, but with no especial prominence, while laws of Rothar and Charlemagne are actually directed against such as should put men or women to death on the charge of witchcraft. In the 11th century, ecclesiastical influence was discouraging the superstitious belief in sorcery. But now a period of reaction set in. The works of the monastic legend and miracle-mongers more and more encouraged a baneful credulity as to the supernatural. In the 13th century, when the spirit of religious persecution had begun to possess all Europe with a dark and cruel madness, the doctrine of witchcraft revived with all its barbaric vigour.[223] That the guilt of thus bringing down Europe intellectually and morally to the level of negro Africa lies in the main upon the Roman Church, the records of Popes Gregory IX. and Innocent VIII., and the history of the Holy Inquisition, are conclusive evidence to prove. To us here the main interest of mediæval witchcraft lies in the extent and accuracy with which the theory of survival explains it. In the very details of the bald conventional accusations that were sworn against the witches, there may be traced tradition often hardly modified from barbarous and savage times. They raised storms by magic rites, they had charms against the hurt of weapons, they had their assemblies on wild heath and mountain-top, they could ride through the air on beasts and even turn into witch-cats and were-wolves themselves, they had familiar spirits, they had intercourse with incubi and succubi, they conveyed thorns, pins, feathers and such things into their victims' bodies, they caused disease by demoniacal possession, they could bewitch by spells and the evil eye, by practising on images and symbols, on food and property. Now all this is sheer survival from præ-Christian ages, 'in errore paganorum revolvitur,' as Burchard of Worms said of the superstition of his time.[224] Two of the most familiar devices used against the mediæval witches may serve to show the place in civilization of the whole craft. The Oriental jinn are in such deadly terror of iron, that its very name is a charm against them; and so in European folk-lore iron drives away fairies and elves, and destroys their power. They are essentially, it seems, creatures belonging to the ancient Stone Age, and the new metal is hateful and hurtful to them. Now as to iron, witches are brought under the same category as elves and nightmares. Iron instruments keep them at bay, and especially iron horseshoes have been chosen for this purpose, as half the stable doors in England still show.[225] Again, one of the best known of English witch ordeals is the trial by 'fleeting' or swimming. Bound hand and foot, the accused was flung into deep water, to sink if innocent and swim if guilty, and in the latter case, as Hudibras has it, to be hanged only for not being drowned. King James, who seems to have had a notion of the real primitive meaning of this rite, says in his Dæmonology, 'It appears that God hath appointed for a supernatural signe of the monstrous impietie of witches, that the water shall refuse to receive them in her bosom that have shaken off them the sacred water of baptism,' &c. Now, in early German history this same trial by water was well known, and its meaning recognized to be that the conscious element rejects the guilty (si aqua illum velut innoxium receperit—innoxii submerguntur aqua, culpabiles supernatant). Already in the 9th century the laws were prohibiting this practice as a relic of superstition. Lastly, the same trial by water is recognized as one of the regular judicial ordeals in the Hindu code of Manu; if the water does not cause the accused to float when plunged into it, his oath is true. As this ancient Indian body of laws was itself no doubt compiled from materials of still earlier date, we may venture to take the correspondence of the water-ordeal among the European and Asiatic branches of the Aryan race as carrying back its origin to a period of remote antiquity.[226]

Let us hope that if the belief in present witchcraft, and the persecution necessarily ensuing upon such belief, once more come into prominence in the civilized world, they may appear in a milder shape than heretofore, and be kept down by stronger humanity and tolerance. But any one who fancies from their present disappearance that they have necessarily disappeared for ever, must have read history to little purpose, and has yet to learn that 'revival in culture' is something more than an empty pedantic phrase. Our own time has revived a group of beliefs and practices which have their roots deep in the very stratum of early philosophy where witchcraft makes its first appearance. This group of beliefs and practices constitutes what is now commonly known as Spiritualism.

Witchcraft and Spiritualism have existed for thousands of years in a closeness of union not unfairly typified in this verse from John Bale's 16th-century Interlude concerning Nature, which brings under one head the art of bewitching vegetables and poultry, and causing supernatural movement of stools and crockery.

'Theyr wells I can up drye,

Cause trees and herbes to dye,

And slee all pulterye,

Whereas men doth me move:

I can make stoles to daunce

And earthen pottes to praunce,

That none shall them enhaunce,

And do but cast my glove.'

The same intellectual movement led to the decline of both witchcraft and spiritualism, till, early in the last century, men thought that both were dying or all but dead together. Now, however, not only are spiritualists to be counted by tens of thousands in America and England, but there are among them several men of distinguished mental power. I am well aware that the problem of the so-called 'spirit-manifestations' is one to be discussed on its merits, in order to arrive at a distinct opinion how far it may be concerned with facts insufficiently appreciated and explained by science, and how far with superstition, delusion, and sheer knavery. Such investigation, pursued by careful observation in a scientific spirit, would seem apt to throw light on some most interesting psychological questions. But though it lies beyond my scope to examine the spiritualistic evidence for itself, the ethnographic view of the matter has, nevertheless, its value. This shows modern spiritualism to be in great measure a direct revival from the regions of savage philosophy and peasant folk-lore. It is not a simple question of the existence of certain phenomena of mind and matter. It is that, in connexion with these phenomena, a great philosophic-religious doctrine, flourishing in the lower culture but dwindling in the higher, has re-established itself in full vigour. The world is again swarming with intelligent and powerful disembodied spiritual beings, whose direct action on thought and matter is again confidently asserted, as in those times and countries where physical science had not as yet so far succeeded in extruding these spirits and their influences from the system of nature.

Apparitions have regained the place and meaning which they held from the level of the lower races to that of mediæval Europe. The regular ghost-stories, in which spirits of the dead walk visibly and have intercourse with corporeal men, are now restored and cited with new examples as 'glimpses of the night-side of nature,' nor have these stories changed either their strength to those who are disposed to believe them, or their weakness to those who are not. As of old, men live now in habitual intercourse with the spirits of the dead. Necromancy is a religion, and the Chinese manes-worshipper may see the outer barbarians come back, after a heretical interval of a few centuries, into sympathy with his time-honoured creed. As the sorcerers of barbarous tribes lie in bodily lethargy or sleep while their souls depart on distant journeys, so it is not uncommon in modern spiritualistic narratives for persons to be in an insensible state when their apparitions visit distant places, whence they bring back information, and where they communicate with the living. The spirits of the living as well as of the dead, the souls of Strauss and Carl Vogt as well as of Augustine and Jerome, are summoned by mediums to distant spirit-circles. As Dr. Bastian remarks, if any celebrated man in Europe feels himself at some moment in a melancholy mood, he may console himself with the idea that his soul has been sent for to America, to assist at the 'rough fixings' of some backwoodsman. Fifty years ago, Dr. Macculloch, in his 'Description of the Western Islands of Scotland,' wrote thus of the famous Highland second-sight: 'In fact it has undergone the fate of witchcraft; ceasing to be believed, it has ceased to exist.' Yet a generation later he would have found it reinstated in a far larger range of society, and under far better circumstances of learning and material prosperity. Among the influences which have combined to bring about the spiritualistic renaissance, a prominent place may, I think, be given to the effect produced on the religious mind of Europe and America by the intensely animistic teachings of Emanuel Swedenborg, in the 18th century. The position of this remarkable visionary as to some of the particular spiritualistic doctrines may be judged of by the following statements from 'The True Christian Religion.' A man's spirit is his mind, which lives after death in complete human form, and this spirit may be conveyed from place to place while the body remains at rest, as on some occasions happened to Swedenborg himself. 'I have conversed,' he says, 'with all my relations and friends, likewise with kings and princes, and men of learning, after their departure out of this life, and this now for twenty-seven years without interruption.' And foreseeing that many who read his 'Memorable Relations' will believe them to be fictions of imagination, he protests in truth they are not fictions, but were really seen and heard; not seen and heard in any state of mind in sleep, but in a state of complete wakefulness.[227]

I shall have to speak elsewhere of some of the doctrines of modern spiritualism, where they seem to fall into their places in the study of Animism. Here, as a means of illustrating the relation of the newer to the older spiritualistic ideas, I propose to glance over the ethnography of two of the most popular means of communicating with the spirit-world by rapping and writing, and two of the prominent spirit-manifestations, the feat of rising in the air, and the trick of the Davenport Brothers.

The elf who goes knocking and routing about the house at night, and whose special German name is the 'Poltergeist,' is an old and familiar personage in European folk-lore.[228] From of old, such unexplained noises have been ascribed to the agency of personal spirits, who more often than not are considered human souls. The modern Dayaks, Siamese, and Singhalese agree with the Esths as to such routing and rapping being caused by spirits.[229] Knockings may be considered mysterious but harmless, like those which in Swabia and Franconia are expected during Advent on the Anklöpferleins-Nächte, or 'Little Knockers' Nights.'[230] Or they may be useful, as when the Welsh miners think that the 'knockers' they hear underground are indicating the rich veins of lead and silver.[231] Or they may be simply annoying, as when, in the ninth century, a malignant spirit infested a parish by knocking at the walls as if with a hammer, but being overcome with litanies and holy water, confessed itself to be the familiar of a certain wicked priest, and to have been in hiding under his cloak. Thus, in the seventeenth century, the famous demon-drummer of Tedworth, commemorated by Glanvil in the 'Saducismus Triumphatus,' thumped about the doors and the outside of the house, and 'for an hour together it would beat *Roundheads and Cuckolds*, the *Tat-too*, and several other *Points of War*, as well as any Drummer.'[232] But popular philosophy has mostly attached to such mysterious noises a foreboding of death, the knock being held as a signal or summons among spirits as among men. The Romans considered that the genius of death thus announced his coming. Modern folk-lore holds either that a knocking or rumbling in the floor is an omen of a death about to happen, or that dying persons themselves announce their dissolution to their friends in such strange sounds. The English rule takes in both cases: 'Three loud and distinct knocks at the bed's head of a sick person, or at the bed's head or door of any of his relations, is an omen of his death.' We happen to have a good means of testing the amount of actual correspondence between omen and event necessary to establish these rules: the illogical people who were (and still are) able to discover a connexion between the ticking of the 'death-watch' beetle and an ensuing death in the house, no doubt found it equally easy to give a prophetic interpretation to any other mysterious knocks.[233] There is a story, dated 1534, of a ghost that answered questions by knocking in the Catholic church of Orleans, and demanded the removal of the provost's Lutheran wife, who had been buried there; but the affair proved to be a trick of a Franciscan friar.[234] The system of working an alphabet by counted raps is a device familiar to prison-cells, where it has long been at once the despair of gaolers and an evidence of the diffusion of education even among the criminal classes. Thus when, in 1847, the celebrated rappings began to trouble the township of Arcadia in the State of New York, the Fox family of Rochester, founders of the modern spiritual movement, had on the one hand only to revive the ancient prevalent belief in spirit-rappings, which had almost fallen into the limbo of discredited superstitions, while, on the other hand, the system of communication with the spirits was ready made to their hand. The system of a rapping-alphabet remains in full use, and numberless specimens of messages thus received are in print, possibly the longest being a novel, of which I can only give the title, 'Juanita, Nouvelle par une Chaise. À l'Imprimerie du Gouvernement, Basse Terre (Guadeloupe), 1853.' In the recorded communications, names, dates, &c., are often alleged to have been stated under remarkable circumstances, while the style of thought, language, and spelling fits with the intellectual quality of the medium. A large proportion of the communications being obviously false and silly, even when the 'spirit' has announced itself in the name of some great statesman, moralist, or philosopher of the past, the theory has been adopted by spiritualists that foolish or lying spirits are apt to personate those of higher degree, and give messages in their names.

Spirit-writing is of two kinds, according as it is done with or without a material instrument. The first kind is in full practice in China, where, like other rites of divination, it is probably ancient. It is called 'descending of the pencil,' and is especially used by the literary classes. When a Chinese wishes to consult a god in this way, he sends for a professional medium. Before the image of the god are set candles and incense, and an offering of tea or mock money. In front of this, on another table, is placed an oblong tray of dry sand. The writing instrument is a V-shaped wooden handle, two or three feet long, with a wooden tooth fixed at its point. Two persons hold this instrument, each grasping one leg of it, and the point resting in the sand. Proper prayers and charms induce the god to manifest his presence by a movement of the point in the sand, and thus the response is written, and there only remains the somewhat difficult and doubtful task of deciphering it. To what state of opinion the rite belongs may be judged from this: when the sacred apricot-tree is to be robbed of a branch to make the spirit-pen an apologetic inscription is scratched upon the trunk.[235] Notwithstanding theological differences between China and England, the art of spirit-writing is much the same in the two countries. A kind of 'planchette' seems to have been known in Europe in the seventeenth century.[236] The instrument, which may now be bought at the toy-shops, is a heart-shaped board some seven inches long, resting on three supports, of which the two at the wide end are castors, and the third at the pointed end is a pencil thrust through a hole in the board. The instrument is placed on a sheet of paper, and worked by two persons laying their fingers lightly on it, waiting till, without conscious effort of the operators, it moves and writes answers to questions. It is not everybody who has the faculty of spirit-writing, but a powerful medium will write alone. Such mediums sometimes consider themselves acted on by some power separate from themselves, in fact, possessed.

Ecclesiastical history commemorates a miracle at the close of the Nicene Council. Two bishops, Chrysanthus and Mysonius, had died during its sitting, and the remaining crowd of Fathers brought the acts, signed by themselves, to the tomb, addressed the deceased bishops as if still alive, and left the document. Next day, returning, they found the two signatures added, to this effect:—'We, Chrysanthus and Mysonius, consenting with all the Fathers in the holy first and œcumenical Nicene Synod, although translated from the body, have also signed the volume with our own hands.'[237] Such spirit-writing without material instrument has lately been renewed by the Baron de Guldenstubbé. This writer confirms by new evidence the truth of the tradition of all peoples as to souls of the dead keeping up their connexion with their mortal remains, and haunting the places where they dwelt 'during their terrestrial incarnation.' Thus Francis I. manifests himself principally at Fontainebleau, while Louis XV. and Marie-Antoinette roam about the Trianons. Moreover, if pieces of blank paper be set out in suitable places, the spirits, enveloped in their ethereal bodies, will concentrate by their force of will electric currents on the paper, and so form written characters. The Baron publishes, in his 'Pneumatologie Positive,' a mass of facsimiles of spirit-writings thus obtained. Julius and Augustus Cæsar give their names near their statues in the Louvre; Juvenal produces a ludicrous attempt at a copy of verses; Héloise at Père-la-Chaise informs the world, in modern French, that Abelard and she are united and happy; St. Paul writes himself ελζιστος αποστολον (meaning, we may suppose, ελαχιστος αποστολων); and Hippokrates the physician (who spells himself Hippōkratĕs) attended M. de Guldenstubbé at his lodgings in Paris, and gave him a signature which of itself cured a sharp attack of rheumatism in a few minutes.[238]

The miracle of rising and floating in the air is one fully recognized in the literature of ancient India. The Buddhist saint of high ascetic rank attains the power called 'perfection' (irdhi), whereby he is able to rise in the air, as also to overturn the earth and stop the sun. Having this power, the saint exercises it by the mere determination of his will, his body becoming imponderous, as when a man in the common human state determines to leap, and leaps. Buddhist annals relate the performance of the miraculous suspension by Gautama himself, as well as by other saints, as, for example, his ancestor Maha Sammata, who could thus seat himself in the air without visible support. Even without this exalted faculty, it is considered possible to rise and move in the air by an effort of ecstatic joy (udwega prîti). A remarkable mention of this feat, as said to be performed by the Indian Brahmans, occurs in the third-century biography of Apollonius of Tyana; these Brahmans are described as going about in the air some two cubits from the ground, not for the sake of miracle (such ambition they despised), but for its being more suitable to solar rites.[239] Foreign conjurers were professing to exhibit this miracle among the Greeks in the second century, as witness Lucian's jocular account of the Hyperborean conjurer:—'Thou art joking, said Kleodemos, but I was once more incredulous than thou about such things, for I thought nothing could have persuaded me to believe them; but when I first saw that foreign barbarian flying—he was of the Hyperboreans, he said—I believed, and was overcome in spite of my resistance. For what was I to do, when I saw him carried through the air in daylight, and walking on the water, and passing leisurely and slowly through the fire? What? (said his interlocutor), you saw the Hyperborean man flying, and walking on the water? To be sure, said he, and he had on undressed leather brogues as they generally wear them; but what's the use of talking of such trifles, considering what other manifestations he showed us,—sending loves, calling up demons, raising the dead, and bringing in Hekate herself visibly, and drawing down the moon?' Kleodemos then goes on to relate how the conjurer first had his four minæ down for sacrificial expenses, and then made a clay Cupid, and sent it flying through the air to fetch the girl whom Glaukias had fallen in love with, and presently, lo and behold, there she was knocking at the door! The interlocutor, however, comments in a sceptical vein on the narrative. It was scarce needful, he says, to have taken the trouble to send for the girl with clay, and a magician from the Hyperboreans, and even the moon, considering that for twenty drachmas she would have let herself be taken to the Hyperboreans themselves; and she seems, moreover, to have been affected in quite an opposite way to spirits, for whereas these beings take flight if they hear the noise of brass or iron, Chrysis no sooner hears the chink of silver anywhere, but she comes toward the sound.[240] Another early instance of the belief in miraculous suspension is in the life of Iamblichus, the great Neo-Platonist mystic. His disciples says Eunapius, told him they had heard a report from his servants, that while in prayer to the gods he had been lifted more than ten cubits from the ground, his body and clothes changing to a beautiful golden colour, but after he ceased from prayer his body became as before, and then he came down to the ground and returned to the society of his followers. They entreated him therefore, 'Why, O most divine teacher, why dost thou do such things by thyself, and not let us partake of the more perfect wisdom?' Then Iamblichus, though not given to laughter, laughed at this story, and said to them, 'It was no fool who tricked you thus, but the thing is not true.'[241]

After a while, the prodigy which the Platonist disclaimed, became a usual attribute of Christian saints. Thus St. Richard, then chancellor to St. Edmund, Archbishop of Canterbury, one day softly opening the chapel door, to see why the archbishop did not come to dinner, saw him raised high in the air, with his knees bent and his arms stretched out; falling gently to the ground, and seeing the chancellor, he complained that he had hindered him of great spiritual delight and comfort. So St. Philip Neri used to be sometimes seen raised several yards from the ground during his rapturous devotions, with a bright light shining from his countenance. St. Ignatius Loyola is declared to have been raised about two feet under the same circumstances, and similar legends of devout ascetics being not only metaphorically but materially 'raised above the earth' are told in the lives of St. Dominic, St. Dunstan, St. Theresa, and other less-known saints. In the last century, Dom Calmet speaks of knowing a good monk who rises sometimes from the ground and remains involuntarily suspended, especially on seeing some devotional image or hearing some devout prayer, and also a nun who has often seen herself raised in spite of herself to a certain distance from the earth. Unfortunately the great commentator does not specify any witnesses as having seen the monk and nun rise in the air. If they only thought themselves thus elevated, their stories can only rank with that of the young man mentioned by De Maistre, who so often seemed to himself to float in the air, that he came to suspect that gravitation might not be natural to man.[242] The hallucination of rising and floating in the air is extremely common, and ascetics of all religions are especially liable to it.

Among modern accounts of diabolic possession, also, the rising in the air is described as taking place not subjectively but objectively. In 1657, Richard Jones, a sprightly lad of twelve years old, living at Shepton Mallet, was bewitched by one Jane Brooks; he was seen to rise in the air and pass over a garden wall some thirty yards, and at other times was found in a room with his hands flat against a beam at the top of the room, and his body two or three feet from the ground, nine people at a time seeing him in this latter position. Jane Brooks was accordingly condemned and executed at Chard Assizes in March, 1658. Richard, the Surrey demoniac of 1689, was hoisted up in the air and let down by Satan; at the beginning of his fits he was, as it were, blown or snatched or borne up suddenly from his chair, as if he would have flown away, but that those who held him hung to his arms and legs and clung about him. One account (not the official medical one) of the demoniacal possessions at Morzine in Savoy, in 1864, relates that a patient was held suspended in the air by an invisible force during some seconds or minutes above the cemetery, in the presence of the archbishop.[243] Modern spiritualists claim this power as possessed by certain distinguished living mediums, who, indeed, profess to rival in sober fact the aerostatic miracles of Buddhist and Catholic legend. The force employed is of course considered to be that of the spirits.

The performances of tied mediums have been specially represented in England by the Davenport Brothers, who 'are generally recognized by Spiritualists as genuine media, and attribute the reverse opinion so deeply rooted in the public mind, to the untruthfulness of the London and many other newspapers.' The performers were bound fast and shut by themselves in a dark cabinet, with musical instruments, whence not only musical sounds proceeded, but the coats of the mediums were taken off and replaced; yet on inspection their bodies were discovered still bound. The spirits would also release the bound mediums from their cords, however carefully tied about them.[244] Now the idea of supernatural unbinding is very ancient, vouched for as it is by no less a personage than the crafty Odysseus himself, in his adventure on board the ship of the Thesprotians:

'Me on the well-benched vessel, strongly bound,

They leave, and snatch their meal upon the beach.

But to my help the gods themselves unwound

My cords with ease, though firmly twisted round.'

In early English chronicle, we find it in a story told by the Venerable Bede. A certain Imma was found all but dead on the field of battle, and taken prisoner, but when he began to recover and was put in bonds to prevent his escaping, no sooner did his binders leave him but he was loose again. The earl who owned him enquired whether he had about him such 'loosening letters' (literas solutorias) as tales were told of; the man replied that he knew naught of such arts; yet when his owner sold him to another master, there was still no binding him. The received explanation of this strange power was emphatically a spiritual one. His brother had sought for his dead body, and finding another like him, buried it and proceeded to say masses for his brother's soul, by the celebration whereof it came to pass that no one could fasten him, for he was out of bonds again directly. So they sent him home to Kent, whence he duly returned his ransom, and his story, it is related, stimulated many to devotion, who understood by it how salutary are masses to the redemption both of soul and body. Again, there prevailed in Scotland up to the 18th century this notion: when the lunatics who had been brought to St. Fillan's Pool to be bathed, were laid bound in the neighbouring church next night, if they were found loose in the morning their recovery was expected, but if at dawn they were still bound, their cure was doubtful.

The untying trick performed among savages is so similar to that of our mountebanks, that when we find the North American Indian jugglers doing both this and the familiar trick of breathing fire, we are at a loss to judge whether they inherited these two feats from their savage ancestors, or borrowed them from the white men. The point is not, however, the mere performance of the untying trick, but its being attributed to the help of spiritual beings. This notion is thoroughly at home in savage culture. It comes out well in the Esquimaux' accounts which date from early in the 18th century. Cranz thus describes the Greenland angekok setting out on his mystic journey to heaven and hell. When he has drummed awhile and made all sorts of wondrous contortions, he is himself bound with a thong by one of his pupils, his head between his legs, and his hands behind his back. All the lamps in the house are put out, and the windows darkened, for no one must see him hold intercourse with his spirit, no one must move or even scratch his head, that the spirit may not be interfered with—or rather, says the missionary, that no one may catch him at his trickery, for there is no going up to heaven in broad daylight. At last, after strange noises have been heard, and a visit has been received or paid to the torngak or spirit, the magician reappears unbound, but pale and excited, and gives an account of his adventures. Castrén's account of the similar proceedings of the Siberian shamans is as follows: 'They are practised' he says, 'in all sorts of conjuring-tricks, by which they know how to dazzle the simple crowd, and inspire greater trust in themselves. One of the most usual juggleries of the shamans in the Government of Tomsk consists of the following hocus-pocus, a wonder to the Russians as well as to the Samoieds. The shaman sits down on the wrong side of a dry reindeer-hide spread in the middle of the floor. There he lets himself be bound hand and foot by the assistants. The shutters are closed, and the shaman begins to invoke his ministering spirits. All at once there arises a mysterious ghostliness in the dark space. Voices are heard from different parts, both within and without the yurt, while on the dry reindeer skin there is a rattling and drumming in regular time. Bears growl, snakes hiss, and squirrels leap about in the room. At last this uncanny work ceases, and the audience impatiently await the result of the game. A few moments pass in this expectation, and behold, the shaman walks in free and unbound from outside. No one doubts that it was the spirits who were drumming, growling, and hissing, who released the shaman from his bonds, and who carried him by secret ways out of the yurt.'[245]

On the whole, the ethnography of spiritualism bears on practical opinion somewhat in this manner. Beside the question of the absolute truth or falsity of the alleged possessions, names-oracles, doubles, brain-waves, furniture movings, and floatings in the air, there remains the history of spiritualistic belief as a matter of opinion. Hereby it appears that the received spiritualistic theory of the alleged phenomena belongs to the philosophy of savages. As to such matters as apparitions or possessions this is obvious, and it holds in more extreme cases. Suppose a wild North American Indian looking on at a spirit-séance in London. As to the presence of disembodied spirits, manifesting themselves by raps, noises, voices, and other physical actions, the savage would be perfectly at home in the proceedings, for such things are part and parcel of his recognized system of nature. The part of the affair really strange to him would be the introduction of such arts as spelling and writing, which do belong to a different state of civilization from his. The issue raised by the comparison of savage, barbaric, and civilized spiritualism, is this: Do the Red Indian medicine-man, the Tatar necromancer, the Highland ghost-seer, and the Boston medium, share the possession of belief and knowledge of the highest truth and import, which, nevertheless, the great intellectual movement of the last two centuries has simply thrown aside as worthless? Is what we are habitually boasting of and calling new enlightenment, then, in fact a decay of knowledge? If so, this is a truly remarkable case of degeneration, and the savages whom some ethnographers look on as degenerate from a higher civilization, may turn on their accusers and charge them with having fallen from the high level of savage knowledge.

Throughout the whole of this varied investigation, whether of the dwindling survival of old culture, or of its bursting forth afresh in active revival, it may perhaps be complained that its illustrations should be chosen so much among things worn out, worthless, frivolous, or even bad with downright harmful folly. It is in fact so, and I have taken up this course of argument with full knowledge and intent. For, indeed, we have in such enquiries continual reason to be thankful for fools. It is quite wonderful, even if we hardly go below the surface of the subject, to see how large a share stupidity and unpractical conservatism and dogged superstition have had in preserving for us traces of the history of our race, which practical utilitarianism would have remorselessly swept away. The savage is firmly, obstinately conservative. No man appeals with more unhesitating confidence to the great precedent-makers of the past; the wisdom of his ancestors can control against the most obvious evidence his own opinions and actions. We listen with pity to the rude Indian as he maintains against civilized science and experience the authority of his rude forefathers. We smile at the Chinese appealing against modern innovation to the golden precepts of Confucius, who in his time looked back with the same prostrate reverence to sages still more ancient, counselling his disciples to follow the seasons of Hea, to ride in the carriage of Yin, to wear the ceremonial cap of Chow.

The nobler tendency of advancing culture, and above all of scientific culture, is to honour the dead without grovelling before them, to profit by the past without sacrificing the present to it. Yet even the modern civilized world has but half learnt this lesson, and an unprejudiced survey may lead us to judge how many of our ideas and customs exist rather by being old than by being good. Now in dealing with hurtful superstitions, the proof that they are things which it is the tendency of savagery to produce, and of higher culture to destroy, is accepted as a fair controversial argument. The mere historical position of a belief or custom may raise a presumption as to its origin which becomes a presumption as to its authenticity. Dr. Middleton's celebrated Letter from Rome shows cases in point. He mentions the image of Diana at Ephesus which fell from the sky, thereby damaging the pretensions of the Calabrian image of St. Dominic, which, according to pious tradition, was likewise brought down from heaven. He notices that as the blood of St. Januarius now melts miraculously without heat, so ages ago the priests of Gnatia tried to persuade Horace, on his road to Brundusium, that the frankincense in their temple had the habit of melting in like manner:

'... dehinc Gnatia lymphis

Iratis exstructa dedit risusque jocosque;

Dum flamma sine thura liquescere limine sacro,

Persuadere cupit: credat Judæus Apella;

Non ego.'[246]

Thus ethnographers, not without a certain grim satisfaction, may at times find means to make stupid and evil superstitions bear witness against themselves.

Moreover, in working to gain an insight into the general laws of intellectual movement, there is practical gain in being able to study them rather among antiquarian relics of no intense modern interest, than among those seething problems of the day on which action has to be taken amid ferment and sharp strife. Should some moralist or politician speak contemptuously of the vanity of studying matters without practical moment, it will generally be found that his own mode of treatment will consist in partizan diatribes on the questions of the day, a proceeding practical enough, especially in confirming those who agree with him already, but the extreme opposite to the scientific way of eliciting truth. The ethnographer's course, again, should be like that of the anatomist who carries on his studies if possible rather on dead than on living subjects; vivisection is nervous work, and the humane investigator hates inflicting needless pain. Thus when the student of culture occupies himself in viewing the bearings of exploded controversies, or in unravelling the history of long-superseded inventions, he is gladly seeking his evidence rather in such dead old history, than in the discussions where he and those he lives among are alive with intense party feeling, and where his judgment is biassed by the pressure of personal sympathy, and even it may be of personal gain or loss. So, from things which perhaps never were of high importance, things which have fallen out of popular significance, or even out of popular memory, he tries to elicit general laws of culture, often to be thus more easily and fully gained than in the arena of modern philosophy and politics.

But the opinions drawn from old or worn-out culture are not to be left lying where they were shaped. It is no more reasonable to suppose the laws of mind differently constituted in Australia and in England, in the time of the cave-dwellers and in the time of the builders of sheet-iron houses, than to suppose that the laws of chemical combination were of one sort in the time of the coal-measures, and are of another now. The thing that has been will be; and we are to study savages and old nations to learn the laws that under new circumstances are working for good or ill in our own development. If it is needful to give an instance of the directness with which antiquity and savagery bear upon our modern life, let it be taken in the facts just brought forward on the relation of ancient sorcery to the belief in witchcraft which was not long since one of the gravest facts of European history, and of savage spiritualism to beliefs which so deeply affect our civilization now. No one who can see in these cases, and in many others to be brought before him in these volumes, how direct and close the connexion may be between modern culture and the condition of the rudest savage, will be prone to accuse students who spend their labour on even the lowest and most trifling facts of ethnography, of wasting their hours in the satisfaction of a frivolous curiosity.

CHAPTER V.
EMOTIONAL AND IMITATIVE LANGUAGE.

> Element of directly expressive Sound in Language—Test by independent correspondence in distinct languages—Constituent processes of Language—Gesture—Expression of feature, &c.—Emotional Tone—Articulate sounds, vowels determined by musical quality and pitch, consonants—Emphasis and Accent—Phrase-melody, Recitative—Sound-Words—Interjections—Calls to Animals—Emotional Cries—Sense-Words formed from Interjections—Affirmative and Negative particles, &c.

In carrying on the enquiry into the development of culture, evidence of some weight is to be gained from an examination of Language. Comparing the grammars and dictionaries of races at various grades of civilization, it appears that, in the great art of speech, the educated man at this day substantially uses the method of the savage, only expanded and improved in the working out of details. It is true that the languages of the Tasmanian and the Chinese, of the Greenlander and the Greek, differ variously in structure; but this is a secondary difference, underlaid by a primary similarity in method, namely, the expression of ideas by articulate sounds habitually allotted to them. Now all languages are found on inspection to contain some articulate sounds of a directly natural and directly intelligible kind. These are sounds of interjectional or imitative character, which have their meaning not by inheritance from parents or adoption from foreigners, but by being taken up directly from the world of sound into the world of sense. Like pantomimic gestures, they are capable of conveying their meaning of themselves, without reference to the particular language they are used in connexion with. From the observation of these, there have arisen speculations as to the origin of language, treating such expressive sounds as the fundamental constituents of language in general, and considering those of them which are still plainly recognizable as having remained more or less in their original state, long courses of adaptation and variation having produced from such the great mass of words in all languages, in which no connexion between idea and sound can any longer be certainly made out. Thus grew up doctrines of a 'natural' origin of language, which, dating from classic times, were developed in the eighteenth century into a system by that powerful thinker, the President Charles de Brosses, and in our own time have been expanded and solidified by a school of philologers, among whom Mr. Hensleigh Wedgwood is the most prominent.[247] These theories have no doubt been incautiously and fancifully worked. No wonder that students who found in nature real and direct sources of articulate speech, in interjectional sounds like *ah! ugh! h'm! sh!* and in imitative sounds like *purr, whiz, tomtom, cuckoo,* should have thought that the whole secret of language lay within their grasp, and that they had only to fit the keys thus found into one hole after another to open every lock. When a philosopher has a truth in his hands, he is apt to stretch it farther than it will bear. The magic umbrella must spread and spread till it becomes a tent wide enough to shelter the king's army. But it must be borne in mind that what criticism touches in these opinions is their exaggeration, not their reality. That interjections and imitative words are really taken up to some extent, be it small or large, into the very body and structure of language, no one denies. Such a denial, if anyone offered it, the advocates of the disputed theories might dispose of in the single phrase, that they would neither be *pooh-poohed* nor *hooted* down. It may be shown within the limits of the most strict and sober argument, that the theory of the origin of language in natural and directly expressive sounds does account for a considerable fraction of the existing copia verborum, while it raises a presumption that, could we trace the history of words more fully, it would account for far more.

In here examining interjectional and imitative sounds with their derivative words, as well as certain other parts of language of a more or less cognate character, I purpose to bring forward as far as possible new evidence derived from the languages of savage and barbarous races. By so doing it becomes practicable to use a check which in great measure stops the main source of uncertainty and error in such enquiries, the habit of etymologizing words off-hand from expressive sounds, by the unaided and often flighty fancy of a philologer. By simply enlarging the survey of language, the province of the imagination is brought within narrower limits. If several languages, which cannot be classed as distinctly of the same family, unite in expressing some notion by a particular sound which may fairly claim to be interjectional or imitative, their combined authority will go far to prove the claim a just one. For if it be objected that such words may have passed into the different languages from a common source, of which the trace is for the most part lost, this may be answered by the question, Why is there not a proportionate agreement between the languages in question throughout the far larger mass of words which cannot pretend to be direct sound-words? If several languages have independently chosen like words to express like meanings, then we may reasonably suppose that we are not deluding ourselves in thinking such words highly appropriate to their purpose. They are words which answered the conditions of original language, conforming as they do to the saying of Thomas Aquinas, that the names of things ought to agree with their natures, 'nomina debent naturis rerum congruere.' Applied in such comparison, the languages of the lower races contribute evidence of excellent quality to the problem. It will at the same time and by the same proofs appear, that savages possess in a high degree the faculty of uttering their minds directly in emotional tones and interjections, of going straight to nature to furnish themselves with imitative sounds, including reproductions of their own direct emotional utterances, as means of expression of ideas, and of introducing into their formal language words so produced. They have clearly thus far the means and power of producing language. In so far as the theories under consideration account for the original formation of language, they countenance the view that this formation took place among mankind in a savage state, and even, for anything appearing to the contrary, in a still lower stage of culture than has survived to our day.[248]

The first step in such investigation is to gain a clear idea of the various elements of which spoken language is made up. These may be enumerated as gesture, expression of feature, emotional tone, emphasis, force, speed, &c. of utterance, musical rhythm and intonation, and the formation of the vowels and consonants which are the skeleton of articulate speech.

In the common intercourse of men, speech is habitually accompanied by gesture, the hands, head, and body aiding and illustrating the spoken phrase. So far as we can judge, the visible gesture and the audible word have been thus used in combination since times of most remote antiquity in the history of our race. It seems, however, that in the daily intercourse of the lower races, gesture holds a much more important place than we are accustomed to see it fill, a position even encroaching on that which articulate speech holds among ourselves. Mr. Bonwick confirms by his experience Dr. Milligan's account of the Tasmanians as using 'signs to eke out the meaning of monosyllabic expressions, and to give force, precision, and character to vocal sounds.' Captain Wilson remarks on the use of gesticulation in modifying words in the Chinook Jargon. There is confirmation to Spix and Martius' description of low Brazilian tribes completing by signs the meaning of their scanty sentences, thus making the words 'wood-go' serve to say 'I will go into the wood,' by pointing the mouth like a snout in the direction meant. The Rev. J. L. Wilson, describing the Grebo language of West Africa, remarks that they have personal pronouns, but seldom use them in conversation, leaving it to gesture to determine whether a verb is to be taken in the first or second person; thus the words 'ni ne' will mean 'I do it,' or 'you do it,' according to the significant gestures of the speaker.[249] Beside such instances, it will hereafter be noticed that the lower races, in counting, habitually use gesture-language for a purpose to which higher races apply word-language. To this prominent condition of gesture as a means of expression among rude tribes, and to the development of pantomime in public show and private intercourse among such peoples as the Neapolitans of our own day, the most extreme contrast may be found in England, where, whether for good or ill, suggestive pantomime is now reduced to so small a compass in social talk, and even in public oratory.

Changes of the bodily attitude, corresponding in their fine gradations with changes of the feelings, comprise conditions of the surface of the body, postures of the limbs, and also especially those expressive attitudes of the face to which our attention is particularly directed when we notice one another. The visible expression of the features is a symptom which displays the speaker's state of mind, his feelings of pleasure or disgust, of pride or humility, of faith or doubt, and so forth. Not that there is between the emotion and its bodily expression any originally intentional connexion. It is merely that a certain action of our physical machinery shows symptoms which we have learnt by experience to refer to a mental cause, as we judge by seeing a man sweat or limp that he is hot or footsore. Blushing is caused by certain emotions, and among Europeans it is a visible expression or symptom of them; not so among South American Indians, whose blushes, as Mr. David Forbes points out, may be detected by the hand or a thermometer, but being concealed by the dark skin cannot serve as a visible sign of feeling.[250] By turning these natural processes to account, men contrive to a certain extent to put on particular physical expressions, frowning or smiling for instance, in order to simulate the emotions which would naturally produce such expressions, or merely to convey the thought of such emotions to others. Now it is well known to every one that physical expression by feature, &c., forming a part of the universal gesture-language, thus serves as an important adjunct to spoken language. It is not so obvious, but on examination will prove to be true, that such expression by feature itself acts as a formative power in vocal language. Expression of countenance has an action beyond that of mere visible gesture. The bodily attitude brought on by a particular state of mind affects the position of the organs of speech, both the internal larynx, &c., and the external features whose change can be watched by the mere looker-on. Even though the expression of the speaker's face may not be seen by the hearer, the effect of the whole bodily attitude of which it forms part is not thereby done away with. For on the position thus taken by the various organs concerned in speech, depends what I have here called 'emotional tone,' whereby the voice carries direct expression of the speaker's feeling.

The ascertaining of the precise physical mode in which certain attitudes of the internal and external face come to correspond to certain moods of mind, is a physiological problem as yet little understood; but the fact that particular expressions of face are accompanied by corresponding and dependent expressions of emotional tone, only requires an observer or a looking-glass to prove it. The laugh made with a solemn, contemptuous, or sarcastic face, is quite different from that which comes from a joyous one; the *ah! oh! ho! hey!* and so on, change their modulations to match the expression of countenance. The effect of the emotional tone does not even require fitness in the meaning of the spoken words, for nonsense or an unknown tongue may be made to convey, when spoken with expressive intonation, the feelings which are displayed upon the speaker's face. This expression may even be recognized in the dark by noticing the tone it gives forth, while the forced character given by the attempt to bring out a sound not matching even the outward play of the features can hardly be hidden by the most expert ventriloquist, and in such forcing, the sound perceptibly drags the face into the attitude that fits with it. The nature of communication by emotional tone seems to me to be somewhat on this wise. It does not appear that particular tones at all belong directly and of themselves to particular emotions, but that their action depends on the vocal organs of the speaker and hearer. Other animals, having vocal organs different from man's, have accordingly, as we know, a different code of emotional tones. An alteration in man's vocal organs would bring a corresponding alteration in the effect of tone in expressing feeling; the tone which to us expresses surprise or anger might come to express pleasure, and so forth. As it is, children learn by early experience that such and such a tone indicates such and such an emotion, and this they make out partly by finding themselves uttering such tones when their feelings have brought their faces to the appropriate attitudes, and partly by observing the expression of voice in others. At three or four years old they are to be seen in the act of acquiring this knowledge, turning round to look at the speaker's face and gesture to make sure of the meaning of the tone. But in later years this knowledge becomes so familiar that it is supposed to have been intuitive. Then, when men talk together, the hearer receives from each emotional tone an indication, a signal, of the speaker's attitude of body, and through this of his state of mind. These he can recognize, and even reproduce in himself, as the operator at one end of a telegraphic wire can follow, by noticing his needles, the action of his colleague at the other. In watching the process which thus enables one man to take a copy of another's emotions through their physical effects on his vocal tone, we may admire the perfection with which a means so simple answers an end so complex, and apparently so remote.

By eliminating from speech all effects of gesture, of expression of face, and of emotional tone, we go far toward reducing it to that system of conventional articulate sounds which the grammarian and the comparative philologist habitually consider as language. These articulate sounds are capable of being roughly set down in signs standing for vowels and consonants, with the aid of accents and other significant marks; and they may then again be read aloud from these written signs, by any one who has learnt to give its proper sound to each letter.

What vowels are, is a matter which has been for some years well understood.[251] They are compound musical tones such as, in the vox humana stop of the organ, are sounded by reeds (vibrating tongues) fitted to organ-pipes of particular construction. The manner of formation of vowels by the voice is shortly this. There are situated in the larynx a pair of vibrating membranes called the vocal chords, which may be rudely imitated by stretching a piece of sheet india-rubber over the open end of a tube, so as to form two half-covers to it, 'like the parchment of a drum split across the middle;' when the tube is blown through, the india-rubber flaps will vibrate as the vocal chords do in the larynx, and give out a sound. In the human voice, the musical effect of the vibrating chords is increased by the cavity of the mouth, which acts as a resonator or sounding-box, and which also, by its shape at any moment, modifies the musical 'quality' or 'timbre' of the sound produced. This, not the less felt because its effects are not registered in musical notation, depends on the harmonic overtones accompanying the fundamental tone which alone musical notation takes account of. It makes the difference between the same note on two instruments, flute and piano for instance, while some instruments, as the violin, can give to one note a wide variation of quality. To such quality the formation of vowels is due. This is perfectly shown by the common Jew's harp, which when struck can be made to utter the vowels a, e, i, o, u, &c., by simply putting the mouth in the proper position for speaking these vowels. In this experiment the player's voice emits no sound, but the vibrating tongue of the Jew's harp placed in front of the mouth acts as a substitute for the vocal chords, and the vowel-sounds are produced by the various positions of the cavity of the mouth, modifying the quality of the note, by bringing out with different degrees of strength the series of harmonic tones of which it is composed. As to musical theory, emotional tone and vowel-tone are connected. In fact, an emotional tone may be defined as a vowel, whose particular musical quality is that produced by the human vocal organs, when adjusted to a particular state of feeling.

Europeans, while using modulation of musical pitch as affecting the force of words in a sentence, know nothing of making it alter the dictionary-meaning of a word. But this device is known elsewhere, especially in South-East Asia, where rises and falls of tone, to some extent like those which serve us in conveying emphasis, question and answer, &c., actually give different signification. Thus in Siamese, *há*=to seek, *hã*=pestilence, *hà*=five. The consequence of this elaborate system of tone-accentuation is the necessity of an accumulation of expletive particles, to supply the place of the oratorical or emphatic intonation, which being thus given over to the dictionary is lost for the grammar. Another consequence is, that the system of setting poetry to music becomes radically different from ours; to sing a Siamese song to a European tune makes the meaning of the syllables alter according to their rise and fall in pitch, and turns their sense into the wildest nonsense.[252] In West Africa, again, the same device appears: thus in Dahoman *so*=stick, *só*=horse, *sò*=thunder; Yoruba, *bá*=with, *bà*=bend.[253] For practical purposes, this linguistic music is hardly to be commended, but theoretically it is interesting, as showing that man does not servilely follow an intuitive or inherited scheme of language, but works out in various ways the resources of sound as a means of expression.

The theory of consonants is much more obscure than that of vowels. They are not musical vibrations as vowels are, but noises accompanying them. To the musician such noises as the rushing of the wind from the organ-pipe, the scraping of the violin, the sputtering of the flute, are simply troublesome as interfering with his musical tones, and he takes pains to diminish them as much as may be. But in the art of language noises of this kind, far from being avoided, are turned to immense account by being used as consonants, in combination with the musical vowels. As to the positions and movements of the vocal organs in producing consonants, an excellent account with anatomical diagrams is given in Professor Max Müller's second series of Lectures. For the present purpose of passing in review the various devices by which the language-maker has contrived to make sound a means of expressing thought, perhaps no better illustration of their nature can be mentioned than Sir Charles Wheatstone's account of his speaking machine;[254] for one of the best ways of studying difficult phenomena is to see them artificially imitated. The instrument in question pronounced Latin, French, and Italian words well: it could say, 'Je vous aime de tout mon cœur,' 'Leopoldus Secundus Romanorum Imperator,' and so forth, but it was not so successful with German. As to the vowels, they were of course simply sounded by suitable reeds and pipes. To affect them with consonants, contrivances were arranged to act like the human organs. Thus *p* was made by suddenly removing the operator's hand from the mouth of the figure, and *b* in the same way, except that the mouth was not quite covered, while an outlet like the nostrils was used in forming *m*; *f* and *v* were rendered by modifying the shape of the mouth by a hand; air was made to rush through small tubes to produce the sibilants *s* and *sh*; and the liquids *r* and *l* were sounded by the action of tremulous reeds. As Wheatstone remarks, the most important use of such ingenious mechanical imitations of speech may be to fix and preserve an accurate register of the pronunciation of different languages. A perfectly arranged speaking machine would in fact represent for us that framework of language which consists of mere vowels and consonants, though without most of those expressive adjuncts which go to make up the conversation of speaking men.

Of vowels and consonants capable of being employed in language, man is able to pronounce and distinguish an enormous variety. But this great stock of possible sounds is nowhere brought into use altogether. Each language or dialect of the world is found in practice to select a limited series of definite vowels and consonants, keeping with tolerable exactness to each, and thus choosing what we may call its phonetic alphabet. Neglecting such minor differences as occur in the speech of individuals or small communities, each dialect of the world may be said to have its own phonetic system, and these phonetic systems vary widely. Our vowels, for instance, differ much from those of French and Dutch. French knows nothing of either of the sounds which we write as *th* in *thin* and *that*, while the Castilian lisped *c*, the so-called *ceceo*, is a third consonant which we must again make shift to write as *th*, though it is quite distinct in sound from both our own. It is quite a usual thing for us to find foreign languages wanting letters even near in sound to some of ours, while possessing others unfamiliar to ourselves. Among such cases are the Chinese difficulty in pronouncing *r*, and the want of *s* and *f* in Australian dialects. When foreigners tried to teach the Mohawks, who have no labials in their language, to pronounce words with *p* and *b* in them, they protested that it was too ridiculous to expect people to shut their mouths to speak; and the Portuguese discoverers of Brazil, remarking that the natives had neither *f*, *l*, nor *r* in their language, neatly described them as a people with neither *fé*, *ley*, nor *rey*, neither faith, law, nor king. It may happen, too, that sounds only used by some nations as interjectional noises, unwritten and unwriteable, shall be turned to account by others in their articulate language. Something of this kind occurs with the noises called 'clicks.' Such sounds are familiar to us as interjections; thus the lateral click made in the cheek (and usually in the left cheek) is continually used in driving horses, while varieties of the dental and palatal click made with the tongue against the teeth and the roof of the mouth, are common in the nursery as expressions of surprise, reproof, or satisfaction. Thus, too, the natives of Tierra del Fuego express 'no' by a peculiar cluck, as do also the Turks, who accompany it with the gesture of throwing back the head; and it appears from the accounts of travellers that the clicks of surprise and admiration among the natives of Australia are much like those we hear at home. But though here these clicking noises are only used interjectionally, it is well known that South African races have taken such sounds up into their articulate speech and have made, as we may say, letters of them. The very name of Hottentots, applied to the Namaquas and other kindred tribes, appears to be not a native name (as Peter Kolb thought) but a rude imitative word coined by the Dutch to express the clicking '*hot* en *tot*,' and the term *Hottentotism* has been thence adopted as a medical description of one of the varieties of stammering. North-West America is another district of the world distinguished for the production of strange clucking, gurgling, and grunting letters, difficult or impossible to European voices. Moreover, there are many sounds capable of being used in articulate speech, varieties of chirping, whistling, blowing, and sucking noises, of which some are familiar to our own use as calls to animals, or interjectional noises of contempt or surprise, but which no tribe is known to have brought into their alphabet. With all the vast phonetic variety of known languages, the limits of possible utterance are far from being reached.

Up to a certain point we can understand the reasons which have guided the various tribes of mankind in the selection of their various alphabets; ease of utterance to the speaker, combined with distinctness of effect to the hearer, have been undoubtedly among the principal of the selecting causes. We may fairly connect with the close uniformity of men's organs of speech all over the world, the general similarity which prevails in the phonetic systems of the most different languages, and which gives us the power of roughly writing down so large a proportion of any one language by means of an alphabet intended for any other. But while we thus account by physical similarity for the existence of a kind of natural alphabet common to mankind, we must look to other causes to determine the selection of sounds used in different languages, and to account for those remarkable courses of change which go on in languages of a common stock, producing in Europe such variations of one original word as *pater, father, vater*, or in the islands of Polynesia offering us the numeral 5 under the strangely-varied forms of *lima, rima, dima, nima*, and *hima*. Changes of this sort have acted so widely and regularly, that since the enunciation of Grimm's law their study has become a main part of philology. Though their causes are as yet so obscure, we may at least argue that such wide and definite operations cannot be due to chance or arbitrary fancy, but must be the result of laws as wide and definite as themselves.

Let us now suppose a book to be written with a tolerably correct alphabet, for instance an ordinary Italian book, or an English one in some good system of phonetic letters. To suppose English written in the makeshift alphabet which we still keep in use, would be of course to complicate the matter in hand with a new and needless difficulty. If, then, the book be written in a sufficient alphabet, and handed to a reader, his office will by no means stop short at rendering back into articulate sounds the vowels and consonants before him, as though he were reading over proofs for the press. For the emotional tone just spoken of has dropped out in writing down the words in letters, and it will be the reader's duty to guess from the meaning of the words what this tone should be, and to put it in again accordingly. He has moreover to introduce emphasis, whether by accent or stress, on certain syllables or words, thereby altering their effect in the sentence; if he says, for example, 'I never sold you that horse,' an emphasis on any one of these six words will alter the import of the whole phrase. Now, in emphatic pronunciation two distinct processes are to be remarked. The effect produced by changes in loudness and duration of words is directly imitative; it is a mere gesture made with the voice, as we may notice by the way in which any one will speak of 'a *short sharp* answer,' 'a *long weary* year,' 'a *loud burst* of music,' 'a *gentle gliding* motion,' as compared with the like manner in which the gesture-language would adapt its force and speed to the kind of action to be represented. Written language can hardly convey but by the context the striking effects which our imitative faculty adds to spoken language, in our continual endeavour to make the sound of each word we speak a sort of echo to its sense. We see this in the difference between writing and telling the little story of the man who was worried by being talked to about 'good books.' 'Do you mean,' he asked, speaking shortly with a face of strong firm approval, '*good* books?' 'or,' with a drawl and a fatuous-benevolent simper, '*goo-d* books?' Musical accent (*accentus*,[255] musical tone) is turned to account as a means of emphasis, as when we give prominence to a particular syllable or word in a sentence by raising or depressing it a semi-tone or more. The reader has to divide his sentences with pauses, being guided in this to some extent by stops; the rhythmic measure in which he will utter prose as well as poetry is not without its effect; and he has again to introduce music by speaking each sentence to a kind of imperfect melody. Professor Helmholtz endeavours to write down in musical notes how a German with a bass voice, speaking on B flat, might say, 'Ich bin spatzieren gegangen.—Bist du spatzieren gegangen?' falling a fourth (to F) at the end of the affirmative sentence, and rising a fifth (to f) in asking the question, thus ranging through an octave.[256] When an English speaker tries to illustrate in his own language the rising and falling tones of Siamese vowels, he compares them with the English ones of question and answer, as in 'Will you go? Yes.'[257] The rules of this imperfect musical intonation in ordinary conversation have been as yet but little studied. But as a means of giving solemnity and pathos to language, it has been more fully developed and even systematized under exact rules of melody, and we thus have on the one hand ecclesiastical intoning and the less conventional half-singing so often to be heard in religious meetings, and on the other the ancient and modern theatrical recitative. By such intermediate stages we may cross the wide interval from spoken prose, with the musical pitch of its vowels so carelessly kept, and so obscured by consonants as to be difficult even to determine, to full song, in which the consonants are as much as possible suppressed, that they may not interfere with the precise and expressive music of the vowels.

Proceeding now to survey such parts of the vocabulary of mankind as appear to have an intelligible origin in the direct expression of sense by sound, let us first examine Interjections. When Horne Tooke spoke, in words often repeated since, of 'the brutish inarticulate Interjection,' he certainly meant to express his contempt for a mode of expression which lay outside his own too narrow view of language. But the epithets are in themselves justifiable enough. Interjections are undoubtedly to a certain extent 'brutish' in their analogy to the cries of animals; and the fact gives them an especial interest to modern observers, who are thus enabled to trace phenomena belonging to the mental state of the lower animals up into the midst of the most highly cultivated human language. It is also true that they are 'inarticulate,' so far at least that the systems of consonants and vowels recognized by grammarians break down more hopelessly than elsewhere in the attempt to write down interjections. Alphabetic writing is far too incomplete and clumsy an instrument to render their peculiar and variously-modulated sounds, for which a few conventionally-written words do duty poorly enough. In reading aloud, and sometimes even in the talk of those who have learnt rather from books than from the living world, we may hear these awkward imitations, *ahem! hein! tush! tut! pshaw!* now carrying the unquestioned authority of words printed in a book, and reproduced letter for letter with a most amusing accuracy. But when Horne Tooke fastens upon an unfortunate Italian grammarian and describes him as 'The industrious and exact Cinonio, who does not appear ever to have had a single glimpse of reason,' it is not easy to see what the pioneer of English philology could find to object to in Cinonio's obviously true assertion, that a single interjection, *ah!* or *ahi!* is capable of expressing more than twenty different emotions or intentions, such as pain, entreaty, threatening, sighing, disdain, according to the tone in which it is uttered.[258] The fact that interjections do thus utter feelings is quite beyond dispute, and the philologist's concern with them is on the one hand to study their action in expressing emotion, and on the other to trace their passage into more fully-formed words, such as have their place in connected syntax and form part of logical propositions.

In the first place, however, it is necessary to separate from proper interjections the many sense-words which, often kept up in a mutilated or old-fashioned guise, come so close to them both in appearance and in use. Among classic examples are φέρε! δεῦτε! *age! macte!* Such a word is *hail!* which as the Gothic Bible shows, was originally an adjective, 'whole, hale, prosperous,' used vocatively, just as the Italians cry *bravo! brava! bravi! brave!* When the African negro cries out in fear or wonder *mámá! mámá!*[259] he might be thought to be uttering a real interjection, 'a word used to express some passion or emotion of the mind,' as Lindley Murray has it, but in fact he is simply calling, grown-up baby as he is, for his mother; and the very same thing has been noticed among Indians of Upper California, who as an expression of pain cry, *aná!* that is 'mother.'[260] Other exclamations consist of a pure interjection combined with a pronoun, as οἴμοι! *oimè! ah me!* or with an adjective, as *alas! hélas!* (ah weary!) With what care interjections should be sifted, to avoid the risk of treating as original elementary sounds of language what are really nothing but sense-words, we may judge from the way in which the common English exclamation *well! well!* approaches the genuine interjectional sound in the Coptic expression 'to make *ouelouele*,' which signifies to wail, Latin *ululare*. Still better, we may find a learned traveller in the 18th century quite seriously remarking, apropos of the old Greek battle-shout, ἀλαλά! ἀλαλά! that the Turks to this day call out *Allah! Allah! Allah!* upon the like occasion.[261]

The calls to animals customary in different countries[262] are to a great extent interjectional in their use, but to attempt to explain them as a whole is to step upon as slippery ground as lies within the range of philology. Sometimes they may be in fact pure interjections, like the *schû schû!* mentioned as an old German cry to scare birds, as we should say *sh sh!*, or the *aá!* with which the Indians of Brazil call their dogs. Or they may be set down as simple imitations of the animal's own cries, as the *clucking* to call fowls in our own farm-yards, or the Austrian calls of *pi pi!* or *tiet tiet!* to chickens, or the Swabian *kauter kaut!* to turkeys, or the shepherd's *baaing* to call sheep in India. In other cases, however, they may be sense-words more or less broken down, as when the creature is spoken to by a sound which seems merely taken from its own common name. If an English countryman meets a stray sheep-dog, he will simply call to him *ship! ship!* So *schäp schäp!* is an Austrian call to sheep, and *köss kuhel köss!* to cows. In German districts *gus gus! gusch gusch! gös gös!* are set down as calls to geese; and when we notice that the Bohemian peasant calls *husy!* to them, we remember that the name for goose in his language is *husa*, a word familiar to English ears in the name of John Huss. The Bohemian, again, will call to his dog *ps ps!* but then *pes* means 'dog.' Other sense-words addressed to animals break down by long repetition into mutilated forms. When we are told that the *to to!* with which a Portuguese calls a dog is short for *toma toma!* (*i.e.*, 'take take!') which tells him to come and take his food, we admit the explanation as plausible; and the *coop coop!* which a cockney might so easily mistake for a pure interjection, is only 'Come up! come up!'

'Come uppe, Whitefoot, come uppe, Lightfoot,

Come uppe, Jetty, rise and follow,

Jetty, to the milking shed.'

But I cannot offer a plausible guess at the origin of such calls as *hüf hüf!* to horses, *hühl hühl!* to geese, *deckel deckel!* to sheep. It is fortunate for etymologists that such trivial little words have not an importance proportioned to the difficulty of clearing up their origin. The word *puss!* raises an interesting philological problem. An English child calling *puss puss!* is very likely keeping up the trace of the old Keltic name for the cat, Irish *pus*, Erse *pusag*, Gaelic *puis*. Similar calls are known elsewhere in Europe (as in Saxony, *pûs pûs!*), and there is some reason to think that the cat, which came to us from the East, brought with it one of its names, which is still current there, Tamil *pûsei!* Afghan *pusha*, Persian *pushak*, &c. Mr. Wedgwood finds an origin for the call in an imitation of the cat's spitting, and remarks that the Servians cry *pis!* to drive a cat away, while the Albanians use a similar sound to call it. The way in which the cry of *puss!* has furnished a name for the cat itself, comes out curiously in countries where the animal has been lately introduced by Englishmen. Thus *boosi* is the recognized word for cat in the Tonga Islands, no doubt from Captain Cook's time. Among Indian tribes of North-West America, *pwsh*, *pish-pish*, appear in native languages with the meaning of cat; and not only is the European cat called a *puss puss* in the Chinook Jargon, but in the same curious dialect the word is applied to a native beast, the cougar, now called 'hyas *puss-puss*,' *i.e.*, 'great cat.'[263]

The derivation of names of animals in this manner from calls to them, may perhaps not have been unfrequent. It appears that *huss!* is a cry used in Switzerland to set dogs on to fight, as *s—s!* might be in England, and that the Swiss call a dog *huss* or *hauss*, possibly from this. We know the cry of *dill! dilly!* as a recognized call to ducks in England, and it is difficult to think it a corruption of any English word or phrase, for the Bohemians also call *dlidli!* to their ducks. Now, though *dill* or *dilly* may not be found in our dictionaries as the name for a duck, yet the way in which Hood can use it as such in one of his best-known comic poems, shows perfectly the easy and natural step by which such transitions can be made:—

'For Death among the water-lilies,

Cried "Duc ad me" to all her dillies.'

In just the same way, because *gee!* is a usual call of the English waggoner to his horses, the word *gee-gee* has become a familiar nursery noun meaning a horse. And neither in such nursery words, nor in words coined in jest, is the evidence bearing on the origin of language to be set aside as worthless; for it may be taken as a maxim of ethnology, that what is done among civilized men in jest, or among civilized children in the nursery, is apt to find its analogue in the serious mental effort of savage, and therefore of primæval tribes.

Drivers' calls to their beasts, such as this *gee! gee-ho!* to urge on horses, and *weh! woh!* to stop them, form part of the vernacular of particular districts. The *geho!* perhaps came to England in the Norman-French, for it is known in France, and appears in the Italian dictionary as *gio!* The traveller who has been hearing the drivers in the Grisons stop their horses with a long *br-r-r!* may cross a pass and hear on the other side a *hü-ü-ü!* instead. The ploughman's calls to turn the leaders of the team to right and left have passed into proverb. In France they say of a stupid clown 'Il n'entend ni à dia! ni à hurhaut!' and the corresponding Platt-Deutsch phrase is 'He weet nich *hutt!* noch *hoh!*' So there is a regular language to camels, as Captain Burton remarks on his journey to Mekka: *ikh ikh!* makes them kneel, *yáhh yáhh!* urges them on, *hai hai!* induces caution, and so forth. In the formation of these quaint expressions, two causes have been at work. The sounds seem sometimes thoroughly interjectional, as the Arab *hai!* of caution, or the French *hue!* North German *jö!* Whatever their origin, they may be made to carry their sense by imitative tones expressive to the ear of both horse and man, as any one will say who hears the contrast between the short and sharp high-pitched *hüp!* which tells the Swiss horse to go faster, and the long-drawn *hü-ü-ü-ü!* which brings him to a stand. Also, the way in which common sense-words are taken up into calls like *gee-up! woh-back!* shows that we may expect to find various old broken fragments of formal language in the list, and such on inspection we find accordingly. The following lines are quoted by Halliwell from the Micro-Cynicon (1599):—

'A base borne issue of a baser syer,

Bred in a cottage, wandering in the myer,

With nailed shooes and whipstaffe in his hand,

Who with a *hey* and *ree* the beasts command.'

This *ree!* is equivalent to 'right' (riddle-me-ree = riddle me right), and tells the leader of the team to bear to the right hand. The *hey!* may correspond with *heit!* or *camether!* which call him to bear 'hither,' *i.e.*, to the left. In Germany *har! här! har-üh!* are likewise the same as 'her,' 'hither, to the left.' So *swude! schwude! zwuder!* 'to the left,' are of course simply 'zuwider,' 'on the contrary way.' Pairs of calls for 'right' and 'left' in German-speaking countries are *hot!—har!* and *hott!—wist!* This *wist!* is an interesting example of the keeping up of ancient words in such popular tradition. It is evidently a mutilated form of an old German word for the left hand, *winistrâ*, Anglo-

Saxon *winstre*, a name long since forgotten by modern High German, as by our own modern English.[264]

As quaint a mixture of words and interjectional cries as I have met with, is in the great French Encyclopædia,[265] which gives a minute description of the hunter's craft, and prescribes exactly what is to be cried to the hounds under all possible contingencies of the chase. If the creatures understood grammar and syntax, the language could not be more accurately arranged for their ears. Sometimes we have what seem pure interjectional cries. Thus, to encourage the hounds to work, the huntsman is to call to them *hà halle halle halle!* while to bring them up before they are uncoupled it is prescribed that he shall call *hau hau!* or *hau tahaut!* and when they are uncoupled he is to change his cry to *hau la y la y la tayau!* a call which suggests the Norman original of the English *tally-ho!* With cries of this kind plain French words are intermixed, *hà bellement là ila, là ila, hau valet!—hau l'ami, tau tau après après, à route à route!* and so on. And sometimes words have broken down into calls whose sense is not quite gone, like the 'vois le ci' and the 'vois le ce l'est' which are still to be distinguished in the shout which is to tell the hunters that the stag they have been chasing has made a return, *vauleci revari vaulecelez!* But the drollest thing in the treatise is the grave set of English words (in very Gallic shape) with which English dogs are to be spoken to, because, as the author says, 'there are many English hounds in France, and it is difficult to get them to work when you speak to them in an unknown tongue, that is, in other terms than they have been trained to.' Therefore, to call them, the huntsman is to cry *here do-do ho ho!* to get them back to the right track he is to say *houpe boy, houpe boy!* when there are several on ahead of the rest of the pack, he is to ride up to them and cry *saf me boy! saf me boy!* and lastly, if they are obstinate and will not stop, he is to make them go back with a shout of *cobat, cobat!*

How far the lower animals may attach any inherent meaning to interjectional sounds is a question not easy to answer. But it is plain that in most of the cases mentioned here they only understand them as recognized signals which have a meaning by regular association, as when they remember that they are fed with one noise and driven away with another, and they also pay attention to the gestures which accompany the cries. Thus the well-known Spanish way of calling the cat is *miz miz!* while *zape zape!* is used to drive it away; and the writer of an old dictionary maintains that there can be no real difference between these words except by custom, for, he declares, he has heard that in a certain monastery where they kept very handsome cats, the brother in charge of the refectory hit upon the device of calling *zape zape!* to them when he gave them their food, and then he drove them away with a stick, crying angrily *miz miz*; and this of course prevented any stranger from calling and stealing them, for only he and the cats knew the secret![266] To philologists, the manner in which such calls to animals become customary in particular districts illustrates the consensus by which the use of words is settled. Each case of the kind indicates that a word has prevailed by selection among a certain society of men, and the main reasons of words holding their ground within particular limits, though it is so difficult to assign them exactly in each case, are probably inherent fitness in the first place, and traditional inheritance in the second.

When the ground has been cleared of obscure or mutilated sense-words, there remains behind a residue of real sound-words, or pure interjections. It has long and reasonably been considered that the place in history of these expressions is a very primitive one. Thus De Brosses describes them as necessary and natural words, common to all mankind, and produced by the combination of man's conformation with the interior affections of his mind. One of the best means of judging the relation between interjectional utterances and the feelings they express, is to compare the voices of the lower animals with our own. To a considerable extent there is a similarity. As their bodily and mental structure has an analogy with our own, so they express their minds by sounds which have to our ears a certain fitness for what they appear to mean. It is so with the bark, the howl, and the whine of the dog, the hissing of geese, the purring of cats, the crowing and clucking of cocks and hens. But in other cases, as with the hooting of owls and the shrieks of parrots and many other birds, we cannot suppose that these sounds are intended to utter anything like the melancholy or pain which such cries from a human being would be taken to convey. There are many animals that never utter any cry but what, according to our notions of the meaning of sounds, would express rage or discomfort; how far are the roars and howls of wild beasts to be thus interpreted? We might as well imagine the tuning violin to be in pain, or the moaning wind to express sorrow. The connexion between interjection and emotion depending on the physical structure of the animal which utters or hears the sound, it follows that the general similarity of interjectional utterance among all the varieties of the human race is an important manifestation of their close physical and intellectual unity.

Interjectional sounds uttered by man for the expression of his own feelings serve also as signs indicating these feelings to another. A long list of such interjections, common to races speaking the most widely various languages, might be set down in a rough way as representing the sighs, groans, moans, cries, shrieks, and growls by which man gives utterance to various of his feelings. Such for instance, are some of the many sounds for which *ah! oh! ahi! aie!* are the inexpressive written representatives; such is the sigh which is written down in the Wolof language of Africa as *hhihhe!* in English as *heigho!* in Greek and Latin as ἒ ἒ! ἒ ἒ! *heu! eheu!* Thus the open-mouthed *wah wah!* of astonishment, so common in the East, reappears in America in the *hwah! hwah-wa!* of the Chinook Jargon; and the kind of groan which is represented in European languages by *weh! ouais! oὐαί! vae!* is given in Coptic by *ouae!* in Galla by *wayo!* in the Ossetic of the Caucasus by *voy!* among the Indians of British Columbia by *woi!* Where the interjections taken down in the vocabularies of other languages differ from those recognized in our own, we at any rate appreciate them and see how they carry their meaning. Thus with the Malagasy *u-u!* of pleasure, the North-American Indian's often-described guttural *ugh!* the *kwish!* of contempt in the Chinook Jargon, the Tunguz *yo yo!* of pain, the Irish *wb wb!* of distress, the native Brazilian's *teh teh!* of wonder and reverence, the *hai-yah!* so well known in the Pigeon-English of the Chinese ports, and even, to take an extreme case, the interjections of surprise among the Algonquin Indians, where men say *tiau!* and women *nyau!* It is much the same with expressions which are not uttered for the speaker's satisfaction, but are calls addressed to another. Thus the Siamese call of *hē!* the Hebrew *he! ha!* for 'lo! behold!' the *hói!* of the Clallam Indians for 'stop!' the Lummi *hái!* for 'hold, enough!'—these and others like them belong just as much to English. Another class of interjections are such as any one conversant with the gesture-signs of savages and deaf-mutes would recognize as being themselves gesture signs, made with vocal sound, in short, voice-gestures. The sound *m'm, m'n*, made with the lips closed, is the obvious expression of the man who tries to speak, but cannot. Even the deaf-and-dumb child, though he cannot hear the sound of his own voice, makes this noise to show that he is dumb, that he is *mu mu*, as the Vei negroes of West Africa would say. To the speaking man, the sound which we write as *mum!* says plainly enough 'hold your tongue!' '*mum's* the word!' and in accordance with this meaning has served to form various imitative words, of which a type is Tahitian *mamu*, to be silent. Often made with a slight effort which aspirates it, and with more or less continuance, this sound becomes what may be indicated as *'m, 'n, h'm, h'n*, &c., interjections which are conventionally written down as words, *hem! ahem! hein!* Their primary sense seems in any case that of hesitation to speak, of 'humming and hawing,' but this serves with a varied intonation to express such hesitation or refraining from articulate words as belongs either to surprise, doubt or enquiry, approbation or contempt. In the vocabulary of the Yorubas of West Africa, the nasal interjection *huñ* is rendered, just as it might be in English, as 'fudge!' Rochefort describes the Caribs listening in reverent silence to their chief's discourse, and testifying their approval with a *hun-hun!* just as in his time (17th century) an English congregation would have saluted a popular preacher.[267] The gesture of blowing, again, is a familiar expression of contempt and disgust, and when vocalized gives the labial interjections which are written *pah! bah! pugh! pooh!* in Welsh *pw!* in Low Latin *puppup!* and set down by travellers among the savages in

Australia as *pooh!* These interjections correspond with the mass of imitative words which express blowing, such as Malay *puput*, to blow. The labial gestures of blowing pass into those of spitting, of which one kind gives the dental interjection *t' t' t'!* which is written in English or Dutch *tut tut!* and that this is no mere fancy, a number of imitative verbs of various countries will serve to show, Tahitian *tutua*, to spit, being a typical instance.

The place of interjectional utterance in savage intercourse is well shown in Cranz's description. The Greenlanders, he says, especially the women, accompany many words with mien and glances, and he who does not well apprehend this may easily miss the sense. Thus when they affirm anything with pleasure they suck down air by the throat with a certain sound, and when they deny anything with contempt or horror, they turn up the nose and give a slight sound through it. And when they are out of humour, one must understand more from their gestures than their words.[268] Interjection and gesture combine to form a tolerable practical means of intercourse, as where the communication between French and English troops in the Crimea is described as 'consisting largely of such interjectional utterances, reiterated with expressive emphasis and considerable gesticulation.'[269] This description well brings before us in actual life a system of effective human intercourse, in which there has not yet arisen the use of those articulate sounds carrying their meaning by tradition, which are the inherited words of the dictionary.

When, however, we look closely into these inherited sense-words themselves, we find that interjectional sounds have actually had more or less share in their formation. Not stopping short at the function ascribed to them by grammarians, of standing here and there outside a logical sentence, the interjections have also served as radical sounds out of which verbs, substantives, and other parts of speech have been shaped. In tracing the progress of interjections upward into fully developed language, we begin with sounds merely expressing the speaker's actual feelings. When, however, expressive sounds like *ah! ugh! pooh!* are uttered not to exhibit the speaker's actual feelings at the moment, but only in order to suggest to another the thought of admiration or disgust, then such interjections have little or nothing to distinguish them from fully formed words. The next step is to trace the taking up of such sounds into the regular forms of ordinary grammar. Familiar instances of such formations may be found among ourselves in nursery language, where to *woh* is found in use with the meaning of to stop, or in that real though hardly acknowledged part of the English language to which belong such verbs as to *boo-hoo*. Among the most obvious of such words are those which denote the actual utterance of an interjection, or pass thence into some closely allied meaning. Thus the Fijian women's cry of lamentation *oile!* becomes the verb *oile* 'to bewail,' *oile-*

taka 'to lament for' (the men cry *ule!*); now this is in perfect analogy with such words as *ululare*, to *wail*. With different grammatical terminations, another sound produces the Zulu verb *gigiteka* and its English equivalent to *giggle*. The Galla *iya*, 'to cry, scream, give the battle-cry' has its analogues in Greek Ιά, Ιή, 'a cry,' Ιήϊος 'wailing, mournful,' &c. Good cases may be taken from a curious modern dialect with a strong propensity to the use of obvious sound-words, the Chinook Jargon of North-West America. Here we find adopted from an Indian dialect the verb to *kish-kish*, that is, 'to drive cattle or horses'; *humm* stands for the word 'stink,' verb or noun; and the laugh, *heehee*, becomes a recognized term meaning fun or amusement, as in *mamook heehee*, 'to amuse' (*i.e.*, 'to make *heehee*') and *heehee house*, 'a tavern.' In Hawaii, *aa* is 'to insult;' in the Tonga Islands, *úi!* is at once the exclamation 'fie!' and the verb 'to cry out against.' In New Zealand, *hé!* is an interjection denoting surprise at a mistake, *hé* as a noun or verb meaning 'error, mistake, to err, to go astray.' In the Quiché language of Guatemala, the verbs *ay, oy, boy*, express the idea of 'to call' in different ways. In the Carajas language of Brazil, we may guess an interjectional origin in the adjective ei, 'sorrowful,' and can scarcely fail to see a derivation from expressive sound in the verb *hai-hai* 'to run away' (the word *aie-aie*, used to mean 'an omnibus' in modern French slang, is said to be a comic allusion to the cries of the passengers whose toes are trodden on). The Camacan Indians, when they wish to express the notion of 'much' or 'many,' hold out their fingers and say *hi*. As this is an ordinary savage gesture expressing multitude, it seems likely that the *hi* is a mere interjection, requiring the visible sign to convey the full meaning.[270] In the Quichua language of Peru, *alalau!* is an interjection of complaint at cold, whence the verb *alalauñini*, 'to complain of the cold.' At the end of each strophe of the Peruvian hymns to the Sun was sung the triumphant exclamation *haylli!* and with this sound are connected the verbs *hayllini* 'to sing,' *hayllicuni*, 'to celebrate a victory.' The Zulu *halala!* of exultation, which becomes also a verb 'to shout for joy,' has its analogues in the Tibetan *alala!* of joy, and the Greek άλαλά, which is used as a noun meaning the battle-cry and even the onset itself, άλαλάζω, 'to raise the war-cry,' as well as Hebrew *hillel*, 'to sing praise,' whence *hallelujah!* a word which the believers in the theory that the Red Indians were the Lost Tribes naturally recognized in the native medicine-man's chant of *hi-le-li-lah!* The Zulu makes his panting *ha!* do duty as an expression of heat, when he says that the hot weather 'says *ha ha*'; his way of pitching a song by a *ha! ha!* is apparently represented in the verb *haya*, 'to lead a song,' *hayo* 'a starting song, a fee given to the singing-leader for the *haya*'; and his interjectional expression *bà bà!* 'as when one smacks his lips from a bitter taste,' becomes a verb-root meaning 'to be bitter or sharp to the taste, to prick, to smart.' The Galla language gives some good examples of interjections passing into words, as where the verbs *birr-djeda* (to say *brr!*) and *birēfada* (to make *brr!*) have the meaning 'to be afraid.' Thus *o!* being the usual answer to a call, and also a cry to drive cattle, there are formed from it by the addition of verbal terminations, the verbs *oada*, 'to answer,' and *ofa*, 'to drive.'

If the magnific and honorific *o* of Japanese grammar can be assigned to an interjectional origin, its capabilities in modifying signification become instructive.[271] It is used before substantives as a prefix of honour; *couni*, 'country,' thus becoming *ocouni*. When a man is talking to his superiors, he puts *o* before the names of all objects belonging to them, while these superiors drop the *o* in speaking of anything of their own, or an inferior's; among the higher classes, persons of equal rank put *o* before the names of each other's things, but not before their own; it is polite to say *o* before the names of all women, and well-bred children are distinguished from little peasants by the way in which they are careful to put it even before the nursery names of father and mother, *o toto, o caca*, which correspond to the *papa* and *mama* of Europe. A distinction is made in written language between *o*, which is put to anything royal, and *oo* which means great, as may be instanced in the use of the word *mets'ké* or 'spy' (literally 'eye-fixer'); *o mets'ké* is a princely or imperial spy, while *oo mets'ké* is the spy in chief. This interjectional adjective *oo*, great, is usually prefixed to the name of the capital city, which it is customary to call *oo Yedo* in speaking to one of its inhabitants, or when officials talk of it among themselves. And lastly, the *o* of honour is prefixed to verbs in all their forms of conjugation, and it is polite to say *ominahai matse*, 'please to see,' instead of the mere plebeian *minahai matse*. Now an English child of six years old would at once understand these formations if taken as interjectional; and if we do not incorporate in our grammar the *o!* of admiration and reverential embarrassment, it is because we have not chosen to take advantage of this rudimentary means of expression. Another exclamation, the cry of *io!* has taken a place in etymology. When added by the German to his cry of 'Fire!' 'Murder!' *Feuerio! Mordio!* it remains indeed as mere an interjection as the *o!* in our street cries of 'Pease-*o!*' 'Dust-*o!*' or the *â!* in old German *wafenâ!* 'to arms!' '*hilfâ!* 'help!' But the Iroquois of North America makes a fuller use of his materials, and carries his *io!* of admiration into the very formation of compound words, adding it to a noun to say that it is beautiful or good; thus, in Mohawk, *garonta* means a tree, *garontio* a beautiful tree; in like manner, *Ohio* means 'river-beautiful;' and *Ontario*, 'hill-rock-beautiful,' is derived in the same way. When, in the old times of the French occupation of Canada, there was sent over a Governor-General of New France, Monsieur de Montmagny, the Iroquois rendered his name from their word *ononte*, 'mountain,' translating him into *Onontio*, or 'Great Mountain,' and thus it came to pass that the name of Onontio was handed down long after, like that of Cæsar, as the title of each succeeding governor, while for the King of France was reserved the yet higher style of 'the great Onontio.'[272]

The quest of interjectional derivations for sense-words is apt to lead the etymologist into very rash speculations. One of his best safeguards is to test forms supposed to be interjectional, by ascertaining whether anything similar has come into use in decidedly distinct languages. For instance, among the familiar sounds which fall on the traveller's ear in Spain is the muleteer's cry to his beasts, *arre! arre!* From this interjection, a family of Spanish words are reasonably supposed to be derived; the verb *arrear*, 'to drive mules,' *arriero*, the name for the 'muleteer' himself, and so forth.[273] Now is this *arre!* itself a genuine interjectional sound? It seems likely to be so, for Captain Wilson found it in use in the Pelew Islands, where the paddlers in the canoes were kept up to their work by crying to them *arree! arree!* Similar interjections are noticed elsewhere with a sense of mere affirmation, as in an Australian dialect where *a-ree!* is set down as meaning 'indeed,' and in the Quichua language where *ari!* means 'yes!' whence the verb *ariñi*, 'to affirm.' Two other cautions are desirable in such enquiries. These are, not to travel too far from the absolute meaning expressed by the interjection, unless there is strong corroborative evidence, and not to override ordinary etymology by treating derivative words as though they were radical. Without these checks, even sound principle breaks down in application, as the following two examples may show. It is quite true that *h'm!* is a common interjectional call, and that the Dutch have made a verb of it, *hemmen*, 'to hem after a person.' We may notice a similar call in West Africa, in the *mma!* which is translated 'hallo! stop!' in the language of Fernando Po. But to apply this as a derivation for German *hemmen*, 'to stop, check, restrain,' to *hem* in, and even to the *hem* of a garment, as Mr. Wedgwood does without even a perhaps,[274] is travelling too far beyond the record. Again, it is quite true that sounds of clicking and smacking of the lips are common expressions of satisfaction all over the world, and words may be derived from these sounds, as where a vocabulary of the Chinook language of North-West America expresses 'good' as *t'k-tok-te*, or *e-tok-te*, sounds which we cannot doubt to be derived from such clicking noises, if the words are not in fact attempts to write down the very clicks themselves. But it does not follow that we may take such words as *deliciæ, delicatus*, out of a highly organized language like Latin, and refer them, as the same etymologist does, to an interjectional utterance of satisfaction, *dlick!*[275] To do this, is to ignore altogether the composition of words; we might as well explain Latin *dilectus* or English *delight* as direct formations from expressive sound. In concluding these remarks on interjections, two or three groups of words may be brought forward as examples of the application of collected evidence from a number of languages, mostly of the lower races.

The affirmative and negative particles, which bear in language such meanings as 'yes!' 'indeed!' and 'no!' 'not,' may have their derivations from many different sources. It is thought that the Australian dialects all belong to a single stock, but so unlike are the sounds they use for 'no!' and 'yes!' that tribes are actually named from these words as a convenient means of distinction. Thus the tribes known as *Gureang, Kamilaroi, Kogai, Wolaroi, Wailwun, Wiratheroi,* have their names from the words they use for 'no,' these being *gure, kamil, ko, wol, wail, wira,* respectively; and on the other hand the *Pikambul* are said to be so called from their word *pika,* 'yes.' The device of naming tribes, thus invented by the savages of Australia, and which perhaps recurs in Brazil in the name of the *Cocatapuya* tribe (*coca* 'no,' *tapuya* 'man') is very curious in its similarity to the mediæval division of *Langue d'oc* and *Langue d'oïl,* according to the words for 'yes!' which prevailed in Southern and Northern France: *oc!* is Latin *hoc,* as we might say 'that's it!' while the longer form *hoc illud* was reduced to *oïl!* and thence to *oui!* Many other of the words for 'yes!' and 'no!' may be sense-words, as, again, the French and Italian *si!* is Latin *sic.* But on the other hand there is reason to think that many of these particles in use in various languages are not sense-words, but sound-words of a purely interjectional kind; or, what comes nearly to the same thing, a feeling of fitness of the sound to the meaning may have affected the choice and shaping of sense-words—a remark of large application in such enquiries as the present. It is an old suggestion that the primitive sound of such words as *non* is a nasal interjection of doubt or dissent.[276] It corresponds in sound with the visible gesture of closing the lips, while a vowel-interjection, with or without aspiration, belongs rather to open-mouthed utterance. Whether from this or some other cause, there is a remarkable tendency among most distant and various languages of the world, on the one hand to use vowel-sounds, with soft or hard breathing, to express 'yes!' and on the other hand to use nasal consonants to express 'no!' The affirmative form is much the commoner. The guttural *i-i!* of the West Australian, the *ēē!* of the Darien, the *a-ah!* of the Clallam, the *é!* of the Yakama Indians, the *e!* of the Basuto, and the *ai!* of the Kanuri, are some examples of a wide group of forms, of which the following are only part of those noted down in Polynesian and South American districts—*ii! é! ia! aio! io! ya! ey!* &c., *h'! heh! he-e! hü! hoehah! ah-ha!* &c. The idea has most weight where pairs of words for 'yes!' and 'no!' are found both conforming. Thus in the very suggestive description by Dobrizhoffer among the Abipones of South America, for 'yes!' the men and youths say *héé!* the women say *háá!* and the old men give a grunt; while for 'no' they all say *yna!* and make the loudness of the sound indicate the strength of the negation. Dr. Martius's collection of vocabularies of Brazilian tribes, philologically very distinct, contains several such pairs of affirmatives and negatives, the equivalents of 'yes!'—'no!' being in Tupi *ayé—aan! aani!*; in Guato *ii!—mau!*; in Jumana, *aeae!—mäiu!*; in Miranha *ha ú!—nani!* The Quichua of Peru affirms by *y! hu!* and expresses 'no,' 'not,' 'not at all,' by *ama! manan!* &c., making from the latter the verb *manamñi*, 'to deny.' The Quiché of Guatemala has *e* or *ve* for the affirmative, *ma, man, mana*, for the negative. In Africa, again, the Galla language has *ee!* for 'yes!' and *hn, hin, hm*, for 'not!'; the Fernandian *ee!* for 'yes!' and *'nt* for 'not;' while the Coptic dictionary gives the affirmative (Latin 'sane') as *eie, ie*, and the negative by a long list of nasal sounds such as *an, emmen, en, mmn*, &c. The Sanskrit particles *hi!* 'indeed, certainly,' *na*, 'not,' exemplify similar forms in Indo-European languages, down to our own *aye!* and *no!*[277] There must be some meaning in all this, for otherwise I could hardly have noted down incidentally, without making any attempt at a general search, so many cases from such different languages, only finding a comparatively small number of contradictory cases.[278]

De Brosses maintained that the Latin *stare*, to *stand*, might be traced to an origin in expressive sound. He fancied he could hear in it an organic radical sign designating fixity, and could thus explain why *st!* should be used as a call to make a man *stand still*. Its connexion with these sounds is often spoken of in more modern books, and one imaginative German philologer describes their origin among primæval men as vividly as though he had been there to see. A man stands beckoning in vain to a companion who does not see him, till at last his effort relieves itself by the help of the vocal nerves, and involuntarily there breaks from him the sound *st!* Now the other hears the sound, turns toward it, sees the beckoning gesture, knows that he is called to stop; and when this has happened again and again, the action comes to be described in common talk by uttering the now familiar *st!* and thus *sta* becomes a root, the symbol of the abstract idea to stand!![279] This is a most ingenious conjecture, but unfortunately nothing more. It would be at any rate strengthened, though not established, if its supporters could prove that the *st!* used to call people in Germany, *pst!* in Spain, is itself a pure interjectional sound. Even this, however, has never been made out. The call has not yet been shown to be in use outside our own Indo-European family of languages; and so long as it is only found in use within these limits, an opponent might even plausibly claim it as an abbreviation of the very *sta!* ('stay! stop!') for which the theory proposes it as an origin.[280]

That it is not unfair to ask for fuller evidence of a sound being purely interjectional than its appearance in a single family of languages, may be shown by examining another group of interjections, which are found among the remotest tribes, and thus have really considerable claims to rank among the primary sounds of language. These are the simple sibilants, *s! sh! h'sh!* used especially to scare birds, and among men to express aversion or call for silence. Catlin describes a party of Sioux Indians, when they came to the portrait of a dead chief, each putting his hand over his mouth with a *hush-sh*; and when he himself wished to approach the sacred 'medicine' in a Mandan lodge, he was called to refrain by the same *hush-sh!* Among ourselves the sibilant interjection passes into two exactly opposite senses, according as it is meant to put the speaker himself to silence, or to command silence for him to be heard; and thus we find the sibilant used elsewhere, sometimes in the one way and sometimes in the other. Among the wild Veddas of Ceylon, *iss!* is an exclamation of disapproval, as in ancient or modern Europe; and the verb *shârak*, to hiss, is used in Hebrew with a like sense, 'they shall hiss him out of his place.' But in Japan reverence is expressed by a hiss, commanding silence. Captain Cook remarked that the natives of the New Hebrides expressed their admiration by hissing like geese. Casalis says of the Basutos, 'Hisses are the most unequivocal marks of applause, and are as much courted in the African parliaments as they are dreaded by our candidates for popular favour.'[281] Among other sibilant interjections, are Turkish *sûsâ!* Ossetic *ss! sos!* 'silence!' Fernandian *sia!* 'listen!' 'tush!' Yoruba *siô!* 'pshaw!' Thus it appears that these sounds, far from being special to one linguistic family, are very widespread elements of human speech. Nor is there any question as to their passage into fully-formed words, as in our verb to *hush*, which has passed into the sense of 'to quiet, put to sleep' (adjectively, 'as *hush* as death'), metaphorically to *hush* up a matter, or Greek σίζω 'to hush, say hush! command silence.' Even Latin *silere* and Gothic *silan*, 'to be silent,' may with some plausibility be explained as derived from the interjectional *s!* of silence.

Sanskrit dictionaries recognize several words which explicitly state their own interjectional derivation; such are *hûṅkâra* (*hûm*-making), 'the utterance of the mystic religious exclamation *hûm!*' and *çiççabda* (*çiç*-sound), 'a hiss.' Besides these obvious formations, the interjectional element is present to some greater or less degree in the list of Sanskrit radicals, which represent probably better than those of any other language the verb-roots of the ancient Aryan stock. In *ru*, 'to roar, cry, wail' and in *kakh*, 'to laugh,' we have the simpler kind of interjectional derivation, that which merely describes a sound. As to the more difficult kind, which carry the sense into a new stage, Mr. Wedgwood makes out a strong case for the connexion of interjections of loathing and aversion, such as *pooh! fie!* &c., with that large group of words which are represented in English by *foul* and *fiend*, in Sanskrit by the verbs *pûy*, 'to become foul, to stink' and *piy, pîy*, 'to revile, to hate.'[282] Further evidence may be here adduced in support of this theory. The languages of the lower races use the sound *pu* to express an evil smell; the Zulu remarks that 'the meat says *pu*' (inyama iti *pu*), meaning that it stinks; the Timorese has *poöp* 'putrid;' the Quiché language has *puh, poh* 'corruption, pus,' *pohir* 'to turn bad, rot,' *puẓ* 'rottenness, what stinks;' the Tupi word for nasty, *puxi*, may be compared with the Latin *putidus*, and the Columbia River name for the 'skunk,' *o-pun-pun*, with similar names of stinking animals; Sanskrit *pûtikâ* 'civet-cat,' and French *putois* 'pole-cat.' From the French interjection *fi!* words have long been formed belonging to the language, if not authenticated by the Academy; in mediæval French 'maistre *fi-fi*' was a recognized term for a scavenger, and *fi-fi* books are not yet extinct.

There has been as yet, unfortunately, too much separation between what may be called generative philology, which examines into the ultimate origins of words, and historical philology, which traces their transmission and change. It will be a great gain to the science of language to bring these two branches of enquiry into closer union, even as the processes they relate to have been going on together since the earliest days of speech. At present the historical philologists of the school of Grimm and Bopp, whose great work has been the tracing of our Indo-European dialects to an early Aryan form of language, have had much the advantage in fulness of evidence and strictness of treatment. At the same time it is evident that the views of the generative philologists, from De Brosses onward, embody a sound principle, and that much of the evidence collected as to emotional and other directly expressive words, is of the highest value in the argument. But in working out the details of such word-formation, it must be remembered that no department of philology lies more open to Augustine's caustic remark on the etymologists of his time, that like the interpretation of dreams, the derivation of words is set down by each man according to his own fancy. (Ut somniorum interpretatio ita verborum origo pro cujusque ingenio prædicatur.)

CHAPTER VI.
EMOTIONAL AND IMITATIVE LANGUAGE
(continued).

> Imitative Words—Human actions named from sound—Animals' names from cries, &c.—Musical Instruments—Sounds reproduced—Words modified to adapt sound to sense—Reduplication—Graduation of vowels to express distance and difference—Children's Language—Sound-words as related to Sense-words—Language an original product of the lower Culture.

From the earliest times of language to our own day, it is unlikely that men ever quite ceased to be conscious that some of their words were derived from imitation of the common sounds heard about them. In our own modern English, for instance, results of such imitation are evident; flies *buzz*, bees *hum*, snakes *hiss*, a cracker or a bottle of ginger-beer *pops*, a cannon or a bittern *booms*. In the words for animals and for musical instruments in the various languages of the world, the imitation of their cries and tones is often to be plainly heard, as in the names of the *hoopoe*, the *ai-ai* sloth, the *kaka* parrot, the Eastern *tomtom*, which is a drum, the African *ulule*, which is a flute, the Siamese *khong-bong*, which is a wooden harmonicon, and in like manner through a host of other words. But these evident cases are far from representing the whole effects of imitation on the growth of language. They form, indeed, the easy entrance to a philological region, which becomes less penetrable the farther it is explored.

The operations of which we see the results before us in the actual languages of the world seem to have been somewhat as follows. Men have imitated their own emotional utterances or interjections, the cries of animals, the tones of musical instruments, the sounds of shouting, howling, stamping, breaking, tearing, scraping, with others which are all day coming to their ears, and out of these imitations many current words indisputably have their source. But these words, as we find them in use, differ often widely, often beyond all recognition, from the original sounds they sprang from. In the first place, man's voice can only make a very rude copy of most sounds his ear receives; his possible vowels are very limited in their range compared with natural tones, and his possible consonants still more helpless as a means of imitating natural noises. Moreover, his voice is only allowed to use a part even of this imperfect imitative power, seeing that each language for its own convenience restricts it to a small number of set vowels and consonants, to which the imitative sounds have to conform, thus becoming conventionalized into articulate words with further loss of imitative accuracy. No class of words have a more perfect imitative origin than those which simply profess to be vocal imitations of sound. How ordinary alphabets to some extent succeed and to some extent fail in writing down these sounds may be judged from a few examples. Thus, the Australian imitation of a spear or bullet striking is given as *toop*; to the Zulu, when a calabash is beaten, it says *boo*; the Karens hear the flitting ghosts of the dead call in the wailing voice of the wind, *re, re, ro, ro*; the old traveller, Pietro della Valle, tells how the Shah of Persia sneered at Timur and his Tartars, with their arrows that went *ter ter*; certain Buddhist heretics maintained that water is alive, because when it boils it says *chichitá, chitichita*, a symptom of vitality which occasioned much theological controversy as to drinking cold and warm water. Lastly, sound-words taken up into the general inventory of a language have to follow its organic changes, and in the course of phonetic transition, combination, decay, and mutilation, to lose ever more and more their original shape. To take a single example, the French *huer* 'to shout' (Welsh *hwa*) may be a perfect imitative verb; yet when it passes into modern English *hue* and cry, our changed pronunciation of the vowel destroys all imitation of the call. Now to the language-makers all this was of little account. They merely wanted recognized words to express recognized thought, and no doubt arrived by repeated trials at systems which were found practically to answer this purpose. But to the modern philologist, who is attempting to work out the converse of the problem, and to follow backward the course of words to original imitative sound, the difficulty is most embarrassing. It is not only that thousands of words really derived from such imitation may now by successive change have lost all safe traces of their history; such mere deficiency of knowledge is only a minor evil. What is far worse is that the way is thrown open to an unlimited number of false solutions, which yet look on the face of them fully as like truth as others which we know historically to be true. One thing is clear, that it is of no use to resort to violent means, to rush in among the words of language, explaining them away right and left as derived each from some remote application of an imitative noise. The advocate of the Imitative Theory who attempts this, trusting in his own powers of discernment, has indeed taken in hand a perilous task, for, in fact, of all judges of the question at issue, he has nourished and trained himself up to become the very worst. His imagination is ever suggesting to him what his judgment would like to find true; like a witness answering the questions of the counsel on his own side, he answers in good faith, but with what bias we all know. It was thus with De Brosses, to whom this department of philology owes so much. It is nothing to say that he had a keen ear for the voice of Nature; she must have positively talked to him in alphabetic language, for he could hear the sound of hollowness in the *sk* of σκάπτω 'to dig,' of hardness in the *cal* of *callosity*, the noise of insertion of a body between two others in the *tr* of *trans, intra*. In enquiries so liable to misleading fancy, no pains should be spared in securing impartial testimony, and it fortunately happens that there are available sources of such evidence, which, when thoroughly worked, will give to the theory of imitative words as near an approach to accuracy as has been attained to in any other wide philological problem. By comparing a number of languages, widely apart in their general system and materials, and whose agreement as to the words in question can only be accounted for by similar formation of words from similar suggestion of sound, we obtain groups of words whose imitative character is indisputable. The groups here considered consist in general of imitative words of the simpler kind, those directly connected with the special sound they are taken from, but their examination to some extent admits of words being brought in, where the connexion of the idea expressed with the sound imitated is more remote. This, lastly, opens the far wider and more difficult problem, how far imitation of sounds is the primary cause of the great mass of words in the vocabularies of the world, between whose sound and sense no direct connexion appears.

Words which express human actions accompanied with sound form a very large and intelligible class. In remote and most different languages, we find such forms as *pu, puf, bu, buf, fu, fuf*, in use with the meaning of *puffing, fuffing*; or blowing; Malay *puput*; Tongan *buhi*; Maori *pupui*; Australian *bobun, bwa-bun*; Galla *bufa, afufa*; Zulu *futa, punga, pupuza* (*fu, pu*, used as expressive particles); Quiché *puba*; Quichua *puhuni*; Tupi *ypeú*; Finnish *puhkia*; Hebrew *puach*; Danish *puste*; Lithuanian *púciu*; and in numbers of other languages;[283] here, grammatical adjuncts apart, the significant force lies in the imitative syllable. Savages have named the European musket when they saw it, by the sound *pu*, describing not the report, but the puff of smoke issuing from the muzzle. The Society Islanders supposed at first that the white men blew through the barrel of the gun, and they called it accordingly *pupuhi*, from the verb *puhi* to blow, while the New Zealanders more simply called it a *pu*. So the Amaxosa of South Africa call it *umpu*, from the imitative sound *pu!* The Chinook Jargon of North-West America uses the phrase *mamook poo* (make *poo*) for a verb 'to shoot,' and a six-chambered revolver is called *tohum poo*, i.e., a 'six-poo.' When a European uses the word *puff* to denote the discharge of a gun, he is merely referring to the smoke blown out, as he would speak of a *puff* of wind, or even a powder-*puff* or a *puff*-ball; and when a pistol is called in colloquial German a *puffer*, the meaning of the word matches that used for it in French Argot, a 'soufflant.' It has often been supposed that the *puff* imitates the actual sound, the *bang* of the gun, and this has been brought forward to show by what extremely different words one and the same sound may be imitated, but this is a mistake.[284] These derivations of the name of the gun from the notion of blowing correspond with those which give names to the comparatively noiseless blow-tube of the bird-hunter, called by the Indians of Yucatan a *pub*, in South America by the Chiquitos a *pucuna*, by the Cocamas a *puna*. Looking into vocabularies of languages which have such verbs 'to blow,' it is usual to find with them other words apparently related to them, and expressing more or less distant ideas. Thus Australian *poo-yu, puyu* 'smoke;' Quichua *puhucuni* 'to light a fire,' *punquini* 'to swell,' *puyu, puhuyu* 'a cloud;' Maori *puku* 'to pant,' *puka* 'to swell;' Tupi *púpú, pupúre* 'to boil;' Galla *bube* 'wind,' *bubiẓa* 'to cool by blowing;' Kanuri (root *fu*) *fungin* 'to blow, swell,' *furúdu* 'a stuffed pad or bolster,' &c., *bubute* 'bellows' (*bubute fungin* 'I blow the bellows'); Zulu (dropping the prefixes) *puku, pukupu* 'frothing, foam,' whence *pukupuku* 'an empty frothy fellow,' *pupuma* 'to bubble, boil,' *fu* 'a cloud,' *fumfu* 'blown about like high grass in the wind,' whence *fumfuta* 'to be confused, thrown into disorder,' *futo* 'bellows,' *fuba* 'the breast, chest,' then figuratively 'bosom, conscience.'

The group of words belonging to the closed lips, of which *mum, mumming, mumble* are among the many forms belonging to European languages,[285] are worked out in like manner among the lower races—Vei *mu mu* 'dumb'; Mpongwe *imamu* 'dumb'; Zulu *momata* (from *moma*, 'a motion with the mouth as in mumbling') 'to move the mouth or lips,' *mumata* 'to close the lips as with a mouthful of water,' *mumuta, mumuẓa* 'to eat mouthfuls of corn, &c., with the lips shut;' Tahitian *mamu* 'to be silent,' *omumu* 'to murmur;' Fijian, *nomo, nomo-nomo* 'to be silent;' Chilian, *ñomn* 'to be silent;' Quiché, *mem* 'mute,' whence *memer* 'to become mute;' Quichua, *amu* 'dumb, silent,' *amullini* 'to have something in the mouth,' *amul-layacuni simicta* 'to mutter, to grumble.' The group represented by Sanskrit *t'hût'hû* 'the sound of spitting,' Persian *thu kerdan* (make *thu*) 'to spit,' Greek πτύω, may be compared with Chinook *mamook toh, tooh*, (make *toh, tooh*); Chilian *tuvcùtun* (make *tuv*); Tahitian *tutua*; Galla *twu*; Yoruba *tu*. Among the Sanskrit verb-roots, none carries its imitative nature more plainly than *kshu* 'to sneeze;' the following analogous forms are from South America:—Chilian, *echiun*; Quichua, *achhini*; and from various languages of Brazilian tribes, *techa-ai, haitschu, atchian, natschun, aritischune*, &c. Another imitative verb is well shown in the Negro-English dialect of Surinam, *njam* 'to eat' (pron. *nyam*), *njam-njam* 'food' ('en hem *njanjam* ben de sprinkhan nanga boesi-honi'—'and his meat was locusts and wild honey'). In Australia the imitative verb 'to eat' reappears as *g'nam-ang*. In Africa the Susu language has *nimnim*, 'to taste,' and a similar formation is observed in the Zulu *nambita* 'to smack the lips after eating or tasting, and thence to be tasteful, to be pleasant to the mind.' This is an excellent instance of the transition of mere imitative sound to the expression of mental emotion, and it corresponds with the imitative way in which the Yakama language, in speaking of little children or pet animals, expresses the verb 'to love' as *nem-no-sha* (to make *n'm-n'*). In more civilized countries these forms are mostly confined to baby-language. The Chinese child's word for eating is *nam*, in English nurseries *nim* is noticed as answering the same purpose, and the Swedish dictionary even recognizes *namnam* 'a tid-bit.'

As for imitative names of animals derived from their cries or noises, they are to be met with in every language from the Australian *twonk* 'frog,' the Yakama *rol-rol* 'lark,' to the Coptic *eeiō* 'ass,' the Chinese *maou* 'cat,' and the English *cuckoo* and *peewit*. Their general principle of formation being acknowledged, their further philological interest turns mostly on cases where corresponding words have thus been formed independently in distant regions, and those where the imitative name of the creature, or its habitual sound, passes to express some new idea suggested by its character. The Sanskrit name of the *kâka* crow reappears in the name of a similar bird in British Columbia, the *káh-káh*; a fly is called by the natives of Australia a *bumberoo*, like Sanskrit *bambharâli* 'fly,' Greek βομ-βύλιος, and our *bumble-bee*. Analogous to the name of the *tse-tse* fly, the terror of African travellers, is *ntsintsi*, the word for 'fly' among the Basutos, which also, by a simple metaphor, serves to express the idea of 'a parasite.' Mr. H. W. Bates's description seems to settle the dispute among naturalists, whether the *toucan* had its name from its cry or not. He speaks of its loud, shrill, yelping cries having 'a vague resemblance to the syllables *tocáno, tocáno*, and hence the Indian name of this genus of birds.' Granting this, we can trace this sound-word into a very new meaning; for it appears that the bird's monstrous bill has suggested a name for a certain large-nosed tribe of Indians, who are accordingly called *Tucanos*.[286] The cock, gallo *quiquiriqui*, as the Spanish nursery-language calls him, has a long list of names from various languages which in various ways imitate his crowing; in Yoruba he is called *koklo*, in Ibo *okoko, akoka*, in Zulu *kuku*, in Finnish *kukko*, in Sanskrit **kukkuta**, and so on. He is mentioned in the Zend-Avesta in a very curious way, by a name which elaborately imitates his cry, but which the ancient Persians seem to have held disrespectful to their holy bird, who rouses men from sleep to good thought, word, and work:—

'The bird who bears the name of Parôdars, O holy Zarathustra;

Upon whom evil-speaking men impose the name *Kabrkataç*.'[287]

The crowing of the cock (Malay *kâluruk, kukuk*) serves to mark a point of time, cockcrow. Other words originally derived from such imitation of crowing have passed into other curiously transformed meanings: Old French *cocart* 'vain;' modern French *coquet* 'strutting like a *cock*, *coquetting*, a *coxcomb*;' *cocarde* 'a *cockade*' (from its likeness to a cock's comb); one of the best instances is *coquelicot*, a name given for the same reason to the wild poppy, and even more distinctly in Languedoc, where *cacaracá* means both the crowing and the flower. The hen in some languages has a name corresponding to that of the cock, as in Kussa *kukuduna* 'cock,' *kukukasi* 'hen;' Ewe *koklo-tsu* 'cock,' *koklo-no* 'hen;' and her *cackle* (whence she has in Switzerland the name of *gugel, güggel*) has passed into language as a term for idle gossip and chatter of women, *caquet, caqueter, gackern*, much as the noise of a very different creature seems to have given rise not only to its name, Italian *cicala*, but to a group of words represented by *cicalar* 'to chirp, chatter, talk sillily.' The *pigeon* is a good example of this kind, both for sound and sense. It is Latin *pipio*, Italian *pippione, piccione, pigione*, modern Greek πιπίνιον, French *pipion* (old), *pigeon*; its derivation is from the young bird's *peep*, Latin *pipire*, Italian *pipiare, pigiolare*, modern Greek πιπινίζω, to chirp; by an easy metaphor, a *pigeon* comes to mean 'a silly young fellow easily caught,' to *pigeon* 'to cheat,' Italian *pipione* 'a silly gull, one that is soon caught and trepanned,' *pippionare* 'to pigeon, to gull one.' In an entirely different family of languages, Mr. Wedgwood points out a curiously similar process of derivation; Magyar *pipegni, pipelni* 'to peep or cheep;' *pipe, pipök* 'a chicken, gosling;' *pipe-ember* (chicken-man), 'a silly young fellow, booby.'[288] The derivation of Greek βοῦς, Latin *bos*, Welsh *bu*, from the ox's lowing, or *booing* as it is called in the north country, has been much debated. With an excessive desire to make Sanskrit answer as a general Indo-European type, Bopp connected Sanskrit *go*, old German *chuo*, English *cow*, with these words, on the unusual and forced assumption of a change from guttural to labial.[289] The direct derivation from sound, however, is favoured by other languages, Cochin-Chinese *bo*, Hottentot *bou*. The beast may almost answer for himself in the words of that Spanish proverb which remarks that people talk according to their nature: 'Habló el *buey*, y dijó *bu!*' 'The ox spoke, and he said *boo!*'

Among musical instruments with imitative names are the following:—the *shee-shee-quoi*, the mystic rattle of the Red Indian medicine-man, an imitative word which reappears in the Darien Indian *shak-shak*, the *shook-shook* of the Arawaks, the Chinook *shugh* (whence *shugh-opoots*, rattletail, *i.e.*, 'rattlesnake;')—the drum, called *ganga* in Haussa, *gañgañ* in the Yoruba country, *gunguma* by the Gallas, and having its analogue in the Eastern *gong*;—the bell, called in Yakama (N. Amer.) *kwa-lal-kwa-lal*, in Yalof (W. Afr.) *walwal*, in Russian *kolokol*. The sound of the horn is imitated in English nurseries as *toot-toot*, and this is transferred to express the 'omnibus' of which the bugle is the signal: with this nursery word is to be classed the Peruvian name for the 'shell-trumpet,' *pututu*, and the Gothic *thuthaurn* (thut-horn), which is even used in the Gothic Bible for the last trumpet of the day of judgement,—'In spêdistin thuthaúrna, thuthaúrneith auk jah daúthans ustandand' (I Cor. xv. 52). How such imitative words, when thoroughly taken up into language, suffer change of pronunciation in which the original sound-meaning is lost, may be seen in the English word *tabor*, which we might not recognize as a sound-word at all, did we not notice that it is French *tabour*, a word which in the form *tambour* obviously belongs to a group of words for drums, extending from the small rattling Arabic *tubl* to the Indian *dundhubi* and the *tombe*, the Moqui drum made of a hollowed log. The same group shows the transfer of such imitative words to objects which are like the instrument, but have nothing to do with its sound; few people who talk of *tambour*-work, and fewer still who speak of a footstool as a *tabouret*, associate these words with the sound of a drum, yet the connexion is clear enough. When these two processes go on together, and a sound-word changes its original sound on the one hand, and transfers its meaning to something else on the other, the result may soon leave philological analysis quite helpless, unless by accident historical evidence is forthcoming. Thus with the English word *pipe*. Putting aside the particular pronunciation which we give the word, and referring it back to its mediæval Latin or French sound in *pipa*, *pipe*, we have before us an evident imitative name of a musical instrument, derived from a familiar sound used also to represent the chirping of chickens, Latin *pipire*, English to *peep*, as in the translation of Isaiah viii. 19: 'Seek ... unto wizards that *peep*, and that mutter.' The Algonquin Indians appear to have formed from this sound *pib* (with a grammatical suffix) their name for the *pib-e-gwun* or native flute. Now just as *tuba*, *tubus*, 'a trumpet' (itself very likely an imitative word) has given a name for any kind of *tube*, so the word *pipe* has been transferred from the musical instrument to which it first belonged, and is used to describe tubes of various sorts, gas-pipes, water-pipes, and pipes in general. There is nothing unusual in these transitions of meaning, which are in fact rather the rule than the exception. The *chibouk* was originally a herdsman's pipe or flute in Central Asia. The *calumet*, popularly ranked with the tomahawk and the mocassin among characteristic Red Indian words, is only the name for a shepherd's pipe (Latin *calamus*) in the dialect of Normandy, corresponding with the *chalumeau* of literary French; for when the early colonists in Canada saw the Indians performing the strange operation of smoking, 'with a hollow piece of stone or wood like a pipe,' as Jacques Cartier has it, they merely gave to the native tobacco-pipe the name of the French musical instrument it resembled. Now changes of sound and of sense like this of the English word *pipe* must have been in continual operation in hundreds of languages where we have no evidence to follow them by, and where we probably may never obtain such evidence. But what little we do know must compel us to do justice to the imitation of sound as a really existing process, capable of furnishing an indefinitely large supply of words for things and actions which have no necessary connexion at all with that sound. Where the traces of the transfer are lost, the result is a stock of words which are the despair of philologists, but are perhaps none the less fitted for the practical use of men who simply want recognized symbols for recognized ideas.

The claim of the Eastern *tomtom* to have its name from a mere imitation of its sound seems an indisputable one; but when it is noticed in what various languages the beating of a resounding object is expressed by something like *tum, tumb, tump, tup*, as in Javan *tumbuk*, Coptic *tmno*, 'to pound in a mortar,' it becomes evident that the admission involves more than at first sight appears. In Malay, *timpa, tampa*, is 'to beat out, hammer, forge;' in the Chinook Jargon *tum-tum* is 'the heart,' and by combining the same sound with the English word 'water,' a name is made for 'waterfall,' *tum-wâta*. The Gallas of East Africa declare that a box on the ear seems to them to make a noise like *tub*, for they call its sound *tubdjeda*, that is, 'to say *tub*.' In the same language, *tuma* is 'to beat,' whence *tumtu*, 'a workman, especially one who beats, a smith.' With the aid of another imitative word, *bufa* 'to blow,' the Gallas can construct this wholly imitative sentence, *tumtun bufa bufti*, 'the smith blows with bellows,' as an English child might say, 'the *tumtum puffs* the *puffer*.' This imitative sound seems to have obtained a footing among the Aryan verb-roots, as in Sanskrit *tup, tubh* 'to smite,' while in Greek, *tup, tump*, has the meaning of 'to beat, to *thump*,' producing for instance τύμπανον, *tympanum*, 'a drum or tomtom.' Again, the verb to *crack* has become in modern English as thorough a root-word as the language possesses. The mere imitation of the sound of breaking has passed into a verb to break; we speak of a *cracked* cup or a *cracked* reputation without a thought of imitation of sound; but we cannot yet use the German *krachen* or French *craquer* in this way, for they have not developed in meaning as our word has, but remain in their purely imitative stage. There are two corresponding Sanskrit words for the saw, *kra-kara, kra-kacha*, that is to say, the '*kra*-maker, *kra*-crier;' and it is to be observed that all such terms, which expressly state that they are imitations of sound, are particularly valuable evidence in these enquiries, for whatever doubt there may be as to other words being really derived from imitative sound, there can, of course, be none here. Moreover, there is evidence of the same sound having given rise to imitative words in other families of language, Dahoman *kra-kra*, 'a watchman's rattle;' Grebo *grikâ* 'a saw;' Aino *chacha* 'to saw;' Malay *graji* 'a saw,' *karat* 'to gnash the teeth,' *karot* 'to make a grating noise;' Coptic *khrij* 'to gnash the teeth,' *khrajrej* 'to grate.' Another form of the imitation is given in the descriptive Galla expression *cacakdjeda*, i.e., 'to say *cacak*,' 'to *crack*, *krachen*.' With this sound corresponds a whole family of Peruvian words, of which the root seems to be the guttural *cca*, coming from far back in the throat; *ccallani*, 'to break,' *ccatatani*, 'to gnash the teeth,' *ccacñiy*, 'thunder,' and the expressive words for 'a thunder-storm,' *ccaccaccahay*, which carries the imitative process so much farther than such European words as thunder-

clap, donner-*klapf*. In Maori, *pata* is 'to *patter* as water dropping, drops of rain.' The Manchu language describes the noise of fruits falling from the trees as *pata pata* (so Hindustani *bhadbhad*); this is like our word *pat*, and we should say in the same manner that the fruit comes *pattering* down, while French *patatra* is a recognized imitation of something falling. Coptic *potpt* is 'to fall,' and the Australian *badbadin* (or *patpatin*) is translated into almost literal English as *pitpatting*. On the strength of such non-Aryan languages, are we to assign an imitative origin to the Sanskrit verb-root *pat*, 'to fall,' and to Greek πίπτω?

Wishing rather to gain a clear survey of the principles of language-making than to plunge into obscure problems, it is not necessary for me to discuss here questions of intricate detail. The point which continually arises is this,—granted that a particular kind of transition from sound to sense is possible in the abstract, may it be safely claimed in a particular case? In looking through the vocabularies of the world, it appears that most languages offer words which, by obvious likeliness or by their correspondence with similar forms elsewhere, may put forward a tolerable claim to be considered imitative. Some languages, as Aztec or Mohawk, offer singularly few examples, while in others they are much more numerous. Take Australian cases: *walle*, 'to *wail*;' *bung-bung-ween*, 'thunder;' *wirriti*, 'to blow, as wind;' *wirrirriti*, 'to storm, rage, as in fight;' *wirri*, *bwirri*, 'the native throwing club,' seemingly so called from its *whir* through the air; *kurarriti*, 'to hum, buzz;' *kurrirrurriri*, 'round about, unintelligible,' &c.; *pitata*, 'to knock, pelt, as rain,' *pitapitata*, 'to knock;' *wiiti*, 'to laugh, rejoice'—as in our own 'Turnament of Tottenham':—

"'*We te he!*' quoth Tyb, and lugh,

"Ye er a dughty man!'"

The so-called Chinook Jargon of British Columbia is a language crowded with imitative words, sometimes adopted from the native Indian languages, sometimes made on the spot by the combined efforts of the white man and the Indian to make one another understand. Samples of its quality are *hōh-hoh*, 'to cough,' *kó-ko*, 'to knock,' *kwa-lal-kwa-lal*, 'to gallop,' *muck-a-muck*, 'to eat,' *chak-chak*, 'the bald eagle' (from its scream), *mamook tsish* (make *tsish*), 'to sharpen on the grindstone.' It has been remarked by Prof. Max Müller that the peculiar sound made in blowing out a candle is not a favourite in civilized languages, but it seems to be recognized here, for no doubt it is what the compiler of the vocabulary is doing his best to write down when he gives *mamook poh* (make *poh*) as the Chinook expression for 'to blow out or extinguish as a candle.' This jargon is in great measure of new growth within the last seventy or eighty years, but its imitative words do not differ in nature from those of the more ordinary and old-established languages of the world. Thus among Brazilian tribes there appear Tupi *cororóng, cururuc,* 'to snore' (compare Coptic *kherkher,* Quichua *ccorcuni (ccor)*), whence it appears that an imitation of a snore may perhaps serve the Carajás Indians to express 'to sleep' as *arourou-cré,* as well as the related idea of 'night,' *roou.* Again Pimenteira *ebaung,* 'to bruise, beat,' compares with Yoruba *gba,* 'to slap,' *gbã* (gbang) 'to sound loudly, to *bang,'* and so forth. Among African languages, the Zulu seems particularly rich in imitative words. Thus *bibiza,* 'to dribble like children, drivel in speaking' (compare English *bib*); *babala,* 'the larger bush-antelope' (from the *baa* of the female); *boba,* 'to babble, chatter, be noisy,' *bobi,* 'a *babbler;' boboni,* 'a throstle' (cries *bo! bo!* compare American *bobolink*); *bomboloza,* 'to rumble in the bowels, to have a bowel-complaint;' *bubula,* 'to *buzz* like bees,' *bubulela,* 'a swarm of bees, a buzzing crowd of people;' *bubuluza,* 'to make a blustering noise, like frothing beer or boiling fat.' These examples, from among those given under one initial letter in one dictionary of one barbaric language, may give an idea of the amount of the evidence from the languages of the lower races bearing on the present problem.

For the present purpose of giving a brief series of examples of the sort of words in which imitative sound seems fairly traceable, the strongest and most manageable evidence is of course found among such words as directly describe sounds or what produces them, such as cries of and names for animals, the terms for action accompanied by sound, and the materials and objects so acted upon. In further investigation it becomes more and more requisite to isolate the sound-type or root from the modifications and additions to which it has been subjected for grammatical and phonetical adaptation. It will serve to give an idea of the extent and intricacy of this problem, to glance at a group of words in one European language, and notice the etymological network which spreads round the German word *klapf,* in Grimm's dictionary, *klappen, klippen, klopfen, kläffen, klimpern, klampern, klateren, kloteren, klitteren, klatzen, klacken,* and more, to be matched with allied forms in other languages. Setting aside the consideration of grammatical inflexion, it belongs to the present subject to notice that man's imitative faculty in language is by no means limited to making direct copies of sound and shaping them into words. It seizes upon ready-made terms of whatever origin, alters and adapts them to make their sound fitting to their sense, and pours into the dictionaries a flood of adapted words of which the most difficult to analyse are those which are neither altogether etymological nor altogether imitative, but partly both. How words, while preserving, so to speak, the same skeleton, may be made to follow the variation of sound, of force, of duration, of size, an imitative group more or less connected with the last will show—*crick, creak, crack, crash, crush, crunch, craunch, scrunch, scraunch.* It does not at all follow that because a word suffers such imitative and symbolic changes it must be, like this, directly imitative in its origin. What, for instance, could sound more imitative than the name of that old-fashioned cannon for throwing grape-shot, the *patterero*? Yet the etymology of the word appears in the Spanish form *pedrero*, French *perrier*; it means simply an instrument for throwing stones (*piedra, pierre*), and it was only when the Spanish word was adopted in England that the imitative faculty caught and transformed it into an apparent sound-word, resembling the verb to *patter*. The propensity of language, especially in slang, to make sense of strange words by altering them into something with an appropriate meaning has been often dwelt upon by philologists, but the propensity to alter words into something with an appropriate sound has produced results immensely more important. The effects of symbolic change of sound acting upon verb-roots seem almost boundless. The verb to *waddle* has a strong imitative appearance, and so in German we can hardly resist the suggestion that imitative sound has to do with the difference between *wandern* and *wandeln*; but all these verbs belong to a family represented by Sanskrit vad, to go, Latin *vado*, and to this root there seems no sufficient ground for assigning an imitative origin, the traces of which it has at any rate lost if it ever had them. Thus, again, to *stamp* with the foot, which has been claimed as an imitation of sound, seems only a 'coloured' word. The root *sta*, 'to stand,' Sanskrit *sthâ*, forms a causative *stap*, Sanskrit sthâpay, 'to make to stand,' English to *stop*, and a foot-*step* is when the foot comes to a stand, a foot-*stop*. But we have Anglo-Saxon *stapan, stæpan, steppan*, English to *step*, varying to express its meaning by sound in to *staup*, to *stamp*, to *stump*, and to *stomp*, contrasting in their violence or clumsy weight with the foot on the Dorset cottage-sill in Barnes's poem:—

'Where love do seek the maïden's evenèn vloor,

Wi' *stip-step light*, an tip-tap slight

Ageän the door.'

By expanding, modifying, or, so to speak, colouring, sound is able to produce effects closely like those of gesture-language, expressing length or shortness of time, strength or weakness of action, and then passing into a further stage to describe greatness or smallness of size or of distance, and thence making its way into the widest fields of metaphor. And it does all this with a force which is surprising when we consider how childishly simple are the means employed. Thus the Bachapin of Africa call a man with the cry *héla!* but according as he is far or farther off the sound of the *héela! hê-ê-la!* is lengthened out. Mr. Macgregor in his 'Rob Roy on the Jordan,' graphically describes this method of expression, "'But where is Zalmouda?"... Then with rough eagerness the strongest of the Dowana faction pushes his long forefinger forward, pointing straight enough—but whither? and with a volley of words ends, *Ah-ah-a-a-a——a-a*. This strange expression had long before puzzled me when first heard from a shepherd in Bashan.... But the simple meaning of this long string of "*ah's?*" shortened, and quickened, and lowered in tone to the end, is merely that the place pointed to is a "very great way off." The Chinook Jargon, as usual representing primitive developments of language, uses a similar device in lengthening the sound of words to indicate distance. The Siamese can, by varying the tone-accent, make the syllable *non*, 'there,' express a near, indefinite, or far distance, and in like manner can modify the meaning of such a word as *ny*, 'little.' In the Gaboon, the strength with which such a word as *mpolu*, 'great,' is uttered serves to show whether it is great, very great, or very very great, and in this way, as Mr. Wilson remarks in his Mpongwe Grammar, 'the comparative degrees of greatness, smallness, hardness, rapidity, and strength, &c., may be conveyed with more accuracy and precision than could readily be conceived.' In Madagascar *ratchi* means 'bad,' but *râtchi* is 'very bad.' The natives of Australia, according to Oldfield, show the use of this process in combination with that of symbolic reduplication: among the Watchandie tribe *jir-rie* signifies 'already or past,' *jir-rie jir-rie* indicates 'a long time ago,' while *jie-r-rie jirrie* (the first syllable being dwelt on for some time) signifies 'an immense time ago.' Again, *boo-rie* is 'small,' *boo-rie-boo-rie* 'very small,' and *b-o-rie boorie* 'exceedingly small.' Wilhelm von Humboldt notices the habit of the southern Guarani dialect of South America of dwelling more or less time on the suffix of the perfect tense, *yma, y—ma*, to indicate the length or shortness of the distance of time at which the action took place; and it is curious to observe that a similar contrivance is made use of among the aboriginal tribes of India, where the Ho language forms a future tense by adding *á* to the root, and prolonging its sound, *kajee* 'to speak,' Amg *kajēēá* 'I will speak.' As might be expected, the languages of very rude tribes show extremely well how the results of such primitive processes pass into the recognized stock of language. Nothing could be better for this than the words by which one of the rudest of living races, the Botocudos of Brazil, express the sea. They have a word for a stream, *ouatou*, and an adjective which means great, *ijipakijiou*; thence the two words 'stream-great,' a little strengthened in the vowels, will give the term for a river, *ouatou-ijipakiiijou*, as it were, 'stream-grea-at,' and this, to express the immensity of the ocean, is amplified into *ouatou-iijipakiijou-ou-ou-ou-ou*. Another tribe of the same family works out the same result more simply; the word *ouatou*, 'stream,' becomes *ouatou-ou-ou-ou*, 'the sea.' The Chavantes very naturally stretch the expression *rom-o-wodi*, 'I go a long way,' into *rom-o-o-o-o-wodi*, 'I go a very long way indeed,' and when they are called upon to count beyond five they say it is *ka-o-o-oki*, by which they evidently mean it is a very great many. The Cauixanas in one vocabulary are described as saying *lawauugabi* for four, and drawling out the same word for five, as if to say 'a long four,' in somewhat the same way as the Aponegicrans, whose word for six is *itawuna*, can expand this into a word for seven, *itawuūna*, obviously thus meaning a 'long six.' In their earlier and simpler stages nothing can be more easy to comprehend than these, so to speak, pictorial modifications of words. It is true that writing, even with the aid of italics and capitals, ignores much of this symbolism in spoken language, but every child can see its use and meaning, in spite of the efforts of book-learning and school-teaching to set aside whatever cannot be expressed by their imperfect symbols, nor controlled by their narrow rules. But when we try to follow out to their full results these methods, at first so easy to trace and appreciate, we soon find them passing out of our grasp. The language of the Sahaptin Indians shows us a process of modifying words which is far from clear, and yet not utterly obscure. These Indians have a way of making a kind of disrespectful diminutive by changing the *n* in a word to *l*; thus *twinwt* means 'tailless,' but to indicate particular smallness, or to express contempt, they make this into *twilwt*, pronounced with an appropriate change of tone; and again, *wana* means 'river,' but this is made into a diminutive *wala* by 'changing *n* into *l*, giving the voice a different tone, putting the lips out in speaking, and keeping them suspended around the jaw.' Here we are told enough about the change of pronunciation to guess at least how it could convey the notions of smallness and contempt. But it is less easy to follow the process by which the Mpongwe language turns an affirmative into a negative verb by 'an intonation upon, or prolongation of the radical vowel,' *tŏnda*, to love, *tōnda*, not to love; *tŏndo*, to be loved, *tōndo*, not to be loved. So Yoruba, *bába*, 'a great thing,' *bàba*, 'a small thing,' contrasted in a proverb, 'Baba bo, baba molle'—'A great matter puts a smaller out of sight.' Language is, in fact, full of phonetic modifications which justify a suspicion that symbolic sound had to do with their production, though it may be hard to say exactly how.

Again, there is the familiar process of reduplication, simple or modified, which produces such forms as *murmur, pitpat, helterskelter*. This action, though much restricted in literary dialects, has such immense scope in the talk of children and savages that Professor Pott's treatise on it[290] has become incidentally one of the most valuable collections of facts ever made with relation to early stages of language. Now up to a certain point any child can see how and why such doubling is done, and how it always adds something to the original idea. It may make superlatives or otherwise intensify words, as in Polynesia *loa* 'long,' *lololoa* 'very long'; Mandingo *ding* 'a child,' *dingding* 'a very little child.' It makes plurals, as Malay *raja-raja* 'princes,' *orang-orang* 'people.' It adds numerals, as Mosquito *walwal* 'four' (two-two), or distributes them, as Coptic *ouai ouai* 'singly' (one-one). These are cases where the motive of doubling is comparatively easy to make out.

As an example of cases much more difficult to comprehend may be taken the familiar reduplication of the perfect tense, Greek γέγραφα from γράφω, Latin *momordi* from *mordeo*, Gothic *haihald* from *haldan*, 'to hold.' Reduplication is habitually used in imitative words to intensify them, and still more, to show that the sound is repeated or continuous. From the immense mass of such words we may take as instances the Botocudo *hou-hou-hou-gitcha* 'to suck' (compare Tongan *hūhū* 'breast'), *kiaku-käck-käck*, 'a butterfly'; Quichua *chiuiuiuiñichi* 'wind whistling in the trees'; Maori *haruru* 'noise of wind'; *hohoro* 'hurry'; Dayak *kakakkaka* 'to go on laughing loud'; Aino *shiriushiriukanni* 'a rasp'; Tamil *murumuru* 'to *murmur*'; Akra *ewiewiewiewie* 'he spoke repeatedly and continually'; and so on, throughout the whole range of the languages of the world.

The device of conveying different ideas of distance by the use of a graduated scale of vowels seems to me one of great philological interest, from the suggestive hint it gives of the proceedings of the language-makers in most distant regions of the world, working out in various ways a similar ingenious contrivance of expression by sound. A typical series is the Javan: *iki* 'this' (close by) *ika* 'that' (at some distance); *iku* 'that' (farther off). It is not likely that the following list nearly exhausts the whole number of cases in the languages of the world, for about half the number have been incidentally noted down by myself without any especial search, but merely in the course of looking over vocabularies of the lower races.[291]

> Javan ... *iki*, this; *ika*, that (intermediate); *iku*, that.
>
> Malagasy ... *ao*, there (at a short distance); *eo*, there (at a shorter distance); *io*, there (close at hand). *atsy*, there (not far off); *etsy*, there (nearer); *itsy*, this or these.
>
> Japanese ... *ko*, here; *ka*, there. *korera*, these; *karera*, they (those).
>
> Canarese ... *ivanu*, this; *uvanu*, that (intermediate); *avanu*, that.
>
> Tamul ... *i*, this; *â*, that.
>
> Rajmahali ... *îh*, this; *âh*, that.
>
> Dhimal ... *isho, ita*, here; *usho, uta*, there. *iti, idong*, this; *uti, udong*, that (of things and persons respectively).
>
> Abchasian ... *abri*, this; *ubri*, that.
>
> Ossetic ... *am*, here; *um*, there.
>
> Magyar ... *ez*, this; *az*, that.
>
> Zulu ... *apa*, here; *apo*, there. *lesi, leso, lesiya*; *abu, abo, abuya*; &c. = this, that, that (in the distance).

Yoruba ... *na*, this; *ni*, that.

Fernandian ... *olo*, this; *ole*, that.

Tumale ... *re*, this; *ri*, that. *ngi*, I; *ngo*, thou; *ngu*, he.

Greenlandish ... *uv*, here, there (where one points to); *iv*, there, up there.

Sujelpa (Coleville Ind.) ... *aa*, this; *ii*, that.

Sahaptin ... *kina*, here; *kuna*, there.

Mutsun ... *ne*, here; *nu*, there.

Tarahumara ... *ibe*, here; *abe*, there.

Guarani ... *nde*, *ne*, thou; *ndi*, *ni*, he.

Botocudo ... *ati*, I; *oti*, thou, you, (prep.) to.

Carib ... *ne*, thou; *ni*, he.

Chilian ... *tva*, *vachi*, this; *tvey*, *veychi*, that.

It is obvious on inspection of this list of pronouns and adverbs that they have in some way come to have their vowels contrasted to match the contrast of here and there, this and that. Accident may sometimes account for such cases. For instance it is well known to philologists that our own *this* and *that* are pronouns partly distinct in their formation, *thi-s* being probably two pronouns run together, but yet the Dutch neuters *dit* 'this,' and *dat* 'that,' have taken the appearance of a single form with contrasted vowels.[292] But accident cannot account for the frequency of such words in pairs, and even in sets of three, in so many different languages. There must have been some common intention at work, and there is evidence that some of these languages do resort to a change of sound as a means of expressing change of distance. Thus the language of Fernando Po can not only express 'this' and 'that' by *olo*, *ole*, but it can even make a change of the pronunciation of the vowel distinguish between *o boehe* 'this month,' and *oh boehe*, 'that month.' In the same way the Grebo can make the difference between 'I' and 'thou,' 'we,' and 'you,' 'solely by the intonation of the voice, which the final *h* of the second persons *mâh* and *ăh* is intended to express.'

mâ di, I eat; *mâh* di, thou eatest;

ă di, we eat; *ăh* di, ye eat.

The set of Zulu demonstratives which express the three distances of near, farther, farthest, are very complex, but a remark as to their use shows how thoroughly symbolic sound enters into their nature. The Zulus not only say *nansi*, 'here is,' *nanso*, 'there is,' *nansiya*, 'there is in the distance,' but they even express the greatness of this distance by the emphasis and prolongation of the *ya*. If we could discern a similar gradation of the vowels to express a corresponding gradation of distance throughout our list, the whole matter would be easier to explain; but it is not so, the *i*-words for instance, are sometimes nearer and sometimes farther off than the *a*-words. We can only judge that, as even children can see that a scale of vowels makes a most expressive scale of distances, many pronouns and adverbs in use in the world have probably taken their shape under the influence of this simple device, and thus there have arisen sets of what we may call contrasted or 'differential' words.

How the differencing of words by change of vowels may be used to distinguish between the sexes, is well put in a remark of Professor Max Müller's: 'The distinction of gender ... is sometimes expressed in such a manner that we can only explain it by ascribing an expressive power to the more or less obscure sound of vowels. *Ukko*, in Finnic, is an old man; *akka*, an old woman.... In Mandshu *chacha* is mas. ... *cheche*, femina. Again, *ama*, in Mandshu, is father; *eme*, mother; *amcha*, father-in-law, *emche*, mother-in-law.'[293] The Coretú language of Brazil has another curiously contrasted pair of words *tsáackö*, 'father,' *tsaacko* 'mother,' while the Carib has *baba* for father, and *bibi* for mother, and the Ibu of Africa has *nna* for father and *nne* for mother. This contrivance of distinguishing the male from the female by a difference of vowels is however but a small part of the process of formation which can be traced among such words as those for father and mother. Their consideration leads into a very interesting philological region, that of 'Children's language.'

If we set down a few of the pairs of words which stand for 'father' and 'mother' in very different and distant languages—*papa* and *mama*; Welsh, *tad* (*dad*) and *mam*; Hungarian, *atya* and *anya*; Mandingo, *fa* and *ba*; Lummi (N. America), *man* and *tan*; Catoquina (S. America), *payú* and *nayú*; Watchandie (Australia), *amo* and *ago*—their contrast seems to lie in their consonants, while many other pairs differ totally, like Hebrew *ab* and *im*; Kuki, *p'ha* and *noo*; Kayan, *amay* and *inei*; Tarahumara, *nono* and *jeje*. Words of the class of *papa* and *mama*, occurring in remote parts of the world, were once freely used as evidence of a common origin of the languages in which they were found alike. But Professor Buschmann's paper on 'Nature-Sound,' published in 1853,[294] effectually overthrew this argument, and settled the view that such coincidence might arise again and again by independent production. It was clearly of no use to argue that Carib and English were allied because the word *papa*, 'father,' belongs to both, or Hottentot and English because both use *mama* for 'mother,' seeing that these childish articulations may be used in just the opposite way, for the Chilian word for mother is *papa*, and the Tlatskanai for father is *mama*. Yet the choice of easy little words for 'father' and 'mother' does not seem to have been quite indiscriminate. The immense list of such words collected by Buschmann shows that the types *pa* and *ta*, with the similar forms *ap* and *at*, preponderate in the world as names for 'father,' while *ma* and *na*, *am* and *an*, preponderate as names for 'mother.' His explanation of this state of things as affected by direct symbolism choosing the hard sound for the father, and the gentler for the mother, has very likely truth in it, but it must not be pushed too far. It cannot be, for instance, the same principle of symbolism which leads the Welshmen to say *tad* for 'father' and *mam* for 'mother,' and the Indian of British Columbia to say *maan*, 'father' and *taan*, 'mother,' or the Georgian to say *mama* 'father' and *deda* 'mother.' Yet I have not succeeded in finding anywhere our familiar *papa* and *mama* exactly reversed in one and the same language; the nearest approach to it that I can give is from the island of Meang, where *mama* meant 'father, man,' and *babi*, 'mother, woman.'[295]

Between the nursery words *papa* and *mama* and the more formal *father* and *mother* there is an obvious resemblance in sound. What, then, is the origin of these words *father* and *mother*? Up to a certain point their history is clear. They belong to the same group of organized words with *vater* and *mutter*, *pater* and *mater*, πατήρ and μήτηρ, *pitar* and *mâtar*, and other similar forms through the Indo-European family of languages. There is no doubt that all these pairs of names are derived from an ancient and common Aryan source, and when they are traced back as far as possible towards that source, they appear to have sprung from a pair of words which may be roughly called *patar* and *matar*, and which were formed by adding *tar*, the suffix of the actor, to the verb-roots *pa* and *ma*. There being two appropriate Sanskrit verbs *pâ* and *mâ*, it is possible to etymologize the two words as *patar*, 'protector,' and *matar*, 'producer.' Now this pair of Aryan words must have been very ancient, lying back at the remote common source from which forms parallel to our English *father* and *mother* passed into Greek and Persian, Norse and Armenian, thus holding fixed type through the eventful course of Indo-European history. Yet, ancient as these words are, they were no doubt preceded by simpler rudimentary words of the children's language, for it is not likely that the primitive Aryans did without baby-words for father and mother until they had an organized system of adding suffixes to verb-roots to express such notions as 'protector' or 'producer.' Nor can it be supposed that it was by mere accident that the root-words thus chosen happened to be the very sounds *pa* and *ma*, whose types so often occur in the remotest parts of the world as names for 'father' and 'mother.' Prof. Adolphe Pictet makes shift to account for the coincidence thus: he postulates first the pair of forms *pâ* and *mâ* as Aryan verb-roots of unknown origin, meaning 'to protect' and 'to create,' next another pair of forms *pa* and *ma*, children's words commonly used to denote father and mother, and lastly he combines the two by supposing that the root-verbs *pâ* and *mâ* were chosen to form the Indo-European words for parents, because of their resemblance to the familiar baby-words already in use. This circuitous process at any rate saves those sacred monosyllables, the Sanskrit verb-roots, from the disgrace of an assignable origin. Yet those who remember that these verb-roots are only a set of crude forms in use in one particular language of the world at one particular period of its development, may account for the facts more simply and more thoroughly. It is a fair guess that the ubiquitous *pa* and *ma* of the children's language were the original forms; that they were used in an early period of Aryan speech as indiscriminately substantive and verb, just as our modern English, which so often reproduces the most rudimentary linguistic processes, can form from the noun 'father' a verb 'to father;' and that lastly they became verb-roots, whence the words *patar* and *matar* were formed by the addition of the suffix.[296]

The baby-names for parents must not be studied as though they stood alone in language. They are only important members of a great class of words, belonging to all times and countries within our experience, and forming a children's language, whose common character is due to its concerning itself with the limited set of ideas in which little children are interested, and expressing these ideas by the limited set of articulations suited to the child's first attempts to talk. This peculiar language is marked quite characteristically among the low savage tribes of Australia; *mamman* 'father,' *ngangan* 'mother,' and by metaphor 'thumb,' 'great toe' (as is more fully explained in *jinnamamman* 'great toe,' i.e. foot's father), *tammin* 'grandfather or grandmother,' *bab-ba* 'bad, foolish, childish,' *bee-bee*, *beep* 'breast,' *pappi* 'father,' *pappa* 'young one,' *pup*, whelp,' (whence is grammatically formed the verb *papparniti* 'to become a young one, to be born.') Or if we look for examples from India, it does not matter whether we take them from non-Hindu or Hindu languages, for in baby-language all races are on one footing. Thus Tamil *appâ* 'father,' *ammâ* 'mother,' Bodo *aphâ* 'father,' *âyâ* 'mother;' the Kocch group *nânâ* and *nâni* 'paternal grandfather and grandmother,' *mâmâ* 'uncle,' *dâdâ* 'cousin,' may be set beside Sanskrit *tata* 'father,' *nanâ* 'mother,' and the Hindustani words of the same class, of which some are familiar to the English ear by being naturalized in Anglo-Indian talk, *bâbâ* 'father,' *bâbû* 'child, prince, Mr.,' *bîbî* 'lady,' *dadâ* 'nurse' (*âyâ* 'nurse' seems borrowed from Portuguese). Such words are continually coming fresh into existence everywhere, and the law of natural selection determines their fate. The great mass of the *nana's* and *dada's* of the nursery die out almost as soon as made. Some few take more root and spread over large districts as accepted nursery words, and now and then a curious philologist makes a collection of them. Of such, many are obvious mutilations of longer words, as French faire *dodo* 'to sleep' (*dormir*), Brandenburg *wiwi*, a common cradle lullaby (*wiegen*). Others, whatever their origin, fall, in consequence of the small variety of articulations out of which they must be chosen, into a curiously indiscriminate and unmeaning mass, as Swiss *bobo* 'a scratch;' *bambam* 'all gone;' Italian *bobò* 'something to drink,' *gogo* 'little boy,' for *dede* 'to play.' These are words quoted by Pott, and for English examples *nana* 'nurse,' *tata!* 'good-bye!' may serve. But all *baby*-words, as this very name proves, do not stop short even at this stage of publicity. A small proportion of them establish themselves in the ordinary talk of grown-up men and women, and when they have once made good their place as constituents of general language, they may pass on by inheritance from age to age. Such examples as have been here quoted of nursery words give a clue to the origin of a mass of names in the most diverse languages, for father, mother, grandmother, aunt, child, breast, toy, doll, &c. The negro of Fernando Po who uses the word *bubboh* for 'a little boy,' is on equal terms with the German who uses *bube*; the Congo-man who uses *tata* for 'father' would understand how the same word could be used in classic Latin for 'father,' and in mediæval Latin for 'pedagogue;' the Carib and the Caroline Islander agree with the Englishman that *papa* is a suitable word to express 'father,' and then it only remains to carry on the word, and make the baby-language name the priests of the Eastern Church and the great *Papa* of the Western. At the same time the evidence explains the indifference with which, out of the small stock of available materials, the same sound does duty for the most different ideas; why *mama* means here 'mother,' there 'father,' there 'uncle,' *maman* here 'mother,' there 'father-in-law,' *dada* here 'father,' there 'nurse,' there 'breast,' *tata* here 'father,' there 'son.' A single group of words may serve to show the character of this peculiar region of language: Blackfoot Indian *ninnah* 'father;' Greek νέννος 'uncle;' νέννα 'aunt;' Zulu *nina*, Sangir *nina*, Malagasy *nini* 'mother;' Javan *nini* 'grandfather or grandmother;' Vayu *nini* 'paternal aunt;' Darien Indian *ninah* 'daughter;' Spanish *niño*, *niña* 'child;' Italian *ninna* 'little girl;' Milanese *ninin* 'bed;' Italian *ninnare* 'to rock the cradle.'

In this way a dozen easy child's articulations, *ba's* and *na's*, *ti's* and *de's*, *pa's* and *ma's*, serve almost as indiscriminately to express a dozen child's ideas as though they had been shaken in a bag and pulled out at random to express the notion that came first, doll or uncle, nurse or grandfather. It is obvious that among words cramped to such scanty choice of articulate sounds, speculations as to derivation must be more than usually unsafe. Looked at from this point of view, children's language may give a valuable lesson to the philologist. He has before him a kind of language, formed, under peculiar conditions, and showing the weak points of his method of philological research, only exaggerated into extraordinary distinctness. In ordinary language, the difficulty of connecting sound with sense lies in great measure in the inability of a small and rigid set of articulations to express an interminable variety of tones and noises. In children's language, a still more scanty set of articulations fails yet more to render these distinctly. The difficulty of finding the derivation of words lies in great measure in the use of more or less similar root-sounds for most heterogeneous purposes. To assume that two words of different meanings, just because they sound somewhat alike, must therefore have a common origin, is even in ordinary language the great source of bad etymology. But in children's language the theory of root-sounds fairly breaks down. Few would venture to assert, for instance, that *papa* and *pap* have a common derivation or a common root. All that we can safely say of connexion between them is that they are words related by common acceptance in the nursery language. As such, they are well marked in ancient Rome as in modern England: *papas* 'nutricius, nutritor,' *pappus* 'senex;' 'cum cibum et potum *buas* ac *papas* dicunt, et matrem *mammam*, patrem *tatam* (or *papam*).'[297]

From children's language, moreover, we have striking proof of the power of consensus of society, in establishing words in settled use without their carrying traces of inherent expressiveness. It is true that children are intimately acquainted with the use of emotional and imitative sound, and their vocal intercourse largely consists of such expression. The effects of this are in some degree discernible in the class of words we are considering. But it is obvious that the leading principle of their formation is not to adopt words distinguished by the expressive character of their sound, but to choose somehow a fixed word to answer a given purpose. To do this, different languages have chosen similar articulations to express the most diverse and opposite ideas. Now in the language of grown-up people, it is clear that social consensus has worked in the same way. Even if the extreme supposition be granted, that the ultimate origin of every word of language lies in inherently expressive sound, this only partly affects the case, for it would have to be admitted that, in actual languages, most words have so far departed in sound or sense from this originally expressive stage, that to all intents and purposes they might at first have been arbitrarily chosen. The main principle of language has been, not to preserve traces of original sound-signification for the benefit of future etymologists, but to fix elements of language to serve as counters for practical reckoning of ideas. In this process much original expressiveness has no doubt disappeared beyond all hope of recovery.

Such are some of the ways in which vocal sounds seem to have commended themselves to the mind of the word-maker as fit to express his meaning, and to have been used accordingly. I do not think that the evidence here adduced justifies the setting-up of what is called the

Interjectional and Imitative Theory as a complete solution of the problem of original language. Valid as this theory proves itself within limits, it would be incautious to accept a hypothesis which can perhaps satisfactorily account for a twentieth of the crude forms in any language, as a certain and absolute explanation of the nineteen-twentieths whose origin remains doubtful. A key must unlock more doors than this, to be taken as the master-key. Moreover, some special points which have come under consideration in these chapters tend to show the positive necessity of such caution in theorizing. Too narrow a theory of the application of sound to sense may fail to include the varied devices which the languages of different regions turn to account. It is thus with the distinction in meaning of a word by its musical accent, and the distinction of distance by graduated vowels. These are ingenious and intelligible contrivances, but they hardly seem directly emotional or imitative in origin. A safer way of putting the theory of a natural origin of language is to postulate the original utterance of ideas in what may be called self-expressive sounds, without defining closely whether their expression lay in emotional tone, imitative noise, contrast of accent or vowel or consonant, or other phonetic quality. Even here, exception of unknown and perhaps enormous extent must be made for sounds chosen by individuals to express some notion, from motives which even their own minds failed to discern, but which sounds nevertheless made good their footing in the language of the family, the tribe, and the nation. There may be many modes even of recognizable phonetic expression, unknown to us as yet. So far, however, as I have been able to trace them here, such modes have in common a claim to belong not exclusively to the scheme of this or that particular dialect, but to wide-ranging principles of formation of language. Their examples are to be drawn with equal cogency from Sanskrit or Hebrew, from the nursery-language of Lombardy, or the half-Indian, half-European jargon of Vancouver's Island; and wherever they are found, they help to furnish groups of sound-words—words which have not lost the traces of their first expressive origin, but still carry their direct significance plainly stamped upon them. In fact, the time has now come for a substantial basis to be laid for Generative Philology. A classified collection of words with any strong claim to be self-expressive should be brought together out of the thousand or so of recognized languages and dialects of the world. In such a Dictionary of Sound-Words, half the cases cited might very likely be worthless, but the collection would afford the practical means of expurgating itself; for it would show on a large scale what particular sounds have manifested their fitness to convey particular ideas, by having been repeatedly chosen among different races to convey them.

Attempts to explain as far as may be the primary formation of speech, by tracing out in detail such processes as have been here described, are likely to increase our knowledge by sure and steady steps wherever imagination does not get the better of sober comparison of facts. But there is one side of this problem of the Origin of Language on which such studies have by no means an encouraging effect. Much of the popular interest in such matters is centred in the question, whether the known languages of the world have their source in one or many primæval tongues. On this subject the opinions of the philologists who have compared the greatest number of languages are utterly at variance, nor has any one brought forward a body of philological evidence strong and direct enough to make anything beyond mere vague opinion justifiable. Now such processes as the growth of imitative or symbolic words form a part, be it small or large, of the Origin of Language, but they are by no means restricted to any particular place or period, and are indeed more or less in activity now. Their operation on any two dialects of one language will be to introduce in each a number of new and independent words, and words even suspected of having been formed in this direct way become valueless as proof of genealogical connexion between the languages in which they are found. The test of such genealogical connexion must, in fact, be generally narrowed to such words or grammatical forms as have become so far conventional in sound and sense, that we cannot suppose two tribes to have arrived at them independently, and therefore consider that both must have inherited them from a common source. Thus the introduction of new sound-words tends to make it practically of less and less consequence to a language what its original stock of words at starting may have been; and the philologist's extension of his knowledge of such direct formations must compel him to strip off more and more of any language, as being possibly of later growth, before he can set himself to argue upon such a residuum as may have come by direct inheritance from times of primæval speech.

In concluding this survey, some general considerations suggest themselves as to the nature and first beginnings of language. In studying the means of expression among men in stages of mental culture far below our own, one of our first needs is to clear our minds of the kind of superstitious veneration with which articulate speech has so commonly been treated, as though it were not merely the principal but the sole means of uttering thought. We must cease to measure the historical importance of emotional exclamations, of gesture-signs, and of picture-writing, by their comparative insignificance in modern civilized life, but must bring ourselves to associate the articulate words of the dictionary in one group with cries and gestures and pictures, as being all of them means of manifesting outwardly the inward workings of the mind. Such an admission, it must be observed, is far from being a mere detail of scientific classification. It has really a most important bearing on the problem of the Origin of Language. For as the reasons are mostly dark to us, why particular words are currently used to express particular ideas, language has come to be looked upon as a mystery, and either occult philosophical causes have been called in to explain its phenomena, or else the endowment of man with the faculties of thought and utterance has been deemed insufficient, and a special revelation has been demanded to put into his mouth the vocabulary of a particular language. In the debate which has been carried on for ages over this much-vexed problem, the saying in the 'Kratylos' comes back to our minds again and again, where Sokrates describes the etymologists who release themselves from their difficulties as to the origin of words by saying that the first words were divinely made, and therefore right, just as the tragedians, when they are in perplexity, fly to their machinery and bring in the gods.[298] Now I think that those who soberly contemplate the operation of cries, groans, laughs, and other emotional utterances, as to which some considerations have been here brought forward, will admit that, at least, our present crude understanding of this kind of expression would lead us to class it among the natural actions of man's body and mind. Certainly, no one who understands anything of the gesture-language or of picture-writing would be justified in regarding either as due to occult causes, or to any supernatural interference with the course of man's intellectual development. Their cause evidently lies in natural operations of the human mind, not such as were effective in some long-past condition of humanity and have since disappeared, but in processes existing amongst us, which we can understand and even practise for ourselves. When we study the pictures and gestures with which savages and the deaf-and-dumb express their minds, we can mostly see at a glance the direct relation between the outward sign and the inward thought which it makes manifest. We may see the idea of 'sleep' shown in gesture by the head with shut eyes, leant heavily against the open hand; or the idea of 'running' by the attitude of the runner, with chest forward, mouth half open, elbows and shoulders well back; or 'candle' by the straight forefinger held up, and as it were blown out; or 'salt' by the imitated act of sprinkling it with thumb and finger. The figures of the child's picture-book, the sleeper and the runner, the candle and the salt-cellar, show their purport by the same sort of evident relation between thought and sign. We so far understand the nature of these modes of utterance, that we are ready ourselves to express thought after thought by such means, so that those who see our signs shall perceive our meaning.

When, however, encouraged by our ready success in making out the nature and action of these ruder methods, we turn to the higher art of speech, and ask how such and such words have come to express such and such thoughts, we find ourselves face to face with an immense problem, as yet but in small part solved. The success of investigation has indeed been enough to encourage us to push vigorously forward in the research, but the present explorations have not extended beyond corners and patches of an elsewhere unknown field. Still the results go far to warrant us in associating expression by gestures and pictures with articulate language as to principles of original formation, much as men associate them in actual life by using gesture and word at once. Of course, articulate speech, in its far more complex and elaborate development, has taken up devices to which the more simple and rude means of communication offer nothing comparable. Still, language, so far as its constitution is understood, seems to have been developed like writing or music, like hunting or fire-making, by the exercise of purely human faculties in purely human ways. This state of things by no means belongs exclusively to rudimentary philological operations, such as the choosing expressive sounds to name corresponding ideas by. In the higher departments of speech, where words already existing are turned to account to express new meanings and shade off new distinctions, we find these ends attained by contrivances ranging from extreme dexterity down to utter clumsiness. For a single instance, one great means of giving new meaning to old sound is metaphor, which transfers ideas from hearing to seeing, from touching to thinking, from the concrete of one kind to the abstract of another, and can thus make almost anything in the world help to describe or suggest anything else. What the German philosopher described as the relation of a cow to a comet, that both have tails, is enough and more than enough for the language-maker. It struck the Australians, when they saw a European book, that it opened and shut like a mussel-shell, and they began accordingly to call books 'mussels' (*müyüm*). The sight of a steam engine may suggest a whole group of such transitions in our own language; the steam passes along 'fifes' or 'trumpets,' that is, *pipes* or *tubes*, and enters by 'folding-doors' or *valves*, to push a 'pestle' or *piston* up and down in a 'roller' or *cylinder*, while the light pours from the furnace in 'staves' or 'poles,' that is, in *rays* or *beams*. The dictionaries are full of cases compared with which such as these are plain and straightforward. Indeed, the processes by which words have really come into existence may often enough remind us of the game of 'What is my thought like?' When one knows the answer, it is easy enough to see what *junketting* and cathedral *canons* have to do with reeds; Latin *juncus* 'a reed,' Low Latin *juncata*, 'cheese made in a reed-basket,' Italian *giuncata* 'cream cheese in a rush frail,' French *joncade* and English *junket*, which are preparations of cream, and lastly *junketting* parties where such delicacies are eaten; Greek κάννη, 'reed, *cane*,' κανῶν, 'measure, rule,' thence *canonicus*, 'a clerk under the ecclesiastical rule or canon.' But who could guess the history of these words, who did not happen to know these intermediate links?

Yet there is about this process of derivation a thoroughly human artificial character. When we know the whole facts of any case, we can generally understand it at once, and see that we might have done the same ourselves had it come in our way. And the same thing is true of the processes of making sound-words detailed in these chapters. Such a view is, however, in no way inconsistent with the attempt to generalize upon these processes, and to state them as phases of the development of language among mankind. If certain men under certain circumstances produce certain results, then we may at least expect that other men much resembling these and placed under roughly similar circumstances will produce more or less like results; and this has been shown over and over again in these pages to be what really happens. Now Wilhelm von Humboldt's view that language is an 'organism' has been considered a great step in philological speculation; and so far as it has led students to turn their minds to the search after general laws, no doubt it has been so. But it has also caused an increase of vague thinking and talking, and thereby no small darkening of counsel. Had it been meant to say that human thought, language, and action generally, are organic in their nature, and work under fixed laws, this would be a very different matter; but this is distinctly not what is meant, and the very object of calling language an organism is to keep it apart from mere human arts and contrivances. It was a hateful thing to Humboldt's mind to 'bring down speech to a mere operation of the understanding.' 'Man,' he says, 'does not so much form language, as discern with a kind of joyous wonder its developments, coming forth as of themselves.' Yet, if the practical shifts by which words are shaped or applied to fit new meanings are not devised by an operation of the understanding, we ought consistently to carry the stratagems of the soldier in the field, or the contrivances of the workman at his bench, back into the dark regions of instinct and involuntary action. That the actions of individual men combine to produce results which may be set down in those general statements of fact which we call laws, may be stated once again as one of the main propositions of the Science of Culture. But the nature of a fact is not altered by its being classed in common with others of the same kind, and a man is not less the intelligent inventor of a new word or a new metaphor, because twenty other intelligent inventors elsewhere may have fallen on a similar expedient.

The theory that the original forms of language are to be referred to a low or savage condition of culture among the remotely ancient human race, stands in general consistency with the known facts of philology. The causes which have produced language, so far as they are understood, are notable for that childlike simplicity of operation which befits the infancy of human civilization. The ways in which sounds are in the first instance chosen and arranged to express ideas, are practical expedients at the level of nursery philosophy. A child of five years old could catch the meaning of imitative sounds, interjectional words, symbolism of sex or distance by contrast of vowels. Just as no one is likely to enter into the real nature of mythology who has not the keenest appreciation of nursery tales, so the spirit in which we guess riddles and play at children's games is needed to appreciate the lower phases of language. Such a state of things agrees with the opinion that such rudimentary speech had its origin among men while in a childlike intellectual condition, and thus the self-expressive branch of savage language affords valuable materials for the problem of primitive speech. If we look back in imagination to an early period of human intercourse, where gesture and self-expressive utterance may have had a far greater comparative importance than among ourselves, such a conception introduces no new element into the problem, for a state of things more or less answering to this is described among certain low savage tribes. If we turn from such self-expressive utterance, to that part of articulate language which carries its sense only by traditional and seemingly arbitrary custom, we shall find no contradiction to the hypothesis. Sound carrying direct meaning may be taken up as an element of language, keeping its first significance recognizable to nations yet unborn. But it may far more probably become by wear of sound and shift of sense an expressionless symbol, such as might have been chosen in pure arbitrariness—a philological process to which the vocabularies of savage dialects bear full witness. In the course of the development of language, such traditional words with merely an inherited meaning have in no small measure driven into the background the self-expressive words, just as the Eastern figures 2, 3, 4, which are not self-expressive, have driven into the background the Roman numerals II, III, IIII, which are—this, again, is an operation which has its place in savage as in cultivated speech. Moreover, to look closely at language as a practical means of expressing thought, is to face evidence of no slight bearing on the history of civilization. We come back to the fact, so full of suggestion, that the languages of the world represent substantially the same intellectual art, the higher nations indeed gaining more expressive power than the lowest tribes, yet doing this not by introducing new and more effective central principles, but by mere addition and improvement in detail. The two great methods of naming thoughts and stating their relation to one another, viz., metaphor and syntax, belong to the infancy of human expression, and are as thoroughly at home in the language of savages as of philosophers. If it be argued that this similarity in principles of language is due to savage tribes having descended from higher culture, carrying down with them in their speech the relics of their former excellence, the answer is that linguistic expedients are actually worked out with as much originality, and more extensively if not more profitably, among savages than among cultured men. Take for example the Algonquin system of compounding words, and the vast Esquimaux scheme of grammatical inflexion. Language belongs in essential principle both to low grades and high of civilization; to which should its origin be attributed? An answer may be had by comparing the methods of language with the work it has to do. Take language all in all over the world, it is obvious that the processes by which words are made and adapted have far less to do with systematic arrangement and scientific classification, than with mere rough and ready ingenuity and the great rule of thumb. Let any one whose vocation it is to realize philosophical or scientific conceptions and to express them in words, ask himself whether ordinary language is an instrument planned for such purposes. Of course it is not. It is hard to say which is the more striking, the want of scientific system in the expression of thought by words, or the infinite cleverness of detail by which this imperfection is got over, so that he who has an idea does somehow make shift to get it clearly in words before his own and other minds. The language by which a nation with highly developed art and knowledge and sentiment must express its thoughts on these subjects, is no apt machine devised for such special work, but an old barbaric engine added to and altered, patched and tinkered into some sort of capability. Ethnography reasonably accounts at once for the immense power and the manifest weakness of language as a means of expressing modern educated thought, by treating it as an original product of low culture, gradually adapted by ages of evolution and selection, to answer more or less sufficiently the requirements of modern civilization.

CHAPTER VII.
THE ART OF COUNTING.

Ideas of Number derived from experience—State of Arithmetic among uncivilized races—Small extent of Numeral-words among low tribes—Counting by fingers and toes—Hand-numerals show derivation of Verbal reckoning from Gesture-counting—Etymology of Numerals—Quinary, Decimal, and Vigesimal notations of the world derived from counting on fingers and toes—Adoption of foreign Numeral-words—Evidence of development of Arithmetic from a low original level of Culture.

Mr. J. S. Mill, in his 'System of Logic,' takes occasion to examine the foundations of the art of arithmetic. Against Dr. Whewell, who had maintained that such propositions as that two and three make five are 'necessary truths,' containing in them an element of certainty beyond that which mere experience can give, Mr. Mill asserts that 'two and one are equal to three' expresses merely 'a truth known to us by early and constant experience: an inductive truth; and such truths are the foundation of the science of Number. The fundamental truths of that science all rest on the evidence of sense; they are proved by showing to our eyes and our fingers that any given number of objects, ten balls for example, may by separation and re-arrangement exhibit to our senses all the different sets of numbers the sum of which is equal to ten. All the improved methods of teaching arithmetic to children proceed on a knowledge of this fact. All who wish to carry the child's mind along with them in learning arithmetic; all who wish to teach numbers, and not mere ciphers—now teach it through the evidence of the senses, in the manner we have described.' Mr. Mill's argument is taken from the mental conditions of people among whom there exists a highly advanced arithmetic. The subject is also one to be advantageously studied from the ethnographer's point of view. The examination of the methods of numeration in use among the lower races not only fully bears out Mr. Mill's view, that our knowledge of the relations of numbers is based on actual experiment, but it enables us to trace the art of counting to its source, and to ascertain by what steps it arose in the world among particular races, and probably among all mankind.

In our advanced system of numeration, no limit is known either to largeness or smallness. The philosopher cannot conceive the formation of any quantity so large or of any atom so small but the arithmetician can keep pace with him, and can define it in a simple combination of written signs. But as we go downwards in the scale of culture, we find that even where the current language has terms for hundreds and thousands, there is less and less power of forming a distinct notion of large numbers, the reckoner is sooner driven to his fingers, and there increases among the most intelligent that numerical indefiniteness that we notice among children—if there were not a thousand people in the street there were certainly a hundred, at any rate there were twenty. Strength in arithmetic does not, it is true, vary regularly with the level of general culture. Some savage or barbaric peoples are exceptionally skilled in numeration. The Tonga Islanders really have native numerals up to 100,000. Not content even with this, the French explorer Labillardière pressed them farther and obtained numerals up to 1000 billions, which were duly printed, but proved on later examination to be partly nonsense-words and partly indelicate expressions,[299] so that the supposed series of high numerals forms at once a little vocabulary of Tongan indecency, and a warning as to the probable results of taking down unchecked answers from question-worried savages. In West Africa, a lively and continual habit of bargaining has developed a great power of arithmetic, and little children already do feats of computation with their heaps of cowries. Among the Yorubas of Abeokuta, to say 'you don't know nine times nine' is actually an insulting way of saying 'you are a dunce.'[300] This is an extraordinary proverb, when we compare it with the standard which our corresponding European sayings set for the limits of stupidity: the German says, 'he can scarce count five'; the Spaniard, 'I will tell you how many make five' (cuantos son cinco); and we have the same saw in England:—

'... as sure as I'm alive,

And knows how many beans make five.'

A Siamese law-court will not take the evidence of a witness who cannot count or reckon figures up to ten; a rule which reminds us of the ancient custom of Shrewsbury, where a person was deemed of age when he knew how to count up to twelve pence.[301]

Among the lowest living men, the savages of the South American forests and the deserts of Australia, 5 is actually found to be a number which the languages of some tribes do not know by a special word. Not only have travellers failed to get from them names for numbers above 2, 3, or 4, but the opinion that these are the real limits of their numeral series is strengthened by the use of their highest known number as an indefinite term for a great many. Spix and Martius say of the low tribes of Brazil, 'They count commonly by their finger joints, so up to three only. Any larger number they express by the word "many."'[302] In a Puri vocabulary the numerals are given as 1. *omi*; 2. *curiri*; 3. *prica*, 'many': in a Botocudo vocabulary, 1. *mokenam*; 2. *uruhú*, 'many.' The numeration of the Tasmanians is, according to Jorgensen, 1. *parmery*; 2. *calabawa*; more than 2, *cardia*; as Backhouse puts it, they count 'one, two, plenty;' but an observer who had specially good opportunities, Dr. Milligan, gives their numerals up to 5, *puggana*, which we shall recur to.[303] Mr. Oldfield (writing especially of Western tribes) says, 'The New Hollanders have no names for numbers beyond *two*. The Watchandie scale of notation is *co-ote-on* (one), *u-tau-ra* (two), *bool-tha* (many), and *bool-tha-bat* (very many). If absolutely required to express the numbers three or four, they say *u-tar-ra coo-te-oo* to indicate the former number, and *u-tar-ra u-tar-ra* to denote the latter.' That is to say, their names for one, two, three, and four, are equivalent to 'one,' 'two,' 'two-one,' 'two-two.' Dr. Lang's numerals from Queensland are just the same in principle, though the words are different: 1. *ganar*; 2. *burla*; 3. *burla-ganar*, 'two-one'; 4. *burla-burla*, 'two-two'; *korumba*, 'more than four, much, great.' The Kamilaroi dialect, though with the same 2 as the last, improves upon it by having an independent 3, and with the aid of this it reckons as far as 6: 1. *mal*; 2. *bularr*; 3. *guliba*; 4. *bularr-bularr*, 'two-two'; 5. *bulaguliba*, 'two-three'; 6. *guliba-guliba* 'three-three.' These Australian examples are at least evidence of a very scanty as well as clumsy numeral system among certain tribes.[304] Yet here again higher forms will have to be noticed, which in one district at least carry the native numerals up to 15 or 20.

It is not to be supposed, because a savage tribe has no current words for numbers above 3 or 5 or so, that therefore they cannot count beyond this. It appears that they can and do count considerably farther, but it is by falling back on a lower and ruder method of expression than speech—the gesture-language. The place in intellectual development held by the art of counting on one's fingers, is well marked in the description which Massieu, the Abbé Sicard's deaf-and-dumb pupil, gives of his notion of numbers in his comparatively untaught childhood: 'I knew the numbers before my instruction, my fingers had taught me them. I did not know the ciphers; I counted on my fingers, and when the number passed 10 I made notches on a bit of wood.'[305] It is thus that all savage tribes have been taught arithmetic by their fingers. Mr. Oldfield, after giving the account just quoted of the capability of the Watchandie language to reach 4 by numerals, goes on to describe the means by which the tribe contrive to deal with a harder problem in numeration.

'I once wished to ascertain the exact number of natives who had been slain on a certain occasion. The individual of whom I made the enquiry, began to think over the names ... assigning one of his fingers to each, and it was not until after many failures, and consequent fresh starts, that he was able to express so high a number, which he at length did by holding up his hand three times, thus giving me to understand that fifteen was the answer to this most difficult arithmetical question.' Of the aborigines of Victoria, Mr. Stanbridge says: 'They have no name for numerals above two, but by repetition they count to five; they also record the days of the moon by means of the fingers, the bones and joints of the arms and the head.'[306] The Bororos of Brazil reckon: 1. *couai*; 2. *macouai*; 3. *ouai*; and then go on counting on their fingers, repeating this *ouai*.[307] Of course it no more follows among savages than among ourselves that, because a man counts on his fingers, his language must be wanting in words to express the number he wishes to reckon. For example it was noticed that when natives of Kamchatka were set to count, they would reckon all their fingers, and then all their toes, so getting up to 20, and then would ask, 'What are we to do next?' Yet it was found on examination that numbers up to 100 existed in their language.[308] Travellers notice the use of finger-counting among tribes who can, if they choose, speak the number, and who either silently count it upon their fingers, or very usually accompany the word with the action; nor indeed are either of these modes at all unfamiliar in modern Europe. Let Father Gumilla, one of the early Jesuit missionaries in South America, describe for us the relation of gesture to speech in counting, and at the same time bring to our minds very remarkable examples (to be paralleled elsewhere) of the action of consensus, whereby conventional rules become fixed among societies of men, even in so simple an art as that of counting on one's fingers. 'Nobody among ourselves,' he remarks, 'except incidentally, would say for instance "one," "two," &c., and give the number on his fingers as well, by touching them with the other hand. Exactly the contrary happens among Indians. They say, for instance, "give me one pair of scissors," and forthwith they raise one finger; "give me two," and at once they raise two, and so on. They would never say "five" without showing a hand, never "ten" without holding out both, never "twenty" without adding up the fingers, placed opposite to the toes. Moreover, the mode of showing the numbers with the fingers differs in each nation. To avoid prolixity, I give as an example the number "three." The Otomacs to say "three" unite the thumb, forefinger, and middle finger, keeping the others down. The Tamanacs show the little finger, the ring finger, and the middle finger, and close the other two. The Maipures, lastly, raise the fore, middle, and ring fingers, keeping the other two hidden.'[309] Throughout the world, the general relation between finger-counting and word-counting may be stated as follows. For readiness and for ease and apprehension of numbers, a palpable arithmetic, such as is worked on finger-joints or fingers,[310] or heaps of pebbles or beans, or the more artificial contrivances of the rosary or the abacus, has so great an advantage over reckoning in words as almost necessarily to precede it. Thus not only do we find finger-counting among savages and uneducated men, carrying on a part of their mental operations where language is only partly able to follow it, but it also retains a place and an undoubted use among the most cultured nations, as a preparation for and means of acquiring higher arithmetical methods.

Now there exists valid evidence to prove that a child learning to count upon its fingers does in a way reproduce a process of the mental history of the human race; that in fact men counted upon their fingers before they found words for the numbers they thus expressed; that in this department of culture, Word-language not only followed Gesture-language, but actually grew out of it. The evidence in question is principally that of language itself, which shows that, among many and distant tribes, men wanting to express 5 in words called it simply by their name for the *hand* which they held up to denote it, that in like manner they said *two hands* or *half a man* to denote 10, that the word *foot* carried on the reckoning up to 15, and to 20, which they described in words as in gesture by the *hands and feet* together, or as *one man*, and that lastly, by various expressions referring directly to the gestures of counting on the fingers and toes, they gave names to these and intermediate numerals. As a definite term is wanted to describe significant numerals of this class, it may be convenient to call them 'hand-numerals' or 'digit-numerals.' A selection of typical instances will serve to make it probable that this ingenious device was not, at any rate generally, copied from one tribe by another or inherited from a common source, but that its working out with original character and curiously varying detail displays the recurrence of a similar but independent process of mental development among various races of man.

Father Gilij, describing the arithmetic of the Tamanacs on the Orinoco, gives their numerals up to 4: when they come to 5, they express it by the word *amgnaitòne*, which being translated means 'a whole hand;' 6 is expressed by a term which translates the proper gesture into words, *itaconò amgnaponà tevinitpe* 'one of the other hand,' and so on up to 9. Coming to 10, they give it in words as *amgna aceponàre* 'both hands.' To denote 11 they stretch out both the hands, and adding the foot they say *puittaponà tevinitpe* 'one to the foot,' and thus up to 15, which is *iptaitòne* 'a whole foot.' Next follows 16, 'one to the other foot,' and so on to 20, *tevin itòto*, 'one Indian;' 21, *itaconò itòto jamgnàr bonà tevinitpe* 'one to the hands of the other Indian;' 40, *acciachè itòto*, 'two Indians;' thence on to 60, 80, 100, 'three, four, five Indians,' and beyond if needful. South America is remarkably rich in such evidence of an early condition of finger-counting recorded in spoken language. Among its many other languages which have recognizable digit-numerals, the Cayriri, Tupi, Abipone, and Carib rival the Tamanac in their systematic way of working out 'hand,' 'hands,' 'foot,' 'feet,' &c. Others show slighter traces of the same process, where, for instance, the numerals 5 or 10 are found to be connected with words for 'hand,' &c., as when the

Omagua uses *pua*, 'hand,' for 5, and reduplicates this into *upapua* for 10. In some South American languages a man is reckoned by fingers and toes up to 20, while in contrast to this, there are two languages which display a miserably low mental state, the man counting only one hand, thus stopping short at 5; the Juri *ghomen apa* 'one man,' stands for 5; the Cayriri *ibichó* is used to mean both 'person' and 5. Digit-numerals are not confined to tribes standing, like these, low or high within the limits of savagery. The Muyscas of Bogota were among the more civilized native races of America, ranking with the Peruvians in their culture, yet the same method of formation which appears in the language of the rude Tamanacs is to be traced in that of the Muyscas, who, when they came to 11, 12, 13, counted *quihicha ata, bosa, mica, i.e.,* 'foot one, two, three.'[311] To turn to North America, Cranz, the Moravian missionary, thus describes about a century ago the numeration of the Greenlanders. 'Their numerals,' he says, 'go not far, and with them the proverb holds that they can scarce count five, for they reckon by the five fingers and then get the help of the toes on their feet, and so with labour bring out twenty,' The modern Greenland grammar gives the numerals much as Cranz does, but more fully. The word for 5 is *tatdlimat*, which there is some ground for supposing to have once meant 'hand;' 6 is *arfinek-attausek*, 'on the other hand one,' or more shortly *arfinigdlit*, 'those which have on the other hand;' 7 is *arfinek-mardluk*, 'on the other hand two;' 13 is *arkanck-pingasut*, 'on the first foot three;' 18 is *arfersanek-pingasut*, 'on the other foot three;' when they reach 20, they can say *inuk nâvdlugo*, 'a man ended,' or *inûp avatai nâvdlugit*,' the man's outer members ended;' in this way by counting several men they reach higher numbers, thus expressing, for example, 53 as *inûp pinga-jugsâne arkanek-pingasut*, 'on the third man on the first foot three.'[312] If we pass from the rude Greenlanders to the comparatively civilized Aztecs, we shall find on the Northern as on the Southern continent traces of early finger-numeration surviving among higher races. The Mexican names for the first four numerals are as obscure in etymology as our own. But when we come to 5 we find this expressed by *macuilli*; and as *ma* (ma-itl) means 'hand,' and *cuiloa* 'to paint or depict,' it is likely that the word for 5 may have meant something like 'hand-depicting.' In 10, *matlactli*, the word *ma*, 'hand,' appears again, while *tlactli* means half, and is represented in the Mexico picture-writings by the figure of half a man from the waist upward; thus it appears that the Aztec 10 means the 'hand-half' of a man, just as among the Towka Indians of South America 10 is expressed as 'half a man,' a whole man being 20. When the Aztecs reach 20 they call it *cempoalli*, 'one counting,' with evidently the same meaning as elsewhere, one whole man, fingers and toes.

Among races of the lower culture elsewhere, similar facts are to be observed. The Tasmanian language again shows the man stopping short at the reckoning of himself when he has held up one hand and counted its fingers; this appears by Milligan's list before mentioned, which ends with *puggana*, 'man,' standing for 5. Some of the West Australian tribes have done much better than this, using their word for 'hand,' *marh-ra*; *marh-jin-bang-ga*, 'half the hands,' is 5; *marh-jin-bang-ga-gudjir-gyn*, 'half the hands and one,' is 6, and so on; *marh-jin-belli-belli-gudjir-jina-bang-ga*, 'the hand on either side and half the feet,' is 15.[313] As an example from the Melanesian languages the Maré will serve; it reckons 10 as *ome re rue tubenine*, apparently 'the two sides' (i.e. both hands), 20 as *sa re ngome*,'one man,' &c.; thus in John v. 5 'which had an infirmity thirty and eight years,' the numeral 38 is expressed by the phrase, 'one man and both sides five and three.'[314] In the Malayo-Polynesian languages, the typical word for 5 is *lima* or *rima*, 'hand,' and the connexion is not lost by the phonetic variations among different branches of this family of languages, as in Malagasy *dimy*, Marquesan *fima*, Tongan *nima*, but while *lima* and its varieties mean 5 in almost all Malayo-Polynesian dialects, its meaning of 'hand' is confined to a much narrower district, showing that the word became more permanent by passing into the condition of a traditional numeral. In languages of the Malayo-Polynesian family, it is usually found that 6, &c., are carried on with words whose etymology is no longer obvious, but the forms *lima-sa*, *lima-zua* 'hand-one,' 'hand-two,' have been found doing duty for 6 and 7.[315] In West Africa, Kölle's account of the Vei language gives a case in point. These negroes are so dependent on their fingers that some can hardly count without, and their toes are convenient as the calculator squats on the ground. The Vei people and many other African tribes, when counting, first count the fingers of their left hand, beginning, be it remembered, from the little one, then in the same manner those of the right hand, and afterwards the toes. The Vei numeral for 20, *mō bánde*, means obviously 'a person (mo) is finished (bande),' and similarly 40, 60, 80, &c. 'two men, three men, four men, &c., are finished,' It is an interesting point that the negroes who used these phrases had lost their original descriptive sense—the words have become mere numerals to them.[316] Lastly, for bringing before our minds a picture of a man counting upon his fingers, and being struck by the idea that if he describes his gestures in words, these words may become an actual name for the number, perhaps no language in the world surpasses the Zulu. The Zulu counting on his fingers begins in general with the little finger of his left hand. When he comes to 5, this he may call *edesanta* 'finish hand;' then he goes on to the thumb of the right hand, and so the word *tatisitupa* 'taking the thumb' becomes a numeral for 6. Then the verb *komba* 'to point,' indicating the forefinger, or 'pointer,' makes the next numeral, 7. Thus, answering the question 'How much did your master give you?' a Zulu would say 'U *kombile*' 'He pointed with his forefinger,' *i.e.*, 'He gave me seven,' and this curious way of using the numeral verb is shown in such an example as 'amahasi *akombile*' 'the horses have pointed,' *i.e.*, 'there were seven of them.' In like manner, *Kijangalobili* 'keep back two fingers,' *i.e.* 8, and *Kijangalolunje* 'keep back one finger,' *i.e.* 9, lead on to *kumi*, 10; at the completion of each ten the two hands with open fingers are clapped together.[317]

The theory that man's primitive mode of counting was palpable reckoning on his hands, and the proof that many numerals in present use are actually derived from such a state of things, is a great step towards discovering the origin of numerals in general. Can we go farther, and state broadly the mental process by which savage men, having no numerals as yet in their language, came to invent them? What was the origin of numerals not named with reference to hands and feet, and especially of the numerals below five, to which such a derivation is hardly appropriate? The subject is a peculiarly difficult one. Yet as to principle it is not altogether obscure, for some evidence is forthcoming as to the actual formation of new numeral words, these being made by simply pressing into the service names of objects or actions in some way appropriate to the purpose.

People possessing full sets of inherited numerals in their own languages have nevertheless sometimes found it convenient to invent new ones. Thus the scholars of India, ages ago, selected a set of words from a memoria technica in order to record dates and numbers. These words they chose for reasons which are still in great measure evident; thus 'moon' or 'earth' expressed 1, there being but one of each; 2 might be called 'eye,' 'wing,' 'arm,' 'jaw,' as going in pairs; for 3 they said 'Rama,' 'fire,' or 'quality,' there being considered to be three Ramas, three kinds of fire, three qualities (guna); for 4 were used 'veda', 'age,' or 'ocean,' there being four of each recognized; 'season' for 6, because they reckoned six seasons; 'sage' or 'vowel' for 7, from the seven sages and the seven vowels; and so on with higher numbers, 'sun' for 12, because of his twelve annual denominations, or 'zodiac' from its twelve signs, and 'nail' for 20, a word incidentally bringing in a finger notation. As Sanskrit is very rich in synonyms, and as even the numerals themselves might be used, it becomes very easy to draw up phrases or nonsense-verses to record series of numbers by this system of artificial memory. The following is a Hindu astronomical formula, a list of numbers referring to the stars of the lunar constellations. Each word stands as the mnemonic equivalent of the number placed over it in the English translation. The general principle on which the words are chosen to denote the numbers is evident without further explanation:—

'Vahni tri rtvishu gunendu kritâgnibhûta

Bânâsvinetra çara bhûku yugabdhi râmâh

Rudrâbdhirâmagunavedaçatâ dviyugma

Dantâ budhairabhihitâh kramaço bhatârâh.'

3 3 6 5 3 1

'Fire, three, season, arrow, quality, moon,

4   3   5

four-side of die, fire, element,

5 2 2 5 1 1 4 4 3

Arrow, Asvin, eye, arrow, earth, earth, age, ocean, Rama,

11 4 3 3 4 100 2 2

Rudra, ocean, Rama, quality, Veda, hundred, two, couple,

32

Teeth: by the wise have been set forth in order the mighty lords.'[318]

It occurred to Wilhelm von Humboldt, in studying this curious system of numeration, that he had before his eyes the evidence of a process very like that which actually produced the regular numeral words denoting *one*, *two*, *three*, &c., in the various languages of the world. The following passage in which, more than sixty years ago, he set forth this view, seems to me to contain a nearly perfect key to the theory of numeral words. 'If we take into consideration the origin of actual numerals, the process of their formation appears evidently to have been the same as that here described. The latter is nothing else than a wider extension of the former. For when 5 is expressed, as in several languages of the Malay family, by "hand" (*lima*), this is precisely the same thing as when in the description of numbers by words, 2 is denoted by "wing." Indisputably there lie at the root of all numerals such metaphors as these, though they cannot always be now traced. But people seem early to have felt that the multiplicity of such signs for the same number was superfluous, too clumsy, and leading to misunderstandings.' Therefore, he goes on to argue, synonyms of numerals are very rare. And to nations with a deep sense of language, the feeling must soon have been present, though perhaps without rising to distinct consciousness, that recollections of the original etymology and descriptive meaning of numerals had best be allowed to disappear, so as to leave the numerals themselves to become mere conventional terms.

The most instructive evidence I have found bearing on the formation of numerals, other than digit-numerals, among the lower races, appears in the use on both sides of the globe of what may be called numeral-names for children. In Australia a well-marked case occurs. With all the poverty of the aboriginal languages in numerals, 3 being commonly used as meaning 'several or many,' the natives in the Adelaide district have for a particular purpose gone far beyond this narrow limit, and possess what is to all intents a special numeral system, extending perhaps to 9. They give fixed names to their children in order of age, which are set down as follows by Mr. Eyre: 1. Kertameru; 2. Warritya; 3. Kudnutya; 4. Monaitya; 5. Milaitya; 6. Marrutya; 7. Wangutya; 8. Ngarlaitya; 9. Pouarna. These are the male names, from which the female differ in termination. They are given at birth, more distinctive appellations being soon afterwards chosen.[319] A similar habit makes its appearance among the Malays, who in some districts are reported to use a series of seven names in order of age, beginning with 1. *Sulung* ('eldest'); 2. *Awang* ('friend, companion'), and ending with *Kechil* ('little one'), or *Bongsu* ('youngest'). These are for sons; daughters have *Meh* prefixed, and nicknames have to be used for practical distinction.[320] In Madagascar, the Malay connexion manifests itself in the appearance of a similar set of appellations given to children in lieu of proper names, which are, however, often substituted in after years. Males; *Lahimatoa* ('first male'), *Lah-ivo* ('intermediate male'); *Ra-fara-lahy* ('last born male'). Females; *Ramatoa* ('eldest female'), *Ra-ivo* ('intermediate'), *Ra-fara-vavy* ('last born female').[321] The system exists in North America. There have been found in use among the Dacotas the following two series of names for sons and daughters in order of birth. Eldest son, *Chaské*; second, *Haparm*; third, *Ha-pe-dah*; fourth, *Chatun*; fifth *Harka*. Eldest daughter, *Wenonah*; second, *Harpen*; third, *Harpstenah*; fourth, *Waska*; fifth, *We-harka*. These mere numeral appellations they retain through childhood, till their relations or friends find occasion to replace them by bestowing some more distinctive personal name.[322] Africa affords further examples.[323]

As to numerals in the ordinary sense, Polynesia shows remarkable cases of new formation. Besides the well-known system of numeral words prevalent in Polynesia, exceptional terms have from time to time grown up. Thus the habit of altering words which sounded too nearly like a king's name, has led the Tahitians on the accession of new chiefs to make several new words for numbers. Thus, wanting a new term for 2 instead of the ordinary *rua*, they for obvious reasons took up the word *piti*, 'together,' and made it a numeral, while to get a new word for 5 instead of *rima*, 'hand,' which had to be discontinued, they substituted *pae*, 'part, division,' meaning probably division of the two hands. Such words as these, introduced in Polynesia for ceremonial reasons, are expected to be dropped again and the old ones replaced, when the reason for their temporary exclusion ceases, yet the new

2 and 5, *piti* and *pae*, became so positively the proper numerals of the language, that they stand instead of *rua* and *rima* in the Tahitian translation of the Gospel of St. John made at the time. Again, various special habits of counting in the South Sea Islands have had their effect on language. The Marquesans, counting fish or fruit by one in each hand, have come to use a system of counting by pairs instead of by units. They start with *tauna*, 'a pair,' which thus becomes a numeral equivalent to 2; then they count onward by pairs, so that when they talk of *takau* or 10, they really mean 10 pair or 20. For bread-fruit, as they are accustomed to tie them up in knots of four, they begin with the word *pona*, 'knot,' which thus becomes a real numeral for 4, and here again they go on counting by knots, so that when they say *takau* or 10, they mean 10 knots or 40. The philological mystification thus caused in Polynesian vocabularies is extraordinary; in Tahitian, &c., *rau* and *mano*, properly meaning 100 and 1,000, have come to signify 200 and 2,000, while in Hawaii a second doubling in their sense makes them equivalent to 400 and 4,000. Moreover, it seems possible to trace the transfer of suitable names of objects still farther in Polynesia in the Tongan and Maori word *tekau*, 10, which seems to have been a word for 'parcel' or 'bunch,' used in counting yams and fish, as also in *tefuhi*, 100, derived from *fuhi*, 'sheaf or bundle.'[324]

In Africa, also, special numeral formations are to be noticed. In the Yoruba language, 40 is called *ogodzi*, 'a string,' because cowries are strung by forties, and 200 is *igba*, 'a heap,' meaning again a heap of cowries. Among the Dahomans in like manner, 40 cowries make a *kade* or 'string,' 50 strings make one *afo* or 'head;' these words becoming numerals for 40 and 2,000. When the king of Dahome attacked Abeokuta, it is on record that he was repulsed with the heavy loss of 'two heads, twenty strings, and twenty cowries' of men, that is to say, 4,820.[325]

Among cultured nations, whose languages are most tightly bound to the conventional and unintelligible numerals of their ancestors, it is likewise usual to find other terms existing which are practically numerals already, and might drop at once into the recognized places of such, if by any chance a gap were made for them in the traditional series. Had we room, for instance, for a new word instead of *two*, then either *pair* (Latin *par*, 'equal') or *couple* (Latin *copula*, 'bond or tie,') is ready to fill its place. Instead of *twenty*, the good English word *score*, 'notch,' will serve our turn, while, for the same purpose, German can use *stiege*, possibly with the original sense of 'a stall full of cattle, a sty;' Old Norse *drótt*, 'a company,' Danish, *snees*. A list of such words used, but not grammatically classed as numerals in European languages, shows great variety: examples are, Old Norse, *flockr* (flock), 5; *sveit*, 6; *drótt* (party), 20; *thiodh* (people), 30; *fölk* (people), 40; *öld* (people), 80; *her* (army), 100; Sleswig, *schilk*, 12 (as though we were to make a numeral out of 'shilling'); Middle High-German, *rotte*, 4; New High-German, *mandel*, 15; *schock* (sheaf), 60. The Letts give a curious parallel to Polynesian cases just cited. They throw crabs and little fish three at a time in counting them, and therefore the word *mettens*, 'a throw,' has come to mean 3; while flounders being fastened in lots of thirty, the word *kahlis*, 'a cord,' becomes a term to express this number.[326]

In two other ways, the production of numerals from merely descriptive words may be observed both among lower and higher races. The Gallas have no numerical fractional terms, but they make an equivalent set of terms from the division of the cakes of salt which they use as money. Thus *tchabnana*, 'a broken piece' (from *tchaba*, 'to break,' as we say 'a fraction'), receives the meaning of one-half; a term which we may compare with Latin *dimidium*, French *demi*. Ordinal numbers are generally derived from cardinal numbers, as *third, fourth, fifth*, from *three, four, five*. But among the very low ones there is to be seen evidence of independent formation quite unconnected with a conventional system of numerals already existing. Thus the Greenlander did not use his 'one' to make 'first,' but calls it *sujugdlek*, 'foremost,' nor 'two' to make 'second,' which he calls *aipâ*, 'his companion;' it is only at 'third' that he takes to his cardinals, and forms *pingajuat* in connexion with *pingasut*, 3. So, in Indo-European languages, the ordinal *prathamas*, πρῶτος, *primus, first*, has nothing to do with a numerical 'one,' but with the preposition *pra*, 'before,' as meaning simply 'foremost;' and although Greeks and Germans call the next ordinal δεύτερος, *zweite*, from δυό, *zwei*, we call it *second*, Latin *secundus*, 'the following' (*sequi*), which is again a descriptive sense-word.

If we allow ourselves to mix for a moment what is with what might be, we can see how unlimited is the field of possible growth of numerals by mere adoption of the names of familiar things. Following the example of the Sleswigers we might make *shilling* a numeral for 12, and go on to express 4 by *groat*; *week* would provide us with a name for 7, and *clover* for 3. But this simple method of description is not the only available one for the purpose of making numerals. The moment any series of names is arranged in regular order in our minds, it becomes a counting-machine. I have read of a little girl who was set to count cards, and she counted them accordingly, January, February, March, April. She might, of course, have reckoned them as Monday, Tuesday, Wednesday. It is interesting to find a case coming under the same class in the language of grown people. We know that the numerical value of the Hebrew letters is given with reference to their place in the alphabet, which was arranged for reasons that can hardly have had anything to do with arithmetic. The Greek alphabet is modified from a Semitic one, but instead of letting the numeral value of their letters follow throughout their newly-arranged alphabet, they reckon α, β, γ, δ, ε, properly, as 1, 2, 3, 4, 5, then put in σ for 6, and so manage to let ι stand for 10, as ʼ does in Hebrew, where it is really the 10th letter. Now, having this conventional arrangement of letters made, it is evident that a Greek who had to give up the regular 1, 2, 3,—εἷς, δύο, τρεῖς, could supply their places at once by adopting the names of the letters which had been settled to stand for them, thus calling 1 *alpha*, 2 *bēta*, 3 *gamma*, and so onward. The thing has actually happened; a remarkable slang dialect of Albania, which is Greek in structure, though full of borrowed and mystified words and metaphors and epithets understood only by the initiated, has, as its equivalent for 'four' and 'ten,' the words δέλτα and ἰῶτα.[327]

While insisting on the value of such evidence as this in making out the general principles of the formation of numerals, I have not found it profitable to undertake the task of etymologizing the actual numerals of the languages of the world, outside the safe limits of the systems of digit-numerals among the lower races, already discussed. There may be in the languages of the lower races other relics of the etymology of numerals, giving the clue to the ideas according to which they were selected for an arithmetical purpose, but such relics seem scanty and indistinct.[328] There may even exist vestiges of a growth of numerals from descriptive words in our Indo-European languages, in Hebrew and Arabic, in Chinese. Such etymologies have been brought forward,[329] and they are consistent with what is known of the principles on which numerals or quasi-numerals are really formed. But so far as I have been able to examine the evidence, the cases all seem so philologically doubtful, that I cannot bring them forward in aid of the theory before us, and, indeed, think that if they succeed in establishing themselves, it will be by the theory supporting them, rather than by their supporting the theory. This state of things, indeed, fits perfectly with the view here adopted, that when a word has once been taken up to serve as a numeral, and is thenceforth wanted as a mere symbol, it becomes the interest of language to allow it to break down into an apparent nonsense-word, from which all traces of original etymology have disappeared.

Etymological research into the derivation of numeral words thus hardly goes with safety beyond showing in the languages of the lower culture frequent instances of digit-numerals, words taken from direct description of the gestures of counting on fingers and toes. Beyond this, another strong argument is available, which indeed covers almost the whole range of the problem. The numerical systems of the world, by the actual schemes of their arrangement, extend and confirm the opinion that counting on fingers and toes was man's original method of reckoning, taken up and represented in language. To count the fingers on one hand up to 5, and then go on with a second five, is a notation by fives, or as it is called, a quinary notation. To count by the use of both hands to 10, and thence to reckon by tens, is a decimal notation. To go on by hands and feet to 20, and thence to reckon by twenties, is a vigesimal notation. Now though in the larger proportion of known languages, no distinct mention of fingers and toes, hands and feet, is observable in the numerals themselves, yet the very schemes of quinary, decimal, and vigesimal notation remain to vouch for such hand-and-foot-counting having been the original method on which they were founded. There seems no doubt that the number of the fingers led to the adoption of the not especially suitable number 10 as a period in reckoning, so that decimal arithmetic is based on human anatomy. This is so obvious, that it is curious to see Ovid in his well-known lines putting the two facts close together, without seeing that the second was the consequence of the first.

'Annus erat, decimum cum luna receperat orbem.

Hic numerus magno tune in honore fuit.

Seu quia tot digiti, per quos numerare solemus:

Seu quia bis quino femina mense parit:

Seu quod adusque decem numero crescente venitur,

Principium spatiis sumitur inde novis.'[330]

In surveying the languages of the world at large, it is found that among tribes or nations far enough advanced in arithmetic to count up to five in words, there prevails, with scarcely an exception, a method founded on hand-counting, quinary, decimal, vigesimal, or combined of these. For perfect examples of the quinary method, we may take a Polynesian series which runs 1, 2, 3, 4, 5, 5·1, 5·2, &c.; or a Melanesian series which may be rendered as 1, 2, 3, 4, 5, 2nd 1, 2nd 2, &c. Quinary leading into decimal is well shown in the Fellata series 1 ... 5, 5·1 ... 10, 10·1 ...10·5, 10·5·1 ... 20, ... 30, ... 40, &c. Pure decimal may be instanced from Hebrew 1, 2 ... 10, 10·1 ... 20, 20·1 ... &c. Pure vigesimal is not usual, for the obvious reason that a set of independent numerals to 20 would be inconvenient; but it takes on from quinary, as in Aztec, which may be analyzed as 1, 2 ... 5, 5·1 ... 10, 10·1 ... 10·5, 10·5·1 ... 20, 20·1 ... 20·10, 20·10·1 ... 40, &c.; or from decimal, as in Basque, 1 ... 10, 10·1 ... 20, 20·1 ... 20·10, 20·10·1 ... 40 &c.[331] It seems unnecessary to bring forward here the mass of linguistic details required for any general demonstration of these principles of numeration among the races of the world. Prof. Pott, of Halle, has treated the subject on elaborate philological evidence, in a special monograph,[332] which is incidentally the most extensive collection of details relating to numerals, indispensable to students occupied with such enquiries. For the present purpose the following rough generalization may suffice, that the quinary system is frequent among the lower races, among whom also the vigesimal system is considerably developed, but the tendency of the higher nations has been to avoid the one as too scanty, and the other as too cumbrous, and to use the intermediate decimal system. These differences in the usage of various tribes and nations do not interfere with, but rather confirm, the general principle which is their common cause, that man originally learnt to reckon from his fingers and toes, and in various ways stereotyped in language the result of this primitive method.

Some curious points as to the relation of these systems may be noticed in Europe. It was observed of a certain deaf-and-dumb boy, Oliver Caswell, that he learnt to count as high as 50 on his fingers, but always 'fived,' reckoning, for instance, 18 objects as 'both hands, one hand, three fingers.'[333] The suggestion has been made that the Greek use of πεμπάζειν, 'to five,' as an expression for counting, is a trace of rude old quinary numeration (compare Finnish *lokket* 'to count,' from *lokke* 'ten'). Certainly, the Roman numerals I, II, ... V, VI ... X, XI ... XV, XVI, &c., form a remarkably well-defined written quinary system. Remains of vigesimal counting are still more instructive. Counting by twenties is a strongly marked Keltic characteristic. The cumbrous vigesimal notation could hardly be brought more strongly into view in any savage race than in such examples as Gaelic *aon deug is da fhichead* 'one, ten, and two twenties,' i.e., 51; or Welsh *unarbymtheg ar ugain* 'one and fifteen over twenty,' i.e., 36; or Breton *unnek ha triugent* 'eleven and three twenties,' i.e., 71. Now French, being a Romance language, has a regular system of Latin tens up to 100; *cinquante, soixante, septante, huitante, nonante*, which are to be found still in use in districts within the limits of the French language, as in Belgium. Nevertheless, the clumsy system of reckoning by twenties has broken out through the decimal system in France. The *septante* is to a great extent suppressed, *soixante-quatorze*, for instance, standing for 74; *quatre-vingts* has fairly established itself for 80, and its use continues into the nineties, *quatre-vingt-treize* for 93; in numbers above 100 we find *six-vingts, sept-vingts, huit-vingts*, for 120, 140, 160, and a certain hospital has its name of Les Quinze-vingts from its 300 inmates. It is, perhaps, the most reasonable explanation of this curious phenomenon, to suppose the earlier Keltic system of France to have held its ground, modelling the later French into its own ruder shape. In England, the Anglo-Saxon numeration is decimal, *hund-seofontig*, 70; *hund-eahtatig*, 80; *hund-nigontig*, 90; *hund-teontig*, 100; *hund-enlufontig*, 110; *hund-twelftig*, 120. It may be here also by Keltic survival that the vigesimal reckoning by the 'score,' *threescore and ten, fourscore and thirteen*, &c., gained a position in English which it has not yet totally lost.[334]

From some minor details in numeration, ethnological hints may be gained. Among rude tribes with scanty series of numerals, combination to make out new numbers is very soon resorted to. Among Australian tribes addition makes 'two-one,' 'two-two,' express 3 and 4; in Guachi 'two-two' is 4; in San Antonio 'four and two-one' is 7. The plan of making numerals by subtraction is known in North America, and is well shown in the Aino language of Yesso, where the words for 8 and 9 obviously mean 'two from ten,' 'one from ten.' Multiplication appears, as in San Antonio, 'two-and-one-two,' and in a Tupi dialect 'two-three,' to express 6. Division seems not known for such purposes among the lower races, and quite exceptional among the higher. Facts of this class show variety in the inventive devices of mankind, and independence in their formation of language. They are consistent at the same time with the general principles of hand-counting. The traces of what might be called binary, ternary, quaternary, senary reckoning, which turn on 2, 3, 4, 6, are mere varieties, leading up to, or lapsing into, quinary and decimal methods.

The contrast is a striking one between the educated European, with his easy use of his boundless numeral series, and the Tasmanian, who reckons 3, or anything beyond 2, as 'many,' and makes shift by his whole hand to reach the limit of 'man,' that is to say, 5. This contrast is due to arrest of development in the savage, whose mind remains in the childish state which the beginning of one of our nursery number-rhymes illustrates curiously. It runs—

'One's none,

Two's some,

Three's a many,

Four's a penny,

Five's a little hundred.'

To notice this state of things among savages and children raises interesting points as to the early history of grammar. W. von Humboldt suggested the analogy between the savage notion of 3 as 'many' and the grammatical use of 3 to form a kind of superlative, in forms of which 'trismegistus,' 'ter felix,' 'thrice blest,' are familiar instances. The relation of single, dual, and plural is well shown pictorially in the Egyptian hieroglyphics, where the picture of an object, a horse for instance, is marked by a single line | if but one is meant, by two lines | | if two are meant, by three lines | | | if three or an indefinite plural number are meant. The scheme of grammatical number in some of the most ancient and important languages of the world is laid down on the same savage principle. Egyptian, Arabic, Hebrew, Sanskrit, Greek, Gothic, are examples of languages using singular, dual, and plural number; but the tendency of higher intellectual culture has been to discard the plan as inconvenient and unprofitable, and only to distinguish singular and plural. No doubt the dual held its place by inheritance from an early period of culture, and Dr. D. Wilson seems justified in his opinion that it 'preserves to us the memorial of that stage of thought when all beyond two was an idea of indefinite number.'[335]

When two races at different levels of culture come into contact, the ruder people adopt new art and knowledge, but at the same time their own special culture usually comes to a standstill, and even falls off. It is thus with the art of counting. We may be able to prove that the lower race had actually been making great and independent progress in it, but when the higher race comes with a convenient and unlimited means of not only naming all imaginable numbers, but of writing them down and reckoning with them by means of a few simple figures, what likelihood is there that the barbarian's clumsy methods should be farther worked out? As to the ways in which the numerals of the superior race are grafted on the language of the inferior, Captain Grant describes the native slaves of Equatorial Africa occupying their lounging hours in learning the numerals of their Arab masters.[336] Father Dobrizhoffer's account of the arithmetical relations between the native Brazilians and the Jesuits is a good description of the intellectual contact between savages and missionaries. The Guaranis, it appears, counted up to 4 with their native numerals, and when they got beyond, they would say 'innumerable.' 'But as counting is both of manifold use in common life, and in the confessional absolutely indispensable in making a complete confession, the Indians were daily taught at the public catechising in the church to count in Spanish. On Sundays the whole people used to count with a loud voice in Spanish, from 1 to 1,000.' The missionary, it is true, did not find the natives use the numbers thus learnt very accurately—'We were washing at a blackamoor,' he says.[337] If, however, we examine the modern vocabularies of savage or low barbarian tribes, they will be found to afford interesting evidence how really effective the influence of higher on lower civilization has been in this matter. So far as the ruder system is complete and moderately convenient, it may stand, but where it ceases or grows cumbrous, and sometimes at a lower limit than this, we can see the cleverer foreigner taking it into his own hands, supplementing or supplanting the scanty numerals of the lower race by his own. The higher race, though advanced enough to act thus on the lower, need not be itself at an extremely high level. Markham observes that the Jivaras of the Marañon, with native numerals up to 5, adopt for higher numbers those of the Quichua, the language of the Peruvian Incas.[338] The cases of the indigenes of India are instructive. The Khonds reckon 1 and 2 in native words, and then take to borrowed Hindi numerals. The Oraon tribes, while belonging to a race of the Dravidian stock, and having had a series of native numerals accordingly, appear to have given up their use beyond 4, or sometimes even 2, and adopted Hindi numerals in their place.[339] The South American Conibos were observed to count 1 and 2 with their own words, and then to borrow Spanish numerals, much as a Brazilian dialect of the Tupi family is noticed in the last century as having lost the native 5, and settled down into using the old native numerals up to 3, and then continuing in Portuguese.[340] In Melanesia, the Annatom language can only count in its own numerals to 5, and then borrows English *siks, seven, eet, nain*, &c. In some Polynesian islands, though the native numerals are extensive enough, the confusion arising from reckoning by pairs and fours as well as units, has induced the natives to escape from perplexity by adopting *huneri* and *tausani*.[341] And though the Esquimaux counting by hands, feet, and whole men, is capable of expressing high numbers, it becomes practically clumsy even when it gets among the scores, and the Greenlander has done well to adopt *untrîte* and *tusinte* from his Danish teachers. Similarity of numerals in two languages is a point to which philologists attach great and deserved importance in the question whether they are to be considered as sprung from a common stock. But it is clear that so far as one race may have borrowed numerals from another, this evidence breaks down. The fact that this borrowing extends as low as 3, and may even go still lower for all we know, is a reason for using the argument from connected numerals cautiously, as tending rather to prove intercourse than kinship.

At the other end of the scale of civilization, the adoption of numerals from nation to nation still presents interesting philological points. Our own language gives curious instances, as *second* and *million*. The manner in which English, in common with German, Dutch, Danish, and even Russian, has adopted Mediæval Latin *dozena* (from *duodecim*) shows how convenient an arrangement it was found to buy and sell by the *dozen*, and how necessary it was to have a special word for it. But the borrowing process has gone farther than this. If it were asked how many sets of numerals are now in use among English-speaking people in England, the probable reply would be one set, the regular *one, two, three*, &c. There exist, however, two borrowed sets as well. One is the well-known dicing-set, *ace, deuce, tray, cater, cinque, size*; thus *size-ace* is '6 and one,' *cinques* or *sinks*, 'double five.' These came to us from France, and correspond with the common French numerals, except *ace*, which is Latin *as*, a word of great philological interest, meaning 'one.' The other borrowed set is to be found in the Slang Dictionary. It appears that the English street-folk have adopted as a means of secret communication a set of Italian numerals from the organ-grinders and image-sellers, or by other ways through which Italian or Lingua Franca is brought into the low neighbourhoods of London. In so doing, they have performed a philological operation not only curious, but instructive. By copying such expressions as, Italian *due soldi, tre soldi*, as equivalent to 'twopence,' 'threepence,' the word *saltee* became a recognized slang term for 'penny,' and pence are reckoned as follows:—

Oney saltee ... 1*d.* uno soldo.

Dooe saltee ... 2*d.* due soldi.

Tray saltee ... 3*d.* tre soldi.

Quarterer saltee ... 4*d.* quattro soldi.

Chinker saltee ... 5*d.* cinque soldi.

Say saltee ... 6*d.* sei soldi.

Say oney saltee or setter saltee ... 7*d.* sette soldi.

Say dooe saltee or otter saltee ... 8*d.* otto soldi.

Say tray saltee or nobba saltee ... 9*d.* nove soldi.

Say quarterer saltee or dacha saltee ... 10*d.* dieci soldi.

Say chinker saltee or dacha oney saltee ... 11*d.* undici soldi.

Oney beong ... 1*s.*

A beong say saltee ... 1*s.* 6*d.*

Dooe beong say saltee or madza caroon ... 2*s.* 6*d.* (half crown, mezza corona.)[342]

One of these series simply adopts Italian numerals decimally. But the other, when it has reached 6, having had enough of novelty, makes 7 by 'six-one,' and so continues. It is for no abstract reason that 6 is thus made the turning-point, but simply because the costermonger is adding pence up to the silver sixpence, and then adding pence again up to the shilling. Thus our duodecimal coinage has led to the practice of counting by sixes, and produced a philological curiosity, a real senary notation.

On evidence such as has been brought forward in this essay, the apparent relations of savage to civilized culture, as regards the Art of Counting, may now be briefly stated in conclusion. The principal methods to which the development of the higher arithmetic are due, lie outside the problem. They are mostly ingenious plans of expressing numerical relation by written symbols. Among them are the Semitic scheme, and the Greek derived from it, of using the alphabet as a series of numerical symbols, a plan not quite discarded by ourselves, at least for ordinals, as in schedules A, B, &c.; the use of initials of numeral words as figures for the numbers themselves, as in Greek Π and Δ for 5 and 10, Roman C and M for 100 and 1,000; the device of expressing fractions, shown in a rudimentary stage in Greek γ', δ', for

1/3, 1/4, γδ for 3/4; the introduction of the cipher or zero, by means of which the Arabic or Indian numerals have their value according to their position in a decimal order corresponding to the succession of the rows of the abacus; and lastly, the modern notation of decimal fractions by carrying down below the unit the proportional order which for ages had been in use above it. The ancient Egyptian and the still-used Roman and Chinese numeration are indeed founded on savage picture-writing,[343] while the abacus and the swan-pan, the one still a valuable school-instrument, and the other in full practical use, have their germ in the savage counting by groups of objects, as when South Sea Islanders count with coco-nut stalks, putting a little one aside every time they come to 10, and a large one when they come to 100, or when African negroes reckon with pebbles or nuts, and every time they come to 5 put them aside in a little heap.[344]

We are here especially concerned with gesture-counting on the fingers, as an absolutely savage art still in use among children and peasants, and with the system of numeral words, as known to all mankind, appearing scantily among the lowest tribes, and reaching within savage limits to developments which the highest civilization has only improved in detail. These two methods of computation by gesture and word tell the story of primitive arithmetic in a way that can be hardly perverted or misunderstood. We see the savage who can only count to 2 or 3 or 4 in words, but can go farther in dumb show. He has words for hands and fingers, feet and toes, and the idea strikes him that the words which describe the gesture will serve also to express its meaning, and they become his numerals accordingly. This did not happen only once, it happened among different races in distant regions, for such terms as 'hand' for 5, 'hand-one' for 6, 'hands' for 10, 'two on the foot' for 12, 'hands and feet' or 'man' for 20, 'two men' for 40, &c., show such uniformity as is due to common principle, but also such variety as is due to independent working-out. These are 'pointer-facts' which have their place and explanation in a development-theory of culture, while a degeneration-theory totally fails to take them in. They are distinct records of development, and of independent development, among savage tribes to whom some writers on civilization have rashly denied the very faculty of self-improvement. The original meaning of a great part of the stock of numerals of the lower races, especially of those from 1 to 4, not suited to be named as hand-numerals, is obscure. They may have been named from comparison with objects, in a way which is shown actually to happen in such forms as 'together' for 2, 'throw' for 3, 'knot' for 4; but any concrete meaning we may guess them to have once had seems now by modification and mutilation to have passed out of knowledge.

Remembering how ordinary words change and lose their traces of original meaning in the course of ages, and that in numerals such breaking down of meaning is actually desirable, to make them fit for pure arithmetical symbols, we cannot wonder that so large a proportion of existing numerals should have no discernible etymology. This is especially true of the 1, 2, 3, 4, among low and high races alike, the earliest to be made, and therefore the earliest to lose their primary significance. Beyond these low numbers the languages of the higher and lower races show a remarkable difference. The hand-and-foot numerals, so prevalent and unmistakable in savage tongues like Esquimaux and Zulu, are scarcely if at all traceable in the great languages of civilization, such as Sanskrit and Greek, Hebrew and Arabic. This state of things is quite conformable to the development-theory of language. We may argue that it was in comparatively recent times that savages arrived at the invention of hand-numerals, and that therefore the etymology of such numerals remains obvious. But it by no means follows from the non-appearance of such primitive forms in cultured Asia and Europe, that they did not exist there in remote ages; they may since have been rolled and battered like pebbles by the stream of time, till their original shapes can no longer be made out. Lastly, among savage and civilized races alike, the general framework of numeration stands throughout the world as an abiding monument of primæval culture. This framework, the all but universal scheme of reckoning by fives, tens, and twenties, shows that the childish and savage practice of counting on fingers and toes lies at the foundation of our arithmetical science. Ten seems the most convenient arithmetical basis offered by systems founded on hand-counting, but twelve would have been better, and duodecimal arithmetic is in fact a protest against the less convenient decimal arithmetic in ordinary use. The case is the not uncommon one of high civilization bearing evident traces of the rudeness of its origin in ancient barbaric life.

CHAPTER VIII.
MYTHOLOGY.

Mythic Fancy based, like other thought, on Experience—Mythology affords evidence for studying laws of Imagination—Change in public opinion as to credibility of Myths—Myths rationalized into Allegory and History—Ethnological import and treatment of Myth—Myth to be studied in actual existence and growth among modern savages and barbarians—Original sources of Myth—Early doctrine of general animation of Nature—Personification of Sun, Moon, and Stars; Water-spout, Sand pillar, Rainbow, Waterfall, Pestilence—Analogy worked into Myth and Metaphor—Myths of Rain, Thunder, &c.—Effect of Language in formation of Myth—Material Personification primary, Verbal Personification secondary—Grammatical Gender, male and female, animate and inanimate, in relation to Myth—Proper Names of objects in relation to Myth—Mental State proper to promote mythic imagination—Doctrine of Werewolves—Phantasy and Fancy.

Among those opinions which are produced by a little knowledge, to be dispelled by a little more, is the belief in an almost boundless creative power of the human imagination. The superficial student, mazed in a crowd of seemingly wild and lawless fancies, which he thinks to have no reason in nature nor pattern in this material world, at first concludes them to be new births from the imagination of the poet, the tale-teller, and the seer. But little by little, in what seemed the most spontaneous fiction, a more comprehensive study of the sources of poetry and romance begins to disclose a cause for each fancy, an education that has led up to each train of thought, a store of inherited materials from out of which each province of the poet's land has been shaped, and built over, and peopled. Backward from our own times, the course of mental history may be traced through the changes wrought by modern schools of thought and fancy, upon an intellectual inheritance handed down to them from earlier generations. And through remoter periods, as we recede more nearly towards primitive conditions of our race, the threads which connect new thought with old do not always vanish from our sight. It is in large measure possible to follow them as clues leading back to that actual experience of nature and life, which is the ultimate source of human fancy. What Matthew Arnold has written of Man's thoughts as he floats along the River of Time, is most true of his mythic imagination:—

'As is the world on the banks
So is the mind of the man.

Only the tract where he sails
He wots of: only the thoughts,
Raised by the objects he passes, are his.'

Impressions thus received the mind will modify and work upon, transmitting the products to other minds in shapes that often seem new, strange, and arbitrary, but which yet result from processes familiar to our experience, and to be found at work in our own individual consciousness. The office of our thought is to develop, to combine, and to derive, rather than to create; and the consistent laws it works by are to be discerned even in the unsubstantial structures of the imagination. Here, as elsewhere in the universe, there is to be recognized a sequence from cause to effect, a sequence intelligible, definite, and where knowledge reaches the needful exactness, even calculable.

There is perhaps no better subject-matter through which to study the processes of the imagination, than the well-marked incidents of mythical story, ranging as they do through every known period of civilization, and through all the physically varied tribes of mankind. Here the divine Maui of New Zealand, fishing up the island with his enchanted hook from the bottom of the sea, will take his place in company with the Indian Vishnu, diving to the depth of the ocean in his avatar of the Boar, to bring up the submerged earth on his monstrous tusks; and here Baiame the creator, whose voice the rude Australians hear in the rolling thunder, will sit throned by the side of Olympian Zeus himself. Starting with the bold rough nature-myths into which the savage moulds the lessons he has learnt from his childlike contemplation of the universe, the ethnographer can follow these rude fictions up into times when they were shaped and incorporated into complex mythologic systems, gracefully artistic in Greece, stiff and monstrous in Mexico, swelled into bombastic exaggeration in Buddhist Asia. He can watch how the mythology of classic Europe, once so true to nature and so quick with her ceaseless life, fell among the commentators to be plastered with allegory or euhemerized into dull sham history. At last, in the midst of modern civilization, he finds the classic volumes studied rather for their manner than for their matter, or mainly valued for their antiquarian evidence of the thoughts of former times; while relics of structures reared with skill and strength by the myth-makers of the past must now be sought in scraps of nursery folk-lore, in vulgar superstitions and old dying legends, in thoughts and allusions carried on from ancient days by the perennial stream of poetry and romance, in fragments of old opinion which still hold an inherited rank gained in past ages of intellectual history. But this turning of mythology to account as a means of tracing the history of laws of mind, is a branch of science scarcely discovered till the nineteenth century. Before entering here on some researches belonging to it, there will be advantage in glancing at the views of older mythologists, to show through what changes their study has at length reached a condition in which it has a scientific value.

It is a momentous phase of the education of mankind, when the regularity of nature has so imprinted itself upon men's minds that they begin to wonder how it is that the ancient legends which they were brought up to hear with such reverent delight, should describe a world so strangely different from their own. Why, they ask, are the gods and giants and monsters no longer seen to lead their prodigious lives on earth—is it perchance that the course of things is changed since the old days? Thus it seemed to Pausanias the historian, that the wide-grown wickedness of the world had brought it to pass that times were no longer as of old, when Lykaon was turned into a wolf, and Niobe into a stone, when men still sat as guests at table with the gods, or were raised like Herakles to become gods themselves. Up to modern times, the hypothesis of a changed world has more or less availed to remove the difficulty of belief in ancient wonder-tales. Yet though always holding firmly a partial ground, its application was soon limited for these obvious reasons, that it justified falsehood and truth alike with even-handed favour, and utterly broke down that barrier of probability which in some measure has always separated fact from fancy. The Greek mind found other outlets to the problem. In the words of Mr. Grote, the ancient legends were cast back into an undefined past, to take rank among the hallowed traditions of divine or heroic antiquity, gratifying to extol by rhetoric, but repulsive to scrutinize in argument. Or they were transformed into shapes more familiar to experience, as when Plutarch, telling the tale of Theseus, begs for indulgent hearers to accept mildly the archaic story, and assures them that he has set himself to purify it by reason, that it may receive the aspect of history.[345] This process of giving fable the aspect of history, this profitless art of transforming untrue impossibilities into untrue possibilities, has been carried on by the ancients, and by the moderns after them, especially according to the two following methods.

Men have for ages been more or less conscious of that great mental district lying between disbelief and belief, where room is found for all mythic interpretation, good or bad. It being admitted that some legend is not the real narrative which it purports to be, they do not thereupon wipe it out from book and memory as simply signifying nothing, but they ask what original sense may be in it, out of what older story it may be a second growth, or what actual event or current notion may have suggested its development into the state in which they find it? Such questions, however, prove almost as easy to answer plausibly as to set; and then, in the endeavour to obtain security that these off-hand answers are the true ones, it becomes evident that the problem admits of an indefinite number of apparent solutions, not only different but incompatible. This radical uncertainty in the speculative interpretation of myths is forcibly stated by Lord Bacon, in the preface to his 'Wisdom of the Ancients.' 'Neither am I ignorant,' he says, 'how fickle and inconsistent a thing fiction is, as being subject to be drawn and wrested any way, and how great the commodity of wit and discourse is, that is able to apply things well, yet so as never meant by the first authors.' The need of such a caution may be judged of from the very treatise to which Bacon prefaced it, for there he is to be seen plunging headlong into the very pitfall of which he had so discreetly warned his disciples. He undertakes, after the manner of not a few philosophers before and after him, to interpret the classic myths of Greece as moral allegories. Thus the story of Memnon depicts the destinies of rash young men of promise; while Perseus symbolizes war, and when of the three Gorgons he attacks only the mortal one, this means that only practicable wars are to be attempted. It would not be easy to bring out into a stronger light the difference between a fanciful application of a myth, and its analysis into its real elements. For here, where the interpreter believed himself to be reversing the process of myth-making, he was in fact only carrying it a stage further in the old direction, and out of the suggestion of one train of thought evolving another connected with it by some more or less remote analogy. Any of us may practise this simple art, each according to his own fancy. If, for instance, political economy happens for the moment to lie uppermost in our mind, we may with due gravity expound the story of Perseus as an allegory of trade: Perseus himself is Labour, and he finds Andromeda, who is Profit, chained and ready to be devoured by the monster Capital; he rescues her and carries her off in triumph. To know anything of poetry or of mysticism is to know this reproductive growth of fancy as an admitted and admired intellectual process. But when it comes to sober investigation of the processes of mythology, the attempt to penetrate to the foundation of an old fancy will scarcely be helped by burying it yet deeper underneath a new one.

Nevertheless, allegory has had a share in the development of myths which no interpreter must overlook. The fault of the rationalizer lay in taking allegory beyond its proper action, and applying it as a universal solvent to reduce dark stories to transparent sense. The same is true of the other great rationalizing process, founded also, to some extent, on fact. Nothing is more certain than that real personages often have mythic incidents tacked on to their history, and that they even figure in tales of which the very substance is mythic. No one disbelieves in the existence of Solomon because of his legendary adventure in the Valley of Apes, nor of Attila because he figures in the Nibelungen Lied. Sir Francis Drake is made not less but more real to us by the cottage tales which tell how he still leads the Wild Hunt over Dartmoor, and still rises to his revels when they beat at Buckland Abbey the drum that he carried round the world. The mixture of fact and fable in traditions of great men shows that legends containing monstrous fancy may yet have a basis in historic fact. But, on the strength of this, the mythologists arranged systematic methods of reducing legend to history, and thereby contrived at once to stultify the mythology they professed to explain, and to ruin the history they professed to develop. So far as the plan consisted in mere suppression of the marvellous, a notion of its trustworthiness may be obtained, as Sir G. W. Cox well puts it, in rationalizing Jack the Giant-Killer by leaving out the giants. So far as it treated legendary wonders as being matter-of-fact disguised in metaphor, the mere naked statement of the results of the method is to our minds its most cruel criticism. Thus already in classic times men were declaring that Atlas was a great astronomer who taught the use of the sphere, and was therefore represented with the world resting on his shoulders. To such a pass had come the decay of myth into commonplace, that the great Heaven-god of the Aryan race, the living personal Heaven himself, Zeus the Almighty, was held to have been a king of Krete, and the Kretans could show to wondering strangers his sepulchre, with the very name of the great departed inscribed upon it. The modern 'euhemerists' (so called from Euhemeros of Messenia, a great professor of the art in the time of Alexander) in part adopted the old interpretations, and sometimes fairly left their Greek and Roman teachers behind in the race after prosaic possibility. They inform us that Jove smiting the giants with his thunderbolts was a king repressing a sedition; Danae's golden shower was the money with which her guards were bribed; Prometheus made clay images, whence it was hyperbolically said that he created man and woman out of clay; and when Daidalos was related to have made figures which walked, this meant that he improved the shapeless old statues, and separated their legs. Old men still remember as the guides of educated opinion in their youth the learned books in which these fancies are solemnly put forth; some of our school manuals still go on quoting them with respect, and a few straggling writers carry on a remnant of the once famous system of which the Abbé Banier was so distinguished an exponent.[346] But it has of late fallen on evil days, and mythologists in authority have treated it in so high-handed a fashion as to bring it into general contempt. So far has the feeling against the abuse of such argument gone, that it is now really desirable to warn students that it has a reasonable as well as an unreasonable side, and to remind them that some wild legends undoubtedly do, and therefore that many others may, contain a kernel of historic truth.

Learned and ingenious as the old systems of rationalizing myth have been, there is no doubt that they are in great measure destined to be thrown aside. It is not that their interpretations are proved impossible, but that mere possibility in mythological speculation is now seen to be such a worthless commodity, that every investigator devoutly wishes there were not such plenty of it. In assigning origins to myths, as in every other scientific enquiry, the fact is that increased information, and the use of more stringent canons of evidence, have raised far above the old level the standard of probability required to produce conviction. There are many who describe our own time as an unbelieving time, but it is by no means sure that posterity will accept the verdict. No doubt it is a sceptical and a critical time, but then scepticism and criticism are the very conditions for the attainment of reasonable belief. Thus, where the positive credence of ancient history has been affected, it is not that the power of receiving evidence has diminished, but that the consciousness of ignorance has grown. We are being trained to the facts of physical science, which we can test and test again, and we feel it a fall from this high level of proof when we turn our minds to the old records which elude such testing, and are even admitted on all hands to contain statements not to be relied on. Historical criticism becomes hard and exacting, even where the chronicle records events not improbable in themselves; and the moment that the story falls out of our scheme of the world's habitual course, the ever repeated question comes out to meet it—Which is the more likely, that so unusual an event should have really happened, or that the record should be misunderstood or false? Thus we gladly seek for sources of history in antiquarian relics, in undesigned and collateral proofs, in documents not written to be chronicles. But can any reader of geology say we are too incredulous to believe wonders, if the evidence carry any fair warrant of their truth? Was there ever a time when lost history was being reconstructed, and existing history rectified, more zealously than they are now by a whole army of travellers, excavators, searchers of old charters, and explorers of forgotten dialects? The very myths that were discarded as lying fables, prove to be sources of history in ways that their makers and transmitters little dreamed of. Their meaning has been misunderstood, but they have a meaning. Every tale that was ever told has a meaning for the times it belongs to; even a lie, as the Spanish proverb says, is a lady of birth ('la mentira es hija de algo'). Thus, as evidence of the development of thought, as records of long past belief and usage, even in some measure as materials for the history of the nations owning them, the old myths have fairly taken their place among historic facts; and with such the modern historian, so able and willing to pull down, is also able and willing to rebuild.

Of all things, what mythologic work needs is breadth of knowledge and of handling. Interpretations made to suit a narrow view reveal their weakness when exposed to a wide one. See Herodotus rationalizing the story of the infant Cyrus, exposed and suckled by a bitch; he simply relates that the child was brought up by a herdsman's wife named Spakô (in Greek Kynô), whence arose the fable that a real bitch rescued and fed him. So far so good—for a single case. But does the story of Romulus and Remus likewise record a real event, mystified in the self-same manner by a pun on a nurse's name, which happened to be a she-beast's? Did the Roman twins also really happen to be exposed, and brought up by a foster-mother who happened to be called Lupa? Positively, the 'Lempriere's Dictionary' of our youth (I quote the 16th edition of 1831) gravely gives this as the origin of the famous legend. Yet, if we look properly into the matter, we find that these two stories are but specimens of a widespread mythic group, itself only a section of that far larger body of traditions in which exposed infants are saved to become national heroes. For other examples, Slavonic folk-lore tells of the she-wolf and she-bear that suckled those superhuman twins, Waligora the mountain-roller and Wyrwidab the oak-uprooter; Germany has its legend of Dieterich, called Wolfdieterich from his foster-mother the she-wolf; in India, the episode recurs in the tales of Satavahana and the lioness, and Sing-Baba and the tigress; legend tells of Burta-Chino, the boy who was cast into a lake, and preserved by a she-wolf to become founder of the Turkish kingdom; and even the savage Yuracarés of Brazil tell of their divine hero Tiri, who was suckled by a jaguar.[347]

Scientific myth-interpretation, on the contrary, is actually strengthened by such comparison of similar cases. Where the effect of new knowledge has been to construct rather than to destroy, it is found that there are groups of myth-interpretations for which wider and deeper evidence makes a wider and deeper foundation. The principles which underlie a solid system of interpretation are really few and simple. The treatment of similar myths from different regions, by arranging them in large compared groups, makes it possible to trace in mythology the operation of imaginative processes recurring with the evident regularity of mental law; and thus stories of which a single instance would have been a mere isolated curiosity, take their place among well-marked and consistent structures of the human mind. Evidence like this will again and again drive us to admit that even as 'truth is stranger than fiction,' so myth may be more uniform than history.

There lies within our reach, moreover, the evidence of races both ancient and modern, who so faithfully represent the state of thought to which myth-development belongs, as still to keep up both the consciousness of meaning in their old myths, and the unstrained unaffected habit of creating new ones. Savages have been for untold ages, and still are, living in the myth-making stage of the human mind. It was through sheer ignorance and neglect of this direct knowledge how and by what manner of men myths are really made, that their simple philosophy has come to be buried under masses of commentators' rubbish. Though never wholly lost, the secret of mythic interpretation was all but forgotten. Its recovery has been mainly due to modern students who have with vast labour and skill searched the ancient language, poetry, and folk-lore of our own race, from the cottage tales collected by the brothers Grimm to the Rig-Veda edited by Max Müller. Aryan language and literature now open out with wonderful range and clearness a view of the early stages of mythology, displaying those primitive germs of the poetry of nature, which later ages swelled and distorted till childlike fancy sank into superstitious mystery. It is not proposed here to enquire specially into this Aryan mythology, of which so many eminent students have treated, but to compare some of the most important developments of mythology among the various races of mankind, especially in order to determine the general relation of the myths of savage tribes to the myths of civilized nations. The argument does not aim at a general discussion of the mythology of the world, numbers of important topics being left untouched which would have to be considered in a general treatise. The topics chosen are mostly such as are fitted, by the strictness of evidence and argument applying to them, to make a sound basis for the treatment of myth as bearing on the general ethnological problem of the development of civilization. The general thesis maintained is that Myth arose in the savage condition prevalent in remote ages among the whole human race, that it remains comparatively unchanged among the modern rude tribes who have departed least from these primitive conditions, while even higher and later grades of civilization, partly by retaining its actual principles, and partly by carrying on its inherited results in the form of ancestral tradition, have continued it not merely in toleration but in honour.

To the human intellect in its early childlike state may be assigned the origin and first development of myth. It is true that learned critics, taking up the study of mythology at the wrong end, have almost habitually failed to appreciate its childlike ideas, conventionalized in poetry or disguised as chronicle. Yet the more we compare the mythic fancies of different nations, in order to discern the common thoughts which underlie their resemblances, the more ready we shall be to admit that in our childhood we dwelt at the very gates of the realm of myth. In mythology, the child is, in a deeper sense than we are apt to use the phrase in, father of the man. Thus, when in surveying the quaint fancies and wild legends of the lower tribes, we find the mythology of the world at once in its most distinct and most rudimentary form, we may here again claim the savage as a representative of the childhood of the human race. Here Ethnology and Comparative Mythology go hand in hand, and the development of Myth forms a consistent part of the development of Culture. If savage races, as the nearest modern representatives of primæval culture, show in the most distinct and unchanged state the rudimentary mythic conceptions thence to be traced onward in the course of civilization, then it is reasonable for students to begin, so far as may be, at the beginning. Savage mythology may be taken as a basis, and then the myths of more civilized races may be displayed as compositions sprung from like origin, though more advanced in art. This mode of treatment proves satisfactory through almost all the branches of the enquiry, and eminently so in investigating those most beautiful of poetic fictions, to which may be given the title of Nature-Myths.

First and foremost among the causes which transfigure into myths the facts of daily experience, is the belief in the animation of all nature, rising at its highest pitch to personification. This, no occasional or hypothetical action of the mind, is inextricably bound in with that primitive mental state where man recognizes in every detail of his world the operation of personal life and will. This doctrine of Animism will be considered elsewhere as affecting philosophy and religion, but here we have only to do with its bearing on mythology. To the lower tribes of man, sun and stars, trees and rivers, winds and clouds, become personal animate creatures, leading lives conformed to human or animal analogies, and performing their special functions in the universe with the aid of limbs like beasts or of artificial instruments like men; or what men's eyes behold is but the instrument to be used or the material to be shaped, while behind it there stands some prodigious but yet half-human creature, who grasps it with his hands or blows it with his breath. The basis on which such ideas as these are built is not to be narrowed down to poetic fancy and transformed metaphor. They rest upon a broad philosophy of nature, early and crude indeed, but thoughtful, consistent, and quite really and seriously meant.

Let us put this doctrine of universal vitality to a test of direct evidence, lest readers new to the subject should suppose it a modern philosophical fiction, or think that if the lower races really express such a notion, they may do so only as a poetical way of talking. Even in civilized countries, it makes its appearance as the child's early theory of the outer world, nor can we fail to see how this comes to pass. The first beings that children learn to understand something of are human beings, and especially their own selves; and the first explanation of all events will be the human explanation, as though chairs and sticks and wooden horses were actuated by the same sort of personal will as nurses and children and kittens. Thus infants take their first step in mythology by contriving, like Cosette with her doll, 'se figurer que quelque chose est quelqu'un;' and the way in which this childlike theory has to be unlearnt in the course of education shows how primitive it is. Even among full-grown civilized Europeans, as Mr. Grote appositely remarks, 'The force of momentary passion will often suffice to supersede the acquired habit, and even an intelligent man may be impelled in a moment of agonizing pain to kick or beat the lifeless object from which he has suffered.' In such matters the savage mind well represents the childish stage. The wild native of Brazil would bite the stone he stumbled over, or the arrow that had wounded him. Such a mental condition may be traced along the course of history, not merely in impulsive habit, but in formally enacted law. The rude Kukis of Southern Asia were very scrupulous in carrying out their simple law of vengeance, life for life; if a tiger killed a Kuki, his family were in disgrace till they had retaliated by killing and eating this tiger, or another; but further, if a man was killed by a fall from a tree, his relatives would take their revenge by cutting the tree down, and scattering it in chips.[348] A modern king of Cochin-China, when one of his ships sailed badly, used to put it in the pillory as he would any other criminal.[349] In classical times, the stories of Xerxes flogging the Hellespont and Cyrus draining the Gyndes occur as cases in point, but one of the regular Athenian legal proceedings is a yet more striking relic. A court of justice was held at the Prytaneum, to try any inanimate object, such as an axe or a piece of wood or stone, which had caused the death of anyone without proved human agency, and this wood or stone, if condemned, was in solemn form cast beyond the border.[350] The spirit of this remarkable procedure reappears in the old English law (repealed within the last reign), whereby not only a beast that kills a man, but a cart-wheel that runs over him, or a tree that falls on him and kills him, is deodand, or given to God, i.e. forfeited and sold for the poor: as Bracton says, 'Omnia quae movent ad mortem sunt Deodanda.' Dr. Reid comments on this law, declaring that its intention was not to punish the ox or the cart as criminal, but 'to inspire the people with a sacred regard to the life of man.'[351] But his argument rather serves to show the worthlessness of off-hand speculations on the origin of law, like his own in this matter, unaided by the indispensable evidence of history and ethnography. An example from modern folklore shows still at its utmost stretch this primitive fancy that inert things are alive and conscious. The pathetic custom of 'telling the bees' when the master or mistress of a house dies, is not unknown in our own country. But in Germany the idea is more fully worked out; and not only is the sad message given to every bee-hive in the garden and every beast in the stall, but every sack of corn must be touched and everything in the house shaken, that they may know the master is gone.[352]

It will be seen presently how Animism, the doctrine of spiritual beings, at once develops with and reacts upon mythic personification, in that early state of the human mind which gives consistent individual life to phenomena that our utmost stretch of fancy only avails to personify in conscious metaphor. An idea of pervading life and will in nature far outside modern limits, a belief in personal souls animating even what we call inanimate bodies, a theory of transmigration of souls as well in life as after death, a sense of crowds of spiritual beings sometimes flitting through the air, but sometimes also inhabiting trees and rocks and waterfalls, and so lending their own personality to such material objects—all these thoughts work in mythology with such manifold coincidence, as to make it hard indeed to unravel their separate action.[353]

Such animistic origin of nature-myths shows out very clearly in the great cosmic group of Sun, Moon, and Stars. In early philosophy throughout the world, the Sun and Moon are alive and as it were human in their nature. Usually contrasted as male and female, they nevertheless differ in the sex assigned to each, as well as in their relations to one another. Among the Mbocobis of South America, the Moon is a man and the Sun his wife, and the story is told how she once fell down and an Indian put her up again, but she fell a second time and set the forest blazing in a deluge of fire.[354] To display the opposite of this idea, and at the same time to illustrate the vivid fancy with which savages can personify the heavenly bodies, we may read the following discussion concerning eclipses, between certain Algonquin Indians and one of the early Jesuit missionaries to Canada in the 17th century, Father Le June:—'Je leur ay demandé d'où venoit l'Eclipse de Lune et de Soleil; ils m'ont respondu que la Lune s'éclipsoit ou paroissoit noire, à cause qu'elle tenoit son fils entre ses bras, qui empeschoit que l'on ne vist sa clarté. Si la Lune a un fils, elle est mariée, ou l'a été, leur dis-je. Oüy dea, me dirent-ils, le Soleil est son mary, qui marche tout le jour, et elle toute la nuict; et s'il s'éclipse, ou s'il s'obscurcit, c'est qu'il prend aussi par fois le fils qu'il a eu de la Lune entre ses bras. Oüy, mais ny la Lune ny le Soleil n'ont point de bras, leur disois-je. Tu n'as point d'esprit; ils tiennent tousiours leurs arcs bandés deuant eux, voilà pourquoy leurs bras ne paroissent point. Et sur qui veulent-ils tirer? Hé qu'en scauons nous?'[355] A mythologically important legend of the same race, the Ottawa story of Iosco, describes Sun and Moon as brother and sister. Two Indians, it is said, sprang through a chasm in the sky, and found themselves in a pleasant moonlit land; there they saw the Moon approaching as from behind a hill, they knew her at the first sight, she was an aged woman with white face and pleasing air; speaking kindly to them, she led them to her brother the Sun, and he carried them with him in his course and sent them home with promises of happy life.[356] As the Egyptian Osiris and Isis were at once brother and sister, and husband and wife, so it was with the Peruvian Sun and Moon, Ynti and Quilla, father and mother of the Incas, whose sister-marriage thus had in their religion at once a meaning and a justification.[357] The myths of other countries, where such relations of sex may not appear, carry on the same lifelike personification in telling the ever-reiterated, never tedious tale of day and night. Thus to the Mexicans it was an ancient hero who, when the old sun was burnt out, and had left the world in darkness, sprang into a huge fire, descended into the shades below, and arose deified and glorious in the east as Tonatiuh the Sun. After him there leapt in another hero, but now the fire had grown dim, and he arose only in milder radiance as Metztli the Moon.[358]

If it be objected that all this may be mere expressive form of speech, like a modern poet's fanciful metaphor, there is evidence which no such objection can stand against. When the Aleutians thought that if anyone gave offence to the moon, he would fling down stones on the offender and kill him,[359] or when the moon came down to an Indian squaw, appearing in the form of a beautiful woman with a child in her arms, and demanding an offering of tobacco and fur robes,[360] what conceptions of personal life could be more distinct than these? When the Apache Indian pointed to the sky and asked the white man, 'Do you not believe that God, this Sun (que Dios, este Sol), sees what we do and punishes us when it is evil?' it is impossible to say that this savage was talking in rhetorical simile.[361] There was something in the Homeric contemplation of the living personal Hêlios, that was more and deeper than metaphor. Even in far later ages, we may read of the outcry that arose in Greece against the astronomers, those blasphemous materialists who denied, not the divinity only, but the very personality of the sun, and declared him a huge hot ball. Later again, how vividly Tacitus brings to view the old personification dying into simile among the Romans, in contrast with its still enduring religious vigour among the German nations, in the record of Boiocalcus pleading before the Roman legate that his tribe should not be driven from their lands. Looking toward the sun, and calling on the other heavenly bodies as though, says the historian, they had been there present, the German chief demanded of them if it were their will to look down upon a vacant soil? (Solem deinde respiciens, et caetera sidera vocans, quasi coram interrogabat, vellentne contueri inane solum?)[362]

So it is with the stars. Savage mythology contains many a story of them, agreeing through all other difference in attributing to them animate life. They are not merely talked of in fancied personality, but personal action is attributed to them, or they are even declared once to have lived on earth. The natives of Australia not only say the stars in Orion's belt and scabbard are young men dancing a corroboree; they declare that Jupiter, whom they call 'Foot of Day' (Ginabong-Bearp), was a chief among the Old Spirits, that ancient race who were translated to heaven before man came on earth.[363] The Esquimaux did not stop short at calling the stars of Orion's belt the Lost Ones, and telling a tale of their being seal-hunters who missed their way home; but they distinctly held that the stars were in old times men and animals, before they went up into the sky.[364] So the North American Indians had more than superficial meaning in calling the Pleiades the Dancers, and the morning-star the Day-bringer; for among them stories are told like that of the Iowas, of the star that an Indian had long gazed upon in childhood, and who came down and talked with him when he was once out hunting, weary and luckless, and led him to a place where there was much game.[365] The Kasia of Bengal declare that the stars were once men: they climbed to the top of a tree (of course the great heaven-tree of the mythology of so many lands), but others below cut the trunk and left them up there in the branches.[366] With such savage conceptions as guides, the original meaning in the familiar classic personification of stars can scarcely be doubted. The explicit doctrine of the animation of stars is to be traced through past centuries, and down to our own. Origen declares that the stars are animate and rational, moved with such order and reason as it would be absurd to say irrational creatures could fulfil. Pamphilius, in his apology for this Father, lays it down that whereas some have held the luminaries of heaven to be animate and rational creatures, while others have held them mere spiritless and senseless bodies, no one may call another a heretic for holding either view, for there is no open tradition on the subject, and even ecclesiastics have thought diversely of it.[367] It is enough to mention here the well-known mediæval doctrine of star-souls and star-angels, so intimately mixed up with the delusions of astrology. In our own time the theory of the animating souls of stars finds still here and there an advocate, and De Maistre, prince and leader of reactionary philosophers, maintains against modern astronomers the ancient doctrine of personal will in astronomic motion, and even the theory of animated planets.[368]

Poetry has so far kept alive in our minds the old animative theory of nature, that it is no great effort to us to fancy the waterspout a huge giant or sea-monster, and to depict in what we call appropriate metaphor its march across the fields of ocean. But where such forms of speech are current among less educated races, they are underlaid by a distinct prosaic meaning of fact. Thus the waterspouts which the Japanese see so often off their coasts are to them long-tailed dragons, 'flying up into the air with a swift and violent motion,' wherefore they call them 'tatsmaki,' 'spouting dragons.'[369] Waterspouts are believed by some Chinese to be occasioned by the ascent and descent of the dragon; although the monster is never seen head and tail at once for clouds, fishermen and sea-side folk catch occasional glimpses of him ascending from the water and descending to it.[370] In the mediæval Chronicle of John of Bromton there is mentioned a wonder which happens about once a month in the Gulf of Satalia, on the Pamphylian coast. A great black dragon seems to come in the clouds, letting down his head into the waves, while his tail seems fixed to the sky, and this dragon draws up the waves to him with such avidity that even a laden ship would be taken up on high, so that to avoid this danger the crews ought to shout and beat boards to drive the dragon off. However, concludes the chronicler, some indeed say that this is not a dragon, but the sun drawing up the water, which seems more true.[371] The Moslems still account for waterspouts as caused by gigantic demons, such as that one described in the 'Arabian Nights:'—'The sea became troubled before them, and there arose from it a black pillar, ascending towards the sky, and approaching the meadow ... and behold it was a Jinnee, of gigantic stature.'[372] The difficulty in interpreting language like this is to know how far it is seriously and how far fancifully meant. But this doubt in no way goes against its original animistic meaning, of which there can be no question in the following story of a 'great sea-serpent' current among a barbarous East African tribe. A chief of the Wanika told Dr. Krapf of a great serpent which is sometimes seen out at sea, reaching from the sea to the sky, and appearing especially during heavy rain. 'I told them,' says the missionary, 'that this was no serpent, but a waterspout.'[373] Out of the similar phenomenon on land there has arisen a similar group of myths. The Moslem fancies the whirling sand-pillar of the desert to be caused by the flight of an evil jinn, and the East African simply calls it a demon (p'hepo). To traveller after traveller who gazes on these monstrous shapes gliding majestically across the desert, the thought occurs that the well-remembered 'Arabian Nights'' descriptions rest upon personifications of the sand-pillars themselves, as the gigantic demons into which fancy can even now so naturally shape them.[374]

Rude and distant tribes agree in the conception of the Rainbow as a living monster. New Zealand myth, describing the battle of the Tempest against the Forest, tells how the Rainbow arose and placed his mouth close to Tane-mahuta, the Father of Trees, and continued to assault him till his trunk was snapt in two, and his broken branches strewed the ground.[375] It is not only in mere nature-myth like this, but in actual awe-struck belief and terror, that the idea of the live Rainbow is worked out. The Karens of Burma say it is a spirit or demon. 'The Rainbow can devour men.... When it devours a person, he dies a sudden or violent death. All persons that die badly, by falls, by drowning, or by wild beasts, die because the Rainbow has devoured their ka-la, or spirit. On devouring persons it becomes thirsty and comes down to drink, when it is seen in the sky drinking water. Therefore when people see the Rainbow, they say, "The Rainbow has come to drink water. Look out, some one or other will die violently by an evil death." If children are playing, their parents will say to them, "The Rainbow has come down to drink. Play no more, lest some accident should happen to you." And after the Rainbow has been seen, if any fatal accident happens to anyone, it is said the Rainbow has devoured him.'[376] The Zulu ideas correspond in a curious way with these. The Rainbow lives with a snake, that is, where it is there is also a snake; or it is like a sheep, and dwells in a pool. When it touches the earth, it is drinking at a pool. Men are afraid to wash in a large pool; they say there is a Rainbow in it, and if a man goes in, it catches and eats him. The Rainbow, coming out of a river or pool and resting on the ground, poisons men whom it meets, affecting them with eruptions. Men say, 'The Rainbow is disease. If it rests on a man, something will happen to him.'[377] Lastly in Dahome, Danh the Heavenly Snake, which makes the Popo beads and confers wealth on man, is the Rainbow.[378]

To the theory of Animism belong those endless tales which all nations tell of the presiding genii of nature, the spirits of cliffs, wells, waterfalls, volcanoes, the elves and wood nymphs seen at times by human eyes when wandering by moonlight or assembled at their fairy festivals. Such beings may personify the natural objects they belong to, as when, in a North American tale, the guardian spirit of waterfalls rushes through the lodge as a raging current, bearing rocks and trees along in its tremendous course, and then the guardian spirit of the islands of Lake Superior enters in the guise of rolling waves covered with silver-sparkling foam.[379] Or they may be guiding and power-giving spirits of nature, like the spirit Fugamu, whose work is the cataract of the Nguyai, and who still wanders night and day around it, though the negroes who tell of him can no longer see his bodily form.[380] The belief prevailing through the lower culture that the diseases which vex mankind are brought by individual personal spirits, is one which has produced striking examples of mythic development. Thus in Burma the Karen lives in terror of the mad 'la,' the epileptic 'la,' and the rest of the seven evil demons who go about seeking his life; and it is with a fancy not many degrees removed from this early stage of thought that the Persian sees in bodily shape the apparition of Al, the scarlet fever:—

'Would you know Al? she seems a blushing maid,
With locks of flame and cheeks all rosy red.'[381]

It is with this deep old spiritualistic belief clearly in view that the ghastly tales are to be read where pestilence and death come on their errand in weird human shape. To the mind of the Israelite, death and pestilence took the personal form of the destroying angel who smote the doomed.[382] When the great plague raged in Justinian's time, men saw on the sea brazen barks whose crews were black and headless men, and where they landed, the pestilence broke out.[383] When the plague fell on Rome in Gregory's time, the saint rising from prayer saw Michael standing with his bloody sword on Hadrian's castle—the archangel stands there yet in bronze, giving the old fort its newer name of the Castle of St. Angelo. Among a whole group of stories of the pestilence seen in personal shape travelling to and fro in the land, perhaps there is none more vivid than this Slavonic one. 'There sat a Russian under a larch-tree, and the sunshine glared like fire. He saw something coming from afar; he looked again—it was the Pest-maiden, huge of stature, all shrouded in linen, striding towards him. He would have fled in terror, but the form grasped him with her long outstretched hand. "Knowest thou the Pest?" she said; "I am she. Take me on thy shoulders and carry me through all Russia; miss no village, no town, for I must visit all. But fear not for thyself, thou shalt be safe amid the dying." Clinging with her long hands, she clambered on the peasant's back; he stepped onward, saw the form above him as he went, but felt no burden. First he bore her to the towns; they found there joyous dance and song; but the form waved her linen shroud, and joy and mirth were gone. As the wretched man looked round, he saw mourning, he heard the tolling of the bells, there came funeral processions, the graves could not hold the dead. He passed on, and coming near each village heard the shriek of the dying, saw all faces white in the desolate houses. But high on the hill stands his own hamlet: his wife, his little children are there, and the aged parents, and his heart bleeds as he draws near. With strong gripe he holds the maiden fast, and plunges with her beneath the waves. He sank: she rose again, but she quailed before a heart so fearless, and fled far away to the forest and the mountain.'[384]

Yet, if mythology be surveyed in a more comprehensive view, it is seen that its animistic development falls within a broader generalization still. The explanation of the course and change of nature, as caused by life such as the life of the thinking man who gazes on it, is but a part of a far wider mental process. It belongs to that great doctrine of analogy, from which we have gained so much of our apprehension of the world around us. Distrusted as it now is by severer science for its misleading results, analogy is still to us a chief means of discovery and illustration, while in earlier grades of education its influence was all but paramount. Analogies which are but fancy to us were to men of past ages reality. They could see the flame licking its yet undevoured prey with tongues of fire, or the serpent gliding along the waving sword from hilt to point; they could feel a live creature gnawing within their bodies in the pangs of hunger; they heard the voices of the hill-dwarfs answering in the echo, and the chariot of the Heaven-god rattling in thunder over the solid firmament. Men to whom these were living thoughts had no need of the schoolmaster and his rules of composition, his injunctions to use metaphor cautiously, and to take continual care to make all similes consistent. The similes of the old bards and orators were consistent, because they seemed to see and hear and feel them: what we call poetry was to them real life, not as to the modern versemaker a masquerade of gods and heroes, shepherds and shepherdesses, stage heroines and philosophic savages in paint and feathers. It was with a far deeper consciousness that the circumstance of nature was worked out in endless imaginative detail in ancient days and among uncultured races.

Upon the sky above the hill-country of Orissa, Pidzu Pennu, the Rain-god of the Khonds, rests as he pours down the showers through his sieve.[385] Over Peru there stands a princess with a vase of rain, and when her brother strikes the pitcher, men hear the shock in thunder and see the flash in lightning.[386] To the old Greeks the rainbow seemed stretched down by Jove from heaven, a purple sign of war and tempest, or it was the personal Iris, messenger between gods and men.[387] To the South Sea Islander it was the heaven-ladder where heroes of old climbed up and down;[388] and so to the Scandinavian it was Bifröst, the trembling bridge, timbered of three hues and stretched from sky to earth; while in German folk-lore it is the bridge where the souls of the just are led by their guardian angels across to paradise.[389] As the Israelite called it the bow of Jehovah in the clouds, it is to the Hindu the bow of Rama,[390] and to the Finn the bow of Tiermes the Thunderer, who slays with it the sorcerers that hunt after men's lives;[391] it is imagined, moreover, as a gold-embroidered scarf, a head-dress of feathers, St. Bernard's crown, or the sickle of an Esthonian deity.[392] And yet through all such endless varieties of mythic conception, there runs one main principle, the evident suggestion and analogy of nature. It has been said of the savages of North America, that 'there is always something actual and physical to ground an Indian fancy on.'[393] The saying goes too far, but within limits it is emphatically true, not of North American Indians alone, but of mankind.

Such resemblances as have just been displayed thrust themselves directly on the mind, without any necessary intervention of words. Deep as language lies in our mental life, the direct comparison of object with object, and action with action, lies yet deeper. The myth-maker's mind shows forth even among the deaf-and-dumb, who work out just such analogies of nature in their wordless thought. Again and again they have been found to suppose themselves taught by their guardians to worship and pray to sun, moon, and stars, as personal creatures. Others have described their early thoughts of the heavenly bodies as analogous to things within their reach, one fancying the moon made like a dumpling and rolled over the tree-tops like a marble across a table, and the stars cut out with great scissors and stuck against the sky, while another supposed the moon a furnace and the stars fire-grates, which the people above the firmament light up as we kindle fires.[394] Now the mythology of mankind at large is full of conceptions of nature like these, and to assume for them no deeper original source than metaphorical phrases, would be to ignore one of the great transitions of our intellectual history.

Language, there is no doubt, has had a great share in the formation of myth. The mere fact of its individualizing in words such notions as winter and summer, cold and heat, war and peace, vice and virtue, gives the myth-maker the means of imagining these thoughts as personal beings. Language not only acts in thorough unison with the imagination whose product it expresses, but it goes on producing of itself, and thus, by the side of the mythic conceptions in which language has followed imagination, we have others in which language has led, and imagination has followed in the track. These two actions coincide too closely for their effects to be thoroughly separated, but they should be distinguished as far as possible. For myself, I am disposed to think (differing here in some measure from Professor Max Müller's view of the subject) that the mythology of the lower races rests especially on a basis of real and sensible analogy, and that the great expansion of verbal metaphor into myth belongs to more advanced periods of civilization. In a word, I take material myth to be the primary, and verbal myth to be the secondary formation. But whether this opinion be historically sound or not, the difference in nature between myth founded on fact and myth founded on word is sufficiently manifest. The want of reality in verbal metaphor cannot be effectually hidden by the utmost stretch of imagination. In spite of this essential weakness, however, the habit of realizing everything that words can describe is one which has grown and flourished in the world. Descriptive names become personal, the notion of personality stretches to take in even the most abstract notions to which a name may be applied, and realized name, epithet, and metaphor pass into interminable mythic growths by the process which Max Müller has so aptly characterized as 'a disease of language.' It would be difficult indeed to define the exact thought lying at the root of every mythic conception, but in easy cases the course of formation can be quite well followed. North American tribes have personified Nipinūkhe and Pipūnūkhe, the beings who bring the spring (nipin) and the winter (pipūn); Nipinūkhe brings the heat and birds and verdure, Pipūnūkhe ravages with his cold winds, his ice and snow; one comes as the other goes, and between them they divide the world.[395] Just such personification as this furnishes the staple of endless nature-metaphor in our own European poetry. In the springtime it comes to be said that May has conquered Winter, his gate is open, he has sent letters before him to tell the fruit that he is coming, his tent is pitched, he brings the woods their summer clothing. Thus, when Night is personified, we see how it comes to pass that Day is her son, and how each in a heavenly chariot drives round the world. To minds in this mythologic stage, the Curse becomes a personal being, hovering in space till it can light upon its victim; Time and Nature arise as real entities; Fate and Fortune become personal arbiters of our lives. But at last, as the change of meaning goes on, thoughts that once had a more real sense fade into mere poetic forms of speech. We have but to compare the effect of ancient and modern personification on our own minds, to understand something of what has happened in the interval. Milton may be consistent, classical, majestic, when he tells how Sin and Death sat within the gates of hell, and how they built their bridge of length prodigious across the deep abyss to earth. Yet such descriptions leave but scant sense of meaning on modern minds, and we are apt to say, as we might of some counterfeit bronze from Naples, 'For a sham antique how cleverly it is done.' Entering into the mind of the old Norseman, we guess how much more of meaning than the cleverest modern imitation can carry, lay in his pictures of Hel, the death-goddess, stern and grim and livid, dwelling in her high and strong-barred house, and keeping in her nine worlds the souls of the departed; Hunger is her dish, Famine is her knife, Care is her bed, and Misery her curtain. When such old material descriptions are transferred to modern times, in spite of all the accuracy of reproduction their spirit is quite changed. The story of the monk who displayed among his relics the garments of St. Faith is to us only a jest; and we call it quaint humour when Charles Lamb, falling old and infirm, once wrote to a friend, 'My bed-fellows are Cough and Cramp; we sleep three in a bed.' Perhaps we need not appreciate the drollery any the less for seeing in it at once a consequence and a record of a past intellectual life.

The distinction of grammatical gender is a process intimately connected with the formation of myths. Grammatical gender is of two kinds. What may be called sexual gender is familiar to all classically-educated Englishmen, though their mother tongue has mostly lost its traces. Thus in Latin not only are such words as *homo* and *femina* classed naturally as masculine and feminine, but such words as *pes* and *gladius* are made masculine, and *biga* and *navis* feminine, and the same distinction is actually drawn between such abstractions as *honos* and *fides*. That sexless objects and ideas should thus be classed as male and female, in spite of a new gender— the neuter or 'neither' gender—having been defined, seems in part explained by considering this latter to have been of later formation, and the original Indo-European genders to have been only masculine and feminine, as is actually the case in Hebrew. Though the practice of attributing sex to objects that have none is not easy to explain in detail, yet there seems nothing mysterious in its principles, to judge from one at least of its main ideas, which is still quite intelligible. Language makes an admirably appropriate distinction between strong and weak, stern and gentle, rough and delicate, when it contrasts them as male and female. It is possible to understand even such fancies as those which Pietro della Valle describes among the mediæval Persians, distinguishing between male and female, that is to say, practically between robust and tender, even in such things as food and cloth, air and water, and prescribing their proper use accordingly.[396] And no phrase could be more plain and forcible than that of the Dayaks of Borneo, who say of a heavy downpour of rain, 'ujatn arai, 'sa!'—'a *he* rain this!'[397] Difficult as it may be to decide how far objects and thoughts were classed in language as male and female because they were personified, and how far they were personified because they were classed as male and female, it is evident at any rate that these two processes fit together and promote each other.[398]

Moreover, in studying languages which lie beyond the range of common European scholarship, it is found that the theory of grammatical gender must be extended into a wider field. The Dravidian languages of South India make the interesting distinction between a 'high-caste or major gender,' which includes rational beings, i.e. deities and men, and a 'caste-less or minor gender,' which includes irrational objects, whether living animals or lifeless things.[399] The distinction between an animate and an inanimate gender appears with especial import in a family of North American Indian languages, the Algonquin. Here not only do all animals belong to the animate gender, but also the sun, moon, and stars, thunder and lightning, as being personified creatures. The animate gender, moreover, includes not only trees and fruits, but certain exceptional lifeless objects which appear to owe this distinction to their special sanctity or power; such are the stone which serves as the altar of sacrifice to the manitus, the bow, the eagle's feather, the kettle, tobacco-pipe, drum, and wampum. Where the whole animal is animate, parts of its body considered separately may be inanimate—hand or foot, beak or wing. Yet even here, for special reasons, special objects are treated as of animate gender; such are the eagle's talons, the bear's claws, the beaver's castor, the man's nails, and other objects for which there is claimed a peculiar or mystic power.[400] If to anyone it seems surprising that savage thought should be steeped through and through in mythology, let him consider the meaning that is involved in a grammar of nature like this. Such a language is the very reflexion of a mythic world.

There is yet another way in which language and mythology can act and re-act on one another. Even we, with our blunted mythologic sense, cannot give an individual name to a lifeless object, such as a boat or a weapon, without in the very act imagining for it something of a personal nature. Among nations whose mythic conceptions have remained in full vigour, this action may be yet more vivid. Perhaps very low savages may not be apt to name their implements or their canoes as though they were live people, but races a few stages above them show the habit in perfection. Among the Zulus we hear of names for clubs, Igumgehle or Glutton, U-nothlola-mazibuko or He-who-watches-the-fords; among names for assagais are Imbubuzi or Groan-causer, U-silo-si-lambile or Hungry Leopard, and the weapon being also used as an implement, a certain assagai bears the peaceful name of U-simbela-banta-bami, He-digs-up-for-my-children.[401] A similar custom prevailed among the New Zealanders. The traditions of their ancestral migrations tell how Ngahue made from his jasper stone those two sharp axes whose names were Tutauru and Hauhau-te-rangi; how with these axes were shaped the canoes Arawa and Tainui; how the two stone anchors of Te Arawa were called Toka-parore or Wrystone, and Tu-te-rangi-haruru or Like-to-the-roaring-sky. These legends do not break off in a remote past, but carry on a chronicle which reaches into modern times. It is only lately, the Maoris say, that the famous axe Tutauru was lost, and as for the ear-ornament named Kaukau-matua, which was made from a chip of the same stone, they declare that it was not lost till 1846, when its owner, Te Heuheu, perished in a landslip.[402] Up from this savage level the same childlike habit of giving personal names to lifeless objects may be traced, as we read of Thor's hammer, Miölnir, whom the giants know as he comes flying through the air, or of Arthur's brand, Excalibur, caught by the arm clothed in white samite when Sir Bedivere flung him back into the lake, or of the Cid's mighty sword Tizona, the Firebrand, whom he vowed to bury in his own breast were she overcome through cowardice of his.

The teachings of a childlike primæval philosophy ascribing personal life to nature at large, and the early tyranny of speech over the human mind, have thus been two great and, perhaps, greatest agents in mythologic development. Other causes, too, have been at work, which will be noticed in connexion with special legendary groups, and a full list, could it be drawn up, might include as contributories many other intellectual actions. It must be thoroughly understood, however, that such investigation of the processes of myth-formation demands a lively sense of the state of men's minds in the mythologic period. When the Russians in Siberia listened to the talk of the rude Kirgis, they stood amazed at the barbarians' ceaseless flow of poetic improvisation, and exclaimed, 'Whatever these people see gives birth to fancies!' Just so the civilized European may contrast his own stiff orderly prosaic thought with the wild shifting poetry and legend of the old myth-maker, and may say of him that everything he saw gave birth to fancy. Wanting the power of transporting himself into this imaginative atmosphere, the student occupied with the analysis of the mythic world may fail so pitiably in conceiving its depth and intensity of meaning, as to convert it into stupid fiction. Those can see more justly who have the poet's gift of throwing their minds back into the world's older life, like the actor who for a moment can forget himself and become what he pretends to be. Wordsworth, that 'modern ancient,' as Max Müller has so well called him, could write of Storm and Winter, or of the naked Sun climbing the sky, as though he were some Vedic poet at the head-spring of his race, 'seeing' with his mind's eye a mythic hymn to Agni or Varuna. Fully to understand an old-world myth needs not evidence and argument alone, but deep poetic feeling.

Yet such of us as share but very little in this rare gift, may make shift to let evidence in some measure stand in its stead. In the poetic stage of thought we may see that ideal conceptions once shaped in the mind must have assumed some such reality to grown-up men and women as they still do to children. I have never forgotten the vividness with which, as a child, I fancied I might look through a great telescope, and see the constellations stand round the sky, red, green, and yellow, as I had just been shown them on the celestial globe. The intensity of mythic fancy may be brought even more nearly home to our minds by comparing it with the morbid subjectivity of illness. Among the lower races, and high above their level, morbid ecstasy brought on by meditation, fasting, narcotics, excitement, or disease, is a state common and held in honour among the very classes specially concerned with mythic idealism, and under its influence the barriers between sensation and imagination break utterly away. A North American Indian prophetess once related the story of her first vision: At her solitary fast at womanhood she fell into an ecstasy, and at the call of the spirits she went up to heaven by the path that leads to the opening of the sky; there she heard a voice, and, standing still, saw the figure of a man standing near the path, whose head was surrounded by a brilliant halo, and his breast was covered with squares; he said, 'Look at me, my name is Oshauwauegeeghick, the Bright Blue Sky!' Recording her experience afterwards in the rude picture-writing of her race, she painted this glorious spirit with the hieroglyphic horns of power and the brilliant halo round his head.[403] We know enough of the Indian pictographs to guess how a fancy with these familiar details of the picture-language came into the poor excited creature's mind; but how far is our cold analysis from her utter belief that in vision she had really seen this bright being, this Red Indian Zeus. Far from being an isolated case, this is scarcely more than a fair example of the rule that any idea shaped and made current by mythic fancy, may at once acquire all the definiteness of fact. Even if to the first shaper it be no more than lively imagination, yet when it comes to be embodied in words and to pass from house to house, those who hear it become capable of the most intense belief that it may be seen in material shape, that it has been seen, that they themselves have seen it. The South African who believes in a god with a crooked leg sees him with a crooked leg in dreams and visions.[404] In the time of Tacitus it was said, with a more poetic imagination, that in the far north of Scandinavia men might see the very forms of the gods and the rays streaming from their heads.[405] In the 6th century the famed Nile-god might still be seen, in gigantic human form, rising waist-high from the waters of his river.[406] Want of originality indeed seems one of the most remarkable features in the visions of mystics. The stiff Madonnas with their crowns and petticoats still transfer themselves from the pictures on cottage walls to appear in spiritual personality to peasant visionaries, as the saints who stood in vision before ecstatic monks of old were to be known by their conventional pictorial attributes. When the devil with horns, hoofs, and tail had once become a fixed image in the popular mind, of course men saw him in this conventional shape. So real had St. Anthony's satyr-demon become to men's opinion, that there is a grave 13th century account of the mummy of such a devil being exhibited at Alexandria; and it is not fifteen years back from the present time that there was a story current at Teignmouth of a devil walking up the walls of the houses, and leaving his fiendish backward footprints in the snow. Nor is it vision alone that is concerned with the delusive realization of the ideal; there is, as it were, a conspiracy of all the senses to give it proof. To take a striking instance: there is an irritating herpetic disease which gradually encircles the body as with a girdle, whence its English name of the *shingles* (Latin, *cingulum*). By an imagination not difficult to understand, this disease is attributed to a sort of coiling snake; and I remember a case in Cornwall where a girl's family waited in great fear to see if the creature would stretch all round her, the belief being that if the snake's head and tail met, the patient would die. But a yet fuller meaning of this fantastic notion is brought out in an account by Dr. Bastian of a physician who suffered in a painful disease, as though a snake were twined round him, and in whose mind this idea reached such reality that in moments of excessive pain he could see the snake and touch its rough scales with his hand.

The relation of morbid imagination to myth is peculiarly well instanced in the history of a widespread belief, extending through savage, barbaric, classic, oriental, and mediæval life, and surviving to this day in European superstition. This belief, which may be conveniently called the Doctrine of Werewolves, is that certain men, by natural gift or magic art, can turn for a time into ravening wild beasts. The origin of this idea is by no means sufficiently explained. What we are especially concerned with is the fact of its prevalence in the world. It may be noticed that such a notion is quite consistent with the animistic theory that a man's soul may go out of his body and enter that of a beast or bird, and also with the opinion that men may be transformed into animals; both these ideas having an important place in the belief of mankind, from savagery onward. The doctrine of werewolves is substantially that of a temporary metempsychosis or metamorphosis. Now it really occurs that, in various forms of mental disease, patients prowl shyly, long to bite and destroy mankind, and even fancy themselves transformed into wild beasts. Belief in the possibility of such transformation may have been the very suggesting cause which led the patient to imagine it taking place in his own person. But at any rate such insane delusions do occur, and physicians apply to them the mythologic term of lycanthropy. The belief in men being werewolves, man-tigers, and the like, may thus have the strong support of the very witnesses who believe themselves to be such creatures. Moreover, professional sorcerers have taken up the idea, as they do any morbid delusion, and pretend to turn themselves and others into beasts by magic art. Through the mass of ethnographic details relating to this subject, there is manifest a remarkable uniformity of principle.

Among the non-Aryan indigenes of India, the tribes of the Garo Hills describe as 'transformation into a tiger' a kind of temporary madness, apparently of the nature of delirium tremens, in which the patient walks like a tiger, shunning society.[407] The Khonds of Orissa say that some among them have the art of 'mleepa,' and by the aid of a god become 'mleepa' tigers for the purpose of killing enemies, one of the man's four souls going out to animate the bestial form. Natural tigers, say the Khonds, kill game to benefit men, who find it half devoured and share it, whereas man-killing tigers are either incarnations of the wrathful Earth-goddess, or they are transformed men.[408] Thus the notion of man-tigers serves, as similar notions do elsewhere, to account for the fact that certain individual wild beasts show a peculiar hostility to man. Among the Ho of Singbhoom it is related, as an example of similar belief, that a man named Mora saw his wife killed by a tiger, and followed the beast till it led him to the house of a man named Poosa. Telling Poosa's relatives of what had occurred, they replied that they were aware that he had the power of becoming a tiger, and accordingly they brought him out bound, and Mora deliberately killed him. Inquisition being made by the authorities, the family deposed, in explanation of their belief, that Poosa had one night devoured an entire goat, roaring like a tiger whilst eating it, and that on another occasion he told his friends he had a longing to eat a particular bullock, and that very night that very bullock was killed and devoured by a tiger.[409] South-eastern Asia is not less familiar with the idea of sorcerers turning into man-tigers and wandering after prey; thus the Jakuns of the Malay Peninsula believe that when a man becomes a tiger to revenge himself on his enemies, the transformation happens just before he springs, and has been seen to take place.[410]

How vividly the imagination of an excited tribe, once inoculated with a belief like this, can realize it into an event, is graphically told by Dobrizhoffer among the Abipones of South America. When a sorcerer, to get the better of an enemy, threatens to change himself into a tiger and tear his tribesmen to pieces, no sooner does he begin to roar, than all the neighbours fly to a distance; but still they hear the feigned sounds. 'Alas!' they cry, 'his whole body is beginning to be covered with tiger-spots!' 'Look, his nails are growing!' the fear-struck women exclaim, although they cannot see the rogue, who is concealed within his tent, but distracted fear presents things to their eyes which have no real existence. 'You daily kill tigers in the plain without dread,' said the missionary; 'why then should you weakly fear a false imaginary tiger in the town?' 'You fathers don't understand these matters,' they reply with a smile. 'We never fear, but kill tigers in the plain, because we can see them. Artificial tigers we do fear, because they can neither be seen nor killed by us.'[411] The sorcerers who induced assemblies of credulous savages to believe in this monstrous imposture, were also the professional spiritualistic mediums of the tribes, whose business it was to hold intercourse with the spirits of the dead, causing them to appear visibly, or carrying on audible dialogues with them behind a curtain. Africa is especially rich in myths of man-lions, man-leopards, man-hyænas. In the Kanuri language of Bornu, there is grammatically formed from the word 'bultu,' a hyæna, the verb 'bultungin,' meaning 'I transform myself into a hyæna;' and the natives maintain that there is a town called Kabutiloa, where every man possesses this faculty.[412] The tribe of Budas in Abyssinia, iron-workers and potters, are believed to combine with these civilized avocations the gift of the evil eye and the power of turning into hyænas, wherefore they are excluded from society and the Christian sacrament. In the 'Life of Nathaniel Pearce,' the testimony of one Mr. Coffin is printed. A young Buda, his servant, came for leave of absence, which was granted; but scarcely was Mr. Coffin's head turned to his other servants, when some of them called out, pointing in the direction the Buda had taken, 'Look, look, he is turning himself into a hyæna.' Mr. Coffin instantly looked round, the young man had vanished, and a large hyæna was running off at about a hundred paces' distance, in full light on the open plain, without tree or bush to intercept the view. The Buda came back next morning, and as usual rather affected to countenance than deny the prodigy. Coffin says, moreover, that the Budas wear a peculiar gold earring, and this he has frequently seen in the ears of hyænas shot in traps, or speared by himself and others; the Budas are dreaded for their magical arts, and the editor of the book suggests that they put ear-rings in hyænas' ears to encourage a profitable superstition.[413] Mr. Mansfield Parkyns' more recent account shows how thoroughly this belief is part and parcel of Abyssinian spiritualism. Hysterics, lethargy, morbid insensibility to pain, and the 'demoniacal possession,' in which the patient speaks in the name and language of an intruding spirit, are all ascribed to the spiritual agency of the Budas. Among the cases described by Mr.

Parkyns was that of a servant-woman of his, whose illness was set down to the influence of one of these blacksmith-hyænas, who wanted to get her out into the forest and devour her. One night, a hyæna having been heard howling and laughing near the village, the woman was bound hand and foot and closely guarded in the hut, when suddenly, the hyæna calling close by, her master, to his astonishment, saw her rise 'without her bonds' like a Davenport Brother, and try to escape.[414] In Ashango-land, M. Du Chaillu tells the following suggestive story. He was informed that a leopard had killed two men, and many palavers were held to settle the affair; but this was no ordinary leopard, but a transformed man. Two of Akondogo's men had disappeared, and only their blood was found, so a great doctor was sent for, who said it was Akondogo's own nephew and heir Akosho. The lad was sent for, and when asked by the chief, answered that it was truly he who had committed the murders, that he could not help it, for he had turned into a leopard, and his heart longed for blood, and after each deed he had turned into a man again. Akondogo loved the boy so much that he would not believe his confession, till Akosho took him to a place in the forest, where lay the mangled bodies of the two men, whom he had really murdered under the influence of this morbid imagination. He was slowly burnt to death, all the people standing by.[415]

Brief mention is enough for the comparatively well-known European representatives of these beliefs. What with the mere continuance of old tradition, what with the tricks of magicians, and what with cases of patients under delusion believing themselves to have suffered transformation, of which a number are on record, the European series of details from ancient to modern ages is very complete. Virgil in the Bucolics shows the popular opinion of his time that the arts of the werewolf, the necromancer or 'medium,' and the witch, were different branches of one craft, where he tells of Mœris as turning into a wolf by the use of poisonous herbs, as calling up souls from the tombs, and as bewitching away crops:—

'Has herbas, atque haec Ponto mihi lecta venena

Ipse dedit Moeris; nascuntur plurima Ponto.

His ego saepe lupum fieri, et se condere sylvis

Moerin, saepe animas imis excire sepulcris,

Atque satas aliò vidi traducere messes.'[416]

Of the classic accounts, one of the most remarkable is Petronius Arbiter's story of the transformation of a 'versipellis' or 'turnskin;' this contains the episode of the wolf being wounded and the man who wore its shape found with a similar wound, an idea not sufficiently proved to belong originally to the lower races, but which becomes a familiar feature in European stories of werewolves and witches. In Augustine's time magicians were persuading their dupes that by means of herbs they could turn them to wolves, and the use of salve for this purpose is mentioned at a comparatively modern date. Old Scandinavian sagas have their werewolf warriors, and shape-changers (hamramr) raging in fits of furious madness. The Danes still know a man who is a werewolf by his eyebrows meeting, and thus resembling a butterfly, the familiar type of the soul, ready to fly off and enter some other body. In the last year of the Swedish war with Russia, the people of Kalmar said the wolves which overran the land were transformed Swedish prisoners. From Herodotus' legend of the Neuri who turned every year for a few days to wolves, we follow the idea on Slavonic ground to where Livonian sorcerers bathe yearly in a river and turn for twelve days to wolves; and widespread Slavonic superstition still declares that the wolves that sometimes in bitter winters dare to attack men, are themselves 'wilkolak,' men bewitched into wolf's shape. The modern Greeks instead of the classic λυκάνθρωπος adopt the Slavonic term βρυκολακας (Bulgarian 'vrkolak'); it is a man who falls into a cataleptic state, while his soul enters a wolf and goes ravening for blood. Modern Germany, especially in the north, still keeps up the stories of wolf-girdles, and in December you must not 'talk of the wolf' by name, lest the werewolves hear you. Our English word 'werewolf,' that is 'man-wolf' (the 'verevulf' of Cnut's Laws), still reminds us of the old belief in our own country, and if it has had for centuries but little place in English folklore, this has been not so much for lack of superstition, as of wolves. To instance the survival of the idea, transferred to another animal, in the more modern witch-persecution, the following Scotch story may serve. Certain witches at Thurso for a long time tormented an honest fellow under the usual form of cats, till one night he put them to flight with his broad-sword, and cut off the leg of one less nimble than the rest; taking it up, to his amazement he found it to be a woman's leg, and next morning he discovered the old hag its owner with but one leg left. In France the creature has what is historically the same name as our 'werewolf;' viz. in early forms 'gerulphus,' 'garoul,' and now pleonastically 'loup-garou.' The parliament of Franche-Comté made a law in 1573 to expel the werewolves; in 1598 the werewolf of Angers gave evidence of his hands and feet turning to wolf's claws; in 1603, in the case of Jean Grenier, the judge declared lycanthropy to be an insane delusion, not a crime. In 1658, a French satirical description of a magician could still give the following perfect account of the witch-werewolf: 'I teach the witches to take the form of wolves and eat children, and when anyone has cut off one of their legs (which proves to be a man's arm) I forsake them when they are discovered, and leave them in the power of justice.' Even in our own day the idea has by no means died out of the French peasant's mind. Not ten years ago in France, Mr. Baring-Gould found it impossible to get a guide after dark across a wild place haunted by a loup-garou, an incident which led him afterwards to write his 'Book of Werewolves,' a monograph of this remarkable combination of myth and madness.[417]

If we judged the myths of early ages by the unaided power of our modern fancy, we might be left unable to account for their immense effect on the life and belief of mankind. But by the study of such evidence as this, it becomes possible to realize a usual state of the imagination among ancient and savage peoples, intermediate between the conditions of a healthy prosaic modern citizen and of a raving fanatic or a patient in a fever-ward. A poet of our own day has still much in common with the minds of uncultured tribes in the mythologic stage of thought. The rude man's imaginations may be narrow, crude, and repulsive, while the poet's more conscious fictions may be highly wrought into shapes of fresh artistic beauty, but both share in that sense of the reality of ideas, which fortunately or unfortunately modern education has proved so powerful to destroy. The change of meaning of a single word will tell the history of this transition, ranging from primæval to modern thought. From first to last, the processes of *phantasy* have been at work; but where the savage could see *phantasms*, the civilized man has come to amuse himself with *fancies*.

CHAPTER IX.
MYTHOLOGY (*continued*).

Nature-myths, their origin, canon of interpretation, preservation of original sense and significant names—Nature-myths of upper savage races compared with related forms among barbaric and civilized nations—Heaven and Earth as Universal Parents—Sun and Moon: Eclipse and Sunset, as Hero or Maiden swallowed by Monster; Rising of Sun from Sea and Descent to Under-World; Jaws of Night and Death, Symplegades; Eye of Heaven, Eye of Odin and the Graiæ—Sun and Moon as mythic civilizers—Moon, her inconstancy, periodical death and revival—Stars, their generation—Constellations, their place in Mythology and Astronomy—Wind and Tempest—Thunder—Earthquake.

From laying down general principles of myth-development, we may now proceed to survey the class of Nature-myths, such especially as seem to have their earliest source and truest meaning among the lower races of mankind.

Science, investigating nature, discusses its facts and announces its laws in technical language which is clear and accurate to trained students, but which falls only as a mystic jargon on the ears of barbarians, or peasants, or children. It is to the comprehension of just these simple unschooled minds that the language of poetic myth is spoken, so far at least as it is true poetry, and not its quaint affected imitation. The poet contemplates the same natural world as the man of science, but in his so different craft strives to render difficult thought easy by making it visible and tangible, above all by referring the being and movement of the world to such personal life as his hearers feel within themselves, and thus working out in far-stretched fancy the maxim that 'Man is the measure of all things.' Let but the key be recovered to this mythic dialect, and its complex and shifting terms will translate themselves into reality, and show how far legend, in its sympathetic fictions of war, love, crime, adventure, fate, is only telling the perennial story of the world's daily life. The myths shaped out of those endless analogies between man and nature which are the soul of all poetry, into those half-human stories still so full to us of unfading life and beauty, are the masterpieces of an art belonging rather to the past than to the present. The growth of myth has been checked by science, it is dying of weights and measures, of proportions and specimens—it is not only dying, but half dead, and students are anatomising it. In this world one must do what one can, and if the moderns cannot feel myth as their forefathers did, at least they can analyse it. There is a kind of intellectual frontier within which he must be who will sympathise with myth, while he must be without who will investigate it, and it is our fortune that we live near this frontier-line, and can go in and out. European scholars can still in a measure understand the belief of Greeks or Aztecs or Maoris in their native myths, and at the same time can compare and interpret them without the scruples of men to whom such tales are history, and even sacred history. Moreover, were the whole human race at a uniform level of culture with ourselves, it would be hard to bring our minds to conceive of tribes in the mental state to which the early growth of nature-myth belongs, even as it is now hard to picture to ourselves a condition of mankind lower than any that has been actually found. But the various grades of existing civilization preserve the landmarks of a long course of history, and there survive by millions savages and barbarians whose minds still produce, in rude archaic forms, man's early mythic representations of nature.

Those who read for the first time the dissertations of the modern school of mythologists, and sometimes even those who have been familiar with them for years, are prone to ask, with half-incredulous appreciation of the beauty and simplicity of their interpretations, can they be really true? Can so great a part of the legendary lore of classic, barbarian, and mediæval Europe be taken up with the everlasting depiction of Sun and Sky, Dawn and Gloaming, Day and Night, Summer and Winter, Cloud and Tempest; can so many of the personages of tradition, for all their heroic human aspect, have their real origin in anthropomorphic myths of nature? Without any attempt to discuss these opinions at large, it will be seen that inspection of nature-mythology from the present point of view tells in their favour, at least as to principle. The general theory that such direct conceptions of nature as are so naïvely and even baldly uttered in the Veda, are among the primary sources of myth, is enforced by evidence gained elsewhere in the world. Especially the traditions of savage races display mythic conceptions of the outer world, primitive like those of the ancient Indian hymns, agreeing with them in their general character, and often remarkably corresponding in their very episodes. At the same time it must be clearly understood that the truth of such a general principle is no warrant for all the particular interpretations which mythologists claim to base upon it, for of these in fact many are wildly speculative, and many hopelessly unsound. Nature-myth demands indeed a recognition of its vast importance in the legendary lore of mankind, but only so far as its claim is backed by strong and legitimate evidence.

The close and deep analogies between the life of nature and the life of man have been for ages dwelt upon by poets and philosophers, who in simile or in argument have told of light and darkness, of calm and tempest, of birth, growth, change, decay, dissolution, renewal. But no one-sided interpretation can be permitted to absorb into a single theory such endless many-sided correspondences as these. Rash inferences which on the strength of mere resemblance derive episodes of myth from episodes of nature must be regarded with utter mistrust, for the student who has no more stringent criterion than this for his myths of sun and sky and dawn, will find them wherever it pleases him to seek them. It may be judged by simple trial what such a method may lead to; no legend, no allegory, no nursery rhyme, is safe from the hermeneutics of a thorough-going mythologic theorist. Should he, for instance, demand as his property the nursery 'Song of Sixpence,' his claim would be easily established: obviously the four-and-twenty blackbirds are the four-and-twenty hours, and the pie that holds them is the underlying earth covered with the overarching sky; how true a touch of nature it is that when the pie is opened, that is, when day breaks, the birds begin to sing; the King is the Sun, and his counting out his money is pouring out the sunshine, the golden shower of Danae; the Queen is the Moon, and her transparent honey the moonlight; the Maid is the 'rosy-fingered' Dawn who rises before the Sun her master, and hangs out the clouds, his clothes, across the sky; the particular blackbird who so tragically ends the tale by snipping off her nose, is the hour of sunrise. The time-honoured rhyme really wants but one thing to prove it a Sun-myth, that one thing being a proof by some argument more valid than analogy. Or if historical characters be selected with any discretion, it is easy to point out the solar episodes embodied in their lives. See Cortès landing in Mexico, and seeming to the Aztecs their very Sun-priest Quetzalcoatl, come back from the East to renew his reign of light and glory; mark him deserting the wife of his youth, even as the Sun leaves the Dawn, and again in later life abandoning Marina for a new bride; watch his sun-like career of brilliant conquest, checkered with intervals of storm, and declining to a death clouded with sorrow and disgrace. The life of Julius Cæsar would fit as plausibly into a scheme of solar myth; his splendid course as in each new land he came, and saw, and conquered; his desertion of Cleopatra; his ordinance of the solar year for men; his death at the hand of Brutus, like Sîfrit's death at the hand of Hagen in the Nibelungen Lied; his falling pierced with many bleeding wounds, and shrouding himself in his cloak to die in darkness. Of Cæsar, better than of Cassius his slayer, it might have been said in the language of sun-myth:

'... O setting sun,

As in thy red rays thou dost sink to-night,

So in his red blood Cassius' day is set;

The sun of Rome is set!'

Thus, in interpreting heroic legend as based on nature-myth, circumstantial analogy must be very cautiously appealed to, and at any rate there is need of evidence more cogent than vague likenesses between human and cosmic life. Now such evidence is forthcoming at its strongest in a crowd of myths, whose open meaning it would be wanton incredulity to doubt, so little do they disguise, in name or sense, the familiar aspects of nature which they figure as scenes of personal life. Even where the tellers of legend may have altered or forgotten its earlier mythic meaning, there are often sufficient grounds for an attempt to restore it. In spite of change and corruption, myths are slow to lose all consciousness of their first origin; as for instance, classical literature retained enough of meaning in the great Greek sun-myth, to compel even Lempriere of the Classical Dictionary to admit that Apollo or Phœbus 'is often confounded with the sun.' For another instance, the Greeks had still present to their thoughts the meaning of Argos Panoptes, Io's hundred-eyed, all-seeing guard who was slain by Hermes and changed into the Peacock, for Macrobius writes as recognizing in him the star-eyed heaven itself;[418] even as Indra, the Sky, is in Sanskrit the 'thousand-eyed' (*sahasrâksha, sahasranayana*). In modern times the thought is found surviving or reviving in a strange region of language: whoever it was that brought argo as a word for 'heaven' into the Lingua Furbesca or Robbers' Jargon of Italy,[419] must have been thinking of the starry sky watching him like Argus with his hundred eyes. The etymology of names, moreover, is at once the guide and safeguard of the mythologist. The obvious meaning of words did much to preserve vestiges of plain sense in classic legend, in spite of all the efforts of the commentators. There was no disputing the obvious facts that Hēlios was the Sun, and Selēnē the Moon; and as for Jove, all the nonsense of pseudo-history could not quite do away the idea that he was really Heaven, for language continued to declare this in such expressions as 'sub Jove frigido.' The explanation of the rape of Persephone, as a nature-myth of the seasons and the fruits of the earth, does not depend alone on analogy of incident, but has the very names to prove its reality, Zeus, Hēlios, Dēmētēr—Heaven, and Sun, and Mother Earth. Lastly, in stories of mythic beings who are the presiding genii of star or mountain, tree or river, or heroes and heroines actually metamorphosed into such objects, personification of nature is still plainly evident; the poet may still as of old see Atlas bear the heavens on his mighty shoulders, and Alpheus in impetuous course pursue the maiden Arethusa.

In a study of the nature-myths of the world, it is hardly practicable to start from the conceptions of the very lowest human tribes, and to work upwards from thence to fictions of higher growth; partly because our information is but meagre as to the beliefs of these shy and seldom quite intelligible folk, and partly because the legends they possess have not reached that artistic and systematic shape which they attain to among races next higher in the scale. It therefore answers better to take as a foundation the mythology of the North American Indians, the South Sea Islanders, and other low-cultured tribes who best represent in modern times the early mythologic period of human history. The survey may be fitly commenced by a singularly perfect and purposeful cosmic myth from New Zealand.

It seems long ago and often to have come into men's minds, that the overarching Heaven and the all-producing Earth are, as it were, a Father and a Mother of the world, whose offspring are the living creatures, men, and beasts, and plants. Nowhere, in the telling of this oft-told tale, is present nature veiled in more transparent personification, nowhere is the world's familiar daily life repeated with more childlike simplicity as a story of long past ages, than in the legend of 'The Children of Heaven and Earth' written down by Sir George Grey among the Maoris about the year 1850. From Rangi, the Heaven, and Papa, the Earth, it is said, sprang all men and things, but sky and earth clave together, and darkness rested upon them and the beings they had begotten, till at last their children took counsel whether they should rend apart their parents, or slay them. Then Tane-mahuta, father of forests, said to his five great brethren, 'It is better to rend them apart, and to let the heaven stand far above us, and the earth lie under our feet. Let the sky become as a stranger to us, but the earth remain close to us as our nursing mother.' So Rongo-ma-tane, god and father of the cultivated food of man, arose and strove to separate the heaven and the earth; he struggled, but in vain, and vain too were the efforts of Tangaroa, father of fish and reptiles, and of Haumia-tikitiki, father of wild-growing food, and of Tu-matauenga, god and father of fierce men. Then slow uprises Tane-mahuta, god and father of forests, and wrestles with his parents, striving to part them with his hands and arms. 'Lo, he pauses; his head is now firmly planted on his mother the earth, his feet he raises up and rests against his father the skies, he strains his back and limbs with mighty effort. Now are rent apart Rangi and Papa, and with cries and groans of woe they shriek aloud.... But Tane-mahuta pauses not; far, far beneath him he presses down the earth; far, far above him he thrusts up the sky.' But Tawhiri-ma-tea, father of winds and storms, had never consented that his mother should be torn from her lord, and now there arose in his breast a fierce desire to war against his brethren. So the Storm-god rose and followed his father to the realms above, hurrying to the sheltered hollows of the boundless skies, to hide and cling and nestle there. Then came forth his progeny, the mighty winds, the fierce squalls, the clouds, dense, dark, fiery, wildly drifting, wildly bursting; and in their midst their father rushed upon his foe. Tane-mahuta and his giant forests stood unconscious and unsuspecting when the raging hurricane burst on them, snapping the mighty trees across, leaving trunks and branches rent and torn upon the ground for the insect and the grub to prey on. Then the father of storms swooped down to lash the waters into billows whose summits rose like cliffs, till Tangaroa, god of ocean and father of all that dwell therein, fled affrighted through his seas. His children, Ika-tere, the father of fish, and Tu-te-wehiwehi, the father of reptiles, sought where they might escape for safety; the father of fish cried, 'Ho, ho, let us all escape to the sea,' but the father of reptiles shouted in answer, 'Nay, nay, let us rather fly inland,' and so these creatures separated, for while the fish fled into the sea, the reptiles sought safety in the forests and scrubs. But the sea-god Tangaroa, furious that his children the reptiles should have deserted him, has ever since waged war on his brother Tane who gave them shelter in his woods, Tane attacks him in return, supplying the offspring of his brother Tu-matauenga, father of fierce men, with canoes and spears and fish-hooks made from his trees, and with nets woven from his fibrous plants, that they may destroy withal the fish, the Sea-god's children; and the Sea-god turns in wrath upon the Forest-god, overwhelms his canoes with the surges of the sea, sweeps with floods his trees and houses into the boundless ocean. Next the god of storms pushed on to attack his brothers the gods and progenitors of the tilled food and the wild, but Papa, the Earth, caught them up and hid them, and so safely were these her children concealed by their mother, that the Storm-god sought for them in vain. So he fell upon the last of his brothers, the father of fierce men, but him he could not even shake, though he put forth all his strength. What cared Tu-matauenga for his brother's wrath? He it was who has planned the destruction of their parents, and had shown himself brave and fierce in war; his brethren had yielded before the tremendous onset of the Storm-god and his progeny; the Forest-god and his offspring had been broken and torn in pieces; the Sea-god and his children had fled to the depths of the ocean or the recesses of the shore; the gods of food had been safe in hiding; but man still stood erect and unshaken upon the bosom of his mother Earth, and at last the hearts of the Heaven and the Storm became tranquil, and their passion was assuaged.

But now Tu-matauenga, father of fierce men, took thought how he might be avenged upon his brethren who had left him unaided to stand against the god of storms. He twisted nooses of the leaves of the whanake tree, and the birds and beasts, children of Tane the Forest-god, fell before him; he netted nets from the flax-plant, and dragged ashore the fish, the children of Tangaroa the Sea-god; he found in the hiding-place underground the children of Rongo-ma-tane, the sweet potato and all cultivated food, and the children of Haumia-tikitiki, the fern-root and all wild-growing food, he dug them up and let them wither in the sun. Yet, though he overcame his four brothers, and they became his food, over the fifth he could not prevail, and Tawhiri-ma-tea, the Storm-god, still ever attacks him in tempest and hurricane, striving to destroy him both by sea and land. It was the bursting forth of the Storm-god's wrath against his brethren that caused the dry land to disappear beneath the waters: the beings of ancient days who thus submerged the land were Terrible-rain, Long-continued-rain, Fierce-hailstorms; and their progeny were Mist, and Heavy-dew, and Light-dew, and thus but little of the dry land was left standing above the sea. Then clear light increased in the world, and the beings who had been hidden between Rangi and Papa before they were parted, now multiplied upon the earth. 'Up to this time the vast Heaven has still ever remained separated from his spouse the Earth. Yet their mutual love still continues; the soft warm sighs of her loving bosom still ever rise up to him, ascending from the woody mountains and valleys, and men call these mists; and the vast Heaven, as he mourns through the long nights his separation from his beloved, drops frequent tears upon her bosom, and men seeing these term them dew-drops.'[420]

The rending asunder of heaven and earth is a far-spread Polynesian legend, well known in the island groups that lie away to the north-east.[421] Its elaboration, however, into the myth here sketched out was probably native New Zealand work. Nor need it be supposed that the particular form in which the English governor took it down among the Maori priests and tale-tellers, is of ancient date. The story carries in itself evidence of an antiquity of character which does not necessarily belong to mere lapse of centuries. Just as the adzes of polished jade and the cloaks of tied flax-fibre, which these New Zealanders were using but yesterday, are older in their place in history than the bronze battle-axes and linen mummy cloths of ancient Egypt, so the Maori poet's shaping of nature into nature-myth belongs to a stage of intellectual history which was passing away in Greece five-and-twenty centuries ago. The myth-maker's fancy of Heaven and Earth as father and mother of all things naturally suggested the legend that they in old days abode together, but have since been torn asunder. In China the same idea of the universal parentage is accompanied by a similar legend of the separation. Whether or not there is historical connexion here between the mythology of Polynesia and China, I will not guess, but certainly the ancient Chinese legend of the separation of heaven and earth in the primæval days of Puang-Ku seems to have taken the very shape of the Polynesian myth: 'Some say a person called Puang-Ku opened or separated the heavens and the earth, they previously being pressed down close together.'[422] As to the mythic details in the whole story of 'The Children of Heaven and Earth,' there is scarcely a thought that is not still transparent, scarcely even a word that has lost its meaning to us. The broken and stiffened traditions which our fathers fancied relics of ancient history, are, as has been truly said, records of a past which was never present; but the simple nature-myth, as we find it in its actual growth, or reconstruct it from its legendary remnants, may be rather called the record of a present which is never past. The battle of the storm against the forest and the ocean is still waged before our eyes; we still look upon the victory of man over the creatures of the land and sea; the food-plants still hide in their mother earth, and the fish and reptiles find shelter in the ocean and the thicket; but the mighty forest-trees stand with their roots firm planted in the ground, while with their branches they push up and up against the sky. And if we have learnt the secret of man's thought in the childhood of his race, we may still realize with the savage the personal being of the ancestral Heaven and Earth.

The idea of the Earth as a mother is more simple and obvious, and no doubt for that reason more common in the world, than the idea of the Heaven as a father. Among the native races of America the Earth-mother is one of the great personages of mythology. The Peruvians worshipped her as Mama-Pacha or 'Mother-Earth,' and the Caribs, when there was an earthquake, said that it was their mother Earth dancing, and signifying to them to dance and make merry likewise, which accordingly they did. Among the North-American Indians the Comanches call on the Earth as their mother, and the Great Spirit as their father. A story told by Gregg shows a somewhat different thought of mythic parentage. General Harrison once called the Shawnee chief Tecumseh for a talk:—'Come here, Tecumseh, and sit by your father!' he said. 'You my father!' replied the chief, with a stern air. 'No! yonder sun (pointing towards it) is my father, and the earth is my mother, so I will rest on her bosom,' and he sat down on the ground. Like this was the Aztec fancy, as it seems from this passage in a Mexican prayer to Tezcatlipoca, offered in time of war: 'Be pleased, O our Lord, that the nobles who shall die in the war be peacefully and joyously received by the Sun and the Earth, who are the loving father and mother of all.'[423] In the mythology of Finns, Lapps, and Esths, Earth-Mother is a divinely honoured personage.[424] Through the mythology of our own country the same thought may be traced, from the days when the Anglo-Saxon called upon the Earth, 'Hâl wes thu folde, fira modor,' 'Hail thou Earth, men's mother,' to the time when mediæval Englishmen made a riddle of her, asking 'Who is Adam's mother?' and poetry continued what mythology was letting fall, when Milton's archangel promised Adam a life to last

'... till like ripe fruit, thou drop

Into thy mother's lap.'[425]

Among the Aryan race, indeed, there stands, wide and firm, the double myth of the 'two great parents,' as the Rig-Veda calls them. They are

Dyaushpitar, Ζεὺς πατήρ, *Jupiter*, the 'Heaven-father,' and *Prthivî mâtar*, the 'Earth-mother;' and their relation is still kept in mind in the ordinance of Brahman marriage according to the Yajur-Veda, where the bridegroom says to the bride, 'I am the sky, thou art the earth, come let us marry.' When Greek poets called Ouranos and Gaia, or Zeus and Dēmētēr, husband and wife, what they meant was the union of Heaven and Earth; and when Plato said that the earth brought forth men, but God was their shaper, the same old mythic thought must have been present to his mind.[426] It reappears in ancient Scythia;[427] and again in China, where Heaven and Earth are called in the Shu-King 'Father and Mother of all things.' Chinese philosophy naturally worked this idea into the scheme of the two great principles of nature, the Yin and Yang, male and female, heavenly and earthly, and from this disposition of nature they drew a practical moral lesson: Heaven, said the philosophers of the Sung dynasty, made man, and earth made woman and therefore woman is to be subject to man as Earth to Heaven.[428]

Entering next upon the world-wide myths of Sun, Moon, and Stars, the regularity and consistency of human imagination may be first displayed in the beliefs connected with eclipses. It is well known that these phenomena, to us now crucial instances of the exactness of natural laws, are, throughout the lower stages of civilization, the very embodiment of miraculous disaster. Among the native races of America it is possible to select a typical series of myths describing and explaining, according to the rules of savage philosophy, these portents of dismay. The Chiquitos of the southern continent thought the Moon was hunted across the sky by huge dogs, who caught and tore her till her light was reddened and quenched by the blood flowing from her wounds, and then the Indians, raising a frightful howl and lamentation, would shoot across into the sky to drive the monsters off. The Caribs, thinking that the demon Maboya, hater of all light, was seeking to devour the Sun and Moon, would dance and howl in concert all night long to scare him away. The Peruvians, imagining such an evil spirit in the shape of a monstrous beast, raised the like frightful din when the Moon was eclipsed, shouting, sounding musical instruments, and beating the dogs to join their howls to the hideous chorus. Nor are such ideas extinct in our own days. In the Tupi language, the proper description of a solar eclipse is 'oarasu jaguaretê vü,' that is, 'Jaguar has eaten Sun;' and the full meaning of this phrase is displayed by tribes who still shout and let fly burning arrows to drive the devouring beast from his prey. On the northern continent, again, some savages believed in a great sun-swallowing dog, while others would shoot up arrows to defend their luminaries against the enemies they fancied attacking them. By the side of these prevalent notions there occur, however, various others; thus the Caribs could imagine the eclipsed Moon hungry, sick, or dying; the Peruvians could fancy the Sun angry and hiding his face, and the sick Moon likely to fall in total darkness, and bring on the end of the world; the Hurons thought the Moon sick, and explained their customary charivari of shouting men and howling dogs as performed to recover her from her complaint. Passing on from these most primitive conceptions, it appears that natives of both South and North America fell upon philosophic myths somewhat nearer the real facts of the case, insomuch as they admit that the Sun and Moon cause eclipses of one another. In Cumana, men thought that the wedded Sun and Moon quarrelled, and that one of them was wounded; and the Ojibwas endeavoured by tumultuous noise to distract the two from such a conflict. The course of progressive science went far beyond this among the Aztecs, who, as part of their remarkable astronomical knowledge, seem to have had an idea of the real cause of eclipses, but who kept up a relic of the old belief by continuing to speak in mythologic phrase of the Sun and Moon being eaten.[429] Elsewhere in the lower culture, there prevailed similar mythic conceptions. In the South Sea Islands some supposed the Sun and Moon to be swallowed by an offended deity, whom they therefore induced, by liberal offerings, to eject the luminaries from his stomach.[430] In Sumatra we have the comparatively scientific notion that an eclipse has to do with the action of the Sun and Moon on one another, and, accordingly, they make a loud noise with sounding instruments to prevent the one from devouring the other.[431] So, in Africa, there may be found both the rudest theory of the Eclipse-monster, and the more advanced conception that a solar eclipse is 'the Moon catching the Sun.'[432]

It is no cause for wonder that an aspect of the heavens so awful as an eclipse should in times of astronomic ignorance have filled men's minds with terror of a coming destruction of the world. It may help us still to realize this thought if we consider how, as Calmet pointed out many years ago, the prophet Joel adopted the plainest words of description of the solar and lunar eclipse, 'The sun shall be turned into darkness and the moon into blood;' nor could the thought of any catastrophe of nature have brought his hearers face to face with a more lurid and awful picture. But to our minds, now that the eclipse has long passed from the realm of mythology into the realm of science, such words can carry but a feeble glimmer of their early meaning. The ancient doctrine of the eclipse has not indeed lost its whole interest. To trace it upward from its early savage stages to the period when astronomy claimed it, and to follow the course of the ensuing conflict over it between theology and science—ended among ourselves but still being sluggishly fought out among less cultured nations—this is to lay open a chapter of the history of opinion, from which the student who looks forward as well as back may learn grave lessons.

There is reason to consider most or all civilized nations to have started from the myth of the Eclipse-monster in forms as savage as those of the

New World. It prevails still among the great Asiatic nations. The Hindus say that the demon Râhu insinuated himself among the gods, and obtained a portion of the amrita, the drink of immortality; Vishnu smote off the now immortal head, which still pursues the Sun and Moon whose watchful gaze detected his presence in the divine assembly. Another version of the myth is that there are two demons, Râhu and Ketu, who devour Sun and Moon respectively, and who are described in conformity with the phenomena of eclipses, Râhu being black, and Ketu red; the usual charivari is raised by the populace to drive them off, though indeed, as their bodies have been cut off at the neck, their prey must of natural course slip out as soon as swallowed. Or Râhu and Ketu are the head and body of the dissevered demon, by which conception the Eclipse-monster is most ingeniously adapted to advanced astronomy, the head and tail being identified with the ascending and descending nodes. The following remarks on the eclipse-controversy, made by Mr. Samuel Davis a century ago in the Asiatick Researches, are still full of interest. 'It is evident, from what has been explained, that the Pūndits, learned in the Jyotish shastrū, have truer notions of the form of earth and the economy of the universe than are ascribed to the Hindoos in general: and that they must reject the ridiculous belief of the common Brahmūns, that eclipses are occasioned by the intervention of the monster Rahoo, with many other particulars equally unscientific and absurd. But as this belief is founded on explicit and positive declarations contained in the védūs and pooranus, the divine authority of which writings no devout Hindoo can dispute, the astronomers have some of them cautiously explained such passages in those writings as disagree with the principles of their own science: and where reconciliation was impossible, have apologized, as well as they could, for propositions necessarily established in the practice of it, by observing, that certain things, as stated in other shastrūs, might have been so formerly, and may be so still; but for astronomical purposes, astronomical rules must be followed.'[433] It is not easy to give a more salient example than this of the consequence of investing philosophy with the mantle of religion, and allowing priests and scribes to convert the childlike science of an early age into the sacred dogma of a late one. Asiatic peoples under Buddhist influence show the eclipse-myth in its different stages. The rude Mongols make a clamour of rough music to drive the attacking Aracho (Râhu) from Sun or Moon. A Buddhist version mentioned by Dr. Bastian describes Indra the Heaven-god pursuing Râhu with his thunderbolt, and ripping open his belly, so that although he can swallow the heavenly bodies, he lets them slip out again.[434] The more civilized nations of South-East Asia, accepting the eclipse-demons Râhu and Ketu, were not quite staggered in their belief by the foreigners' power of foretelling eclipses, nor even by learning roughly to do the same themselves. The Chinese have official announcement of an eclipse duly made beforehand, and then proceed to encounter the ominous monster, when he comes, with gongs and bells and the regularly appointed prayers. Travellers of a century or two ago relate curious details of such combined belief in the dragon and the almanac, culminating in an ingenious argument to account for the accuracy of the Europeans' predictions. These clever people, the Siamese said, know the monster's mealtimes, and can tell how hungry he will be, that is, how large an eclipse will be required to satisfy him.[435]

In Europe popular mythology kept up ideas, either of a fight of sun or moon with celestial enemies, or of the moon's fainting or sickness; and especially remnants of such archaic belief are manifested in the tumultuous clamour raised in defence or encouragement of the afflicted luminary. The Romans flung firebrands into the air, and blew trumpets, and clanged brazen pots and pans, 'laboranti succurrere lunae.' Tacitus, relating the story of the soldiers' mutiny against Tiberius, tells how their plan was frustrated by the moon suddenly languishing in a clear sky (luna claro repente coelo visa languescere): in vain by clang of brass and blast of trumpet they strove to drive away the darkness, for clouds came up and covered all, and the plotters saw, lamenting, that the gods turned away from their crime.[436] In the period of the conversion of Europe, Christian teachers began to attack the pagan superstition, and to urge that men should no longer clamour and cry 'vince luna!' to aid the moon in her sore danger; and at last there came a time when the picture of the sun or moon in the dragon's mouth became a mere old-fashioned symbol to represent eclipses in the calendar, and the saying, 'Dieu garde la lune des loups' passed into a mocking proverb against fear of remote danger. Yet the ceremonial charivari is mentioned in our own country in the seventeenth century: 'The Irish or Welsh during eclipses run about beating kettles and pans, thinking their clamour and vexations available to the assistance of the higher orbes.' In 1654 Nuremberg went wild with terror of an impending solar eclipse; the markets ceased, the churches were crowded with penitents, and a record of the event remains in the printed thanksgiving which was issued (Danckgebeth nach vergangener höchstbedrohlich und hochschädlicher Sonnenfinstenuss), which gives thanks to the Almighty for granting to poor terrified sinners the grace of covering the sky with clouds, and sparing them the sight of the awful sign in heaven. In our own times, a writer on French folklore was surprised during a lunar eclipse to hear sighs and exclamations, 'Mon Dieu, qu'elle est souffrante!' and found on enquiry that the poor moon was believed to be the prey of some invisible monster seeking to devour her.[437] No doubt such late survivals have belonged in great measure to the ignorant crowd, for the educated classes of the West have never suffered in its extreme the fatal Chinese union of scepticism and superstition. Yet if it is our mood to bewail the slowness with which knowledge penetrates the mass of mankind, there stand dismal proofs before us here. The eclipse remained an omen of fear almost up to our own century, and could rout a horror-stricken army, and fill Europe with dismay, a thousand years after Pliny had written in memorable words his eulogy of the astronomers; those great men, he said, and above ordinary mortals, who, by discovering the laws of the heavenly bodies, had freed the miserable mind of men from terror at the portents of eclipses.

Day is daily swallowed up by Night, to be set free again at dawn, and from time to time suffers a like but shorter durance in the maw of the Eclipse and the Storm-cloud; Summer is overcome and prisoned by dark Winter, to be again set free. It is a plausible opinion that such scenes from the great nature-drama of the conflict of light and darkness are, generally speaking, the simple facts, which in many lands and ages have been told in mythic shape, as legends of a Hero or maiden devoured by a Monster, and hacked out again or disgorged. The myths just displayed show with absolute distinctness, that myth can describe eclipse as the devouring and setting free of the personal sun and moon by a monster. The following Maori legend will supply proof as positive that the episode of the Sun's or the Day's death in sunset may be dramatized into a tale of a personal solar hero plunging into the body of the personal Night.

Maui, the New Zealand cosmic hero, at the end of his glorious career came back to his father's country, and was told that here, perhaps, he might be overcome, for here dwelt his mighty ancestress, Hine-nui-te-po, Great-Daughter-of-Night, whom 'you may see flashing, and as it were opening and shutting there, where the horizon meets the sky; what you see yonder shining so brightly-red, are her eyes, and her teeth are as sharp and hard as pieces of volcanic glass; her body is like that of a man; and as for the pupils of her eyes, they are jasper; and her hair is like the tangles of long sea-weed, and her mouth is like that of a barra-couta.' Maui boasted of his former exploits, and said, 'Let us fearlessly seek whether men are to die or live for ever;' but his father called to mind an evil omen, that when he was baptizing Maui he had left out part of the fitting prayers, and therefore he knew that his son must perish. Yet he said, 'O, my last-born, and the strength of my old age, ... be bold, go and visit your great ancestress, who flashes so fiercely there where the edge of the horizon meets the sky.' Then the birds came to Maui to be his companions in the enterprise, and it was evening when they went with him, and they came to the dwelling of Hine-nui-te-po, and found her fast asleep. Maui charged the birds not to laugh when they saw him creep into the old chieftainess, but when he had got altogether inside her, and was coming out of her mouth, then they might laugh long and loud. So Maui stripped off his clothes, and the skin on his hips, tattooed by the chisel of Uetonga, looked mottled and beautiful, like a mackerel's, as he crept in. The birds kept silence, but when he was in up to his waist, the little tiwakawaka could hold its laughter in no longer, and burst out loud with its merry note; then Maui's ancestress awoke, closed on him and caught him tight, and he was killed. Thus died Maui, and thus death came into the world, for Hine-nui-te-po is the goddess both of night and death, and had Maui entered into her body and passed safely through her, men would have died no more. The New Zealanders hold that the Sun descends at night into his cavern, bathes in the Wai Ora Tane, the Water of Life, and returns at dawn from the under-world; hence we may interpret the thought that if Man could likewise descend into Hades and return, his race would be immortal.[438] Further evidence that Hine-nui-te-po is the deity of Night or Hades, appears in another New Zealand myth. Tane, descending to the shades below in pursuit of his wife, comes to the Night (Po) of Hine-a-te-po, Daughter-of-Night, who says to him, 'I have spoken thus to her "Return from this place, as I, Hine-a-te-po, am here. I am the barrier between night and day."'[439] It is seldom that solar characteristics are more distinctly marked in the several details of a myth than they are here.

In the list of myths of engulfing monsters, there are others which seem to display, with a clearness almost approaching this, an origin suggested by the familiar spectacle of Day and Night, or Light and Darkness. The simple story of the Day may well be told in the Karen tale of Ta Ywa, who was born a tiny child, and went to the Sun to make him grow; the Sun tried in vain to destroy him by rain and heat, and then blew him up large till his head touched the sky; then he went forth and travelled from his home far over the earth; and among the adventures which befell him was this—a snake swallowed him, but they ripped the creature up, and Ta Ywa came back to life,[440] like the Sun from the ripped up serpent-demon in the Buddhist eclipse-myth. In North American Indian mythology, a principal personage is Manabozho, an Algonquin hero or deity whose solar character is well brought into view in an Ottawa myth which tells us that Manabozho (whom it calls Na-na-bou-jou) is the elder brother of Ning-gah-be-ar-nong Manito, the Spirit of the West, god of the country of the dead in the region of the setting sun. Manabozho's solar nature is again revealed in the story of his driving the West, his father, across mountain and lake to the brink of the world, though he cannot kill him. This sun-hero Manabozho, when he angled for the King of Fishes, was swallowed, canoe and all; then he smote the monster's heart with his war-club till he would fain have cast him up into the lake again, but the hero set his canoe fast across the fish's throat inside, and finished slaying him; when the dead monster drifted ashore, the gulls pecked an opening for Manabozho to come out. This is a story familiar to English readers from its introduction into the poem of Hiawatha. In another version, the tale is told of the Little Monedo of the Ojibwas, who also corresponds with the New Zealand Maui in being the

Sun-Catcher; among his various prodigies, he is swallowed by the great fish, and cut out again by his sister.[441] South Africa is a region where there prevail myths which seem to tell the story of the world imprisoned in the monster Night, and delivered by the dawning Sun. The Basutos have their myth of the hero Litaolane; he came to man's stature and wisdom at his birth; all mankind save his mother and he had been devoured by a monster; he attacked the creature and was swallowed whole, but cutting his way out he set free all the inhabitants of the world. The Zulus tell stories as pointedly suggestive. A mother follows her children into the maw of the great elephant, and finds forests and rivers and highlands, and dogs and cattle, and people who had built their villages there; a description which is simply that of the Zulu Hades. When the Princess Untombinde was carried off by the Isikqukqumadevu, the 'bloated, squatting, bearded monster,' the King gathered his army and attacked it, but it swallowed up men, and dogs, and cattle, all but one warrior; he slew the monster, and there came out cattle, and horses, and men, and last of all the princess herself. The stories of these monsters being cut open imitate, in graphic savage fashion, the cries of the imprisoned creatures as they came back from darkness into daylight. 'There came out first a fowl, it said, "Kukuluku! I see the world!" For, for a long time it had been without seeing it. After the fowl there came out a man, he said "Hau! I at length see the world!"' and so on with the rest.[442]

The well-known modern interpretation of the myth of Perseus and Andromeda, or of Herakles and Hesione, as a description of the Sun slaying the Darkness, has its connexion with this group of legends. It is related in a remarkable version of this story, that when the Trojan King Laomedon had bound his daughter Hesione to the rock, a sacrifice to Poseidon's destroying sea-monster, Herakles delivered the maiden, springing full-armed into the fish's gaping throat, and coming forth hairless after three days' hacking within. This singular story, probably in part of Semitic origin, combines the ordinary myth of Hesione or Andromeda with the story of Jonah's fish, for which indeed the Greek sculpture of Andromeda's monster served as the model in early Christian art, while Joppa was the place where vestiges of Andromeda's chains on a rock in front of the town were exhibited in Pliny's time, and whence the bones of a whale were carried to Rome as relics of Andromeda's monster. To recognize the place which the nature-myth of the Man swallowed by the Monster occupies in mythology, among remote and savage races and onward among the higher nations, affects the argument on a point of Biblical criticism. It strengthens the position of the critics who, seeing that the Book of Jonah consists of two wonder-episodes adapted to enforce two great religious lessons, no longer suppose intention of literal narrative in what they may fairly consider as the most elaborate parable of the Old

Testament. Had the Book of Jonah happened to be lost in old times, and only recently recovered, it is indeed hardly likely that any other opinion of it than this would find acceptance among scholars.[443]

The conception of Hades as a monster swallowing men in death, was actually familiar to Christian thought. Thus, to take instances from different periods, the account of the Descent into Hades in the Apocryphal Gospel of Nicodemus makes Hades speak in his proper personality, complaining that his belly is in pain, when the Saviour is to descend and set free the saints imprisoned in it from the beginning of the world; and in mediæval representations of this deliverance, the so-called 'Harrowing of Hell,' Christ is depicted standing before a huge fish-like monster's open jaws, whence Adam and Eve are coming forth first of mankind.[444] With even more distinctness of mythical meaning, the man-devouring monster is introduced in the Scandinavian Eireks-Saga. Eirek, journeying toward Paradise, comes to a stone bridge guarded by a dragon, and entering into its maw, finds that he has arrived in the world of bliss.[445] But in another wonder-tale, belonging to that legendary growth which formed round early Christian history, no such distinguishable remnant of nature-myth survives. St. Margaret, daughter of a priest of Antioch, had been cast into a dungeon, and there Satan came upon her in the form of a dragon and swallowed her alive:

'Maiden Mergrete tho Loked her beside,

And sees a loathly dragon, Out of an hirn glide:

His eyen were full griesly, His mouth opened wide,

And Margrete might no where flee There she must abide,

Maiden Margrete Stood still as any stone,

And that loathly worm, To her-ward gan gone

Took her in his foul mouth, And swallowed her flesh and bone.

Anon he brast—Damage hath she none!

Maiden Mergrete Upon the dragon stood;

Blyth was her harte, And joyful was her mood.'[446]

Stories belonging to the same group are not unknown to European folk-lore. One is the story of Little Red Ridinghood, mutilated in the English nursery version, but known more perfectly by old wives in Germany, who can tell that the lovely little maid in her shining red satin cloak was swallowed with her grandmother by the Wolf, but they both came out safe and sound when the hunter cut open the sleeping beast. Any one who can fancy with prince Hal, 'the blessed sun himself a fair hot wench in flame-coloured taffeta,' and can then imagine her swallowed up by Sköll, the Sun-devouring Wolf of Scandinavian mythology, may be inclined to class the tale of Little Red Ridinghood as a myth of sunset and sunrise. There is indeed another story in Grimm's Märchen, partly the same as this one, which we can hardly doubt to have a quaint touch of sun-myth in it. It is called the Wolf and Seven Kids, and tells of the Wolf swallowing the kids all but the youngest of the seven, who was hidden in the clock-case. As in Little Red Ridinghood, they cut open the Wolf and fill him with stones. This tale, which took its present shape since the invention of clocks, looks as though the tale-teller was thinking, not of real kids and wolf, but of days of the week swallowed by night, or how should he have hit upon such a fancy as that the wolf could not get at the youngest of the seven kids, because it was hidden (like to-day) in the clock case?[447]

It may be worth while to raise the question apropos of this nursery tale, does the peasant folk-lore of modern Europe really still display episodes of nature-myth, not as mere broken-down and senseless fragments, but in full shape and significance? In answer it will be enough to quote the story of Vasilissa the Beautiful, brought forward by Mr. W. Ralston in one of his lectures on Russian Folk-lore. Vasilissa's stepmother and two sisters, plotting against her life, send her to get a light at the house of Bába Yagá, the witch, and her journey contains the following history of the Day, told in truest mythic fashion. Vasilissa goes and wanders, wanders in the forest. She goes, and she shudders. Suddenly before her bounds a rider, he himself white, and clad in white, the horse under him white, and the trappings white. And day began to dawn. She goes farther, when a second rider bounds forth, himself red, clad in red, and on a red horse. The sun began to rise. She goes on all day, and towards evening arrives at the witch's house. Suddenly there comes again a rider, himself black, clad all in black, and on a black horse; he bounded to the gates of the Bába Yagá and disappeared as if he had sunk through the earth. Night fell. After this, when Vasilissa asks the witch, who was the white rider, she answers, 'That is my clear Day;' who was the red rider, 'That is my red Sun;' who was the black rider, 'That is my black Night; they are all my trusty friends.' Now, considering that the story of Little Red Ridinghood belongs to the same class of folk-lore tales as this story of Vasilissa the Beautiful, we need not be afraid to seek in the one for traces of the same archaic type of nature-myth which the other not only keeps up, but keeps up with the fullest consciousness of meaning.

The development of nature-myth into heroic legend seems to have taken place among the barbaric tribes of the South Sea Islands and North America much as it took place among the ancestors of the classic nations of the Old World. We are not to expect accurate consistency or proper sequence of episodes in the heroic cycles, but to judge from the characteristics of the episodes themselves as to the ideas which suggested them. As regards the less cultured races, a glance at two legendary cycles, one from Polynesia and the other from North America, will serve to give an idea of the varieties of treatment of phases of sun-myth. The New Zealand myth of Maui, mixed as it may be with other fancies, is in its most striking features the story of Day and Night. The story of the Sun's birth from the ocean is thus told. There were five brothers, all called Maui, and it was the youngest Maui who had been thrown into the sea by Taranga his mother, and rescued by his ancestor Tama-nui-ki-te-Rangi, Great-Man-in-Heaven, who took him to his house, and hung him in the roof. Then is given in fanciful personality the tale of the vanishing of Night at dawn. One night, when Taranga came home, she found little Maui with his brothers, and when she knew her last-born, the child of her old age, she took him to sleep with her, as she had been used to take the other Mauis his brothers, before they were grown up. But the little Maui grew vexed and suspicious, when he found that every morning his mother rose at dawn and disappeared from the house in a moment, not to return till nightfall. So one night he crept out and stopped every crevice in the wooden window and the doorway, that the day might not shine into the house; then broke the faint light of early dawn, and then the sun rose and mounted into the heavens, but Taranga slept on, for she knew not it was broad day outside. At last she sprang up, pulled out the stopping of the chinks, and fled in dismay. Then Maui saw her plunge into a hole in the ground and disappear, and thus he found the deep cavern by which his mother went down below the earth as each night departed. After this, follows the episode of Maui's visit to his ancestress Muri-ranga-whenua, at that western Land's End where Maori souls descend into the subterranean region of the dead. She sniffs as he comes towards her, and distends herself to devour him, but when she has sniffed round from south by east to north, she smells his coming by the western breeze, and so knows that he is a descendant of hers. He asks for her wondrous jawbone, she gives it to him, and it is his weapon in his next exploit when he catches the sun, Tama-nui-te-Ra, Great-Man-Sun, in the noose, and wounds him and makes him go slowly. With a fishhook pointed with the miraculous jawbone, and smeared with his own blood for bait, Maui next performs his most famous feat of fishing up New Zealand, still called Te-Ika-a-Maui, the fish of Maui. To understand this, we must compare the various versions of the story in these and other Pacific Islands, which show that it is a general myth of the rising of dry land from beneath the ocean. It is said elsewhere that it was Maui's grandfather, Rangi-Whenua, Heaven-Earth, who gave the jawbone. More distinctly, it is also said that Maui had two sons, whom he slew when young to take their jawbones; now these two sons must be the Morning and Evening, for Maui made the morning and evening stars from an eye of each; and it was with the jawbone of the eldest that he drew up the land from the deep. It is related that when Maui pulled up his fish, he found it was land, on which were houses, and stages on which to put food, and dogs barking, and fires burning, and people working. It appears, moreover, that the submarine region out of which the land was lifted was the under-world of Night, for Maui's hook had caught the gable of the house of Hine-nui-te-po, Great-Daughter-of-Night, and when the land came up her house was on it, and she was standing near. Another Maori legend tells how Maui takes fire in his hands, it burns him, and he springs with it into the sea: 'When he sank in the waters, the sun for the first time set, and darkness covered the earth. When he found that all was night, he immediately pursued the sun, and brought him back in the morning.' When Maui carried or flung the fire into the sea, he set a volcano burning. It is told, again, that when Maui had put out all fires on earth, his mother sent him to get new fire from her ancestress Mahuika. The Tongans, in their version of the myth, relate how the youngest Maui discovers the cavern that leads to Bulotu, the west-land of the dead, and how his father, another Maui, sends him to the yet older Maui who sits by his great fire; the two wrestle, and Maui brings away fire for men, leaving the old earthquake-god lying crippled below. The legendary group thus dramatizes the birth of the sun from the ocean and the departure of the night, the extinction of the light at sunset and its return at dawn, and the descent of the sun to the western Hades, the under-world of night and death, which is incidentally identified with the region of subterranean fire and earthquake. Here, indeed, the characteristics of true nature-myth are not indistinctly marked, and Maui's death by his ancestress the Night fitly ends his solar career.[448]

It is a sunset-story, very differently conceived, that begins the beautiful North American Indian myth of the Red Swan. The story belongs to the Algonquin race. The hunter Ojibwa had just killed a bear and begun to skin him, when suddenly something red tinged all the air around. Reaching the shore of a lake, the Indian saw it was a beautiful red swan, whose plumage glittered in the sun. In vain the hunter shot his shafts, for the bird floated unharmed and unheeding, but at last he remembered three magic arrows at home, which had been his father's. The first and second arrow flew near and nearer, the third struck the swan, and flapping its wings, it flew off slowly towards the sinking of the sun. With full sense of the poetic solar meaning of this episode Longfellow has adapted it as a sunset picture, in one of his Indian poems:

'Can it be the sun descending

O'er the level plain of water?
Or the Red Swan floating, flying,
Wounded by the magic arrow,

Staining all the waves with crimson,
With the crimson of its life-blood,
Filling all the air with splendour,
With the splendour of its plumage?'

The story goes on to tell how the hunter speeds westward in pursuit of the Red Swan. At lodges where he rests, they tell him she has often passed there, but those who followed her have never returned. She is the daughter of an old magician who has lost his scalp, which Ojibwa succeeds in recovering for him and puts back on his head, and the old man rises from the earth, no longer aged and decrepit, but splendid in youthful glory. Ojibwa departs, and the magician calls forth the beautiful maiden, now not his daughter but his sister, and gives her to his victorious friend. It was in after days, when Ojibwa had gone home with his bride, that he travelled forth, and coming to an opening in the earth, descended and came to the abode of departed spirits; there he could behold the bright western region of the good, and the dark cloud of wickedness. But the spirits told him that his brethren at home were quarrelling for the possession of his wife, and at last, after long wandering, this Red Indian Odysseus returned to his mourning constant Penelope, laid the magic arrows to his bow, and stretched the wicked suitors dead at his feet.[449] Thus savage legends from Polynesia and America, possibly indeed shaped under European influence, agree with the theory[450] that Odysseus visiting the Elysian fields, or Orpheus descending to the land of Hades to bring back the 'wide-shining' Eurydikê, are but the Sun himself descending to, and ascending from, the world below.

Where Night and Hades take personal shape in myth, we may expect to find conceptions like that simply shown in a Sanskrit word for evening, '**rajanîmukha**,' i.e., 'mouth of night.' Thus the Scandinavians told of Hel the death-goddess, with mouth gaping like the mouth of Fenrir her brother, the moon-devouring wolf; and an old German poem describes Hell's abyss yawning from heaven to earth:

'der was der Hellen gelîch

diu daz abgrunde

begenit mit ir munde

unde den himel zuo der erden.'[451]

The sculptures on cathedrals still display for the terror of the wicked the awful jaws of Death, the mouth of Hell wide yawning to swallow its victims. Again, where barbaric cosmology accepts the doctrine of a firmament arching above the earth, and of an under world whither the sun descends when he sets and man when he dies, here the conception of gates or portals, whether really or metaphorically meant, has its place. Such is the great gate which the Gold Coast negro describes the Heaven as opening in the morning for the Sun; such were the ancient Greek's gates of Hades, and the ancient Jew's gates of Sheol. There are three mythic descriptions connected with these ideas found among the Karens, the Algonquins, and the Aztecs, which are deserving of special notice. The Karens of Burma, a race among whom ideas are in great measure borrowed from the more cultured Buddhists they have been in contact with, have precedence here for the distinctness of their statement. They say that in the west there are two massive strata of rocks which are continually opening and shutting, and between these strata the sun descends at sunset, but how the upper stratum is supported, no one can describe. The idea comes well into view in the description of a Bghai festival, where sacrificed fowls are thus addressed,— 'The seven heavens, thou ascendest to the top; the seven earths, thou descendest to the bottom. Thou arrivest at Khu-the; thou goest unto Tha-ma [i.e., Yama, the Judge of the Dead in Hades.] Thou goest through the crevices of rocks, thou goest through the crevices of precipices. At the opening and shutting of the western gates of rock, thou goest in between; thou goest below the earth where the Sun travels. I employ thee, I exhort thee. I make thee a messenger, I make thee an angel, &c.'[452] Passing from Burma to the region of the North American lakes, we find a corresponding description in the Ottawa tale of Iosco, already quoted here for its clearly marked personification of Sun and Moon. This legend, though modern in some of its description of the Europeans, their ships, and their far-off land across the sea, is evidently founded on a myth of Day and Night. Iosco seems to be Ioskeha, the White One, whose contest with his brother Tawiscara, the Dark One, is an early and most genuine Huron nature-myth of Day and Night. Iosco and his friends travel for years eastward and eastward to reach the sun, and come at last to the dwelling of Manabozho near the edge of the world, and then, a little beyond, to the chasm to be passed on the way to the land of the Sun and Moon. They began to hear the sound of the beating sky, and it seemed near at hand, but they had far to travel before they reached the place. When the sky came down, its pressure would force gusts of wind from the opening, so strong that the travellers could hardly keep their feet, and the sun passed but a short distance above their heads, The sky would come down with violence, but it would rise slowly and gradually. Iosco and one of his friends stood near the edge, and with a great effort leapt through and gained a foothold on the other side; but the other two were fearful and undecided, and when their companions called to them through the darkness, 'Leap! leap! the sky is on its way down,' they looked up and saw it descending, but paralyzed by fear they sprang so feebly that they only reached the other side with their hands, and the sky at the same moment striking violently on the earth with a terrible sound, forced them into the dreadful black abyss.[453] Lastly, in the funeral ritual of the Aztecs there is found a like description of the first peril that the shade had to encounter on the road leading to that subterranean Land of the Dead, which the sun lights when it is night on earth. Giving the corpse the first of the passports that were to carry him safe to his journey's end, the survivors said to him, 'With these you will pass between the two mountains that smite one against the other.'[454] On the suggestion of this group of solar conceptions and that of Maui's death, we may perhaps explain as derived from a broken-down fancy of solar myth that famous episode of Greek legend, where the good ship Argo passed between the Symplêgades, those two huge cliffs that opened and closed again with swift and violent collision.[455] Can any effort of baseless fancy have brought into the poet's mind a thought so quaint in itself, yet so fitting with the Karen and Aztec myths of the gates of Night and Death? With the Maori legend, the Argonautic tale has a yet deeper coincidence. In both the event is to determine the future; but this thought is worked out in two converse ways. If Maui passed through the entrance of Night and returned to Day, death should not hold mankind; if the Argo passed the Clashers, the way should lie open between them for ever. The Argo sped through in safety, and the Symplêgades can clash no longer on the passing ship; Maui was crushed, and man comes not forth again from Hades.

There is another solar metaphor which describes the sun, not as a personal creature, but as a member of a yet greater being. He is called in Java and Sumatra 'Mata-ari,' in Madagascar 'Maso-andro,' the 'Eye of Day.' If we look for translation of this thought from metaphor into myth, we may find it in the New Zealand stories of Maui setting his own eye up in heaven as the Sun, and the eyes of his two children as the Morning and the Evening Stars.[456] The nature-myth thus implicitly and explicitly stated is one widely developed on Aryan ground. It forms part of that macrocosmic description of the universe well known in Asiatic myth, and in Europe expressed in that passage of the Orphic poem which tells of Jove, at once the world's ruler and the world itself: his glorious head irradiates the sky where hangs his starry hair, the waters of the sounding ocean are the belt that girds his sacred body the earth omniparent, his eyes are sun and moon, his mind, moving and ruling by counsel all things, is the royal æther that no voice nor sound escapes:

'Sunt oculi Phœbus, Phœboque adversa recurrens

Cynthia. Mens verax nullique obnoxius æther

Regius interitu', qui cuncta movetque regitque

Consilio. Vox nulla potest, sonitusve, nec ullus

Hancce Jovis sobolem strepitus, nec fama latere.

Sic animi sensum, et caput immortale beatus

Obtinet: illustre, immensum, immutabile pandens,

Atque lacertorum valido stans robore certus.'[457]

Where the Aryan myth-maker takes no thought of the lesser light, he can in various terms describe the sun as the eye of heaven. In the Rig-Veda it is the 'eye of Mitra, Varuna, and Agni'—'**chakshuh Mitrasya Varunasyah Agneh.**'[458] In the Zend-Avesta it is 'the shining sun with the swift horses, the eye of Ahura-Mazda;' elsewhere both eyes, apparently sun and moon, are praised.[459] To Hesiod it is the 'all-seeing eye of Zeus'—'πάντα ἰδὼν Διὸς ὀφθαλμός;' Macrobius speaks of antiquity calling the sun the eye of Jove—'τί ἥλιος; οὐράνιος ὀφθαλμός.'[460] The old Germans, in calling the sun 'Wuotan's eye,'[461] recognized Wuotan, Woden Odhin, as being himself the divine Heaven. These mythic expressions are of the most unequivocal type. By the hint they give, conjectural interpretations may be here not indeed asserted, but suggested, for two of the quaintest episodes of ancient European myth. Odin, the All-father, say the old skalds of Scandinavia, sits among his Æsir in the city Asgard, on his high throne Hlidskialf (Lid-shelf), whence he can look down over the whole world discerning all the deeds of men. He is an old man wrapped in his wide cloak, and clouding his face with his wide hat, 'os pileo ne cultu proderetur obnubens,' as Saxo Grammaticus has it. Odin is one-eyed; he desired to drink from Mimir's well, but he had to leave there one of his eyes in pledge, as it is said in the Völuspa:

'All know I, Odin! Where thou hiddest thine eye

In Mimir's famous well.

Mead drinks Mimir every morning

From Wale-father's pledge—Wit ye what this is?'

As Odin's single eye seems certainly to be the sun in heaven, one may guess what is the lost eye in the well—perhaps the sun's own reflection in any pool, or more likely that of the moon, which in popular myth is told of as found in the well.[462] Possibly, too, some such solar fancy may explain part of the myth of Perseus. There are three Scandinavian Norns, whose names are Urdhr, Verdhandi, and Skuld—Was, and Is, and Shall-be—and these three maidens are the 'Weird sisters' who fix the lifetime of all men. So the Fates, the Parkai, daughters of the inevitable Anágkē, divide among them the periods of time: Lachesis sings the past, Klôthô the present, Atropos the future. Now is it allowable to consider these fatal sisters as of common nature with two other mythic sister-triads—the Graiai and their kinsfolk the Gorgons?[463] If it be so, it is easy to understand why of the three Gorgons one alone was mortal, whose life her two immortal sisters could not save, for the deathless past and future cannot save the ever-dying present. Nor would the riddle be hard to read, what is the one eye that the Graiai had between them, and passed from one to another?—the eye of day—the sun, that the past gives up to the present, and the present to the future.

Compared with the splendid Lord of Day, the pale Lady of Night takes, in myth as in nature, a lower and lesser place. Among the wide legendary group which associates together Sun and Moon, two striking examples are to be seen in the traditions by which half-civilized races of South America traced their rise from the condition of the savage tribes around them. These legends have been appealed to even by modern writers as gratefully remembered records of real human benefactors, who carried long ago to America the culture of the Old World. But happily for historic truth, mythic tradition tells its tales without expurgating the episodes which betray its real character to more critical observation. The Muyscas of the high plains of Bogota were once, they said, savages without agriculture, religion, or law; but there came to them from the East an old and bearded man, Bochica, the child of the Sun, and he taught them to till the fields, to clothe themselves, to worship the gods, to become a nation. But Bochica had a wicked, beautiful wife, Huythaca, who loved to spite and spoil her husband's work; and she it was who made the river swell till the land was covered by a flood, and but a few of mankind escaped to the mountain-tops. Then Bochica was wroth, and he drove the wicked Huythaca from the earth, and made her the Moon, for there had been no moon before; and he cleft the rocks and made the mighty cataract of Tequendama, to let the deluge flow away. Then, when the land was dry, he gave to the remnant of mankind the year and its periodic sacrifices, and the worship of the Sun. Now the people who told this myth had not forgotten, what indeed we might guess without their help, that Bochica was himself Zuhé, the Sun, and Huythaca the Sun's wife, the Moon.[464]

Like to this in meaning, though different in fancy, is the civilization-myth of the Incas. Men, said this Quichua legend, were savages dwelling in caves like wild beasts devouring wild roots and fruit and human flesh, covering themselves with leaves and bark or skins of animals. But our father the Sun took pity on them, and sent two of his children, Manco Ccapac and his sister-wife, Mama Occllo these rose from the lake of Titicaca, and gave to the uncultured hordes law and government, marriage and moral order, tillage and art and science. Thus was founded the great Peruvian empire, where in after ages each Inca and his sister-wife, continuing the mighty race of Manco Ccapac and Mama Occllo, represented in rule and religion not only the first earthly royal ancestors, but the heavenly father and mother of whom we can see these to be personifications, namely, the Sun himself, and his sister-wife the Moon.[465] Thus the nations of Bogota and Peru, remembering their days of former savagery, and the association of their culture with their national religion, embodied their traditions in myths of an often-recurring type, ascribing to the gods themselves, in human shape, the establishment of their own worship.

The 'inconstant moon' figures in a group of characteristic stories. Australian legend says that Mityan, the Moon, was a native cat, who fell in love with some one else's wife, and was driven away to wander ever since.[466] The Khasias of the Himalaya say that the Moon falls monthly in love with his mother-in-law, who throws ashes in his face, whence his spots.[467] Slavonic legend, following the same track, says that the Moon, King of Night and husband of the Sun, faithlessly loved the Morning Star, wherefore he was cloven through in punishment, as we see him in the sky.[468] By a different train of thought, the Moon's periodic death and revival has suggested a painful contrast to the destiny of man, in one of the most often-repeated and characteristic myths of South Africa, which is thus told among the Namaqua. The Moon once sent the Hare to Men to give this message, 'Like as I die and rise to life again, so you also shall die and rise to life again,' but the Hare went to the Men and said, 'Like as I die and do not rise again, so you shall also die and not rise to life again.' Then the Hare returned and told the Moon what he had done, and the Moon struck at him with a hatchet and slit his lip, as it has remained ever since, and some say the Hare fled and is still fleeing, but others say he clawed at the Moon's face and left the scars that are still to be seen on it, and they also say that the reason why the Namaqua object to eating the hare (a prejudice which in fact they share with very different races) is because he brought to men this evil message.[469] It is remarkable that a story so closely resembling this, that it is difficult not to suppose both to be versions from a common original, is told in the distant Fiji Islands. There was a dispute between two gods as to how man should die: 'Ra Vula (the Moon) contended that man should be like himself—disappear awhile and then live again. Ra Kalavo (the Rat) would not listen to this kind proposal, but said, "Let man die as a rat dies." And he prevailed.' The dates of the versions seem to show that the presence of these myths among the Hottentots and Fijians, at the two opposite sides of the globe, is at any rate not due to transmission in modern times.[470]

There is a very elaborate savage nature-myth of the generation of the Stars, which may unquestionably serve as a clue connecting the history of two distant tribes. The rude Mintira of the Malayan Peninsula express in plain terms the belief in a solid firmament, usual in the lower grades of civilization; they say the sky is a great pot held over the earth by a cord, and if this cord broke, everything on earth would be crushed. The Moon is a woman, and the Sun also: the Stars are the Moon's children, and the Sun had in old times as many. Fearing, however, that mankind could not bear so much brightness and heat, they agreed each to devour her children; but the Moon, instead of eating up her stars, hid them from the Sun's sight, who believing them all devoured, ate up her own; no sooner had she done it, than the Moon brought her family out of their hiding-place. When the Sun saw them, filled with rage she chased the Moon to kill her; the chase has lasted ever since, and sometimes the Sun even comes near enough to bite the Moon, and that is an eclipse; the Sun, as men may still see, devours his Stars at dawn, and the Moon hides hers all day while the Sun is near, and only brings them out at night when her pursuer is far away. Now among a tribe of North East India, the Ho of Chota-Nagpore, the myth reappears, obviously from the same source, but with a varied ending; the Sun cleft the Moon in twain for her deceit, and thus cloven and growing whole again she remains, and her daughters with her which are the Stars.[471]

From savagery up to civilization, there may be traced in the mythology of the Stars a course of thought, changed indeed in application, yet never broken in its evident connexion from first to last. The savage sees individual stars as animate beings, or combines star-groups into living celestial creatures, or limbs of them, or objects connected with them; while at the other extremity of the scale of civilization, the modern astronomer keeps up just such ancient fancies, turning them to account in useful survival, as a means of mapping out the celestial globe. The savage names and stories of stars and constellations may seem at first but childish and purposeless fancies; but it always happens in the study of the lower races, that the more means we have of understanding their thoughts, the more sense and reason do we find in them. The aborigines of Australia say that Yurree and Wanjel, who are the stars we call Castor and Pollux, pursue Purra the Kangaroo (our Capella), and kill him at the the beginning of the great heat and the mirage is the smoke of the fire they roast him by. They say also that Marpean-Kurrk and Neilloan (Arcturus and Lyra) were the discoverers of the ant-pupas and the eggs of the loan-bird, and taught the aborigines to find them for food. Translated into the language of fact, these simple myths record the summer place of the stars in question, and the seasons of ant-pupas and loan-eggs, which seasons are marked by the stars who are called their discoverers.[472] Not less transparent is the meaning in the beautiful Algonquin myth of the Summer-maker. In old days eternal winter reigned upon the earth, till a sprightly little animal called the Fisher, helped by other beasts his friends, broke an opening through the sky into the lovely heaven-land beyond, let the warm winds pour forth and the summer descend to earth, and opened the cages of the prisoned birds: but when the dwellers in heaven saw their birds let loose and their warm gales descending, they started in pursuit, and shooting their arrows at the Fisher, hit him at last in his one vulnerable spot at the tip of his tail; thus he died for the good of the inhabitants of earth, and became the constellation that bears his name, so that still at the proper season men see him lying as he fell toward the north on the plains of heaven, with the fatal arrow still sticking in his tail.[473] Compare these savage stories with Orion pursuing the Pleiad sisters who take refuge from him in the sea, and the maidens who wept themselves to death and became the starry cluster of the Hyades, whose rising and setting betokened rain: such mythic creatures might for simple significance have been invented by savages, even as the savage constellation-myths might have been made by ancient Greeks. When we consider that the Australians who can invent such myths, and invent them with such fulness of meaning, are savages who put two and one together to make their numeral for three, we may judge how deep in the history of culture those conceptions lie, of which the relics are still represented in our star-maps by Castor and Pollux, Arcturus and Sirius, Boötes and Orion, the Argo and the Charles's Wain, the Toucan and the Southern Cross. Whether civilized or savage, whether ancient or new made after the ancient manner, such names are so like in character that any tribe of men might adopt them from any other, as American tribes are known to receive European names into their own skies, and as our constellation of the Royal Oak is said to have found its way, in new copies of the old Hindu treatises, into the company of the Seven Sages and the other ancient constellations of Brahmanic India.

Such fancies are so fanciful, that two peoples seldom fall on the same name for a constellation, while, even within the limits of the same race, terms may differ altogether. Thus the stars which we call Orion's Belt are in New Zealand either the Elbow of Maui, or they form the stem of the Canoe of Tamarerete, whose anchor dropped from the prow is the Southern Cross.[474] The Great Bear is equally like a Wain, Orion's Belt serves as well for Frigga's or Mary's Spindle, or Jacob's Staff. Yet sometimes natural correspondences occur. The seven sister Pleiades seem to the Australians a group of girls playing to a corroboree; while the North American Indians call them the Dancers; and the Lapps the Company of Virgins.[475] Still more striking is the correspondence between savages and cultured nations in fancies of the bright starry band that lies like a road across the sky. The Basutos call it the 'Way of the Gods;' the Ojis say it is the 'Way of Spirits,' which souls go up to heaven by.[476] North American tribes know it as 'the Path of the Master of Life,' the 'Path of Spirits,' 'the Road of Souls,' where they travel to the land beyond the grave, and where their camp-fires may be seen blazing as brighter stars.[477] Such savage imaginations of the Milky Way fit with the Lithuanian myth of the 'Road of the Birds,' at whose end the souls of the good, fancied as flitting away at death like birds, dwell free and happy.[478] That souls dwell in the Galaxy was a thought familiar to the Pythagoreans, who gave it on their master's word that the souls that crowd there descend, and appear to men as dreams,[479] and to the Manichæans whose fancy transferred pure souls to this 'column of light,' whence they could come down to earth and again return.[480] It is a fall from such ideas of the Galaxy to the Siamese 'Road of the White Elephant,' the Spaniards' 'Road of Santiago,' or the Turkish 'Pilgrims' Road,' and a still lower fall to the 'Straw Road' of the Syrian, the Persian, and the Turk, who thus compare it with their lanes littered with the morsels of straw that fall from the nets they carry it in.[481] But of all the fancies which have attached themselves to the celestial road, we at home have the quaintest. Passing along the short and crooked way from St. Paul's to Cannon Street, one thinks to how small a remnant has shrunk the name of the great street of the Wætlingas, which in old days ran from Dover through London into Wales. But there is a Watling Street in heaven as well as on earth, once familiar to Englishmen, though now almost forgotten even in local dialect. Chaucer thus speaks of it in his 'House of Fame:' —

'Lo there (quod he) cast up thine eye

Se yondir, lo, the Galaxie,

The whiche men clepe The Milky Way,

For it is white, and some parfay,

Ycallin it han Watlynge strete.'[482]

Turning from the mythology of the heavenly bodies, a glance over other districts of nature-myth will afford fresh evidence that such legend has its early home within the precincts of savage culture. It is thus with the myths of the Winds. The New Zealanders tell how Maui can ride upon the other Winds or imprison them in their caves, but he cannot catch the West wind nor find its cave to roll a stone against the mouth, and therefore it prevails, yet from time to time he all but overtakes it, and hiding in its cave for shelter it dies away.[483] Such is the fancy in classic poetry of Aeolus holding the prisoned winds in his dungeon cave:—

'Hic vasto rex Aeolus antro

Luctantes ventos, tempestatesque sonoras

Imperio premit, ac vinclis et carcere fraenat.'[484]

The myth of the Four Winds is developed among the native races of America with a range and vigour and beauty scarcely rivalled elsewhere in the mythology of the world. Episodes belonging to this branch of Red Indian folklore are collected in Schoolcraft's 'Algic Researches,' and thence rendered with admirable taste and sympathy, though unfortunately not with proper truth to the originals, in Longfellow's masterpiece, the 'Song of Hiawatha.' The West Wind Mudjekeewis is Kabeyun, Father of the Winds, Wabun is the East Wind, Shawondasee the South Wind, Kabibonokka the North Wind. But there is another mighty wind not belonging to the mystic quaternion, Manabozho the North-West Wind, therefore described with mythic appropriateness as the unlawful child of Kabeyun. The fierce North Wind, Kabibnokka, in vain strives to force Shingebis, the lingering diver-bird, from his warm and happy winter-lodge; and the lazy South Wind, Shawondasee, sighs for the maiden of the prairie with her sunny hair, till it turns to silvery white, and as he breathes upon her, the prairie dandelion has vanished.[485] Man naturally divides his horizon into four quarters, before and behind, right and left, and thus comes to fancy the world a square, and to refer the winds to its four corners. Dr. Brinton, in his 'Myths of the New World,' has well traced from these ideas the growth of legend after legend among the native races of America, where four brother heroes, or mythic ancestors or divine patrons of mankind, prove, on closer view, to be in personal shape the Four Winds.[486]

The Vedic hymns to the Maruts, the Storm Winds, who tear asunder the forest kings and make the rocks shiver, and assume again, after their wont, the form of new-born babes, the mythic feats of the child Hermes in the Homeric hymn, the legendary birth of Boreas from Astraios and Eôs, Starry Heaven and Dawn, work out, on Aryan ground, mythic conceptions that Red Indian tale-tellers could understand and rival.[487] The peasant who keeps up in fireside talk the memory of the Wild Huntsman, Wodejäger, the Grand Veneur of Fontainebleau, Herne the Hunter of Windsor Forest, has almost lost the significance of this grand old storm-myth. By mere force of tradition, the name of the 'Wish' or 'Wush' hounds of the Wild Huntsman has been preserved through the west of England; the words must for ages past have lost their meaning among the country folk, though we may plainly recognize in them Woden's ancient well-known name, old German 'Wunsch.' As of old, the Heaven-God drives the clouds before him in raging tempest across the sky, while, safe within the cottage walls, the taleteller unwittingly describes in personal legendary shape this same Wild Hunt of the Storm.[488]

It has many a time occurred to the savage poet or philosopher to realize the thunder, or its cause, in myths of a Thunder-bird. Of this wondrous creature North American legend has much to tell. He is the bird of the great Manitu, as the eagle is of Zeus, or he is even the great Manitu himself incarnate. The Assiniboins not only know of his existence, but have even seen him, and in the far north the story is told how he created the world. The Ahts of Vancouver's Island talk of Tootooch, the mighty bird dwelling aloft and far away, the flap of whose wings makes the thunder (Tootah), and his tongue is the forked lightning. There were once four of these birds in the land, and they fed on whales; but the great deity Quawteaht, entering into a whale, enticed one thunder-bird after another to swoop down and seize him with his talons, when plunging to the bottom of the sea he drowned it. Thus three of them perished, but the last one spread his wings and flew to the distant height where he has since remained. The meaning of the story may probably be that thunderstorms come especially from one of the four quarters of heaven. Of such myths, perhaps that told among the Dacotas is the quaintest: Thunder is a large bird, they say: hence its velocity. The old bird begins the thunder; its rumbling noise is caused by an immense quantity of young birds, or thunders, who continue it, hence the long duration of the peals. The Indian says it is the young birds, or thunders, that do the mischief; they are like the young mischievous men who will not listen to good counsel. The old thunder or bird is wise and good, and does not kill anybody, nor do any kind of mischief. Descending southward to Central America, there is found mention of the bird Voc, the messenger of Hurakan, the Tempest-god (whose name has been adopted in European languages as *huracano*, *ouragan*, *hurricane*) of the Lightning and of the Thunder. So among Caribs, Brazilians, Hervey Islanders and Karens, Bechuanas and Basutos, we find legends of a flapping or flashing Thunderbird, which seem simply to translate into myth the thought of thunder and lightning descending from the upper regions of the air, the home of the eagle and the vulture.[489]

The Heaven-god dwells in the regions of the sky, and thus what form could be fitter for him and for his messengers than the likeness of a bird? But to cause the ground to quake beneath our feet, a being of quite different nature is needed, and accordingly the office of supporting the solid earth is given in various countries to various monstrous creatures, human or animal in character, who make their office manifest from time to time by a shake given in negligence or sport or anger to their burden. Wherever earthquakes are felt, we are likely to find a version of the great myth of the Earth-bearer. Thus in Polynesia the Tongans say that Maui upholds the earth on his prostrate body, and when he tries to turn over into an easier posture there is an earthquake, and the people shout and beat the ground with sticks to make him lie still. Another version forms part of the interesting myth lately mentioned, which connects the under-world whither the sun descends at night, with the region of subterranean volcanic fire and of earthquake. The old Maui lay by his fire in the dead-land of Bulotu, when his grandson Maui came down by the cavern entrance; the young Maui carried off the fire, they wrestled, the old Maui was overcome, and has lain there bruised and drowsy ever since, underneath the earth, which quakes when he turns over in his sleep.[490] In Celebes we hear of the world-supporting Hog, who rubs himself against a tree, and then there is an earthquake.[491] Among the Indians of North America, it is said that earthquakes come of the movement of the great world-bearing Tortoise. Now this Tortoise seems but a mythic picture of the Earth itself, and thus the story only expresses in mythic phrase the very fact that the earth quakes; the meaning is but one degree less distinct than among the Caribs, who say when there is an earthquake that their Mother Earth is dancing.[492] Among the higher races of the continent, such ideas remain little changed in nature; the Tlascalans said that the tired world-supporting deities shifting their burden to a new relay caused the earthquake;[493] the Chibchas said it was their god Chibchacum moving the earth from shoulder to shoulder.[494] The myth ranges in Asia through as wide a stretch of culture. The Kamchadals tell of Tuil the Earthquake-god, who sledges below ground, and when his dog shakes off fleas or snow there is an earthquake;[495] Ta Ywa, the solar hero of the Karens, set Shie-oo beneath the earth to carry it, and there is an earthquake when he moves.[496] The world-bearing elephants of the Hindus, the world-supporting frog of the Mongol Lamas, the world-bull of the Moslems, the gigantic Omophore of the Manichæan cosmology, are all creatures who carry the earth on their backs or heads, and shake it when they stretch or shift.[497] Thus in European mythology the Scandinavian Loki, strapped down with thongs of iron in his subterranean cavern, writhes when the overhanging serpent drops venom on him; or Prometheus struggles beneath the earth to break his bonds; or the Lettish Drebkuls or Poseidon the Earth-shaker makes the ground rock beneath men's feet.[498] From thorough myths of imagination such as most of these, it may be sometimes possible to distinguish philosophic myths like them in form, but which appear to be attempts at serious explanation without even a metaphor. The Japanese think that earthquakes are caused by huge whales creeping underground, having been probably led to this idea by finding the fossil bones which seem the remains of such subterranean monsters, just as we know that the Siberians who find in the ground the mammoth-bones and tusks account for them as belonging to huge burrowing beasts, and by force of this belief, have brought themselves to think they can sometimes see the earth heave and sink as the monsters crawl below. Thus, in investigating the earthquake myths of the world, it appears that two processes, the translation into mythic language of the phenomenon itself, and the crude scientific theory to account for it by a real moving animal underground, may result in legends of very striking similarity.[499]

In thus surveying the mythic wonders of heaven and earth, sun, moon, and stars, wind, thunder, and earthquake, it is possible to set out in investigation under conditions of actual certainty. So long as such beings as Heaven or Sun are consciously talked of in mythic language, the meaning of their legends is open to no question, and the actions ascribed to them will as a rule be natural and apposite. But when the phenomena of nature take a more anthropomorphic form, and become identified with personal gods and heroes, and when in after times these beings, losing their first consciousness of origin, become centres round which floating fancies cluster, then their sense becomes obscure and corrupt, and the consistency of their earlier character must no longer be demanded. In fact, the unreasonable expectation of such consistency in nature-myths, after they have passed into what may be called their heroic stage, is one of the mythologist's most damaging errors. The present examination of nature-myths has mostly taken them in their primitive and unmistakable condition, and has only been in some degree extended to include closely-corresponding legends in a less easily interpretable state. It has lain beyond my scope to enter into any systematic discussion of the views of Grimm, Grote, Max Müller, Kuhn, Schirren, Cox, Bréal, Dasent, Kelly, and other mythologists. Even the outlines here sketched out have been purposely left without filling in surrounding detail which might confuse their shape, although this strictness has caused the neglect of many a tempting hint to work out episode after episode, by tracing their relation to the myths of far-off times and lands. It has rather been my object to bring prominently into view the nature-mythology of the lower races, that their clear and fresh mythic conceptions may serve as a basis in studying the nature-myths of the world at large. The evidence and interpretation here brought forward, imperfect as they are, seem to countenance a strong opinion as to the historical development of legends which describe in personal shape the life of nature. The state of mind to which such imaginative fictions belong is found in full vigour in the savage condition of mankind, its growth and inheritance continue into the higher culture of barbarous or half-civilized nations, and at last in the civilized world its effects pass more and more from realized belief into fanciful, affected, and even artificial poetry.

CHAPTER X.
MYTHOLOGY (*continued*).

> Philosophical Myths: inferences become pseudo-history—Geological Myths—Effect of doctrine of Miracles on Mythology—Magnetic Mountain—Myths of relation of Apes to Men by development or degeneration—Ethnological import of myths of Ape-men, Men with tails, Men of the woods—Myths of Error, Perversion, and Exaggeration: stories of Giants, Dwarfs, and Monstrous Tribes of men—Fanciful explanatory Myths—Myths attached to legendary or historical Personages—Etymological Myths on names of places and persons—Eponymic Myths on names of tribes, nations, countries, &c.; their ethnological import—Pragmatic Myths by realization of metaphors and ideas—Allegory—Beast-Fable—Conclusion.

Although the attempt to reduce to rule and system the whole domain of mythology would as yet be rash and premature, yet the piecemeal invasion of one mythic province after another proves feasible and profitable. Having discussed the theory of nature-myths, it is worth while to gain in other directions glimpses of the crude and child-like thought of mankind, not arranged in abstract doctrines, but embodied by mythic fancy. We shall find the result in masses of legends, full of interest as bearing on the early history of opinion, and which may be roughly classified under the following headings: myths philosophical or explanatory; myths based on real descriptions misunderstood, exaggerated, or perverted; myths attributing inferred events to legendary or historical personages; myths based on realization of fanciful metaphor; and myths made or adapted to convey moral or social or political instruction.

Man's craving to know the causes at work in each event he witnesses, the reasons why each state of things he surveys is such as it is and no other, is no product of high civilization, but a characteristic of his race down to its lowest stages. Among rude savages it is already an intellectual appetite whose satisfaction claims many of the moments not engrossed by war or sport, food or sleep. Even to the Botocudo or Australian, scientific speculation has its germ in actual experience: he has learnt to do definite acts that definite results may follow, to see other acts done and their results following in course, to make inference from the result back to the previous action, and to find his inference verified in fact. When one day he has seen a deer or a kangaroo leave footprints in the soft ground, and the next day he has found new footprints and inferred that such an animal made them, and has followed up the track and killed the game, then he knows that he has reconstructed a history of past events by inference from their results. But in the early stages of knowledge the confusion is extreme between actual tradition of events, and ideal reconstruction of them. To this day there go about the world endless stories told as matter of known reality, but which a critical examination shows to be mere inferences, often utterly illusory ones, from facts which have stimulated the invention of some curious enquirer. Thus a writer in the Asiatick Researches at the end of the 18th century relates the following account of the Andaman islanders, as a historical fact of which he had been informed: 'Shortly after the Portuguese had discovered the passage to India round the Cape of Good Hope, one of their ships, on board of which were a number of Mozambique negroes, was lost on the Andaman islands, which were till then uninhabited. The blacks remained in the island and settled it: the Europeans made a small shallop in which they sailed to Pegu.' Many readers must have had their interest excited by this curious story, but at the first touch of fact it dissolves into a philosophic myth, made by the easy transition from what might have been to what was. So far from the islands having been uninhabited at the time of Vasco de Gama's voyage, their population of naked blacks with frizzled hair had been described six hundred years earlier, and the story, which sounded reasonable to people puzzled by the appearance of a black population in the Andaman islands, is of course repudiated by ethnologists aware of the wide distribution of the negroid Papuans, really so distinct from any race of African negroes.[500] Not long since, I met with a very perfect myth of this kind. In a brickfield near London, there had been found a number of fossil elephant bones, and soon afterwards a story was in circulation in the neighbourhood somewhat in this shape: 'A few years ago, one of Wombwell's caravans was here, an elephant died, and they buried him in the field, and now the scientific gentlemen have found his bones, and think they have got a præ-Adamite elephant.' It seemed almost cruel to spoil this ingenious myth by pointing out that such a prize as a living mammoth was beyond the resources even of Wombwell's menagerie. But so exactly does such a story explain the facts to minds not troubled with nice distinctions between existing and extinct species of elephants, that it was on another occasion invented elsewhere under similar circumstances. This was at Oxford, where Mr. Buckland found the story of the Wombwell's caravan and dead elephant current to explain a similar find of fossil bones.[501] Such explanations of the finding of fossils are easily devised and used to be freely made, as when fossil bones found in the Alps were set down to Hannibal's elephants, or when a petrified oyster-shell found near Mont Cenis set Voltaire reflecting on the crowd of pilgrims on their way to Rome, or when theologians supposed such shells on mountains to have been left on their slopes and summits by a rising deluge. Such theoretical explanations are unimpeachable in their philosophic spirit, until further observation may prove them to be unsound. Their disastrous effect on the historic conscience of mankind only begins when the inference is turned upside down, to be told as a recorded fact.

In this connexion brief notice may be taken of the doctrine of miracles in its special bearing on mythology. The mythic wonder-episodes related by a savage tale-teller, the amazing superhuman feats of his gods and heroes, are often to his mind miracles in the original popular sense of the word, that is, they are strange and marvellous events; but they are not to his mind miracles in a frequent modern sense of the word, that is, they are not violations or supersessions of recognized laws of nature. Exceptio probat regulam; to acknowledge anything as an exception is to imply the rule it departs from; but the savage recognizes neither rule nor exception. Yet a European hearer, brought up to use a different canon of evidence, will calmly reject this savage's most revered ancestral traditions, simply on the ground that they relate events which are impossible. The ordinary standards of possibility, as applied to the credibility of tradition, have indeed changed vastly in the course of culture through its savage, barbaric, and civilized stages. What concerns us here is that there is an important department of legend which this change in public opinion, generally so resistless, left to a great extent unaltered. In the middle ages the long-accepted practice rose to its height, of allowing the mere assertion of supernatural influence by angels or devils, saints or sorcerers, to override the rules of evidence and the results of experience. The consequence was that the doctrine of miracles became as it were a bridge along which mythology travelled from the lower into the higher culture. Principles of myth-formation belonging properly to the mental state of the savage, were by its aid continued in strong action in the civilized world. Mythic episodes which Europeans would have rejected contemptuously if told of savage deities or heroes, only required to be adapted to appropriate local details, and to be set forth as miracles in the life of some superhuman personage, to obtain as of old a place of credit and honour in history.

From the enormous mass of available instances in proof of this let us take two cases belonging to the class of geological myths. The first is the well-known legend of St. Patrick and the serpents. It is thus given by Dr. Andrew Boorde in his description of Ireland and the Irish in Henry VIII.'s time. 'Yet in Ierland is stupendyous thynges; for there is neyther Pyes nor venymus wormes. There is no Adder, nor Snake, nor Toode, nor Lyzerd, nor no Euyt, nor none such lyke. I haue sene stones the whiche haue had the forme and shap of a snake and other venimus wormes. And the people of the countre sayth that suche stones were wormes, and they were turned into stones by the power of God and the prayers of saynt Patryk. And Englysh marchauntes of England do fetch of the erth of Irlonde to caste in their gardens, to kepe out and to kyll venimus wormes.'[502] In treating this passage, the first step is to separate pieces of imported foreign myth, belonging properly not to Ireland, but to islands of the Mediterranean; the story of the earth of the island of Krete being fatal to venomous serpents is to be found in Ælian,[503] and St. Honoratus clearing the snakes from his island (one of the Lerins opposite Cannes)[504] seems to take precedence of the Irish saint. What is left after these deductions is a philosophic myth accounting for the existence of fossil ammonites as being petrified snakes, to which myth a historical position is given by claiming it as a miracle, and ascribing it to St. Patrick. The second myth is valuable for the historical and geological evidence which it incidentally preserves. At the celebrated ruins of the temple of Jupiter Serapis at Pozzuoli, the ancient Puteoli, the marble columns, encircled half-way up by borings of lithodomi, stand to prove that the ground of the temple must have been formerly submerged many feet below the sea, and afterwards upheaved to become again dry land. History is remarkably silent as to the events demonstrated by this conclusive geological evidence; between the recorded adornment of the temple by Roman emperors from the second to the third century, and the mention of its existence in ruins in the 16th century, no documentary information was till lately recognized. It has now been pointed out by Mr. Tuckett that a passage in the Apocryphal Acts of Peter and Paul, dating apparently more or less before the end of the 9th century, mentions the subsidence of the temple, ascribing it to a miracle of St. Paul. The legend is as follows: 'And when he (Paul) came out of Messina he sailed to Didymus, and remained there one night. And having sailed thence, he came to Pontiole (Puteoli) on the second day. And Dioscorus the shipmaster, who brought him to Syracuse, sympathizing with Paul because he had delivered his son from death, having left his own ship in Syracuse, accompanied him to Pontiole. And some of Peter's disciples having been found there, and having received Paul, exhorted him to stay with them. And he stayed a week in hiding, because of the command of Cæsar (that he should be put to death). And all the toparchs were waiting to seize and kill him. But Dioscorus the shipmaster, being himself also bald, wearing his shipmaster's dress, and speaking boldly, on the first day went out into the city of Pontiole. Thinking therefore that he was Paul, they seized him and beheaded him, and sent his head to Cæsar.... And Paul, being in Pontiole, and having heard that Dioscorus had been beheaded, being grieved with great grief, gazing into the height of the heaven, said: "O Lord Almighty in Heaven, who hast appeared to me in every place whither I have gone on account of Thine only-begotten Word, our Lord Jesus Christ, punish this city, and bring out all who have believed in God and followed His word." He said to them, therefore, "Follow me." And going forth from Pontiole with those who had believed in the word of God, they came to a place called Baias (Baiæ), and looking up with their eyes, they all see that city called Pontiole sunk into the sea-shore about one fathom; and there it is until this day, for a remembrance, under the sea.... And those who had been saved out of the city of Pontiole, that had been swallowed up, reported to Cæsar in Rome that Pontiole had been swallowed up with all its multitude.'[505]

Episodes of popular myth, which are often items of the serious belief of the times they belong to, may serve as important records of intellectual history. As an example belonging to the class of philosophical or explanatory myths, let us glance at an Arabian Nights' story, which at first sight may seem an effort of the wildest imagination, but which is nevertheless traceable to a scientific origin; this is the story of the Magnetic Mountain. The Third Kalenter relates in his tale how a contrary wind drove his ships into a strange sea, and there, by the attraction of their nails and other ironwork, they were violently drawn towards a mountain of black loadstone, till at last the iron flew out to the mountain, and the ships went to pieces in the surf. The episode is older than the date when the 'Thousand and One Nights' were edited. When, in Henry of Veldeck's 12th century poem, Duke Ernest and his companions sail into the Klebermeer, they see the rock that is called Magnes, and are themselves dragged in below it among 'many a work of keels,' whose masts stand like a forest.[506] Turning from tale-tellers to grave geographers and travellers who talk of the loadstone mountain, we find El Kazwini, like Serapion before him, believing such boats as may be still seen in Ceylon, pegged and sewn without metal nails, to be so built lest the magnetic rock should attract them from their course at sea. This quaint notion is to be found in 'Sir John Mandeville': 'In an isle clept Crues, ben schippes with-outen nayles of iren, or bonds, for the rockes of the adamandes; for they ben alle fulle there aboute in that see, that it is marveyle to spaken of. And gif a schipp passed by the marches, and hadde either iren bandes or iren nayles, anon he sholde ben perishet. For the adamande of this kinde draws the iren to him; and so wolde it draw to him the schipp, because of the iren; that he sholde never departen fro it, ne never go thens.'[507] Now it seems that accounts of the magnetic mountain have been given not only as belonging to the southern seas, but also to the north, and that men have connected with such notions the pointing of the magnetic needle, as Sir Thomas Browne says, 'ascribing thereto the cause of the needle's direction, and conceeving the effluxions from these mountains and rocks invite the lilly toward the north.'[508] On this evidence we have, I think, fair ground for supposing that hypotheses of polar magnetic mountains were first devised to explain the action of the compass, and that these gave rise to stories of such mountains exerting what would be considered their proper effect on the iron of passing ships.

The argument is clenched by the consideration that Europeans, who colloquially say the needle points to the north, naturally required their loadstone mountain in high northern latitudes while on the other hand it was as natural that Orientals should place this wondrous rock in the south, for they say it is to the south that the needle points. The conception of magnetism among peoples who had not reached the idea of double polarity may be gathered from the following quaint remarks in the 17th century cyclopædia of the Chinese emperor Kang-hi. 'I now hear the Europeans say it is towards the North pole that the compass turns; the ancients said it was toward the South; which have judged most rightly? Since neither give any reason why, we come to no more with the one side than with the other. But the ancients are the earlier in date, and the farther I go the more I perceive that they understood the mechanism of nature. All movement languishes and dies in proportion as it approaches the north; it is hard to believe it to be from thence that the movement of the magnetic needle comes.'[509]

To suppose that theories of a relation between man and the lower mammalia are only a product of advanced science, would be an extreme mistake. Even at low levels of culture, men addicted to speculative philosophy have been led to account for the resemblance between apes and themselves by solutions satisfactory to their own minds, but which we must class as philosophic myths. Among these, stories which embody the thought of an upward change from ape to man, more or less approaching the last-century theory of development, are to be found side by side with others which in the converse way account for apes as degenerate from a previous human state.

Central American mythology works out the idea that monkeys were once a human race.[510] In South-East Africa, Father Dos Santos remarked long since that 'they hold that the apes were anciently men and women, and thus they call them in their tongue the first people.' The Zulus still tell the tale of an Amafeme tribe who became baboons. They were an idle race who did not like to dig, but wished to eat at other people's houses, saying, 'We shall live, although we do not dig, if we eat the food of those who cultivate the soil.' So the chief of that place, of the house of Tusi, assembled the tribe, and they prepared food and went out into the wilderness. They fastened on behind them the handles of their now useless digging picks, these grew and became tails, hair made its appearance on their bodies, their foreheads became overhanging, and so they became baboons, who are still called 'Tusi's men.'[511] Mr. Kingsley's story of the great and famous nation of the Doasyoulikes, who degenerated by natural selection into gorillas, is the civilized counterpart of this savage myth. Or monkeys may be transformed aborigines, as the Mbocobis relate in South America: in the great conflagration of their forests a man and woman climbed a tree for refuge from the fiery deluge, but the flames singed their faces and they became apes.[512] Among more civilized nations these fancies have graphic representatives in Moslem legends, of which one is as follows:—There was a Jewish city which stood by a river full of fish, but the cunning creatures, noticing the habits of the citizens, ventured freely in sight on the Sabbath, though they carefully kept away on working-days. At last the temptation was too strong for the Jewish fishermen, but they paid dearly for a few days' fine sport by being miraculously turned into apes as a punishment for Sabbath-breaking. In after times, when Solomon passed through the Valley of Apes, between Jerusalem and Mareb, he received from their descendants, monkeys living in houses and dressed like men, an account of their strange history.[513] So, in classic times, Jove had chastised the treacherous race of the Cercopes; he took from them the use of tongues born but to perjure, leaving them to bewail in hoarse cries their fate, transformed into the hairy apes of the Pithecusæ, like and yet unlike the men they had been:—

'In deforme viros animal mutavit, ut idem

Dissimiles homini possent similesque videri.'[514]

Turning from degeneration to development, it is found that legends of the descent of human tribes from apes are especially applied to races despised as low and beast-like by some higher neighbouring people, and the low race may even acknowledge the humiliating explanation. Thus the aboriginal features of the robber-caste of the Marawars of South India are the justification for their alleged descent from Rama's monkeys, as for the like genealogy of the Kathkuri, or catechu-gatherers, which these small, dark, low-browed, curly-haired tribes actually themselves believe in. The Jaitwas of Rajputana, a tribe reckoned politically as Rajputs, nevertheless trace their descent from the monkey-god Hanuman, and confirm it by alleging that their princes still bear its evidence in a tail-like prolongation of the spine; a tradition which has probably a real ethnological meaning, pointing out the Jaitwas as of non-Aryan race.[515] Wild tribes of the Malay peninsula, looked down on as lower animals by the more warlike and civilized Malays, have among them traditions of their own descent from a pair of the 'unka puteh,' or 'white monkeys,' who reared their young ones and sent them into the plains, and there they perfected so well that they and their descendants became men, but those who returned to the mountains still remained apes.[516] Thus Buddhist legend relates the origin of the flat-nosed, uncouth tribes of Tibet, offspring of two miraculous apes, transformed to people the snow-kingdom. Taught to till the ground, when they had grown corn and eaten it their tails and hair gradually disappeared, they began to speak, became men, and clothed themselves with leaves. The population grew closer, the land was more and more cultivated, and at last a prince of the race of Sakya, driven from his home in India, united their isolated tribes into a single kingdom.[517] In these traditions the development from ape to man is considered to have come in successive generations, but the negroes are said to attain the result in the individual, by way of metempsychosis. Froebel speaks of negro slaves in the United States believing that in the next world they shall be white men and free, nor is there anything strange in their cherishing a hope so prevalent among their kindred in West Africa. But from this the traveller goes on to quote another story, which, if not too good to be true, is a theory of upward and downward development, almost thorough enough for a Buddhist philosopher. He says, 'A German whom I met here told me that the blacks believe the damned among the negroes to become monkeys; but if in this state they behave well, they are advanced to the state of a negro again, and bliss is eventually possible to them, consisting in their turning white, becoming winged, and so on.'[518]

To understand these stories (and they are worth some attention for the ethnological hints they contain), it is necessary that we should discard the results of modern scientific zoology, and bring our minds back to a ruder condition of knowledge. The myths of human degeneration and development have much more in common with the speculations of Lord Monboddo than with the anatomical arguments of Professor Huxley. On the one hand, uncivilized men deliberately assign to apes an amount of human quality which to modern naturalists is simply ridiculous. Everyone has heard the story of the negroes declaring that apes really can speak, but judiciously hold their tongues lest they should be made to work; but it is not so generally known that this is found as serious matter of belief in several distant regions—West Africa, Madagascar, South America, &c.—where monkeys or apes are found.[519] With this goes another widely-spread anthropoid story, which relates how great apes like the gorilla and the orang-utan carry off women to their homes in the woods, much as the Apaches and Comanches of our own time carry off to their prairies the women of North Mexico.[520] And on the other hand, popular opinion has under-estimated the man as much as it has over-estimated the monkey. We know how sailors and emigrants can look on savages as senseless, ape-like brutes, and how some writers on anthropology have contrived to make out of the moderate intellectual difference between an Englishman and a negro something equivalent to the immense interval between a negro and a gorilla. Thus we can have no difficulty in understanding how savages may seem mere apes to the eyes of men who hunt them like wild beasts in the forests, who can only hear in their language a sort of irrational gurgling and barking, and who fail totally to appreciate the real culture which better acquaintance always shows among the rudest tribes of man. It is well known that when Sanskrit legend tells of the apes who fought in the army of King Hanuman, it really refers to those aborigines of the land who were driven by the Aryan invaders to the hills and jungles, and whose descendants are known to us as Bhils, Kols, Sonthals, and the like, rude tribes such as the Hindu still speaks of as 'monkey-people.'[521] One of the most perfect identifications of the savage and the monkey in Hindustan is the following description of the *bunmanus*, or 'man of the woods' (Sanskr. *vana* = wood, *manusha* = man). 'The *bunmanus* is an animal of the monkey kind. His face has a near resemblance to the human; he has no tail, and walks erect. The skin of his body is black, and slightly covered with hair.' That this description really applies not to apes, but to the dark-skinned, non-Aryan aborigines of the land, appears further in the enumeration of the local dialects of Hindustan, to which, it is said, 'may be added the jargon of the bunmanus, or wild men of the woods.'[522] In the islands of the Indian Archipelago, whose tropical forests swarm both with high apes and low savages, the confusion between the two in the minds of the half-civilized inhabitants becomes almost inextricable. There is a well-known Hindu fable in the Hitopadesa, which relates as a warning to stupid imitators the fate of the ape who imitated the carpenter, and was caught in the cleft when he pulled out the wedge; this fable has come to be told in Sumatra as a real story of one of the indigenous savages of the island.[523] It is to rude forest-men that the Malays habitually give the name of *orang-utan*, i.e., 'man of the woods.' But in Borneo this term is applied to the miyas ape, whence we have learnt to call this creature the orang-utan, and the Malays themselves are known to give the name in one and the same district to both the savage and the ape.[524] This term 'man of the woods' extends far beyond Hindu and Malay limits. The Siamese talk of the *khon pa*, 'men of the wood,' meaning apes;[525] the Brazilians of *cauiari*, or 'wood-men,' meaning a certain savage tribe.[526] The name of the *Bosjesman*, so amusingly mispronounced by Englishmen, as though it were some outlandish native word, is merely the Dutch equivalent for *Bush-man*, 'man of the woods or bush.'[527] In our own language the 'homo *silvaticus*' or 'forest-man' has become the '*salvage* man' or *savage*. European opinion of the native tribes of the New World may be judged of by the fact that, in 1537, Pope Paul III. had to make express statement that these Indians were really men (attendentes Indos ipsos utpote veros homines).[528] Thus there is little cause to wonder at the circulation of stories of ape-men in South America, and at there being some indefiniteness in the local accounts of the *selvage* or 'savage,' that hairy wild man of the woods who, it is said, lives in the trees, and sometimes carries off the native women.[529] The most perfect of these mystifications is to be found in a Portuguese manuscript quoted in the account of Castelnau's expedition, and giving, in all seriousness, the following account of the people called *Cuatas*: 'This populous nation dwells east of the Juruena, in the neighbourhood of the rivers San Joâo and San Thome, advancing even to the confluence of the Juruena, and the Arinos. It is a very remarkable fact that the Indians composing it walk naturally like the quadrupeds, with their hands on the ground; they have the belly, breast, arms, and legs covered with hair, and are of small stature; they are fierce, and use their teeth as weapons; they sleep on the ground, or among the branches of trees; they have no industry, nor agriculture, and live only on fruits, wild roots, and fish.'[530] The writer of this record shows no symptom of being aware that *cuata* or *coata* is the name of the large black Simia Paniscus, and that he has been really describing, not a tribe of Indians, but a species of apes.

Various reasons may have led to the growth of another quaint group of legends, describing human tribes with tails like beasts. To people who at once believe monkeys a kind of savages, and savages a kind of monkeys, men with tails are creatures coming under both definitions. Thus the Homo caudatus, or satyr, often appears in popular belief as a half-human creature, while even in old-fashioned works on natural history he may be found depicted on the evident model of an anthropoid ape. In East Africa, the imagined tribe of long-tailed men are also monkey-faced,[531] while in South America the *coata tapuya*, or 'monkey-men,' are as naturally described as men with tails.[532] European travellers have tried to rationalize the stories of tailed men which they meet with in Africa and the East. Thus Dr. Krapf points to a leather appendage worn behind from the girdle by the Wakamba, and remarks, 'It is no wonder that people say there are men with tails in the interior of Africa,' and other writers have called attention to hanging mats or waist-cloths, fly-flappers or artificial tails worn for ornament, as having made their wearers liable to be mistaken at a distance for tailed men.[533] But these apparently silly myths have often a real ethnological significance, deeper at any rate than such a trivial blunder. When an ethnologist meets in any district with the story of tailed men, he ought to look for a despised tribe of aborigines, outcasts, or heretics, living near or among a dominant population, who look upon them as beasts, and furnish them with tails accordingly. Although the aboriginal Miau-tsze, or 'children of the soil,' come down from time to time into Canton to trade, the Chinese still firmly believe them to have short tails like monkeys;[534] the half-civilized Malays describe the ruder forest tribes as tailed men;[535] the Moslem nations of Africa tell the same story of the Niam-Nam of the interior.[536] The outcast race of Cagots, about the Pyrenees, were said to be born with tails; and in Spain the mediæval superstition still survives that the Jews have tails, like the devil, as they say.[537] In England the notion was turned to theological profit by being claimed as a judgment on wretches who insulted St. Augustine and St. Thomas of Canterbury. Horne Tooke quotes thus from that zealous and somewhat foul-mouthed reformer, Bishop Bale: 'Johan Capgrave and Alexander of Esseby sayth, that for castynge of fyshe tayles at thys Augustyne, Dorsett Shyre menne hadde tayles ever after. But Polydorus applieth it unto Kentish men at Stroud by Rochester, for cuttinge of Thomas Becket's horse's tail. Thus hath England in all other land a perpetuall infamy of tayles by theyr wrytten legendes of lyes, yet can they not well tell where to bestowe them truely ... an Englyshman now cannot travayle in an other land, by way of marchandyse or any other honest occupyinge, but it is most contumeliously thrown in his tethe, that al Englishmen have tailes.'[538] The story at last sank into a commonplace of local slander between shire and shire, and the Devonshire belief that Cornishmen had tails lingered at least till a few years ago.[539] Not less curious is the tradition among savage tribes, that the tailed state was an early or original condition of man. In the Fiji Islands there is a legend of a tribe of men with tails like dogs, who perished in the great deluge, while the Tasmanians declared that men originally had tails and no knee-joints. Among the natives of Brazil, it is related by a Portuguese writer of about 1600, after a couple have been married, the father or father-in-law cuts a wooden stick with a sharp flint, imagining that by this ceremony he cuts off the tails of any future grandchildren, so that they will be born tailless.[540] There seems no evidence to connect the occasional occurrence of tail-like projections by malformation with the stories of tailed human tribes.[541]

Anthropology, until modern times, classified among its facts the particulars of monstrous human tribes, gigantic or dwarfish, mouthless or headless, one-eyed or one-legged, and so forth. The works of ancient geographers and naturalists abound in descriptions of these strange creatures; writers such as Isidore of Seville and Roger Bacon collected them, and sent them into fresh and wider circulation in the middle ages, and the popular belief of uncivilized nations retains them still. It was not till the real world had been so thoroughly explored as to leave little room in it for the monsters, that about the beginning of the present century science banished them to the ideal world of mythology. Having had to glance here at two of the principal species in this amazing semi-human menagerie, it may be worth while to look among the rest for more hints as to the sources of mythic fancy.[542]

That some of the myths of giants and dwarfs are connected with traditions of real indigenous or hostile tribes is settled beyond question by the evidence brought forward by Grimm, Nilsson, and Hanusch. With all the difficulty of analyzing the mixed nature of the dwarfs of European folklore, and judging how far they are elves, or gnomes, or such like nature-spirits, and how far human beings in mythic aspect, it is impossible not to recognize the element derived from the kindly or mischievous aborigines of the land, with their special language, and religion, and costume. The giants appear in European folklore as Stone-Age heathen, shy of the conquering tribes of men, loathing their agriculture and the sound of their church-bells. The rude native's fear of the more civilized intruder in his land is well depicted in the tale of the giant's daughter, who found the boor ploughing his field and carried him home in her apron for a plaything—plough, and oxen, and all; but her mother bade her carry them back to where she found them, for, said she, they are of a people that can do the Huns much ill. The fact of the giant tribes bearing such historic names as Hun or Chud is significant, and Slavonic men have, perhaps, not yet forgotten that the dwarfs talked of in their legends were descended from the aborigines whom the Old-Prussians found in the land. Beyond a doubt the old Scandinavians are describing the ancient and ill-used Lapp population, once so widely spread over Northern Europe, when their sagas tell of the dwarfs, stunted and ugly, dressed in reindeer kirtle and coloured cap, cunning and cowardly, shy of intercourse even with friendly Norsemen, dwelling in caves or in the mound-like Lapland 'gamm,' armed only with arrows tipped with stone and bone, yet feared and hated by their conquerors for their fancied powers of witchcraft.[543] Moslem legend relates that the race of Gog and Magog (Yajuj and Majuj) are of tiny stature, but with ears like elephants; they are a numerous people, and ravaged the world; they dwell in the East, separated from Persia by a high mountain, with but one pass; and the nations their neighbours, when they heard of Alexander the Great (Dhû 'l-Karnain) traversing the world, paid tribute to him, and he made them a wall of bronze and iron, to keep in the nation of Gog and Magog.[544] Who can fail to recognize in this a mystified description of the Tatars of High Asia? Professor Nilsson tries to account in a general way for the huge or tiny stature of legendary tribes, as being mere exaggeration of their actual largeness or smallness. We must admit that this sometimes really happens. The accounts which European eye-witnesses brought home of the colossal stature of the Patagonians, to whose waists they declared their own heads reached, are enough to settle once for all the fact that myths of giants may arise from the sight of really tall men,[545] and it is so, too, with the dwarf-legends of the same region, as where Knivet, the old traveller, remarks of the little people of Rio de la Plata, that they are 'not so very little as described.'[546]

Nevertheless, this same group of giant and dwarf myths may serve as a warning not to stretch too widely a partial explanation, however sound within its proper limits. There is plenty of evidence that giant-legends are sometimes philosophic myths, made to account for the finding of great fossil bones. To give but a single instance of such connexion, certain huge jaws and teeth, found in excavating on the Hoe at Plymouth, were recognized as belonging to the giant Gogmagog, who in old times fought his last fight there against Corineus, the eponymic hero of Cornwall.[547] As to the dwarfs, again, stories of them are curiously associated with those long-enduring monuments of departed races—their burial-cysts and dolmens. Thus, in the United States, ranges of rude stone cysts, often only two or three feet long, are connected with the idea of a pygmy race buried in them. In Brittany, the dolmens are the abodes and treasuries of the dwarfs who built them, and likewise in India it is a usual legend of such prehistoric burial-places, that they were dwarfs' houses—the dwellings of the ancient pygmies, who here again appear as representatives of prehistoric tribes.[548] But a very different meaning is obvious in a mediæval traveller's account of the hairy, man-like creatures of Cathay, one cubit high, and that do not bend their knees as they walk, or in an Arab geographer's description of an island people in the Indian seas, four spans high, naked, with red downy hair on their faces, and who climb up trees and shun mankind. If any one could possibly doubt the real nature of these dwarfs, his doubt may be resolved by Marco Polo's statement that in his time monkeys were regularly embalmed in the East Indies, and sold in boxes to be exhibited over the world as pygmies.[549] Thus various different facts have given rise to stories of giants and dwarfs, more than one mythic element perhaps combining to form a single legend—a result perplexing in the extreme to the mythological interpreter.

Descriptions of strange tribes made in entire good faith may come to be understood in new extravagant senses, when carried among people not aware of the original facts. The following are some interpretations of this kind, among which some far-fetched cases are given, to show that the method must not be trusted too much. The term 'nose-less' is apt to be misunderstood, yet it was fairly enough applied to flat-nosed tribes, such as Turks of the steppes, whom Rabbi Benjamin of Tudela thus depicts in the twelfth century:—'They have no noses, but draw breath through two small holes.'[550] Again, among the common ornamental mutilations of savages is that of stretching the ears to an enormous size by weights or coils, and it is thus verbally quite true that there are men whose ears hang down upon their shoulders. Yet without explanation such a phrase would be understood to describe, not the appearance of a real savage with his ear-lobes stretched into pendant fleshy loops, but rather that of Pliny's *Panotii*, or of the Indian *Karnaprâvarana*, 'whose ears serve them for cloaks,' or of the African dwarfs, said to use their ears one for mattress and the other for coverlet when they lie down. One of the most extravagant of these stories is told by Fray Pedro Simon in California, where in fact the territory of *Oregon* has its name from the Spanish term of *Orejones*, or 'Big-Ears,' given to the inhabitants from their practice of stretching their ears with ornaments.[551] Even purely metaphorical descriptions, if taken in a literal sense, are capable of turning into catches, like the story of the horse with its head where its tail should be. I have been told by a French Protestant from the Nismes district that the epithet of *gorgeo negro*, or 'black-throat,' by which

Catholics describe a Huguenot, was taken so literally that heretic children were sometimes forced to open their mouths to satisfy the orthodox of their being of the usual colour within. On examining the description of savage tribes by higher races, it appears that several of the epithets usually applied only need literalizing to turn into the wildest of the legendary monster-stories. Thus the Burmese speak of the rude Karens as 'dog-men;'[552] Marco Polo describes the Angaman (Andaman) islanders as brutish and savage cannibals, with heads like dogs.[553] Ælian's account of the dog-headed people of India is on the face of it an account of a savage race. The Kynokephali, he says, are so called from their bodily appearance, but otherwise they are human, and they go dressed in the skins of beasts; they are just, and harm not men; they cannot speak, but roar, yet they understand the language of the Indians; they live by hunting, being swift of foot, and they cook their game not by fire, but by tearing it into fragments and drying it in the sun; they keep goats and sheep, and drink the milk. The naturalist concludes by saying that he mentions these fitly among the irrational animals, because they have not articulate, distinct, and human language.[554] This last suggestive remark well states the old prevalent notion that barbarians have no real language, but are 'speechless,' 'tongueless,' or even mouthless.[555] Another monstrous people of wide celebrity are Pliny's Blemmyæ, said to be headless, and accordingly to have their mouths and eyes in their breasts creatures over whom Prester John reigned in Asia, who dwelt far and wide in South American forests, and who to our mediæval ancestors were as real as the cannibals with whom Othello couples them:—

'The Anthropophagi, and men whose heads

Do grow beneath their shoulders.'

If, however, we look in dictionaries for the *Acephali*, we may find not actual headless monsters, but heretics so called because their original head or founder was not known; and when the kingless Turkoman hordes say of themselves 'We are a people without a head,' the metaphor is even more plain and natural.[556] Moslem legend tells of the Shikk and the Nesnas, creatures like one half of a split man, with one arm, leg, and eye. Possibly it was thence that the Zulus got their idea of a tribe of half-men, who in one of their stories found a Zulu maiden in a cave and thought she was two people, but on closer inspection of her admitted, 'The thing is pretty! But oh the two legs!' These realistic fancies coincide with the simple metaphor which describes a savage as only 'half a man,' *semihomo*, as Virgil calls the ferocious Cacus.[557] Again, when the Chinese compared themselves to the outer barbarians, they said 'We see with two eyes, the Latins with one, and all other nations are blind.' Such metaphors, proverbial among ourselves, verbally correspond with legends of one-eyed tribes, such as the savage cave-dwelling Kyklopes.[558] Verbal coincidence of this kind, untrustworthy enough in these latter instances, passes at last into the vaguest fancy. The negroes called Europeans 'long-headed,' using the phrase in our familiar metaphorical sense; but translate it into Greek, and at once Hesiod's *Makrokephaloi* come into being.[559] And, to conclude the list, one of the commonest of the monster-tribes of the Old and New World is that distinguished by having feet turned backward. Now there is really a people whose name, memorable in scientific controversy, describes them as 'having feet the opposite way,' and they still retain that ancient name of *Antipodes*.[560]

Returning from this digression to the region of philosophic myth, we may examine new groups of explanatory stories, produced from that craving to know causes and reasons which ever besets mankind. When the attention of a man in the myth-making stage of intellect is drawn to any phenomenon or custom which has to him no obvious reason, he invents and tells a story to account for it, and even if he does not persuade himself that this is a real legend of his forefathers, the story-teller who hears it from him and repeats it is troubled with no such difficulty. Our task in dealing with such stories is made easy when the criterion of possibility can be brought to bear upon them. It has become a mere certainty to moderns that asbestos is not really salamander's wool; that morbid hunger is not really caused by a lizard or a bird in a man's stomach; that a Chinese philosopher cannot really have invented the fire-drill by seeing a bird peck at the branches of a tree till sparks came. The African Wakuafi account for their cattle-lifting proclivities by the calm assertion that Engai, that is, Heaven, gave all cattle to them, and so wherever there is any it is their call to go and seize it.[561] So in South America the fierce Mbayas declare they received from the Caracara a divine command to make war on all other tribes, killing the men and adopting the women and children.[562] But though it may be consistent with the notions of these savages to relate such explanatory legends, it is not consistent with our notions to believe them. Fortunately, too, the ex post facto legends are apt to come into collision with more authentic sources of information, or to encroach on the domain of valid history. It is of no use for the Chinese to tell their stupid story of written characters having been invented from the markings on a tortoise's shell, for the early forms of such characters, plain and simple pictures of objects, have been preserved in China to this day. Nor can we praise anything but ingenuity in the West Highland legend that the Pope once laid an interdict on the land, but forgot to curse the hills, so the people tilled them, this story being told to account for those ancient traces of tillage still to be seen on the wild hill-sides, the so-called 'elf-furrows.'[563] The most embarrassing cases of explanatory tradition are those which are neither impossible enough to condemn, nor probable enough to receive. Ethnographers who know how world-wide is the practice of defacing the teeth among the lower races, and how it only dies gradually out in higher civilization, naturally ascribe the habit to some general reason in human nature, at a particular stage of development. But the mutilating tribes themselves have local legends to account for local customs; thus the Penongs of Burmah and the Batoka of East Africa both break their front teeth, but the one tribe says its reason is not to look like apes, the other that it is to be like oxen and not like zebras.[564] Of the legends of tattooing, one of the oldest is that told to account for the fact that while the Fijians tattoo only the women, their neighbours, the Tongans, tattoo only the men. It is related that a Tongan, on his way from Fiji to report to his countrymen the proper custom for them to observe, went on his way repeating the rule he had carefully learnt by heart, 'Tattoo the women, but not the men,' but unluckily he tripped over a stump, got his lesson wrong, and reached Tonga repeating 'Tattoo the men, but not the women,' an ordinance which they observed ever after. How reasonable such an explanation seemed to the Polynesian mind, may be judged from the Samoans having a version with different details, and applied to their own instead of the Tongan islands.[565]

All men feel how wanting in sense of reality is a story with no personal name to hang it to. This want is thus graphically expressed by Sprenger the historian in his life of Mohammed: 'It makes, on me at least, quite a different impression when it is related that "the Prophet said to Alkama," even if I knew nothing whatever else of this Alkama, than if it were merely stated that "he said to somebody."' The feeling which this acute and learned critic thus candidly confesses, has from the earliest times, and in the minds of men troubled with no such nice historic conscience, germinated to the production of much mythic fruit. Thus it has come to pass that one of the leading personages to be met with in the tradition of the world is really no more than—Somebody. There is nothing this wondrous creature cannot achieve, no shape he cannot put on; one only restriction binds him at all, that the name he assumes shall have some sort of congruity with the office he undertakes, and even from this he oftentimes breaks loose. So rife in our own day is this manufacture of personal history, often fitted up with details of place and date into the very semblance of real chronicle, that it may be guessed how vast its working must have been in days of old. Thus the ruins of ancient buildings, of whose real history and use no trustworthy tradition survives in local memory, have been easily furnished by myth with a builder and a purpose. In Mexico the great Somebody assumes the name of Montezuma, and builds the aqueduct of Tezcuco; to the Persian any huge and antique ruin is the work of the heroic Antar; in Russia, says Dr. Bastian, buildings of the most various ages are set down to Peter the Great, as in Spain to Boabdil or Charles V.; and European folklore may attribute to the Devil any old building of unusual massiveness, and especially those stone structures which antiquaries now class as præ-historic monuments. With a more graceful thought, the Indians of North America declare that the imitative tumuli of Ohio, great mounds laid out in rude imitation of animals, were shaped in old days by the great Manitu himself, in promise of a plentiful supply of game in the world of spirits. The New Zealanders tell how the hero Kupe separated the North and South Islands, and formed Cook's Straits. Greek myth placed at the gate of the Mediterranean the twin pillars of Herakles; in more recent times the opening of the Straits of Gibraltar became one of the many feats of Alexander of Macedon.[566] Such a group of stories as this is no unfair test of the value of mere traditions of personal names which simply answer the questions that mankind have been asking for ages about the origin of their rites, laws, customs, arts. Some such traditions are of course genuine, and we may be able, especially in the more modern cases, to separate the real from the imaginary. But it must be distinctly laid down that, in the absence of corroborative evidence, every tradition stands suspect of mythology, if it can be made by the simple device of fitting some personal name to the purely theoretical assertion that somebody must have introduced into the world fire-making, or weapons, or ornaments, or games, or agriculture, or marriage, or any other of the elements of civilization.

Among the various matters which have excited curiosity, and led to its satisfaction by explanatory myths, are local names. These, when the popular ear has lost their primitive significance, become in barbaric times an apt subject for the myth-maker to explain in his peculiar fashion. Thus the Tibetans declare that their lake *Chomoriri* was named from a woman (*chomo*) who was carried into it by the yak she was riding, and cried in terror *ri-ri!* The Arabs say the founders of the city of *Sennaar* saw on the river bank a beautiful woman with teeth glittering like fire, whence they called the place *Sinnâr*, i.e., 'tooth of fire.' The Arkadians derived the name of their town *Trapezus* from the table (*trapeza*), which Zeus overturned when the wolfish Lykaon served a child on it for a banquet to him.[567] Such crude fancies in no way differ in nature from English local legends current up to recent times, such as that which relates how the Romans, coming in sight of where *Exeter* now stands, exclaimed in delight, '*Ecce terra!*' and thus the city had its name. Not long ago, a curious enquirer wished to know from the inhabitants of *Fordingbridge*, or as the country people call it, *Fardenbridge*, what the origin of this name might be, and heard in reply that the bridge was thought to have been built when wages were so cheap that masons worked for a 'farden' a day. The Falmouth folks' story of Squire Pendarvis and his ale is well known, how his servant excused herself for selling it to the sailors, because, as she said, 'The *penny come* so *quick*,' whence the place came to be called *Pennycomequick*; this nonsense being invented to account for an ancient Cornish name, probably *Penycumgwic*, 'head of the creek valley.' Mythic fancy had fallen to a low estate when it dwindled to such remnants as this.

That personal names may pass into nouns, we, who talk of *broughams* and *bluchers*, cannot deny. But any such etymology ought to have contemporary document or some equally forcible proof in its favour, for this is a form of explanation taken by the most flagrant myths. David the painter, it is related, had a promising pupil named *Chicque*, the son of a fruiterer; the lad died at eighteen, but his master continued to hold him up to later students as a model of artistic cleverness, and hence arose the now familiar term of *chic*. Etymologists, a race not wanting in effrontery, have hardly ever surpassed this circumstantial canard; the word *chic* dates at anyrate from the seventeenth century.[568] Another word with which similar liberty has been taken, is *cant*. Steele, in the 'Spectator,' says that some people derive it from the name of one Andrew *Cant*, a Scotch minister, who had the gift of preaching in such a dialect that he was understood by none but his own congregation, and not by all of them. This is, perhaps, not a very accurate delineation of the real Andrew Cant, who is mentioned in 'Whitelock's Memorials,' and seems to have known how to speak out in very plain terms indeed. But at any rate he flourished about 1650, whereas the verb to *cant* was then already an old word. To *cante*, meaning to speak, is mentioned in Harman's 'List of Rogues' Words,' in 1566, and in 1587 Harrison says of the beggars and gypsies that they have devised a language among themselves, which they name *canting*, but others 'Pedlars' Frenche.'[569] Of all etymologies ascribed to personal names, one of the most curious is that of the Danse *Macabre*, or Dance of Death, so well known from Holbein's pictures. Its supposed author is thus mentioned in the 'Biographie Universelle:' 'Macaber, poëte allemand, serait tout-à-fait inconnu sans l'ouvrage qu'on a sous son nom.' This, it may be added, is true enough, for there never was such a person at all, the Danse *Macabre* being really Chorea *Machabæorum*, the Dance of the *Maccabees*, a kind of pious pantomime of death performed in churches in the fifteenth century. Why the performance received this name, is that the rite of Mass for the dead is distinguished by the reading of that passage from the twelfth chapter of Book II. of the *Maccabees*, which relates how the people betook themselves to prayer, and besought the Lord that the sin of those who had been slain among them might be wholly blotted out; for if Judas had not expected that the slain should rise again, it had been superfluous and vain to pray for the dead.[570] Traced to its origin, it is thus seen that the Danse *Macabre* is neither more nor less than the Dance of the Dead.

It is not an unusual thing for tribes and nations to be known by the name of their chief, as in books of African travel we read of 'Eyo's people,' or 'Kamrazi's people.' Such terms may become permanent, like the name of the *Osmanli* Turks taken from the great *Othman*, or *Osman*. The notions of kinship and chieftainship may easily be combined, as where some individual Brian or Alpine may have given his name to a clan of *O'Briens* or *Mac Alpines*. How far the tribal names of the lower races may have been derived from individual names of chiefs or forefathers, is a question on which distinct evidence is difficult to obtain. In Patagonia bands or subdivisions of tribes are designated by the names of temporary chiefs, every roving party having such a leader, who is sometimes even styled 'yank,' i.e. 'father.'[571] The Zulus and Maoris were races who paid great attention to the traditional genealogies of their clan-ancestors, who were, indeed, not only their kinsfolk but their gods; and they distinctly recognize the possibility of tribes being named from a deceased ancestor or chief. The Kafir tribe of *Ama-Xosa* derives its name from a chief, *U-Xosa*;[572] and the Maori tribes of *Ngate-Wakaue* and *Nga-Puhi* claim descent from chiefs called *Wakaue* and *Puhi*.[573] Around this nucleus of actuality, however, there gathers an enormous mass of fiction simulating its effects. The myth-maker, curious to know how many people or country gained its name, had only to conclude that it came from a great ancestor or ruler, and then the simple process of turning a national or local title into a personal name at once added a new genealogy to historical tradition. In some cases, the name of the imagined ancestor is invented in such form that the local or gentile name may stand as grammatically derived from it, as usually happens in real cases, like the derivation of *Cæsarea* from *Cæsar*, or of the *Benedictines* from *Benedict*. But in the fictitious genealogy or history of the myth-maker, the mere unaltered name of the nation, tribe, country, or city often becomes without more ado the name of the eponymic hero. It has to be remembered, moreover, that countries and nations can be personified by an imaginative process which has not quite lost its sense in modern speech. *France* is talked of by politicians as an individual being, with particular opinions and habits, and may even be embodied as a statue or picture with suitable attributes. And if one were to say that *Britannia* has two daughters, *Canada* and *Australia*, or that she has gone to keep house for a decrepit old aunt called *India*, this would be admitted as plain fact expressed in fantastic language. The invention of ancestries from eponymic heroes or name-ancestors has, however, often had a serious effect in corrupting historic truth, by helping to fill ancient annals with swarms of fictitious genealogies. Yet, when surveyed in a large view, the nature of the eponymic fictions is patent and indisputable, and so regular are their forms, that we could scarcely choose more telling examples of the consistent processes of imagination, as shown in the development of myths.

The great number of the eponymic ancestors of ancient Greek tribes and nations makes it easy to test them by comparison, and the test is a destructive one. Treat the heroic genealogies they belong to as traditions founded on real history, and they prove hopelessly independent and incompatible; but consider them as mostly local and tribal myths and such independence and incompatibility become their proper features. Mr. Grote, whose tendency is to treat all myths as fictions not only unexplained but unexplainable, here makes an exception, tracing the eponymic ancestors from whom Greek cities and tribes derived their legendary parentage to mere embodied local and gentile names. Thus, of the fifty sons of Lykaôn, a whole large group consists of personified cities of Arkadia, such as *Mantinêus, Phigalos, Tegeatês*, who, according to the simply inverting legend, are called founders of *Mantinêa, Phigalia, Tegea*. The father of King Æakos was Zeus, his mother his own personified land, *Ægina*; the city of *Mykênai* had not only an ancestress *Mykênê*, but an eponymic ancestor as well, *Mykêneus*. Long afterwards, mediæval Europe, stimulated by the splendid genealogies through which Rome had attached herself to Greece and the Greek gods and heroes, discovered the secret of rivalling them in the chronicles of Geoffry of Monmouth and others, by claiming as founders of *Paris* and *Tours* the Trojans *Paris* and *Turnus*, and connecting *France* and *Britain* with the Trojan war through *Francus*, son of Hector, and *Brutus*, great grandson of Æneas. A remarkably perfect eponymic historical myth accounting for the Gypsies or Egyptians, may be found cited seriously in 'Blackstone's Commentaries:' when Sultan Selim conquered Egypt in 1517, several of the natives refused to submit to the Turkish yoke, and revolted under one *Zinganeus*, whence the Turks called them *Zinganees*, but, being at length surrounded and banished, they agreed to disperse in small parties over the world, &c., &c. It is curious to watch Milton's mind emerging, but not wholly emerging, from the state of the mediæval chronicler. He mentions in the beginning of his 'History of Britain,' the 'outlandish figment' of the four kings, *Magus, Saron, Druis,* and *Bardus*; he has no approval for the giant *Albion*, son of Neptune, who subdued the island and called it after his own name; he scoffs at the four sons of Japhet, called *Francus, Romanus, Alemannus,* and *Britto*. But when he comes to *Brutus* and the Trojan legends of old English history, his sceptical courage fails him: 'those old and inborn names of successive kings, never any to have bin real persons, or don in their lives at least som part of what so long hath bin remember'd, cannot be thought without too strict an incredulity.'[574]

Among ruder races of the world, asserted genealogies of this class may be instanced in South American tribes called the *Amoipira* and *Potyuara*,[575] Khond clans called *Baska* and *Jakso*,[576] Turkoman hordes called *Yomut, Tekke,* and *Chaudor*,[577] all of them professing to derive their designations from ancestors or chiefs who bore as individuals these very names. Where criticism can be brought to bear on these genealogies, its effect is often such as drove Brutus and his Trojans out of English history. When there appear in the genealogy of Haussa, in West Africa, plain names of towns like *Kano* and *Katsena*,[578] it is natural to consider these towns to have been personified into mythic ancestors. Mexican tradition assigns a whole set of eponymic ancestors or chiefs to the various races of the land, as *Mexi* the founder of *Mexico*, *Chichimecatl* the first king of the *Chichimecs*, and so forth, down to *Otomitl* the ancestor of the *Otomis*, whose very name by its termination betrays its Aztec invention.[579] The Brazilians account for the division of the *Tupis* and *Guaranis*, by the legend of two ancestral brothers, *Tupi* and *Guarani*, who quarrelled and separated, each with his followers: here an eponymic origin of the story is made likely by the word *Guarani* not being an old national name at all, but merely the designation of 'warriors' given by the missionaries to certain tribes.[580] And when such facts are considered as that North American clans named after animals, *Beaver*, *Crayfish*, and the like, account for these names by simply claiming the very creatures themselves as ancestors,[581] the tendency of general criticism will probably be not so much in favour of real forefathers and chiefs who left their names to their tribes, as of eponymic ancestors created by backwards imitation of such inheritance.

The examination of eponymic legend, however, must by no means stop short at the destructive stage. In fact, when it has undergone the sharpest criticism, it only displays the more clearly a real historic value, not less perhaps than if all the names it records were real names of ancient chiefs. With all their fancies, blunders, and shortcomings, the heroic genealogies preserve early theories of nationality, traditions of migration, invasion, connexion by kindred or intercourse. The ethnologists of old days, borrowing the phraseology of myth, stated what they looked on as the actual relations of races, in a personifying language of which the meaning may still be readily interpreted. The Greek legend of the twin brothers *Danaos* and *Ægyptos*, founders of the nations of the *Danaoi* or Homeric Greeks and of the *Ægyptians*, represents a distinct though weak ethnological theory. Their eponymic myth of *Hellēn*, the personified race of the *Hellēnes*, is another and more reasonable ethnological document stating kinship among four great branches of the Greek race: the three sons of *Hellēn*, it relates, were *Aiolos*, *Dōros*, and *Xouthos*; the first two gave their names to the *Æolians* and *Dorians*, the third had sons called *Achaios* and *Iōn*, whose names passed as a heritage to the *Achaioi* and *Ionians*. The belief of the *Lydians*, *Mysians*, and *Karians* as to their national kinship is well expressed in the genealogy in Herodotus, which traces their descent from the three brothers *Lydos*, *Mysos*, and *Kar*.[582] The Persian legend of Feridun (Thraetaona) and his three sons, *Irej*, *Tur*, and *Selm*, distinguishes the two nationalities of *Iranian* and *Turanian*, i.e. Persian and Tatar.[583] The national genealogy of the Afghans is worthy of remark. It runs thus: Melik Talut (King Saul) had two sons, Berkia and Irmia (Berekiah and Jeremiah), who served David; the son of Berkia was *Afghan*, and the son of Irmia was *Usbek*. Thanks to the aquiline noses of the Afghans, and to their use of Biblical personal names derived from Biblical sources, the idea of their being descendants of the lost tribes of Israel found great credence among European scholars up to the present century.[584] Yet the pedigree is ethnologically absurd, for the whole source of the imagined cousinship of the Aryan *Afghan* and the Turanian *Usbek*, so distinct both in feature and in language, appears to be in their union by common Mohammedanism, while the reckless jumble of sham history, which derives both from a Semitic source, is only too characteristic of Moslem chronicle. Among the Tatars is found a much more reasonable national pedigree; in the 13th century, William of Ruysbroek relates, as sober circumstantial history, that they were originally called *Turks* from *Turk* the eldest son of Japhet, but one of their princes left his dominions to his twin sons, *Tatar* and *Mongol* which gave rise to the distinction that has ever since prevailed between these two nations.[585] Historically absurd, this legend states what appears the unimpeachable ethnological fact, that the *Turks*, *Mongols*, and *Tatars* are closely-connected branches of one national stock, and we can only dispute in it what seems an exorbitant claim on the part of the *Turk* to represent the head of the family, the ancestor of the *Mongol* and the *Tatar*. Thus these eponymic national genealogies, mythological in form but ethnological in substance, embody opinions of which we may admit or deny the truth or value, but which we must recognize as distinctly ethnological documents.[586]

It thus appears that early ethnology is habitually expressed in a metaphorical language, in which lands and nations are personified, and their relations indicated by terms of personal kinship. This description applies to that important document of ancient ethnology, the table of nations in the 10th chapter of Genesis. In some cases it is a problem of minute and difficult criticism to distinguish among its ancestral names those which are simply local or national designations in personal form. But to critics conversant with the ethnic genealogies of other peoples, such as have here been quoted, simple inspection of this national list may suffice to show that part of its names are not names of real men, but of personified cities, lands, and races. The city *Zidon* (צידן) is brother to Heth (חת) the father of the *Hittites*, and next follow in person the Jebusite and the Amorite. Among plain names of countries, *Cush* or Æthiopia (כוש) begets Nimrod, *Asshur* or *Assyria* (אשור) builds Nineveh, and even the dual *Mizraim* (מצרים), the 'two Egypts,' usually regarded as signifying Upper and Lower Egypt, appears in the line of generations as a personal son and brother of other countries, and ancestor of populations. The Aryan stock is clearly recognized in personifications of at least two of its members, *Madai* (מדי) the *Mede*, and *Javan* (יון) the *Ionian*. And as regards the family to which the Israelites themselves belong, if *Canaan* (כנען), the father of *Zidon* (צידן), be transferred to it to represent the Phœnicians, by the side of *Asshur* (אשור), *Aram* (ארם), *Eber* (עבר), and the other descendants of Shem, the result will be mainly to arrange the Semitic stock according to the ordinary classification of modern comparative philology.

Turning now from cases where mythologic phrase serves as a medium for expressing philosophic opinion, let us quickly cross the district where fancy assumes the semblance of explanatory legend. The mediæval schoolmen have been justly laughed at for their habit of translating plain facts into the terms of metaphysics, and then solemnly offering them in this scientific guise as explanations of themselves—accounting for opium making people sleep, by its possession of a dormitive virtue. The myth-maker's proceedings may in one respect be illustrated by comparing them with this. Half mythology is occupied, as many a legend cited in these chapters has shown, in shaping the familiar facts of daily life into imaginary histories of their own cause and origin, childlike answers to those world-old questions of whence and why, which the savage asks as readily as the sage. So familiar is the nature of such description in the dress of history, that its easier examples translate off-hand. When the Samoans say that ever since the great battle among the plantains and bananas, the vanquished have hung down their heads, while the victor stands proudly erect,[587] who can mistake the simple metaphor which compares the upright and the drooping plants to a conqueror standing among his beaten foes? In simile just as obvious lies the origin of another Polynesian legend, which relates the creation of the coco-nut from a man's head, the chestnuts from his kidneys, and the yams from his legs.[588] To draw one more example from the mythology of plants, how transparent is the Ojibwa fancy of that heavenly youth with green robe and waving feathers, whom for the good of men the Indian overcame and buried, and who sprang again from his grave as the Indian corn, Mondamin, the 'Spirit's grain.'[589] The New Forest peasant deems that the marl he digs is still red with the blood of his ancient foes the Danes; the Maori sees on the red cliffs of Cook's Straits the blood-stains that Kupe made when, mourning for the death of his daughter, he cut his forehead with pieces of obsidian; in the spot where Buddha offered his own body to feed the starved tigress's cubs, his blood for ever reddened the soil and the trees and flowers. The modern Albanian still sees the stain of slaughter in streams running red with earth, as to the ancient Greek the river that flowed by Byblos bore down in its summer floods the red blood of Adonis. The Cornishman knows from the red filmy growth on the brook pebbles that murder has been done there; John the Baptist's blood still grows in Germany on his day, and peasants still go out to search for it; the red meal fungus is blood dropped by the flying Huns when they hurt their feet against the high tower-roofs. The traveller in India might see on the ruined walls of Ganga Raja the traces of the blood of the citizens spilt in the siege, and yet more marvellous to relate, at St. Denis's church in Cornwall, the blood-stains on the stones fell there when the saint's head was cut off somewhere else.[590] Of such translations of descriptive metaphor under thin pretence of history, every collection of myth is crowded with examples, but it strengthens our judgment of the combined consistency and variety of what may be called the mythic language, to extract from its dictionary such a group as this, which in variously imaginative fashion describes the appearance of a blood-red stain.

The merest shadowy fancy or broken-down metaphor, when once it gains a sense of reality, may begin to be spoken of as an actual event. The Moslems have heard the very stones praise Allah, not in simile only but in fact, and among them the saying that a man's fate is written on his forehead has been materialized into a belief that it can be deciphered from the letter-like markings of the sutures of his skull. One of the miraculous passages in the life of Mohammed himself is traced plausibly by Sprenger to such a pragmatized metaphor. The angel Gabriel, legend declares, opened the prophet's breast, and took a black clot from his heart, which he washed with Zemzem water and replaced; details are given of the angel's dress and golden basin, and Anas ibn Malik declared he had seen the very mark where the wound was sewn up. We may venture with the historian to ascribe this marvellous incident to the familiar metaphor that Mohammed's heart was divinely opened and cleansed, and indeed he does say in the Koran that God opened his heart.[591] A single instance is enough to represent the same habit in Christian legend. Marco Polo relates how in 1225 the Khalif of Bagdad commanded the Christians of his dominions, under penalty of death or Islam, to justify their Scriptural text by removing a certain mountain. Now there was among them a shoemaker, who, having been tempted to excess of admiration for a woman, had plucked out his offending eye. This man commanded the mountain to remove, which it did to the terror of the Khalif and all his people, and since then the anniversary of the miracle has been kept holy. The Venetian traveller, after the manner of mediæval writers, records the story without a symptom of suspicion;[592] yet to our minds its whole origin so obviously lies in three verses of St. Matthew's gospel, that it is needless to quote them. To modern taste such wooden fictions as these are far from attractive. In fact the pragmatizer is a stupid creature; nothing is too beautiful or too sacred to be made dull and vulgar by his touch, for it is through the very incapacity of his mind to hold an abstract idea that he is forced to embody it in a material incident. Yet wearisome as he may be, it is none the less needful to understand him, to acknowledge the vast influence he has had on the belief of mankind, and to appreciate him as representing in its extreme abuse that tendency to clothe every thought in a concrete shape, which has in all ages been a mainspring of mythology.

Though allegory cannot maintain the large place often claimed for it in mythology, it has yet had too much influence to be passed over in this survey. It is true that the search for allegorical explanation is a pursuit that has led many a zealous explorer into the quagmires of mysticism. Yet there are cases in which allegory is certainly used with historical intent, as for instance in the apocryphal Book of Enoch, with its cows and sheep which stand for Israelites, and asses and wolves for Midianites and Egyptians, these creatures figuring in a pseudo-prophetic sketch of Old Testament chronicles. As for moral allegory, it is immensely plentiful in the world, although its limits are narrower than mythologists of past centuries have supposed. It is now reasonably thought preposterous to interpret the Greek legends as moral apologues, after the manner of Herakleides the philosopher, who could discern a parable of repentant prudence in Athene seizing Achilles when just about to draw his sword on Agamemnon.[593] Still, such a mode of interpretation has thus much to justify it, that numbers of the fanciful myths of the world are really allegories. There is allegory in the Hesiodic myth of Pandora, whom Zeus sent down to men, decked with golden band and garland of spring flowers, fit cause of longing and the pangs of love, but using with a dog-like mind her gifts of lies and treachery and pleasant speech. Heedless of his wiser brother's words, the foolish Epimetheus took her; she raised the lid of the great cask and shook out the evils that wander among mankind, and the diseases that by day and night come silently bringing ill; she set on the lid again and shut hope in, that evil might be ever hopeless to mankind. Shifted to fit a different moral, the allegory remained in the later version of the tale, that the cask held not curses but blessings; these were let go and lost to men when the vessel was too curiously opened, while Hope alone was left behind for comfort to the luckless human race.[594] Yet the primitive nature of such legends underlies the moral shape upon them. Zeus is no allegoric fiction, and Prometheus, unless modern mythologists judge him very wrongly, has a meaning far deeper than parable. Xenophon tells after Prodikos the story of Herakles choosing between the short and easy path of pleasure and the long and toilsome path of virtue,[595] but though the mythic hero may thus be made to figure in a moral apologue, an imagination so little in keeping with his unethic nature jars upon the reader's mind.

The general relation of allegory to pure myth can hardly be brought more clearly into view than in a class of stories familiar to every child, the Beast-fables. From the ordinary civilized point of view the allegory in such fictions seems fundamental, the notion of a moral lesson seems bound up with their very nature, yet a broader examination tends to prove the allegorical growth as it were parasitic on an older trunk of myth without moral. It is only by an effort of intellectual reaction that a modern writer can imitate in parable the beast of the old Beast-fable. No wonder, for the creature has become to his mind a monster, only conceivable as a caricature of man made to carry a moral lesson or a satire. But among savages it is not so. To their minds the semi-human beast is no fictitious creature, invented to preach or sneer, he is all but a reality. Beast-fables are not nonsense to men who ascribe to the lower animals a power of speech, and look on them as partaking of moral human nature; to men in whose eyes any hyæna or wolf may probably be a man-hyæna or a werewolf; to men who so utterly believe 'that the soul of our grandam might haply inhabit a bird' that they will really regulate their own diet so as to avoid eating an ancestor; to men an integral part of whose religion may actually be the worship of beasts. Such beliefs belong even now to half mankind, and among such the beast-stories had their first home. Even the Australians tell their quaint beast-tales, of the Rat, the Owl, and the fat Blackfellow, or of Pussy-brother who singed his friends' noses while they were asleep.[596] The Kamchadals have an elaborate myth of the adventures of their stupid deity Kutka with the Mice who played tricks upon him, such as painting his face like a woman's, so that when he looked in the water he fell in love with himself.[597] Beast-tales abound among such races as the Polynesians and the North American Indians, who value in them ingenuity of incident and neat adaptation of the habits and characters of the creatures. Thus in a legend of the Flathead Indians, the Little Wolf found in Cloudland his grandsires the Spiders with their grizzled hair and long crooked nails, and they spun balls of thread to let him down to earth; when he came down and found his wife the Speckled Duck, whom the Old Wolf had taken from him, she fled in confusion, and that is why she lives and dives alone to this very day.[598] In Guinea, where beast-fable is one of the great staples of native conversation, the following story is told as a type of the tales which in this way account for peculiarities of animals. The great Engena-monkey offered his daughter to be bride of the champion who should perform the feat of drinking a whole barrel of rum. The dignified Elephant, the graceful Leopard, the surly Boar, tried the first mouthful of the fire-water, and retreated. Then the tiny Telinga-monkey came, who had cunningly hidden in the long grass thousands of his fellows; he took his first glass and went away, but instead of his coming back, another just like him came for the second, and so on till the barrel was emptied and Telinga walked off with the Monkey-king's daughter. But in the narrow path the Elephant and Leopard attacked him and drove him off and he took refuge in the highest boughs of the trees, vowing never more to live on the ground and suffer such violence and injustice. This is why to this day the little telingas are only found in the highest tree-tops.[599] Such stories have been collected by scores from savage tradition in their original state, while as yet no moral lesson has entered into them. Yet the easy and natural transition from the story into the parable is made among savages, perhaps without help from higher races. In the Hottentot Tales, side by side with the myth of the cunning Jackal tricking the Lion out of the best of the carcase, and getting the black stripe burnt on his own back by carrying off the Sun, there occurs the moral apologue of the Lion who thought himself wiser than his Mother, and perished by the Hunter's spear, for want of heed to her warning against the deadly creature whose head is in a line with his breast and shoulders.[600] So the Zulus have a thorough moral apologue in the story of the hyrax, who did not go to fetch his tail on the day when tails were given out, because he did not like to be out in the rain; he only asked the other animals to bring it for him, and so he never got it.[601] Among the North American legends of Manabozho, there is a fable quite Æsopian in its humour. Manabozho, transformed into a Wolf, killed a fat moose, and being very hungry sat down to eat. But he fell into great doubts as to where to begin, for, said he, if I begin at the head, people will laugh and say, he ate him backwards, but if I begin at the side they will say, he ate him sideways. At last he made up his mind, and was just putting a delicate piece into his mouth, when a tree close by creaked. Stop, stop! said he to the tree, I cannot eat with such a noise, and in spite of his hunger he left the meat and climbed up to quiet the creaking, but was caught between two branches and held fast, and presently he saw a pack of wolves coming. Go that way! Go that way! he cried out, whereupon the wolves said, he must have something there, or he would not tell us to go another way. So they came on, and found the moose, and ate it to the bones while Manabozho looked wistfully on. The next heavy blast of wind opened the branches and let him out, and he went home thinking to himself, 'See the effect of meddling with frivolous things when I had certain good in my possession.'[602]

In the Old World, the moral Beast-fable was of no mean antiquity, but it did not at once supplant the animal-myths pure and simple. For ages the European mind was capable at once of receiving lessons of wisdom from the Æsopian crows and foxes, and of enjoying artistic but by no means edifying beast-stories of more primitive type. In fact the Babrius and Phædrus collections were over a thousand years old, when the genuine Beast-Epic reached its fullest growth in the incomparable 'Reynard the Fox,' traceable in Jakob Grimm's view to an original Frankish composition of the 12th century, itself containing materials of far earlier date.[603] Reynard is not a didactic poem, at least if a moral hangs on to it here and there it is oftenest a Macchiavellian one; nor is it essentially a satire, sharply as it lashes men in general and the clergy in particular. Its creatures are incarnate qualities, the Fox of cunning, the Bear of strength, the Ass of dull content, the Sheep of guilelessness. The charm of the narrative, which every class in mediæval Europe delighted in, but which we have allowed to drop out of all but scholars' knowledge, lies in great measure in he cleverly sustained combination of the beast's nature and the man's. How great the influence of the Reynard Epic was in the middle ages, may be judged from *Reynard, Bruin, Chanticleer*, being still names familiar to people who have no idea of their having been originally names of the characters in the great beast-fable. Even more remarkable are its traces in modern French. The donkey has its name of *baudet* from *Baudoin*, Baldwin the Ass. Common French dictionaries do not even contain the word *goupil* (*vulpes*), so effectually has the Latin name of the fox been driven out of use by his Frankish title in the Beast-Epic, *Raginhard* the Counsellor, *Reinhart, Reynard, Renart, renard*. The moralized apologues like Æsop's which Grimm contemptuously calls 'fables thinned down to mere moral and allegory,' 'a fourth watering of the old grapes into an insipid moral infusion,' are low in æsthetic quality as compared with the genuine beast-myths. Mythological critics will be apt to judge them after the manner of the child who said how convenient it was to have 'Moral' printed in Æsop's fables, that everybody might know what to skip.

The want of power of abstraction which has ever had such disastrous effect on the beliefs of mankind, confounding myth and chronicle, and crushing the spirit of history under the rubbish of literalized tradition, comes very clearly into view in the study of parable. The state of mind of the deaf, dumb, and blind Laura Bridgman, so instructive in illustrating the mental habits of uneducated though full-sensed men, displays in an extreme form the difficulty such men have in comprehending the unreality of any story. She could not be made to see that arithmetical problems were anything but statements of concrete fact, and when her teacher asked her, 'If you can buy a barrel of cider for four dollars, how much can you buy for one dollar?' she replied quite simply, 'I cannot give much for cider, because it is very sour.'[604] It is a surprising instance of this tendency to concretism, that among people so civilized as the Buddhists, the most obviously moral beast-fables have become literal incidents of sacred history. Gautama, during his 550 jatakas or births, took the form of a frog, a fish, a crow, an ape, and various other animals, and so far were the legends of these transformations from mere myth to his followers, that there have been preserved as relics in Buddhist temples the hair, feathers, and bones of the creatures whose bodies the great teacher inhabited. Now among the incidents which happened to Buddha during his series of animal births, he appeared as an actor in the familiar fable of the Fox and the Stork, and it was he who, when he was a Squirrel, set an example of parental virtue by trying to dry up the ocean with his tail, to save his young ones whose nest had drifted out to sea, till his persevering courage was rewarded by a miracle.[605] To our modern minds, a moral which seems the very purpose of a story is evidence unfavourable to its truth as fact. But if even apologues of talking birds and beasts have not been safe from literal belief, it is clear that the most evident moral can have been but slight protection to parables told of possible and life-like men. It was not a needless precaution to state explicitly of the New Testament parables that they were parables, and even this guard has not availed entirely. Mrs. Jameson relates some curious experience in the following passage:—'I know that I was not very young when I entertained no more doubt of the substantial existence of Lazarus and Dives than of John the Baptist and Herod; when the Good Samaritan was as real a personage as any of the Apostles; when I was full of sincerest pity for those poor foolish Virgins who had forgotten to trim their lamps, and thought them—in my secret soul—rather hardly treated. This impression of the literal actual truth of the parables I have since met with in many children, and in the uneducated but devout hearers and readers of the Bible; and I remember that when I once tried to explain to a good old woman the proper meaning of the word parable, and that the story of the Prodigal Son was not a fact, she was scandalized—she was quite sure that Jesus would never have told anything to his disciples that was not true. Thus she settled the matter in her own mind, and I thought it best to leave it there undisturbed.'[606] Nor, it may be added, has such realization been confined to the minds of the poor and ignorant. St. Lazarus, patron saint of lepers and their hospitals, and from whom the *lazzarone* and the *lazzaretto* take their name, obviously derives these qualities from the Lazarus of the parable.

The proof of the force and obstinacy of the mythic faculty, thus given by the relapse of parable into pseudo-history, may conclude this dissertation on mythology. In its course there have been examined the processes of animating and personifying nature, the formation of legend by exaggeration and perversion of fact, the stiffening of metaphor by mistaken realization of words, the conversion of speculative theories and still less substantial fictions into pretended traditional events, the passage of myth into miracle-legend, the definition by name and place given to any floating imagination, the adaptation of mythic incident as moral example, and the incessant crystallization of story into history. The investigation of these intricate and devious operations has brought ever more and more broadly into view two principles of mythologic science. The first is that legend, when classified on a sufficient scale, displays a regularity of development which the notion of motiveless fancy quite fails to account for, and which must be attributed to laws of formation whereby every story, old and new, has arisen from its definite origin and sufficient cause. So uniform indeed is such development, that it becomes possible to treat myth as an organic product of mankind at large, in which individual, national, and even racial distinctions stand subordinate to universal qualities of the human mind. The second principle concerns the relation of myth to history. It is true that the search for mutilated and mystified traditions of real events, which formed so main a part of old mythological researches, seems to grow more hopeless the farther the study of legend extends. Even the fragments of real chronicle found embedded in the mythic structure are mostly in so corrupt a state, that, far from their elucidating history, they need history to elucidate them. Yet unconsciously, and as it were in spite of themselves, the shapers and transmitters of poetic legend have preserved for us masses of sound historical evidence. They moulded into mythic lives of gods and heroes their own ancestral heirlooms of thought and word, they displayed in the structure of their legends the operations of their own minds, they placed on record the arts and manners, the philosophy and religion of their own times, times of which formal history has often lost the very memory. Myth is the history of its authors, not of its subjects; it records the lives, not of superhuman heroes, but of poetic nations.

CHAPTER XI.
ANIMISM.

Religious ideas generally appear among low races of Mankind—Negative statements on this subject frequently misleading and mistaken: many cases uncertain—Minimum definition of Religion—Doctrine of Spiritual Beings, here termed Animism—Animism treated as belonging to Natural Religion—Animism divided into two sections, the philosophy of Souls, and of other Spirits—Doctrine of Souls, its prevalence and definition among the lower races—Definition of Apparitional Soul or Ghost-Soul—It is a theoretical conception of primitive Philosophy, designed to account for phenomena now classed under Biology, especially Life and Death, Health and Disease, Sleep and Dreams, Trance and Visions—Relation of Soul in name and nature to Shadow, Blood, Breath—Division of Plurality of Souls—Soul cause of Life; its restoration to body when supposed absent—Exit of Soul in Trances—Dreams and Visions: theory of exit of dreamer's or seer's own soul; theory of visits received by them from other souls—Ghost-Soul seen in Apparitions—Wraiths and Doubles—Soul has form of body; suffers mutilation with it—Voice of Ghost—Soul treated and defined as of Material Substance; this appears to be the original doctrine—Transmission of Souls to service in future life by Funeral Sacrifice of wives, attendants, &c.—Souls of Animals—Their transmission by Funeral Sacrifice—Souls of Plants—Souls of Objects—Their transmission by Funeral Sacrifice—Relation of doctrine of Object-Souls to Epicurean theory of Ideas—Historical development of Doctrine of Souls, from the Ethereal Soul of primitive Biology to the Immaterial Soul of modern Theology.

Are there, or have there been, tribes of men so low in culture as to have no religious conceptions whatever? This is practically the question of the universality of religion, which for so many centuries has been affirmed and denied, with a confidence in striking contrast to the imperfect evidence on which both affirmation and denial have been based. Ethnographers, if looking to a theory of development to explain civilization, and regarding its successive stages as arising one from another, would receive with peculiar interest accounts of tribes devoid of all religion. Here, they would naturally say, are men who have no religion because their forefathers had none, men who represent a præ-religious condition of the human race, out of which in the course of time religious conditions have arisen. It does not, however, seem advisable to start from this ground in an investigation of religious development. Though the theoretical niche is ready and convenient, the actual statue to fill it is not forthcoming. The case is in some degree similar to that of the tribes asserted to exist without language or without the use of fire; nothing in the nature of things seems to forbid the possibility of such existence, but as a matter of fact the tribes are not found. Thus the assertion that rude non-religious tribes have been known in actual existence, though in theory possible, and perhaps in fact true, does not at present rest on that sufficient proof which, for an exceptional state of things, we are entitled to demand.

It is not unusual for the very writer who declares in general terms the absence of religious phenomena among some savage people, himself to give evidence that shows his expressions to be misleading. Thus Dr. Lang not only declares that the aborigines of Australia have no idea of a supreme divinity, creator, and judge, no object of worship, no idol, temple, or sacrifice, but that 'in short, they have nothing whatever of the character of religion, or of religious observance, to distinguish them from the beasts that perish.' More than one writer has since made use of this telling statement, but without referring to certain details which occur in the very same book. From these it appears that a disease like small-pox, which sometimes attacks the natives, is ascribed by them 'to the influence of Budyah, an evil spirit who delights in mischief;' that when the natives rob a wild bees' hive, they generally leave a little of the honey for Buddai; that at certain biennial gatherings of the Queensland tribes, young girls are slain in sacrifice to propitiate some evil divinity; and that, lastly, according to the evidence of the Rev. W. Ridley, 'whenever he has conversed with the aborigines, he found them to have definite traditions concerning supernatural beings— Baiame, whose voice they hear in thunder, and who made all things, Turramullum the chief of demons, who is the author of disease, mischief, and wisdom, and appears in the form of a serpent at their great assemblies, &c.'[607] By the concurring testimony of a crowd of observers, it is known that the natives of Australia were at their discovery, and have since remained, a race with minds saturated with the most vivid belief in souls, demons, and deities. In Africa, Mr. Moffat's declaration as to the Bechuanas is scarcely less surprising—that 'man's immortality was never heard of among that people,' he having remarked in the sentence next before, that the word for the shades or manes of the dead is 'liriti.'[608] In South America, again, Don Felix de Azara comments on the positive falsity of the ecclesiastics' assertion that the native tribes have a religion. He simply declares that they have none; nevertheless in the course of his work he mentions such facts as that the Payaguas bury arms and clothing with their dead and have some notions of a future life, and that the Guanas believe in a Being who rewards good and punishes evil. In fact, this author's reckless denial of religion and law to the lower races of this region justifies D'Orbigny's sharp criticism, that, 'this is indeed what he says of all the nations he describes, while actually proving the contrary of his thesis by the very facts he alleges in its support.'[609]

Such cases show how deceptive are judgments to which breadth and generality are given by the use of wide words in narrow senses. Lang, Moffat, and Azara are authors to whom ethnography owes much valuable knowledge of the tribes they visited, but they seem hardly to have recognized anything short of the organized and established theology of the higher races as being religion at all. They attribute irreligion to tribes whose doctrines are unlike theirs, in much the same manner as theologians have so often attributed atheism to those whose deities differed from their own, from the time when the ancient invading Aryans described the aboriginal tribes of India as *adeva*, i.e. 'godless,' and the Greeks fixed the corresponding term ἄθεοι on the early Christians as unbelievers in the classic gods, to the comparatively modern ages when disbelievers in witchcraft and apostolical succession were denounced as atheists; and down to our own day, when controversialists are apt to infer, as in past centuries, that naturalists who support a theory of development of species therefore necessarily hold atheistic opinions.[610] These are in fact but examples of a general perversion of judgment in theological matters, among the results of which is a popular misconception of the religions of the lower races, simply amazing to students who have reached a higher point of view. Some missionaries, no doubt, thoroughly understand the minds of the savages they have to deal with, and indeed it is from men like Cranz, Dobrizhoffer, Charlevoix, Ellis, Hardy, Callaway, J. L. Wilson, T. Williams, that we have obtained our best knowledge of the lower phases of religious belief. But for the most part the 'religious world' is so occupied in hating and despising the beliefs of the heathen whose vast regions of the globe are painted black on the missionary maps, that they have little time or capacity left to understand them. It cannot be so with those who fairly seek to comprehend the nature and meaning of the lower phases of religion. These, while fully alive to the absurdities believed and the horrors perpetrated in its name, will yet regard with kindly interest all record of men's earnest seeking after truth with such light as they could find. Such students will look for meaning, however crude and childish, at the root of doctrines often most dark to the believers who accept them most zealously; they will search for the reasonable thought which once gave life to observances now become in seeming or reality the most abject and superstitious folly. The reward of these enquirers will be a more rational comprehension of the faiths in whose midst they dwell, for no more can he who understands but one religion understand even that religion, than the man who knows but one language can understand that language. No religion of mankind lies in utter isolation from the rest, and the thoughts and principles of modern Christianity are attached to intellectual clues which run back through far præ-Christian ages to the very origin of human civilization, perhaps even of human existence.

While observers who have had fair opportunities of studying the religion of savages have thus sometimes done scant justice to the facts before their eyes, the hasty denials of others who have judged without even facts can carry no great weight. A 16th-century traveller gave an account of the natives of Florida which is typical of such: 'Touching the religion of this people, which wee have found, for want of their language wee could not understand neither by signs nor gesture that they had any religion or lawe at all.... We suppose that they have no religion at all, and that they live at their own libertie.'[611] Better knowledge of these Floridans nevertheless showed that they had a religion, and better knowledge has reversed many another hasty assertion to the same effect; as when writers used to declare that the natives of Madagascar had no idea of a future state, and no word for soul or spirit;[612] or when Dampier enquired after the religion of the natives of Timor, and was told that they had none;[613] or when Sir Thomas Roe landed in Saldanha Bay on his way to the court of the Great Mogul, and remarked of the Hottentots that 'they have left off their custom of stealing, but know no God or religion.'[614] Among the numerous accounts collected by Lord Avebury as evidence bearing on the absence or low development of religion among low races,[615] some may be selected as lying open to criticism from this point of view. Thus the statement that the Samoan Islanders had no religion cannot stand, in face of the elaborate description by the Rev. G. Turner of the Samoan religion itself; and the assertion that the Tupinambas of Brazil had no religion is one not to be received on merely negative evidence, for the religious doctrines and practices of the Tupi race have been recorded by Lery, De Laet, and other writers. Even with much time and care and knowledge of language, it is not always easy to elicit from savages the details of their theology. They try to hide from the prying and contemptuous foreigner their worship of gods who seem to shrink, like their worshippers, before the white man and his mightier Deity. Mr. Sproat's experience in Vancouver's Island is an apt example of this state of things. He says: 'I was two years among the Ahts, with my mind constantly directed towards the subject of their religious beliefs, before I could discover that they possessed any ideas as to an overruling power or a future state of existence. The traders on the coast, and other persons well acquainted with the people, told me that they had no such ideas, and this opinion was confirmed by conversation with many of the less intelligent savages; but at last I succeeded in getting a satisfactory clue.'[616] It then appeared that the Ahts had all the time been hiding a whole characteristic system of religious doctrines as to souls and their migrations, the spirits who do good and ill to men, and the great gods above all. Thus, even where no positive proof of religious ideas among any particular tribe has reached us, we should distrust its denial by observers whose acquaintance with the tribe in question has not been intimate as well as kindly. It is said of the Andaman Islanders that they have not the rudest elements of a religious faith; yet it appears that the natives did not even display to the foreigners the rude music which they actually possessed, so that they could scarcely have been expected to be communicative as to their theology, if they had any.[617] In our time the most striking negation of the religion of savage tribes is that published by Sir Samuel Baker, in a paper read in 1866 before the Ethnological Society of London, as follows: 'The most northern tribes of the White Nile are the Dinkas, Shillooks, Nuehr, Kytch, Bohr, Aliab, and Shir. A general description will suffice for the whole, excepting the Kytch. Without any exception, they are without a belief in a Supreme Being, neither have they any form of worship or idolatry; nor is the darkness of their minds enlightened by even a ray of superstition.' Had this distinguished explorer spoken only of the Latukas, or of other tribes hardly known to ethnographers except through his own intercourse with them, his denial of any religious consciousness to them would have been at least entitled to stand as the best procurable account, until more intimate communication should prove or disprove it. But in speaking thus of comparatively well known tribes such as the Dinkas, Shilluks and Nuehr, Sir S. Baker ignores the existence of published evidence, such as describes the sacrifices of the Dinkas, their belief in good and evil spirits (adjok and djyok), their good deity and heaven-dwelling creator, Dendid, as likewise Néar the Deity of the Nuehr, and the Shilluk's creator, who is described as visiting, like other spirits, a sacred wood or tree. Kaufmann, Brun-Rollet, Lejean, and other observers, had thus placed on record details of the religion of these White Nile tribes, years before Sir S. Baker's rash denial that they had any religion at all.[618]

The first requisite in a systematic study of the religions of the lower races, is to lay down a rudimentary definition of religion. By requiring in this definition the belief in a supreme deity or of judgment after death, the adoration of idols or the practice of sacrifice, or other partially-diffused doctrines or rites, no doubt many tribes may be excluded from the category of religious. But such narrow definition has the fault of identifying religion rather with particular developments than with the deeper motive which underlies them. It seems best to fall back at once on this essential source, and simply to claim, as a minimum definition of Religion, the belief in Spiritual Beings. If this standard be applied to the descriptions of low races as to religion, the following results will appear. It cannot be positively asserted that every existing tribe recognizes the belief in spiritual beings, for the native condition of a considerable number is obscure in this respect, and from the rapid change or extinction they are undergoing, may ever remain so. It would be yet more unwarranted to set down every tribe mentioned in history, or known to us by the discovery of antiquarian relics, as necessarily having passed the defined minimum of religion. Greater still would be the unwisdom of declaring such a rudimentary belief natural or instinctive in all human tribes of all times; for no evidence justifies the opinion that man, known to be capable of so vast an intellectual development, cannot have emerged from a non-religious condition, previous to that religious condition in which he happens at present to come with sufficient clearness within our range of knowledge. It is desirable, however, to take our basis of enquiry in observation rather than from speculation. Here, so far as I can judge from the immense mass of accessible evidence, we have to admit that the belief in spiritual beings appears among all low races with whom we have attained to thoroughly intimate acquaintance; whereas the assertion of absence of such belief must apply either to ancient tribes, or to more or less imperfectly described modern ones. The exact bearing of this state of things on the problem of the origin of religion may be thus briefly stated. Were it distinctly proved that non-religious savages exist or have existed, these might be at least plausibly claimed as representatives of the condition of Man before he arrived at the religious state of culture. It is not desirable, however, that this argument should be put forward, for the asserted existence of the non-religious tribes in question rests, as we have seen, on evidence often mistaken and never conclusive. The argument for the natural evolution of religious ideas among mankind is not invalidated by the rejection of an ally too weak at present to give effectual help. Non-religious tribes may not exist in our day, but the fact bears no more decisively on the development of religion, than the impossibility of finding a modern English village without scissors or books or lucifer-matches bears on the fact that there was a time when no such things existed in the land.

I propose here, under the name of Animism, to investigate the deep-lying doctrine of Spiritual Beings, which embodies the very essence of Spiritualistic as opposed to Materialistic philosophy. Animism is not a new technical term, though now seldom used.[619] From its special relation to the doctrine of the soul, it will be seen to have a peculiar appropriateness to the view here taken of the mode in which theological ideas have been developed among mankind. The word Spiritualism, though it may be, and sometimes is, used in a general sense, has this obvious defect to us, that it has become the designation of a particular modern sect, who indeed hold extreme spiritualistic views, but cannot be taken as typical representatives of these views in the world at large. The sense of Spiritualism in its wider acceptation, the general belief in spiritual beings, is here given to Animism.

Animism characterizes tribes very low in the scale of humanity, and thence ascends, deeply modified in its transmission, but from first to last preserving an unbroken continuity, into the midst of high modern culture. Doctrines adverse to it, so largely held by individuals or schools, are usually due not to early lowness of civilization, but to later changes in the intellectual course, to divergence from, or rejection of, ancestral faiths; and such newer developments do not affect the present enquiry as to the fundamental religious condition of mankind. Animism is, in fact, the groundwork of the Philosophy of Religion, from that of savages up to that of civilized men. And although it may at first sight seem to afford but a bare and meagre definition of a minimum of religion, it will be found practically sufficient; for where the root is, the branches will generally be produced. It is habitually found that the theory of Animism divides into two great dogmas, forming parts of one consistent doctrine; first, concerning souls of individual creatures, capable of continued existence after the death or destruction of the body; second, concerning other spirits, upward to the rank of powerful deities. Spiritual beings are held to affect or control the events of the material world, and man's life here and hereafter; and it being considered that they hold intercourse with men, and receive pleasure or displeasure from human actions, the belief in their existence leads naturally, and it might almost be said inevitably, sooner or later to active reverence and propitiation. Thus Animism in its full development, includes the belief in souls and in a future state, in controlling deities and subordinate spirits, these doctrines practically resulting in some kind of active worship. One great element of religion, that moral element which among the higher nations forms its most vital part, is indeed little represented in the religion of the lower races. It is not that these races have no moral sense or no moral standard, for both are strongly marked among them, if not in formal precept, at least in that traditional consensus of society which we call public opinion, according to which certain actions are held to be good or bad, right or wrong. It is that the conjunction of ethics and Animistic philosophy, so intimate and powerful in the higher culture, seems scarcely yet to have begun in the lower. I propose here hardly to touch upon the purely moral aspects of religion, but rather to study the animism of the world so far as it constitutes, as unquestionably it does constitute, an ancient and world-wide philosophy, of which belief is the theory and worship is the practice. Endeavouring to shape the materials for an enquiry hitherto strangely undervalued and neglected, it will now be my task to bring as clearly as may be into view the fundamental animism of the lower races, and in some slight and broken outline to trace its course into higher regions of civilization. Here let me state once for all two principal conditions under which the present research is carried on. First, as to the religious doctrines and practices examined, these are treated as belonging to theological systems devised by human reason, without supernatural aid or revelation; in other words, as being developments of Natural Religion. Second, as to the connexion between similar ideas and rites in the religions of the savage and the civilized world. While dwelling at some length on doctrines and ceremonies of the lower races, and sometimes particularizing for special reasons the related doctrines and ceremonies of the higher nations, it has not seemed my proper task to work out in detail the problems thus suggested among the philosophies and creeds of Christendom. Such applications, extending farthest from the direct scope of a work on primitive culture, are briefly stated in general terms, or touched in slight allusion, or taken for granted without remark. Educated readers possess the information required to work out their general bearing on theology, while more technical discussion is left to philosophers and theologians specially occupied with such arguments.

The first branch of the subject to be considered is the doctrine of human and other Souls, an examination of which will occupy the rest of the present chapter. What the doctrine of the soul is among the lower races, may be explained in stating the animistic theory of its development. It seems as though thinking men, as yet at a low level of culture, were deeply impressed by two groups of biological problems. In the first place, what is it that makes the difference between a living body and a dead one; what causes waking, sleep, trance, disease, death? In the second place, what are those human shapes which appear in dreams and visions? Looking at these two groups of phenomena, the ancient savage philosophers probably made their first step by the obvious inference that every man has two things belonging to him, namely, a life and a phantom. These two are evidently in close connexion with the body, the life as enabling it to feel and think and act, the phantom as being its image or second self; both, also, are perceived to be things separable from the body, the life as able to go away and leave it insensible or dead, the phantom as appearing to people at a distance from it. The second step would seem also easy for savages to make, seeing how extremely difficult civilized men have found it to unmake. It is merely to combine the life and the phantom. As both belong to the body, why should they not also belong to one another, and be manifestations of one and the same soul? Let them then be considered as united, and the result is that well-known conception which may be described as an apparitional-soul, a ghost-soul. This, at any rate, corresponds with the actual conception of the personal soul or spirit among the lower races, which may be defined as follows: It is a thin unsubstantial human image, in its nature a sort of vapour, film, or shadow; the cause of life and thought in the individual it animates; independently possessing the personal consciousness and volition of its corporeal owner, past or present; capable of leaving the body far behind, to flash swiftly from place to place; mostly impalpable and invisible, yet also manifesting physical power, and especially appearing to men waking or asleep as a phantasm separate from the body of which it bears the likeness; continuing to exist and appear to men after the death of that body; able to enter into, possess, and act in the bodies of other men, of animals, and even of things. Though this definition is by no means of universal application, it has sufficient generality to be taken as a standard, modified by more or less divergence among any particular people. Far from these world-wide opinions being arbitrary or conventional products, it is seldom even justifiable to consider their uniformity among distant races as proving communication of any sort. They are doctrines answering in the most forcible way to the plain evidence of men's senses, as interpreted by a fairly consistent and rational primitive philosophy. So well, indeed, does primitive animism account for the facts of nature, that it has held its place into the higher levels of education. Though classic and mediæval philosophy modified it much, and modern philosophy has handled it yet more unsparingly, it has so far retained the traces of its original character, that heirlooms of primitive ages may be claimed in the existing psychology of the civilized world. Out of the vast mass of evidence, collected among the most various and distant races of mankind, typical details may now be selected to display the earlier theory of the soul, the relation of the parts of this theory, and the manner in which these parts have been abandoned, modified, or kept up, along the course of culture.

To understand the popular conceptions of the human soul or spirit, it is instructive to notice the words which have been found suitable to express it. The ghost or phantasm seen by the dreamer or the visionary is an unsubstantial form, like a shadow or reflexion, and thus the familiar term of the *shade* comes in to express the soul. Thus the Tasmanian word for the shadow is also that for the spirit;[620] the Algonquins describe a man's soul as *otahchuk*, 'his shadow;'[621] the Quiché language uses *natub* for 'shadow, soul;'[622] the Arawak *ueja* means 'shadow, soul, image;'[623] the Abipones made the one word *loákal* serve for 'shadow, soul, echo, image.'[624] The Zulus not only use the word *tunzi* for 'shadow, spirit, ghost,' but they consider that at death the shadow of a man will in some way depart from the corpse, to become an ancestral spirit.[625] The Basutos not only call the spirit remaining after death the *seriti* or 'shadow,' but they think that if a man walks on the river bank, a crocodile may seize his shadow in the water and draw him in;[626] while in Old Calabar there is found the same identification of the spirit with the *ukpon* or 'shadow,' for a man to lose which is fatal.[627] There are thus found among the lower races not only the types of those familiar classic terms, the *skia* and *umbra*, but also what seems the fundamental thought of the stories of shadowless men still current in the folklore of Europe, and familiar to modern readers in Chamisso's tale of Peter Schlemihl. Thus the dead in Purgatory knew that

Dante was alive when they saw that, unlike theirs, his figure cast a shadow on the ground.[628] Other attributes are taken into the notion of soul or spirit, with especial regard to its being the cause of life. Thus the Caribs, connecting the pulses with spiritual beings, and especially considering that in the heart dwells man's chief soul, destined to a future heavenly life, could reasonably use the one word *iouanni* for 'soul, life, heart.'[629] The Tongans supposed the soul to exist throughout the whole extension of the body, but particularly in the heart. On one occasion, the natives were declaring to a European that a man buried months ago was nevertheless still alive. 'And one, endeavouring to make me understand what he meant, took hold of my hand, and squeezing it, said, "This will die, but the life that is within you will never die;" with his other hand pointing to my heart.'[630] So the Basutos say of a dead man that his heart is gone out, and of one recovering from sickness that his heart is coming back.[631] This corresponds to the familiar Old World view of the heart as the prime mover in life, thought, and passion. The connexion of soul and blood, familiar to the Karens and Papuas, appears prominently in Jewish and Arabic philosophy.[632] To educated moderns the idea of the Macusi Indians of Guiana may seem quaint, that although the body will decay, 'the man in our eyes' will not die, but wander about.[633] Yet the association of personal animation with the pupil of the eye is familiar to European folklore, which not unreasonably discerned a sign of bewitchment or approaching death in the disappearance of the image, pupil, or baby, from the dim eyeballs of the sick man.[634]

The act of breathing, so characteristic of the higher animals during life, and coinciding so closely with life in its departure, has been repeatedly and naturally identified with the life or soul itself. Laura Bridgman showed in her instructive way the analogy between the effects of restricted sense and restricted civilization, when one day she made the gesture of taking something away from her mouth: 'I dreamed,' she explained in words, 'that God took away my breath to heaven.'[635] It is thus that West Australians used one word *waug* for 'breath, spirit, soul;[636] that in the Netela language of California, *piuts* means 'life, breath, soul;'[637] that certain Greenlanders reckoned two souls to man, namely his shadow and his breath;[638] that the Malays say the soul of the dying man escapes through his nostrils, and in Java use the same word *ñawa* for 'breath, life, soul.'[639] How the notions of life, heart, breath, and phantom unite in the one conception of a soul or spirit, and at the same time how loose and vague such ideas are among barbaric races, is well brought into view in the answers to a religious inquest held in 1528 among the natives of Nicaragua. 'When they die, there comes out of their mouth something that resembles a person, and is called *julio* [Aztec *yuli*==to live]. This being goes to the place where the man and woman are. It is like a person, but does not die, and the body remains here.' *Question.* 'Do those who go up on high keep the same body, the same face, and the same limbs, as here below?' *Answer.* 'No; there is only the heart.' *Question.* 'But since they tear out their hearts [i.e. when a captive was sacrificed], what happens then?' *Answer.* 'It is not precisely the heart, but that in them which makes them live, and that quits the body when they die.' Or, as stated in another interrogatory, 'It is not their heart that goes up above, but what makes them live, that is to say, the breath that issues from their mouth and is called *julio*.'[640] The conception of the soul as breath may be followed up through Semitic and Aryan etymology, and thus into the main streams of the philosophy of the world. Hebrew shows *nephesh*, 'breath,' passing into all the meanings of 'life, soul, mind, animal,' while *ruach* and *neshamah* make the like transition from 'breath' to 'spirit'; and to these the Arabic *nefs* and *ruh* correspond. The same is the history of Sanskrit *âtman* and *prâna*, of Greek *psychē* and *pneuma*, of Latin *animus*, *anima*, *spiritus*. So Slavonic *duch* has developed the meaning of 'breath' into that of soul or spirit; and the dialects of the Gypsies have this word *dūk* with the meanings of 'breath, spirit, ghost,' whether these pariahs brought the word from India as part of their inheritance of Aryan speech, or whether they adopted it in their migration across Slavonic lands.[641] German *geist* and English *ghost*, too, may possibly have the same original sense of breath. And if any should think such expressions due to mere metaphor, they may judge the strength of the implied connexion between breath and spirit by cases of most unequivocal significance. Among the Seminoles of Florida, when a woman died in childbirth, the infant was held over her face to receive her parting spirit, and thus acquire strength and knowledge for its future use. These Indians could have well understood why at the death-bed of an ancient Roman, the nearest kinsman leant over to inhale the last breath of the departing (et excipies hanc animam ore pio). Their state of mind is kept up to this day among Tyrolese peasants, who can still fancy a good man's soul to issue from his mouth at death like a little white cloud.[642]

It will be shown that men, in their composite and confused notions of the soul, have brought into connexion a list of manifestations of life and thought even more multifarious than this. But also, seeking to avoid such perplexity of combination, they have sometimes endeavoured to define and classify more closely, especially by the theory that man has a combination of several kinds of spirit, soul, or image, to which different functions belong. Already in the barbaric world such classification has been invented or adopted. Thus the Fijians distinguished between a man's 'dark spirit' or shadow, which goes to Hades, and his 'light spirit' or reflexion in water or a mirror, which stays near where he dies.[643] The Malagasy say that the *saina* or mind vanishes at death, the *aina* or life becomes mere air, but the *matoatoa* or ghost hovers round the tomb.[644] In North America, the duality of the soul is a strongly marked Algonquin belief; one soul goes out and sees dreams while the other remains behind; at death one of the two abides with the body, and for this the survivors leave offerings of food, while the other departs to the land of the dead. A division into three souls is also known, and the Dakotas say that man has four souls, one remaining with the corpse, one staying in the village, one going in the air, and one to the land of spirits.[645] The Karens distinguish between the 'là' or 'kelah,' the personal life-phantom, and the 'thah,' the responsible moral soul.[646] More or less under Hindu influence, the Khonds have a fourfold division, as follows: the first soul is that capable of beatification or restoration to Boora the Good Deity; the second is attached to a Khond tribe on earth and is reborn generation after generation, so that at the birth of each child the priest asks who has returned; the third goes out to hold spiritual intercourse, leaving the body in a languid state, and it is this soul which can pass for a time into a tiger, and transmigrates for punishment after death; the fourth dies on the dissolution of the body.[647] Such classifications resemble those of higher nations, as for instance the three-fold division of shade, manes, and spirit:

'Bis duo sunt homini, manes, caro, spiritus, umbra:

Quatuor ista loci bis duo suscipiunt.

Terra tegit carnem, tumulum circumvolat umbra,

Orcus habet manes, spiritus astra petit.'

Not attempting to follow up the details of such psychical division into the elaborate systems of literary nations, I shall not discuss the distinction which the ancient Egyptians seem to have made in the Ritual of the Dead between the man's *ba, akh, ka, khaba,* translated by Dr. Birch as his 'soul,' 'mind,' 'image,' 'shade,' or the Rabbinical division into what may be roughly described as the bodily, spiritual, and celestial souls, or the distinction between the emanative and genetic souls in Hindu philosophy, or the distribution of life, apparition, ancestral spirit, among the three souls of the Chinese, or the demarcations of the *nous, psychē,* and *pneuma,* or of the *anima* and *animus,* or the famous classic and mediæval theories of the vegetal, sensitive, and rational souls. Suffice it to point out here that such speculation dates back to the barbaric condition of our race, in a state fairly comparing as to scientific value with much that has gained esteem within the precincts of higher culture. It would be a difficult task to treat such classification on a consistent logical basis. Terms corresponding with those of life, mind, soul, spirit, ghost, and so forth, are not thought of as describing really separate entities, so much as the several forms and functions of one individual being. Thus the confusion which here prevails in our own thought and language, in a manner typical of the thought and language of mankind in general, is in fact due not merely to vagueness of terms, but to an ancient theory of substantial unity which underlies them. Such ambiguity of language, however, will be found to interfere little with the present enquiry, for the details given of the nature and action of spirits, souls, phantoms, will themselves define the exact sense such words are to be taken in.

The early animistic theory of vitality, regarding the functions of life as caused by the soul, offers to the savage mind an explanation of several bodily and mental conditions, as being effects of a departure of the soul or some of its constituent spirits. This theory holds a wide and strong position in savage biology. The South Australians express it when they say of one insensible or unconscious, that he is 'wilyamarraba,' i.e., 'without soul.'[648] Among the Algonquin Indians of North America, we hear of sickness being accounted for by the patient's 'shadow' being unsettled or detached from his body, and of the convalescent being reproached for exposing himself before his shadow was safely settled down in him; where we should say that a man was ill and recovered, they would consider that he died, but came again. Another account from among the same race explains the condition of men lying in lethargy or trance; their souls have travelled to the banks of the River of Death, but have been driven back and return to reanimate their bodies.[649] Among the Fijians, 'when any one faints or dies, their spirit, it is said, may sometimes be brought back by calling after it; and occasionally the ludicrous scene is witnessed of a stout man lying at full length, and bawling out lustily for the return of his own soul.'[650] To the negroes of North Guinea, derangement or dotage is caused by the patient being prematurely deserted by his soul, sleep being a more temporary withdrawal.[651] Thus, in various countries, the bringing back of lost souls becomes a regular part of the sorcerer's or priest's profession. The Salish Indians of Oregon regard the spirit as distinct from the vital principle, and capable of quitting the body for a short time without the patient being conscious of its absence; but to avoid fatal consequences it must be restored as soon as possible, and accordingly the medicine-man in solemn form replaces it down through the patient's head.[652] The Turanian or Tatar races of Northern Asia strongly hold the theory of the soul's departure in disease, and among the Buddhist tribes the Lamas carry out the ceremony of soul-restoration in most elaborate form. When a man has been robbed by a demon of his rational soul, and has only his animal soul left, his senses and memory grow weak and he falls into a dismal state. Then the Lama undertakes to cure him, and with quaint rites exorcises the evil demon. But if this fails, then it is the patient's soul itself that cannot or will not find its way back. So the sick man is laid out in his best attire and surrounded with his most attractive possessions, the friends and relatives go thrice round the dwelling, affectionately calling back the soul by name, while as a further inducement the Lama reads from his book descriptions of the pains of hell, and the dangers incurred by a soul which wilfully abandons its body, and then at last the whole assembly declare with one voice that the wandering spirit has returned and the patient will recover.[653] The Karens of Burma will run about pretending to catch a sick man's wandering soul, or as they say with the Greeks and Slavs, his 'butterfly' (leip-pya), and at last drop it down upon his head. The Karen doctrine of the 'là' is indeed a perfect and well-marked vitalistic system. This là, soul, ghost, or genius, may be separated from the body it belongs to, and it is a matter of the deepest interest to the Karen to keep his là with him, by calling it, making offerings of food to it, and so forth. It is especially when the body is asleep, that the soul goes out and wanders; if it is detained beyond a certain time, disease ensues, and if permanently, then its owner dies. When the 'wee' or spirit-doctor is employed to call back the departed shade or life of a Karen, if he cannot recover it from the region of the dead, he will sometimes take the shade of a living man and transfer it to the dead, while its proper owner, whose soul has ventured out in a dream, sickens and dies. Or when a Karen becomes sick, languid and pining from his là having left him, his friends will perform a ceremony with a garment of the invalid's and a fowl which is cooked and offered with rice, invoking the spirit with formal prayers to come back to the patient.[654] This ceremony is perhaps ethnologically connected, though it is not easy to say by what manner of diffusion or when, with a rite still practised in China. When a Chinese is at the point of death, and his soul is supposed to be already out of his body, a relative may be seen holding up the patient's coat on a long bamboo, to which a white cock is often fastened, while a Tauist priest by incantations brings the departed spirit into the coat, in order to put it back into the sick man. If the bamboo after a time turns round slowly in the holder's hands, this shows that the spirit is inside the garment.[655]

Such temporary exit of the soul has a world-wide application to the proceedings of the sorcerer, priest, or seer himself. He professes to send forth his spirit on distant journeys, and probably often believes his soul released for a time from its bodily prison, as in the case of that remarkable dreamer and visionary Jerome Cardan, who describes himself as having the faculty of passing out of his senses as into ecstasy whenever he will, feeling when he goes into this state a sort of separation near the heart as if his soul were departing, this state beginning from his brain and passing down his spine, and he then feeling only that he is out of himself.[656] Thus the Australian native doctor is alleged to obtain his initiation by visiting the world of spirits in a trance of two or three days' duration;[657] the Khond priest authenticates his claim to office by remaining from one to fourteen days in a languid and dreamy state, caused by one of his souls being away in the divine presence;[658] the Greenland angekok's soul goes forth from his body to fetch his familiar demon;[659] the Turanian shaman lies in lethargy while his soul departs to bring hidden wisdom from the land of spirits.[660] The literature of more progressive races supplies similar accounts. A characteristic story from old Scandinavia is that of the Norse chief Ingimund, who shut up three Finns in a hut for three nights, that they might visit Iceland and inform him of the lie of the country where he was to settle; their bodies became rigid, they sent their souls on the errand, and awakening after the three days they gave a description of the Vatnsdæl.[661] The typical classic case is the story of Hermotimos, whose prophetic soul went out from time to time to visit distant regions, till at last his wife burnt the lifeless body on the funeral pile, and when the poor soul came back, there was no longer a dwelling for it to animate.[662] A group of the legendary visits to the spirit-world; which will be described in the next chapter, belong to this class. A typical spiritualistic instance may be quoted from Jung-Stilling, who says that examples have come to his knowledge of sick persons who, longing to see absent friends, have fallen into a swoon during which they have appeared to the distant objects of their affection.[663] As an illustration from our own folklore, the well-known superstition may serve, that fasting watchers on St. John's Eve may see the apparitions of those doomed to die during the year come with the clergyman to the church door and knock; these apparitions are spirits who come forth from their bodies, for the minister has been noticed to be much troubled in his sleep while his phantom was thus engaged, and when one of a party of watchers fell into a sound sleep and could not be roused, the others saw his apparition knock at the church door.[664] Modern Europe has indeed kept closely enough to the lines of early philosophy, for such ideas to have little strangeness to our own time. Language preserves record of them in such expressions as 'out of oneself,' 'beside oneself,' 'in an ecstasy,' and he who says that his spirit goes forth to meet a friend, can still realize in the phrase a meaning deeper than metaphor.

This same doctrine forms one side of the theory of dreams prevalent among the lower races. Certain of the Greenlanders, Cranz remarks, consider that the soul quits the body in the night and goes out hunting, dancing, and visiting; their dreams, which are frequent and lively, having brought them to this opinion.[665] Among the Indians of North America, we hear of the dreamer's soul leaving his body and wandering in quest of things attractive to it. These things the waking man must endeavour to obtain, lest his soul be troubled, and quit the body altogether.[666] The New Zealanders considered the dreaming soul to leave the body and return, even travelling to the region of the dead to hold converse with its friends.[667] The Tagals of Luzon object to waking a sleeper, on account of the absence of his soul.[668] The Karens, whose theory of the wandering soul has just been noticed, explain dreams to be what this là sees and experiences in its journeys when it has left the body asleep. They even account with much acuteness for the fact that we are apt to dream of people and places which we knew before; the leip-pya, they say, can only visit the regions where the body it belongs to has been already.[669] Onward from the savage state, the idea of the spirit's departure in sleep may be traced into the speculative philosophy of higher nations, as in the Vedanta system, and the Kabbala.[670] St. Augustine tells one of the double narratives which so well illustrate theories of this kind. The man who tells Augustine the story relates that, at home one night before going to sleep, he saw coming to him a certain philosopher, most well known to him, who then expounded to him certain Platonic passages, which when asked previously he had refused to explain. And when he (afterwards) enquired of this philosopher why he did at his house what he had refused to do when asked at his own: 'I did not do it,' said the philosopher, 'but I dreamt I did.' And thus, says Augustine, that was exhibited to one by phantastic image while waking, which the other saw in a dream.[671] European folklore, too, has preserved interesting details of this primitive dream-theory, such as the fear of turning a sleeper over lest the absent soul should miss the way back. King Gunthram's legend is one of a group interesting from the same point of view. The king lay in the wood asleep with his head in his faithful henchman's lap; the servant saw as it were a snake issue from his lord's mouth and run to the brook, but it could not pass, so the servant laid his sword across the water, and the creature ran along it and up into a mountain; after a while it came back and returned into the mouth of the sleeping king, who waking told him how he had dreamt that he went over an iron bridge into a fountain full of gold.[672] This is one of those instructive legends which preserve for us, as in a museum, relics of an early intellectual condition of our Aryan race, in thoughts which to our modern minds have fallen to the level of quaint fancy, but which still remain sound and reasonable philosophy to the savage. A Karen at this day would appreciate every point of the story; the familiar notion of spirits not crossing water which he exemplifies in his Burmese forests by stretching threads across the brook for the ghosts to pass along; the idea of the soul going forth embodied in an animal; and the theory of the dream being a real journey of the sleeper's soul. Finally, this old belief still finds, as such beliefs so often do, a refuge in modern poetry:

'Yon child is dreaming far away,

And is not where he seems.'

This opinion, however, only constitutes one of several parts of the theory of dreams in savage psychology. Another part has also a place here, the view that human souls come from without to visit the sleeper, who sees them as dreams. These two views are by no means incompatible. The

North American Indians allowed themselves the alternative of supposing a dream to be either a visit from the soul of the person or object dreamt of, or a sight seen by the rational soul, gone out for an excursion while the sensitive soul remains in the body.[673] So the Zulu may be visited in a dream by the shade of an ancestor, the itongo, who comes to warn him of danger, or he may himself be taken by the itongo in a dream to visit his distant people, and see that they are in trouble; as for the man who is passing into the morbid condition of the professional seer, phantoms are continually coming to talk to him in his sleep, till he becomes, as the expressive native phrase is, 'a house of dreams.'[674] In the lower range of culture, it is perhaps most frequently taken for granted that a man's apparition in a dream is a visit from his disembodied spirit, which the dreamer, to use an expressive Ojibwa idiom, 'sees when asleep.' Such a thought comes out clearly in the Fijian opinion that a living man's spirit may leave the body, to trouble other people in their sleep;[675] or in a recent account of an old Indian woman of British Columbia sending for the medicine-man to drive away the dead people who came to her every night.[676] A modern observer's description of the state of mind of the negroes of West Africa in this respect is extremely characteristic and instructive. 'All their dreams are construed into visits from the spirits of their deceased friends. The cautions, hints, and warnings which come to them through this source are received with the most serious and deferential attention, and are always acted upon in their waking hours. The habit of relating their dreams, which is universal, greatly promotes the habit of dreaming itself, and hence their sleeping hours are characterized by almost as much intercourse with the dead as their waking are with the living. This is, no doubt, one of the reasons of their excessive superstitiousness. Their imaginations become so lively that they can scarcely distinguish between their dreams and their waking thoughts, between the real and the ideal, and they consequently utter falsehood without intending, and profess to see things which never existed.'[677]

To the Greek of old, the dream-soul was what to the modern savage it still is. Sleep, loosing cares of mind, fell on Achilles as he lay by the sounding sea, and there stood over him the soul of Patroklos, like to him altogether in stature, and the beauteous eyes, and the voice, and the garments that wrapped his skin; he spake, and Achilles stretched out to grasp him with loving hands, but caught him not, and like a smoke the soul sped twittering below the earth. Along the ages that separate us from Homeric times, the apparition in dreams of men living or dead has been a subject of philosophic speculation and of superstitious fear.[678] Both the phantom of the living and the ghost of the dead figure in Cicero's typical tale. Two Arcadians came to Megara together, one lodged at a friend's house, the other at an inn. In the night this latter appeared to his fellow-traveller, imploring his help, for the innkeeper was plotting his death; the sleeper sprang up in alarm, but thinking the vision of no consequence went to sleep again. Then a second time his companion appeared to him, to entreat that though he had failed to help, he would at least avenge, for the innkeeper had killed him and hidden his body in a dung-cart, wherefore he charged his fellow-traveller to be early next morning at the city-gate before the cart passed out. Struck with this second dream, the traveller went as bidden, and there found the cart; the body of the murdered man was in it, and the innkeeper was brought to justice. 'Quid hoc somnio dici potest divinius!'[679] Augustine discusses with reference to the nature of the soul various dream-stories of his time, where the apparitions of men dead or living are seen in dreams. In one of the latter he himself figured, for when a disciple of his, Eulogius the rhetor of Carthage, once could not get to sleep for thinking of an obscure passage in Cicero's Rhetoric, that night Augustine came to him in a dream and explained it. But Augustine's tendency was toward the modern theory of dreams, and in this case he says it was certainly his image that appeared, not himself, who was far across the sea, neither knowing nor caring about the matter.[680] As we survey the immense series of dream-stories of similar types in patristic, mediæval, and modern literature, we may find it difficult enough to decide which are truth and which are fiction. But along the course of these myriad narratives of human phantoms appearing in dreams to cheer or torment, to warn or inform, or to demand fulfilment of their own desires, the problem of dream-apparitions may be traced in progress of gradual determination, from the earlier conviction that a disembodied soul really comes into the presence of the sleeper, toward the later opinion that such a phantasm is produced in the dreamer's mind without the perception of any external objective figure.

The evidence of visions corresponds with the evidence of dreams in their bearing on primitive theories of the soul,[681] and the two classes of phenomena substantiate and supplement one another. Even in healthy waking life, the savage or barbarian has never learnt to make that rigid distinction between subjective and objective, between imagination and reality, to enforce which is one of the main results of scientific education. Still less, when disordered in body and mind he sees around him phantom human forms, can he distrust the evidence of his very senses. Thus it comes to pass that throughout the lower civilization men believe, with the most vivid and intense belief, in the objective reality of the human spectres which they see in sickness, exhaustion, or excitement. As will be hereafter noticed, one main reason of the practices of fasting, penance, narcotising by drugs, and other means of bringing on morbid exaltation, is that the patients may obtain the sight of spectral beings, from whom they look to gain spiritual knowledge and even worldly power. Human ghosts are among the principal of these phantasmal figures. There is no doubt that honest visionaries describe ghosts as they really appear to their perception, while even the impostors who pretend to see them conform to the descriptions thus established; thus, in West Africa, a man's *kla* or soul, becoming at his death a *sisa* or ghost, can remain in the house with the corpse, but is only visible to the wong-man, the spirit-doctor.[682] Sometimes the phantom has the characteristic quality of not being visible to all of an assembled company. Thus the natives of the Antilles believed that the dead appeared on the roads when one went alone, but not when many went together;[683] thus among the Finns the ghosts of the dead were to be seen by the shamans, but not by men generally unless in dreams.[684] Such is perhaps the meaning of the description of Samuel's ghost, visible to the witch of Endor, but not to Saul, for he has to ask her what it is she sees.[685] Yet this test of the nature of an apparition is one which easily breaks down. We know well how in civilized countries a current rumour of some one having seen a phantom is enough to bring a sight of it to others whose minds are in a properly receptive state. The condition of the modern ghost-seer, whose imagination passes on such slight excitement into positive hallucination is rather the rule than the exception among uncultured and intensely imaginative tribes, whose minds may be thrown off their balance by a touch, a word, a gesture, an unaccustomed noise. Among savage tribes, however, as among civilized races who have inherited remains of early philosophy formed under similar conditions, the doctrine of visibility or invisibility of phantoms has been obviously shaped with reference to actual experience. To declare that souls or ghosts are necessarily either visible or invisible, would directly contradict the evidence of men's senses. But to assert or imply, as the lower races do, that they are visible sometimes and to some persons, but not always or to every one, is to lay down an explanation of facts which is not indeed our usual modern explanation, but which is a perfectly rational and intelligible product of early science.

Without discussing on their merits the accounts of what is called 'second sight,' it may be pointed out that they are related among savage tribes, as when Captain Jonathan Carver obtained from a Cree medicine-man a true prophecy of the arrival of a canoe with news next day at noon; or when Mr. J. Mason Brown, travelling with two voyageurs on the Coppermine River, was met by Indians of the very band he was seeking, these having been sent by their medicine-man, who, on enquiry, stated that 'He saw them coming, and heard them talk on their journey.'[686] These are analogous to accounts of the Highland second-sight, as when Pennant heard of a gentleman of the Hebrides, said to have the convenient gift of foreseeing visitors in time to get ready for them, or when Dr. Johnson was told by another laird that a labouring man of his had predicted his return to the island, and described the peculiar livery his servant had been newly dressed in.[687]

As a general rule, people are apt to consider it impossible for a man to be in two places at once, and indeed a saying to that effect has become a popular saw. But the rule is so far from being universally accepted, that the word 'bilocation' has been invented to express the miraculous faculty possessed by certain Saints of the Roman Church, of being in two places at once; like St. Alfonso di Liguori, who had the useful power of preaching his sermon in church while he was confessing penitents at home.[688] The reception and explanation of these various classes of stories fit perfectly with the primitive animistic theory of apparitions, and the same is true of the following most numerous class of the second-sight narratives.

Death is the event which, in all stages of culture, brings thought to bear most intensely, though not always most healthily, on the problems of psychology. The apparition of the disembodied soul has in all ages been thought to bear especial relation to its departure from its body at death. This is well shown by the reception not only of a theory of ghosts, but of a special doctrine of 'wraiths' or 'fetches.' Thus the Karens say that a man's spirit, appearing after death, may thus announce it.[689] In New Zealand it is ominous to see the figure of an absent person, for if it be shadowy and the face not visible, his death may ere long be expected, but if the face be seen he is dead already. A party of Maoris (one of whom told the story) were seated round a fire in the open air, when there appeared, seen only by two of them, the figure of a relative left ill at home; they exclaimed, the figure vanished, and on the return of the party it appeared that the sick man had died about the time of the vision.[690] Examining the position of the doctrine of wraiths among the higher races, we find it especially prominent in three intellectual districts, Christian hagiology, popular folklore, and modern spiritualism. St. Anthony saw the soul of St. Ammonius carried to heaven in the midst of choirs of angels, the same day that the holy hermit died five days' journey off in the desert of Nitria; when St. Ambrose died on Easter Eve, several newly-baptized children saw the holy bishop, and pointed him out to their parents, but these with their less pure eyes could not behold him; and so forth.[691] Folklore examples abound in Silesia and the Tyrol, where the gift of wraith-seeing still flourishes, with the customary details of funerals, churches, four-cross-roads, and headless phantoms, and an especial association with New Year's Eve. The accounts of 'second-sight' from North Britain mostly belong to a somewhat older date. Thus the St. Kilda people used to be haunted by their own spectral doubles, forerunners of impending death, and in 1799 a traveller writes of the peasants of Kirkcudbrightshire, 'It is common among them to fancy that they see the wraiths of persons dying, which will be visible to one and not to others present with him. Within these last twenty years, it was hardly possible to meet with any person who had not seen many wraiths and ghosts in the course of his experience.' Those who discuss the authenticity of the second-sight stories as actual evidence, must bear in mind that they prove a little too much; they vouch not only for human apparitions, but for such phantoms as demon-dogs, and for still more fanciful symbolic omens. Thus a phantom shroud seen in spiritual vision on a living man predicts his death, immediate if it is up to his head, less nearly approaching if it is only up to his waist; and to see in spiritual vision a spark of fire fall upon a person's arm or breast, is a forerunner of a dead child to be seen in his arms.[692] As visionaries often see phantoms of living persons without any remarkable event coinciding with their hallucinations, it is naturally admitted that a man's phantom or 'double' may be seen without portending anything in particular. The spiritualistic theory specially insists on cases of apparition where the person's death corresponds more or less nearly with the time when some friend perceives his phantom.[693] Narratives of this class, which I can here only specify without arguing on them, are abundantly in circulation. Thus, I have an account by a lady, who 'saw, as it were, the form of some one laid out,' near the time when a brother died at Melbourne, and who mentions another lady known to her, who thought she saw her own father look in at the church window at the moment he was dying in his own house. Another account is sent me by a Shetland lady, who relates that about twenty years ago she and a girl leading her pony recognized the familiar figure of one Peter Sutherland, whom they knew to be at the time in ill-health in Edinburgh; he turned a corner and they saw no more of him, but next week came the news of his sudden death.

That the apparitional human soul bears the likeness of its fleshly body, is the principle implicitly accepted by all who believe it really and objectively present in dreams and visions. My own view is that nothing but dreams and visions could have ever put into men's minds such an idea as that of souls being ethereal images of bodies. It is thus habitually taken for granted in animistic philosophy, savage or civilized, that souls set free from the earthly body are recognized by a likeness to it which they still retain, whether as ghostly wanderers on earth or inhabitants of the world beyond the grave. Man's spirit, says Swedenborg, is his mind, which lives after death in complete human form, and this is the poet's dictum in 'In Memoriam:'

'Eternal form shall still divide

The eternal soul from all beside;

And I shall know him when we meet.'

This world-wide thought, coming into view here in a multitude of cases from all grades of culture, needs no collection of ordinary instances to illustrate it.[694] But a quaint and special group of beliefs will serve to display the thoroughness with which the soul is thus conceived as an image of the body. As a consistent corollary to such an opinion, it is argued that the mutilation of the body will have a corresponding effect upon the soul, and very low savage races have philosophy enough to work out this idea. Thus it was recorded of the Indians of Brazil by one of the early European visitors, that they 'believe that the dead arrive in the other world wounded or hacked to pieces, in fact just as they left this.'[695] Thus, too, the Australian who has slain his enemy will cut off the right thumb of the corpse, so that although the spirit will become a hostile ghost, it cannot throw with its mutilated hand the shadowy spear, and may be safely left to wander, malignant but harmless.[696] The negro fears long sickness before death, such as will send him lean and feeble into the next world. His theory of the mutilation of soul with body could not be brought more vividly into view than in that ugly story of the West Indian planter, whose slaves began to seek in suicide at once relief from present misery and restoration to their native land; but the white man was too cunning for them, he cut off the heads and hands of the corpses, and the survivors saw that not even death could save them from a master who could maim their very souls in the next world.[697] The same rude and primitive belief continues among nations risen far higher in intellectual rank. The Chinese hold in especial horror the punishment of decapitation, considering that he who quits this world lacking a member will so arrive in the next, and a case is recorded lately of a criminal at Amoy who for this reason begged to die instead by the cruel death of crucifixion, and was crucified accordingly.[698] The series ends as usual in the folklore of the civilized world. The phantom skeleton in chains that haunted the house at Bologna, showed the way to the garden where was buried the real chained fleshless skeleton it belonged to, and came no more when the remains had been duly buried. When the Earl of Cornwall met the fetch of his friend William Rufus carried black and naked on a black goat across the Bodmin moors, he saw that it was wounded through the midst of the breast; and afterwards he heard that at that very hour the king had been slain in the New Forest by the arrow of Walter Tirell.[699]

In studying the nature of the soul as conceived among the lower races, and in tracing such conceptions onward among the higher, circumstantial details are available. It is as widely recognized among mankind that souls or ghosts have voices, as that they have visible forms, and indeed the evidence for both is of the same nature. Men who perceive evidently that souls do talk when they present themselves in dream or vision, naturally take for granted at once the objective reality of the ghostly voice, and of the ghostly form from which it proceeds. This is involved in the series of narratives of spiritual communications with living men, from savagery onward to civilization, while the more modern doctrine of the subjectivity of such phenomena recognizes the phenomena themselves, but offers a different explanation of them. One special conception, however, requires particular notice. This defines the spirit-voice as being a low murmur, chirp, or whistle, as it were the ghost of a voice. The Algonquin Indians of North America could hear the shadow-souls of the dead chirp like crickets.[700] The divine spirits of the New Zealand dead, coming to converse with the living, utter their words in whistling tones, and such utterances by a squeaking noise are mentioned elsewhere in Polynesia.[701] The Zulu diviner's familiar spirits are ancestral manes, who talk in a low whistling tone short of a full whistle, whence they have their name of 'imilozi' or whistlers.[702] These ideas correspond with classic descriptions of the ghostly voice, as a 'twitter or 'thin murmur:'

Ψυχὴ δὲ κατὰ χθονὸς ἠύτε καπνὸς,

Ψχετο τετριγυῖα.'[703]

'Umbra cruenta Remi visa est assistere lecto,

Atque haec exiguo murmure verba loqui.'[704]

As the attributes of the soul or ghost extend to other spiritual beings, and the utterances of such are to a great extent given by the voice of mediums, we connect these accounts with the notion that the language of demons is also a low whistle or mutter, whence the well-known practice of whispering or murmuring charms, the 'susurrus necromanticus' of sorcerers, to whom the already cited description of 'wizards that peep (i.e. chirp) and mutter' is widely applicable.[705]

The conception of dreams and visions as caused by present objective figures, and the identification of such phantom souls with the shadow and the breath, has led to the treatment of souls as substantial material beings. Thus it is a usual proceeding to make openings through solid materials to allow souls to pass. The Iroquois in old times used to leave an opening in the grave for the lingering soul to visit its body, and some of them still bore holes in the coffin for the same purpose.[706] The Malagasy sorcerer, for the cure of a sick man who had lost his soul, would make a hole in a burial-house to let out a spirit which he would catch in his cap and so convey to the patient's head.[707] The Chinese make a hole in the roof to let out the soul at death.[708] And lastly, the custom of opening a window or door for the departing soul when it quits the body is to this day a very familiar superstition in France, Germany, and England.[709] Again, the souls of the dead are thought susceptible of being beaten, hurt and driven like any other living creatures. Thus the Queensland aborigines would beat the air in an annual mock fight, held to scare away the souls that death had let loose among the living since last year.[710] Thus North American Indians, when they had tortured an enemy to death, ran about crying and beating with sticks to scare the ghost away; they have been known to set nets round their cabins to catch and keep out neighbours' departed souls; fancying the soul of a dying man to go out at the wigwam roof, they would habitually beat the sides with sticks to drive it forth; we even hear of the widow going off from her husband's funeral followed by a person flourishing a handful of twigs about her head like a flyflapper, to drive off her husband's ghost and leave her free to marry again.[711] With a kindlier feeling, the Congo negroes abstained for a whole year after a death from sweeping the house, lest the dust should injure the delicate substance of the ghost;[712] the Tonquinese avoided house-cleaning during the festival when the souls of the dead came back to their houses for the New Year's visit;[713] and it seems likely that the special profession of the Roman 'everriatores' who swept the houses out after a funeral, was connected with a similar idea.[714] To this day, it remains a German peasants' saying that it is wrong to slam a door, lest one should pinch a soul in it.[715] The not uncommon practice of strewing ashes to show the footprints of ghosts or demons takes for granted that they are substantial bodies. In the literature of animism, extreme tests of the weight of ghosts are now and then forthcoming. They range from the declaration of a Basuto diviner that the late queen had been bestriding his shoulders, and he never felt such a weight in his life, to Glanvil's story of David Hunter the neat-herd, who lifted up the old woman's ghost, and she felt just like a bag of feathers in his arms, or the pathetic German superstition that the dead mother's coming back in the night to suckle the baby she has left on earth, may be known by the hollow pressed down in the bed where she lay, and at last down to the alleged modern spiritualistic reckoning of the weight of a human soul at from 3 to 4 ounces.[716]

Explicit statements as to the substance of soul are to be found both among low and high races, in an instructive series of definitions. The Tongans imagined the human soul to be the finer or more aeriform part of the body, which leaves it suddenly at the moment of death; something comparable to the perfume and essence of a flower as related to the more solid vegetable fibre.[717] The Greenland seers described the soul as they habitually perceived it in their visions; it is pale and soft, they said, and he who tries to seize it feels nothing, for it has no flesh nor bone nor sinew.[718] The Caribs did not think the soul so immaterial as to be invisible, but said it was subtle and thin like a purified body.[719] Turning to higher races, we may take the Siamese as an example of a people who conceive of souls as consisting of subtle matter escaping sight and touch, or as united to a swiftly moving aerial body.[720] In the classic world, it is recorded as an opinion of Epicurus that 'they who say the soul is incorporeal talk folly, for it could neither do nor suffer anything were it such.'[721] Among the Fathers, Irenæus describes souls as incorporeal in comparison with mortal bodies,[722] and Tertullian relates a vision or revelation of a certain Montanist prophetess, of the soul seen by her corporeally, thin and lucid, aerial in colour and human in form.[723] For an example of mediæval doctrine, may be cited a 14th-century English poem, the 'Ayenbite of Inwyt' (i.e. 'Remorse of Conscience') which points out how the soul, by reason of the thinness of its substance, suffers all the more in purgatory:

'The soul is more tendre and nesche

Than the bodi that hath bones and fleysche;

Thanne the soul that is so tendere of kinde,

Mote nedis hure penaunce hardere y-finde,

Than eni bodi that evere on live was.'[724]

The doctrine of the ethereal soul passed on into more modern philosophy, and the European peasant holds fast to it still; as Wuttke says, the ghosts of the dead have to him a misty and evanescent materiality, for they have bodies as we have, though of other kind: they can eat and drink, they can be wounded and killed.[725] Nor was the ancient doctrine ever more distinctly stated than by a modern spiritualistic writer, who observes that 'a spirit is no immaterial substance; on the contrary, the spiritual organization is composed of matter ... in a very high state of refinement and attenuation.'[726]

Among rude races, the original conception of the human soul seems to have been that of ethereality, or vaporous materiality, which has held so large a place in human thought ever since. In fact, the later metaphysical notion of immateriality could scarcely have conveyed any meaning to a savage. It is moreover to be noticed that, as to the whole nature and action of apparitional souls, the lower philosophy escapes various difficulties which down to modern times have perplexed metaphysicians and theologians of the civilized world. Considering the thin ethereal body of the soul to be itself sufficient and suitable for visibility, movement, and speech, the primitive animists required no additional hypotheses to account for these manifestations; they had no place for theories such as detailed by Calmet, as that immaterial souls have their own vaporous bodies, or occasionally have such vaporous bodies provided for them by supernatural means to enable them to appear as spectres, or that they possess the power of condensing the circumambient air into phantom-like bodies to invest themselves in, or of forming from it vocal instruments.[727] It appears to have been within systematic schools of civilized philosophy that the transcendental definitions of the immaterial soul were obtained, by abstraction from the primitive conception of the ethereal-material soul, so as to reduce it from a physical to a metaphysical entity.

Departing from the body at the time of death, the soul or spirit is considered set free to linger near the tomb, to wander on earth or flit in the air, or to travel to the proper region of spirits—the world beyond the grave. The principal conceptions of the lower psychology as to a Future Life will be considered in the following chapters, but for the present purpose of investigating the theory of souls in general, it will be well to enter here upon one department of the subject. Men do not stop short at the persuasion that death releases the soul to a free and active existence, but they quite logically proceed to assist nature, by slaying men in order to liberate their souls for ghostly uses. Thus there arises one of the most widespread, distinct, and intelligible rites of animistic religion—that of funeral human sacrifice for the service of the dead. When a man of rank dies and his soul departs to its own place, wherever and whatever that place may be, it is a rational inference of early philosophy that the souls of attendants, slaves, and wives, put to death at his funeral, will make the same journey and continue their service in the next life, and the argument is frequently stretched further, to include the souls of new victims sacrificed in order that they may enter upon the same ghostly servitude. It will appear from the ethnography of this rite that it is not strongly marked in the very lowest levels of culture, but that, arising in the lower barbaric stage, it develops itself in the higher, and thenceforth continues or dwindles in survival.

Of the murderous practices to which this opinion leads, remarkably distinct accounts may be cited from among tribes of the Indian Archipelago. The following account is given of the funerals of great men among the rude Kayans of Borneo:—'Slaves are killed in order that they may follow the deceased and attend upon him. Before they are killed the relations who surround them enjoin them to take great care of their master when they join him, to watch and shampoo him when he is indisposed, to be always near him, and to obey all his behests. The female relatives of the deceased then take a spear and slightly wound the victims, after which the males spear them to death.' Again, the opinion of the Idaan is 'that all whom they kill in this world shall attend them as slaves after death. This notion of future interest in the destruction of the human species is a great impediment to an intercourse with them, as murder goes farther than present advantage or resentment. From the same principle they will purchase a slave, guilty of any capital crime, at fourfold his value, that they may be his executioners.' With the same idea is connected the ferocious custom of 'head-hunting,' so prevalent among the Dayaks before Rajah Brooke's time. They considered that the owner of every human head they could procure would serve them in the next world, where, indeed, a man's rank would be according to his number of heads in this. They would continue the mourning for a dead man till a head was brought in, to provide him with a slave to accompany him to the 'habitation of souls;' a father who lost his child would go out and kill the first man he met, as a funeral ceremony; a young man might not marry till he had procured a head, and some tribes would bury with a dead man the first head he had taken, together with spears, cloth, rice, and betel. Waylaying and murdering men for their heads became, in fact, the Dayaks' national sport, and they remarked 'the white men read books, we hunt for heads instead.'[728] Of such rites in the Pacific islands, the most hideously purposeful accounts reach us from the Fiji group. Till lately, a main part of the ceremony of a great man's funeral was the strangling of wives, friends, and slaves, for the distinct purpose of attending him into the world of spirits. Ordinarily the first victim was the wife of the deceased, and more than one if he had several, and their corpses, oiled as for a feast, clothed with new fringed girdles, with heads dressed and ornamented, and vermilion and turmeric powder spread on their faces and bosoms, were laid by the side of the dead warrior. Associates and inferior attendants were likewise slain, and these bodies were spoken of as 'grass for bedding the grave.' When Ra Mbithi, the pride of Somosomo, was lost at sea, seventeen of his wives were killed; and after the news of the massacre of the Namena people, in 1839, eighty women were strangled to accompany the spirits of their murdered husbands. Such sacrifices took place under the same pressure of public opinion which kept up the widow-burning in modern India. The Fijian widow was worked upon by her relatives with all the pressure of persuasion and of menace; she understood well that life to her henceforth would mean a wretched existence of neglect, disgrace, and destitution; and tyrannous custom, as hard to struggle against in the savage as in the civilized world, drove her to the grave. Thus, far from resisting, she became importunate for death, and the new life to come, and till public opinion reached a more enlightened state, the missionaries often used their influence in vain to save from the strangling-cord some wife whom they could have rescued, but who herself refused to live. So repugnant to the native mind was the idea of a chieftain going unattended into the other world, that the missionaries' prohibition of the cherished custom was one reason of the popular dislike to Christianity. Many of the nominal Christians, when once a chief of theirs was shot from an ambush, esteemed it most fortunate that a stray shot at the same time killed a young man at a distance from him, and thus provided a companion for the spirit of the slain chief.[729]

In America, the funeral human sacrifice makes its characteristic appearance. A good example may be taken from among the Osages, whose habit was sometimes to plant in the cairn raised over a corpse a pole with an enemy's scalp hanging to the top. Their notion was that by taking an enemy and suspending his scalp over the grave of a deceased friend, the spirit of the victim became subjected to the spirit of the buried warrior in the land of spirits. Hence the last and best service that could be performed for a deceased relative was to take an enemy's life, and thus transmit it by his scalp.[730] The correspondence of this idea with that just mentioned among the Dayaks is very striking. With a similar intention, the Caribs would slay on the dead master's grave any of his slaves they could lay hands on.[731] Among the native peoples risen to considerably higher grades of social and political life, these practices were not suppressed but exaggerated, in the ghastly sacrifices of warriors, slaves, and wives, who departed to continue their duteous offices at the funeral of the chief or monarch in Central America[732] and Mexico,[733] in Bogota[734] and Peru.[735] It is interesting to notice, in somewhat favourable contrast with these customs of comparatively cultured American nations, the practice of certain rude tribes of the North-West. The Quakeolths, for instance, did not actually sacrifice the widow, but they made her rest her head on her husband's corpse while it was being burned, until at last she was dragged more dead than alive from the flames; if she recovered, she collected her husband's ashes and carried them about with her for three years, during which any levity or deficiency of grief would render her an outcast. This looks like a mitigated survival from an earlier custom of actual widow-burning.[736]

Of such funeral rites, carried out to the death, graphic and horrid descriptions are recorded in the countries across Africa—East, Central, and West. A headman of the Wadoe is buried sitting in a shallow pit, and with the corpse a male and female slave alive, he with a bill-hook in his hand to cut fuel for his lord in the death-world, she seated on a little stool with the dead chief's head in her lap. A chief of Unyamwezi is entombed in a vaulted pit, sitting on a low stool with a bow in his right hand, and provided with a pot of native beer; with him are shut in alive three women slaves, and the ceremony is concluded with a libation of beer on the earth heaped up above them all. The same idea which in Guinea makes it common for the living to send messages by the dying to the dead, is developed in Ashanti and Dahome into a monstrous system of massacre. The King of Dahome must enter Deadland with a ghostly court of hundreds of wives, eunuchs, singers, drummers, and soldiers. Nor is this all. Captain Burton thus describes the yearly 'Customs:'—'They periodically supply the departed monarch with fresh attendants in the shadowy world. For unhappily these murderous scenes are an expression, lamentably mistaken but perfectly sincere, of the liveliest filial piety.' Even this annual slaughter must be supplemented by almost daily murder:—'Whatever action, however trivial, is performed by the King, it must dutifully be reported to his sire in the shadowy realm. A victim, almost always a war-captive, is chosen; the message is delivered to him, an intoxicating draught of rum follows it, and he is dispatched to Hades in the best of humours.'[737] In southern districts of Africa, accounts of the same class begin in Congo and Angola with the recorded slaying of the dead man's favourite wives, to live with him in the other world, a practice still in vogue among the Chevas of the Zambesi district, and formerly known among the Maravis; while the funeral sacrifice of attendants with a chief is a thing of the past among the Barotse, as among the Zulus, who yet have not forgotten the days when the chief's servants and attendant warriors were cast into the fire which had consumed his body, that they might go with him, and prepare things beforehand, and get food for him.[738]

If now we turn to the records of Asia and Europe, we shall find the sacrifice of attendants for the dead widely prevalent in both continents in old times, while in the east its course may be traced continuing onward to our own day. The two Mohammedans who travelled in Southern Asia in the ninth century relate that on the accession of certain kings a quantity of rice is prepared, which is eaten by some three or four hundred men, who present themselves voluntarily to share it, thereby undertaking to burn themselves at the monarch's death. With this corresponds Marco Polo's thirteenth-century account in Southern India of the king of Maabar's guard of horsemen, who, when he dies and his body is burnt, throw themselves into the fire to do him service in the next world.[739] In the seventeenth century the practice is described as still prevailing in Japan, where, on the death of a nobleman, from ten to thirty of his servants put themselves to death by the 'hara kari,' or ripping-up, having indeed engaged during his lifetime, by the solemn compact of drinking wine together, to give their bodies to their lord at his death. Yet already in ancient times such funeral sacrifices were passing into survival, when the servants who followed their master in death were replaced by clay images set up at the tomb.[740] Among the Ossetes of the Caucasus, an interesting relic of widow-sacrifice is still kept up: the dead man's widow and his saddle-horse are led thrice round the grave, and no man may marry the widow or mount the horse thus devoted.[741] In China, legend preserves the memory of the ancient funeral human sacrifice. The brother of Chin Yang, a disciple of Confucius, died, and his widow and steward wished to bury some living persons with him, to serve him in the regions below. Thereupon the sage suggested that the proper victims would be the widow and steward themselves, but this not precisely meeting their views, the matter dropped, and the deceased was interred without attendants. This story at least shows the rite to have been not only known but understood in China long ago. In modern China, the suicide of widows to accompany their husbands is a recognized practice, sometimes even performed in public. Moreover, the ceremonies of providing sedan-bearers and an umbrella-bearer for the dead, and sending mounted horsemen to announce beforehand his arrival to the authorities of Hades, although these bearers and messengers are only made of paper and burnt, seem to represent survivals of a more murderous reality.[742]

The Aryan race gives striking examples of the rite of funeral human sacrifice in its sternest shape, whether in history or in myth, that records as truly as history the manners of old days.[743] The episodes of the Trojan captives laid with the horses and hounds on the funeral pile of Patroklos, and of Evadne throwing herself into the funeral pile of her husband, and Pausanias's narrative of the suicide of the three Messenian widows, are among its Greek representatives.[744] In Scandinavian myth, Baldr is burnt with his dwarf foot-page, his horse and saddle; Brynhild lies on the pile by her beloved Sigurd, and men and maids follow after them on the hell-way.[745] The Gauls in Cæsar's time burned at the dead man's sumptuous funeral whatever was dear to him, animals also, and much-loved slaves and clients.[746] Old mentions of Slavonic heathendom describe the burning of the dead with clothing and weapons, horses and hounds, with faithful servants, and above all, with wives. Thus St. Boniface says that 'the Wends keep matrimonial love with so great zeal, that the wife may refuse to survive her husband, and she is held praiseworthy among women who slays herself by her own hand, that she may be burnt on one pyre with her lord.'[747] This Aryan rite of widow-sacrifice has not only an ethnographic and antiquarian interest, but even a place in modern politics. In Brahmanic India the widow of a Hindu of the Brahman or the Kshatriya caste was burnt on the funeral pile with her husband, as a *sati* or 'good woman,' which word has passed into English as *suttee*. Mentioned in classic and mediæval times, the practice was in full vigour at the beginning of the last century.[748] Often one dead husband took many wives with him. Some went willingly and gaily to the new life, many were driven by force of custom, by fear of disgrace, by family persuasion, by priestly threats and promises, by sheer violence. When the rite was suppressed under modern British rule, the priesthood resisted to the uttermost, appealing to the Veda, as sanctioning the ordinance, and demanding that the foreign rulers should respect it. Yet in fact, as Prof. H. H. Wilson proved, the priests had actually falsified their sacred Veda in support of a rite enjoined by long and inveterate prejudice, but not by the traditional standards of Hindu faith. The ancient Brahmanic funeral rites have been minutely detailed from the Sanskrit authorities in an essay by Prof. Max Müller. Their directions are that the widow is to be set on the funeral pile with her husband's corpse, and if he be a warrior his bow is to be placed there too. But then a brother-in-law or adopted child or old servant is to lead the widow down again at the summons, 'Rise, woman, come to the world of life; thou sleepest nigh unto him whose life is gone. Come to us. Thou hast thus fulfilled thy duties of a wife to the husband who once took thy hand, and made thee a mother.' The bow, however, is to be broken and thrown back upon the pile, and the dead man's sacrificial instruments are to be laid with him and really consumed. While admitting that the modern ordinance of Suttee-burning is a corrupt departure from the early Brahmanic ritual, we may nevertheless find reason to consider the practice as not a new invention by the later Hindu priesthood, but as the revival, under congenial influences, of an ancient Aryan rite belonging originally to a period even earlier than the Veda. The ancient authorized ceremony looks as though, in a primitive form of the rite, the widow had been actually sent with the dead, for which real sacrifice a humaner law substituted a mere pretence. This view is supported by the existence of an old and express prohibition of the wife being sacrificed, a prohibition seemingly directed against a real custom, 'to follow the dead husband is prohibited, so says the law of the Brahmans. With regard to the other castes this law for women may be or may not be.'[749] To treat the Hindu widow-burning as a case of survival and revival seems to me most in accordance with a general ethnographic view of the subject. Widow-sacrifice is found in various regions of the world under a low state of civilization, and this fits with the hypothesis of its having belonged to the Aryan race while yet in an early and barbarous condition. Thus the prevalence of a rite of suttee like that of modern India among ancient Aryan nations settled in Europe, Greeks, Scandinavians, Germans, Slaves, may be simply accounted for by direct inheritance from the remote common antiquity of them all. If this theory be sound, it will follow that ancient as the Vedic ordinances may be, they represent in this matter a reform and a reaction against a yet more ancient barbaric rite of widow-sacrifice, which they prohibited in fact, but yet kept up in symbol. The history of religion displays but too plainly the proneness of mankind to relapse, in spite of reformation, into the lower and darker condition of the past. Stronger and more tenacious than even Vedic authority, the hideous custom of the suttee may have outlived an attempt to suppress it in early Brahmanic times, and the English rulers, in abolishing it, may have abolished a relic not merely of degenerate Hinduism, but of the far more remotely ancient savagery out of which the Aryan civilization had grown.

In now passing from the consideration of the souls of men to that of the souls of the lower animals, we have first to inform ourselves as to the savage man's idea, which is very different from the civilized man's, of the nature of these lower animals. A remarkable group of observances customary among rude tribes will bring this distinction sharply into view. Savages talk quite seriously to beasts alive or dead as they would to men alive or dead, offer them homage, ask pardon when it is their painful duty to hunt and kill them. A North American Indian will reason with a horse as if rational. Some will spare the rattlesnake, fearing the vengeance of its spirit if slain; others will salute the creature reverently, bid it welcome as a friend from the land of spirits, sprinkle a pinch of tobacco on its head for an offering, catch it by the tail and dispatch it with extreme dexterity, and carry off its skin as a trophy. If an Indian is attacked and torn by a bear, it is that the beast fell upon him intentionally in anger, perhaps to revenge the hurt done to another bear. When a bear is killed, they will beg pardon of him, or even make him condone the offence by smoking the peace-pipe with his murderers, who put the pipe in his mouth and blow down it, begging his spirit not to take revenge.[750] So in Africa, the Kafirs will hunt the elephant, begging him not to tread on them and kill them, and when he is dead they will assure him that they did not kill him on purpose, and they will bury his trunk, for the elephant is a mighty chief, and his trunk is his hand that he may hurt withal. The Congo people will even avenge such a murder by a pretended attack on the hunters who did the deed.[751] Such customs are common among the lower Asiatic tribes. The Stiens of Kambodia ask pardon of the beast they have killed;[752] the Ainos of Yesso kill the bear, offer obeisance and salutation to him, and cut up his carcase.[753] The Koriaks, if they have slain a bear or wolf, will flay him, dress one of their people in the skin, and dance round him, chanting excuses that they did not do it, and especially laying the blame on a Russian. But if it is a fox, they take his skin, wrap his dead body in hay, and sneering tell him to go to his own people and say what famous hospitality he has had, and how they gave him a new coat instead of his old one.[754] The Samoyeds excuse themselves to the slain bear, telling him it was the Russians who did it, and that a Russian knife will cut him up.[755] The Goldi will set up the slain bear, call him 'my lord' and do ironical homage to him, or taking him alive will fatten him in a cage, call him 'son' and 'brother,' and kill and eat him as a sacrifice at a solemn festival.[756] In Borneo, the Dayaks, when they have caught an alligator with a baited hook and rope, address him with respect and soothing till they have his legs fast, and then mocking call him 'rajah' and 'grandfather.'[757] Thus when the savage gets over his fears, he still keeps up in ironical merriment the reverence which had its origin in trembling sincerity. Even now the Norse hunter will say with horror of a bear that will attack man, that he can be 'no Christian bear.'

The sense of an absolute psychical distinction between man and beast, so prevalent in the civilized world, is hardly to be found among the lower races. Men to whom the cries of beasts and birds seem like human language, and their actions guided as it were by human thought, logically enough allow the existence of souls to beasts, birds, and reptiles, as to men. The lower psychology cannot but recognize in beasts the very characteristics which it attributes to the human soul, namely, the phenomena of life and death, will and judgment, and the phantom seen in vision or in dream. As for believers, savage or civilized, in the great doctrine of metempsychosis, these not only consider that an animal may have a soul, but that this soul may have inhabited a human being, and thus the creature may be in fact their own ancestor or once familiar friend. A line of facts, arranged as waymarks along the course of civilization, will serve to indicate the history of opinion from savagery onward, as to the souls of animals during life and after death. North American Indians held every animal to have its spirit, and these spirits their future life; the soul of the Canadian dog went to serve his master in the other world; among the Sioux, the prerogative of having four souls was not confined to man, but belonged also to the bear, the most human of animals.[758] The Greenlanders considered that a sick human soul might be replaced by the sorcerer with a fresh healthy soul of a hare, a reindeer, or a young child.[759] Maori tale-tellers have heard of the road by which the spirits of dogs descend to Reinga, the Hades of the departed; the Hovas of Madagascar know that the ghosts of beasts and men, dwelling in a great mountain in the south called Ambondrombe, come out occasionally to walk among the tombs or execution-places of criminals.[760] The Kamchadals held that every creature, even the smallest fly, would live again in the under-world.[761] The Kukis of Assam think that the ghost of every animal a Kuki kills in the chase or for the feast will belong to him in the next life, even as the enemy he slays in the field will then become his slave. The Karens apply the doctrine of the spirit or personal life-phantom, which is apt to wander from the body and thus suffer injury, equally to men and to animals.[762] The Zulus say the cattle they kill come to life again, and become the property of the dwellers in the world beneath.[763] The Siamese butcher, when in defiance of the very principles of his Buddhism he slaughters an ox, before he kills the creature has at least the grace to beseech its spirit to seek a happier abode.[764] In connexion with such transmigration, Pythagorean and Platonic philosophy gives to the lower animals undying souls, while other classic opinion may recognize in beasts only an inferior order of soul, only the 'anima' but not the human 'animus' besides. Thus Juvenal:

'Principio indulsit communis conditor illis

Tantum animas; nobis animum quoque....'[765]

Through the middle ages, controversy as to the psychology of brutes has lasted on into our own times, ranging between two extremes; on the one the theory of Descartes which reduced animals to mere machines, on the other what Mr. Alger defines as 'the faith that animals have immaterial and deathless souls.' Among modern speculations may be instanced that of Wesley, who thought that in the next life animals will be raised even above their bodily and mental state at the creation, 'the horridness of their appearance will be exchanged for their primæval beauty,' and it even may be that they will be made what men are now, creatures capable of religion. Adam Clarke's argument for the future life of animals rests on abstract justice: whereas they did not sin, but yet are involved in the sufferings of sinful man, and cannot have in the present state the happiness designed for them, it is reasonable that they must have it in another.[766] Although, however, the primitive belief in the souls of animals still survives to some extent in serious philosophy, it is obvious that the tendency of educated opinion on the question whether brutes have soul, as distinguished from life and mind, has for ages been in a negative and sceptical direction. The doctrine has fallen from its once high estate. It belonged originally to real, though rude science. It has now sunk to become a favourite topic in that mild speculative talk which still does duty so largely as intellectual conversation, and even then its propounders defend it with a lurking consciousness of its being after all a piece of sentimental nonsense.

Animals being thus considered in the primitive psychology to have souls like human beings, it follows as the simplest matter of course that tribes who kill wives and slaves, to dispatch their souls on errands of duty with their departed lords, may also kill animals in order that their spirits may do such service as is proper to them. The Pawnee warrior's horse is slain on his grave to be ready for him to mount again, and the Comanche's best horses are buried with his favourite weapons and his pipe, all alike to be used in the distant happy hunting-grounds.[767] In South America not only do such rites occur, but they reach a practically disastrous extreme. Patagonian tribes, says D'Orbigny, believe in another life, where they are to enjoy perfect happiness, therefore they bury with the deceased his arms and ornaments, and even kill on his tomb all the animals which belonged to him, that he may find them in the abode of bliss; and this opposes an insurmountable barrier to all civilization, by preventing them from accumulating property and fixing their habitations.[768] Not only do Pope's now hackneyed lines express a real motive with which the Indian's dog is buried with him, but on the North American continent the spirit of the dog has another remarkable office to perform. Certain Esquimaux, as Cranz relates, would lay a dog's head in a child's grave, that the soul of the dog, who is everywhere at home, might guide the helpless infant to the land of souls. In accordance with this, Captain Scoresby in Jameson's Land found a dog's skull in a small grave, probably a child's. Again, in the distant region of the Aztecs, one of the principal funeral ceremonies was to slaughter a techichi, or native dog; it was burnt or buried with the corpse, with a cotton thread fastened to its neck, and its office was to convey the deceased across the deep waters of Chiuhnahuapan, on the way to the Land of the Dead.[769] The dead Buraet's favourite horse, led saddled to the grave, killed, and flung in, may serve for a Tatar example.[770] In Tonquin, even wild animals have been customarily drowned at funeral ceremonies of princes, to be at the service of the departed in the next world.[771] Among Semitic tribes, an instance of the custom may be found in the Arab sacrifice of a camel on the grave, for the dead man's spirit to ride upon.[772] Among the nations of the Aryan race in Europe, the prevalence of such rites is deep, wide, and full of purpose. Thus, warriors were provided in death with horses and housings, with hounds and falcons. Customs thus described in chronicle and legend, are vouched for in our own time by the opening of old barbaric burial-places. How clear a relic of savage meaning lies here may be judged from a Livonian account as late as the fourteenth century, which relates how men and women slaves, sheep and oxen, with other things, were burnt with the dead, who, it was believed, would reach some region of the living, and find there, with the multitude of cattle and slaves, a country of life and happiness.[773] As usual, these rites may be traced onward in survival. The Mongols, who formerly slaughtered camels and horses at their owner's burial, have been induced to replace the actual sacrifice by a gift of the cattle to the Lamas.[774] The Hindus offer a black cow to the Brahmans, in order to secure their passage across the Vaitaranî, the river of death, and will often die grasping the cow's tail as if to swim across in herdsman's fashion, holding on to a cow.[775] It is mentioned as a belief in Northern Europe that he who has given a cow to the poor will find a cow to take him over the bridge of the dead, and a custom of leading a cow in the funeral procession is said to have been kept up to modern times.[776] All these rites probably belong together as connected with ancient funeral sacrifice, and the survival of the custom of sacrificing the warrior's horse at his tomb is yet more striking. Saint-Foix long ago put the French evidence very forcibly. Mentioning the horse led at the funeral of Charles VI., with the four valets-de-pied in black, and bareheaded, holding the corners of its caparison, he recalls the horses and servants killed and buried with præ-Christian kings. And that his readers may not think this an extraordinary idea, he brings forward the records of property and horses being presented at the offertory in Paris, in 1329, of Edward III. presenting horses at King John's funeral in London, and of the funeral service for Bertrand Duguesclin, at St. Denis, in 1389, when horses were offered, the Bishop of Auxerre laid his hand on their heads, and they were afterwards compounded for.[777] Germany retained the actual sacrifice within the memory of living men. A cavalry general, Count Friedrich Kasimir Boos von Waldeck, was buried at Treves in 1781 according to the forms of the Teutonic Order; his horse was led in the procession, and the coffin having been lowered into the grave the horse was killed and thrown in upon it.[778] This was, perhaps, the last occasion when such a sacrifice was consummated in solemn form in Europe. But that pathetic incident of a soldier's funeral, the leading of the saddled and bridled charger in the mournful procession, keeps up to this day a lingering reminiscence of the grim religious rite now passed away.

Plants, partaking with animals the phenomena of life and death, health and sickness, not unnaturally have some kind of soul ascribed to them. In fact, the notion of a vegetable soul, common to plants and to the higher organisms possessing an animal soul in addition, was familiar to mediæval philosophy, and is not yet forgotten by naturalists. But in the lower ranges of culture, at least within one wide district of the world, the souls of plants are much more fully identified with the souls of animals. The Society Islanders seem to have attributed 'varua,' i.e. surviving soul or spirit, not to men only but to animals and plants.[779] The Dayaks of Borneo not only consider men and animals to have a spirit or living principle, whose departure from the body causes sickness and eventually death, but they also give to the rice its 'samangat padi,' or 'spirit of the paddy,' and they hold feasts to retain this soul securely, lest the crop should decay.[780] The Karens say that plants as well as men and animals have their 'là' ('kelah'), and the spirit of sickly rice is here also called back like a human spirit considered to have left the body. Their formulas for the purpose have even been written down, and this is part of one:—'O come, rice kelah, come. Come to the field. Come to the rice.... Come from the West. Come from the East. From the throat of the bird, from the maw of the ape, from the throat of the elephant.... From all granaries come. O rice kelah, come to the rice.'[781] There is reason to think that the doctrine of the spirits of plants lay deep in the intellectual history of South-East Asia, but was in great measure superseded under Buddhist influence. The Buddhist books show that in the early days of their religion, it was matter of controversy whether trees had souls, and therefore whether they might lawfully be injured. Orthodox Buddhism decided against the tree-souls, and consequently against the scruple to harm them, declaring trees to have no mind or sentient principle, though admitting that certain dewas or spirits do reside in the body of trees, and speak from within them. Buddhists also relate that a heterodox sect kept up the early doctrine of the actual animate life of trees, in connexion with which may be remembered Marco Polo's somewhat doubtful statement as to certain austere Indians objecting to green herbs for such a reason, and some other passages from later writers. The subject of the spirits of plants is an obscure one, whether from the lower races not having definite opinions, or from our not finding it easy to trace them.[782] The evidence from funeral sacrifices, so valuable as to most departments of early psychology, fails us here, from plants not being thought suitable to send for the service of the dead.[783] Yet, as we shall see more fully elsewhere, there are two topics which bear closely on the matter. On the one hand, the doctrine of transmigration widely and clearly recognises the idea of trees or smaller plants being animated by human souls; on the other, the belief in tree-spirits and the practice of tree-worship involve notions more or less closely coinciding with that of tree-souls, as when the classic hamadryad dies with her tree, or when the Talein of South-East Asia, considering every tree to have a demon or spirit, offers prayers before he cuts one down.

Thus far the details of the lower animistic philosophy are not very unfamiliar to modern students. The primitive view of the souls of men and beasts, as asserted or acted on in the lower and middle levels of culture, so far belongs to current civilized thought, that those who hold the doctrine to be false, and the practices based upon it futile, can nevertheless understand and sympathise with the lower nations to whom they are matters of the most sober and serious conviction. Nor is even the notion of a separable spirit or soul as the cause of life in plants too incongruous with ordinary ideas to be readily appreciable. But the theory of souls in the lower culture stretches beyond this limit, to take in a conception much stranger to modern thought. Certain high savage races distinctly hold, and a large proportion of other savage and barbarian races make a more or less close approach to, a theory of separable and surviving souls or spirits belonging to stocks and stones, weapons, boats, food, clothes, ornaments, and other objects which to us are not merely soulless but lifeless.

Yet, strange as such a notion may seem to us at first sight, if we place ourselves by an effort in the intellectual position of an uncultured tribe, and examine the theory of object-souls from their point of view, we shall hardly pronounce it irrational. In discussing the origin of myth, some account has been already given of the primitive stage of thought in which personality and life are ascribed not to men and beasts only, but to things. It has been shown how what we call inanimate objects—rivers, stones, trees, weapons, and so forth—are treated as living intelligent beings, talked to, propitiated, punished for the harm they do. Hume, whose 'Natural History of Religion' is perhaps more than any other work the source of modern opinions as to the development of religion, comments on the influence of this personifying stage of thought. 'There is an universal tendency among mankind to conceive all beings like themselves, and to transfer to every object those qualities with which they are familiarly acquainted, and of which they are intimately conscious.... The *unknown causes*, which continually employ their thought, appearing always in the same aspect, are all apprehended to be of the same kind or species. Nor is it long before we ascribe to them thought and reason, and passion, and sometimes even the limbs and figures of men, in order to bring them nearer to a resemblance with ourselves.' Auguste Comte has ventured to bring such a state of thought under terms of strict definition in his conception of the primary mental condition of mankind—a state of 'pure fetishism, constantly characterized by the free and direct exercise of our primitive tendency to conceive all external bodies soever, natural or artificial, as animated by a life essentially analogous to our own, with mere differences of intensity.'[784] Our comprehension of the lower stages of mental culture depends much on the thoroughness with which we can appreciate this primitive, childlike conception, and in this our best guide may be the memory of our own childish days. He who recollects when there was still personality to him in posts and sticks, chairs, and toys, may well understand how the infant philosophy of mankind could extend the notion of vitality to what modern science only recognises as lifeless things; thus one main part of the lower animistic doctrine as to souls of objects is accounted for. The doctrine requires for its full conception of a soul not only life, but also a phantom or apparitional spirit; this development, however, follows without difficulty, for the evidence of dreams and visions applies to the spirits of objects in much the same manner as to human ghosts. Everyone who has seen visions while lightheaded in fever, everyone who has ever dreamt a dream, has seen the phantoms of objects as well as of persons. How then can we charge the savage with far-fetched absurdity for taking into his philosophy and religion an opinion which rests on the very evidence of his senses? The notion is implicitly recognized in his accounts of ghosts, which do not come naked, but clothed, and even armed; of course there must be spirits of garments and weapons, seeing that the spirits of men come bearing them. It will indeed place savage philosophy in no unfavourable light, if we compare this extreme animistic development of it with the popular opinion still surviving in civilized countries, as to ghosts and the nature of the human soul as connected with them. When the ghost of Hamlet's father appeared armed cap-a-pe,

'Such was the very armour he had on,

When he the ambitious Norway combated.'

And thus it is a habitual feature of the ghost-stories of the civilized, as of the savage world, that the ghost comes dressed, and even dressed in well-known clothing worn in life. Hearing as well as sight testifies to the phantoms of objects: the clanking of ghostly chains and the rustling of ghostly dresses are described in the literature of apparitions. Now by the savage theory, according to which the ghost and his clothes are alike real and objective, and by the modern scientific theory, according to which both ghost and garment are alike imaginary and subjective, the facts of apparitions are rationally met. But the modern vulgar who ignore or repudiate the notion of ghosts of things, while retaining the notion of ghosts of persons, have fallen into a hybrid state of opinion which has neither the logic of the savage nor of the civilized philosopher.

Among the lower races of mankind, three have been observed to hold most explicitly and distinctly the doctrine of object-souls. These are the Algonquin tribes, extending over a great district of North America, the islanders of the Fijian group, and the Karens of Burma. Among the Indians of North America, Father Charlevoix wrote, souls are, as it were, the shadows and the animated images of the body, and it is by a consequence of this principle that they believe everything to be animate in the universe. This missionary was especially conversant with the Algonquins, and it was among one of their tribes, the Ojibwas, that Keating noticed the opinion that not only men and beasts have souls, but inorganic things, such as kettles, &c., have in them a similar essence. In the same district Father Le Jeune had described, in the seventeenth century, the belief that the souls, not only of men and animals, but of hatchets and kettles, had to cross the water to the Great Village, out where the sun sets.[785] In interesting correspondence with this quaint thought is Mariner's description of the Fiji doctrine—'If an animal or a plant die, its soul immediately goes to Bolotoo; if a stone or any other substance is broken, immortality is equally its reward; nay, artificial bodies have equal good luck with men, and hogs, and yams. If an axe or a chisel is worn out or broken up, away flies its soul for the service of the gods. If a house is taken down or any way destroyed, its immortal part will find a situation on the plains of Bolotoo; and, to confirm this doctrine, the Fiji people can show you a sort of natural well, or deep hole in the ground, at one of their islands, across the bottom of which runs a stream of water, in which you may clearly perceive the souls of men and women, beasts and plants, of stocks and stones, canoes and houses, and of all the broken utensils of this frail world, swimming, or rather tumbling along one over the other pell-mell into the regions of immortality.' A full generation later the Rev. Thomas Williams, while remarking that the escape of brutes and lifeless substances to the spirit-land of Mbulu does not receive universal credit among the Fijians, nevertheless confirms the older account of it:—'Those who profess to have seen the souls of canoes, houses, plants, pots, or any artificial bodies, swimming with other relics of this frail world on the stream of the Kauvandra well, which bears them into the regions of immortality, believe this doctrine as a matter of course; and so do those who have seen the footmarks left about the same well by the ghosts of dogs, pigs, &c.'[786] The theory among the Karens is stated by the Rev. E. B. Cross, as follows:—'Every object is supposed to have its "kelah." Axes and knives, as well as trees and plants, are supposed to have their separate "kelahs."' 'The Karen, with his axe and cleaver, may build his house, cut his rice, and conduct his affairs, after death as before.'[787]

As so many races perform funeral sacrifices of men and animals, in order to dispatch their souls for the service of the soul of the deceased, so tribes who hold this doctrine of object-souls very rationally sacrifice objects, in order to transmit these souls. Among the Algonquin tribes, the sacrifice of objects for the dead was a habitual rite, as when we read of a warrior's corpse being buried with musket and war-club, calumet and war-paint, and a public address being made to the body at burial concerning his future path; while in like manner a woman would be buried with her paddle and kettle, and the carrying-strap for the everlasting burden of her heavily-laden life. That the purpose of such offerings is the transmission of the object's spirit or phantom to the possession of the man's is explicitly stated as early as 1623 by Father Lallemant; when the Indians buried kettles, furs, &c., with the dead, they said that the bodies of the things remained, but their souls went to the dead who used them. The whole idea is graphically illustrated in the following Ojibwa tradition or myth. Gitchi Gauzini was a chief who lived on the shores of Lake Superior, and once, after a few days' illness, he seemed to die. He had been a skilful hunter, and had desired that a fine gun which he possessed should be buried with him when he died. But some of his friends not thinking him really dead, his body was not buried; his widow watched him for four days, he came back to life, and told his story. After death, he said, his ghost travelled on the broad road of the dead toward the happy land, passing over great plains of luxuriant herbage, seeing beautiful groves, and hearing the songs of innumerable birds, till at last, from the summit of a hill, he caught sight of the distant city of the dead, far across an intermediate space, partly veiled in mist, and spangled with glittering lakes and streams. He came in view of herds of stately deer and moose, and other game, which with little fear walked near his path. But he had no gun, and remembering how he had requested his friends to put his gun in his grave, he turned back to go and fetch it. Then he met face to face the train of men, women, and children who were travelling toward the city of the dead. They were heavily laden with guns, pipes, kettles, meats, and other articles; women were carrying basket-work and painted paddles, and little boys had their ornamented clubs and their bows and arrows, the presents of their friends. Refusing a gun which an overburdened traveller offered him, the ghost of Gitchi Gauzini travelled back in quest of his own, and at last reached the place where he had died. There he could see only a great fire before and around him, and finding the flames barring his passage on every side, he made a desperate leap through, and awoke from his trance. Having concluded his story, he gave his auditors this counsel, that they should no longer deposit so many burdensome things with the dead, delaying them on their journey to the place of repose, so that almost everyone he met complained bitterly. It would be wiser, he said, only to put such things in the grave as the deceased was particularly attached to, or made a formal request to have deposited with him.[788]

With purpose no less distinct, when a dead Fijian chief is laid out oiled and painted and dressed as in life, a heavy club is placed ready near his right hand, which holds one or more of the much-prized carved 'whale's tooth' ornaments. The club is to serve for defence against the adversaries who await his soul on the road to Mbulu, seeking to slay and eat him. We hear of a Fijian taking a club from a companion's grave, and remarking in explanation to a missionary who stood by, 'The ghost of the club has gone with him.' The purpose of the whale's tooth is this; on the road to the land of the dead, near the solitary hill of Takiveleyawa, there stands a ghostly pandanus-tree, and the spirit of the dead man is to throw the spirit of the whale's tooth at this tree, having struck which he is to ascend the hill and await the coming of the spirits of his strangled wives.[789] The funeral rites of the Karens complete the present group. They kept up what seems a clear survival from actual human and animal sacrifice, fastening up near an important person's grave a slave and a pony; these invariably released themselves, and the slave became henceforth a free man. Moreover, the practice of placing food, implements and utensils, and valuables of gold and silver, near the remains of the deceased, was general among them.[790]

Now the sacrifice of property for the dead is one of the great religious rites of the world; are we then justified in asserting that all men who abandon or destroy property as a funeral ceremony believe the articles to have spirits, which spirits are transmitted to the deceased? Not so; it is notorious that there are people who recognize no such theory but who nevertheless deposit offerings with the dead. Affectionate fancy or symbolism, a horror of the association of death leading the survivors to get rid of anything that even suggests the dreadful thought, a desire to abandon the dead man's property, an idea that the hovering ghost may take pleasure in or make use of the gifts left for him, all these are or may be efficient motives.[791] Yet, having made full allowance for all this, we shall find good reason to judge that many other peoples, though they may never have stated the theory of object-souls in the same explicit way as the Algonquins, Fijians, and Karens, have recognized it with more or less distinctness. It has given me the more confidence in this opinion to find it held, under proper reservation, by Mr. W. R. Alger, an American investigator, who in a treatise entitled 'A Critical History of the Doctrine of a Future Life' has discussed the ethnography of his subject with remarkable learning and sagacity. 'The barbarian brain,' he writes, 'seems to have been generally impregnated with the feeling that everything else has a ghost as well as man.... The custom of burning or burying things with the dead probably arose, in some cases at least, from the supposition that every object, has its *manes*.'[792] It will be desirable briefly to examine further the subject of funeral offerings, as bearing on this interesting question of early psychology.

A wide survey of funeral sacrifices over the world will plainly show one of their most usual motives to be a more or less defined notion of benefiting the deceased, whether out of kindness to him or from fear of his displeasure. How such an intention may have taken this practical shape we can perhaps vaguely guess, familiar as we are with a state of mind out of which funeral sacrifices could naturally have sprung. The man is dead, but it is still possible to fancy him alive, to take his cold hand, to speak to him, to place his chair at the table, to bury suggestive mementoes in his coffin, to throw flowers into his grave, to hang wreaths of everlastings on his tomb. The Cid may be set on Babieca with his sword Tizona in his hand, and carried out to do battle as of old against the unbeliever; the dead king's meal may be carried in to him in state, although the chamberlain must announce that the king does not dine to-day. Such childlike ignoring of death, such childlike make-believe that the dead can still do as heretofore, may well have led the savage to bury with his kinsman the weapons, clothes, and ornaments that he used in life, to try to feed the corpse, to put a cigar in the mouth of the skull before its final burial, to lay playthings in the infant's grave. But one thought beyond would carry this dim blind fancy into the range of logical reasoning. Granted that the man is dead and his soul gone out of him, then the way to provide that departed soul with food or clothes or weapons is to bury or burn them with the body, for whatever happens to the man may be taken to happen to the objects that lie beside him and share his fate, while the precise way in which the transmission takes place may be left undecided. It is possible that the funeral sacrifice customary among mankind may have rested at first, and may to some extent still rest, on vague thoughts and imaginations like these, as yet fitted into no more definite and elaborate philosophic theory.

There are, however, two great groups of cases of funeral sacrifice, which so logically lead up to or involve the notion of souls or spirits of objects, that the sacrificer himself could hardly answer otherwise a point-blank question as to their meaning. The first group is that in which those who sacrifice men and beasts with the intention of conveying their souls to the other world, also sacrifice lifeless things indiscriminately with them. The second group is that in which the phantoms of the objects sacrificed are traced distinctly into the possession of the human phantom.

The Caribs, holding that after decease man's soul found its way to the land of the dead, sacrificed slaves on a chief's grave to serve him in the new life, and for the same purpose buried dogs with him, and also weapons.[793] The Guinea negroes, at the funeral of a great man, killed several wives and slaves to serve him in the other world, and put fine clothes, gold fetishes, coral, beads, and other valuables, into the coffin, to be used there too.[794] When the New Zealand chief had slaves killed at his death for his service, and the mourning family gave his chief widow a rope to hang herself with in the woods and so rejoin her husband,[795] it is not easy to discern here a motive different from that which induced them at the same time to provide the dead man also with his weapons. Nor can an intellectual line well be drawn between the intentions with which the Tunguz has buried with him his horse, his bow and arrows, his smoking apparatus and kettle. In the typical description which Herodotus gives of the funeral of the ancient

Scythian chiefs, the miscellaneous contents of the burial-mound, the strangled wife and household servants, the horses, the choice articles of property, the golden vessels, fairly represent the indiscriminate purpose which actuated the barbaric sacrifice of creatures and things.[796] So in old Europe, the warrior with his sword and spear, the horse with his saddle, the hunter's hound and hawk and his bow and arrow, the wife with her gay clothes and jewels, lie together in the burial-mound. Their common purpose has become one of the most undisputed inferences of Archæology.

As for what becomes of the objects sacrificed for the dead there are on record the most distinct statements taken from the sacrificers themselves. Although the objects rot in the grave or are consumed on the pile, they nevertheless come in some way into the possession of the disembodied souls they are intended for. Not the material things themselves, but phantasmal shapes corresponding to them, are carried by the souls of the dead on their far journey beyond the grave, or are used in the world of spirits; while sometimes the phantoms of the dead appear to the living, bearing property which they have received by sacrifice, or demanding something that has been withheld. The Australian will take his weapons with him to his paradise.[797] A Tasmanian, asked the reason of a spear being deposited in a native's grave, replied 'To fight with when he is asleep.'[798] Many Greenlanders thought that the kayak and arrows and tools laid by a man's grave, the knife and sewing implements laid by a woman's, would be used in the next world.[799] The instruments buried with the Sioux are for him to make a living with hereafter; the paints provided for the dead Iroquois were to enable him to appear decently in the other world.[800] The Aztec's water-bottle was to serve him on the journey to Mictlan, the land of the dead; the bonfire of garments and baskets and spoils of war was intended to send them with him, and somehow to protect him against the bitter wind; the offerings to the warrior's manes on earth would reach him on the heavenly plains.[801] Among the old Peruvians, a dead prince's wives would hang themselves in order to continue in his service, and many of his attendants would be buried in his fields or places of favourite resort, in order that his soul, passing through those places, might take their souls along with him for future service. In perfect consistency with these strong animistic notions, the Peruvians declared that their reason for sacrifice of property to the dead was that they 'have seen, or thought they saw, those who have long been dead walking, adorned with the things that were buried with them, and accompanied by their wives who had been buried alive.'[802]

As definite an implication of the spirit or phantom of an object appears in a recent account from Madagascar, where things are buried to become in some way useful to the dead. When King Radama died, it was reported and firmly believed that his ghost was seen one night in the garden of his country seat, dressed in one of the uniforms which had been buried with him, and riding one of the best horses killed opposite his tomb.[803] Turanian tribes of North Asia avow that the motive of their funeral offerings of horses and sledges, clothes and axes and kettles, flint and steel and tinder, meat and butter, is to provide the dead for his journey to the land of souls, and for his life there.[804] Among the Esths of Northern Europe, the dead starts properly equipped on his ghostly journey with needle and thread, hairbrush and soap, bread and brandy and coin; a toy, if it is a child. And so full a consciousness of practical meaning survived till lately, that now and then a soul would come back at night to reproach its relations with not having provided properly for it, but left it in distress.[805] To turn from these now Europeanized Tatars to a rude race of the Eastern Archipelago, among the Orang Binua of Sambawa there prevails this curious law of inheritance; not only does each surviving relative, father, mother, son, brother, and so forth, take his or her proper share, but the deceased inherits one share from himself, which is devoted to his use by eating the animals at the funeral feast, burning everything else that will burn, and burying the remainder.[806] In Cochin China, the common people object to celebrating their feast of the dead on the same day with the upper classes, for this excellent reason, that the aristocratic souls might make the servant souls carry home their presents for them. These people employ all the resources of their civilization to perform with the more lavish extravagance the savage funeral sacrifices. Here are details from an account published in 1849 of the funeral of a late king of Cochin China. 'When the corpse of Thien Tri was deposited in the coffin, there were also deposited in it many things for the use of the deceased in the other world, such as his crown, turbans, clothes of all descriptions, gold, silver, and other precious articles, rice and other provisions.' Meals were set out near the coffin, and there was a framed piece of damask with woollen characters, the abode of one of the souls of the defunct. In the tomb, an enclosed edifice of stone, the childless wives of the deceased were to be perpetually shut up to guard the sepulchre, 'and prepare daily the food and other things of which they think the deceased has need in the other life.' At the time of the deposit of the coffin in a cavern behind the tomb building, there were burnt there great piles of boats, stages, and everything used in the funeral, 'and moreover of all the objects which had been in use by the king during his lifetime, of chessmen, musical instruments, fans, boxes, parasols, mats, fillets, carriages, &c., &c., and likewise a horse and an elephant of wood and pasteboard.' 'Some months after the funeral, at two different times, there were constructed in a forest near a pagoda two magnificent palaces of wood with rich furnishings, in all things similar to the palace which the defunct monarch had inhabited. Each palace was composed of twenty rooms, and the most scrupulous attention was given in order that nothing might be awanting necessary for a palace, and these palaces were burned with great pomp, and it is thus that immense riches have been given to the flames from the foolish belief that it would serve the dead in the other world.'[807]

Though the custom is found among the Beduins of arraying the dead with turban, girdle, and sword, yet funeral offerings for the service of the dead are by no means conspicuous among Semitic nations. The mention of the rite by Ezekiel, while showing a full sense of its meaning, characterizes it as not Israelite, but Gentile: 'The mighty fallen of the uncircumcised, which are gone down to Hades with weapons of war, and they have laid their swords under their heads.'[808] Among the Aryan nations, on the contrary, such funeral offerings are known to have prevailed widely and of old, while for picturesqueness of rite and definiteness of purpose they can scarcely be surpassed even among savages. Why the Brahman's sacrificial instruments are to be burnt with him on the funeral pile, appears from this line of the Veda recited at the ceremony: '**Yadâ gachâhatyasunîtimetâmathâ devânâm vasanîrbhavâti,**'—'When he cometh unto that life, faithfully will he do the service of the gods.'[809] Lucian is sarcastic, but scarcely unfair, in his comments on the Greek funeral rites, speaking of those who slew horses and slave-girls and cupbearers, and burned or buried clothes and ornaments, as for use and service in the world below; of the meat and drink offerings on the tombs which serve to feed the bodiless shades in Hades; of the splendid garments and the garlands of the dead, that they might not suffer cold upon the road, nor be seen naked by Kerberos. For Kerberos was intended the honey-cake deposited with the dead; and the obolus placed in the mouth was the toll for Charon, save at Hermione in Argolis, where men thought there was a short descent to Hades, and therefore provided the dead with no coin for the grim ferryman. How such ideas could be realized, may be seen in the story of Eukrates, whose dead wife appeared to him to demand one of her golden sandals, which had been dropped underneath the chest, and so not burnt for her with the rest of her wardrobe; or in the story of Periander, whose dead wife Melissa refused to give him an oracular response, for she was shivering and naked, because the garments buried with her had not been burnt, and so were of no use, wherefore Periander plundered the Corinthian women of their best clothes, which he burned in a great trench with prayer, and now obtained his answer.[810] The ancient Gauls were led, by their belief in another life, to burn and bury with the dead things suited to the living; nor is the record improbable that they transferred to the world below the repayment of loans, for even in modern centuries the Japanese would borrow money in this life, to be repaid with heavy interest in the next.[811] The souls of the Norse dead took with them from their earthly home servants and horses, boats and ferry-money, clothes and weapons. Thus, in death as in life, they journeyed, following the long dark 'hell-way' (helvegr). The 'hell-shoon' (helskó) were bound upon the dead man's feet for the toilsome journey; and when King Harald was slain in the battle of Bravalla, they drove his war-chariot, with the corpse upon it into the great burial-mound, and there they killed the horse, and King Hring gave his own saddle beside, that the fallen chief might ride or drive to Walhalla, as it pleased him.[812] Lastly, in the Lithuanian and old Prussian district, where Aryan heathendom held its place in Europe so firmly and so late, accounts of funeral sacrifice of men, and beasts, and things, date on even beyond the middle ages. Even as they thought that men would live again in the resurrection rich or poor, noble or peasant, as on earth, so 'they believed that the things burned would rise again with them, and serve them as before.' Among these people lived the Kriwe Kriweito, the great priest, whose house was on the high steep mountain Anafielas. All the Souls of their dead must clamber up this mountain, wherefore they burned with them claws of bears and lynxes for their help. All the souls must pass through the Kriwe's house, and he could describe to the surviving relatives of each the clothes, and horse, and weapons he had seen him come with, and even show, for greater certainty, some mark made with lance or other instrument by the passing soul.[813] Such examples of funeral rites show a common ceremony, and to a great degree a common purpose, obtaining from savagery through barbarism, and even into the higher civilization. Now could we have required from all these races a distinct answer to the question, whether they believed in spirits of all things, from men and beasts down to spears and cloaks, sticks and stones, it is likely that we might have often received the same acknowledgment of fully developed animism which stands on record in North America, Polynesia, and Burma. Failing such direct testimony, it is at least justifiable to say that the lower culture, by practically dealing with object-souls, goes far towards acknowledging their existence.

Before quitting the discussion of funeral offerings for transmission to the dead, the custom must be traced to its final decay. It is apt not to die out suddenly, but to leave surviving remnants, more or less dwindled in form and changed in meaning. The Kanowits of Borneo talk of setting a man's property adrift for use in the next world, and even go so far as to lay out his valuables by the bier, but in fact they only commit to the frail canoe a few old things not worth plundering.[814] So in North America, the funeral sacrifice of the Winnebagos has come down to burying a pipe and tobacco with the dead, and sometimes a club in a warrior's grave, while the goods brought and hung up at the burial-place are no longer left there, but the survivors gamble for them.[815] The Santals of Bengal put two vessels, one for rice and the other for water, on the dead man's couch, with a few rupees, to enable him to appease the demons on the threshold of the shadowy world, but when the funeral pile is ready these things are removed.[816] The fanciful art of replacing costly offerings by worthless imitations is at this day worked out into the quaintest devices in China. As the men and horses dispatched by fire for the service of the dead are but paper figures, so offerings of clothes and money may be represented likewise. The imitations of Spanish pillar-dollars in pasteboard covered with tinfoil, the sheets of tinfoil-paper which stand for silver money, and if coloured yellow for gold, are consumed in such quantities that the sham becomes a serious reality, for the manufacture of mock-money is the trade of thousands of women and children in a Chinese city. In a similar way trunks full of property are forwarded in the care of the newly deceased, to friends who are gone before. Pretty paper houses, 'replete with every luxury,' as our auctioneers say, are burnt for the dead Chinaman to live in hereafter, and the paper keys are burnt also, that he may unfasten the paper locks of the paper chests that hold the ingots of gold-paper and silver-paper, which are to be realized as current gold and silver in the other world, an idea which, however, does not prevent the careful survivors from collecting the ashes to re-extract the tin from them in this.[817] Again, when the modern Hindu offers to his dead parent funeral cakes with flowers and betel, he presents a woollen yarn which he lays across the cake, and naming the deceased says, 'May this apparel, made of woollen yarn, be acceptable to thee.'[818] Such facts as these suggest a symbolic meaning in the practically useless offerings which Sir John Lubbock groups together—the little models of kayaks and spears in Esquimaux graves, the models of objects in Egyptian tombs, and the flimsy unserviceable jewelry buried with the Etruscan dead.[819]

Just as people in Borneo, after they had become Mohammedans, still kept up the rite of burying provisions for the dead man's journey, as a mark of respect,[820] so the rite of interring funeral offerings survived in Christian Europe. The ancient Greek burial of the dead with the obolus in his mouth for Charon's toll is represented in the modern Greek world, where Charon and the funeral coin are both familiar. As the old Prussians furnished the dead with spending-money to buy refreshment on his weary journey, so to this day German peasants bury a corpse with money in his mouth or hand, a fourpenny-piece or so. Similar little funeral offerings of coin are recorded in the folklore books elsewhere in Europe.[821] Christian funeral offerings of this kind are mostly trifling in value, and doubtful as to the meaning with which they were kept up. The early Christians retained the heathen custom of placing in the tomb such things as articles of the toilette and children's playthings; modern Greeks would place oars on a shipman's grave, and other such tokens for other crafts; the beautiful classic rite of scattering flowers over the dead still holds its place in Europe.[822] Whatever may have been the thoughts which first prompted these kindly ceremonies, they were thoughts belonging to far præ-Christian ages. The change of sacrifice from its early significance is shown among the Hindus, who have turned it to account for purposes of priestcraft: he who gives water or shoes to a Brahman will find water to refresh him, and shoes to wear, on the journey to the next world, while the gift of a present house will secure him a future palace.[823] In interesting correspondence with this, is a transition from pagan to Christian folklore in our own land. The Lyke-Wake Dirge, the not yet forgotten funeral chant of the North Country, tells, like some savage or barbaric legend, of the passage over the Bridge of Death and the dreadful journey to the other world. But though the ghostly traveller's feet are still shod with the old Norseman's hell-shoon, he gains them no longer by funeral offering, but by his own charity in life:—

'This a nighte, this a nighte

Every night and alle;

Fire and fleet and candle-light,

And Christe receive thy saule.

When thou from hence away are paste

Every night and alle;

To Whinny-moor thou comes at laste,

And Christe receive thy saule.

If ever thou gave either hosen or shoon,

Every night and alle;

Sit thee down and put them on,

And Christe receive thy saule.

But if hosen nor shoon thou never gave neean,

Every night and alle;

The Whinnes shall prick thee to the bare beean,

And Christe receive thy saule.

From Whinny-moore when thou may passe,

Every night and alle;

To Brig o' Dread thou comes at laste,

And Christe receive thy saule.

From Brig o' Dread when thou are paste,

Every night and alle;

To Purgatory Fire thou comes at laste,

And Christe receive thy saule.

If ever thou gave either milke or drink,

Every night and alle;

The fire shall never make thee shrinke,

And Christe receive thy saule.

But if milk nor drink thou never gave neean,

Every night and alle;

The fire shall burn thee to the bare beean

And Christe receive thy saule.'[824]

What reader, unacquainted with the old doctrine of offerings for the dead, could realize the meaning of its remnants thus lingering in peasants' minds? The survivals from ancient funeral ceremony may here again serve as warnings against attempting to explain relics of intellectual antiquity by viewing them from the changed level of modern opinion.

Having thus surveyed at large the theory of spirits or souls of objects, it remains to point out what, to general students, may seem the most important consideration belonging to it, namely, its close relation to one of the most influential doctrines of civilized philosophy. The savage thinker, though occupying himself so much with the phenomena of life, sleep, disease, and death, seems to have taken for granted, as a matter of course, the ordinary operations of his own mind. It hardly occurred to him to think about the machinery of thinking. Metaphysics is a study which first assumes clear shape at a comparatively high level of intellectual culture. The metaphysical philosophy of thought taught in our modern European lecture-rooms is historically traced back to the speculative psychology of classic Greece. Now one doctrine which there comes into view is especially associated with the name of Democritus, the philosopher of Abdera, in the fifth century B.C. When Democritus propounded the great problem of metaphysics, 'How do we perceive external things?'—thus making, as Lewes says, an era in the history of philosophy,—he put forth, in answer to the question, a theory of thought. He explained the fact of perception by declaring that things are always throwing off images εἴδωλα of themselves, which images, assimilating to themselves the surrounding air, enter a recipient soul, and are thus perceived. Now, supposing Democritus to have been really the originator of this famed theory of ideas, how far is he to be considered its inventor? Writers on the history of philosophy are accustomed to treat the doctrine as actually made by the philosophical school which taught it. Yet the evidence here brought forward shows it to be really the savage doctrine of object-souls, turned to a new purpose as a method of explaining the phenomena of thought. Nor is the correspondence a mere coincidence, for at this point of junction between classic religion and classic philosophy the traces of historical continuity may be still discerned. To say that Democritus was an ancient Greek is to say that from his childhood he had looked on at the funeral ceremonies of his country, beholding the funeral sacrifices of garments and jewels and money and food and drink, rites which his mother and his nurse could tell him were performed in order that the phantasmal images of these objects might pass into the possession of forms shadowy like themselves, the souls of dead men. Thus Democritus, seeking a solution of his great problem of the nature of thought, found it by simply decanting into his metaphysics a surviving doctrine of primitive savage animism. This thought of the phantoms or souls of things, if simply modified to form a philosophical theory of perception, would then and there become his doctrine of Ideas. Nor does even this fully represent the closeness of union which connects the savage doctrine of flitting object-souls with the Epicurean philosophy. Lucretius actually makes the theory of film-like images of things (simulacra, membranæ) account both for the apparitions which come to men in dreams, and the images which impress their minds in thinking. So unbroken is the continuity of philosophic speculation from savage to cultured thought. Such are the debts which civilized philosophy owes to primitive animism.

The doctrine of ideas, thus developed in the classic world, has, indeed, by no means held its course thenceforth unchanged through metaphysics, but has undergone transition somewhat like that of the doctrine of the soul itself. Ideas, fined down to the abstract forms or species of material objects, and applied to other than visible qualities, have at last come merely to denote subjects of thought. Yet to this day the old theory has not utterly died out, and the retention of the significant term 'idea' (ἰδέα, visible form) is accompanied by a similar retention of original meaning. It is still one of the tasks of the metaphysician to display and refute the old notion of ideas as being real images, and to replace it by more abstract conceptions. It is a striking instance that Dugald Stewart can cite from the works of Sir Isaac Newton the following distinct recognition of 'sensible species:' 'Is not the sensorium of animals, the place where the sentient substance is present; and to which the sensible species of things are brought, through the nerves and brain, that there they may be perceived by the mind present in that place?' Again, Dr. Reid states the original theory of ideas, while declaring that he conceives it 'to have no solid foundation, though it has been adopted very generally by philosophers.... This notion of our perceiving external objects, not immediately, but in certain images or species of them conveyed by the senses, seems to be the most ancient philosophical hypothesis we have on the subject of perception, and to have, with small variations, retained its authority to this day.' Granted that Dr. Reid exaggerated the extent to which metaphysicians have kept up the notion of ideas as real images of things, few will deny that it does linger much in modern minds, and that people who talk of ideas do often, in some hazy metaphorical way, think of sensible images.[825] One of the shrewdest things ever said about either ideas or ghosts was Bishop Berkeley's retort upon Halley, who bantered him about his idealism. The bishop claimed the mathematician as an idealist also, his 'ultimate ratios' being ghosts of departed quantities, appearing when the terms that produced them vanished.

It remains to sum up in few words the doctrine of souls, in the various phases it has assumed from first to last among mankind. In the attempt to trace its main course through the successive grades of man's intellectual history, the evidence seems to accord best with a theory of its development, somewhat to the following effect. At the lowest levels of culture of which we have clear knowledge, the notion of a ghost-soul animating man while in the body, and appearing in dream and vision out of the body, is found deeply ingrained. There is no reason to think that this belief was learnt by savage tribes from contact with higher races, nor that it is a relic of higher culture from which the savage tribes have degenerated; for what is here treated as the primitive animistic doctrine is thoroughly at home among savages, who appear to hold it on the very evidence of their senses, interpreted on the biological principle which seems to them most reasonable. We may now and then hear the savage doctrines and practices concerning souls claimed as relics of a high religious culture pervading the primæval race of man. They are said to be traces of remote ancestral religion, kept up in scanty and perverted memory by tribes degraded from a nobler state. It is easy to see that such an explanation of some few facts, sundered from their connexion with the general array, may seem plausible to certain minds. But a large view of the subject can hardly leave such argument in possession. The animism of savages stands for and by itself; it explains its own origin. The animism of civilized men, while more appropriate to advanced knowledge, is in great measure only explicable as a developed product of the older and ruder system. It is the doctrines and rites of the lower races which are, according to their philosophy, results of point-blank natural evidence and acts of straightforward practical purpose. It is the doctrines and rites of the higher races which show survival of the old in the midst of the new, modification of the old to bring it into conformity with the new, abandonment of the old because it is no longer compatible with the new. Let us see at a glance in what general relation the doctrine of souls among savage tribes stands to the doctrine of souls among barbaric and cultured nations. Among races within the limits of savagery, the general doctrine of souls is found worked out with remarkable breadth and consistency. The souls of animals are recognized by a natural extension from the theory of human souls; the souls of trees and plants follow in some vague partial way; and the souls of inanimate objects expand the general category to its extremest boundary. Thenceforth, as we explore human thought onward from savage into barbarian and civilized life, we find a state of theory more conformed to positive science, but in itself less complete and consistent. Far on into civilization, men still act as though in some half-meant way they believed in souls or ghosts of objects, while nevertheless their knowledge of physical science is beyond so crude a philosophy. As to the doctrine of souls of plants, fragmentary evidence of the history of its breaking down in Asia has reached us. In our own day and country, the notion of souls of beasts is to be seen dying out. Animism, indeed, seems to be drawing in its outposts, and concentrating itself on its first and main position, the doctrine of the human soul. This doctrine has undergone extreme modification in the course of culture. It has outlived the almost total loss of one great argument attached to it,—the objective reality of apparitional souls or ghosts seen in dreams and visions. The soul has given up its ethereal substance, and become an immaterial entity, 'the shadow of a shade.' Its theory is becoming separated from the investigations of biology and mental science, which now discuss the phenomena of life and thought, the senses and the intellect, the emotions and the will, on a ground-work of pure experience. There has arisen an intellectual product whose very existence is of the deepest significance, a 'psychology' which has no longer anything to do with 'soul.' The soul's place in modern thought is in the metaphysics of religion, and its especial office there is that of furnishing an intellectual side to the religious doctrine of the future life. Such are the alterations which have differenced the fundamental animistic belief in its course through successive periods of the world's culture. Yet it is evident that, notwithstanding all this profound change, the conception of the human soul is, as to its most essential nature, continuous from the philosophy of the savage thinker to that of the modern professor of theology. Its definition has remained from the first that of an animating, separable, surviving entity, the vehicle of individual personal existence. The theory of the soul is one principal part of a system of religious philosophy which unites, in an unbroken line of mental connexion, the savage fetish-worshipper and the civilized Christian. The divisions which have separated the great religions of the world into intolerant and hostile sects are for the most part superficial in comparison with the deepest of all religious schisms, that which divides Animism from Materialism.

END OF VOL. I.

Footnotes

1. Fortnightly Review: 'Origin of Language,' April 15, 1866; 'Religion of Savages,' August 15, 1866. Lectures at Royal Institution: 'Traces of the Early Mental Condition of Man,' March 15, 1867; 'Survival of Savage Thought in Modern Civilization,' April 23, 1869. Lecture at University College, London: 'Spiritualistic Philosophy of the Lower Races of Mankind,' May 8, 1869. Paper read at British Association, Nottingham, 1866: 'Phenomena of Civilization Traceable to a Rudimental Origin among Savage Tribes.' Paper read at Ethnological Society of London, April 26, 1870: 'Philosophy of Religion among the Lower Races of Mankind,' &c., &c.

2. Blackstone, 'Commentaries on the Laws of England,' bk. II., ch. 3. The above example replaces that given in former editions. Another example may be found in his explanation of the origin of deodand, bk. I., ch. 8, as designed, in the blind days of popery, as an expiation for the souls of such as were snatched away by sudden death; see below, p. 287. [Note to 3rd ed.]

3. G. W. Earl, 'Papuans,' p. 79; A. R. Wallace, 'Eastern Archipelago.'

4. Rochefort, 'Iles Antilles,' pp. 400-480.

5. Gibbon, 'Decline and Fall of the Roman Empire,' ch. xxxviii.

6. De Maistre, 'Soirées de St. Pétersbourg,' vol. ii. p. 150.

7. De Brosses, 'Dieux Fétiches,' p. 15; 'Formation des Langues,' vol. i. p. 49; vol. ii. p. 32.

8. Goguet, 'Origine des Lois, des Arts,' &c., vol. i. p. 88.

9. Whately, 'Essay on the Origin of Civilisation,' in Miscellaneous Lectures, &c. His evidence is examined in detail in my 'Early History of Mankind,' ch. vii. See also W. Cooke Taylor, 'Natural History of Society.'

10. Goguet, vol. iii. p. 270.

11. Lecret. v. 923, &c.; see Hor. Sat. i. 3.

12. 'Avesta,' trans. Spiegel & Bleeck, vol. ii. p. 50.

13. Hardy, 'Manual of Budhism,' pp. 64, 128.

14. Niebuhr, 'Römische Geschichte,' part i. p. 88: 'Nur das haben sie übersehen, dasz kein einziges Beyspiel von einem wirklich wilden Volk aufzuweisen ist, welches frey zur Cultur übergegangen wäre.'

15. Whately, 'Essay on Origin of Civilisation.'

16. Ovid. Ex Ponto, iii. 8; see Grote, 'History of Greece,' vol. xii. p. 641.

17. W. C. Taylor, 'Nat. Hist. of Society,' vol. i. p. 202.

18. Fynes Moryson, 'Itinerary;' London, 1617, part iii. p. 162, &c.; J. Evans in 'Archæologia,' vol. xli. See description of hide-boiling, &c., among the wild Irish, about 1550, in Andrew Boorde, 'Introduction of Knowledge,' ed. by F. J. Furnivall, Early English Text Soc. 1870.

19. Buchanan, 'Rerum Scoticarum Historia;' Edinburgh, 1528, p. 7. See 'Early History of Mankind,' 2nd ed. p. 272.

20. Martin, 'Description of Western Islands,' in Pinkerton, vol. iii. p. 639.

21. Barrow, 'Mutiny of the Bounty'; W. Brodie, 'Pitcairn's Island.'

22. Wallace, 'Malay Archipelago,' vol. i. pp. 42, 471; vol. ii. pp. 11, 43, 48; Latham, 'Descr. Eth.,' vol. ii. pp. 492-5; D. and C. Livingstone, 'Exp. to Zambesi,' p. 45.

23. Southey, 'History of Brazil,' vol. iii. p. 422.

24. J. L. Wilson, 'W. Afr.,' p. 189.

25. Waitz, 'Anthropologie,' vol. ii. p. 359, see 91; Du Chaillu, 'Ashangoland,' p. 116; T. H. Bent, 'Ruined Cities of Mashonaland.'

26. Charlevoix, 'Nouvelle France,' vol. vi. p. 51.

27. Irving, 'Astoria,' vol. ii. ch. v.

28. Milton and Cheadle, 'North West Passage by Land,' p. 241; Waitz, vol. iii. pp. 74-6.

29. 'Early History of Mankind,' p. 187.

30. Schoolcraft, 'Algic Res.,' vol. i. p. 50.

31. Steller, 'Kamtschatka,' p. 272.

32. See G. Campbell, 'Ethnology of India,' in Journ. As. Soc. Bengal, 1866 part ii.

33. J. Bailey, 'Veddahs,' in Tr. Eth. Soc., vol. ii. p. 278; see vol. iii. p. 70; Knox, 'Historical Relation of Ceylon,' London, 1681, part iii. chap. i. See A. Thomson, 'Osteology of the Veddas,' in Journ. Anthrop. Inst. 1889, vol. xix. p. 125; L. de Zoysa, 'Origin of Veddas,' in Journ. Ceylon Branch Royal Asiatic Soc., vol. vii.; B. F. Hartshorne in Fortnightly Rev., Mar. 1876. [Note to 3rd edition.]

34. Journ. Ind. Archip., vol. i. pp. 295-9; vol. ii. p. 237.

35. For the connexion between the Aztec language and the Sonoran family extending N. W. toward the sources of the Missouri, see Buschmann, 'Spuren der Aztekischen Sprache im Nördlichen Mexico,' &c., in Abh. der Akad. der Wissensch, 1854; Berlin, 1859; also Tr. Eth. Soc., vol. ii. p. 130. For the connexion between the Natchez and Maya languages see Daniel G. Brinton, in 'American Historical Magazine,' 1867, vol. i. p. 16; and 'Myths of the New World,' p. 28.

36. J. H. Lamprey, in Trans. of Prehistoric Congress, Norwich, 1868, p. 60; J. Linton Palmer, in Journ. Eth. Soc., vol. i. 1869.

37. Squier and Davis, 'Mon. of Mississippi Valley,' &c., in Smithsonian Contr., vol. i. 1848; Lubbock, 'Prehistoric Times,' chap. vii.; Waitz, 'Anthropologie,' vol. iii. p. 72; Bartram, 'Creek and Cherokee Ind.,' in Tr. Amer. Ethnol. Soc., vol. iii. part i. See Petrie, 'Inductive Metrology,' 1877, p. 122. [Note to 3rd ed.]

38. St. John, 'Life in Forests of Far East,' vol. ii. p. 327.

39. Rafn, 'Americas Arctiske Landes Gamle Geographic,' pl. vii., viii.

40. Lubbock (Lord Avebury), in 'Report of British Association, 1867,' p. 121.

41. Lyell, 'Antiquity of Man,' chap. xix.

42. Frere, in 'Archæologia,' 1800.

43. J. Evans, in 'Archæologia,' 1861; Lubbock, 'Prehistoric Times,' 2nd ed., p. 335.

44. See 'Early History of Mankind,' 2nd ed. chap. viii.

45. Argyll, 'Primeval Man,' p. 129.

46. Lecret. De Rerum Natura, v. 1281.

47. See Lyell, 'Antiquity of Man,' 3rd ed. 1863; Lubbock, 'Prehistoric Times, 2nd ed. 1870; 'Trans. of Congress of Prehistoric Archæology' (Norwich, 1868); Stevens, 'Flint Chips, &c.,' 1870; Nilsson, 'Primitive Inhabitants of Scandinavia' (ed. by Lubbock, 1868); Falconer, 'Palæontological Memoirs, &c.'; Lartet and Christy, 'Reliquiæ Aquitanicæ' (ed. by T. R. Jones); Keller, 'Lake Dwellings' (Tr. and Ed. by J. E. Lee), &c., &c.

48. Wallace, 'Indian Archipelago,' vol. i. p. 357.

49. 'Early History of Mankind,' pp. 192, 243, &c., &c.

50. Nilsson, 'Primitive Inhabitants of Scandinavia,' p. 104.

51. Klemm, 'Allg. Culturwissenschaft,' part ii., Werkzeuge und Waffen.

52. Lane Fox (Pitt-Rivers), 'Lectures on Primitive Warfare,' Journ. United Service Inst., 1867-9.

53. Evans in 'Trans. of Congress of Prehistoric Archæology' (Norwich, 1868), p. 191; Rau in 'Smithsonian Reports,' 1868; Sir E. Belcher in Tr. Eth. Soc., vol. i. p. 129.

54. See details in 'Early History of Mankind,' chap. vii.-ix.

55. Will. de Rubruquis in Pinkerton, vol. vii. pp. 46, 67, 132; Michie, 'Siberian Overland Route,' p. 96.

56. Ovid. Fast. v. 487. For modern Italy and France, see Edélestane du Méril, 'Études d'Archéol.' p. 121.

57. 'Journ. Ind. Archip.' (ed. by J. R. Logan), vol. ii. p. liv.

58. Klemm, 'Cultur-Geschichte,' vol. ii. p. 209.

59. Oldfield in 'Tr. Eth. Soc.' vol. iii. p. 266; Dumont d'Urville, 'Voy. de l'Astrolabe,' vol. i. p. 411.

60. Strutt, 'Sports and Pastimes,' book ii. chap. ii.

61. Polack, 'New Zealanders,' vol. ii. p. 171.

62. Polack, ibid.; Wilkes, 'U. S. Exp.' vol. i. p. 194. See the account of the game of liagi in Mariner, 'Tonga Is.' vol. ii. p. 339; and Yate, 'New Zealand,' p. 113.

63. Petron. Arbitri Satiræ rec. Büchler, p. 64 (other readings are *buccæ* or *bucco*).

64. Compare Davis, 'Chinese,' vol. i. p. 317; Wilkinson, Ancient Egyptians, vol. i. p. 188; Facciolati, Lexicon, s.v. 'micare'; &c.

65. Jamieson, 'Dict. of Scottish Lang.' s.v.

66. 'Early History of Mankind,' p. 244, &c.; Grimm, 'Deutsche Myth.,' p. 573.

67. Grimm, *ibid.*, p. 1200.

68. Halliwell, 'Popular Rhymes,' p. 112; Grimm, 'D. M.' p. 812. Bastian, 'Mensch,' vol. iii. p. 106. Johannis Philosophi Ozniensis Opera (Aucher), Venice, 1834, pp. 78-89. 'Infantium sanguini similam commiscentes illegitimam communionem deglutiunt; quo pacto porcorum suos fœtus immaniter vescentium exsuperant edacitatem. Quique illorum cadavera super tecti culmen celantes, ac sursum oculis in cœlum defixis respicientes, jurant alieno verbo ac sensu: *Altissimus novit.* Solem vero deprecari volentes, ajunt: *Solicule, Lucicule*; atque aëreos, vagosque dæmones clam invocant, juxta Manichæorum Simonisque incantatoris errores. Similiter et primum parientis fœminæ puerum de manu in manum inter eos invicem projectum, quum pessimâ morte occiderint, illum, in cujus manu exspiraverit puer, ad primam sectæ dignitatem provectum venerantur; atque per utriusque nomen audent insane jurare; *Juro*, dicunt, *per unigenitum filium*: et iterum: *Testem habeo tibi gloriam ejus, in cujus manum unigenitus filius spiritum suum tradidit....* Contra hos [the orthodox] audacter evomere præsumunt impietatis suæ bilem, atque insanientes, ex mali spiritus blasphemiâ, *Sculpticolas* vocant.'

69. Polack, vol. i. p. 270.

70. Bosman, 'Guinese Kust,' letter x.; Eng. Trans. in Pinkerton, vol. xvi. p. 399.

71. Homer, Iliad, vii. 171; Pindar, Pyth. iv. 338.

72. Tacit. Germania. 10.

73. Smith's 'Dic. of Gr. and Rom. Ant.,' arts. 'oraculum,' 'sortes.'

74. Roberts, 'Oriental Illustrations,' p. 163.

75. Gataker, pp. 91, 141; see Lecky, 'History of Rationalism,' vol. i. p. 307.

76. Jeremy Taylor, 'Ductor Dubitantium,' in Works, vol. xiv. p. 337.

77. See Wuttke, 'Deutsche Volksaberglaube,' pp. 95, 115, 178.

78. Mariner, 'Tonga Islands,' vol. ii. p. 239; Turner, 'Polynesia,' p. 214; Williams, 'Fiji,' vol. i. p. 228. Compare Cranz, 'Grönland,' p. 231.

79. R. Taylor, 'New Zealand,' pp. 206, 348, 387.

80. Smith's Dic., art. 'talus.'

81. Brand, 'Popular Antiquities,' vol. ii. p. 412.

82. D. & C. Livingstone, 'Exp. to Zambesi,' p. 51.

83. Doolittle, 'Chinese,' vol. ii. pp. 108, 285-7; see 384; Bastian, 'Oestl. Asien,' vol. iii. pp. 76, 125.

84. Smith's Dic., art. 'cottabos.'

85. Grimm, 'Deutsche Myth.' p. 222.

86. Plin. viii. 54.

87. From a letter of Mr. H. J. Stokes, Negapatam, to Mr. F. M. Jennings. General details of the Couvade in 'Early History of Mankind.' p. 293.

88. Hâvamâl, 138.

89. Jamieson, 'Scottish Dictionary,' s.v. 'coals'; R. Hunt, 'Popular Romances,' 1st ser. p. 83.

90. Wuttke, 'Volksaberglaube,' p. 131.

91. Rochholz, 'Deutscher Glaube und Brauch,' vol. i. p. 120; R. Chambers, 'Popular Rhymes of Scotland,' Miscellaneous; Grimm, pp. 969, 976; Wuttke, p. 115.

92. Mendes, 'Service for the First Nights of Passover,' London, 1862 (in the Jewish interpretation the word *shunra*,—'cat,' is compared with *shinâr*). Halliwell, 'Nursery Rhymes,' p. 288; 'Popular Rhymes,' p. 6.

93. Williams, 'Fiji,' vol. i. p. 110.

94. Shortland, 'Traditions of N. Z.' p. 196.

95. Casalis, 'Études sur la langue Séchuana.'

96. R. F. Burton, 'Wit and Wisdom from West Africa.' See also Waitz, vol. ii. p. 245.

97. Callaway, 'Nursery Tales, &c. of Zulus,' vol. i. p. 364, &c.

98. Casalis, 'Etudes sur la langue Séchuana,' p. 91; 'Basutos,' p. 337.

99. Steere, 'Swahili Tales,' p. 418.

100. Burton, 'Wit and Wisdom from West Africa,' p. 212.

101. Turner, 'Polynesia,' p. 216. See Polack, 'New Zealanders,' vol. ii. p. 171.

102. Sahagun, 'Historia de Nueva España,' in Kingsborough's 'Antiquities, of Mexico,' vol. vii. p. 178.

103. Grimm, p. 699.

104. Diog. Laert. i. 91; Athenagoras. x, 451.

105. Mannhardt's 'Zeitschr. für Deutsche Mythologie,' vol. iii. p. 2, &c.:

'Nóg er forthun nösgás vaxin,

Barngiorn su er bar bútimbr saman;

Hlifthu henni halms bitskálmir,

Thó lá drykkjar drynhrönn yfir.'

106. See Grote, 'Hist. of Greece,' vol. ii. p. 5.

107. Mannhardt's 'Zeitschr.' l.c.

108. E. A. W. Zimmermann, 'Geographische Geschichte des Menschen,' &c., 1778-83, vol. iii. See Professor Rolleston's Inaugural Address, British Association, 1870.

109. Earl of Chesterfield, 'Letters to his Son,' vol. ii. No. lxviii.

110. See Hylten-Cavallius, 'Wärend och Wirdarne,' vol. i. pp. 161-70 Grimm, pp. 52-5, 1201; Brand, vol. ii. pp. 314, 325, &c.

111. Callaway, 'Religion of Amazulu,' pp. 64, 222-5, 263.

112. Godignus, 'Vita Patris Gonzali Sylveriæ.' Col. Agripp. 1616; lib. ii. c. x.

113. Bosman, 'Guinea,' letter xviii. in Pinkerton, vol. xvi. p. 478.

114. Burton, 'Wit and Wisdom from West Africa,' p. 373.

115. Shortland, 'Trads. of New Zealand,' p. 131.

116. Turner, 'Polynesia,' p. 348; see also Williams, 'Fiji,' vol. i. p. 250.

117. Mariner, 'Tonga Is.' vol. i. p. 456.

118. Garcilaso de la Vega, 'Hist. de la Florida,' vol. iii. ch. xli.

119. Among dissertations on the subject, see especially Sir Thos. Browne 'Pseudodoxia Epidemica' (Vulgar Errors), book iv. chap. ix.;

Brand 'Popular Antiquities,' vol. iii. p. 119, &c.; R. G. Haliburton, 'New Materials for the History of Man.' Halifax, N. S. 1863; 'Encyclopædia Britannica,' (5th ed.) art. 'sneezing,' Wernsdorf, 'De Ritu Sternutantibus bene precandi.' Leipzig, 1741; see also Grimm, D. M. p. 1070, note.

120. Homer, Odyss. xvii. 541.

121. Xenophon, Anabasis, iii. 2, 9.

122. Aristot. Problem. xxxiii. 7.

123. Anthologia Græca, Brunck, vol. iii. p. 95.

124. Petron. Arb. Sat. 98.

125. Plin. xxviii. 5.

126. Noel, 'Dic. des Origines;' Migne, 'Dic. des Superstitions,' &c.; Bastian, 'Oestl. Asien,' vol. ii. p. 129.

127. Ward, 'Hindoos,' vol. i. p. 142; Dubois, 'Peuples de l'Inde,' vol. i. p. 465; Sleeman, 'Ramaseeana,' p. 120.

128. Buxtorf, 'Lexicon Chaldaicum;' Tendlau, 'Sprichwörter, &c. Deutsch-Jüdischer Vorzeit.' Frankf. a. M., 1860, p. 142.

129. Lane, 'Modern Egyptians,' vol. i. p. 282. See Grant, in 'Tr. Eth. Soc.' vol. iii. p. 90.

130. Grimm, 'D. M.' pp. 1070, 1110.

131. 'Manuel des Pecchés,' in Wedgwood, 'Dic. English Etymology,' s.v., 'wassail.'

132. Brand, vol. iii. p. 126.

133. Callaway, p. 263.

134. Ward, l.c.

135. 'Pend-Nameh,' tr. de Sacy, ch. lxiii.; Maury, 'Magie,' &c., p. 302; Lane, l.c.

136. G. Brecher, 'Das Transcendentale im Talmud,' p. 168; Joseph. Ant. Jud. viii. 2, 5.

137. Migne, 'Dic. des Hérésies,' s.v.

138. Bastian, 'Mensch,' vol. ii. pp. 115, 322.

139. Wuttke, 'Deutsche Volksaberglaube,' p. 137.

140. Haliburton, op. cit.

141. Powell and Magnussen, 'Legends of Iceland,' 2nd ser. p. 448.

142. The cases in which a sneeze is interpreted under special conditions, as with reference to right and left, early morning, &c. (see Plutarch, De Genio Socratis, &c.), are not considered here, as they belong to ordinary omen-divination.

143. W. Scott, 'Minstrelsy of Scottish Border;' Forbes Leslie, 'Early Races of Scotland,' vol. i. pp. 194, 487; Grimm, 'Deutsche Mythologie,' pp. 972, 1095; Bastian, 'Mensch,' vol. ii. pp. 92, 407, vol. iii. pp. 105, 112; Bowring, 'Servian Popular Poetry,' p. 64. A review of the First Edition of the present work in 'Nature,' June 15, 1871, contains the following:—'It is not, for example, many years since the present Lord Leigh was accused of having built an obnoxious person—one account, if we remember right, said eight obnoxious persons—into the foundation of a bridge at Stoneleigh. Of course so preposterous a charge carried on its face its own sufficient refutation; but the fact that it was brought at all is a singular instance of the almost incredible vitality of old traditions.'

144. Waitz, vol. ii. p. 197.

145. Ellis, 'Polyn. Res.' vol. i. p. 346; Tyerman and Bennet, vol. ii. p. 39.

146. St. John, 'Far East,' vol. i. p. 46; see Bastian, vol. ii. p. 407. I am indebted to Mr. R. K. Douglas for a perfect example of one meaning of the foundation-sacrifice, from the Chinese book, 'Yūh hea ke' ('Jewelled Casket of Divination'): 'Before beginning to build, the workmen should sacrifice to the gods of the neighbourhood, of the earth and wood. Should the carpenters be very apprehensive of the building falling, they, when fixing a post, should take something living and put it beneath, and lower the post on it, and to liberate [the evil influences] they should strike the post with an axe and repeat—

"It is well, it is well,

May those who live within

Be ever warm and well fed."'

147. Caron, 'Japan,' in Pinkerton, vol. vii. p. 623.

148. F. Mason, 'Burmah,' p. 100; Bastian, 'Oestl. Asien,' vol. i. pp. 193, 214; vol. ii. pp. 91, 270; vol. iii. p. 16; Roberts, 'Oriental Illustrations,' p. 283.

149. Bastian, 'Mensch,' vol. iii. p. 107. A modern Arnaut story is given by Prof. Liebrecht in 'Philologus,' vol. xxiii. (1865), p. 682.

150. Bastian, 'Mensch,' vol. iii. p. 210; Ward, 'Hindoos,' vol. ii. p. 318.

151. Kracheninnikow, 'Descr. du Kamchatka, Voy. en Sibérie,' vol. iii. p. 72.

152. Steller, 'Kamtschatka,' pp. 265, 274.

153. J. V. Grohmann, 'Aberglauben und Gebräuche aus Böhmen,' p. 12.

154. Chap. XVIII.

155. Eastman, 'Dacotah,' pp. 118, 125.

156. R. Taylor, 'New Zealand,' p. 48.

157. Bastian, 'Oestl. Asien,' vol. iii. p. 34.

158. Hanusch, 'Wissenschaft des Slawischen Mythus,' p. 299.

159. Grimm, 'Deutsche Myth,' p. 462.

160. Bastian, 'Oestl. Asien,' vol. i. p. 119.

161. 'Life of Nath. Pearce,' ed. by J. J. Halls, vol. i. p. 286.

162. 'Journ. Ind. Archip.' vol. i. p. 328; vol. ii. p. 273; see vol. iv. p. 425.

163. Muir, 'Sanskrit Texts,' part ii. p. 435.

164. Dalton, 'Kols,' in 'Tr. Eth. Soc.' vol. vi. p. 6; see p. 16.

165. Jas. Gardner, 'Faiths of the World,' s.v. 'Exorcism.'

166. Shortt, 'Tribes of Neilgherries,' in 'Tr. Eth. Soc.' vol. vii. pp. 247, 277; Sir W. Elliot in 'Trans. Congress of Prehistoric Archæology,' 1868, p. 253.

167. F. Rühs, 'Finland,' p. 296; Bastian, 'Mensch,' vol. iii. p. 202.

168. Brand, 'Pop. Ant.' vol. iii. pp. 81-3; see p. 313.

169. Wuttke, 'Deutsche Volksaberglaube,' p. 128; see p. 239.

170. For an examination of numerous magical arts, mostly coming under this category, see 'Early History of Mankind,' chaps. vi. and x.

171. Stanbridge, 'Abor. of Victoria,' in 'Tr. Eth. Soc.' vol. i. p. 299; Ellis, 'Polyn. Res.' vol. i. p. 364; J. L. Wilson, 'W. Africa,' p. 215;

Spiegel, 'Avesta,' vol. i. p. 124; Wuttke, 'Deutsche Volksaberglaube,' p. 195; general references in 'Early History of Mankind,' p. 129.

172. Burton, 'W. and W. from West Africa,' p. 411.

173. W. Gregory, 'Letters on Animal Magnetism,' p. 128.

174. Eyre, 'Australia,' vol. ii. p. 361; Collins, 'New South Wales,' vol. i. pp. 561, 594.

175. Shortt, in 'Tr. Eth. Soc.' vol. vi. p. 278.

176. Bastian, 'Mensch,' vol. iii. p. 117.

177. See Grote, vol. iii. pp. 113, 351.

178. Hardy, 'Eastern Monachism,' p. 241.

179. Oldfield, in 'Tr. Eth. Soc.' vol. iii. p. 246.

180. Grout, 'Zulu-land,' p. 134.

181. See specimen and description in the Christy Museum.

182. Macpherson, 'India,' pp. 130, 363.

183. Wuttke, 'Volksaberglaube,' p. 31.

184. R. Hunt, 'Pop. Rom. of W. of England,' 2nd ser. p. 165; Brand, 'Pop. Ant.' vol. ii. p. 231.

185. Wuttke, p. 100.

186. Grimm, 'D. M.' p. 560.

187. Brand, vol. iii. p. 240.

188. Hunt, *ibid.* p. 148.

189. Wuttke, p. 165; Brand, vol. iii. p. 305.

190. Magalhanes de Gandavo, p. 125; D'Orbigny, vol. ii. p. 168.

191. St. John, 'Far East,' vol. i. p. 202; 'Journ. Ind. Archip.' vol. ii. p. 357.

192. Yate, 'New Zealand,' p. 90; Polack, vol. i. p. 248.

193. Klemm, 'Cultur-Gesch.' vol. iii. p. 202.

194. Burton, 'Wit and Wisdom from West Africa,' p. 381.

195. See Cornelius Agrippa, 'De Occulta Philosophia,' i. 53; 'De Vanitate Scient.' 37; Grimm, 'D. M.' p. 1073; Hanusch, 'Slaw. Myth.' p. 285; Brand, vol. iii. pp. 184-227.

196. Oldfield in 'Tr. Eth. Soc.' vol. iii. p. 241.

197. Steller, 'Kamtschatka,' p. 279.

198. Callaway, 'Rel. of Amazulu,' pp. 236, 241; R. Taylor, 'N. Z.' p. 334.

199. Artemidorus, 'Oneirocritica;' Cockayne, 'Leechdoms, &c., of Early England,' vol. iii.; Seafield, 'Literature, &c., of Dreams;' Brand, vol. iii.; Halliwell, 'Pop. Rhymes, &c.,' p. 217, &c., &c.

200. St. John, 'Far East,' vol. i. pp. 74, 115; Ellis, 'Polyn. Res.' vol. iv. p. 150; Polack, 'New Zealanders,' vol. i. p. 255.

201. Georgi, 'Reise im Russ. Reich,' vol. i. p. 281; Hooker, 'Himalayan Journals,' vol. i. p. 135; 'As. Res.' vol. iii. p. 27; Latham, 'Descr. Eth.' vol. i. p. 61.

202. Cieza de Leon, p. 289; Rivero and Tschudi, 'Peru,' p. 183.

203. Burton, 'Central Afr.' vol. ii. p. 32; Waitz, vol. ii. pp. 417, 518.

204. Plin. xi. 73. See Cic. de Divinatione, ii. 12.

205. Wuttke, 'Volksaberglaube,' p. 32.

206. Le Jeune, 'Nouvelle France,' vol. i. p. 90.

207. J. H. Plath, 'Rel. d. alten Chinesen,' part i. p. 89; Klemm, 'Cultur. Gesch.' vol. iii. pp. 109, 199; vol. iv. p. 221; Rubruquis, in Pinkerton, vol. vii. p. 65; Grimm, 'D. M.' p. 1067; R. F. Burton, 'Sindh,' p. 189; M. A. Walker, 'Macedonia,' p. 169.

208. Brand, vol. iii. p. 339; Forbes Leslie, vol. ii. p. 491.

209. Maury, 'Magie, &c.', p. 74; Brand, vol. iii. p. 348, &c. See figure in Cornelius Agrippa, 'De Occult. Philosoph.,' ii. 27.

210. R. Taylor, 'New Zealand,' p. 205; Shortland, p. 139; Callaway, 'Religion of Amazulu,' p. 330, &c.; Theophylact. in Brand, vol. iii. p. 332. Compare mentions of similar devices; Herodot. iv. 67 (Scythia); Burton, 'Central Africa,' vol. ii. p. 350.

211. Migne's 'Dic. des Sciences Occultes.'

212. Mason, 'Karens,' in 'Journ. As. Soc. Bengal,' 1865, part ii. p. 200; Bastian, 'Oestl. Asien,' vol. i. p. 146.

213. Hodgson, 'Abor. of India,' p. 170. See Macpherson, p. 106 (Khonds).

214. Ammian. Marcellin. xxix. 1.

215. Chevreul, 'De la Baguette Divinatoire, du Pendule dit Explorateur et des Tables Tournantes,' Paris, 1854; Brand, vol. iii. p. 332; Grimm, 'D. M.' p. 926; H. B. Woodward, in 'Geological Mag.,' Nov. 1872; Wuttke, p. 94.

216. Cornelius Agrippa, 'De Speciebus Magiæ,' xxi.; Brand, vol. iii. p. 351; Grimm, 'D. M.' p. 1062.

217. De Maistre, 'Soirées de St. Petersbourg,' vol. ii. p. 212.

218. Shortland, 'Trads., &c. of New Zealand,' p. 138.

219. See Cicero, 'De Div.' i.; Lucian, 'De Astrolog.'; Cornelius Agrippa, 'De Occulta Philosophia;' Sibly, 'Occult Sciences;' Brand, vol. iii.

220. Plin. xvi. 75; xviii. 75; Grimm, 'D. M.' p. 676; Brand, vol. ii. p. 169; vol. iii. p. 144.

221. Bacon, 'Novum Organum.' The original story is that of Diagoras; see Cicero, 'De Natura Deorum,' iii. 37; Diog. Laërt. lib. vi., Diogenes, 6.

222. Du Chaillu, 'Ashango-land,' pp. 428, 435; Burton, 'Central Afr.' vol. i. pp. 57, 113, 121.

223. See Grimm, 'D. M.' ch. xxxiv.; Lecky, 'Hist. of Rationalism,' vol. i. chap. i.; Horst, 'Zauber-Bibliothek;' Raynald, 'Annales Ecclesiastici,' vol. ii., Greg. IX. (1233), xli.-ii.; Innoc. VIII. (1484), lxxiv.

224. See also Dasent, 'Introd. to Norse Tales;' Maury, 'Magie, &c.,' ch. vii.

225. Lane, 'Thousand and One Nights,' vol. i. p. 30; Grimm, 'D. M.' pp. 435, 465, 1056; Bastian, 'Mensch,' vol. ii. pp. 265, 287; vol. iii. p. 204; D. Wilson, 'Prehistoric Annals of Scotland,' vol. ii. p. 126; Wuttke, 'Volksaberglaube,' pp. 15, 20, 122, 220.

226. Brand, 'Pop. Ant.' vol. iii. pp. 1-43; Wuttke, 'Volksaberglaube,' p. 50; Grimm, 'Deutsche Rechtsalterthümer,' p. 923; Pictet, 'Origines Indo-Europ.' part ii. p. 459; Manu, viii., 114-5; see Plin. vii. 2.

227. Swedenborg, 'The True Christian Religion,' London, 1855, Nos. 156, 157, 281, 851.

228. Grimm, 'Deutsche Myth,' pp. 473, 481.

229. St. John, 'Far East,' vol. i. p. 82; Bastian, 'Psychologie,' p. 111; 'Oestl. Asien.' vol. iii. pp. 232, 259, 288; Boecler, 'Ehsten Aberglaube,' p. 147.

230. Bastian, 'Mensch,' vol. ii. p. 74.

231. Brand, vol. ii. p. 486.

232. Glanvil, 'Saducismus Triumphatus,' part ii. The invisible drummer appears to have been one William Drury; see 'Pepys' Diary,' vol. i. p. 227.

233. Brand, vol. iii. pp. 225, 233; Grimm, pp. 801, 1089, 1141; Wuttke, pp. 38-9, 208; Shortland, 'Trads. of New Zealand,' p. 137 (ominous ticking of insect, doubtful whether idea native, or introduced by foreigners).

234. Bastian, 'Mensch,' vol. ii. p. 393.

235. Doolittle, 'Chinese,' vol. ii. p. 112; Bastian, 'Oestl. Asien,' vol. iii. p. 252; 'Psychologie,' p. 159.

236. Toehla, 'Aurifontina Chymica,' cited by K. R. H. Mackenzie, in 'Spiritualist,' Mar. 15, 1870.

237. Nicephor. Callist. Ecclesiast. Hist. viii. 23; Stanley, 'Eastern Church,' p. 172.

238. 'Pneumatologie Positive et Expérimentale; La Réalité des Esprits et le Phénomène Merveilleux de leur Écriture Directe démontrés,' par le Baron L. de Guldenstubbé. Paris, 1857.

239. Hardy, 'Manual of Budhism,' pp. 38, 126, 150; 'Eastern Monachism,' pp. 272, 285, 382; Köppen, 'Religion des Buddha,' vol. i. p. 412; Bastian, 'Oestl. Asien,' vol. iii. p. 390; Philostrati Vita Apollon. Tyan. iii. 15. See the mention among the Saadhs of India (17th century), by Trant, in 'Missionary Register,' July, 1820, pp. 294-6.

240. Lucian, Philopseudes, 13.

241. Eunapius in Iambl.

242. Alban Butler, 'Lives of the Saints,' vol. i. p. 674; Calmet, 'Diss. sur les Apparitions, &c.,' chap. xxi.; De Maistre, 'Soirées de St. Pétersbourg,' vol. ii. pp. 158, 175. See also Bastian, 'Mensch,' vol. ii. p. 578; 'Psychologie,' p. 159.

243. Glanvil, 'Saducismus Triumphatus,' part ii.; Bastian, 'Psychologie,' p. 161.

244. 'Spiritualist,' Feb. 15, 1870. Orrin Abbott, 'The Davenport Brothers,' New York, 1864.

245. Homer, Odyss. xiv. 345 (Worsley's Trans.); Beda, 'Historia Ecclesiastica,' iv. 22; Grimm, 'D. M.,' p. 1180 (an old German loosing-charm is given from the Merseburg MS.); J. Y. Simpson, in 'Proc. Ant. Soc. Scotland,' vol. iv.; Keating, 'Long's Exp. to St. Peter's River,' vol. ii. p. 159; Egede, 'Greenland,' p. 189; Cranz, 'Grönland,' p. 269; Castrén, 'Reiseberichte,' 1845-9, p. 173.

246. Conyers Middleton, 'A Letter from Rome,' 1729; Hor. Sat. I. v. 98.

247. C. de Brosses, 'Traité de la Formation Mécanique des Langues,' &c. (1st ed. 1765); Wedgwood, 'Origin of Language' (1866); 'Dic. of English Etymology' (1859, 2nd ed. 1872); Farrar, 'Chapters on Language' (1865).

248. Among the principal savage and barbaric languages here used for evidence, are as follows:—Africa: Galla (Tutschek, Gr. and Dic.), Yoruba (Bowen, Gr. and Dic.), Zulu (Döhne, Dic.). Polynesia, &c.: Maori (Kendall, Vocab., Williams, Dic.), Tonga (Mariner, Vocab.), Fiji (Hazlewood, Dic.), Melanesia (Gabelentz, Melan. Spr.). Australia (Grey, Moore, Schürmann, Oldfield, Vocabs.). N. America: Pima, Yakama, Clallam, Lummi, Chinuk, Mohawk, Micmac (Smithson. Contr. vol. iii.), Chinook Jargon (Gibbs, Dic.), Quiché (Brasseur, Gr. and Dic.). S. America: Tupi (Diaz, Dic.), Carib (Rochefort, Vocab.), Quichua (Markham, Gr. and Dic.), Chilian (Febres, Dic.), Brazilian tribes (Martius, 'Glossaria linguarum Brasiliensium'). Many details in Pott, 'Doppelung,' &c.

249. Bonwick, 'Daily Life of Tasmanians,' p. 140; Capt. Wilson, in 'Tr. Eth. Soc.,' vol. iv. p. 322, &c.; J. L. Wilson, in 'Journ. Amer. Oriental Soc.,' vol. i. 1849, No. 4; also Cranz., 'Grönland,' p. 279 (cited below, p. 186). For other accounts, see 'Early Hist. of Mankind,' p. 77.

250. Forbes, 'Aymara Indians,' in Journ. Eth. Soc. 1870, vol. ii. p. 208.

251. See Helmholtz, 'Tonempfindungen,' 2nd ed. p. 163; McKendrick, Text Book of Physiology, p. 681, &c., 720, &c.; Max Müller, 'Lectures,' 2nd series, p. 95, &c.

252. See Pallegoix, 'Gramm. Ling. Thai.'; Bastian, in 'Monatsb. Berlin. Akad.' June 6, 1867, and 'Roy. Asiatic Soc.,' June, 1867.

253. Burton, in 'Mem. Anthrop. Soc.,' vol. i. p. 313; Bowen, 'Yoruba Gr. and Dic.' p. 5; see J. L. Wilson, 'W. Afr.,' p. 461.

254. C. W., in 'London and Westminster Review,' Oct. 1837.

255. 'Accentus est etiam in dicendo cantus obscurior.'—Cic. de Orat.

256. Helmholtz, p. 364.

257. Caswell, in Bastian, 'Berlin. Akad.' l.c.

258. Horne Tooke, 'Diversions of Purley,' 2nd ed. London, 1798, pt. i. pp. 60-3.

259. R. F. Burton, 'Lake Regions of Central Africa,' vol. ii. p. 333; Livingstone, 'Missionary Tr. in S. Africa,' p. 298; 'Gr. of Mpongwe lang,' A. B. C. F. Missions, Rev. J. L. Wilson, p. 27. See Callaway, 'Zulu Tales,' vol. i. p. 59.

260. Arroyo de la Cuesta, 'Gr. of Mutsun Lang.' p. 39, in Smithsonian Contr., vol. iii.; Neapolitan *mamma mia!* exclamation of wonder, &c., Liebrecht in Götting. Gel. Anz. 1872, p. 1287.

261. Shaw, 'Travels in Barbary,' in Pinkerton, vol. xv. p. 669.

262. Some of the examples here cited, will be found in Grimm, 'Deutsche Gr.' vol. iii. p. 308; Pott, 'Doppelung.' p. 27; Wedgwood, 'Origin of Language.'

263. See Pictet, 'Origines Indo-Europ.' part i. p. 382; Caldwell, 'Gr. of Dravidian Langs.' p. 465; Wedgwood, Dic. s.v. 'puss,' &c.; Mariner, 'Tonga Is. (Vocab.)'; Gibbs, 'Dic. of Chinook Jargon,' Smithsonian Coll. No. 161; Pandosy, 'Gr. and Dic. of Yakama,' Smithson. Contr. vol. iii.; compare J. L. Wilson, 'Mpongwe Gr.' p. 57. The Hindu child's call to the cat *mun mun!* may be from Hindust. *mâno* = cat. It. *micio,* Fr. *mite, minon,* Ger. *mieze,* &c. = 'cat,' and Sp. *miz!* Ger. *minz!* &c. = 'puss!' are from imitations of a *mew.*

264. For lists of drivers' words, see Grimm, l.c.; Pott, 'Zählmethode,' p. 261; Halliwell, 'Dic. of Archaic and Provincial English,' s.v. 'ree;' Brand, vol. ii. p. 15; Pictet, part ii. p. 489.

265. 'Encyclopédie, ou Dictionnaire Raisonné des Sciences, &c.' Recueil de Planches, Paris, 1763, art. 'Chasses.' The traditional cries are still more or less in use. See 'A Week in a French Country-house.'

266. Aldrete, 'Lengua Castellana,' Madrid, 1673, s.vv. *harre, exe.*

267. 'There prevailed in those days an indecent custom; when the preacher touched any favourite topick in a manner that delighted his audience, their approbation was expressed by a loud hum, continued in proportion to their zeal or pleasure. When Burnet preached, part of his congregation hummed so loudly and so long, that he sat down to enjoy it, and rubbed his face with his handkerchief. When Sprat preached, he likewise was honoured with the like animating hum, but he stretched out his hand to the congregation, and cried, "Peace, peace; I pray you, peace."' Johnson, 'Life of Sprat.'

268. Cranz, 'Grönland,' p. 279.

269. D. Wilson, 'Prehistoric Man,' p. 65.

270. Compare, in the same district, Camé *ii*, Cotoxó *biebie*, *eubiähiä*, multus, -a, -um.

271. J. H. Donker Curtius, 'Essai de Grammaire Japonaise,' p. 34, &c. 199. In former editions of the present work, the directly interjectional character of the *o* is held in an unqualified manner. Reference to the grammars of Prof. B. H. Chamberlain and others, where this particle (*on*, *o*) is connected with other forms implying a common root, leaves the argument to depend wholly or partly on the supposition of an interjectional source for this root. [Note to 3rd ed.]

272. Bruyas, 'Mohawk Lang.,' p. 16, in Smithson. Contr. vol. iii. Schoolcraft, 'Indian Tribes,' Part iii. p. 328, 502, 507. Charlevoix, 'Nouv. France,' vol. i. p. 350.

273. The *arre!* may have been introduced into Europe by the Moors, as it is used in Arabic, and its use in Europe corresponds nearly with the limits of the Moorish conquest, in Spain *arre!* in Provence *arri!*

274. Wedgwood, 'Origin of Language,' p. 92.

275. Ibid., p. 72.

276. De Brosses, vol. i. p. 203. See Wedgwood.

277. Also Oraon *hae—ambo*; Micmac *é—mw*.

278. A double contradiction in Carib *anhan!* = 'yes!' *oua!* = 'no!' Single contradictions in Catoquina *hang!* Tupi *eém!* Botocudo *hemhem!* Yoruba *eñ!* for 'yes!' Culino *aiy!* Australian *yo!* for 'no!' &c. How much these sounds depend on peculiar intonation, we, who habitually use *h'm!* either for 'yes!' or 'no!' can well understand.

279. (Charles de Brosses) 'Traité de la Formation Mécanique des Langues, &c.' Paris, An. ix., vol. i. p. 238; vol. ii. p. 313. Lazarus and Steinthal, 'Zeitschrift für Völkerpsychologie,' &c., vol. i. p. 421. Heyse, 'System der Sprachwissenschaft,' p. 73. Farrar, 'Chapters on Language,' p. 202.

280. Similar sounds are used to command silence, to stop speaking as well as to stop going. English *husht! whist! hist!* Welsh *ust!* French *chut!* Italian *zitto!* Swedish *tyst!* Russian *st'!* and the Latin *st!* so well described in the curious old line quoted by Mr. Farrar, which compares it with the gesture of the finger on the lips:—

'Isis, et Harpocrates digito qui significat *st!*'

This group of interjections, again, has not been proved to be in use outside Aryan limits.

281. Catlin, 'North American Indians,' vol. i. pp. 221, 39, 151, 162. Bailey in 'Tr. Eth. Soc.,' vol. ii. p. 318. Job xxvii. 23. (The verb *shârak* also signifies to call by a hiss, 'and he will hiss unto them from the end of the earth, and behold, they shall come with speed,' Is. v. 26; Jer. xix. 8.) Alcock, 'The Capital of the Tycoon,' vol. i. p. 394. Cook, '2nd Voy.' vol. ii. p. 36. Casalis, 'Basutos,' p. 234.

282. Wedgwood, 'Origin of Language,' p. 83, 'Dictionary,' Introd. p. xlix. and s.v. 'foul.' Prof. Max Müller, 'Lectures,' 2nd series, p. 92, protests against the indiscriminate derivation of words directly from such cries and interjections, without the intervention of determinate roots. As to the present topic, he points out that Latin *pus, putridus,* Gothic *fuls,* English *foul,* follow Grimm's law as if words derived from a single root. Admitting this, however, the question has to be raised, how far pure interjections and their direct derivatives, being self-expressive and so to speak living sounds, are affected by phonetic changes such as that of Grimm's law, which act on articulate sounds no longer fully expressive in themselves, but handed down by mere tradition. Thus *p* and *f* occur in one and the same dialect in interjections of disgust and aversion, *puh! fi!* being used in Venice or Paris, just as similar sounds would be in London. In tracing this group of words from early Aryan forms, it must also be noticed that Sanskrit is a very imperfect guide, for its alphabet has no *f,* and it can hardly give the rule in this matter to languages possessing both *p* and *f,* and thus capable of nicer appreciation of this class of interjections.

283. Mpongwe *punjina*; Basuto *foka*; Carib *phoubäe*; Arawac *appüdün* (ignem sufflare). Other cases are given by Wedgwood, 'Or. of Lang.' p. 83.

284. See Wedgwood, 'Dic.' Introd. p. viii.

285. See Wedgwood, Dic., s.v. 'mum,' &c.

286. Bates, 'Naturalist on the Amazons,' 2nd ed., p. 404; Markham in 'Tr. Eth. Soc.,' vol. iii. p. 143.

287. 'Avesta,' Farg. xviii. 34-5.

288. Wedgwood, Dic., s.v. 'pigeon;' Diez, 'Etym. Wörterb.,' s.v. 'piccione.'

289. Bopp, 'Gloss. Sanscr.,' s.v. 'go.' See Pott, 'Wurzel-Wörterb. der Indo-Germ. Spr.,' s.v. 'gu,' 'Zählmethode,' p. 227.

290. Pott, 'Doppelung (Reduplication, Gemination) als eines der wichtigsten Bildungsmittel der Sprache,' 1862. Frequent use has been here made of this work.

291. For authorities see especially Pott, 'Doppelung,' p. 30, 47-49; W. v. Humboldt, 'Kawi-Spr.' vol. ii. p. 36; Max Müller in Bunsen, 'Philos. of Univ. Hist.' vol. i. p. 329; Latham, 'Comp. Phil.' p. 200; and the grammars and dictionaries of the particular languages. The Guarani and Carib on authority of D'Orbigny, 'L'Homme Américain,' vol. ii. p. 268; Dhimal of Hodgson, 'Abor. of India,' p. 69, 79, 115; Colville Ind. of Wilson in 'Tr. Eth. Soc.' vol. iv. p. 331; Botocudo of Martius, 'Gloss. Brasil.'

292. Also Old High German *diz* and *daz*.

293. Max Müller, l.c.

294. J. C. E. Buschmann, 'Ueber den Naturlaut,' Berlin, 1853; and in 'Abh. der K. Akad. d. Wissensch,' 1852. An English trans. in 'Proc. Philological Society,' vol. vi. See De Brosses, 'Form. des L.,' vol. i. p. 211.

295. One family of languages, the Athapascan, contains both *appá* and *mama* as terms for 'father,' in the Tahkali and Tlatskanai.

296. See Pott, 'Indo-Ger. Wurzelwörterb.' s.v. 'pâ'; Böhtlingk and Roth, 'Sanskrit-Wörterb.' s.v. *mâtar*; Pictet, 'Origines Indo-Europ.,' part ii. p. 349; Max Müller, 'Lectures,' 2nd series, p. 212.

297. Facciolati, 'Lexicon;' Varro, ap. Nonn., ii. 97.

298. Plato, 'Cratylus', 90.

299. Mariner, 'Tonga Islands,' vol. ii. p. 390.

300. Crowther, 'Yoruba Vocab.'; Burton, 'W. & W. from W. Africa,' p. 253. 'O daju danu, o ko mo essan messan.—You (may seem) very clever, (but) you can't tell 9 × 9.'

301. Low in 'Journ. Ind. Archip.' vol. i. p. 408; 'Year-Books Edw. I.' (xx.-i.) ed. Horwood, p. 220.

302. Spix and Martius, 'Reise in Brazilien,' p. 387.

303. 'Tasmanian Journal,' vol. i.; Backhouse, 'Narr.' p. 104; Milligan in 'Papers, &c., Roy. Soc. Tasmania,' vol. iii. part ii. 1859.

304. Oldfield in 'Tr. Eth. Soc.'; vol. iii. p. 291; Lang, 'Queensland,' p. 433; 'Latham, Comp. Phil.' p. 352. Other terms in Bonwick, l. c.

305. Sicard, 'Théorie des Signes pour l'Instruction des Sourds-Muets,' vol. ii. p. 634.

306. Stanbridge in 'Tr. Eth. Soc.' vol. i. p. 304.

307. Martius, 'Gloss. Brasil,' p. 15.

308. Kracheninnikow, 'Kamtchatka,' p. 17.

309. Gumilla, 'Historia del Orenoco,' vol. iii. ch. xlv.; Pott, 'Zählmethode,' p. 16.

310. The Eastern brokers have used for ages, and still use, the method of secretly indicating numbers to one another in bargaining, 'by snipping fingers under a cloth.' 'Every joynt and every finger hath his signification,' as an old traveller says, and the system seems a more or less artificial development of ordinary finger-counting, the thumb and little finger stretched out, and the other fingers closed, standing for 6 or 60, the addition of the fourth finger making 7 or 70, and so on. It is said that between two brokers settling a price by thus snipping with the fingers, cleverness in bargaining, offering a little more, hesitating, expressing an obstinate refusal to go farther, &c., comes out just as in chaffering in words.

311. Gilij; 'Saggio di Storia Americana,' vol. ii. p. 332 (Tamanac, Maypure). Martius, 'Gloss. Brasil,' (Cayriri, Tupi, Carib, Omagua, Juri, Guachi, Coretu, Cherentes, Maxuruna, Caripuna, Cauixana, Carajás, Coroado, &c.); Dobrizhoffer, 'Abipones,' vol. ii. p. 168; Humboldt, 'Monumens,' pl. xliv. (Muysca).

312. Cranz, 'Grönland,' p. 286; Kleinschmidt, 'Gr. der Grönl. Spr.;' Rae in 'Tr. Eth. Soc.' vol. iv. p. 145.

313. Milligan, l. c.; G. F. Moore, 'Vocab. W. Australia.' Compare a series of quinary numerals to 9, from Sydney, in Pott, 'Zählmethode,' p. 46.

314. Gabelentz, 'Melanesiche Sprachen,' p. 183.

315. W. v. Humboldt, 'Kawi-Spr.' vol. ii. p. 308; corroborated by 'As. Res.' vol. vi. p. 90; 'Journ. Ind. Archip.' vol. iii. p. 182, &c.

316. Kölle, 'Gr. of Vei Lang.' p. 27.

317. Schreuder, 'Gr. for Zulu Sproget,' p. 30; Döhne, 'Zulu Dic.'; Grout, 'Zulu Gr.' See Hahn, 'Gr. des Herero.'

318. Sir W. Jones in 'As. Res.' vol. ii. 1790, p. 296; E. Jacquet in 'Nouv. Journ. Asiat.' 1835; W. v. Humboldt, 'Kawi-Spr.' vol. i. p. 19. This system of recording dates, &c., extended as far as Tibet and the Indian Archipelago. Many important points of Oriental chronology depend on such formulas. Unfortunately their evidence is more or less vitiated by inconsistencies in the use of words for numbers.

319. Eyre, 'Australia,' vol. ii. p. 324; Schürmann, 'Vocab. of Parnkalla Lang.,' gives forms partially corresponding.

320. 'Journ. Ind. Archip.' New Ser. vol. ii. 1858, p. 118 (Sulong, Awang, Itam ('black'), Puteh ('white'), Allang, Pendeh, Kechil or Bongsu); Bastian, 'Oestl. Asien,' vol. ii. p. 494. The details are imperfectly given, and seem not all correct.

321. Ellis, 'Madagascar,' vol. i. p. 154. Also Andriampaivo, or Lahi-Zandrina, for last male; Andrianivo for intermediate male. Malagasy *lahy*, 'male'= Malay *laki*; Malagasy *vavy*, 'female' = Tongan *fafine*, Maori *wahine*, 'woman;' comp. Malay *bâtina*, 'female.'

322. M. Eastman, 'Dahcotah; or, Life and Legends of the Sioux,' p. xxv.

323. 'Journ. Ethnol. Soc.' vol. iv. (Akra); Ploss, 'Das Kind,' vol. i. p. 139 (Elmina).

324. H. Hale, 'Ethnography and Philology,' vol. vi. of Wilkes, U.S. Exploring Exp., Philadelphia, 1846, pp. 172, 289. (N.B.—The ordinary editions do not contain this important volume.)

325. Bowen, 'Gr. and Dic. of Yoruba.' Burton in 'Mem. Anthrop. Soc.,' vol. i. p. 314.

326. See Pott, 'Zählmethode,' pp. 78, 99, 124, 161; Grimm, 'Deutsche Rechtsalterthümer,' ch. v.

327. Francisque-Michel, 'Argot,' p. 483.

328. Of evidence of this class, the following deserves attention:—Dobrizhoffer, 'Abipones,' vol. ii. p. 169, gives *geyenkñatè*, 'ostrich-toes,' as the numeral for 4, their ostrich having three toes before and one behind, and *neènhalek*, 'a five-coloured spotted hide,' as the numeral 5. D'Orbigny, 'L'Homme Américain,' vol. ii. p. 163, remarks:—'Les Chiquitos ne savent compter que jusqu'à un (*tama*), n'ayant plus ensuite que des termes de comparaison.' Kölle, 'Gr. of Vei Lang.,' notices that *féra* means both 'with' and 2, and thinks the former meaning original (compare the Tah. *piti*, 'together,' thence 2). Quichua *chuncu*, 'heap,' *chunca*, 10, may be connected. Aztec, *ce*, 1, *centli*, 'grain,' may be connected. On possible derivations of 2 from hand, &c., especially Hottentot, *t'koam*, 'hand, 2,' see Pott, 'Zählmethode,' p. 29.

329. See Farrar, 'Chapters on Language,' p. 223. Benloew, 'Recherches sur l'Origine des Noms de Nombre;' Pictet, 'Origines Indo-Europ.' part ii. ch. ii.; Pott, 'Zählmethode,' p. 128, &c.; A. v. Humboldt's plausible comparison between Skr. *pancha*, 5, and Pers. *penjeh*, 'the palm of the hand with the fingers spread out; the outspread foot of a bird,' as though 5 were called *pancha* from being like a hand, is erroneous. The Persian *penjeh* is itself derived from the numeral 5, as in Skr. the hand is called *panchaçâkha*, 'the five-branched.' The same formation is found in English; slang describes a man's hand as his 'fives,' or 'bunch of fives,' thence the name of the game of fives, played by striking the ball with the open hand, a term which has made its way out of slang into accepted language. Burton describes the polite Arab at a meal, calling his companion's attention to a grain of rice fallen into his beard. 'The gazelle is in the garden,' he says, with a smile. 'We will hunt her with the *five*,' is the reply.

330. Ovid, Fast. iii. 121.

331. The actual word-numerals of the two quinary series are given as examples. Triton's Bay, 1, *samosi*; 2, *roëeti*; 3, *touwroe*; 4, *faat*; 5, *rimi*; 6, *rim-samos*; 7, *rim-roëeti*; 8, *rim-touwroe*; 9, *rim-faat*; 10, *woetsja*. Lifu, 1, *pacha*; 2, *lo*; 3, *kun*; 4, *thack*; 5, *thabumb*; 6, *lo-acha*; 7, *lo-a-lo*; 8, *lo-kunn*; 9, *lo-thack*; 10, *te-bennete*.

332. A. F. Pott, 'Die Quinäre und Vigesimale Zählmethode bei Völkern aller Welttheile,' Halle, 1847; supplemented in 'Festgabe zur xxv. Versammlung Deutscher Philologen, &c., in Halle' (1867).

333. 'Account of Laura Bridgman,' London, 1845, p. 159.

334. Compare the Rajmahali tribes adopting Hindi numerals, yet reckoning by twenties. Shaw, l.c. The use of a 'score' as an indefinite number in England, and similarly of 20 in France, of 40 in the Hebrew of the Old Testament and the Arabic of the Thousand and One Nights, may be among other traces of vigesimal reckoning.

335. D. Wilson, 'Prehistoric Man,' p. 616.

336. Grant in 'Tr. Eth. Soc.' vol. iii. p. 90.

337. Dobrizhoffer, 'Gesch. der Abiponer,' p. 205; Eng. Trans. vol. ii. p. 171.

338. Markham in 'Tr. Eth. Soc.' vol. iii. p. 166.

339. Latham, 'Comp. Phil.' p. 186; Shaw in 'As. Res.' vol. iv. p. 96; 'Journ. As. Soc. Bengal,' 1866, part ii. pp. 27, 204, 251.

340. St. Cricq in 'Bulletin de la Soc. de Géog.' 1853, p. 286; Pott, 'Zählmethode,' p. 7.

341. Gabelentz, p. 89; Hale, l.c.

342. J. C. Hotten, 'Slang Dictionary,' p. 218.

343. 'Early History of Mankind,' p. 106.

344. Ellis, 'Polyn. Res.' vol. i. p. 91; Klemm, C. G. vol. iii. p. 383.

345. Grote, 'History of Greece,' vol. i. chaps. ix. xi.; Pausanias viii. 2; Plutarch. Theseus 1.

346. See Banier, 'La Mythologie et les Fables expliquées par l'Histoire,' Paris, 1738; Lempriere, 'Classical Dictionary,' &c.

347. Hanusch, 'Slav. Myth.' p. 323; Grimm, D. M. p. 363; Latham, 'Descr. Eth.' vol. ii. p. 448; I. J. Schmidt, 'Forschungen,' p. 13; J. G. Müller, 'Amer. Urrelig.' p. 268. See also Plutarch. Parallela xxxvi.; Campbell, 'Highland Tales,' vol. i. p. 278; Max Müller, 'Chips,' vol. ii. p. 169; Tylor, 'Wild Men and Beast-children,' in Anthropological Review, May 1863.

348. Macrae in 'As. Res.' vol. vii. p. 189.

349. Bastian, 'Oestl. Asien,' vol. i. p. 51.

350. Grote, vol. iii. p. 104; vol. v. p. 22; Herodot. i. 189; vii. 34; Porphyr. de Abstinentia, ii. 30; Pausan. i. 28; Pollux, 'Onomasticon.'

351. Reid, 'Essays,' vol. iii. p. 113.

352. Wuttke, 'Volksaberglaube,' p. 210.

353. See chap. xi.

354. D'Orbigny, 'L'Homme Américain,' vol. ii. p. 102. See also De la Borde, 'Caraibes,' p. 525.

355. Le Jeune in 'Relations des Jésuites dans la Nouvelle France,' 1634, p. 26. See Charlevoix, 'Nouvelle France,' vol. ii. p. 170.

356. Schoolcraft, 'Algic Researches,' vol. ii. p. 54; compare 'Tanner's Narrative,' p. 317; see also 'Prose Edda,' i. 11; 'Early Hist. of Mankind,' p. 327.

357. Prescott, 'Peru,' vol. i. p. 86; Garcilaso de la Vega, 'Comm. Real.' i. c. 15; iii. c. 21.

358. Torquemada, 'Monarquia Indiana,' vi. 42; Clavigéro, vol. ii. p. 9; Sahagun in Kingsborough, 'Antiquities of Mexico.'

359. Bastian, 'Mensch,' vol. ii. p. 59.

360. Le Jeune, in 'Relations des Jésuites dans la Nouvelle France,' 1639, p. 88.

361. Froebel, 'Central America,' p. 490.

362. Tac. Ann. xiii. 55.

363. Stanbridge, in 'Tr. Eth. Soc.' vol. i. p. 301.

364. Cranz, 'Grönland,' p. 295; Hayes, 'Arctic Boat Journey,' p. 254.

365. Schoolcraft, 'Indian Tribes,' part iii. p. 276; see also De la Borde, 'Caraibes,' p. 525.

366. H. Yule in 'Journ. As. Soc. Bengal,' vol. xiii. (1844), p. 628.

367. Origen, de Principiis, i. 7, 3; Pamphil. Apolog. pro Origine, ix. 84.

368. De Maistre, 'Soirées de Saint-Pétersbourg,' vol. ii. p. 210, see 184.

369. Kaempfer, 'Japan,' in Pinkerton, vol. vii. p. 684.

370. Doolittle, 'Chinese,' vol. ii. p. 265; see Ward, 'Hindoos,' vol. i. p. 140 (Indra's elephants drinking).

371. Chron. Joh. Bromton, in 'Hist. Angl. Scriptores,' x. Ric. I. p. 1216.

372. Lane, 'Thousand and one N.' vol. i. p. 30, 7.

373. Krapf, 'Travels,' p. 198.

374. Lane, *ibid.* pp. 30, 42; Burton, 'El Medinah and Meccah,' vol. ii. p. 69; 'Lake Regions,' vol. i. p. 297; J. D. Hooker, 'Himalayan Journals,' vol. i. p. 79; Tylor, 'Mexico,' p. 30; Tyerman and Bennet, vol. ii. p. 362. (Hindu piçâcha = demon, whirlwind.)

375. Taylor, 'New Zealand,' p. 121.

376. Mason, 'Karens,' in 'Journ. As. Soc. Bengal,' 1865, part ii. p. 217.

377. Callaway, 'Zulu Tales,' vol. i. p. 294.

378. Burton, 'Dahome,' vol. ii. p. 148; see 242.

379. Schoolcraft, 'Algic Res.' vol. ii. p. 148.

380. Du Chaillu, 'Ashango-land,' p. 106.

381. Jas. Atkinson, 'Customs of the Women of Persia,' p. 49.

382. 2 Sam. xxiv. 16; 2 Kings xix. 35.

383. G. S. Assemanni, 'Bibliotheca Orientalis,' ii. 86.

384. Hanusch, 'Slav. Mythus,' p. 322. Compare Torquemada, 'Monarquia Indiana,' i. c. 14 (Mexico); Bastian, 'Psychologie,' p. 197.

385. Macpherson, 'India,' p. 357.

386. Markham, 'Quichua Gr. and Dic.' p. 9.

387. Welcker, 'Griech. Götterl.' vol. i. p. 690.

388. Ellis, 'Polyn. Res.' vol. i. p. 231; Polack, 'New Z.' vol. i. p. 273.

389. Grimm, 'D. M.' pp. 694-6.

390. Ward, 'Hindoos,' vol. i. p. 140.

391. Castren, 'Finnische Mythologie,' pp. 48, 49.

392. Delbrück in Lazarus and Steinthal's Zeitschrift, vol. iii. p. 269.

393. Schoolcraft, part iii. p. 520.

394. Sicard, 'Théorie des Signes, &c.' Paris 1808, vol. ii. p. 634; 'Personal Recollections' by Charlotte Elizabeth, London, 1841, p. 182; Dr. Orpen, 'The Contrast,' p. 25. Compare Meiners, vol. i. p. 42.

395. Le Jeune, in 'Rel. des Jés. dans la Nouvelle France,' 1634, p. 13.

396. Pietro della Valle, 'Viaggi,' letter xvi.

397. 'Journ. Ind. Archip.' vol. ii. p. xxvii.

398. See remarks on the tendency of sex-denoting language to produce myth in Africa, in W. H. Bleek, 'Reynard the Fox in S. Afr.' p. xx.; 'Origin of Lang.' p. xxiii.

399. Caldwell, 'Comp. Gr. of Dravidian Langs.' p. 172.

400. Schoolcraft, 'Indian Tribes,' part ii. p. 366. For other cases see especially Pott in Ersch and Gruber's 'Allg. Encyclop.' art. 'Geschlecht;' also D. Forbes, 'Persian Gr.' p. 26; Latham, 'Descr. Eth.' vol. ii. p. 60.

401. Callaway, 'Relig. of Amazulu,' p. 166.

402. Grey, 'Polyn. Myth.' pp. 132, &c., 211; Shortland, 'Traditions of N. Z.' p. 15.

403. Schoolcraft, 'Indian Tribes,' part i. p. 391 and pl. 55.

404. Livingstone, 'S. Afr.' p. 124.

405. Tac. Germania, 45.

406. Maury, 'Magie, &c.' p. 175.

407. Eliot in 'As. Res.' vol. iii. p. 32.

408. Macpherson, 'India,' pp. 92, 99, 108.

409. Dalton, 'Kols of Chota-Nagpore' in 'Tr. Eth. Soc.' vol. vi. p. 32.

410. J. Cameron, 'Malayan India,' p. 393; Bastian, 'Oestl. Asien,' vol. i. p. 119; vol. iii. pp. 261, 273; 'As. Res.' vol. vi. p. 173.

411. Dobrizhoffer, 'Abipones,' vol. ii. p. 77. See J. G. Müller, 'Amer. Urrelig.' p. 63; Martius, 'Ethn. Amer.' vol. i. p. 652; Oviedo, 'Nicaragua,' p. 229; Piedrahita, 'Nuevo Reyno de Granada,' part i. lib. c. 3.

412. Kölle, 'Afr. Lit. and Kanuri Vocab.' p. 275.

413. 'Life and Adventures of Nathaniel Pearce' (1810-9), ed. by J. J. Halls, London, 1831, vol. i. p. 286; also 'Tr. Eth. Soc.' vol. vi. p. 288; Waitz, vol. ii. p. 504.

414. Parkyns, 'Life in Abyssinia' (1853), vol. ii. p. 146.

415. Du Chaillu, 'Ashango-land,' p. 52. For other African details, see Waitz, vol. ii. p. 343; J. L. Wilson, 'W. Afr.' pp. 222, 365, 398; Burton, 'E. Afr.' p. 57; Livingstone, 'S. Afr.' pp. 615, 642; Magyar, 'S. Afr.' p. 136.

416. Virg. Bucol. ecl. viii. 95.

417. For collections of European evidence, see W. Hertz, 'Der Werwolf;' Baring-Gould, 'Book of Werewolves;' Grimm, 'D. M.' p. 1047; Dasent, 'Norse Tales,' Introd. p. cxix.; Bastian, 'Mensch.' vol. ii. pp. 32, 566; Brand, 'Pop. Ant.' vol. i. p. 312, vol. iii. p. 32; Lecky, 'Hist. of Rationalism,' vol. i. p. 82. Particular details in Petron. Arbiter, Satir. lxii.; Virgil. Eclog. viii. 97; Plin. viii. 34; Herodot. iv. 105; Mela ii. 1; Augustin. De Civ. Dei, xviii. 17; Hanusch, 'Slav. Myth.' pp. 286, 320; Wuttke, 'Deutsche Volksaberglaube,' p. 118.

418. Macrob. 'Saturn.' i. 19, 12. See Eurip. Phœn. 1116, &c. and Schol.; Welcker, vol. i. p. 336; Max Müller, 'Lectures,' vol. ii. p. 380.

419. Francisque-Michel, 'Argot,' p. 425.

420. Sir G. Grey, 'Polynesian Mythology,' p. i. &c., translated from the original Maori text published by him under the title of 'Ko nga Mahinga a nga Tupuna Maori, &c.' London, 1854. Compare with Shortland, 'Trads. of N. Z.' p. 55, &c.; R. Taylor, 'New Zealand,' p. 114, &c.

421. Schirren, 'Wandersagen der Neuseeländer, &c.' p. 42; Ellis, 'Polyn. Res.' vol. i. p. 116; Tyerman and Bennet, p. 526; Turner, 'Polynesia,' p. 245.

422. Premare in Pauthier, 'Livres Sacrés de l'Orient,' p. 19; Doolittle, 'Chinese,' vol. ii. p. 396.

423. J. G. Müller, 'Amer. Urrelig.' pp. 108, 110, 117, 221, 369, 494, 620; Rivero and Tschudi, 'Ant. of Peru,' p. 161; Gregg, 'Journal of a Santa Fé Trader,' vol. ii. p. 237; Sahagun, 'Retorica, &c., Mexicana,' cap. 3, in Kingsborough, 'Ant. of Mexico,' vol. v.

424. Castrén, 'Finn. Myth.' p. 86.

425. Grimm, 'D. M.' pp. xix. 229-33, 608; Halliwell, 'Pop. Rhymes,' p. 153; Milton, 'Paradise Lost,' ix. 273, i. 535; see Lucretius, i. 250.

426. Pictet, 'Origines Indo-Europ.' part ii. pp. 663-7; Colebrooke, 'Essays,' vol. i. p. 220. Plato, Repub. iii. 414-5; 'ἡ γῆ αὐτοὺς μήτηρ οὖσα ἀνῆκε—ἀλλ' ὁ θεὸς πλάττων.'

427. Herod. iv. 59.

428. Plath, 'Religion der alten Chinesen' part i. p. 37; Davis, 'Chinese,' vol. ii. p. 64; Legge, 'Confucius,' p. 106; Bastian, 'Mensch,' vol. ii. p. 437, vol. iii. p. 302.

429. J. G. Müller, 'Amer. Urrelig.' pp. 53, 219, 231, 255, 395, 420; Martius 'Ethnog. Amer.' vol. i. pp. 329, 467, 585, vol. ii. p. 109; Southey, 'Brazil,' vol. i. p. 352, vol. ii. p. 371; De la Borde, 'Caraibes,' p. 525; Dobrizhoffer 'Abipones,' vol. ii. p. 84; Smith and Lowe, 'Journey from Lima to Para,' p. 230; Schoolcraft, 'Indian Tribes of N. A.' part i. p. 271; Charlevoix, 'Nouv. France,' vol. vi. p. 149; Cranz, 'Grönland,' p. 295; Bastian, 'Mensch,' vol. iii. p. 191; 'Early Hist, of Mankind,' p. 163.

430. Ellis, 'Polyn. Res.' vol. i. p. 331.

431. Marsden, 'Sumatra,' p. 194.

432. Grant in 'Tr. Eth. Soc.' vol. iii. p. 90; Kölle, 'Kanuri Proverbs, &c.' p. 207.

433. H. H. Wilson, 'Vishnupurana,' pp. 78, 140; Skr. Dic. s.v. râhu; Sir W. Jones in 'As. Res.' vol. ii. p. 290; S. Davis, *ibid.*, p. 258; Pictet, 'Origines Indo-Europ.' part ii. p. 584; Roberts, 'Oriental Illustrations,' p. 7; Hardy, 'Manual of Buddhism.'

434. Castrén, 'Finn. Myth,' p. 63; Bastian, 'Oestl. Asien,' vol. ii. p. 344.

435. Klemm, 'C. G.' vol. vi. p. 449; Doolittle, 'Chinese,' vol. i. p. 308; Turpin, Richard, and Borri in Pinkerton, vol. iv. pp. 579, 725, 815; Bastian, 'Oestl. Asien,' vol. ii. p. 109, vol. iii. p. 242. See Eisenmenger, 'Entdecktes Judenthum,' vol. i. p. 398 (Talmudic myth).

436. Plutarch, de Facie in Orbe Lunae; Juvenal, Sat. vi. 441; Plin. ii. 9; Tacit. Annal. i. 28.

437. Grimm, 'D. M.' pp. 668-78, 224; Hanusch, 'Slaw. Myth,' p. 268; Brand, 'Pop. Ant.' vol. iii. p. 152; Horst, 'Zauber-Bibliothek,' vol. iv. p. 350; D. Monnier, 'Traditions populaires comparées,' p. 138; see Migne, 'Dic. des Superstitions,' art. 'Eclipse'; Cornelius Agrippa, 'De Occulta Philosophia,' ii. c. 45, gives a picture of the lunar eclipse-dragon.

438. Grey, 'Polyn. Myth.' pp. 54-58; in his Maori texts, Ko nga Mahinga, pp. 28-30, Ko nga Mateatea, pp. xlviii.-ix. I have to thank Sir G. Grey for a more explicit and mythologically more consistent translation of the story of Maui's entrance into the womb of Hine-nui-te-po and her crushing him to death between her thighs, than is given in his English version. Compare R. Taylor, 'New Zealand,' p. 132; Schirren, 'Wandersagen der Neuseel.' p. 33; Shortland, 'Trads.

of N. Z.' p. 63 (a version of the myth of Maui's death); see also pp. 171, 180, and Baker in 'Tr. Eth. Soc.' vol. i. p. 53.

439. John White, 'Ancient History of the Maori,' vol. i. p. 146. In former editions a statement received from New Zealand was inserted, that the cry or laugh of the tiwakawaka or pied fantail is only heard at sunset. This, however does not agree with the accounts of Sir W. Lawry Buller, who, in his 'Birds of New Zealand,' vol. i. p. 69, supplemented by his answer to my enquiry, makes it clear that the bird sings in the daytime. Thus the argument connecting the sunset-song with the story as a sunset-myth falls away. In another version of Maui's death, in White, vol. ii. p. 112, the laughing bird is the patatai or little swamp-rail, which cries at and after nightfall and in the early morning (Buller, vol. ii. p. 98). Note to 3rd ed.

440. Mason, 'Karens,' in 'Journ. As. Soc. Bengal,' 1865, part ii. p. 178, &c.

441. Schoolcraft, 'Indian Tribes,' part iii. p. 318; 'Algic Res.' vol. i. p. 135, &c., 144; John Tanner, 'Narrative,' p. 357; see Brinton, 'Myths of New World,' p. 166. For legends of Sun-Catcher, see 'Early Hist. of Mankind,' ch. xii.

442. Casalis, 'Basutos,' p. 347; Callaway, 'Zulu Tales,' vol. i. pp. 56, 69, 84, 334 (see also the story, p. 241, of the frog who swallowed the princess and carried her safe home). See Cranz, p. 271 (Greenland angekok swallowed by bear and walrus and thrown up again), and Bastian, 'Mensch,' vol. ii. pp. 506-7; J. M. Harris in 'Mem. Anthrop. Soc.' vol. ii. p. 31 (similar notions in Africa and New Guinea).

443. Tzetzes ap. Lycophron, Cassandra, 33. As to connexion with Joppa and Phœnicia, see Plin. v. 14; ix. 4; Mela, i. 11; Strabo, xvi. 2, 28; Movers, Phönizier, vol. i. pp. 422-3. The expression in Jonah, ii. 2, 'out of the belly of Hades' (mibten sheol, ἐκ κοιλίας ᾅδου) seems a relic of the original meaning of the myth.

444. 'Apocr. Gosp.' Nicodemus, ch. xx.; Mrs. Jameson, 'History of our Lord in Art,' vol. ii. p. 258.

445. Eireks Saga, 3, 4, in 'Flateyjarbok,' vol. i., Christiania, 1859; Baring-Gould, 'Myths of the Middle Ages,' p. 238.

446. Mrs. Jameson, 'Sacred and Legendary Art,' vol. ii. p. 138.

447. J. and W. Grimm, 'Kinder und Hausmärchen,' vol. i. pp. 26, 140; vol. iii. p. 15. (See ref. to these two stories, 'Early Hist. of M.' 1st ed. (1865) p. 338.) I find that Sir G. W. Cox, 'Mythology' (1870), vol. i. p. 358, had noticed the Wolf and Seven Kids as a myth of the

days of the week (Note to 2nd ed.). For mentions of the wolf of darkness, see Hanusch, p. 192; Edda, 'Gylfaginning,' 12; Grimm, 'D. M.' pp. 224, 668. With the episode of the stones substituted compare the myth of Zeus and Kronos. For various other stories belonging to the group of the Man swallowed by the Monster, see Lucian, Historiæ Veræ I.; Hardy, 'Manual of Buddhism,' p. 501; Lane, 'Thousand and One Nights,' vol. iii. p. 104; Halliwell, 'Pop. Rhymes,' p. 98; 'Nursery Rhymes,' p. 48; 'Early Hist. of Mankind,' p. 337.

448. Grey, 'Polyn. Myth.' p. 16, &c., see 144; Jas. White, 'Ancient History of the Maori,' vol. ii. pp. 76, 115. Other details in Schirren, 'Wandersagen der Neuseeländer,' pp. 32-7, 143-51; R. Taylor, 'New Zealand,' p. 124, &c.; compare 116, 141, &c., and volcano-myth, p. 248; Yate, 'New Zealand,' p. 142; Polack, 'M. and C. of New Z.' vol. i. p. 15; S. S. Farmer, 'Tonga Is.' p. 134. See also Turner, 'Polynesia,' pp. 252, 527 (Samoan version). In comparing the group of Maui-legends it is to be observed that New Zealand Mahuika and Maui-Tikitiki correspond to Tongan Mafuike and Kijikiji, Samoan Mafuie and Tiitii.

449. Schoolcraft, 'Algic Res.' vol. ii. pp. 1-33. The three arrows recur in Manabozho's slaying the Shining Manitu, vol. i. p. 153. See the remarkably corresponding three magic arrows in Orvar Odd's Saga; Nilsson, 'Stone Age,' p. 197. The Red-Swan myth of sunset is introduced in George Eliot's 'Spanish Gypsy,' p. 63; Longfellow, 'Hiawatha,' xii.

450. See Kuhn's 'Zeitschrift,' 1860, vol. ix. p. 212; Max Müller, 'Chips,' vol. ii. p. 127; Cox, 'Mythology,' vol. i. p. 256, vol. ii. p. 239.

451. Grimm, 'D. M.' pp. 291, 767.

452. Mason, 'Karens,' in 'Journ. As. Soc. Bengal,' 1865, part ii. pp. 233-4. Prof. Liebrecht, in his notice of the 1st ed. of the present work, in 'Gött. Gel. Anz.' 1872, p. 1290, refers to a Burmese legend in Bastian, O. A. vol. ii. p. 515, and a Mongol legend, Gesser Chan, book iv.

453. Schoolcraft, 'Algic Researches,' vol. ii. p. 40, &c.; Loskiel, 'Gesch. der Mission,' Barby, 1789, p. 47 (the English edition, part i. p. 35, is incorrect). See also Brinton, 'Myths of New World,' p. 63. In an Esquimaux tale, Giviok comes to the two mountains which shut and open; paddling swiftly between, he gets through, but the mountains clashing together crush the stern of his kayak: Rink, 'Eskimoische Eventyr og Sagn,' p. 98, referred to by Liebrecht, l.c.

454. Kingsborough, 'Antiquities of Mexico,' vol. i.; Torquemanda, 'Monarquia Indiana,' xiii. 47; 'Con estos has de pasar por medio de dos Sierras, que se estan batiendo, y encontrando la una con la otra.' Clavigero, vol. ii. p. 94.

455. Apollodor. i. 9, 22; Appollon. Rhod. Argonautica, ii. 310-616; Pindar, 'Pythia Carm.' iv. 370.

456. Polack, 'Manners of N. Z.' vol. i. p. 16; 'New Zealand,' vol. i. p. 358; Yate, p. 142; Schirren, pp. 88, 165.

457. Euseb. Præp. Evang. iii. 9.

458. Rig-Veda, i. 115; Böhtlingk and Roth, s.v. 'mitra.'

459. Avesta, tr. Spiegel, 'Yaçna,' i. 35; iii., lxvii., 61-2; compare Burnouf, 'Yaçna.'

460. Macrob. Saturnal. i. 21, 13. See Max Müller, 'Chips,' vol. ii. p. 85.

461. Grimm, 'Deutsche Myth.' p. 665. See also Hanusch, 'Slaw. Myth.' p. 213.

462. Edda, 'Völuspa,' 22; 'Gylfaginning,' 15. See Grimm, 'D. M.' p. 133; 'Reinhart Fuchs.'

463. As to the identification of the Norns and the Fates, see Grimm, 'D. M.' pp. 376-86; Max Müller, 'Chips,' vol. ii. p. 154. It is to be observed in connexion with the Perseus-myth, that another of its obscure episodes, the Gorgon's head turning those who look on it into stone, corresponds with myths of the sun itself. In Hispaniola, men came out of two caves (thus being born of their mother Earth); the giant who guarded these caves strayed one night, and the rising sun turned him into a great rock called Kauta, just as the Gorgon's head turned Atlas the Earth-bearer into the mountain that bears his name; after this, others of the early cave-men were surprised by the sunlight, and turned into stones, trees, plants or beasts (Friar Roman Pane in 'Life of Columbus' in Pinkerton, vol. xii. p. 80; J. G. Müller, 'Amer. Urrelig.' p. 179). In Central America a Quiché legend relates how the ancient animals were petrified by the Sun (Brasseur, 'Popol Vuh,' p. 245). Thus the Americans have the analogue of the Scandinavian myths of giants and dwarfs surprised by daylight outside their hiding-places, and turned to stones. Such fancies appear connected with the fancied human shapes of rocks or 'standing stones' which peasants still account for as transformed creatures. Thus in Fiji, two rocks are a male and female deity turned to stone at daylight, Seemann, 'Viti,' p. 66; see Liebrecht in

'Heidelberg. Jahrb.' 1864, p. 216. This idea is brought also into the Perseus-myth, for the rocks abounding in Seriphos are the islanders thus petrified by the Gorgon's head.

464. Piedrahita, 'Hist. Gen. de las Conquistas del Nuevo Reyno de Granada,' Antwerp, 1688, part i. lib. i. c. 3; Humboldt, 'Monumens,' pl. vi.; J. G. Müller, 'Amer. Urrelig.' pp. 423-30.

465. Garcilaso de la Vega, 'Commentarios Reales,' i. c. 15; Prescott, 'Peru,' vol. i. p. 7; J. G. Müller, pp. 303-8, 328-39. Other Peruvian versions show the fundamental solar idea in different mythic shapes (Tr. of Cieza de Leon, tr. and ed. by C. R. Markham, Hakluyt Soc. 1864, pp. xlix. 298, 316, 372). W. B. Stevenson ('Residence in S. America,' vol. i. p. 394) and Bastian ('Mensch,' vol. iii. p. 347) met with a curious perversion of the myth, in which *Inca Manco Ccapac*, corrupted into *Ingasman Cocapac*, gave rise to a story of an *Englishman* figuring in the midst of Peruvian mythology.

466. Stanbridge, 'Abor. of Australia,' in 'Tr. Eth. Soc.' vol. i. p. 301.

467. H. Yule, 'Journ. As. Soc. Bengal,' vol. xiii. p. 628.

468. Hanusch, 'Slaw. Myth.' p. 269.

469. Bleek, 'Reynard in S. Africa,' pp. 69-74; C. J. Andersson, 'Lake Ngami,' p. 328; see Grout, 'Zulu-land,' p. 148; Arbousset and Daumas, p. 471. As to connexion of the moon with the hare, cf. Skr. 'çaçanka;' and in Mexico, Sahagun, book vii. c. 2, in Kingsborough, vol. vii.

470. Williams, 'Fiji,' vol. i. p. 205. Compare the Caroline Island myth that in the beginning men only quitted life on the last day of the waning moon, and resuscitated as from a peaceful sleep when she reappeared; but the evil spirit Erigirers inflicted a death from which there is no revival: De Brosses, 'Hist. des Navig. aux Terres Australes,' vol. ii. p. 479. Also in a song of the Indians of California it is said, that even as the moon dies and returns to life, so they shall be re-born after death; Duflot de Mofras in Bastian, 'Rechtsverhältnisse,' p. 385, see 'Psychologie,' p. 54.

471. 'Journ. Ind. Archip.' vol. i. p. 284; vol. iv. p. 333; Tickell in 'Journ. As. Soc.' Bengal, vol. ix. part ii. p. 797; Latham, 'Descr. Eth.' vol. ii. p. 422.

472. Stanbridge in 'Tr. Eth. Soc.' vol. i. pp. 301-3.

473. Schoolcraft, 'Algic Res.' vol. i. pp. 57-66. The story of the hero or deity invulnerable like Achilles save in one weak spot, recurs in

the tales of the slaying of the Shining Manitu, whose scalp alone was vulnerable, and of the mighty Kwasind, who could be killed only by the cone of the white pine wounding the vulnerable place on the crown of his head (vol. i. p. 153; vol. ii. p. 163).

474. Taylor, 'New Zealand,' p. 363.

475. Stanbridge, l.c.; Charlevoix, vol. vi. p. 148; Leems, 'Lapland,' in Pinkerton, vol. i. p. 411. The name of the Bear occurring in North America in connexion with the stars of the Great and Little Bear (Charlevoix, l.c.; Cotton Mather in Schoolcraft, 'Tribes,' vol. i. p. 284) has long been remarked on (Goguet, vol. i. p. 262; vol. ii. p. 366, but with reference to Greenland, see Cranz, p. 294). See observations on the history of the Aryan name in Max Müller, 'Lectures,' 2nd series, p. 361.

476. Casalis, p. 196; Waitz, vol. ii. p. 191.

477. Long's Exp. vol. i. p. 288; Schoolcraft, part i. p. 272; Le Jeune in 'Rel. des Jés. de la Nouvelle France,' 1634, p. 18; Loskiel, part i. p. 35; J. G. Müller, p. 63.

478. Hanusch, pp. 272, 407, 415.

479. Porphyr. de Antro Nympharum, 28; Macrob. de Somn. Scip. 1. 12.

480. Beausobre, 'Hist. de Manichée,' vol. ii. p. 513.

481. Bastian, 'Oestl. Asien,' vol. iii. p. 341; 'Chronique de Tabari,' tr. Dubeux, p. 24; Grimm, 'D.M.' p. 330, &c.

482. Chaucer, 'House of Fame,' ii. 427. With reference to questions of Aryan mythology illustrated by the savage galaxy-myths, see Pictet, 'Origines,' part ii. p. 582, &c. Mr. J. Jeremiah informs me that 'Watling Street' is still (1871) a name for the Milky Way in Scotland; see also his paper on 'Welsh names of the Milky Way,' Philological Soc., Nov. 17, 1871. The corresponding name 'London Road' is used in Suffolk.

483. Yate, 'New Zealand,' p. 144, see Ellis, 'Polyn. Res.' vol. ii. p. 417.

484. Virg. Aeneid, i. 56; Homer, Odyss. x. 1.

485. Schoolcraft, 'Algic Res.' vol. i. p. 200; vol. ii. pp. 122, 214; 'Indian Tribes,' part iii. p. 324.

486. Brinton, 'Myths of the New World,' ch. iii.

487. 'Rig-Veda,' tr. by Max Müller, vol. i. (Hymns to Maruts); Welcker, 'Griech. Götterl.' vol. iii. p. 67; Cox, 'Mythology of Aryan Nations,' vol. ii. ch. v.

488. Grimm, 'D. M.' pp. 126, 599, 894; Hunt, 'Pop. Rom.' 1st ser. p. xix.; Baring-Gould, 'Book of Werewolves,' p. 101; see 'Myths of the Middle Ages,' p. 25; Wuttke, 'Deutsche Volksaberglaube,' pp. 13, 236; Monnier, 'Traditions,' pp. 75, &c., 741, 747.

489. Pr. Max v. Wied, 'Reise in N. A.' vol. i. pp. 446, 455; vol. ii. pp. 152, 223; Sir Alex. Mackenzie, 'Voyages,' p. cxvii.; Sproat, 'Scenes of Savage Life' (Vancouver's I.), pp. 177, 213; Irving, 'Astoria,' vol. ii. ch. xxii.; Le Jeune, op. cit. 1634, p. 26; Schoolcraft, 'Indian Tribes,' part iii. p. 233, 'Algic Res.' vol. ii. pp. 114-6, 199; Catlin, vol. ii. p. 164; Brasseur, 'Popol Vuh,' p. 71 and Index, 'Hurakan;' J. G. Müller, 'Amer. Urrel.' pp. 222, 271; Ellis, 'Polyn. Res.' vol. ii. p. 417; Jno. Williams, 'Missionary Enterprise,' p. 93; Mason, l.c. p. 217; Moffat, 'South Africa,' p. 338; Casalis, 'Basutos,' p. 266; Callaway, 'Religion of Amazulu,' p. 119.

490. Mariner, 'Tonga Is.' vol. ii. p. 120; S. S. Farmer, 'Tonga,' p. 135; Schirren, pp. 35-7.

491. 'Journ. Ind. Archip.' vol. ii. p. 837.

492. J. G. Müller, 'Amer. Urrelig.' pp. 61, 122.

493. Brasseur, 'Mexique,' vol. iii. p. 482.

494. Pouchet, 'Plurality of Races,' p. 2.

495. Steller, 'Kamtschatka,' p. 267.

496. Mason, 'Karens,' l.c. p. 182.

497. Bell, 'Tr. in Asia,' in Pinkerton, vol. vii. p. 369; Bastian, 'Oestl. Asien,' vol. ii. p. 168; Lane, 'Thousand and one Nights,' vol. i. p. 21; see Latham, 'Descr. Eth.' vol. ii. p. 171; Beausobre, 'Manichée,' vol. i. p. 243.

498. Edda, 'Gylfaginning,' 50; Grimm, 'D. M.' p. 777, &c.

499. Kaempfer, 'Japan,' in Pinkerton, vol. vii. p. 684; see mammoth-myths in 'Early Hist, of Mankind,' p. 315.

500. Hamilton in 'As. Res.' vol. ii. p. 344; Colebrooke, ibid. vol. iv. p. 385; Earl in 'Journ. Ind. Archip.' vol. iii. p. 682; vol. iv. p. 9. See Renaudot, 'Travels of Two Mahommedans,' in Pinkerton, vol. vii. p. 183.

501. F. Buckland, 'Curiosities of Nat. Hist.' 3rd series, vol. ii. p. 39.

502. Andrew Boorde, 'Introduction of Knowledge,' ed. by F. J. Furnivall, Early Eng. Text Soc. 1870, p. 133.

503. Ælian, De Nat. Animal, v. 2, see 8.

504. Acta Sanctorum Bolland. Jan. xvi.

505. 'Acts of Peter and Paul,' trans. by A. Walker, in Ante-Nicene Library, vol. xvi. p. 257; F. F. Tuckett in 'Nature,' Oct. 20, 1870. See Lyell, 'Principles of Geology,' ch. xxx.; Phillips, 'Vesuvius,' p. 244.

506. Lane, 'Thousand and One N.' vol. i. pp. 161, 217; vol. iii. p. 78; Hole, 'Remarks on the Ar. N.' p. 104; Heinrich von Veldeck, 'Herzog Ernst's von Bayern Erhöhung, &c.' ed. Rixner, Amberg, 1830, p. 65; see Ludlow, 'Popular Epics of Middle Ages,' p. 221.

507. Sir John Maundevile, 'Voiage and Travaile.'

508. Sir Thomas Browne, 'Vulgar Errours,' ii. 3.

509. 'Mémoires conc. l'Hist., &c., des Chinois,' vol. iv. p. 457. Compare the story of the magnetic (?) horseman in 'Thousand and One N.' vol. iii. p. 119, with the old Chinese mention of magnetic cars with a movable-armed pointing figure, A. v. Humboldt, 'Asie Centrale,' vol. i. p. xl.; Goguet, vol. iii. p. 284. (The loadstone mountain has its power from a turning brazen horseman on the top.)

510. Brasseur, 'Popol Vuh,' pp. 23-31. Compare this Central American myth of the ancient senseless mannikins who become monkeys, with a Pottowatomi legend in Schoolcraft, 'Indian Tribes,' part i. p. 320.

511. Dos Santos, 'Ethiopia Oriental,' Evora, 1609, part i. chap. ix.; Callaway, 'Zulu Tales,' vol. i. p. 177. See also Burton, 'Footsteps in E. Afr.' p. 274; Waitz, 'Anthropologie,' vol. ii. p. 178 (W. Afr.).

512. D'Orbigny, 'L'Homme Américain,' vol. ii. p. 102.

513. Weil, 'Bibl. Leg. der Muselmänner,' p. 267; Lane, 'Thousand and One N.' vol. iii. p. 350; Burton, 'El Medinah, &c.' vol. ii. p. 343.

514. Ovid, 'Metamm.' xiv. 89-100; Welcker, 'Griechische Götterlehre,' vol. iii. p. 108.

515. Campbell in 'Journ. As. Soc. Bengal,' 1866, part ii. p. 132; Latham, 'Descr. Eth.' vol. ii. p. 456; Tod, 'Annals of Rajasthan,' vol. i. p. 114.

516. Bourien in 'Tr. Eth. Soc.' vol. iii. p. 73; see 'Journ. Ind. Archip.' vol. ii. p. 271.

517. Bastian, 'Oestl. Asien,' vol. iii. p. 435; 'Mensch,' vol. iii. pp. 347, 349, 387, Koeppen, vol. ii. p. 44; J. J. Schmidt, 'Völker Mittel-Asiens,' p. 210.

518. Froebel, 'Central America,' p. 220; see Bosman, 'Guinea,' in Pinkerton, vol. xvi. p. 401. For other traditions of human descent from apes, see Farrar, 'Chapters on Language,' p. 45.

519. Bosman, 'Guinea,' p. 440; Waitz, vol. ii. p. 178; Cauche, 'Relation de Madagascar,' p. 127; Dobrizhoffer, 'Abipones,' vol. i. p. 288; Bastian, 'Mensch,' vol. ii. p. 44; Pouchet, 'Plurality of Human Race,' p. 22.

520. Monboddo, 'Origin and Progress of Lang.' 2nd ed. vol. i. p. 277; Du Chaillu, 'Equatorial Africa,' p. 61; St. John, 'Forests of Far East,' vol. i. p. 17; vol. ii. p. 239.

521. Max Müller in Bunsen, 'Phil. Univ. Hist.' vol. i. p. 340; 'Journ. As. Soc. Bengal,' vol. xxiv. p. 207. See Marsden in 'As. Res.' vol. iv. p. 226; Fitch in Pinkerton, vol. ix. p. 415; Bastian, 'Oestl. Asien,' vol. i. p. 465; vol. ii. p. 201.

522. Ayeen Akbaree, trans. by Gladwin; 'Report of Ethnological Committee Jubbulpore Exhibition, 1866-7,' part i. p. 3. See the mention of the *ban-manush* in 'Kumaon and Nepal,' Campbell; 'Ethnology of India,' in 'Journ. As. Soc. Bengal,' 1866, part ii. p. 46.

523. Marsden, 'Sumatra,' p. 41.

524. Logan in 'Journ. Ind. Archip.' vol. i. p. 246; vol. iii. p. 490; Thomson, ibid. vol. i. p. 350; Crawfurd, ibid. vol. iv. p. 186.

525. Bastian, 'Oestl. Asien,' vol. i. p. 123; vol. iii. p. 435.

526. Martius, 'Ethnog. Amer.' vol. i. pp. 425, 471.

527. Its analogue is *bosjesbok*, 'bush-goat,' the African antelope. The derivation of the *Bosjesman's* name from his nest-like shelter in a bush, given by Kolben and others since, is newer and far-fetched.

528. Martius, vol. i. p. 50.

529. Humboldt and Bonpland, vol. v. p. 81; Southey, 'Brazil,' vol. i. p. xxx.; Bates, 'Amazons,' vol. i. p. 73; vol. ii. p. 204.

530. Castelnau, 'Exp. dans l'Amér. du Sud,' vol. iii. p. 118. See Martius, vol. i. pp. 248, 414, 563, 633.

531. Petherick, 'Egypt, &c.' p. 367.

532. Southey, 'Brazil,' vol. i. p. 685; Martius, vol. i. pp. 425, 633.

533. Krapf, p. 142; Baker, 'Albert Nyanza,' vol. i. p. 83; St. John, vol. i. pp. 51, 405; and others.

534. Lockhart, 'Abor. of China,' in 'Tr. Eth. Soc.' vol. i. p. 181.

535. 'Journ. Ind. Archip.' vol. ii. p. 358; vol. iv. p. 374; Cameron, 'Malayan India,' p. 120; Marsden, p. 7; Antonio Galvano, pp. 120, 218.

536. Davis, 'Carthage,' p. 230; Bostock and Riley's Pliny (Bohn's ed.), vol. ii. p. 134, note.

537. Francisque-Michel, 'Races Maudites,' vol. i. p. 17; 'Argot,' p. 349; Fernan Caballero, 'La Gaviota,' vol. i. p. 59.

538. Horne Tooke, 'Diversions of Purley,' vol. i. p. 397.

539. Baring-Gould, 'Myths,' p. 137.

540. Williams, 'Fiji,' vol. i. p. 252; Backhouse, 'Austr.' p. 557; Purchas, vol. iv. p. 1290; De Laet, 'Novus Orbis,' p. 543.

541. For various other stories of tailed men, see 'As. Res.' vol. iii. p. 149; 'Mem. Anthrop. Soc.' vol. i. p. 454; 'Journ. Ind. Archip.' vol. iii. p. 261, &c. (Nicobar Islands); Klemm, 'C. G.' vol. ii. pp. 246, 316 (Sarytschew Is.); 'Letters of Columbus,' Hakluyt Soc. p. 11 (Cuba), &c., &c.

542. Details of monstrous tribes have been in past centuries specially collected in the following works: 'Anthropometamorphosis: Man Transformed, or the Artificiall Changeling, &c.,' scripsit J. B. cognomento Chirosophus, M.D., London, 1653; Calovius, 'De Thaumatanthropologia, vera pariter atque ficta tractatus historico-physicus,' Rostock, 1685; J. A. Fabricius, 'Dissertatio de hominibus orbis nostri incolis, &c.,' Hamburg, 1721. Only a few principal references are here given.

543. Grimm, 'D. M.' ch. xvii. xviii.; Nilsson, 'Primitive Inhabitants of Scandinavia,' ch. vi.; Hanusch, 'Slaw. Myth.' pp. 230, 325-7; Wuttke, 'Volksabergl.' p. 231.

544. 'Chronique de Tabari,' tr. Dubeux, part i. ch. viii. See Koran, xviii. 92.

545. Pigafetta in Pinkerton, vol. xi. p. 314. See Blumenbach, 'De Generis Humanæ Varietate;' Fitzroy, 'Voy. of Adventure and Beagle,' vol. i.; Waitz, 'Anthropologie,' vol. iii. p. 488.

546. Knivet in Purchas, vol. iv. p. 1231; compare Humboldt and Bonpland, vol. v. p. 564, with Martius, 'Ethnog. Amer.' p. 424; see also Krapf, 'East Africa,' p. 51; Du Chaillu, 'Ashango-land,' p. 319.

547. 'Early Hist. of Mankind,' ch. xi.; Hunt, 'Pop. Rom.' 1st series, pp. 18, 304.

548. Squier, 'Abor. Monuments of N. Y.' p. 68; Long's 'Exp.' vol. i. pp. 62, 275; Hersart de Villemarqué, 'Chants Populaires de la Bretagne,' p. liv., 35; Meadows Taylor in 'Journ. Eth. Soc.' vol. i. p. 157.

549. Gul. de Rubruquis in Pinkerton, vol. vii. p. 69; Lane, 'Thousand and One N.' vol. iii. pp. 81, 91, see 24, 52, 97; Hole, p. 63; Marco Polo, book iii. ch. xii.

550. Benjamin of Tudela, 'Itinerary,' ed. and tr. by Asher, 83; Plin. vii. 2. See Max Müller in Bunsen 'Philos. Univ. Hist.,' vol. i. pp. 346, 358.

551. Plin. iv. 27; Mela, iii. 6; Bastian, 'Oestl. Asien,' vol. i. p. 120; vol. ii. p. 93; St. John, vol. ii. p. 117; Marsden, p. 53; Lane, 'Thousand and One N.' vol. iii. pp. 92, 305; Petherick, 'Egypt, &c.' p. 367; Burton, 'Central Afr.' vol. i. p. 235; Pedro Simon, 'Indias Occidentales,' p. 7.

552. Bastian, 'Oestl. Asien,' vol i. p. 133.

553. Marco Polo, book iii. ch. xviii.

554. Ælian, iv. 46; Plin. vi. 35; vii. 2. See for other versions, Purchas, vol. iv. p. 1191; vol. v. p. 901; Cranz, p. 267; Lane, 'Thousand and One Nights,' vol. iii. pp. 36, 94, 97, 305; Davis, 'Carthage,' p. 230; Latham, 'Descr. Eth.' vol. ii. p. 83.

555. Plin. v. 8; vi. 24, 35; vii. 2; Mela, iii. 9; Herberstein in Hakluyt, vol. i. p. 593; Latham, 'Descr. Eth.' vol. i. p. 483; Davis, l.c.; see 'Early Hist. of Mankind,' p. 77.

556. Plin. v. 8; Lane, vol. i. p. 33; vol. ii. p. 377; vol. iii. p. 81; Eisenmenger, vol. ii. p. 559; Mandeville, p. 243; Raleigh in Hakluyt, vol. iii. pp. 652, 665; Humboldt and Bonpland, vol. v. p. 176; Purchas, vol. iv. p. 1285; vol. v. p. 901; Isidor. Hispal. s.v. 'Acephali;' Vambéry, p. 310, see p. 436.

557. Lane, vol. i. p. 33; Callaway, 'Zulu Tales,' vol. i. pp. 199, 202. Virg. Æn. viii. 194; a similar metaphor is the name of the *Nimchas*, from Persian nim—half, 'Journ. Eth. Soc.' vol. i. p. 192, cf. French *demi-monde*. Compare the 'one-legged' tribes, Plin. vii. 2; Schoolcraft, 'Indian Tribes,' part iii. p. 521; Charlevoix, vol. i. p. 25. The Australians use the metaphor 'of one leg' (matta gyn) to describe tribes as of one stock, G. F. Moore, 'Vocab.' pp. 5, 71.

558. Hayton in Purchas, vol. iii. p. 108; see Klemm, 'C. G.' vol. vi. p. 129; Vambéry, p. 49; Homer. Odyss. ix.; Strabo, i. 2, 12; see Scherzer, 'Voy. of Novara,' vol. ii. p. 40; C. J. Andersson, 'Lake Ngami, &c.,' p. 453; Du Chaillu, 'Equatorial Africa,' p. 440; Sir J. Richardson, 'Polar Regions,' p. 300. For tribes with more than two eyes, see Pliny's metaphorically explained Nisacæthæ and Nisyti, Plin. vi. 35; also Bastian, 'Mensch,' vol. ii. p. 414; 'Oestl. Asien,' vol. i. pp. 25, 76; Petherick, l.c.; Bowen, 'Yoruba Gr.' p. xx.; Schirren, p. 196.

559. Kölle, 'Vei Gr.' p. 229; Strabo, i. 2, 35. The artificially elongated skulls of real Μακροκέφαλοι (Hippokrates, 'De Aeris,' 14.) are found in the burial-places of Kertch.

560. Plin., vii. 2.; Humboldt and Bonpland, vol. v. p. 81.

561. Krapf, p. 359.

562. Southey, 'Brazil,' vol. iii. p. 390.

563. D. Wilson, 'Archæology, &c. of Scotland,' p. 123.

564. Bastian, 'Oestl. Asien,' vol. i. p. 128; Livingstone, p. 532.

565. Williams, 'Fiji,' p. 160; Seemann, 'Viti,' p. 113; Turner, 'Polynesia,' p. 182 (a similar legend told by the Samoans). Another tattooing legend in Latham, 'Descr. Eth.' vol. i. p. 152; Bastian, 'Oestl. Asien,' vol. i. p. 112.

566. Bastian, 'Mensch,' vol. iii. pp. 167-8; Wilkinson in Rawlinson's 'Herodotus,' vol. ii. p. 79; Grimm, 'D. M.' pp. 972-6; W. G. Palgrave, 'Arabia,' vol. i. p. 251; Squier and Davis, 'Monuments of Mississippi Valley,' p. 134; Taylor, 'New Zealand,' p. 258.

567. Latham, 'Descr. Eth.' vol. i. p. 43; Lejean in 'Rev. des Deux Mondes,' 15 Feb. 1862, p. 856; Apollodor. iii. 8. Compare the derivation of *Arequipa* by the Peruvians from the words *ari! quepay*== 'yes! remain,' said to have been addressed to the colonists by the Inca: Markham, 'Quichua Gr. and Dic.;' also the supposed etymology of *Dahome, Danh-ho-men*== 'on the belly of Danh,' from

the story of King Dako building his palace on the body of the conquered King Danh: Burton, in 'Tr. Eth. Soc.' vol. iii. p. 401.

568. Charnock, 'Verba Nominalia,' s.v. 'chic;' see Francisque-Michel, 'Argot,' s.v.

569. 'Spectator,' No. 147; Brand, 'Pop. Ant.' vol. iii. p. 93; Hotten, 'Slang Dictionary,' p. 3; Charnock, s.v. 'cant.' As to the real etymology, that from the beggar's whining *chaunt* is defective, for the beggar drops this tone exactly when he *cants*, i.e., talks jargon with his fellows. If *cant* is directly from Latin *cantare*, it will correspond with Italian *cantare* and French *chanter*, both used as slang words for to speak (Francisque-Michel, 'Argot'). A Keltic origin is more probable, Gaelic and Irish *cainnt*, *caint* == talk, language, dialect (see Wedgwood 'Etymological Dictionary'). The Gaelic equivalents for pedlars' French or tramps' slang, are 'Laidionn nan ceard,' '*cainnt* cheard,' i.e., tinkers' Latin or jargon, or exactly 'cairds' *cant*.' A deeper connexion between *cainnt* and *cantare* does not affect this.

570. See also Francisque-Michel, 'Argot,' s.v. 'maccabe, macchabée'==noyé.

571. Musters, 'Patagonians,' pp. 69, 184.

572. Döhne, 'Zulu Dic.' p. 417; Arbousset and Daumas, p. 269; Waitz, vol. ii. pp. 349, 352.

573. Shortland, 'Trads. of N. Z.' p. 224.

574. On the adoption of imaginary ancestors as connected with the fiction of a common descent, and the important political and religious effects of these proceedings, see especially Grote, 'History of Greece,' vol. i.; McLennan, 'Primitive Marriage;' Maine, 'Ancient Law.' Interesting details on eponymic ancestors in Pott, 'Anti-Kaulen, oder Mythische Vorstellungen vom Ursprnge der Völker and Sprachen.'

575. Martius, 'Ethnog. Amer.' vol. i. p. 54; see p. 283.

576. Macpherson, 'India,' p. 78.

577. Vambéry, 'Central Asia,' p. 325; see also Latham, 'Descr. Eth.' vol. i. p. 456 (Ostyaks); Georgi, 'Reise im Russ. Reich,' vol. i. 242 (Tunguz).

578. Barth, 'N. & Centr. Afr.' vol. ii. p. 71.

579. J. G. Müller, 'Amer. Urrelig.' p. 574.

580. Martius, vol. i. pp. 180-4; Waitz, vol. iii. p. 416.

581. Schoolcraft, 'Indian Tribes,' part i. p. 319, part iii. p. 268, see part ii. p. 49; Catlin, vol. ii. p. 128; J. G. Müller, pp. 134, 327.

582. Grote, 'Hist. of Greece;' Pausan. iii. 20; Diod. Sic. v.; Apollodor. Bibl. i. 7, 3, vi. 1, 4; Herodot. i. 171.

583. Max Müller in Bunsen, vol. i. p. 338; Tabari, part i. ch. xlv., lxix.

584. Sir W. Jones in 'As. Res.' vol. ii. p. 24; Vansittart, ibid. p. 67; see Campbell, in 'Journ. As. Soc. Bengal,' 1866, part ii. p. 7.

585. Will, de Rubruquis in Pinkerton, vol. vii. p. 23; Gabelentz in 'Zeitschr. für die Kunde des Morgenlandes,' vol. ii. p. 73; Schmidt, 'Völker Mittel-Asien,' p. 6.

586. See also Pott, 'Anti-Kaulen,' pp. 19, 23; 'Rassen,' pp. 70, 153; and remarks on colonization-myths in Max Müller, 'Chips,' vol. ii. p. 68.

587. Seemann, 'Viti,' p. 311; Turner, 'Polynesia,' p. 252.

588. Ellis, 'Polyn. Res.' vol. i. p. 69.

589. Schoolcraft, 'Algic Res.' vol. i. p. 122; 'Indian Tribes,' part i. p. 320, part ii. p. 230.

590. J. R. Wise, 'The New Forest,' p. 160; Taylor, 'New Zealand,' p. 268; Max Müller, 'Chips,' vol. i. p. 249; M. A. Walker, 'Macedonia,' p. 192; Movers, 'Phönizier,' vol. i. p. 665; Lucian. de Deâ Syriâ, 8; Hunt, 'Pop. Rom.' 2nd Series, p. 15; Wuttke, 'Volksaberglaube,' pp. 16, 94; Bastian, 'Mensch,' vol. ii. p. 59, vol. iii. p. 185; Buchanan, 'Mysore, &c.' in Pinkerton, vol. viii. p. 714.

591. Sprenger, 'Leben des Mohammad,' vol. i. pp. 78, 119, 162, 310.

592. Marco Polo, book i. ch. viii.

593. Grote, vol. i. p. 347.

594. Welcker, vol. i. p. 756.

595. Xenoph. Memorabilia, ii. 1.

596. Oldfield in 'Tr. Eth. Soc.' vol. iii. p. 259.

597. Steller, 'Kamtschatka,' p. 255.

598. Wilson in 'Tr. Eth. Soc.' vol. iv. p. 306.

599. J. L. Wilson, 'W. Afr.' p. 382.

600. Bleek, 'Reynard in S. Afr.' pp. 5, 47, 67 (these are not among the stories which seem recently borrowed from Europeans). See 'Early History of Mankind,' p. 10.

601. Callaway, 'Zulu Tales,' vol. i. p. 355.

602. Schoolcraft, 'Algic Res.' vol. i. p. 160; see pp. 43, 51.

603. Jakob Grimm, 'Reinhart Fuchs,' Introd.

604. Account of Laura Bridgman, p. 120.

605. Bowring, 'Siam,' vol. i. p. 313; Hardy, 'Manual of Budhism,' p. 98. See the fable of the 'Crow and Pitcher,' in Plin. x. 60, and Bastian, 'Mensch,' vol. i. p. 76.

606. Jameson, 'History of Our Lord in Art,' vol. i. p. 375.

607. J. D. Lang, 'Queensland,' pp. 340, 374, 380, 388, 444 (Buddai appears, p. 379, as causing a deluge; he is probably identical with Budyah).

608. Moffat, 'South Africa,' p. 261.

609. Azara, 'Voy. dans l'Amérique Méridionale,' vol. ii. pp. 3, 14, 25, 51, 60, 91, 119, &c.; D'Orbigny, 'L'Homme Américain,' vol. ii. p. 318.

610. Muir, 'Sanskrit Texts,' part ii. p. 435; Euseb. 'Hist. Eccl.' iv. 15; Bingham, book i. ch. ii.; Vanini, 'De Admirandis Naturae Arcanis,' dial. 37; Lecky, 'Hist. of Rationalism,' vol. i. p. 126; Encyclop. Brit. (5th ed.) s.v. 'Superstition.'

611. J. de Verrazano in Hakluyt, vol. iii. p. 300.

612. See W. Ellis, 'Hist. of Madagascar,' vol. i. p. 429; Flacourt, 'Hist. de Madagascar,' p. 59.

613. Dampier, 'Voyages,' vol. ii. part ii. p. 76.

614. Roe in Pinkerton, vol. viii. p. 2.

615. Lubbock, 'Prehistoric Times,' p. 564: see also 'Origin of Civilization,' p. 138.

616. Sproat, 'Scenes and Studies of Savage Life,' p. 205.

617. Mouat, 'Andaman Islanders,' pp. 2, 279, 303. Since the above was written, the remarkable Andaman religion has been described by Mr. E. H. Man, in 'Journ. Anthrop. Inst.' vol. xii. (1883) p. 156. (Note to 3rd ed.)

618. Baker, 'Races of the Nile Basin,' in Tr. Eth. Soc. vol. v. p. 231; 'The Albert Nyanza,' vol. i. p. 246. See Kaufmann, 'Schilderungen aus Central-afrika,' p. 123; Brun-Rollet, 'Le Nil Blanc et le Soudan,' pp. 100, 222, also pp. 164, 200, 234; G. Lejean in 'Rev. des Deux M.' April 1, 1862, p. 760; Waitz, 'Anthropologie,' vol. ii. pp. 72-5; Bastian, 'Mensch,' vol. iii. p. 208. Other recorded cases of denial of religion of savage tribes on narrow definition or inadequate evidence may be found in Meiners, 'Gesch. der Rel.' vol. i. pp. 11-15 (Australians and Californians); Waitz, 'Anthropologie,' vol. i. p. 323 (Aru Islanders, &c.); Farrar in 'Anthrop. Rev.' Aug. 1864, p. ccxvii, (Kafirs, &c.); Martius, 'Ethnog. Amer.' vol. i. p. 583 (Manaos); J. G. Palfrey, 'Hist. of New England,' vol. i. p. 46 (New England tribes).

619. The term has been especially used to denote the doctrine of Stahl, the promulgator also of the phlogiston-theory. The Animism of Stahl is a revival and development in modern scientific shape of the classic theory identifying vital principle and soul. See his 'Theoria Medica Vera,' Halle, 1737; and the critical dissertation on his views, Lemoine, 'Le Vitalisme et l'Animisme de Stahl,' Paris, 1864.

620. Bonwick, 'Tasmanians,' p. 182.

621. Tanner's 'Narr.' p. 291, Cree atchâk==soul.

622. Brasseur, 'Langue Quichée,' s.v.

623. Martius, 'Ethnog. Amer.' vol. i. p. 705; vol. ii. p. 310.

624. Dobrizhoffer, 'Abipones,' vol. ii. p. 194.

625. Döhne, 'Zulu Dic.' s.v. 'tunzi;' Callaway, 'Rel. of Amazulu,' pp. 91, 126; 'Zulu Tales,' vol. i. p. 342.

626. Casalis, 'Basutos,' p. 245; Arbousset and Daumas, 'Voyage,' p. 12.

627. Goldie, 'Efik Dictionary,' s.v.; see Kölle, 'Afr. Native Lit.' p. 324 (Kanuri). Also 'Journ. Ind. Archip.' vol. v. p. 713 (Australian).

628. Dante, 'Div. Comm. Purgatorio,' canto iii. Compare Grohmann, 'Aberglauben aus Böhmen,' p. 221. See *ante*, p. 85.

629. Rochefort, pp. 429, 516; J. G. Müller, p. 207.

630. Mariner, 'Tonga Is.' vol. ii. p. 135; S. S. Farmer, 'Tonga,' &c. p. 131.

631. Casalis, l.c. See also Mariner, ibid.

632. Bastian, 'Psychologie,' pp. 15-23.

633. J. H. Bernau, 'Brit. Guiana,' p. 134.

634. Grimm, 'D. M.' pp. 1028, 1133. Anglo-Saxon *man-lica*.

635. Lieber, 'Laura Bridgman,' in Smithsonian Contrib. vol. ii. p. 8.

636. G. F. Moore, 'Vocab. of W. Australia,' p. 103.

637. Brinton, p. 50, see p. 235; Bastian, 'Psychologie,' p. 15.

638. Cranz, 'Grönland,' p. 257.

639. Crawfurd, 'Malay Gr. and Dic.' s.v.; Marsden, 'Sumatra,' p. 386.

640. Oviedo, 'Hist. du Nicaragua,' pp. 21-51.

641. Pott, 'Zigeuner,' vol. ii. p. 306; 'Indo-Germ. Wurzel-Wörterbuch,' vol. i. p. 1073; Borrow, 'Lavengro,' vol. ii. ch. xxvi. 'write the lil of him whose *dook* gallops down that hill every night,' see vol. iii. ch. iv.

642. Brinton, 'Myths of New World,' p. 253; Comm. in Virg. Æn. iv. 684; Cic. Verr. v. 45; Wuttke, 'Volksaberglaube,' p. 210; Rochholz, 'Deutscher Glaube,' &c. vol. i. p. 111.

643. Williams, 'Fiji,' vol. i. p. 241.

644. Ellis, 'Madagascar,' vol. i. p. 393.

645. Charlevoix, 'Nouvelle France,' vol. vi. pp. 75-8; Schoolcraft, 'Indian Tribes,' part i. pp. 33, 83, part iv. p. 70; Waitz, vol. iii. p. 194; J. G. Müller, pp. 66, 207-8.

646. Cross in 'Journ. Amer. Oriental Soc.' vol. iv. p. 310.

647. Macpherson, pp. 91-2. See also Klemm, 'C. G.' vol. iii. p. 71 (Lapp); St. John, 'Far East,' vol. i. p. 189 (Dayaks).

648. Shürmann, 'Vocab. of Parnkalla Lang.' s.v.

649. Tanner's 'Narr.' p. 291; Keating, 'Narr. of Long's Exp.' vol. ii. p. 154.

650. Williams, 'Fiji,' vol. i. p. 242; see the converse process of catching away a man's soul, causing him to pine and die, p. 250.

651. J. L. Wilson, 'W. Afr.' p. 220.

652. Bastian, 'Mensch,' vol. ii. p. 319; also Sproat, p. 213 (Vancouver's I.).

653. Bastian, 'Psychologie,' p. 34; Gmelin, 'Reisen durch Sibirien,' vol. ii. p. 359 (Yakuts); Ravenstein, 'Amur,' p. 351 (Tunguz).

654. Bastian, 'Oestl. Asien,' vol. i. p. 143; vol. ii. pp. 388, 418; vol. iii. p. 236. Mason, 'Karens,' l.c. p. 196, &c.; Cross, 'Karens,' in 'Journ. Amer. Oriental Soc.' vol. iv. 1854, p. 307. See also St. John, 'Far East,' l.c. (Dayaks).

655. Doolittle, 'Chinese,' vol. i. p. 150.

656. Cardan, 'De Varietate Rerum,' Basel, 1556, cap. xliii.

657. Stanbridge, 'Abor. of Victoria,' in 'Tr. Eth. Soc.' vol. i. p. 300.

658. Macpherson, 'India,' p. 103.

659. Cranz, 'Grönland,' p. 269. See also Sproat, l.c.

660. Rühs, 'Finland,' p. 303; Castrén, 'Finn. Myth.' p. 134; Bastian, 'Mensch,' vol. ii. p. 319.

661. Vatnsdæla Saga; Baring-Gould, 'Werewolves,' p. 29.

662. Plin. vii. 53; Lucian. Hermotimus, Musc. Encom. 7.

663. R. D. Owen, 'Footfalls on the Boundary of another World,' p. 259. See A. R. Wallace, 'Scientific Aspect of the Supernatural,' p. 43.

664. Brand, 'Pop. Ant.' vol. i. p. 331, vol. iii. p. 236. See Calmet, 'Diss. sur les Esprits;' Maury, 'Magie,' part ii. ch. iv.

665. Cranz, 'Grönland,' p. 257.

666. Waitz, vol. iii. p. 195.

667. Taylor, 'New Zealand,' pp. 104, 184, 333; Baker in 'Tr. Eth. Soc.' vol. i. p. 57.

668. Bastian, 'Mensch,' vol. ii. p. 319; Jagor in 'Journ. Eth. Soc.,' vol. ii. p. 175.

669. Mason, 'Karens,' l.c. p. 199; Cross, l.c.; Bastian, 'Oestl. Asien,' vol. i. p. 144, vol. ii. p. 389, vol. iii. p. 266.

670. Bastian, 'Psychologie,' pp. 16-20; Eisenmenger, vol. i. p. 458, vol. ii. pp. 13, 20, 453; Franck, 'Kabbale,' p. 235.

671. Augustin. De Civ. Dei, xviii. 18.

672. Grimm, 'D. M.' p. 1036.

673. Charlevoix, 'Nouvelle France,' vol. vi. p. 78; Lafitau, 'Mœurs des Sauvages,' vol. i. p. 363.

674. Callaway, 'Relig. of Amazulu,' pp. 228, 260, 316; 'Journ. Anthrop. Inst.' vol. i. p. 170. See also St. John, 'Far East,' vol. i. p. 199 (Dayaks).

675. Williams, 'Fiji,' vol. i. p. 242.

676. Mayne, 'Brit. Columbia,' p. 261; see Sproat, l.c.

677. J. L. Wilson, 'W. Africa,' pp. 210, 395; M. H. Kingsley, 'W. African Studies,' p. 205. See also Ellis, 'Polyn. Res.' vol. i. p. 396; J. G. Müller, 'Amer. Urrel.' p. 287; Buchanan, 'Mysore,' in Pinkerton, vol. viii. p. 677; 'Early Hist. of Mankind,' p. 8.

678. Homer. Il. xxiii. 59. See also Odyss. xi. 207, 222; Porphyr. De Antro Nympharum; Virgil. Æn. ii. 794; Ovid. Fast. v. 475.

679. Cicero De Divinatione, i. 27.

680. Augustin. De Curâ pro Mortuis, x.-xii. Epist. clviii.

681. Compare Voltaire's remarks, 'Dict. Phil.' art. 'ame,' &c.

682. Steinhauser, 'Religion des Negers,' in 'Magazin der Evang. Missionen', Basel, 1856, No. 2, p. 135.

683. 'Historie del S. D. Fernando Colombo,' tr. Alfonso Ulloa, Venice, 1571, p. 127, Eng. Tr. in Pinkerton, vol. xii. p. 80.

684. Castrén, 'Finn. Myth.' p. 120.

685. 1 Sam. xxviii. 12.

686. Brinton, 'Myths of New World,' p. 269.

687. Pennant, '2nd Tour in Scotland,' in Pinkerton, vol. iii. p. 315; Johnson, 'Journey to the Hebrides.'

688. J. Gardner, 'Faiths of the World,' s.v. 'bilocation.'

689. Mason, 'Karens,' l.c. p. 198.

690. Shortland, 'Trads. of New Zealand,' p. 140; Polack, 'M. and C. of New Zealanders,' vol. i. p. 268. See also Ellis, 'Madagascar,' vol. i. p. 393; J. G. Müller, p. 261.

691. Calmet, 'Diss. sur les Esprits,' vol. i. ch. xl.

692. Wuttke, 'Volksaberglaube,' pp. 44, 56, 208; Brand, 'Popular Antiquities,' vol. iii. pp. 155, 235; Johnson, 'Journey to the Hebrides;' Martin, 'Western Islands of Scotland,' in Pinkerton, vol. iii. p. 670.

693. See R. D. Owen, 'Footfalls on the Boundary of another World;' Mrs. Crowe, 'Night-Side of Nature;' Howitt's Tr. of Ennemoser's 'Magic,' &c.

694. The conception of the soul as a small human image is found in various districts; see Eyre, 'Australia,' vol. ii. p. 356; St. John, 'Far East,' vol. i. p. 189 (Dayaks); Waitz, vol. iii. p. 194 (N. A. Ind.). The idea of a soul as a sort of 'thumbling' is familiar to the Hindus and to German folklore; compare the representations of tiny souls in mediæval pictures.

695. Magalhanes de Gandavo, p. 110; Maffei, 'Indie Orientali,' p. 107.

696. Oldfield in 'Tr. Eth. Soc.' vol. iii. p. 287.

697. Waitz, vol. ii. p. 194; Römer, 'Guinea,' p. 42.

698. Meiners, vol. ii. pp. 756, 763; Purchas, vol. iii. p. 495; J. Jones in 'Tr. Eth. Soc.' vol. iii. p. 138.

699. Calmet, vol. i. ch. xxxvi.; Plin. Ep. vii. 27; Hunt, 'Pop. Romances,' vol. ii. p. 156.

700. Le Jeune in 'Rel. des Jésuites,' 1639, p. 43; see 1634, p. 13.

701. Shortland, 'Trads. of N. Z.' p. 92; Yate, p. 140; R. Taylor, pp. 104, 153; Ellis, 'Polyn. Res.' vol. i. p. 406.

702. Callaway, 'Rel. of Amazulu,' pp. 265, 348, 370.

703. Homer, Il. xxiii. 100.

704. Ovid, Fast. v. 457.

705. Isaiah viii. 19; xxix. 4. The Arabs hate whistling (el sifr), it is talking to devils (Burton, 'First Footsteps in East Africa,' p. 142). 'Nicolaus Remigius, whose "Daemonolatreia" is one of the ghastliest volumes in the ghastly literature of witchcraft, cites Hermolaus Barbarus as having heard the voice *sub-sibilantis daemonis*, and, after giving other instances, adduces the authority of Psellus to prove that the devils generally speak very low and confusedly in order not to be caught fibbing,' Dr Sebastian Evans in 'Nature,' June 22, 1871, p. 140. (Nicolai Remigii Daemonolatreia, Col. Agripp. 1596, lib. i. c. 8, 'pleraeque aliae vocem illis esse aiunt qualem emittunt qui os in dolium aut restam rimosam insertum habent'—'ut Daemones e pelvi stridulâ voce ac tenui sibilo verba ederent').

706. Morgan, 'Iroquois,' p. 176.

707. Flacourt, 'Madagascar,' p. 101.

708. N. B. Dennys, 'Folk-Lore of China,' p. 22.

709. Monnier, 'Traditions Populaires,' p. 142; Wuttke, 'Volksaberglaube,' p. 209; Grimm, 'D. M.' p. 801; Meiners, vol. ii. p. 761.

710. Lang, 'Queensland,' p. 441; Bonwick, 'Tasmanians,' p. 187.

711. Charlevoix, 'Nouvelle France,' vol. vi. pp. 76, 122; Le Jeune in 'Rel. des Jésuites,' 1634, p. 23; 1639, p. 44; Tanner's 'Narr.' p. 292; Peter Jones, 'Hist. of Ojebway Indians,' p. 99.

712. Bastian, 'Mensch,' vol. ii. p. 323.

713. Meiners, vol. i. p. 318.

714. Festus, s.v. 'everriatores;' see Bastian, l.c., and compare Hartknoch, cited below, vol. ii. p. 40.

715. Wuttke, 'Volksaberglaube,' pp. 132, 216.

716. Casalis, 'Basutos,' p. 285; Glanvil, 'Saducismus Triumphatus,' part ii. p. 161; Wuttke, p. 216; Bastian 'Psychologie' p. 192.

717. Mariner, 'Tonga Is.' vol. ii. p. 135.

718. Cranz, 'Grönland,' p. 257.

719. Rochefort, 'Iles Antilles,' p. 429.

720. Loubere, 'Siam,' vol. i. p. 458; Bastian, 'Oestl. Asien,' vol. iii. p. 259; see p. 278.

721. Diog. Laert. x. 67-8; see Serv. ad. Æn. iv. 654.

722. Irenæus contra Hæres. v. 7, 1; see Origen, De Princep. ii. 3, 2.

723. Tertull. De Anima, 9.

724. Hampole, 'Ayenbite of Inwyt.'

725. Wuttke, 'Volksaberglaube,' pp. 216, 226.

726. A. J. Davis, 'Philosophy of Spiritual Intercourse,' New York, 1851, p. 49.

727. Calmet, vol. i. ch. xli. &c.

728. 'Journ. Ind. Archip.' vol. ii. p. 359; vol. iii. pp. 104, 556; Earl, 'Eastern Seas,' p. 266; St. John, 'Far East,' vol. i. pp. 52, 73, 79, 119; Mundy, 'Narr. from Brooke's Journals,' p. 203. Heads were taken as funeral offerings by the Garos of N. E. India, Eliot in 'As. Res.' vol.

iii. p. 28, Dalton, 'Descr. Ethnol. of Bengal,' p. 67; see also pp. 46-7 (Kukis).

729. T. Williams, 'Fiji,' vol. i. pp. 188-204; Mariner, 'Tonga Is.' vol. ii. p. 220. For New Zealand accounts, see R. Taylor, 'New Zealand,' pp. 218, 227; Polack, 'New Zealanders,' vol. i. pp. 66, 78, 116.

730. J. M'Coy, 'Hist. of Baptist Indian Mission,' p. 360; Waitz, vol. iii. p. 200.

731. Rochefort, 'Iles Antilles,' pp. 429, 512; see also J. G. Müller, pp. 174, 222.

732. Oviedo, 'Hist. de las Indias,' lib. xxix. c. 31; Charlevoix, 'Nouv. Fr.' vol. vi. p. 178 (Natchez); Waitz, vol. iii. p. 219. See Brinton, 'Myths of New World,' p. 239.

733. Brasseur, 'Mexique,' vol. iii. p. 573.

734. Piedrahita, 'Nuevo Reyno de Granada,' part i. lib. i. c. 3.

735. Cieza de Leon, p. 161; Rivero and Tschudi, 'Peruv. Ant.' p. 200; Prescott, 'Peru,' vol. i. p. 29. See statements as to effigies, J. G. Müller, p. 379.

736. Simpson, 'Journey,' vol. i. p. 190; similar practice among Takulli or Carrier Ind., Waitz, vol. iii. p. 200.

737. Burton, 'Central Afr.' vol. i. p. 124; vol. ii. p. 25; 'Dahome,' vol. ii. p. 18, &c.; 'Tr. Eth. Soc.' vol. iii. p. 403; J. L. Wilson, 'W. Afr.' pp. 203, 219, 394. See also H. Rowley, 'Mission to Central Africa,' p. 229.

738. Cavazzi, '1st. Descr. de' tre Regni Congo, Matamba, et Angola,' Bologna, 1687, lib. i. 264; Waitz, vol. ii. pp. 419-21; Callaway, 'Religion of Amazulu,' p. 212.

739. Renaudot, 'Acc. by two Mohammedan Travellers,' London, 1733, p. 81; and in Pinkerton, vol. vii. p. 215; Marco Polo, book iii. chap. xx.; and in Pinkerton, vol. vii. p. 162.

740. Caron, 'Japan,' ibid., p. 622; Siebold, 'Nippon,' v. p. 22.

741. 'Journ. Ind. Archip.' new series, vol. ii. p. 374.

742. Legge, 'Confucius,' p. 119; Doolittle, 'Chinese,' vol. i. pp. 108, 174, 192. The practice of attacking or killing all persons met by a funeral procession is perhaps generally connected with funeral human sacrifice; any one met on the road by the funeral of a Mongol prince was slain and ordered to go as escort; in the

Kimbunda country, any one who meets a royal funeral procession is put to death with the other victims at the grave (Magyar, 'Süd. Afrika,' p. 353); see also Mariner, 'Tonga Is.' vol. i. p. 403; Cook, 'First Voy.' vol. i. pp. 146, 236 (Tahiti).

743. Jakob Grimm, 'Verbrennen der Leichen,' contains an instructive collection of references and citations.

744. Homer, Il. xxiii. 175; Eurip. Suppl.; Pausanias, iv. 2.

745. Edda, 'Gylfaginning,' 49; 'Brynhildarqvitha,' &c.

746. Cæsar., Bell. Gall. vi. 19.

747. Hanusch, 'Slaw. Myth.' p. 145.

748. Strabo, xv. 1, 62; Cic. Tusc. Disp. v. 27, 78; Diod. Sic. xvii. 91; xix. 33, &c.; Grimm, 'Verbrennen,' p. 261; Renaudot, 'Two Mohammedans,' p. 4; and in Pinkerton, vol. vii. p. 194. See Buchanan, ibid. pp. 675, 682; Ward, 'Hindoos,' vol. ii. pp. 298-312.

749. H. H. Wilson, 'On the supposed Vaidik authority for the Burning of Hindu Widows,' in 'Journ. Roy. As. Soc.' vol. xvi. (1854) p. 201; in his 'Works,' vol. ii. p. 270. Max Müller, 'Todtenbestattung bei den Brahmanen,' in 'Zeitschr. der Deutsch. Morgenl. Ges.' vol. ix.; 'Chips,' vol. ii. p. 34.

750. Schoolcraft, 'Indian Tribes,' part i. p. 543; part iii. pp. 229, 520; Waitz, vol. iii. pp. 191-3.

751. Klemm, 'Cultur-Gesch.' vol. iii. pp. 355, 364; Waitz, vol. ii. p. 178.

752. Mouhot, 'Indo-China,' vol. i. p. 252.

753. Wood in 'Tr. Eth. Soc.' vol. iv. p. 36.

754. Bastian, 'Mensch,' vol. iii. p. 26.

755. De Brosses, 'Dieux Fétiches,' p. 61.

756. Ravenstein, 'Amur,' p. 382; T. W. Atkinson, p. 483.

757. St. John, 'Far East,' vol. ii. p. 253 (Dayaks).

758. Charlevoix, 'Nouvelle France,' vol. vi. p. 78; Sagard, 'Hist. du Canada,' p. 497; Schoolcraft, 'Indian Tribes,' part iii. p. 229.

759. Cranz, 'Grönland,' p. 257.

760. Taylor, 'New Zealand,' p. 271; Ellis, 'Madagascar,' vol. i. p. 429.

761. Steller, 'Kamtschatka,' p. 269.

762. Stewart, 'Notes on Northern Cachar,' in 'Journ. As. Soc. Bengal,' vol. xxiv. p. 632; Cross, 'Karens,' l.c.; Mason, 'Karens,' l.c.

763. Callaway, 'Zulu Tales,' vol. i. p. 317.

764. Low in 'Journ. Ind. Archip.' vol. i. p. 426. See Meiners, vol. i. p. 220; vol. ii. p. 791.

765. Juvenal, Sat. xv. 148.

766. Alger, 'Future Life,' p. 632, and see 'Bibliography,' appendix ii.; Wesley, 'Sermon on Rom. viii. 19-22;' Adam Clarke, 'Commentary,' on same text. This, by the way, is the converse view to Bellarmine's, who so patiently let the fleas bite him, saying, 'We shall have heaven to reward us for our sufferings, but these poor creatures have nothing but the enjoyment of the present life.'—Bayle 'Biog. Dic.' The argument in Butler's 'Analogy,' part i. ch. i. puts the evidence for souls of brutes on much the same footing as that for souls of men.

767. Schoolcraft, 'Indian Tribes,' part i. pp. 237, 262; part ii. p. 68.

768. D'Orbigny, 'L'Homme Américain,' vol. i. p. 196; vol. ii. pp. 23, 78; Falkner, 'Patagonia,' p. 118; Musters, 'Patagonians,' p. 178.

769. Egede, 'Greenland,' p. 152; Cranz, p. 301: sec Nilsson, p. 140. Torquemada, 'Monarquia Indiana,' xiii. ch. 47; Clavigero, 'Messico,' vol. ii. pp. 94-6.

770. Georgi, 'Reise im Russ. R.' vol. i. p. 312.

771. Baron, 'Tonquin,' in Pinkerton, vol. ix. p. 704.

772. W. G. Palgrave, 'Arabia,' vol. i. p. 10; Bastian, 'Mensch,' vol. ii. p. 334; Waitz, vol. ii. p. 519 (Gallas).

773. Grimm, 'Verbrennen der Leichen.' A curious correspondence in the practice of cutting off a fowl's head as a funeral rite is to be noticed among the Yorubas of W. Africa (Burton, 'W. and W.' p. 220), Chuwashes of Siberia (Castrén, 'Finn. Myth.' p. 120), old Russians (Grimm, 'Verbrennen,' p. 254).

774. Bastian, 'Mensch,' vol. ii. p. 335.

775. Colebrooke, 'Essays,' vol. i. p. 177; Ward, 'Hindoos,' vol. ii. pp. 62, 284, 331.

776. Mannhardt, 'Götterwelt der Deutschen, &c.' vol. i. p. 319.

777. Saint-Foix, 'Œuvres,' Maestricht, 1778, vol. iv. p. 150.

778. Chr. von Stramberg, 'Rheinischer Antiquarius,' i. vol. i., Coblence, 1851, p. 203; J. M. Kemble, 'Horæ Ferales,' p. 66.

779. Moerenhout, 'Voy. Aux Iles du Grand Océan,' vol. i. p. 430.

780. St. John 'Far East,' vol. i. p. 187.

781. Mason, 'Karens,' in 'Journ. As. Soc. Bengal,' 1865, part ii. p. 202; Cross in 'Journ. Amer. Oriental Soc.' vol. iv. p. 309. See comparison of Siamese and Malay ideas; Low in 'Journ. Ind. Archip.' vol. i. p. 340.

782. Hardy, 'Manual of Budhism,' pp. 291, 443; Bastian, 'Oestl. Asien,' vol. ii. p. 184; Marco Polo, book iii. ch. xxii. (compare various readings); Meiners, vol. i. p. 215; vol. ii. p. 799.

783. Malay evidence has since been noticed by Wilken, 'Het Animisme bij den Volken van den Indischen Archipel.' p. 104. (Note to 3rd edition.)

784. Hume, 'Nat. Hist. of Rel.' sec. ii.; Comte, 'Philosophie Positive,' vol. v. p. 30.

785. Charlevoix, vol. vi. p. 74; Keating, 'Long's Exp.' vol. ii. p. 154; Le Jeune, 'Nouvelle France,' p. 59; also Waitz, vol. iii. p. 199; Gregg, 'Commerce of Prairies,' vol. ii. p. 244; see Addison's No. 56 of the 'Spectator.'

786. Mariner, 'Tonga Is.' vol. ii. p. 129; Williams, 'Fiji,' vol. i. p. 242. Similar ideas in Tahiti, Cook's 3rd Voy. vol. ii. p. 166.

787. Cross, l.c. pp. 309, 313; Mason, l.c. p. 202. Compare Meiners, vol. i. p. 144; Castrén, 'Finn. Myth.' pp. 161-3.

788. Schoolcraft, 'Indian Tribes,' part ii. p. 68; 'Algec Res.' vol. ii. p. 128; Lallemant in 'Rel. des Jésuites dans la Nouvelle France,' 1626, p. 3.

789. Williams, 'Fiji,' vol. i. pp. 188, 243, 246; Alger, p. 82; Seemann, 'Viti,' p. 229.

790. 'Journ. Ind. Archip.' new series, vol. ii. p. 421.

791. For some cases in which horror or abnegation are assigned as motives for abandonment of the dead man's property, see Humboldt and Bonpland, vol. v. p. 626; Dalton in 'Journ. As. Soc. Bengal,' 1866, part ii. p. 191, &c.; Earl, 'Papuans,' p. 108; Callaway, 'Rel. of Amazulu,' p. 13; Egede, 'Greenland,' p. 151; Cranz, p. 301;

Loskiel, 'Ind. N. A.' part i. p. 64, but see p. 76. The destruction or abandonment of the whole property of the dead may plausibly, whether justly or not, be explained by horror or abnegation; but these motives do not generally apply to cases where only part of the property is sacrificed, or new objects are provided expressly, and here the service of the dead seems the reasonable motive. Thus, at the funeral of a Garo girl, earthen vessels were broken as they were thrown in above the buried ashes. 'They said, the spirit of the girl would not benefit by them if they were given unbroken, but for her the fragments would unite again.' (Dalton, 'Descriptive Ethnology of Bengal,' p. 67.) The mere fact of breaking or destruction of objects at funerals does not carry its own explanation, for it is equally applicable to sentimental abandonment and to practical transmission of the spirit of the object, as a man is killed to liberate his soul. For good cases of the breaking of vessels and utensils given to the dead, see 'Journ. Ind. Archip.' vol. i. p. 325 (Mintira); Grey, 'Australia,' vol. i. p. 322; G. F. Moore, 'Vocab. W. Australia,' p. 13 (Australians); Markham in 'Tr. Eth. Soc.' vol. iii. p. 188 (Ticunas); St. John, vol. i. p. 68 (Dayaks); Ellis, 'Madagascar,' vol. i. p. 254; Schoolcraft, 'Indian Tribes,' part i. p. 84 (Appalachicola); D. Wilson, 'Prehistoric Man,' vol. ii. p. 196 (N. A. I. and ancient graves in England). Cases of formal sacrifice where objects are offered to the dead and taken away again, are generally doubtful as to motive; see Spix and Martius, vol. i. p. 383; Martius, vol. i. p. 485 (Brazilian Tribes); Moffat, 'S. Africa,' p. 308 (Bechuanas); 'Journ. Ind. Archip.' vol. iii. p. 149 (Kayans).

792. Alger, 'Future Life,' p. 81. He treats, however (p. 76), as intentionally symbolic the rite of the Winnebagos, who light fires on the grave to provide night after night camp-fires for the soul on its far journey (Schoolcraft, 'Ind. Tr.' vol. iv. p. 55; the idea is introduced in Longfellow's 'Hiawatha,' xix.). I agree with Dr. Brinton ('Myths of New World,' p. 241) that to look for recondite symbolic meaning in these simple childish rites is unreasonable. There was a similar Aztec rite (Clavigero, vol. ii. p. 94). The Mintira light fires on the grave for the spirit to warm itself at ('Journ. Ind. Archip.' vol. i. p. 325, see p. 271, and compare Martius, vol. i. p. 491). So Australians will light a fire near their camp at night for the ghost of some lately dead relative to sit by (Millett, 'Australian Parsonage,' p. 76.)

793. J. G. Müller, 'Amer. Urrelig.' p. 222, see 420.

794. Bosman, 'Guinea,' in Pinkerton, vol. xvi. p. 430.

795. Polack, 'M. of New Zealanders,' vol. ii. pp. 66, 78, 116, 127.

796. Georgi, 'Russ. R.' vol. i. p. 266; Herodot. iv. 71, see note in Rawlinson's Tr. &c. &c.

797. Oldfield in 'Tr. Eth. Soc.' vol. iii. pp. 228, 245.

798. Bonwick, 'Tasmanians,' p. 97.

799. Cranz, 'Grönland,' pp. 263, 301.

800. Schoolcraft, 'Indian Tribes,' part iv. pp. 55, 65; J. G. Müller, 'Amer. Urrel.' pp. 88, 287.

801. Sahagun, book iii. App. in Kingsborough, 'Antiquities of Mexico,' vol. vii.; Clavigero, vol. ii. p. 94; Brasseur, vol. iii. pp. 497, 569.

802. Cieza de Leon, p. 161; Rivero and Tschudi, 'Peruvian Antiquities,' pp. 186, 200.

803. Ellis, 'Hist, of Madagascar,' vol. i. pp. 254, 429; see Flacourt, p. 60.

804. Castrén, 'Finn. Myth,' p. 118; J. Billings, 'Exp. to N. Russia,' p. 129; see 'Samoiedia' in Pinkerton, vol. i. p. 532, and Leems, 'Lapland,' ibid. p. 484.

805. Boecler, 'Ehsten Gebraüche,' p. 69.

806. 'Journ. Ind. Archip.' vol. ii. p. 691; see vol. i. pp. 297, 349.

807. Bastian, 'Psychologie,' p. 89; 'Journ. Ind. Archip.' vol. iii. p. 337. For other instances, see Bastian, 'Mensch,' vol. ii. p. 332, &c.; Alger, 'Future Life,' part ii.

808. Klemm, 'C. G.' vol. iv. p. 159; Ezek. xxxii. 27.

809. Max Müller, 'Todtenbestattung der Brahmanen,' in D. M. Z. vol. ix. pp. vii.-xiv.

810. Lucian. De Luctu, 9, &c.; Philopseudes, 27; Strabo, viii. 6, 12; Herodot. v. 92; Smith's 'Dic. Gr. and Rom. Ant.' art. 'funus.'

811. Valer. Max. ii.; Mela, iii. 2. Froius (1565) in Maffei, 'Histor. Indicarum,' lib. iv.

812. Grimm, 'Verbrennen der Leichen,' pp. 232, &c., 247, &c.; 'Deutsche Myth.' pp. 795-800.

813. Dusburg, 'Chronicon Prussiæ,' iii. c. v.; Hanusch, 'Slaw. Myth.' pp. 898, 415 (Anafielas is the glass-mountain of Slavonic and

German myth, see Grimm, 'D. M.' p. 796). Compare statement in St. Clair and Brophy, 'Bulgaria,' p. 61; as to food transmitted to dead in other world, with more probable explanation, p. 77.

814. St. John, 'Far East,' vol. i. pp. 54, 68. Compare Bosman, 'Guinea,' in Pinkerton, vol. xvi. p. 430.

815. Schoolcraft, 'Indian Tribes,' part iv. p. 54.

816. Hunter, 'Rural Bengal,' p. 210.

817. Davis, 'Chinese,' vol. i. p. 276; Doolittle, vol. i. p. 193; vol. ii. p. 275; Bastian, 'Mensch,' vol. ii. p. 334; see Marco Polo, book ii. ch. lxviii.

818. Colebrooke, 'Essays,' vol. i. pp. 161, 169.

819. Lubbock, 'Prehistoric Times,' p. 142; Wilkinson, 'Ancient Eg.' vol. ii. p. 319.

820. Beeckmann, 'Voy. to Borneo,' in Pinkerton, vol. xi. p. 110.

821. Politis, 'Neohellen. Mythologia,' vol. i. part i. p. 266; Hartknoch, 'Alt. und Neues Preussen,' part i. p. 181; Grimm, 'D. M.' pp. 791-5; Wuttke, 'Deutsche Volksaberglaube,' p. 212; Rochholz, 'Deutscher Glaube,' &c. vol. i. p. 187, &c.; Maury, 'Magie,' &c. p. 158 (France).

822. Maitland, 'Church in the Catacombs,' p. 137; Forbes Leslie, vol. ii. p. 502; Meiners, vol. ii. p. 750; Brand, 'Pop. Ant.', vol. ii. p. 307.

823. Ward, 'Hindoos,' vol. ii. p. 284.

824. From the collated and annotated text in J. C. Atkinson, 'Glossary of Cleveland Dialect,' p. 595 (a = one, neean = none, beean = bone). Other versions in Scott, 'Minstrelsy of the Scottish Border,' vol. ii. p. 367; Kelly, 'Indo-European Folk-lore,' p. 115; Brand, 'Pop. Ant.' vol. ii. p. 275. Two verses have perhaps been lost between the fifth and sixth. J. C. A. reads 'meate' in vv. 7 and 8; the usual reading 'milke' is retained here. The sense of these two verses may be that the liquor sacrificed in life will quench the fire: an idea parallel to that known to folklore, that he who gave bread in his lifetime will find it after death ready for him to cast into the hellhound's jaws (Mannhardt, 'Götterwelt der Deutschen und Nordischen Völker,' p. 319), a sop to Cerberus.

825. Lewes, 'Biographical History of Philosophy,' Democritus (and see his remarks on Reid); Lucretius, lib. iv.; 'Early Hist. of Mankind,'

p. 8; Stewart, 'Philosophy of Human Mind,' vol. i. chap. i. sec. 2; Reid, 'Essays,' ii. chaps. iv. xiv.; see Thos. Browne, 'Philosophy of the Mind,' lect. 27.